LAW AND RELIGION IN EUROPE

A Comparative Introduction

GW00673846

Law and Religion in Europe

A Comparative Introduction

NORMAN DOE

Professor of Law and Director
Centre for Law and Religion
Law School, Cardiff University

OXFORD
UNIVERSITY PRESS

OXFORD
UNIVERSITY PRESS

Great Clarendon Street, Oxford OX2 6DP

Oxford University Press is a department of the University of Oxford.
It furthers the University's objective of excellence in research, scholarship,
and education by publishing worldwide in

Oxford New York

Auckland Cape Town Dar es Salaam Hong Kong Karachi
Kuala Lumpur Madrid Melbourne Mexico City Nairobi
New Delhi Shanghai Taipei Toronto

With offices in

Argentina Austria Brazil Chile Czech Republic France Greece
Guatemala Hungary Italy Japan Poland Portugal Singapore
South Korea Switzerland Thailand Turkey Ukraine Vietnam

Oxford is a registered trade mark of Oxford University Press
in the UK and in certain other countries

Published in the United States
by Oxford University Press Inc., New York

British Library Cataloguing in Publication Data
Data available

Library of Congress Cataloging in Publication Data
Data available

Typeset by SPI Publisher Services, Pondicherry, India
Printed in Great Britain
on acid-free paper by
CPI Antony Rowe

ISBN 978–0–19–960401–2 (Hbk)
ISBN 978–0–19–960400–5 (Pbk)

1 3 5 7 9 10 8 6 4 2

This book is dedicated, for their hard work and good cheer, to the members of the European Consortium for Church and State Research.

Preface

This book has grown mainly out of my work with the European Consortium for Church and State Research (founded in 1989). The Consortium brings together scholars and practitioners from across the European Union (and beyond) to study the national laws on religion in the Member States and to disseminate its research in the universities of Europe. It was my pleasure and honour to serve as President of the Consortium in 2010—and it was Professor David McClean of Sheffield who first introduced me to the Consortium in the mid-1990s. Without the hard work of the Consortium members, over the years, this book would not have been possible. I have relied very heavily on experiences at the annual Consortium conferences, teaching and other collaborations with Consortium colleagues, the proceedings and journal of the Consortium, the volumes published in its Law and Religion Series (all published by Peeters, Leuven), as well as explanations and translations of material by Consortium members. Professors Ferrari (Milan), Robbers (Trier), Ibán (Madrid), and Basdevant-Gaudemet (Paris), in particular, have played the role of scholastic mentors superbly.

I have enjoyed the good fortune of the patience of students at Cardiff Law School—on the undergraduate module Comparative Law of Religion and the postgraduate LLM in Canon Law—for experiments with ideas and materials. To my colleagues at the Centre for Law and Religion at Cardiff Law School I owe a particular debt of gratitude for commenting on draft chapters: Dr Russell Sandberg, Professor Mark Hill QC (a fellow Consortium member), Dr Augur Pearce, Eithne D'Auria, Frank Cranmer, Anthony Jeremy, and Bishop Paul Colton. Cardiff Law School, under its then head Professor Gillian Douglas, was kind enough to grant me study leave for 2010–11—this allowed me to spend the autumn of 2010 writing up sections of the book. Similarly, I am extremely grateful to the President and Fellows of Trinity College, Oxford, for having awarded me a visiting fellowship for the Hilary term 2011 which enabled me to put the finishing touches to the book before embarking on another study whilst at the college. Research assistance from Louise Edmunds and Maria Clara Ho was invaluable. At the postgraduate office, Sharron Alldred, Sarah Kennedy, and Helen Calvert have as always provided first-class support. At Oxford University Press Alex Flach and Natasha Knight are to be especially thanked for their continued faith in the project, as are Fiona Stables and Alison Floyd with invaluable assistance at the stage of production.

Finally, I should like to thank my family—my wife Heather (a doctor), our children Rachel (law), Elizabeth (architecture), and Edward (physiotherapy), my mother, father, and brother Martin (also a lawyer) for their constant support.

I make no apology for the density of the footnotes, which some may find a bore—as my doctoral supervisors Professors Ullmann and Milsom at Cambridge (Trinity and St John's respectively) used to suggest, more often than not it is there we find the legal evidence—but any errors in these, and the text, are needless to say my sole responsibility.

CND

Visiting Fellow
Trinity College
Oxford
Hilary 2011

Contents

List of Abbreviations

AB	Administratiefrechtelijke Beslissingen, Decisions of Administrative Agencies (Netherlands)
Admin Ct	Administrative Court (eg Bulgaria)
A-G	Attorney-General (eg Portugal, UK)
AGG	Allgemeines Gleichbehandlungsgesetz, General Act on Equal Treatment (Germany)
AJDA	Actualité Juridique Droit Administratif, Periodical on Administrative Law (France)
ALPRC	Act on the Legal Position of Religious Communities (Slovenia)
Ann dr Lux	Annales du Droit Luxembourgeois (Luxembourg)
Arb	Arbeitsgericht, Labour Court (Austria)
B&C	Barnewall & Cresswell's King's Bench Reports (UK, England and Wales)
BekGG	Bekenntnisgemeinschaften, Law on Religious Communities (Germany)
BGBI	Bundesgesetzblatt, Austrian Law Gazette (Austria)
BH	Birósági Határozatok, Court Decisions (Hungary)
BHRC	Butterworths Human Rights Cases
BrB	Brottsbalken, Criminal Code (Sweden)
BS	Belgisch Staatsblad, Official Journal (Belgium)
Bull Civ	Bulletin des Arrêts de la Chambre Civile de la Cour de Cassation, Bulletin of the Judgments of the Civil Chamber of the Court of Cassation (France)
Bull Crim	Bulletin des Arrêts de la Chambre Criminelle de la Court de Cassation, Bulletin of the Judgments of the Criminal Chamber of the Court of Cassation (France)
BVerfGE	Bundesverfassungsgericht, Federal Constitutional Court (Germany)
B-VG	Bundes-Verfassungsgesetz, Constitutional Law (Austria)
BvL	Bundesverwaltungsgericht, Federal Administrative Court (Germany)
CA	Court of Appeal
Cass	Cour de Cassation, Court of Cassation (Luxembourg, France)
CC	Civil Code
CCl	Conseil Constitutionnel, Constitutional Council (France)
CCA	Churches and Congregations Act (Estonia)
CCP	Code of Civil Procedure
CCt	Constitutional Court
CD	Collection of Decisions of the European Commission on Human Rights
CE	Conseil d'État, Council of State (France)
CFR	Charter of Fundamental Rights (EU)
CFRF	Charter of Fundamental Rights and Freedoms (Czech Republic)
CLR	Cyprus Law Reports (Cyprus)
COE	Council of Europe
COMECE	Commission des Épiscopats de la Communauté Européenne (Commission of Catholic Episcopal Conferences in Europe)
Coll	Collection
COS	Council of State

CR App R	Criminal Appeals Reports (UK)
CRSL	Churches and Religious Societies Law (Czech Republic)
CSJ	Cour Supérieure de Justice, Supreme Court (Luxembourg)
D	Recueil Dalloz, De Doctrine, de jurisprudence et de législation (France)
D&R	Decisions & Reports (European Commission of Human Rights)
DC	District Court
DES	Department of Education and Science (Ireland)
DL	Decree-Law (Italy, Portugal, Spain)
Doc	Document
DR	Dowling & Ryland's King's Bench Reports (UK, England and Wales)
DzU	Dziennik Ustaw, Official Journal of Laws (Poland)
EA	Education Act
EAT	Employment Appeals Tribunal (UK)
EC	European Commission
EccLJ	Ecclesiastical Law Journal
ECHR	European Convention for the Protection of Human Rights and Fundamental Freedoms (Council of Europe)
ECRI	European Commission against Racism and Intolerance
ECtHR	European Court of Human Rights
EEA	European Economic Area
EHRR	European Human Rights Reports
EJCSR	European Journal for Church and State Research
ENLENDF	European Network of Legal Experts in the Non-Discrimination Field
EOO	Equal Opportunities Ombudsman (Lithuania)
ET	Employment Tribunal
ETA	Equal Treatment Act (or Law) (eg Austria)
ETC	Equal Treatment Commission (Netherlands)
Eur Comm	European Commission on Human Rights
EURT	European Union Reform Treaty
FEREDE	Federation of Evangelical Religious Entities of Spain
FLR	Family Law Reports (UK, England and Wales)
FLSCC	Federal Law on the Status of Confessional Communities (Austria)
FRA	Freedom of Religion Act (Finland, Slovenia)
G	Gesetz, Law (Germany)
GA	General Assembly (UN)
GETA	General Equal Treatment Act (Netherlands)
GG	Grundgesetz, Basic Law of the Federal Republic (Germany)
Hag Eccl	Haggard's Ecclesiastical Reports (UK, England and Wales)
HALDE	High Authority against Discrimination and for Equality (France)
HC	High Court
HE	Hallituksen esitys, Government Bill (Finland)
HL	House of Lords (UK)
HR	Hoge Raad, Supreme Court (Netherlands)
ICCPR	International Covenant on Civil and Political Rights (UN)
ICESR	International Covenant on Economic and Social Rights (UN)
ICR	Industrial Cases Reports (UK, England and Wales)
IEHC	High Court (Ireland)
IESC	Supreme Court (Ireland)
ILRM	Irish Law Reports Monthly

IR	Irish Reports
IRFR	International Religious Freedom Report
JCP	Jurisclasseur Périodique (France)
K	Kodeks (Poland)
KB	King's Bench Law Reports (UK, England and Wales)
KKO	Korkein Oikeus, Supreme Court (Finland)
KZP	Konstytucyjnego Prawo, Constitutional Law (Poland)
LD	Legislative Decree (eg Greece)
Lagen	Law, Sweden
LC	Labour Code
LEA	Local Education Authority (UK, England and Wales)
LFCRC	Law on Freedom of Conscience, Religion and Churches (Hungary)
LORCA	Law on Religious Communities and Associations (Lithuania)
LORF	Law on Religious Freedom (Portugal, Spain)
LORO	Law on Religious Organisations (Latvia)
LR A&E	Law Reports, Admiralty and Ecclesiastical (UK, England and Wales)
LR P&D	Law Reports, Probate & Divorce Cases (UK, England and Wales)
LR Sc & Div	Law Reports, House of Lords Scottish & Divorce Appeal Cases
LRCP	Law Reports, Common Pleas Division (UK, England and Wales)
LTL	Litas (Lithuania)
Lux	Luxembourg
M&W	Meeson & Welsby's Exchequer Reports (UK, England and Wales)
MLR	Modern Law Review (UK)
NCCD	National Council on Combating Discrimination (Romania)
NJ	Nederlandse Jurisprudentie, Dutch Case Law (Netherlands)
NJA	Nytt Juridiskt Arkiv, Supreme Court (Sweden)
NSA	Naczelny Sad Administracyjny, Supreme Administrative Court (Poland)
NUJ	National Union of Journalists (UK)
OG	Official Gazette
OGH	Oberster Gerichtshof, Supreme Court (Austria)
OGH SZ	Sammlung der Entscheidungen des Osterreichischen Obersten Gerichtshofs in Zivil-und Justizverwaltungssachen, Collection of Decisions of the Supreme Court in Civil and Judicial Administration Matters (Austria)
OJ	Official Journal
OSNKW	Orzecznictwo Sadu Najwyzszego Izba Karna i Wojskowa, Criminal and Military Chamber (Poland)
OSP	Orzecznictwo Sadu Polskich, Polish Court of Law (Poland)
OTK	Orzecznictwo Trybunalu Konstytucyjnego, Official Digest of the Constitutional Tribunal (Poland)
PADC	Protection against Discrimination Commission (Bulgaria)
Pas	Pasicrisie Luxembourgeoise (Luxembourg)
PC	Penal or Criminal Code
PD	Presidential Decree (eg Greece, Italy)
PECCSR	Proceedings of the European Consortium for Church and State Research
PeVL	Perustuslakivaliokunta, Constitutional Law Committee (Finland)
PL	Public Law (UK)
PrivSchG	Privatschulgesetz, Private School Law (Germany)
Prot	Protocol

Rb	Rechtbank, District Court (Netherlands)
RCA	Recognition of Churches Act (Austria)
RCLP	Religious Communities Law (Slovenia)
RD	Royal Decree (eg Italy)
RDA	Religious Denominations Act (Bulgaria)
Rec	Recommendation
Reg	Regulation
RelUG	Religionsunterrichtsgesetz, Religious Education Law (Austria)
Rep	Republic
Res	Resolution
RFDA	Revue Française de Droit Administratif, French Administrative Law Journal
RT	Riigi Teataja, State Gazette (Estonia)
RTVE	Ente Publico Radiotelevision Española (Spain)
RVDW	Rechtspraak Van De Week, Law of the Week Periodical (Netherlands)
SACRE	Standing Advisory Council for Religious Education (UK, England and Wales)
Sb	Sbirka, Collection of Laws (Czech Republic)
SC	Supreme Court
SchOG	Schulorganisationsgesetz, Law on School Organization (Austria)
SchZG	Schulzeitgesetz, Law on Schooling (Austria)
Sent	Sentence, Court Judgment (Italy)
SFCR	Statute on Freedom of Conscience and Religion (Poland)
SFS	Svensk Forfattningssamling, Swedish Code of Statutes (Sweden)
SG	State Gazette (Bulgaria)
SI	Statutory Instrument (UK)
SoS	Secretary of State (UK)
SOU	Staters Offentliga Utredningar, Government Reports (Sweden)
SRS	Socialist Republic of Slovenia
SSFA	School Standards and Framework Act 1998 (UK, England and Wales)
StGG	Staatsgrundgesetz, Constitution (Austria)
STJ	Supremo Tribunal de Justicia, Supreme Court of Justice (Spain)
Strfl	Straffeloven, Penal Code (Denmark)
Sygn	Sygnatura, File Reference (Poland)
TFEU	Treaty on the Functioning of the European Union
TLR	Times Law Reports (UK, England and Wales)
U	Ugeskrift for Retsvaesen, Law Journal (Denmark)
UDHR	Universal Declaration on Human Rights (UN)
UKHL	United Kingdom House of Lords
UKSC	United Kingdom Supreme Court
UNCRC	United Nations Committee on the Rights of the Child
UNDID	UN Declaration on the Elimination of All Forms of Intolerance and Discrimination based on Religion or Belief
UNGA	United Nations General Assembly
UNHCR	United Nations High Commissioner for Refugees
UNHRC	United Nations Human Rights Committee
UNSR	United Nations Special Rapporteur
US	Ustavni Soud, Constitutional Court (Czech Republic)
Vfslg	Verfassungssammlung, Constitutional Court (Austria)

VR	Verkeersrecht, Law Journal (Netherlands)
VwGHSlg	Verwaltungsgerichtshof, Administrative Court (Austria)
WPflG	Wehrpflichtgesetz, National Service Act (Germany)
WRV	Verfassung der Weimarer Republik, Constitution of the Weimar Republic (Germany)
YB	Year Book
Zb	Zbierka, Act (Slovakia)
Zz	Zmena, Collection (Slovakia)

Table of Cases

Germany

CCt

Italy

CCt
Court of Cassation

Lithuania

CCt

Introduction

Each State in Europe has its own national law affecting religion. These national laws also function in wider legal environments. The European Union (EU) has laws and other regulatory instruments on religion directed to both the EU institutions and its twenty-seven Member States.[1] Similarly, the Council of Europe has norms on religion in the European Convention on Human Rights (ECHR) and the case-law of the European Court of Human Rights applicable to its forty-seven Member States.[2] These systems of religion law—State and international laws on religion—are distinct from systems of religious law—the normative systems of religious organizations and traditions.[3] The principal focus of this book is national religion laws in the Member States of the European Union, though it also takes into account a selection of other States in the wider Council of Europe; all the States studied are signatories of the ECHR.[4] The book examines these national laws comparatively, their similarities and differences—it describes them, explains them, and evaluates them, where appropriate, in the context of EU law, the ECHR, and global international law on religion,[5] and the standards which these promote in terms of democracy, freedom, and equality.

On the basis of a study of these national laws, this book proposes that there are principles of religion law common to the States of Europe. Whilst there are real and

[1] The European Union is governed by the European Parliament (which represents EU citizens), the Council of the EU (with one minister representing each State)—together these legislate for the EU—the European Commission (composed of commissioners and the civil service; it may propose laws and monitor their application), the European Council (composed of heads of State, this sets the general direction of the EU), and the European Court of Justice; the member states retain national sovereignty. See generally TC Hartley, *The Foundations of European Union Law* (Oxford: OUP, 7th edn, 2010).

[2] The Council of Europe (founded in 1949 and based in Strasbourg) covers almost the whole of the European continent; it seeks to develop throughout Europe common and democratic principles based on the ECHR and other instruments. See generally RCA White and C Ovey, *Jacobs, White and Ovey: The European Convention on Human Rights* (Oxford: OUP, 5th edn, 2010).

[3] The expressions 'religion law' and 'religious law' are increasingly used in secondary literature in the field of law and religion, which is itself starting to be seen as involving the study of both state law on religion (international and national) and religious law (such as the canon law or other regulatory systems of Christian churches, Jewish law, and Islamic law). This book examines aspects of religious law only when necessary to elucidate elements of religion law. For the concept of religious law, see eg the studies in A Huxley (ed), *Religion, Law and Tradition* (London: Routledge, 2002).

[4] Whilst all the States of the EU are studied, occasional reference is made to States in the wider Council of Europe, usually to the extent that they are relevant to Strasbourg cases decided under the ECHR.

[5] ie primarily, the instruments of the United Nations and its various institutions.

significant differences of detail, the similarities between national laws are also profound. From these similarities may be induced shared principles of religion law.[6] These common principles suggest a homogeneous European approach to the legal accommodation of religion in contemporary society.[7] Often, the juridical similarities, and the principles which flow from them, are stimulated by shared historical experiences, or contemporary social and political demands common to the States (such as the need to accommodate religious pluralism). Needless to say, the laws of States may also be unified through common compliance with EU law, the ECHR, and global international law. National differences, too, exist by virtue of divergent historical, political, and social factors, as well as by the margin of appreciation afforded by these international instruments.[8] This comparative study presents the legal evidence for the similarities and differences between national laws. In so doing it re-assesses the classical doctrine that there are three basic models of state-religion relations in Europe: state-church; separation; and cooperation. The book proposes on the legal evidence, particularly in terms of laws beneath the constitutional level, that the dominant model in Europe is that of cooperation between State and religion.[9]

To this end, the book introduces the key areas of national religion laws. Chapter 1 examines the sources of laws on religion, which also tell us about the scope and subject-matter of religion laws, legal definitions of religion, and systems of national laws on religion—in terms of the posture of States towards religion. Chapters 2 and 3 examine religious freedom and the individual (Chapter 2), and how this is applied in the field of religious discrimination law and the growing laws on religious hatred (Chapter 3). Religious discrimination law also impacts on religious organizations, and the extent to which they may discriminate (for example on grounds of religion, sex, or sexual orientation). Religious organizations are the principal focus of the next four chapters: their legal position and legal personality (Chapter 4), their autonomy and the status and functions of ministers of religion (Chapter 5), their doctrines and worship (Chapter 6), and their property and finances (Chapter 7). The book then concentrates on religion in the public sphere, in schools, prisons, hospitals, and the armed forces (Chapter 8), and religion in the private world of marriage and the upbringing of children (Chapter 9). Chapter 10 explores the increasing volume of religion law in the European Union and seeks to articulate its fundamental principles. The study ends with conclusions about the principles of religion law common to the States of Europe (a tentative statement of which appears in the Appendix), whether these may be used as a material or inspirational source for the development of EU law on religion, and how the study of law and

---

[6] For a discussion of the concept, see N Doe, 'Towards a "Common Law" on Religion in the European Union' in LN Leustean and JTS Madeley (eds), *Religion, Politics and Law in the European Union* (London: Routledge, 2010) 141–60.

[7] eg Grace Davie, the sociologist of religion, suggests that sociological, historical, and legal evidence reveals a basic common 'European' approach to religion: G Davie, *Religion in Modern Europe: A Memory Mutates* (Oxford: OUP, 2000); see more fully General Conclusion, which follows Ch 10 below.

[8] The margin of appreciation is a concept developed by the European Court of Human Rights to allow States a degree of freedom in their application of the ECHR in the light of national conditions.

[9] See Ch 1 below for the various models and a critique of them.

religion in Europe may learn from, as well as be of value to, disciplines beyond law—not least the sociology of religion.[10]

The relationship between law and religion has attracted a great deal of attention in recent years, politically and academically. This mirrors an increase both in the volume of national laws on religion and in litigation which invokes nationally or at Strasbourg the provisions of the ECHR on religion. The focus to-date of public and academic debate has been on whether national laws accommodate religion in modern pluralistic societies. In the political sphere, the 'soul for Europe' movement, the furore over the Danish cartoons depicting the prophet Mohammed, crucifixes in Italian schools, investigations into child protection in the Catholic Church in Ireland, and papal pronouncements about religion and equality laws in the States of Europe, for example, have very much placed law and religion on the agenda for public debate throughout Europe.[11] The development of structures for dialogue between government and religious organizations, at national and international level, also underscores the need for society and religion to be in partnership, given the role that religions can play in the promotion of social cohesion and respect.[12]

In the academic sphere, national studies on law and religion in the individual States of Europe have blossomed,[13] such as those on religion law in the United Kingdom.[14] There is also a growing literature on international law and religion, particularly on religious freedom under the ECHR,[15] as well as the posture of the institutions of the European Union towards religion.[16] However, there is no

---

[10] It would be interesting to determine the degree to which national laws are also, in some fundamental sense, re-presentations of religious law—most religions would not see the principles set out in the Appendix as inconsistent with their own laws and doctrines or their own views on the role of the State.

[11] Indeed, on 16 November 2009, the EU Council of Ministers underlined 'the strong commitment of the European Union to the promotion and protection of freedom of religion or belief'.

[12] For the EU, see Ch 10 below; see also eg COE, Parliamentary Assembly, Res 1743 (2010) on Islam, Islamism and Islamophobia in Europe, especially para 3 (on the contribution of religions to the promotion of fundamental values) and para 6 (on the social roles played by religions).

[13] eg a country-by-country series on national religion laws has been launched as part of the *International Encyclopaedia of Laws* (Dordrecht: Kluwer Law International, 2010). But much of the literature is not in the English language. Indeed, journals such as *Daimon: annuario di diritto camparato delle religioni* (Bologna), *Anuario de derecho eclesiástico del estado* (Madrid), *Österreichisches Archiv für recht & religion* (Vienna), and *L'Année Canonique* (Paris) sometimes have comparative studies on national religion laws, but they are rarely comprehensive and pan-continental; see also eg 'État et religion en Europe: les systèmes de reconnaissance' (2004) *Revue de droit canonique* 54.

[14] R Sandberg, *Law and Religion* (Cambridge: CUP, 2011), J Rivers, *The Law of Organized Religion* (Oxford: OUP, 2010), S Knights, *Freedom of Religion, Minorities and the Law* (Oxford: OUP, 2007), PW Edge, *Legal Responses to Religious Difference* (Dordrecht: Kluwer Law International, 2001) and *Religion and Law: An Introduction* (Aldershot: Ashgate, 2006), R Ahdar and I Leigh, *Religious Freedom in the Liberal State* (Oxford: OUP, 2005), A Bradney, *Law and Faith in a Sceptical Age* (Abingdon: Routledge Cavendish, 2009), and M Hill, *Ecclesiastical Law* (Oxford: OUP, 3rd edn, 2007).

[15] C Evans, *Freedom of Religion under the European Convention on Human Rights* (Oxford: OUP, 2001), PM Taylor, *Freedom of Religion* (Cambridge: CUP, 2005), and MD Evans, *Religious Liberty and International Law in Europe* (Cambridge: CUP, 1997).

[16] See eg the excellent study by R McCrea, *Religion and the Public Order of the European Union* (Oxford: OUP, 2010); see also J Rivers, 'In pursuit of pluralism: the ecclesiastical policy of the European Union' (2004) 7 EccLJ 267, and the study by M Ventura, *La Laicità dell'Unione Europea: Diritti, Mercato, Religione* (Turin: G Giappichelli Editore, 2001).

widely-accessible book dedicated to a comprehensive, comparative, and thematic study of national religion laws in Europe.[17] Be that as it may, the work of the European Consortium for Church and State Research is an invaluable resource for such a comparative study.[18] The Consortium's *State and Church in the European Union*, edited by Gerhard Robbers (and in its second edition), is the leading European text (in English) on the religion laws of the Member States of the European Union.[19] Nevertheless, this is a volume of national reports each written by a member of the Consortium from the country in question—national laws are not compared thematically, though there is a short comparison by Gerhard Robbers in the final chapter.[20] The same generally applies to the published annual proceedings of the Consortium,[21] though these also carry occasional comparative studies on single topics.[22] By way of contrast, there is a vibrant comparative literature on religion in Europe outside the discipline of law in the fields of sociology of religion, political studies, and history.[23]

Needless to say, the connection between law and religion is an important part of the juridical history of Europe.[24] Whilst a legal history of religion in Europe, in the context of its religious history, is beyond the scope of this book, a general acquaintance with its main themes is essential to understand more fully modern

---

[17] Exceptions include the edited volume in Spanish by A Fernández-Coronado González (editor in chief), *El derecho de la libertad de conciencia en el marco de la Unión Europea: pluralismo y monorías* (Madrid: Editorial Colex, 2002) and, in German, S Mückl, *Europäisierung des Staatskirchenrechts* (Baden-Baden: Nomos, 2005). There is also a strong comparative dimension to S Ferrari and IC Ibán, *Diritto e religione in Europa occidentale* (Bologna: Il Mulino, 1997) and F Margiotta Broglio, C Mirabelli, and F Onida, *Religioni e sistemi giuridici: introduzione al diritto ecclesiastico comparato* (Bologna: Il Mulino, 1997).

[18] The Consortium publishes the proceedings of its annual conference, sponsors a Law and Religion Series, and runs the *European Journal for Church and State Research* (all by Peeters of Leuven). I have relied heavily on translations of national laws into English by colleagues in the Consortium, as well as compendia of legal texts such as S Berlingò (ed), *Code Européen: Droit et Religions* (Milan Dott A Giuffrè Editore, 2001) and those found on links from its website at <http://www.church-state-europe.org>.

[19] G Robbers (ed), *State and Church in the European Union* (Baden-Baden: Nomos, 2nd edn, 2005).

[20] He has also developed the comparative theme well in G Robbers, 'Diversity of state-religion relations and European Union unity' (2004) 7 EccLJ 304.

[21] It also applies to Consortium-related studies: see eg H Warnink (ed), *Legal Position of Churches and Church Autonomy* (Leuven: Peeters, 2001) and G Robbers (ed), *Church Autonomy* (Frankfurt am Main: Peter Lang, 2001).

[22] See eg N Doe, 'Religion and media law in Europe: a comparative study' in N Doe (ed), *The Portrayal of Religion in Europe: The Media and the Arts* (Leuven: Peeters, 2004) 287, B Schanda, 'Covenantal cooperation of state and religions in the post-communist member countries of the EU' in R Puza and N Doe (eds), *Religion and Law in Dialogue* (Leuven: Peeters, 2006) 251, and S Ferrari, 'Church and state in post-communist Europe' in S Ferrari and WC Durham (eds), *Law and Religion in Post-Communist Europe* (Leuven: Peeters, 2003) 411.

[23] This literature is helpfully reviewed by LN Leustean and JTS Madeley (eds), *Religion, Politics and Law in the European Union* (London: Routledge, 2010) 1–16.

[24] European legal history has been dominated by the civilian tradition (and reception) of Roman law alongside local customary law (with the exception of Scandinavia and the common law of England), the medieval expansion of canon law, the rise of nation states, and the influence of the Napoleonic code: see generally R Lesaffer (trans by J Arriens), *European Legal History: A Cultural and Political Perspective—The Civil Law Tradition in Context* (Cambridge: CUP, 2009).

national religion laws. A historical overview is particularly valuable in order to appreciate the evolution of what is commonly understood today as the three modern postures of European States towards religion.[25] The so-called state-church system operates in the largely Protestant countries of Scandinavia and the United Kingdom, with their national, folk, or established churches and in Greece, with its prevailing religion of Orthodox Christianity. In the separation systems of France and Ireland, religion has no formal place in the constitutional life of the State. The cooperation systems of Spain, Portugal, and Italy, and most central and eastern countries have a basic separation of State and religion but there are also formal agreements between the State and certain religious organizations (such as the Catholic Church). The legal evolution of these religion-state models, and how they accommodate religious freedom, has been shaped directly by the religious and political history of Europe.

In very broad terms, the adoption of Christianity in the fourth century by Constantine as the official religion of the Roman Empire and his inauguration of Constantinople (formerly Byzantium) as its capital set the scene for two important initiatives. One was the emergence of imperial law on religion and the development of the canon law of the church.[26] The other was the migration of the western Latin Christianity of Rome to central and northern Europe, and that of the eastern Orthodox Christianity of Byzantium along a south to north corridor in the east.[27] Doctrinal disagreement in the church of the east and west eventually culminated in the Great Schism between the Latin and Byzantine churches in 1054, and the separation brought about by it persists today in the divisions between the Catholic Church (of Rome) and the Orthodox Church.[28] In the Mediterranean, Orthodox Christianity was sometimes displaced by Latin Christianity and, particularly after the fall of Constantinople in 1453, by Islam and its law under the Ottomans.[29]

---

[25] For the standard understanding that there are three models at work in Europe, see eg G Robbers, 'State and church in the European Union' in G Robbers (ed), *State and Church in the European Union* (Baden-Baden: Nomos, 2nd edn, 2005) 577, 578 *et seq*.

[26] The so-called Edict of Milan 313 provided for religious freedom; Constantine inaugurated Constantinople as his capital in the east on the site of the city of Byzantium in 330; the early councils of the church, initially convened under imperial patronage, led to the promulgation of canons on a host of aspects of church life, governance, ministry, doctrine, and ritual. For an introduction to these events, and references to the relevant secondary literature, see FL Cross and EA Livingstone (eds), *The Oxford Dictionary of the Christian Church* (Oxford: OUP, 3rd edn (revsd), 2005) 408–10.

[27] MD Goodman, *Mission and Conversion: Proselytizing in the Religious History of the Roman Empire* (Oxford: OUP, 1994), RE Sullivan, *Christian Missionary Activity in the Early Middle Ages* (Aldershot: Variorum, 1994), and N Berend, *Christianization and the Rise of Christian Monarchy: Scandinavia, Central Europe and Rus' c. 900–1200* (Cambridge: CUP, 2007). eg whilst Wales and Scotland were already Christian, Augustine was sent by Rome in 597 to convert the English; Denmark became Christian, *c* 960, Poland, *c* 966, Hungary, *c* 1000, Sweden, *c* 1008, Estonia, in the 13th century, and Lithuania *c* 1387.

[28] See generally H Chadwick, *East and West: The Making of a Rift in the Church* (Oxford: OUP, 2003); see also JM Hussey and A Louth, *The Orthodox Church in the Byzantine Empire* (Oxford: OUP, 2010).

[29] eg Cyprus was part of the Byzantine Empire (325–1191) but Orthodoxy was displaced by Latin Christianity (1191–1489, and during Venetian rule, 1489–1571)—the Ottomans ruled during the period 1571–1878; Bulgaria embraced Orthodoxy *c* 864 (it fell to Byzantium in 1018 and to the Ottoman Empire, 1396–1876); Slovakia, *c* 863 (from the 10th century it was part of Hungary until

Moreover, medieval Europe saw the rise of secular jurisdictions based either on Roman (civil) law or indigenous laws (or both) alongside ecclesiastical jurisdictions based on canon law, deriving in the west from the authority of the pope or in the east from patriarchs and synods of bishops. Sometimes the jurisdictions co-existed in their own temporal and spiritual spheres, and sometimes the laws of secular rulers fused with those of the church—often they clashed.[30]

Discontent with and protests against the beliefs and practices of the medieval western Church of Rome led to the Protestant Reformation in the sixteenth century.[31] This made its mark predominantly in northern Europe with the termination of the jurisdiction of the Roman pontiff, the development of the principle that subjects should follow the religion of their ruler (*cuius regio eius religio*), and the establishment of state churches rooted in Lutheranism in present-day Germany,[32] Denmark,[33] Sweden,[34] and Finland.[35] Calvinism emerged in Switzerland,[36] and (what became) Anglicanism as the established religion of England.[37] However, the Reformation, Counter-Reformation (the revival of the Roman Catholic Church from the mid-sixteenth century), and Thirty Years War (between Catholic and

the 16th century). See also eg WM Watt, *The Influence of Islam in Medieval Europe* (Edinburgh: Edinburgh University Press, 1994): 1492 saw the expulsion of Islam from Spain and 1683 the Ottoman siege of Vienna.

[30] See eg J Witte and FS Alexander (eds), *Christianity and Law: An Introduction* (Cambridge: CUP, 2008); JA Brundage, *Medieval Canon Law* (London: Longman, 1995); RH Helmholz, *The Spirit of Classical Canon Law* (Athens, GA and London: University of Georgia Press, 1996); and J Herrin, *Byzantium: The Surprising Life of a Medieval Empire* (London: Allen Lane, 2007). For the interplay between canonical and common law ideas in England, see N Doe, *Fundamental Authority in Late Medieval English Law* (Cambridge: CUP, 1990).

[31] See generally E Cameron, *The European Reformation* (Oxford: Clarendon Press, 1991). For juridical aspects, see J Witte, *Law and Protestantism: The Legal Teachings of the Lutheran Reformation* (Cambridge: CUP, 2002).

[32] Inspired by Martin Luther (from 1517), the Protestant *Landeskirchen* emerged under the presidency of local rulers; however, the Catholic archbishops of Trier, Cologne, and Mainz were Prince Electors of the Holy Roman Empire (governed by the Habsburg dynasty and claiming its origins from Charlemagne who had been crowned as emperor by Pope Leo III in 800). The Peace of Augsburg, 1555, recognized the equality of Protestants and Catholics and the maxim *cuius regio eius religio*.

[33] Rome was dominant until 1536 when Christian III was crowned as a Lutheran king; he (and his council) issued a Church Ordinance (1537–9) on the Evangelical Lutheran Church as the state church; the *Lex Regia* 1665 gave the king competence over religious matters, and the Code Book (*Danske Lov*) 1683 (in book two) established the constitution of the church.

[34] The Augsburg Confession 1530 (the Lutheran confession of faith) was embraced in 1593 and the Evangelical-Lutheran Church was the established church in Sweden until 2000.

[35] The Lutheran Church displaced Rome *c* 1530, with the king as its head and a Church Code 1686.

[36] From 1541, John Calvin balanced ecclesiastical autonomy and civil authority in Geneva; Reformed Protestantism (often called Calvinism) became influential in parts of Germany, France, the Netherlands, and Scotland; the work of Zwingli was important in Zurich. 'Erastianism', the competence of the State over ecclesiastical matters, is named after the Swiss theologian Thomas Erastus (1524–85).

[37] In England, statutes from the 1530s established the Church of England with the monarch as its head; from *c* 1558, the church was conceived as both catholic and reformed. In Scotland, the Reformation (1560) resulted in the Presbyterian Church of Scotland being the national church (as it is today).

Protestant rulers in central Europe, 1618–48), each stimulated the introduction of intolerant laws.[38] Roman Catholicism suffered in a series of legal measures in England and Wales in the latter part of the reign of Elizabeth I (1558–1603), and it was banned by law in Latvia in 1621.[39] Equally, Protestantism suffered in, for example, present-day Lithuania and Poland, where the building of Protestant churches was forbidden in 1716 and the constitution of 1792 affirmed Catholicism as the 'national religion'.[40]

After the religious violence of the previous century and beyond, the eighteenth century heralded the entry of so-called Josephinism, which advocated religious toleration and the responsibility of the State to regulate religious conflict.[41] This stimulated the repeal of some laws which discriminated against religious minorities, as occurred in England, though in France tolerance came as a result of anti-clericalism towards the Catholic Church.[42] In turn, the nineteenth century witnessed the development of constitutional rights to religious freedom,[43] re-negotiation of the position of churches,[44] and in some States the separation of church and State.[45] However, elsewhere the bonds between State and church were strengthened, while at the same time formal safeguards of religious freedom were introduced to protect minorities. After the War of Independence (1821) the Orthodox Church became the prevailing religion in Greece (but its autonomy

---

[38] MR O'Connell, *The Counter Reformation 1559–1610* (London: Harper and Row, 1974); G Parker (ed), *The Thirty Years' War* (London: Routledge, 1984). The war ended with the Peace of Westphalia 1648—its two treaties used the Peace of Augsburg 1555 principle, *cuius regio eius religio* (see n 32 above).

[39] In England and Wales, anti-Catholic laws were made in the reign of Elizabeth I (1558–1603); but, for the survival of Roman canon law, see RH Helmholz, *Roman Canon Law in Reformation England* (Cambridge: CUP, 1990); Lutheran Sweden conquered parts of Latvia in 1621.

[40] Lithuania: anti-Protestant laws were enacted in 1630, 1648, 1666, and 1674; in 1791 the country was declared Catholic but when Russia annexed it in 1795, the Catholic Church was forbidden eg to publish literature and appoint bishops; after an uprising of 1863 its properties were confiscated.

[41] Josephinism expresses the principles which stimulated the reforms of Joseph II (Holy Roman Emperor 1765–90); see SK Padover, *The Revolutionary Emperor Joseph II of Austria 1741–1790* (London: Archon Books, 2nd edn, 1967).

[42] English intolerance towards dissenters was addressed by the Toleration Act 1689 and eg the Roman Catholic Relief Act 1829. The French Declaration of the Rights of Man and of the Citizen (1789) included freedom of belief (Art 10) and the Constitution (1791) religious freedom (Title 1); a Decree of 2 November 1789 nationalized church property (in return the State met clergy expenses); and the Civil Constitution of the Clergy (12 July 1790) rendered the church a public service; Poland: religious tolerance was introduced in a law of 1768 (prior to partition in 1772, 1793, and 1795).

[43] Belgium did so in its Constitution of 1831; Luxembourg, 1848; the Netherlands, 1814, 1815, and 1848 (prompting restoration of the Catholic hierarchy in 1853); Hungary, 1895. For international agreements which may have stimulated these developments, see MD Evans, *Religious Liberty and International Law in Europe* (Cambridge: CUP, 1997) chs 1 and 2.

[44] Napoleon Bonaparte negotiated a concordat between France and the Holy See in 1801 (elements of it remain today), but with severe limits on the church; some anti-clerical laws of the 1880s are still in force today. Italian unification (1860–70) led to tensions with the Catholic Church.

[45] The Irish Church Act 1869 disestablished the Church of Ireland; the Austrian Constitutional Act 1867 introduced state neutrality toward religion (retained in the Federal Constitution of 1920).

fluctuated with constitutional changes and religious freedom was guaranteed).[46]
Much the same happened later in Romania.[47] Similarly, Catholicism became the
national religion in Portugal under the constitution of 1822.[48] New legislation was
introduced in Denmark, where the Lutheran state church became the folk church
in 1849;[49] and in Finland (under Russian rule from 1809) a new Lutheran Code
was enacted in 1869 with religious freedom for dissenters in 1889.[50] The legal
implications of earlier Muslim expansion were also adjusted to political changes; for
instance, in Cyprus, Ottoman governance was displaced by the British common
law but elements of Islamic law continued.[51]

In the early twentieth century alongside guarantees of religious freedom in,
for example, Latvia, Lithuania, Germany, and Finland,[52] we see the introduction
of laws to separate further the State from religion in France (in 1905), with the
exception of its three eastern *départements*,[53] and to disestablish the Church of
England in Wales (in 1914).[54] However, the dominant theme after the First World
War is the legal consolidation of national religion. The Catholic Church was given
a special constitutional position in Malta (1921),[55] Poland (1921),[56] Ireland

[46] 'State-law rule' over the Orthodox Church (from a Decree of 1833) was repeated in the
Constitution 1844 but not in subsequent constitutions (1864–1952); but the 1968 and (current)
1975 constitutions recognized Orthodoxy as the prevailing religion.

[47] A statute of 1858 established the Metropolitan of the Romanian Orthodox Church as president
of the parliament; in 1866 a new constitution guaranteed religious freedom (Arts 5 and 21) but
recognized the Orthodox Church as the 'dominant religion in the state' (Art 21) and its metropolitan
and bishops were members of the Senate (Art 76).

[48] The constitution of 1822 provided that 'the religion of the Portuguese nation is Roman Catholic';
the Constitution of 1826 forbad religious persecution provided the State religion was respected.

[49] The 1849 constitution guaranteed religious freedom, and monarch and parliament assumed
competence over (what was by now known as) the Folk Church (*Folkekirke*).

[50] These laws were passed under the (Russian) Orthodox Grand Dukes.

[51] During British rule (1878–1960), the Ottoman Sultan retained ownership of the island and
Cypriots remained Ottoman subjects; the Ottoman decree Hatt-i-Humayun (1856) continued to
apply to religious authorities; the Orthodox Church functioned as both a religious organization of
Orthodox Christians and the political coalition for Greeks under foreign sovereignty.

[52] Latvia: decree on religious freedom 1906; Lithuania gained independence in 1918, and the 1922
Constitution promoted religious liberty; Germany: the Weimar Constitution of 1919 established
separation of State and church; Finland's independence from Russia (1919) led to the creation of new
religious freedom law (1922); the Czechoslovak Rep Constitution of 1920 also guaranteed religious
freedom.

[53] Law of Separation 1905; diplomatic relations with the Holy See were cut in 1904; the law does
not apply to Haut-Rhin, Bas-Rhin, or Moselle, which were formerly under German rule but returned
to France in 1918.

[54] Welsh Church Act 1914; disestablishment was postponed until after the First World War and
took place in 1920: see N Doe, *The Law of the Church in Wales* (Cardiff: University of Wales Press,
2002) ch 1.

[55] Invaded by France in 1798, under British rule (1814–1964) the position of the Catholic Church
was guaranteed; the instrument of self-government in 1921 did not provide for a state religion but the
first act of the Maltese legislative Assembly provided that Catholicism was the religion of Malta, and
this was repeated in the Constitution of 1964 after independence from Britain.

[56] The 1921 constitution invoked God and the first concordat with the Holy See was signed in
1925.

(1922),[57] Italy (1929),[58] Portugal (1935–71),[59] and Spain (1939–78).[60] Similarly, the Romanian Orthodox and Greek Catholic churches were given a special place in Romania, with the former having a more prominent legal position (1923),[61] and the newly founded Slovak Republic defined itself constitutionally as Christian in 1939.[62] Elsewhere, the legal regimes developed in the nineteenth century continued much as they were.

If the early twentieth century was significant for the consolidation or promotion of national religion, the aftermath of the Second World War saw a move in parts of Europe towards a greater formal separation between church and State. This was never more evident than under communism in the countries of central and eastern Europe, where atheism became official state policy and religion was suppressed.[63] In France, too, new constitutions reiterated the secular posture of the State towards religion.[64] However, at the same time, legal reforms facilitated greater cooperation between government and religion in Austria[65] and in Germany.[66] Indeed, the late twentieth century saw the emergence of international law standards on religion, the demise of communism, and an increase in formal separation but greater cooperation between State and religion.[67] In former communist countries, after 1989, new

[57] The Irish Free State Const 1922 provided for religious freedom and that 'all lawful authority comes from God to the people'; Const, 1937 invoked 'the Name of the Most Holy Trinity' and Art 44.1.2 provided: 'The State recognises the special position of the Holy Catholic Apostolic and Roman Church as the guardian of the Faith professed by the great majority of the citizens'; Art 44 also recognized the Church of Ireland, Presbyterian Church in Ireland, Methodist Church in Ireland, Religious Society of Friends in Ireland, and Jewish Congregations and other religious denominations; following a referendum, the Fifth Amendment of the Constitution Act 1972 deleted these two provisions.

[58] Entry to power of the Fascist party in 1922 led, under the Lateran Treaties 1929, to the creation of the Vatican State, and to a new law of 1929 on religious organizations.

[59] While separation followed the Republican revolution in 1910, the reinstatement of Catholicism led to concordats with the Holy See in 1940 (amended 1975) and 2004.

[60] Const 1931, Art 3 had established that Spain has no official religion; a concordat with the Holy See was signed in 1953.

[61] Const 1923, Art 7; Art 22: 'Orthodoxy is the religion of the majority, the Orthodox Church is the dominant church and the Greek Catholic Church has priority over the other religions' (this also placed the Orthodox Church under state control); Art 72: bishops and heads of other religions (if their members number over 200,000), and the Muslim leader were members of Senate; Const 1938 repeated these provisions.

[62] Const 1939, Preamble.

[63] S Ferrari and WC Durham (eds), *Law and Religion in Post-Communist Europe* (Leuven: Peeters, 2003). eg after its alliance with Germany, Bulgaria came under the Soviet Union in 1946—state and religion were separated and atheism became a state policy with severe religious repression; Czech Rep: a law of 1 November 1949 required state permission for religious activity and criminal prosecution if such permission was not obtained; Romania: the constitutions of 1947–89 removed earlier provisions on the dominant religion (Orthodoxy) but provided for religious freedom, though in practice there was hostility to religion (church schools were closed and church buildings demolished).

[64] Const 1946, Preamble, guarantees freedom of belief, and Const 1958, Art 2, provides that France is *laïque* (secular).

[65] After the reconstitution of Austria in 1945, the Concordat with the Holy See (1934) was recognized in 1957; legislation on recognized churches (1874) still operates alongside laws for the Protestants (1961), Orthodox (1967), and Jews (1982).

[66] Accepting responsibility for the mass murder of European Jews by Nazi-Germany in the 1940s—the Jewish religious community plays a specific role today.

[67] eg in the Netherlands, the 1983 constitutional revision protected religious freedom but state-funding of clergy salaries ended by agreement.

constitutions developed religious freedom and new laws were created for religious organizations.[68] Similarly, in Spain the demise of fascism resulted in separation with cooperation on the basis of a new constitution (1978) and statute (1980).[69] Much the same happened in Portugal[70] and Italy (where there are agreements with certain religious groups).[71] Nor have the national churches been immune from actual or potential legal reforms: the disestablishment debate is active in England;[72] the Swedish national church was disestablished in 2000;[73] and the position of the Finnish national church has been adjusted with a move towards greater autonomy.[74] As will be seen, the laws of the European Union, the United Nations, and the Council of Europe (with its European Convention on Human Rights) have also impacted greatly on religion.[75]

Today, the greater mobility and migration of people have increased the religious pluralism of Europe—this is particularly notable in the case of Islam.[76] But the historical patterns of religious demography persist.[77] Catholicism still predominates in Italy (90 per cent), Ireland (88 per cent), Portugal (85 per cent), Spain (80 per cent), France (80 per cent), Austria (73 per cent), and Belgium (70 per cent); it is also the majority religion in Luxembourg and Malta.[78] Protestantism predominates in Finland (85 per cent Lutheran, 1 per cent Orthodox), Denmark (84 per cent Lutheran), Sweden (80 per cent Lutheran), and the United Kingdom (where 71 per cent consider themselves 'Christian').[79] However, there are broadly equal numbers

---

[68] Anti-religious legislation was repealed in the Czech Rep (by Act of 13 December 1989), with religious freedom being protected under the Charter of Fundamental Rights and Liberties (1991) and Federal Act no 308/1991. New constitutions and laws on religious freedom and organizations have appeared eg in: Bulgaria (Const 1991, new laws, 2002); Latvia (Const 1998, new laws, 1995); Poland (1989, with a new concordat with the Holy See in 1993 and a new constitution in 1997).

[69] Following the death of Franco in 1975, a new concordat with the Holy See (1976) replaced that of 1953; the Constitution of 1978 guaranteed full religious freedom; there are agreements with the Holy See, Protestants, Jews, and Muslims, and a law on religious freedom was passed in 1980.

[70] The Const of 1976 and Law of Religious Liberty 2001 established separation and cooperation.

[71] A new Const of 1948 provided for religious liberty, a new agreement with the Holy See was concluded in 1984, and agreements have been signed with other religious groups since the 1980s.

[72] RM Morris (ed), *Church and State in 21st Century Britain: The Future of Church Establishment* (London: Palgrave Macmillan, 2009); in Northern Ireland (part of the UK since the 1920s) relations between Roman Catholics and Protestants still shape the political agenda.

[73] Political debate on the matter ended with disestablishment on 1 January 2000.

[74] The Lutheran and Orthodox Churches still enjoy public law status, unlike other faith groups; since 1993, the Lutheran Church has been regulated by a state-made Church Code (on church-state relations) and a church-made Church Ordinance (on its internal life and doctrine); since 2000, its bishops ceased being state officials; clergy are now church-funded (not state-funded). The new Const 1999 guarantees religious freedom (and is supplemented by a law of 2003).

[75] See Chs 1 and 2 (for the ECHR and UN) and Ch 10 (for the EU).

[76] See eg RJ Pauly, *Islam in Europe: Integration or Marginalisation?* (Aldershot: Ashgate, 2004), and J Klausen, *The Islamic Challenge: Politics and Religion in Western Europe* (Oxford: OUP, 2005).

[77] The following percentages are approximations; they are from G Robbers (ed), *State and Church in the European Union* (Baden-Baden: Nomos, 2nd edn, 2005) and the website of European Studies on Religion and State Interaction: <http://www.euresisnet.eu/Pages/Religion-State.aspx>.

[78] There are also significant minorities in these countries: eg in France Islam is the second largest religion with about 6m adherents; and Belgium has approximately 400,000 Muslims.

[79] Census, 2001 (England, Wales, Scotland); approximately 71% Christian, 16% non-religious, and 7.5% state no religious affiliation; *c* 5.5% belong to smaller denominations: Islam (2.78%), Hinduism (0.98%), Sikhism (0.59%), Judaism (0.47%), Buddhism (0.26%). In England, the Church

of Protestants and Catholics in Germany[80] and the Netherlands.[81] There are substantial Orthodox Christian majorities in Greece (95 per cent), and Cyprus (94 per cent). In the countries of central and eastern Europe, Orthodox Christianity predominates in Romania (86.8 per cent), and Bulgaria (83.7 per cent Christian, of which 82.6 per cent are Orthodox, and 12.2 per cent Muslim), but there are Catholic majorities in Poland (90 per cent), Lithuania (79 per cent), Slovakia (69 per cent), Slovenia (57.8 per cent), and Hungary (54.5 per cent, with 15.9 per cent belonging to Reformed churches). There are broadly equal numbers of Orthodox and Lutheran Christians in Latvia;[82] the same applies in Estonia, though here the majority claim no religious affiliation,[83] as is also the case in the Czech Republic, but here of those who do claim a religion, the majority is Catholic.[84] With these figures in mind, it is not surprising that, as will be seen, tensions abound concerning the rights of religious minorities under the contemporary national laws of Europe; and Strasbourg recognizes the continuing importance of historical approaches to religion.[85]

Each of the phases in the religious legal history of Europe has in its own way impacted on the long tradition of study in this field.[86] The coexistence of temporal and spiritual jurisdictions in the middle ages meant that the systematic study of the canon law of the western Christian church, alongside the civilian tradition of the study of Roman law, was prominent in the faculties of the medieval universities of Europe.[87] However, in countries affected by the Protestant Reformation in the sixteenth century and beyond, the teaching of Roman canon law was abandoned or replaced with study of State law applicable to the new national churches.[88] During the nineteenth century, the law of church-state relations

---

of England has *c* 1.4m members, the Roman Catholic Church *c* 0.93m, and other churches together *c* 1.28m.

[80] Population 82.5m; approximately 26.5m Catholics; 26.2m Protestants (the Lutheran and Reformed Churches, *Landeskirchen*, form the Evangelical Church of Germany (EKD)); Islam, 3.2m; Jewish, more than 100,000; Orthodox Christians, 1.2m.

[81] Catholics, 31%; United Reformed and Lutheran churches 21%; Muslims 886,000; and Hindus 95,000.

[82] Orthodox, 25%; Lutherans, 25%; Catholics 21%; non-believers, 12%.

[83] Of these, 23% are members of Christian churches: 11% belong to the Estonian Evangelical Lutheran Church, and 10% to the Orthodox Church.

[84] Population 10.3m: over 6m regard themselves as non-denominational (58.3% of the population); the Catholic Church has 2.7m; and the Evangelical Church of Czech Brethren about 117,000.

[85] *Dahlab v Switzerland*, App no 42393/98, 15 February 2001: 'It is not possible to discern throughout Europe a uniform conception of the significance of religion in society, and the meaning or impact of the public expression of a religious belief will differ according to time and context. Rules in this sphere will consequently vary from one country to another according to national traditions'.

[86] For an excellent overview, see the studies in JM González del Valle and A Hollerbach (eds), *The Teaching of Church-State Relations in European Universities* (Leuven: Peeters, 2005).

[87] See eg W Ullmann, *Law and Politics in the Middle Ages: An Introduction to the Sources of Medieval Political Ideas* (London: The Sources of History Limited, 1975), and RC van Caenegem, *Judges, Legislators and Professors: Chapters in European Legal History* (Cambridge: CUP, 1987).

[88] In England, the canon law faculties at Oxford and Cambridge were dissolved in the 1530s and in Germany the study of *kirchenstaatsrecht* originated in the Reformation, but discussions about canon law persisted in eg Italy and France in the works of jurists such as GB de Luca (d 1683), *Theatrum veritatis, etc* (23 vols, Rome, 1669–81); Anaclet Reiffenstuel (d 1703), *Jus canonicum universum* (6 vols,

emerges as a distinct academic discipline among scholars at universities in, for example, Germany,[89] Denmark,[90] Greece,[91] and Portugal.[92] This ebb and flow of national religion, separation, and cooperation between State and religion generated study on law and religion in the early twentieth century in Italy,[93] Spain,[94] and, later in the century, in France[95] and the United Kingdom.[96] Today universities across Europe (in their law schools or their theology faculties) teach at least aspects of national laws on church-state relations,[97] and the demise of communism has stimulated academic research in the subject in central and eastern Europe.[98] There are also now specialized institutes, research clusters, and learned societies devoted to the study of law and religion at national level, as well as international postgraduate programmes.[99]

Venice, 1763–66); Lucius Ferraris (d *c* 1763), *Prompta bibliotheca canonica* (3 vols, Bologna, 1746); and Durand de Maillane (d 1814), *Dictionnaire de droit canonique* (Lyon, 2nd edn, 1710).

[89] Scholars include Paul Hinschius (1835–98, Kiel and Berlin), *Das kirchenrecht der katholiken und protestanten in Deutschland* (6 vols, Berlin, 1869–77); Emil Albert Friedberg (1837–1910, Leipzig and Strasbourg), *Lehrbuch des katholischen und evangelischen Kirchenrechts* (6 vols, Leipzig, 1903); and Rudolph Sohm (1841–1917, Freiburg, Strasbourg, and Leipzig), 'Das Verhältnis von Staat und Kirche aus dem Begriff von Staat und Kirche entwickelt' (1872) 11 *Zeitschrift fürt Kirchenrecht* 157–84.

[90] See eg CD Hedegaard (d 1781), *Danske Lov* (1775, a commentary on the Danish church law book of 1683); Hedegaard built on the work of JLA Kolderup-Rosenvinge (d 1850), *Grundrids af den danske kirkeret* (2 vols, 1838–40); EF Larsen, *Den danske kirkeret* (1901–12); church law was introduced into the law faculty of the University of Copenhagen in 1821 (until 1871).

[91] The first ecclesiastical law professor at the law faculty of Athens was M Potlis (1855–62), see eg his *Syntagma of the Holy Canons* (6 vols, Athens, 1852–59).

[92] Portuguese ecclesiastical law was introduced at the University of Coimbra in 1859 but this was suppressed by a Decree of 16 November 1910 (on the republican separation between church and State).

[93] Italian scholars in the early 20th century included Francesco Scaduto (1858–1942), *Il diritto ecclesiastico vigente in Italia* (2 vols, Turin, 189–1); and Arturo Carlo Jemolo (1891–1981), *Lezioni di diritto ecclesiastico* (Milan, 4th edn, 1979); both were stimulated by the concordat signed with the Holy See in 1929.

[94] Initially, Catholic canon lawyers became interested in the subject following the signing of the concordat with the Holy See in 1953; these included Pedro Lombardía (1930–86), *Derecho eclesiástico del estado* (5 vols, Pampelune, 1980–91).

[95] Whilst there was no such tradition in French law schools, scholars such as Gabriel le Bras (1891–1970) and Jean Gaudemet (1908–2001) worked on the history of canon law and state religion law.

[96] See R Sandberg, *Law and Religion* (Cambridge: CUP, 2011) ch 1.

[97] For a historical overview and modern studies in this field, see JM González del Valle and A Hollerbach (eds), *The Teaching of Church-State Relations in European Universities* (Leuven: Peeters, 2005) 63 *et seq*, 105 *et seq*, 174 *et seq*, eg in Germany traditionally, *kirchenrecht* (the history of church law and church-state relations) is studied in theology faculties, and *staatskirchenrecht* (law on church-state relations) as part of public law in law schools.

[98] The scholars include Jiří Rajmund Tretera (Czech Republic), M Kiviorg (Estonia), Ringolds Balodis (Latvia), J Kuznecoviene (Lithuania), B Schanda (Hungary), M Rynkowski (Poland), L Šturm (Slovenia), and M Moravčíková (Slovakia); see the Bibliography for their works.

[99] eg Austria has an *Institut für Recht und Religion* at the Vienna Law Faculty. In the UK, the Law and Religion Scholars Network (LARSN) was set up in 2008 under the auspices of the Centre for Law and Religion established at Cardiff Law School in 1998. There is the Society for Church Law in Denmark (*Selskab for Kirkeret*, est 1989), the Church Law Society of the Czech Republic, and, in the UK, the Ecclesiastical Law Society (est 1987). The International Consortium for Law and Religion Studies (ICLARS) was set up in 2008.

This book seeks to compare the national laws on religion in Europe, in the context of the wider legal environment of EU law and the ECHR. As has been seen, its focus is a subject close to the heart of the legal, political, and religious history of Europe–it is also part and parcel of a long tradition of academic study in this field. However, the subject brings its own methodological challenges–not least in terms of the volume and variety of laws studied. Indeed, in the quest for shared principles, the study concentrates on primary legal sources rather than secondary national commentaries (see, for example, those in G Robbers (ed), *State and Church in the European Union* (Baden-Baden: Nomos, 2nd edn, 2005)). In consequence, each chapter that follows carries extensive footnotes which refer to the primary legal materials.[100] These are designed not only to provide the legal evidence for propositions which appear in the text, but also to allow national laws to speak for themselves. Unless the text or context provide otherwise, references to national legal sources in the footnotes are merely examples—when legal provisions are unique to one State, this is indicated. Secondary literature is listed in the Bibliography which, in addition to the principal works in the English language on national laws on religion, carries a list of studies for further reading in the languages of each country examined. An Appendix of the principles of religion law common to the States of Europe is included towards the end of this book. These, it is suggested, are what emerge from a study of national laws on religion in Europe.

---

[100] Alongside references to constitutions and legislation, there are very many references to judicial decisions. However, it is important to distinguish here between the case-law of ordinary courts and that of Constitutional Courts. This distinction is clarified throughout the book in the references, lest the impression be given of juridical equivalence between these essentially different species of case-law. This is because, of course, in the civilian tradition judicial decisions are not binding precedents as they are in the common law tradition—cases cited in this book from the former are illustrative of, among other things, the ways in which legislation is applied to concrete factual circumstances.

1

The Scope, Sources, and Systems of Religion Law

The historical forces—political, religious, and social—which have shaped the religious complexion of modern Europe continue in one way or another to affect the character of national laws. This is the case with regard to the sources and subject-matter of national religion laws, the legal definitions of religion, and the postures which States have towards state-religion relations. The formal sources used by States to regulate religion are much the same as they were a century ago, but international law has now made its mark alongside domestic sources. The same applies to the subjects treated by national laws—religious freedom and the autonomy of religious organizations persist as regulated topics—but the rise of religious pluralism has led to an increase in laws on religious discrimination and hatred, for example. The emergence of the separation of church and State, and in many countries greater cooperation between government and religions (especially in the twentieth century), also account for the contemporary understanding that there are now three state-religion models at work in Europe: state-church; separation; and cooperation. Even the expressions used across Europe to represent state law on religion echo the historical role of Christianity: the terms ecclesiastical law, church law, confessional law, and the law of church and State being still the most common.[1] The following seeks to elucidate principles of religion law common to the States of Europe in terms of their scope, sources, and postures.

The sources of religion law

States regulate religion by means of two basic sources: internal—national domestic laws; and external—international laws which have been domesticated by means of ratification or incorporation into national law (often with constitutional status). Identifying formal legal sources also reveals the subject-matter of religion law.

---

[1] eg in Spain, *el derecho eclesiástico del estado* is the law of the State which deals with all religions not simply Christian churches; in Denmark, *kirkeret* (church law) is used similarly; in Poland, law on religion is *prawo wyznaniowe*—confessional law; in Germany, it is *staatskirchenrecht*; but in England, 'ecclesiastical law' applies only to the established Church of England: N Doe, *The Legal Framework of the Church of England* (Oxford: Clarendon Press, 1996) ch 1.

Internal sources: domestic religion laws

The principal domestic instruments which States employ to regulate religion are constitutions; sub-constitutional laws, case-law, or jurisprudence; and, in some countries, agreements, and regional laws.[2] European constitutions generally deal with the fundamentals of relations between the State and religion,[3] and, occasionally, the rule of law and religion.[4] In their treatment of fundamental rights they address religious freedom,[5] or aspects of this such as freedom of belief,[6] or freedom of worship,[7] as well as religious discrimination,[8] or the equality of religions.[9] Constitutions may also regulate religious organizations,[10] including national churches,[11] the funding of religion,[12] religious education in public schools,[13] and conscientious objection.[14] Equally, sub-constitutional laws (enacted under legislative powers conferred by the constitution, and often designed to complement it), treat a wide range of religious subjects, including: religious freedom,[15] religious organizations,[16] both topics sometimes addressed in a single statute,[17] religious

---

[2] We shall also see that States increasingly use quasi-legislation—informal rules to supplement formal laws on religion (such as circulars or guidance); see generally N Doe, 'Ecclesiastical quasi-legislation' in N Doe, M Hill, and R Ombres (eds), *English Canon Law* (Cardiff: University of Wales Press, 1998) 93.

[3] Cyprus: Const, Art 109; Ireland: Const, Art 44.2.2; Poland: Const, Art 25.

[4] Denmark: Const, Art 71: no person shall be committed to prison by reason of their religious conviction; Lithuania: Const, Art 28: religion does not justify the violation of law.

[5] Finland: Const, Art 11; Denmark: Const, Art 67; Greece: Const, Art 13; Ireland: Const, Art 44.2.1; Spain: Const, Art 16; Italy: Const, Art 19; Hungary: Const, Art 60; Latvia: Const, Art 99; Lithuania: Const, Arts 25, 26; Netherlands: Const, Art 6; Poland: Const, Art 53.

[6] France: Const, 1958, Preamble: this refers to the Declaration of the Rights of Man and of the Citizen 1789 and to the preamble of the Const 1946 on freedom of belief; Art 2: France 'assures the equality before the law of all its citizens without distinction of origin, race or religion. It respects all beliefs'.

[7] Denmark: Const, Art 68; Belgium: Const, Arts 19, 20; Italy: Const, Art 20; Luxembourg: Const, Art 19; Malta: Const, Art 40.

[8] Denmark: Const, Art 70; Cyprus: Const, Art 28; Spain: Const, Art 14(2); Ireland: Const, Art 44.2.3; Italy: Const, Art 3(1); Malta: Const, Art 32; Netherlands: Const, Art 1; Slovenia: Const, Art 14; Finland: Const, Art 6.

[9] Cyprus: Const, Arts 18, 23, 28; Italy: Const, Art 8.1.

[10] Austria: StGG, Art 15; Belgium: Const, Art 21; Cyprus: Const, Art 110; Ireland: Const, Art 44.2.5; Italy: Const, Art 7; Slovenia: Const, Art 7; Sweden: Const, Art 8.6.

[11] Denmark: Arts 4, 69; Finland: Const, Art 76; Malta: Const, Art 2; Greece: Const, Art 3.

[12] Luxembourg: Const, Art 106; Ireland: Const, Art 44.2.2.

[13] Germany: GG, Art 7; Netherlands: Const, Art 23; Poland: Const, Art 48.

[14] Slovenia: Const, 1991, Art 46; Finland: Const, Art 127(2).

[15] France: Law of 1905, Art 1: 'The republic assures freedom of conscience. It guarantees the free exercise of religion subject only to the restrictions mentioned hereafter in the interest of public order'; Spain: LORF, Organic Law 7/1980 of 5 July.

[16] Austria: RCA 1874, FLSCC 1998 (BeKGG), Interconfessional Relations Act 1868.

[17] Czech Rep: Act no 3/2002 Sb; Hungary: Act 4/1990; Latvia: LORO 1995, Art 7; Poland: Law of 17 May 1989 (Dz U (OJ) 1989, no 29, Item 55; Portugal: Law 16/2001 of 22 June; Slovenia: ALPRC—OG, SRS, Nos 15/76, 42/86, 22/91; Slovakia: Act no 308/1991 Zb (amended by Act no 394/2000 Zz), Act no 192/1992 Zb; Finland: Act 453 of 2003; Spain: LORF, Law 7/1980 of 5 July, Art 7(1); Sweden: Religious Communities Act 1998, Lagen (1998:1593) and (1998:1591).

education,[18] religious property,[19] the financing of religion,[20] chaplaincies,[21] religious dress,[22] and religious marriages.[23] There are also laws of general applicability to wider fields with specific provisions which affect religion within those fields, such as: discrimination law and religious equality,[24] criminal law and the vilification of religion,[25] heritage and planning law and places of worship,[26] taxation law and religious exemptions,[27] education law and religious education,[28] abortion law and rights of medical personnel to refrain on religious grounds from participating in abortions,[29] and military law and conscientious objections to military service.[30]

Needless to say, judicial decisions are a fundamental source of law on religion for States which participate in the common law tradition, such as the United Kingdom, Ireland, and Cyprus.[31] However, case-law on religion is important across Europe,[32] including in States of the civilian tradition, like Italy and Spain,[33] and it is active in the States of central and eastern Europe, such as on the constitutionality of law on religion;[34] the jurisprudence of the German Constitutional Court is

---

[18] Latvia: LORO, Art 6; Lithuania: LORCA, Art 14; Portugal: Decree-Law 323/83 of 5 July, Ordinance 333/86 of 2 July, through to Decree-Law 329/98 of 2 November.

[19] Lithuania: LORCA, Arts 13, 16, 17, 18 (property and labour relations); Slovakia: Act no 282/1993 Zz; and for financing of churches and ministers' salaries, Government Decree no 578/1990 Zb.

[20] France: Law of 1905, Art 2; Hungary: Act 32/1991 (property), Act 124/1997 (finance); Sweden: Act on Levies to Religious Denominations, Lagen (1999:291) and Act on Contributions to Denominations, Lagen (1999:932): other than to the Church of Sweden.

[21] Portugal: DL 79/83 of 9 February, 345/85 of 23 August, 34-A/90 of 24 January, 93/91 of 26 February.

[22] France: Law of 15 March 2004 on the display of religious symbols in public schools.

[23] Sweden: Act on Officiating of Marriages within Denominations other than the Church of Sweden, Lagen (1993:305); UK: Marriage Act 1949; see also Divorce (Religious Marriages) Act 2002.

[24] Denmark: Const, Art 70; Act on Prohibition of Discrimination in the Labour Market (459/1996).

[25] Malta: PC, Arts 163–165; Belgium: PC, Arts 143, 144, 268; Luxembourg: PC, Arts 145, 268.

[26] Malta: Act VI of 2002; Ireland: Planning and Development Act 2000, s 4(2), Regs 2001 (SI no 600) Art 10; Sweden: Cultural Heritage Act, Lagen (1988:950).

[27] Greece: LD 1249/1982; UK: Sharing of Church Buildings Act 1969.

[28] Austria: RelUG, s 1(2), PrivSchG, s 20; Luxembourg: Law of 31 May 1982.

[29] Austria: Strafgesetzbuch, s 97 (abortion), FortpflanzungsG, s 6 (medically assisted procreation).

[30] Austria: ZivildienstG, s 291; Greece: Law 1763/1988, Art 6; Portugal: Law 7/92 of 12 May.

[31] eg Ireland: *McGrath and O Ruairc v Trustees of the College of Maynooth* [1979] ILRM 166: the autonomy of religious organizations; *Campaign to Separate Church and State Ltd v Minister for Education* [1998] 3 IR 321, [1998] 2 ILRM 81: funding chaplains in schools.

[32] Denmark: HC, Case U 2000.2350: religious headscarves in the work place; Netherlands: SC, HR, 19 January 1962, NJ 1962, 107: the then existing constitutional prohibition on religious processions was held compatible with ECHR, Art 9; Greece: COS, Decision 1444/1991 on the Ancient Calanderists.

[33] Italy: CCt, Decision no 195, 27 April 1993 (on the Church of Scientology); Spain: CCt, Judgment 46/2001, 15 February (defining religion); Portugal: CCt, Decisions 92/84 of 7 November, 423/87 of 26 November, and 174/93 of 17 February; and France: CCl, Decision CC, no 77–87 DC 23.11.1977 (religious freedom).

[34] Czech Rep: CCt, 27 November 2002 no Pl US 6/02, overturning elements of a 2002 Act on registration of religious organizations; Lithuania: CCt, Ruling, 13 June 2000 no 49-1424: 'naming churches . . . as traditional is not an act establishing them as [such]' but simply states their factual status in society; Slovenia: CCt, Decision no U-I-68/98 (November 2001); and no Rm-1/02-21 (November 2003): the agreement with the Holy See was consistent with the constitution; Slovakia: CCt, Decision no Pl U 18/95 24 May 1995 on exemption from military service under Const, Art 25(2)); CCt, Decision no III US 156/05–5, 1 June 2005 on employment law and churches.

particularly rich in this field.[35] Agreements between a State and a religious organization, such as the Holy See,[36] or other religious entity, may also be a source of legal rules, when the agreement is ratified by law.[37] These agreements deal with a variety of subjects, such as pastoral care in prisons and the armed forces,[38] or education.[39] Federalism in some States, and devolution in others, has also led to a rise in regional laws on religion: this is the case in Belgium, Spain, and the United Kingdom;[40] regional law which forbids religious discrimination is found in Austria;[41] and there are agreements between religious organizations and regional government below federal level in Germany.[42] The variety of legal instruments used to regulate religion, and the range of matters regulated, indicate the pervasiveness of religion in society, the extent of the competence assumed by States over religion, and the level at which such matters are best treated.

External sources of religion law: international law

There are three main external sources for national religion laws in Europe: the law of the European Union (which is dealt with in Chapter 10),[43] the European Convention on Human Rights (of the Council of Europe), and the global international law of the United Nations.[44] Along with other matters associated with religion,[45] the European Convention on Human Rights (ECHR) protects religious freedom, and the right to hold and to manifest religious belief, as well as the authority of the State to limit the exercise of the right to manifest religion.[46]

---

[35] Particularly on religious freedom and the autonomy of religious organizations, see Chs 2 and 5 below.

[36] Concordats with the Holy See (a juridical person in international law) have the status of treaties under international law; they include Luxembourg: Concordat 1801; Germany: Reichskonkordat 1933; Portugal: Concordat 7 May 1940 as amended 15 February 1975, and 18 May 2004; see below.

[37] Spain: LORF, Organic Law 7/1980 of 5 July, Art 7: cooperation agreements must be ratified by statute; Netherlands: an agreement of 1983 to terminate government funding of ministers of religion was ratified by statute; Poland: Law of 20 February 1997 ratifies an agreement with the Pentecostal Church.

[38] Czech Rep: agreement on pastoral service in prisons between the Prison Administration, Ecumenical Council of Churches and Catholic Bishops' Conference (1999).

[39] Lithuania: agreement with the Holy See (5 May 2000).

[40] Belgium: Law of 13 July 2001, Art 4; Spain: see JG Oliva and D Lambert, 'Regional ecclesiastical law: religion and devolution in Spain and Wales' in N Doe and R Sandberg (eds), *Law and Religion: New Horizons* (Leuven: Peeters, 2010) 219.

[41] Austria: eg the Viennese Agricultural Labour Equal Treatment Act, Viennese Provincial Law Gazette Nos 25/1980 and 38/2008: this deals with the religion of agricultural and forestry workers.

[42] Germany: many aspects of religion-state relations are governed by the laws of the *Bundesländer* (Federal States), and agreements between these and religious organizations; see Ch 4 below.

[43] Reference is also made to this in other chapters when EU law is implemented by national laws, such as in the field of religion and data protection (Ch 2), and religious discrimination (Ch 3).

[44] For historical antecedents to both the ECHR and UN law, see MD Evans, *Religious Liberty and International Law in Europe* (Cambridge: CUP, 1997) esp chs 1–7.

[45] ECHR, Art 14: discrimination; Art 2 First Protocol: education; see Chs 3 and 9 below.

[46] ECHR, Art 9: '1. Everyone has the right to freedom of thought, conscience and religion; this right includes freedom to change his religion or belief and freedom, either alone or in community with others and in public or private, to manifest his religion or belief, in worship, teaching, practice and observance. 2. Freedom to manifest one's religion or beliefs shall be subject only to such limitations as

The importance of the ECHR for religious liberty is recognized by most commentators,[47] particularly the role of the European Court of Human Rights,[48] though some question its value today.[49] All States of the EU have ratified the ECHR, though its status within national laws varies from State to State: in States with a monist approach to international law, the ECHR is applicable directly on ratification without further enactment by the state legislature,[50] but in those with a dualist system, ratification must be followed by legislation for incorporation in national law.[51] In turn, in many States the ECHR is part of the constitutional order and as such may have primacy over national law,[52] but in others it is not: in Ireland, the courts may make a declaration of incompatibility between any statutory provision or rule of law and the ECHR but such a declaration does not make the law unconstitutional or otherwise invalid and so susceptible to judicial challenge; the United Kingdom is similar.[53]

ECHR provisions and abundant jurisprudence on religion have played a greater role in the courts of some States than in others.[54] For example, it has been invoked in relation to religious education in public schools (in Poland),[55] religious freedom (in Romania),[56] and corporal punishment (in the United Kingdom).[57] Indeed, the Austrian Constitutional Court has held that national constitutional and ECHR protection of religious freedom are to be understood as an integrated whole.[58] However, whilst the ECHR may be commonly invoked, remarkably little use has

---

are prescribed by law and are necessary in a democratic society in the interests of public safety, for the protection of public order, health or morals, or for the protection of the rights and freedoms of others.'

[47] See eg J Martinez-Torrón, 'Religious liberty in European jurisprudence' in M Hill (ed), *Religious Liberty and Human Rights* (Cardiff: University of Wales Press, 2002) 99–100.

[48] M Janis, R Kay, and A Bradley, *European Human Rights Law* (Oxford: OUP, 2nd edn, 2000) vii, 30.

[49] PM Taylor, *Freedom of Religion: UN and European Human Rights Law and Practice* (Cambridge: CUP, 2005) xi: 'The escalating religious intolerance of recent years, both through State violation and by non-State entities, is most conspicuous in events following the collapse of the former Soviet Union, in religious conflict in many parts of the world, and, of course, in the attacks of 11 September 2001. This has caused speculation whether the international instruments which were developed more than half a century ago . . . are sufficient to meet present and foreseeable demands.'

[50] Estonia: Const, Arts 3, 123; it ratified the ECHR in 1996; France, in 1974.

[51] Cyprus: Law, no 39/1962; Hungary: Act XXXI/1993; Italy: Const, Art 10: 'The legal system of Italy conforms to the generally recognized principles of international law'; Art 80 (ratification).

[52] Austria: ratified 1958 as part of the constitutional order: BGBl 219/1958, BVG BGBl 59/1964; Luxembourg: Law of Ratification 29 August 1953; for the cases see Cass, 14 July 1954, Pas Lux 16, 150, 152; Cour d'Appel, 13 November 2001, *Ann dr lux* 12 (2002) 455; Romania: ratified by Law no 30 1994; Finland: ratified 1990 (under Const, Art 95.2); Sweden ratified 1952, incorporated 1995.

[53] Ireland, Const Art 29.6: 'no international agreement shall be part of the domestic law of the State save as may be determined by the Oireachtas'; ratified 1953, incorporated by ECHR Act 2003, ss 1–4; UK: Human Rights Act 1998; see also Cyprus: T Hadjanastassiou, 'The European Convention on Human Rights applicable in Cyprus' (1976) 3 Cyprus Law Tribune 97.

[54] C Evans, *Freedom of Religion under the European Convention on Human Rights* (Oxford: OUP, 2001).

[55] Poland: CCt, Case U 12/92; since then Art 9 has been rarely invoked: CCt, Case K 44/2002 (but only in passing in a dissenting judgment).

[56] Romania: SC, Decision no 1934, 7.7.1999.

[57] UK: *R v Secretary of State for Education and Employment and ors, ex p Williamson* [2005] UKHL 15.

[58] Austria: VfSlg 16.054/2000; cf VfSlg 15.680/1999; VfSlg 15.394/1998; VfSlg 15.592/1999.

been made of Strasbourg jurisprudence on religion by courts in France,[59] Estonia,[60] Italy,[61] and Ireland, where it has been understood that provisions of the ECHR on religion 'guarantee substantially the same rights with regard to free practice of religion' as those contained in the Irish constitution.[62] This is not surprising—domestic protection of religious freedom is now deeply embedded in the legal cultures of Europe: some constitutional provisions are ancient and many pre-date the ECHR,[63] and they operate regardless of whether the country has a state church,[64] a system of separation,[65] or one of cooperation.[66] Nevertheless, the ECHR has influenced the development of constitutional texts in several States as evidenced by the similarities between these and the text of the ECHR.[67] Moreover, in several States Article 9 and Strasbourg jurisprudence enjoyed persuasive authority prior to formal ratification of the ECHR.[68]

In the wider environment of global international law, European States are also subject to the standards set by the United Nations, with its Human Rights Committee and Special Rapporteur on religion or belief (who examines incidents inconsistent with international standards). The United Nations has four instruments relevant to the field of religion.[69] Article 18 of the Universal Declaration of Human Rights 1948 provides for religious freedom and limitations on its exercise, and is almost identical to Article 9 ECHR,[70] as is Article 18 of the International

---

[59] France: CCl, Decision no 77-87 DC 23.11.1977 (religious education).

[60] Estonia: SC, Cases no III-4/A-4/93, 4.11.1993 (RT III 1993, 72/73, 1052); no III-4/A-1/94, 12.1.1994 (RT III 1994, 8, 129); no III-4/A-2/94, 12.1.1994 (RT III 1994, 8, 130).

[61] Italy: CCt, Decision no 388 of 1999: 'human rights protected by universal or regional conventions signed by Italy are expressed—and protected with the same intensity—by the Constitution'. However, the draft law on religious freedom of the Constitutional Affairs Commission, Chamber of Deputies, July 2007, explicitly refers to the ECHR.

[62] Ireland: Report of the Constitution Review Group (1996) 380; see eg *Murphy v Independent Radio and Television Commission* [1999] 1 IR 12: this involved advertisements claimed to be offensive to religion and was resolved under ECHR, Art 10.

[63] Belgium: Const (1831), Art 19; France: Declaration of the Rights of Man etc (1789), Art 10; Const 1946, Preamble, 5: no one can be wronged in his work or employment by reason of his origins, opinions or beliefs; Const, 1958, Art 1.

[64] Finland: Const (2000), Art 11; Denmark: Const, Art 67; Greece: Const, Art 13.

[65] Ireland: Const, Art 44. 2.1.

[66] Germany: GG, Art 4: 'Freedom of faith and of conscience, and freedom to profess a religious or philosophical creed, shall be inviolable'; Italy: Const, Art 19.

[67] Czech Rep: Const, Arts 15 and 16 are almost identical to Art 9 ECHR; see also Hungary: Const, Art 60; Slovenia: Const, Art 41.1; Bulgaria: Const, Art 13(1)–(4).

[68] Cyprus: *AG v Ibrahim* [1964] CLR 195, 225; UK: *Ahmad v Inner London Education Authority* [1978] QB 36; but even post-incorporation, Strasbourg case-law enjoys only persuasive not binding authority—the courts must consult but have no duty to follow it: Human Rights Act 1998, s 2(1); Ireland: the following cases on religion were resolved under Const, Art 44 not the ECHR: *Quinn's Supermarket v Attorney General* [1972] IR 1; *Campaign to Separate Church and State Ltd v Minister for Education* [1998] 2 ILRM 81; *Corway v Independent Newspapers (Ireland) Ltd* [1999] 4 IR 484.

[69] See MD Evans, *Religious Liberty and International Law in Europe* (Cambridge: CUP, 1997) chs 8 and 9. For comparison of UN law and the ECHR, see PM Taylor, *Freedom of Religion* (Cambridge: CUP, 2005).

[70] 'Everyone has the right to freedom of thought, conscience and religion; this right includes freedom to change his religion or belief, and freedom, either alone or in community with others and in public or private, to manifest his religion or belief in teaching, practice, worship and observance'; States may impose limits on the right to manifest religion on the basis of Art 29.2: 'In the exercise of his rights

Covenant on Civil and Political Rights 1966.[71] Alongside this binding treaty law, there is the non-binding Declaration on Elimination of All Forms of Intolerance and Discrimination Based on Religion or Belief 1981, which deals in Article 1 with religious freedom and in Article 2 with religious discrimination.[72] The Convention on the Rights of the Child 1989 deals with religious freedom of parents and children as well as religious discrimination against children.[73] Most European States have ratified these,[74] and they are occasionally invoked by national courts.[75]

Legal definitions of religion

An understanding of the nature of religion is implicit in global international law in its treatment of the elements of religious freedom—religion involves belief which may be manifested in teaching, practice, worship, and observance.[76] Equally implicit are the notions that religion involves choice,[77] individual or collective action,[78] and a host of activities such as the maintenance of sacred places, charitable initiatives, rituals and customs, dissemination of belief, training, appointment and functions of leaders, observance of holy days, and adherence to principles in the

and freedoms, everyone shall be subject only to such limitations as are determined by law solely for the purpose of securing due recognition and respect for the rights and freedoms of others and of meeting the just requirements of morality, public order and the general welfare in a democratic society.'

[71] ICCPR (1966) UN HR Cn; Art 18: '1. Everyone shall have the right to freedom of thought, conscience and religion. This right shall include freedom to have or adopt a religion or belief of his choice, and freedom, either individually or in community with others and in public or private, to manifest his religion or belief in worship, observance, practice and teaching. 2. No one shall be subject to coercion which would impair his freedom to have or to adopt a religion or belief of his choice. 3. Freedom to manifest one's religion or belief may be subject to such limitations as are prescribed by law and necessary to protect public safety, order, health or morals or the fundamental rights and freedoms of others. 4. The States Parties to the present Covenant undertake to have respect for the liberty of parents and, where applicable, legal guardians to ensure the religious and moral education of their children in conformity with their own convictions.'

[72] UNDID, Art 1: '1. Everyone shall have the right to freedom of thought, conscience and religion. This right shall include freedom to have a religion or whatever belief of his choice, and freedom, either individually or in community with others and in public or private, to manifest his religion or belief in worship, observance, practice and teaching. 2. No one shall be subject to coercion which would impair his freedom to have a religion or belief of his choice. 3. Freedom to manifest one's religion or belief may be subject only to such limitations as are prescribed by law and are necessary to protect public safety, order, health or morals or the fundamental rights and freedoms of others.'

[73] For the UNCRC, see S Langlaude, *The Right of the Child to Religious Freedom in International Law* (Leiden: Martinus Nijhoff Publishers, 2007); see Ch 9 below.

[74] eg ICCPR and UNCRC have been ratified and are court-enforceable in Belgium, Bulgaria, Cyprus, the Czech Republic, Denmark, Estonia, Finland, Germany, Greece, Hungary, Latvia, Lithuania, the Netherlands, Poland, Spain; ICCPR has been ratified but is not enforceable in Austria, France, Ireland, Italy, Luxembourg, Sweden; the same applies to UNCRC in Austria, Ireland, and Sweden.

[75] Romania: HC of Cassation, Decision 1088/2006 invoked ICCPR, Art 18; Netherlands: HR 19 January 1962, NJ 1962, 107 (also invoking Art 18); Poland: CCt, K 26/00 (Art 22).

[76] UDHR, Art 18 (see n 70 above).

[77] ICCPR, Art 18 (see n 71 above).

[78] UNDID, Art 1 (see n 72 above).

lives of believers.[79] Similarly, Article 9 ECHR associates religion with belief and the manifestation of belief in teaching, worship, practice, and observance, but Strasbourg is often criticized for its failure to define 'religion'.[80] Nevertheless, to attract protection, for Strasbourg beliefs must have 'a certain level of cogency, serious reflection and importance',[81] not simply being 'mere opinions or deeply held feelings', but rather spiritual or philosophical convictions with an identifiable formal content.[82] Strasbourg takes a liberal approach to the definition of belief: its institutions have considered claims concerning, for example, scientology, druidism, pacifism, and atheism.[83]

The criteria used to recognize religion

At the national level, it may be necessary to define 'religion' in order to determine whether legal benefits and burdens apply in particular circumstances, for example whether a claim is properly one of religious freedom, whether an exception to discrimination law is religious, or whether an activity is for the advancement of religion.[84] However, the States of Europe do not generally define 'religion' in their constitutions or other formal legislation, but, rather, leave it to the courts to determine whether something is 'religion'.[85] Consequently, the nature of religion is most usually elucidated in case-law, though sometimes also in statements issued

---

[79] ibid Art 6: freedom of religion shall include, *inter alia*, 'the following freedoms: (a) To worship or assemble in connection with a religion or belief, and to establish and maintain places for these purposes; (b) To establish and maintain appropriate charitable or humanitarian institutions; (c) To make, acquire and use to an adequate extent the necessary articles and materials related to the rites or customs of a religion or belief; (d) To write, issue and disseminate relevant publications in these areas; (e) To teach a religion or belief in places suitable for these purposes; (f) To solicit and receive voluntary financial and other contributions from individuals and institutions; (g) To train, appoint, elect or designate by succession appropriate leaders called for by the requirements and standards of any religion or belief; (h) To observe days of rest and to celebrate holidays and ceremonies in accordance with the precepts of one's religion or belief; (i) To establish and maintain communications with individuals and communities in matters of religion and belief at the national and international levels'.

[80] R Ahdar and I Leigh, *Religious Freedom in the Liberal State* (Oxford: OUP, 2005) 122, 124: 'It is a frequent criticism of the jurisprudence on Article 9 . . . that it has failed almost entirely to confront the issue of defining religion . . . The reason why . . . may be [that] courts harbour a general unwillingness to differentiate religion from other beliefs deemed worthwhile'. See also C Evans, *Freedom of Religion under the European Convention on Human Rights* (Oxford: OUP, 2001) 53.

[81] *Campbell and Cosans v UK* (1982) 4 EHRR 293. See also: The Office for Democratic Institutions and Human Rights, *Guidelines for Review of Legislation Pertaining to Religion or Belief* (2004) Section A, para 3: 'The "belief" aspect typically pertains to deeply held conscientious beliefs that are fundamental about the human condition and the world. Thus, atheism and agnosticism, for example, are generally held to be entitled to the same protection as religious beliefs.'

[82] *McFeeley v UK* (1980) 3 EHRR 161; see also *X v UK* App no 7291/75 (1977) 11 D&R 55.

[83] *X and Church of Scientology v Sweden* App no 7805/77 (1978) 16 D&R 68; druidism: *Chappell v UK* App no 12587/86 (1987) 53 D&R 241; pacifism: *Arrowsmith v UK* (1978) 3 EHRR 218; atheism: *Angelini v Sweden* (1988) 10 EHRR 123; Moon sect: *X v Austria* App no 8652/79 (1981) 26 D&R 89; *X v UK* App no 7291/75 (1977) 11 D&R 55: the applicant failed 'to establish the existence of the Wicca religion'.

[84] See Chs 2, 3, and 4 below.

[85] Romania: SC, Decisions 769, 7 March 2000 and 1124, 28 March 2000; Germany: CCt, BVerfGE 84, 341. This approach was taken in Sweden on a discrimination bill in 2003: Proposition 2002/03:65, p 82.

by executive bodies or in the course of parliamentary debate.[86] Yet courts may decline to define 'religion' for a variety of reasons, typified in recent British case-law: it may be unnecessary to do so, as when it is sufficient to determine that a 'belief' is asserted;[87] it is obvious that something is 'religion';[88] or it is too difficult to define 'religion', particularly 'in an age of increasingly multicultural societies' where there is a trend towards 'a newer more expansive reading of religion'.[89] In turn, States are generally agreed that 'religion' must be interpreted in a broad manner;[90] '"religion" is not restricted to churches and officially recognised religious communities';[91] and some national courts warn against too Judeo-Christian an understanding of religion.[92]

States agree that to be religion the phenomenon must satisfy some 'minimum' or 'objective' criteria. There is, however, divergence as to what criteria; and some States simply look to Strasbourg.[93] Italian criteria include 'public recognition', 'common opinion', and 'self-perception'.[94] In Portugal whether it is embedded in society is important.[95] It used to be the case in Germany that the religious belief or practice had to be linked to well-established faiths.[96] However, in German jurisprudence today whether a belief or activity is religious is to be determined objectively by reference to 'spiritual content and external appearance';[97] but

---

[86]　eg religion is defined in Austria in the explanatory notes produced by the government on the various statutes which deal with religion; in Portugal by a statement of the Attorney-General; in Sweden in parliamentary debate; in the UK, by the Charity Commission (see below).

[87]　UK: *R v Secretary of State for Education, ex p Williamson* [2005] UKHL 15, para 24, *per* Lord Nicholls: '[Article 9] leaves on one side the difficult question of the criteria to be applied in deciding whether a belief is to be characterised as religious. This question will seldom, if ever, arise under the [ECHR] . . . Article 9 embraces freedom of thought, conscience and religion. The atheist, the agnostic, and the sceptic are as much entitled to freedom to hold and manifest their beliefs as the theist. These beliefs are placed on an equal footing for the purpose of this guaranteed freedom.'

[88]　ibid Lord Walker, paras 55–56: 'it is not in dispute that Christianity is a religion'.

[89]　ibid para 54: 'it is certainly not necessary, and is probably not useful . . . to try to reach a precise definition [of 'religion']. Courts in different jurisdictions . . . have almost always remarked on its difficulty. . . . The trend of authority (unsurprisingly in an age of increasingly multicultural societies and increasing respect for human rights) is towards a "newer, more expansive, reading" of religion'.

[90]　Slovenia: FRA 2007: its definition of religious freedom implies that religion involves belief and its expression in 'a mass, class, practice or religious ritual', or conscientious objection to a duty required by law that seriously contradicts religious belief.

[91]　Austria: ETA, Explanatory Notes: 'Religion is any religious, confessional belief'.

[92]　Spain: CCt, Judgment 46/2001 of 15 February: until this case, 'religion' was implicitly understood to come from the Judeo-Christian tradition, and to a more limited extent, from Islam.

[93]　Romania: CCt, Decision 72 (18 July 1995); UK: *R v Secretary of State for Education, ex p Williamson* [2005] UKHL 15, paras 23–24: 'The belief must be consistent with basic standards of human dignity or integrity . . . [and] relate to matters more than merely trivial. It must possess an adequate degree of seriousness and importance . . . it must be a belief on a fundamental problem. With religious belief this requisite is readily satisfied. [It must] be coherent in the sense of being intelligible and capable of being understood. But, again, too much should not be demanded in this regard.'

[94]　Italy: CCt, Dec no 195, 27 April 1993: the Church of Scientology met the criteria of public recognition (*pubblici riconoscimenti*), common opinion (*comune considerazione*), and self-perception.

[95]　Portugal: 'Churches are large communities that are well established in society': A-G, Proclamation no 54/95, DR II Série, no 222, 24/09/96. The Committee for Religious Freedom has not as yet defined 'religion' (*religião*) or 'belief' (*crença*).

[96]　Germany: CCt, BVerfGE 12, 1(4).

[97]　Germany: CCt, BVerfGE 84, 341: 'The mere claim and self-understanding that a community professes a religion . . . cannot justify for it and its members [religious freedom]; rather there must actually be a religion and religious community in terms of spiritual content and external appearance.'

religious 'self-understanding' must also be considered,[98] and on occasion it may be 'self-evident' that something (such as Bahá'í) is a religion.[99] As such, States speak of sham religions, usually in the context of sects,[100] which they consider are not religions properly so-called;[101] this approach may lead to negative definitions of religion.[102]

Religion as belief and practice

There is little to distinguish between European States in terms of the core elements of their understanding of religion—religion is transcendent belief in divinity and action based upon it in the world. States are in agreement that religion involves 'belief', 'a set of beliefs', 'a statement of belief', or 'a specifically formulated belief'.[103] Some States link religion to 'faith', 'a structure of convictions', or faith based on convictions.[104] Beliefs are religious by virtue of their object—'a supreme being',[105] 'transcendence, a higher being of divinity',[106] or 'the dependence of human beings on a power over the human race'.[107] Religion seeks both 'to explain humankind and the world in its transcendent meaning',[108] and to address 'the ultimate questions of human society and individual life' including the quest for salvation.[109] Religious belief, a common category in national laws,[110] therefore offers a particular 'world view'[111] about the whole of life (its origin and purpose) which gives sense to

---

[98] Germany: CCt, BVerfGE 24, 236 (247f): this is required by the principle of autonomy; see Ch 4 below.

[99] Germany: CCt, BVerfGE 83, 341 (353); see also Hungary: CCt, Decision 4/1993 (II.12) AB.

[100] Belgium: Act of 2 June 1998: a sect is 'any group with a religious or philosophical vocation, or pretending to have such a vocation, which in its organisation or practice performs illegal and damaging activities . . . to individuals or to the community or violates human dignity'.

[101] For sects see Ch 3 below.

[102] Spain: LORF, Art 3.2: 'activities, intentions and entities relating to or engaging in the study of and experimentation on psychic or parapsychological phenomena or the dissemination of humanistic or spiritual values or other similar non-religious aims do not qualify for the protection provided in this Act'; they may be excluded from the Register of Religious Associations.

[103] Bulgaria: RDA, Art 1; Austria: ETA, Explanatory Notes; Denmark: Guidelines of the Standing Advisory Committee on Religious Communities (January 2002).

[104] UK: for religion as 'faith and worship', see *Re South Place Ethical Society, Barralet v AG* [1980] 1 WLR 1565; *R v Registrar General, ex p Segerdal* [1970] 3 WLR 479; France: Lyon CA, 28 July 1997: 'common faith'; Austria: FLSCC, Explanatory Notes: religion is 'a structure of convictions'; Sweden: for debate on 'belief' signified by 'worship' (*religion*) or 'religious faith' (*trosuppfattning*) and its connection to 'conviction' (*övertygelse*), see government Proposition 2002/03:65, pp 81–2.

[105] UK: *Re The Druid Network* [2010] Charity Commission Decision (21 September 2010): the Druid Network had a combination of belief in a supreme being and notions of 'sacred nature'.

[106] Spain: the General Directorate for Religious Affairs (Ministry of Justice) adopted the idea that the concept of religion consists of 'an organic whole of dogma or beliefs related to transcendence, a higher being or a divinity', but this approach was criticized in CCt, Judgment 46/2001 of 15 February.

[107] Denmark: Guidelines, Standing Advisory Committee on Religious Communities (January 2002).

[108] Austria: FLSCC, Explanatory Notes.

[109] Austria: ETA, Explanatory Notes.

[110] Slovenia: FRA (2 February 2007): religious freedom includes conscientious objection against an obligation required by law that seriously contradicts religious belief of a person.

[111] Denmark: Explanatory Notes to Draft no 384 SE (11th Riigikogu).

human life and transcends the world.[112] However, the broad approach to religion has led to the idea that religion may embrace 'theistic, non-theistic or atheistic' beliefs.[113] In other words, religion is not confined to belief in (or the relation of humans to) a Creator but refers 'to theistic, non-theistic, and atheistic convictions. It includes convictions such as agnosticism, free thinking, pacifism, atheism and rationalism'.[114] Religious belief is often treated as a species of belief in general, but distinguished from other beliefs, such as those that are philosophical, political, or ideological.[115]

Another fundamental concept in national laws is that religion is capable of expression, representation, or manifestation in outward 'acts of a religious character' through 'individual or collective behaviour' which results from or is otherwise related to religious belief.[116] The outward acts of religious belief may take a wide variety of forms. One form of expression is teaching,[117] the profession of faith,[118] dogma,[119] or doctrine.[120] Such teaching results in visible religious practices,[121] which themselves may symbolize the beliefs upon which they are based.[122] Consequently, religion is commonly viewed as an individual or a group activity,[123]

---

[112] Germany: CCt, BVerfGE 90, 112 (115); see also CCt, BVerfGE 24, 236 (247f).
[113] Poland: 'religion shall in particular include . . . having theistic, non-theistic or atheistic beliefs' Law on the Protection of Aliens, 18 March 2008 (Journal of Law 2008, no 70, item 416), Art 14.2.
[114] Cyprus: *Pitsillides v The Republic of Cyprus* [1983] 2 CLR 374; UK: Charities Act 2006, s 2(2) (c) and (h): schemes for 'the advancement of religion' and for 'reconciliation or the promotion of religious . . . harmony or equality and diversity' are charitable; s 2(3): 'religion' includes 'a religion which involves belief in more than one god' and 'a religion which does not involve belief in a god'.
[115] Austria: ETA, Explanatory Notes: belief embraces 'all religious, ideological, political and other leading perceptions of life and of the world' as well as 'an orientation of the personal and societal position for the individual understanding of life'; belief is 'a system of interpretation consisting of personal convictions concerning the basic structure, modality and functions of the world; it is not a scientific system'; see also Germany: CCt, BVerfGE 90, 112 (115): religion transcends the world whereas philosophical belief is not a metaphysical but an immanent system of convictions; Sweden: Government Proposition 2002/03:65, pp 81–2 (on the now repealed Prohibition on Discrimination Act 2003); SOU 2000:43, p 155; Legislative Council, Official Statement 2003-03-06, Proposition 2002/03:65, p 344; SOU 2006:22, p 311.
[116] Poland: Law on the Protection of Aliens, Act of 18 March 2008 (Journal of Law 2008, no 70, item 416), Art 14.2; Austria: FLSCC, Explanatory Notes (representation); Bulgaria: RDA, Art 1.
[117] In global international law, teaching (or practice) 'includes acts integral to the conduct by religious groups of their basic affairs, such as, *inter alia*, the freedom to choose their own religious leaders, priests and teachers, the freedom to establish seminaries or religious schools and the freedom to prepare and distribute religious texts and publications': UNHRC (1993), General Comment 22.
[118] Czech Rep: CCt: 27 November 2002 Pl US 6/02.
[119] Austria: ETA, Explanatory Notes; Spain: dogma was a criterion for the General Directorate for Religious Affairs, but this was criticized by the CCt, Judgment 46/2001 of 15 February.
[120] Portugal: A-G, Proclamation no 54/95, published in DR II Série, no 222, 24/09/96.
[121] Austria: ETA, Explanatory Notes. See also UNHRC (1993), General Comment 22: religion 'may include not only ceremonial acts but also such customs as the observance of dietary regulations, the wearing of distinctive clothing or headcoverings, participation in rituals associated with certain stages of life, and the use of a particular language customarily spoken by a group'.
[122] Austria: FLSCC, Explanatory Notes: practices as 'symbols' of belief.
[123] Indeed, religious groups may also claim an ethnic dimension: in Cyprus, the Maronites complained that the Constitution classifies them merely as a 'religious group', whilst they consider themselves also as 'a specific ethnic group'; the Latin community, too, is dissatisfied with the term 'Latin' as it does not properly reflect their Catholic religious identity: see Opinion on Cyprus by the Advisory Committee on the Framework Convention for the Protection of National Minorities 2001.

carried out voluntarily,[124] in public or private.[125] Religious groups (or confessions) are 'social aggregates', unified by a common faith,[126] or by common membership of a religious community,[127] which consists of 'a body of adherents'.[128] This idea often represents the 'objective element' of religion, whether the community is small[129] or large.[130] Such religious groups may or may not have formal structures,[131] internal rules, and governing bodies,[132] and the latter may in turn be bureaucratic or hierarchical.[133]

Key to national understandings of religion is worship.[134] Religion consists of 'concrete and definite acts of worship', an external expression of the relationship between the adherents to a religion and a higher being or divinity.[135] Some States see this as the primary medium for the expression of religious belief,[136] or indeed as the principal characteristic of religion itself.[137] Rituals and ceremonies are also commonly associated with religious practice and worship.[138] Performed in public or in private, individually or collectively,[139] religious rituals include, for example, participation in a Mass or a religious class.[140] Such activities may involve 'communication' with a

---

[124] Bulgaria: religion involves a 'voluntary union of natural persons for purposes of manifestation of a certain religion': RDA, Art 1.

[125] Slovenia: FRA (2 February 2007).

[126] Portugal: 'A religious confession can be defined as a community based on a doctrine, manifested in a cult, and established according to rules addressed to the human group of followers'; 'Religious confessions are social aggregates unified by the communion of faith of their members; the religious confession has a doctrine, the fundaments of faith are the religious principles accepted by the believers': A-G, Proclamation no 54/95, published in DR II Série, no 222, 24/09/96.

[127] Austria: ETA, Explanatory Notes.

[128] Spain: the General Directorate for Religious Affairs considered that religion involves 'ritual practice, whether individual or collective (worship), constituting the adherents' institutional means of communication with the higher being;' this was criticized in CCt Judgment 46/2001 of 15 February.

[129] France: Lyon CA, Decision of 28 July 1997: a community is the objective element of religion.

[130] Portugal: A-G, Proclamation no 54/95, published in DR II Série, no 222, 24/09/96.

[131] Spain: this view of the General Directorate for Religious Affairs was discussed by the CCt, Judgment 46/2001 of 15 February: the Unification Church was held to be religious under LORF.

[132] Bulgaria: RDA, Art 1: a religious institution has 'governing bodies and statutes'.

[133] Portugal: 'Churches are large communities that are well established in society, with a formal structure that is bureaucratic and hierarchical'; 'Sects are in principle smaller and less organised': Office of A-G, Proclamation no 54/95, published in DR II Série, no 222, 24 September 1996.

[134] The idea also appears in global international law: UNHRC (1993), General Comment 22: worship 'extends to ritual and ceremonial acts giving direct expression to belief, as well as various practices integral to such acts, including the building of places to worship, the use of ritual formulae and objects, the display of symbols, and the observance of holidays and days of rest'.

[135] Spain: the General Directorate for Religious Affairs proposed 'as a consequence of the existence of acts of worship, although this is not an essential element, ownership of places to which the adherents may go to perform such acts'; this was criticized by the CCt in Judgment 46/2001 of 15 February.

[136] See n 104 above.

[137] UK: *Re The Druid Network* [2010] Charity Commission Decision (21 September 2010): the Network had elements of common worship; Luxembourg: CCt, Judgment 3/1998 of 20.11.98, Mémorial (OG) A of 18 January 1999, no 002/1999; Sweden: Government Proposition 2002/03:65, pp 81–2 (on the now repealed Prohibition on Discrimination Act 2003).

[138] Bulgaria: RDA, Art 1: the 'performance of worship, religious rituals and ceremonies'.

[139] Poland: Law on Aliens, Act of 18 March 2008 (Journal of Law 2008, no 70, item 416), Art 14.2.

[140] Slovenia: FRA (2 February 2007).

higher being,[141] or 'reverence' to a dominant power in the form of 'submission to the object worshipped, veneration of that object, praise, thanksgiving, prayer or intercession',[142] or 'communal or personal worship, supplication and meditation'.[143] They may include abstention from work on certain days, wearing prescribed forms of dress, rituals connected with the preparation of food, and abstinence from certain types of food or drink.[144] However, not all rituals may be protected by religious liberty but only those required by a religious duty.[145]

Importantly, religion also involves the observance of norms of conduct.[146] Religious belief generates 'principles',[147] 'rules',[148] 'rules for [a] way of life',[149] or 'a body of moral rules', and these regulate the individual and social behaviour of its adherents.[150] Such norms may represent an 'identifiable positive, beneficial, moral and ethical framework',[151] and they may include the laws of nature and other guidelines for human ethics and morality.[152] As adherents to religion may 'pattern their whole behaviour on the teachings of their faith and act according to their inner beliefs',[153] so 'religious faiths call for more than belief'—'To a greater or lesser extent adherents are required or encouraged to act in certain ways' not only to 'affect the entirety of a believer's way of life' but also to 'impact on others'.[154] Indeed, the Constitutional Court of the Czech Republic is notable for its recognition of the wider social impact of religion; organized religion involves values which go beyond the profession of belief: 'the task of [religious] entities cannot...be reduced to the mere profession of a particular religious faith...but their role in society is considerably wider and also consists of radiating religious values externally, not only through religious activities but also, e.g. charitable, humanitarian and general educational activities'.[155]

---

[141] Spain: the General Directorate for Religious Affairs considered that religion involves 'ritual practice, whether individual or collective (worship), constituting the adherents' institutional means of communication with the higher being:' see CCt Judgment 46/2001 of 15 February.

[142] UK: *R v Registrar General, ex p Segerdal* [1970] 3 ALL ER 886, *per* Winn LJ.

[143] UK: *R v Secretary of State for Education, ex p Williamson* [2005] UKHL 15, paras 16–17.

[144] ibid.

[145] Estonia: Tartu DC, Case no 3-07-701 (2 May 2007): candles were an important part of Buddhist rituals, but Buddhism did not require a prisoner to burn them in his cell.

[146] For the notion of 'customs' and 'dietary regulations' in international law, see n 121 above.

[147] Bulgaria: RDA, Art 1: 'a set of beliefs and principles'; Austria: FLSCC, Explanatory Notes: religion provides rituals, for example, 'with basic principles and doctrine'.

[148] Portugal: a religious confession may have 'rules addressed to the human group of followers (believers)' as well as 'religious principles accepted by the believers': Office of the A-G, Proclamation no 54/95, published in DR II Série, no 222, 24 September 1996.

[149] Austria: ETA, Explanatory Notes: 'rules for the way of life'.

[150] Spain: for the General Directorate for Religious Affairs, religion consists of 'a body of moral rules regulating the individual and social behaviour of the adherents to a religious denomination, derived from that dogma'; this was criticized by the CCt in Judgment 46/2001 of 15 February.

[151] UK: *Re The Druid Network* [2010] Charity Commission Decision (21 September 2010).

[152] Denmark: Guidelines of the Standing Advisory Committee on Religious Communities (January 2002).

[153] Germany: CCt, BVerfGE, 98 (106).

[154] UK: *R v Secretary of State for Education, ex p Williamson* [2005] UKHL 15, paras 16–17, *per* Lord Nicholls: precepts such as the duty to love one's neighbour impact on others in addition to abstinence from work, food, and drink, and holy days and times 'impact on others'.

[155] Czech Rep: CCt, 22 November 2002, no Pl US 6/02.

Whilst the above seeks to draw together the core of religion from a wide range of national laws, it might be helpful to present some complete juridical definitions in order to illustrate the spectrum of approaches used in terms of their detail and focus. At one end is the minimalist approach of France: 'a religion can be defined by the convergence of two elements, an objective element, the existence of a community even limited, and a subjective element, a common faith'.[156] Other minimalist approaches focus on the transcendence of faith: in Denmark, religion is seen as 'a specifically formulated belief in the dependence of human beings on a power over the human race [which] provides guidelines for human ethics and morality'.[157] At the other end of the spectrum is the more detailed and expansive approach of Austria: 'for a religion there are minimum requirements concerning a statement of belief, rules for a way of life and a cult';[158] religion is a 'structure of convictions whose content is capable of representation [which] has been growing in history to explain humankind and the world in its transcendent meaning and to accompany [this] with specific rites and symbols [giving] them orientation in accordance with basic principles and doctrine'.[159] Between these two extremes is the tripartite approach of Poland:

...the concept of religion shall in particular include: (a) having theistic, non-theistic or atheistic beliefs, (b) participation, or refraining from engaging in religious rituals, performed in public or private, individually or collectively, [and] (c) other acts of a religious character, beliefs expressed [in the form] of individual or collective behaviour as a result of religious beliefs or related to them.[160]

Occasionally, States propose understandings of particular religions. In Spain, for example, Catholicism is understood to involve mission, worship, teaching, and the exercise of jurisdiction through institutions;[161] evangelical Christianity is understood to involve duties of worship, the administration of the sacraments, pastoral care, preaching the Gospel and religious teaching;[162] Judaism involves Jewish law and tradition, worship, rituals, teaching the Jewish religion, providing spiritual support, and the exercise of rabbinic office;[163] and Islam is understood to involve Islamic law and tradition as these issue from the Qu'ran and Sunna, as well as rituals

---

[156] France: Lyon CA, Decision of 28 July 1997; see also Portugal: 'A religious confession [is] a community based on a doctrine, manifested in a cult, and established according to rules addressed to the human group of followers': A-G, Proclamation no 54/95, DR II Série, no 222, 24/09/96.
[157] Guidelines of the Standing Advisory Committee on Religious Communities (January 2002).
[158] ETA, Explanatory Notes: religion is 'a system to address in its dogma, practice and social manifestations the ultimate questions of human society and individual life'; it involves ideas about salvation and the means to achieve salvation, 'personal (god, gods) and impersonal (rules, cognition, knowledge) transcendence'.
[159] FLSCC, Explanatory Notes.
[160] Law on Aliens, Act of 18 March 2008, Art 14.2.
[161] Agreement with the Holy See on Legal Affairs, 4 December 1979, Art 1.1.
[162] Agreement with FEREDE, Law 24/1992, 10 November, Art 6.
[163] Agreement with Israelite Communities, Law 25/1992, 10 November, Art 6: 'functions set out under Jewish law and tradition shall be considered to be the functions characteristic of the Jewish religion, including the religious functions deriving from the rabbinic office, worship, administration of ritual services, rabbi training, teaching the Jewish religion and tendering spiritual support'.

and pastoral assistance.[164] Indeed, Strasbourg portrays Islam as concerned with the divine, law, stability, and the whole of life (public and private), but Strasbourg also has concerns about how Islam may or may not be reconciled with pluralism and democracy.[165] This was echoed recently by the Parliamentary Assembly of the Council of Europe: 'Islam is not only a religion but also a social, legal and political code of conduct'; it can be 'violent or mainstream and peaceful, but in both cases it does not accept the separation between religion and State which is a fundamental principle of the democratic and pluralistic societies'; the assembly also underlines the profound contribution of Islam to European culture and values of human dignity.[166]

   Given the need to know when a belief or activity is religious for the purpose of applying legal rights or duties to concrete claims, it is perhaps surprising that most national laws do not define 'religion'. However, given what seems to be a consensus that religion is to be understood broadly, it is perhaps not surprising that States employ somewhat rough and ready but generally objective criteria to define religion—though the subjective understanding of claimants also has a part to play. In those States whose laws address the nature of religion, definitions range from the brief to the detailed—yet, at their core is the idea of religion both as belief in a transcendental worldview and as practice in teaching, worship, and norms of conduct. Such an approach seems to be consistent with that of international law. This flexible strategy—do not define 'religion' at all or else define it minimally—could be justified on the basis of the need to make the law inclusive. This may be especially desirable in societies which today are increasingly characterized by religious pluralism.

The systems of religion law: state postures

Academic lawyers frequently distinguish between three models of religion-state relations in Europe: state church systems, separation systems, and hybrid systems.[167]

---

[164] Agreement with the Islamic Commission of Spain, Law 26/1992 of 10 November, Art 6: 'practices conducted in accordance with Islamic law and tradition, issuing from the Qu'ran or the Sunna and protected under the General Act on Religious Liberty shall be considered to be Islamic religious services or training or religious assistance'.

[165] *Refah Partisi (The Welfare Party) and ors v Turkey* (2003) 37 EHRR 1, para 123: 'sharia, which faithfully reflects the dogmas and divine rules laid down by religion, is stable and invariable. Principles such as pluralism in the political sphere or the constant evolution of public freedoms have no place in it ... the introduction of sharia [is] difficult to reconcile with the fundamental principles of democracy ... particularly with regard to its criminal law and criminal procedure, its rules on the legal status of women and the way it intervenes in all spheres of private and public life in accordance with religious precepts'.

[166] Res 1743 (2010) paras 2 and 3; moreover: 'Islam, Judaism and Christianity—the three monotheist religions—share the same historic and cultural roots and recognise the same fundamental values, in particular the paramount value of human life and dignity, the ability and freedom to express thoughts, the respect for others and their property, the importance of social welfare' (values which are themselves reflected in the ECHR: ibid para 3); see also Res 1162 (1991).

[167] G Robbers (ed), *State and Church in the European Union* (Baden-Baden: Nomos, 2nd edn, 2005) 577.

State church systems are characterized by the existence of close constitutional links between the State and a particular religious community, its 'national', 'established', or 'folk' church, or 'prevailing religion' or 'traditional religion'; examples include England, Denmark, Greece, Finland, Malta, and (historically) Sweden. Systems which separate State and religion, with constitutional statements of the secular character of the State and prohibitions against state financial support for religion, include France, Ireland, Slovenia, and the Netherlands. The so-called hybrid systems are also known as cooperation systems—constitutional separation of State and religion is coupled with the recognition of a multitude of common tasks which link State and religious activity, and cooperation between the State and individual religious groups is often organized on the basis of agreements, including concordats with the Holy See (which have status in international law); examples include Spain, Italy, Germany, Belgium, Austria, Portugal, and Baltic and central and eastern States. While global international law tends to view state-church systems as permissible (provided they facilitate religious freedom),[168] the Council of Europe prefers States to have a secular posture,[169] with neutrality and separation between State and religion,[170] but at the same time promoting dialogue with religion.[171] However, the European Union formally respects the national church-state postures of its Member States.[172]

---

[168] UNHRC (1993), General Comment 22, para 9: 'The fact that a religion is recognized as a state religion or that it is established as official or traditional or that its followers comprise the majority of the population, shall not result in any impairment of the enjoyment of any of the rights under the [ICCPR] . . . nor in any discrimination against adherents to other religions or non-believers.'

[169] *Refah Partisi (The Welfare Party) and ors v Turkey* (2003) 37 EHRR 1, para 93: 'the principle of secularism is certainly one of the fundamental principles of the State which are in harmony with the rule of law and respect for human rights and democracy. An attitude which fails to respect that principle will not necessarily be accepted as being covered by . . . Article 9 of the Convention'; see also *Lautsi v Italy*, App no 30814/06 (ECtHR, 3 November 2009).

[170] *Darby v Sweden* (1991) 13 EHRR 774; *Refah Partisi v Turkey* (2003) 37 EHRR 1: 'the State's role as the neutral and impartial organiser of the exercise of various religions, faiths and beliefs' and its 'duty of neutrality and impartiality'; see also *Yanasik v Turkey* App no 14524/89 (1993) 74 D&R 14.

[171] The Parliamentary Assembly of the Council of Europe encourages dialogue with religion: see eg Doc 6732 (1993), Rec 1202 (1993); Doc 8270 (1998), Rec 1396 (1999); Doc 10970 (2006), Rec 1510 (2006); Doc 11298 (2007), Rec 1804 (2007); Doc 12266 (2010), Rec 1743 (2010): 'Recalling its [Rec] 1804 (2007) on state, religion, secularity and human rights, the Assembly emphasises that democratic standards require a separation of the state and its organs from religions and religious organisations. Governments, parliaments and public administrations that democratically reflect and serve their society as a whole must be neutral towards all religious, agnostic or atheist beliefs. Nevertheless, religion and democracy are not incompatible, in particular as religions may play a beneficial social role. Member states should therefore encourage religious organisations to support actively peace, tolerance, solidarity and intercultural dialogue'; see also the white paper on intercultural dialogue, *Living Together as Equals in Dignity* (May 2008) launched by the Ministers of Foreign Affairs of the Council of Europe: the Council of Europe 'has frequently recognised inter-religious dialogue . . . as part of intercultural dialogue and encouraged religious communities to engage actively in promoting human rights, democracy and the rule of law in a multicultural Europe. Inter-religious dialogue can also contribute to a stronger consensus regarding the solutions to social problems'; for discussion, see F Cranmer, 'Religion, human rights and the Council of Europe: a note' (2009) 162 Law and Justice 36. For dialogue between religions and the EU, see Ch 10 below.

[172] Treaty of Amsterdam 1997, Appendix, Declaration on the Status of Churches and Non-confessional Organisations: 'The European Union respects and does not prejudice the status under

The state church model

States within this model are distinctive by virtue of the special constitutional position of a particular Christian church and special benefits and burdens resulting from that position. Such churches may be subject to varying degrees of state control. In Denmark, there is a high degree of control. The constitution provides that: 'The Evangelical Lutheran Church shall be the Folk Church of Denmark, and as such shall be supported by the State'; moreover, the monarch shall be a member of that church.[173] However, the Danish folk church has no synod, no legal personality as a corporate body, and its constitution is to be laid down by statute (but this has not yet occurred).[174] The church is subject to direct state control. The Ministry of Ecclesiastical Affairs determines rules on church membership, the creation of new parishes, and the appointment and dismissal of its clergy (who have the status of civil servants).[175] Local church units (the parishes) operate as state agencies performing various administrative functions for the State, and all taxpayers who are members of the national church pay a church tax.[176] Nevertheless, Danish law also provides for religious freedom, prohibitions against religious discrimination, and the operation of other religious organizations which may function freely in society.[177]

Other state church systems in Europe differ substantially from the Danish model. In Greece, state control is minimal. The constitution provides that the prevailing religion is that of the Orthodox Church of Greece; united with the Ecumenical Patriarchate of Constantinople, the church is autocephalous and administered by its Holy Synods.[178] The church has personality in public law

---

national laws of churches and religious associations or communities in the Member States.' See Ch 10 below.

[173] Const, Art 4; Art 6: 'The King shall be a member of the Evangelical Lutheran Church'.

[174] Const, Art 66: 'The constitution of the established Church shall be laid down by statute', no such statute has actually been enacted despite several commissions.

[175] 'The Ministry of Ecclesiastical Affairs is the governing body of the Danish National Evangelical Lutheran Church and [administers] grants and appropriations to that part of the Danish national Church funded out of the National Budget. The most important task of the Ministry of Ecclesiastical Affairs is to [administer] the [church] in conformity with current legislation': Statement, Ministry of Ecclesiastical Affairs, 2009. The Standing Advisory Committee on Religious Communities is independent of the Ministry of Ecclesiastical Affairs and has guidelines for approval of groups as religious communities for the purposes of marriage law; see Ch 9 below.

[176] Since 1903, all members of the Danish National Church over the age of 18 have been eligible to vote and stand for election to Parochial Church Councils the functions of which include the upkeep of registers and buildings; for its property and finances, see Ch 7 below.

[177] Const, Art 69: 'Rules for religious bodies dissenting from the established church shall be laid down by statute'; they function as private associations.

[178] Const, Art 3.1: 'The prevailing religion in Greece is that of the Eastern Orthodox Church of Christ. The Orthodox Church of Greece, acknowledging our Lord Jesus Christ as its head, is inseparably united in doctrine with the Great Church of Christ in Constantinople and with every other Church of Christ of the same doctrine, observing unwaveringly, as they do, the holy apostolic and synodal canons and sacred traditions. It is autocephalous and is administered by the Holy Synod of serving Bishops and the Permanent Holy Synod originating thereof and assembled as specified by the Statutory Charter of the Church in compliance with the provisions of the Patriarchal Tome of June 29, 1850 and the Synodal Act of September 4, 1928'—the Patriarchal Tome 1850 provides that the Holy

and a statutory charter approved by parliament; its holy canons are invulnerable from challenge in state courts as to doctrine and liturgy.[179] The church is funded by the State.[180] Moreover, the President of Greece and members of parliament must take Christian oaths.[181] Nevertheless, religious freedom is protected for other 'known religions' (those which do not have secret doctrines and worship).[182] There are several agreements with various minority religions and laws on specific groups ratify or otherwise implement these.[183] Indeed, in Thrace there is protection for the Islamic minority and limited scope is given to Muslim law.[184] However, Strasbourg has criticized Greek law which deals with proselytizing,[185] as well as the treatment of the Catholic Church.[186]

The juxtaposition of church-state relations in Denmark and Greece indicates the breadth of the state-church category. These States may be contrasted with Finland, where two churches have special treatment. The Evangelical Lutheran Church enjoys constitutional status,[187] and the Orthodox Church, the second largest religious community, is subject to special law;[188] but some decisions taken in both churches must be approved by the State.[189] The Evangelical Lutheran Church is governed by church law enacted on the exclusive initiative of its General Synod— the government cannot interfere in the content of ecclesiastical bills introduced by the synod; parliament enacts the law but may only approve or reject the bill; the church and its parishes are autonomous; bishops are no longer appointed by the

---

Synod administers 'Church matters according to the divine and holy canons freely and unrestrainedly from all temporal interventions'; Art 3.2: 'The ecclesiastical regime existing in certain districts of the State shall not be deemed contrary to the provisions of the preceding paragraph'; Art 3.3: 'The text of the Holy Scriptures shall be maintained unaltered. Official translation of the text into any other form of language, without prior sanction by the Autocephalous Church of Greece and the Great Church of Christ in Constantinople, is prohibited'.

[179] For the statutory charter, see Law 590/1977, Art 1(4) (under Const, Art 3 in conjunction with Art 72); see the Charter, Arts 4, 6, and 9, for the competences of the Permanent Holy Synod and Holy Synod of the Hierarchy. The statutory charter of the Church of Crete is also state law: Law 4149/1961.

[180] Funding takes various forms (eg grants, clergy salaries, tax exemptions); see Ch 7 below.

[181] Const, Art 33: the President on taking office must take a Christian oath 'in the name of the Holy and Consubstantial and Indivisible Trinity'; Art 59: 'Members of Parliament who are of a different religion or creed shall take the same oath according to the form of their own religion or creed.'

[182] Const, Art 13: religious freedom for known religions.

[183] London Protocol 22.1/3.2.1830 between Great Britain, France and Russia (on Catholics)—see now Law 2731/15-7-1991; Treaty of Athens (9/14-11-1913), Art 11 (ratified by Law 4213 4 November 1913): this requires Greece to respect religious minorities; Treaty of Sèvres, 28.7/ 10.8.1920 (on the protection of minorities). There are laws for the Jewish community (L 2456/ 1920 and 367/1947, and royal decree 29/29 March 1949); Muslim community (L 2345/1920 and 1920/1991).

[184] Treaty of Lausanne 1923 ratified by DL 25/25, August 1923.

[185] *Kokkinakis v Greece* (1994) 17 EHRR 397; see also *Larissis and ors v Greece* (1998) Series A no 65: the convictions of three Pentecostal Air Force officers for proselytizing servicemen were held not to violate ECHR, Art 9 but the measures taken by them to proselytize civilians were unjustified and in breach of ECHR, Art 9.

[186] *Canea Catholic Church v Greece* (1999) 27 EHRR 521.

[187] Const, Art 76 (The Church Act)—which came into force on 1 March 2000.

[188] Law 521/1969 (a skeleton law) and the (supplementary) Law 179/1970.

[189] The Orthodox Church is subject ecclesiastically to the Ecumenical Patriarch, and decisions of the Lutheran Synod and Orthodox General Assembly have legal effect only if approved by the State.

State; and its ministers are no longer state-funded.[190] The Orthodox Church is regulated by specific parliamentary law; the synod presents bills to parliament and the government may alter the bill prior to its approval by parliament without the consent of the church.[191] Both churches enjoy a church tax.[192] Nevertheless, Finnish law provides for religious freedom, prohibits religious discrimination, and enables religious groups to associate freely.[193] Iceland,[194] Norway,[195] and Lichtenstein[196] have similar arrangements.

Whilst in the United Kingdom several government bodies engage in dialogue with religion,[197] in England, the Church of England was established by a series of ancient parliamentary statutes.[198] Its position is not dissimilar to that of the Lutheran Church in Finland. Though it is not a department of State,[199] but a

---

[190] Const, Art 76 (The Church Act): 'Provisions on the organisation and administration of the Evangelical Lutheran Church are laid down in the Church Act. The legislative procedure for enactment of the Church Act and the right to submit legislative proposals relating to the Church Act are governed by the specific provisions in that Code.' The church has created for itself a Church Ordinance 1993.

[191] Law 521/1969; new legislation was due in 2007 to effect greater autonomy, allowing the synod to create its own constitution and ending state-payment of church expenses.

[192] See Ch 7 below.

[193] Const, Art 11: religious freedom; Art 6: religious discrimination; FRA, Act 453 of 2003.

[194] Const, Art 62: 'The Evangelical Lutheran Church shall be the State Church in Iceland and, as such, it shall be supported and protected by the State' (the State pays the salaries of its clergy and whilst the church elects its bishops, it is the President of Iceland who signs the candidate into office)—the church has an Assembly, and its highest authority is its Council (with two clergy and two lay persons presided over by the bishop); Art 63: 'All persons have the right to form religious associations and to practise their religion in conformity with their individual convictions. Nothing may however be preached or practised which is prejudicial to good morals or public order'; Art 64 guarantees religious freedom; a church tax is payable but non-members may pay an equivalent sum to the University of Iceland.

[195] Const, Art 2: the Evangelical Lutheran Church is the 'official religion of the State' (*statens offentlige religion*); the king is its titular head and it is administered by the Ministry of Culture and Church Affairs; it is regulated by law enacted by parliament (*Storting*), above all by the Act Concerning the Administration of the Church of Norway 1953.

[196] Const, Art 37: 'The Roman Catholic Church is the State Church and as such enjoys the full protection of the State; other confessions shall be entitled to practise their creeds and to hold religious services to the extent consistent with morality and public order'; Art 37.1: religious freedom; Art 38: this guarantees religious autonomy.

[197] The Department for Communities and Local Government has a Race, Cohesion and Faiths Directorate; within this there is a Cohesion and Faiths Unit which has advised on several legal reforms in the field of religion; the Equality and Human Rights Commission (set up under the Equality Act 2006) is to promote equality which includes religion or belief; the Charity Commission for England and Wales also has a Faith and Social Cohesion Unit and a Faith Advisory Group. The Churches' Legislation Advisory Service (composed of representatives from churches as well as the United Synagogue) liaises between these and government.

[198] The Church of England 'established according to the laws of this realm under the Queen's Majesty, belongs to the true and apostolic Church of Christ' (Canon A1); the church is 'an aggregate of individuals . . . including all persons who adhere and conform to the liturgy and ordinances of the Church of England as by law established, or it may be considered as an organised operative institution' (*Re Barnes, Simpson v Barnes* [1930] 2 Ch 80); the Reformation legislation of the 1530s resulted in the foundation (through a series of Acts of Parliament) of the Church of England.

[199] 'A Church which is established is not thereby made a department of State. The process of establishment means that the State has accepted the Church as a religious body in its opinion truly teaching the Christian faith, and given to it a certain legal position, and its decrees, if rendered under certain legal conditions, certain legal sanctions': *Marshall v Graham* [1907] 2 KB 112.

religious organization,[200] the church is subject to the royal supremacy;[201] the monarch is supreme governor[202] and appoints its bishops, some of whom sit in the House of Lords.[203] People who are resident in parishes of the Church of England have rights to baptism, marriage, and burial.[204] Legislation of its General Synod (its central legislature of bishops, clergy, and laity) in the form of a Measure must receive parliamentary and royal approval before it acquires the same authority and invulnerability from judicial challenge as an Act of Parliament.[205] A Canon must receive royal assent and not be inconsistent with common law, statute, and prerogative.[206] There is a constitutional convention that Parliament will not legislate for the church without its consent—but this is not judicially enforceable.[207] However, in Wales the Church of England was disestablished in 1920 and replaced with the autonomous Church in Wales,[208] and in Scotland the national (Presbyterian) Church of Scotland enjoys greater spiritual autonomy,[209] as is also the position with the Roman Catholic Church in Malta.[210] In Sweden the national (Lutheran) Church of Sweden has recently been disestablished but some links with the State remain, though religious freedom is provided for.[211]

The separation model

On the surface, separation systems are characterized by the secular constitutional posture of the State, its religious indifference or neutrality, the absence of state funding for religion, non-intervention in religious affairs, and the promotion of

---

[200] *Aston Cantlow and Wilmcote with Billesley Parochial Church Council v Wallbank* [2004] 1 AC 546, especially para 13, *per* Lord Nicholls: 'As the established church it still has special links with central government. But the Church of England remains an essentially religious organisation'; para 156, *per* Lord Roger: 'The mission of the Church is a religious mission, distinct from the secular mission of government'—'the Church seeks to serve the purposes of God, not those of the government'; links with the State 'do not include any funding of the Church by the government'.

[201] Canons of the Church of England, Canon A7: 'We acknowledge that the Queen's excellent Majesty, acting according to the laws of the realm, is the highest power under God in this kingdom, and has supreme authority over all persons in all causes, as well ecclesiastical as civil.'

[202] The heir apparent must be 'protestant' and the monarch 'shall join in communion with the Church of England as by law established': Act of Settlement 1700; a declaration must be made that they will uphold and maintain the church: Accession Declaration Act 1910; Coronation Oath Act 1689.

[203] Appointment of Bishops Act 1533; M Hill, *Ecclesiastical Law* (Oxford: OUP, 3rd edn, 2007) para 1.21.

[204] See generally Doe (n 1 above) 357–68, and 385 *et seq.*

[205] Church of England Assembly (Powers) Act 1919.

[206] Synodical Government Measure 1969.

[207] Lord Sainsbury, 19 July 2005 GC 192–3.

[208] Welsh Church Act 1914, Welsh Church (Temporalities) Act 1919; see N Doe, *The Law of the Church in Wales* (Cardiff: University of Wales Press, 2002) ch 1: but duties to marry and bury continue as vestiges.

[209] Church of Scotland Act 1921; see JL Weatherhead (ed), *The Constitution and Laws of the Church of Scotland* (Edinburgh: Board of Practice and Procedure, 1997).

[210] Malta: Const, Art 2: 'The Religion of Malta is the Roman Catholic Apostolic Religion'.

[211] Religious Communities Act 1998; Church of Sweden Act 1998; see L Friedner, 'State and church in Sweden 2000' (2001) 8 EJCSR, 255.

religious freedom for all.[212] France is seen as a separation system par excellence: constitutionally, 'France is a Republic which is indivisible, secular (*laïque*), democratic and social. It guarantees equality before the law to all its citizens, without distinction of origin, race or religion. It respects all forms of belief'.[213] This *laïcité* of the State is spelt out in the 1905 *Loi de la Séparation*: 'The Republic assures freedom of conscience. It guarantees the free exercise of religion subject only to the restrictions mentioned hereafter in the interest of public order', and 'The Republic does not recognize, remunerate, or subsidize any religious denomination'.[214] The regime is supervised by the *Bureau des Cultes* of the Ministry of the Interior.[215] *Laïcité* is perhaps most vividly expressed in the ban on the wearing of religious symbols in schools.[216] However, the doctrine of *laïcité positive* enables the exercise of religious liberty—and, perhaps paradoxically, the doctrine generates cooperation between State and religion: religious groups may function as private law associations; assistance is given to the maintenance of historic places of worship; and funding is available for spiritual assistance in schools, hospitals, prisons, and the armed forces;[217] moreover, the president is consulted about the appointment of Catholic bishops.[218] Above all, the separation law does not apply to the three eastern French *départements* where there are cooperation agreements with various religious organizations.[219]

Although the apparent paradoxes of the French system of *laïcité positive* raise questions about the usefulness of the separation category, Ireland illustrates its limitations.[220] The Irish constitution spells out the basics of separation and neutrality: 'The State guarantees not to endow any religion'; it 'shall not impose any disabilities or make any discrimination on the ground of religious profession, belief or status'; and every religious denomination has 'the right to manage its own affairs'.[221] The anti-endowment provision has been held to prohibit concurrent endowment (the conferral of financial benefits on all religions) as well as the establishment of religion.[222] However, the Irish constitution also expressly recognizes the value of religion: 'The State acknowledges that the homage of public worship is due to Almighty God. It shall hold His Name in reverence, and shall respect and honour religion'.[223] This provision has been interpreted as underpin-

---

[212] R Ahdar and I Leigh, *Religious Freedom in the Liberal State* (Oxford: OUP, 2005) 72 *et seq.*

[213] Const, 1958, Art 2.

[214] Law of 9 December 1905, Arts 1 and 2.

[215] The bureau was created in 1918; there is also a *conseiller pour les affaires religieuses* for the Minister of Foreign Affairs.

[216] Law of 15 March 2004; see Ch 8 below.

[217] See Chs 4, 7, and 8 below.

[218] This position remains under the Napoleonic Concordat with the Holy See (15 July 1801).

[219] Namely Huat-Rhin, Bas-Rhin, and Moselle, which were under German rule until 1918.

[220] Robbers (n 167 above) 578: Ireland is a 'separation system' because separation exists 'to a great extent'.

[221] Const, Art 44.2.2 (endowment), Art 44.2.3 (disabilities), Art 44.2.5 (denominations).

[222] *Campaign to Separate Church and State v Minister for Education* [1998] 3 IR 321.

[223] Const, Art 44.1; the Constitutional Review Group in 1996 called for Art 44.1 to be replaced by the phrase 'The State guarantees to respect religion', but this has not occurred.

ning Christianity,[224] but its benefits are not confined to Christians,[225] and 'the State is not placed in the position of an arbiter of religious truth'.[226] Indirect financial aid is provided to religious groups.[227] This has led some commentators to see Irish religion-state relations as being characterized by 'inextricable interdependence', typified in the field of education, most of which is provided by church schools.[228] Slovenia and the Netherlands are also States which exist at the separatist end of the spectrum.[229]

The cooperation model

The most prevalent model in Europe is the so-called hybrid or cooperation model, characterized by a basic separation of State and religion and the secular posture of the State, but where relations with a religious organization and matters of common concern are addressed usually in the form of agreements.[230] Portugal, Spain, and Italy are seen as the classic examples. Portuguese law provides that: 'churches and other religious communities are separate from the State'; moreover: 'The State neither adopts any religion whatsoever nor pronounces on religious issues';[231] however, whilst, for example, ministers of religion are excluded from membership of public bodies and education must be non-confessional,[232] there are agreements with religious organizations.[233] Similarly, the Spanish constitution provides that: 'No religion shall have a state character. Public authorities shall take the religious beliefs of Spanish society into account and shall in consequence maintain appropriate cooperation with the Catholic Church and the other religious communities.'[234] As such, under the auspices of the Directorate for Religious Affairs at the Ministry of Justice, there are agreements with the Catholic Church

---

[224] *Norris v Attorney General* [1984] IR 36.

[225] *Corway v Independent Newspapers (Ireland) Ltd* [1999] 4 IR 484: '[The] State acknowledges that the homage of public worship is due to Almighty God . . . At the same time it guarantees freedom of conscience, the free profession and practice of religion and equality before the law to all citizens, be they Roman Catholics, Protestants, Jews, Muslims, agnostics or atheists.'

[226] ibid: 'Its only function is to protect public order and morality'; see also *Flynn v Power and Sisters of the Holy Faith* [1985] IR 648: a religious body may require higher standards than those applying to average employees.

[227] eg ministers of religion are liable to income tax (*Dolan v K* [1944] IR 470), but income to a religious organization by way of a gift or bequest which qualifies as charitable is tax exempt.

[228] Colton: PECCSR (2006) 111. See Ch 8 below.

[229] eg both forbid solemnization of religious marriages before a civil marriage; see Ch 9 below.

[230] Robbers (n 167 above) 579: a formal agreement is merely a reflection of the cooperationist nature of the system rather than proof of its existence.

[231] LORF 2002 (Law no 16/2001), implemented by DL 134/2003, Art 3: the 'Principle of separation'; Art 4: the 'Principle of the non-denominational State'; see also Art 4.2: 'The non-denominational principle shall be respected in official ceremonies and State protocol'. There is a government Committee for Religious Freedom.

[232] DL 701-B/76 of 29 September, Art 4, which renders ministers of religion ineligible for election to parliament and other state and municipal bodies, and Law 14/79 of 16 May, Art 6, on regional parliaments; LORF, Art 4.4: 'State education shall be non-confessional'; see Ch 8 below.

[233] eg Concordat with the Holy See, 7 May 1940, amended 15 February 1975, and Concordat 18 May 2004.

[234] Const, Art 16.1.

(a concordat which has status in international law), and covenants with Evangelical (Protestant), Jewish, and Muslim communities which have been ratified by law.[235] Equally, however, religious freedom is afforded to all Spaniards.[236] Italy safeguards the liberty and equality of individuals in religious matters whilst simultaneously guaranteeing cooperation between the State and religious bodies.[237] The constitution provides that both the State and the Roman Catholic Church are 'according to its own order, independent and sovereign' and that their 'relations are ruled by the Lateran Treaties'; all other religious denominations 'are equally free before the law' and their relations with the State are to be defined 'on the basis of agreements with their respective representatives'; some have agreements, others do not, and the latter are governed by particular law.[238] The Cypriot constitution also operates a cooperation system.[239]

Cooperation, by way of agreements with and/or laws directed to specific religious organizations, is also the key characteristic of state-religion relations in Austria (with its recognized religions, public and private),[240] Belgium (also with recognized religions),[241] Luxembourg (where ministers of religion are state-paid),[242] and Germany (with its judicially-recognized neutrality, and public and private religious bodies, as well as numerous agreements at the level of the *länder*).[243]

---

[235] Agreement with the Holy See on Legal Affairs, 4 December 1979; Agreement with the Evangelical Religious Entities, Law 24/1992, 10 November; Agreement with Israelite Communities, Law 25/1992, 10 November; Agreement with the Islamic Commission of Spain, Law 26/1992, 10 November.

[236] Const, Art 16.1; LORF, Law 7/1980 of 5 July; Art 7 deals with cooperation agreements with registered religious organizations; see Ch 4 below.

[237] Const, Art 3: all citizens are 'equal before the law, regardless of . . . religion'; Art 19: everyone has the right to 'profess faith freely' and to 'exercise worship in public or private, provided that the rites involved do not offend common decency'.

[238] Const, Art 7 (Catholic Church); Art 8 (other denominations); Agreement with the Holy See 1984 replaced the Lateran Concordat 1929 and subsequent agreements have been entered (eg on church holidays (1985) and cultural and religious heritage (1996)); also agreements with eg Seventh-Day Adventists (1986); other denominations are governed by Law no 1159 of 24 June 1929 (no action has been taken on a proposal for its reform approved by the Council of Ministers in 1990).

[239] Const, Art 2; Art 110 recognizes the Orthodox Church and Turkish Cypriot religious trust (Muslim); the law also recognizes the Armenian, Maronite and Latin Catholic churches; see Ch 4 below; Const, Art 18: religious freedom.

[240] Const, Art 7.1: religious equality; RCA 1874 (with public corporation status—eg Catholic, Lutheran, Reformed churches, Islamic and Jewish communities); FLSCC 1998 (eg Baha'I, Baptists, Seventh-Day Adventists, Hindus); agreements with the Holy See are subject to incorporation in domestic law: B-VG, Art 50.

[241] Const, Art 21: the State cannot intervene in the nomination of ministers of religion; Art 19: freedom of worship; there are particular laws on each of the recognized religions (eg Roman Catholics, Law of 8 April 1802; Protestants, Law of 8 April 1802; Jews, Law of 4 March 1870; Muslims, Law of 19 July 1974; Orthodox, Law of 17 April 1985); see Ch 4 below.

[242] Const, Art 19: religious liberty; Art 106: funding ministers of religion on the basis of agreements signed with the State; in 1801 Luxembourg was a department of France, and as a result the Concordat of that year between France and the Holy See is still in some sense in force.

[243] Federal CCt, BVerfGE 24, 236 (247f): 'Admittedly, the state is neutral in religious matters and has to interpret constitutional terms on neutral, general grounds, and not on those found in the particular belief or philosophy'; for public religious corporations, see Ch 4 below; a Reichskonkordat was signed with the Catholic Church in 1933. Agreements have been entered between the Protestant church and the *länder*: eg Saxony (1994), Thuringia (1994), and Brandenburg (1996); and with the Catholic Church: eg Saxony (1996), Thuringia (1997), and Brandenburg (2003); and with smaller

The constitutions of the central and eastern States of Europe present the terms of both separation and cooperation formally. Some also illustrate the ambiguities of separation. The Czech Republic 'must not be bound either by any exclusive ideology or by a particular religion'—religious affairs are the responsibility of the Department of Churches at the Ministry of Culture, religious freedom is guaranteed, religious discrimination forbidden, religious associations may be registered (with consequential rights), and there are agreements with some religious organizations.[244] The same applies in Hungary (separation),[245] Romania (autonomy of religion),[246] Slovakia (the State is not bound by any religion),[247] and Slovenia (separation).[248] Similar arrangements—separation-with-cooperation—are also found in Poland,[249] Estonia,[250] Latvia,[251] and Lithuania.[252] However, the Bulgarian

religious communities (eg the Association of Jewish Congregations of Lower Saxony (1983); there is also an agreement between the Federal Republic of Germany and the Central Council of Jews (2003).

[244] CFRF 1992, Art 2.1; Arts 15, 16: religious freedom; CRSL 2002: registration; there is an agreement on cooperation between Czech Radio, the Ecumenical Council of Churches, and the Catholic Bishops' Conference (1999).

[245] Const, Art 60.3: 'The church and the State shall operate in separation in the Republic of Hungary'; Art 60.1–2: religious freedom; LFCRC 1990 regulates registered religious associations; there are agreements on specific issues (but not a general one) with the Holy See (on military chaplaincies, 10 January 1994; on finance, 20 June 1997).

[246] Const, Art 29.1: religious freedom; Art 29.2: it must be manifested in a spirit of tolerance and mutual respect; Art 29.5: religious organisations 'shall be autonomous from the State and shall enjoy support from it, including the facilitation of religious assistance in the armed forces, hospitals, prisons, homes and orphanages'; Art 29.4: religious enmity is forbidden; Art 29.3: 'All religions shall be free and organised in accordance with their own statutes, under the terms laid down by law'.

[247] Const, Art 1: the Republic is not bound by any ideology or religious belief; Art 24: religious freedom; a Law of 2007 regulates registration (and the register is kept by the Church Department of the Ministry of Culture); there are agreements with the Holy See, no 326/2001, no 648/2002 Zz; for agreements with registered churches, etc, see Act no 394/2000.

[248] Const, Art 7: 'The State and religious communities are separate. Religious communities enjoy equal rights and freedom of activity'; Art 41: religious freedom; Law of 2007 (registration); there are agreements with the Holy See 2001 and the Protestant Church 2000.

[249] Const, Art 25.3: 'The relationship between the State and churches and other religious organisations shall be based on the principle of respect for their autonomy and the mutual independence of each in its own sphere, as well as the principle of cooperation for the individual and the common good'; Art 25.4: 'The relations between [Poland] and the Roman Catholic Church shall be determined by international treaty concluded with the Holy See, and by statute'; Art 25.5: 'The relations between [Poland] and other churches and religious organisations shall be determined by statutes adopted pursuant to agreements concluded between their appropriate representatives and the Council of Ministers'; Art 53: religious freedom; see also the Statute on the Relationship between the Catholic Church and the State 1989, and the Statute on Freedom of Conscience and Religion 1989; there is a concordat with the Holy See 1993; Law of 20 February 1997 ratifies an agreement with the Pentecostal Church.

[250] Const, Art 40: 'There is no state church'; this article also deals with religious freedom; CCA 2002, RT I 2002, 24, 135; RT I 2002, 61, 375 deals with registered religious associations; there is an informal agreement with the Catholic Church (12 March 1999). There is also a Religious Affairs Department in the Ministry of Internal Affairs.

[251] Const, Art 99: 'The church shall be separate from the State' (but religious freedom is guaranteed); LORO 1995 (as amended) governs the registration, etc of religious organizations; there are agreements with the Holy See (ratified 25 October 2002) and with seven traditional religions (2004).

[252] Const, Art 43: 'There shall not be a state religion in Lithuania'; the article provides for the autonomy of religious organizations under statutes established by agreement or by law; Art 26: religious freedom; LORCA 1995 (registration of religious organizations and agreements) and Art 5

constitution provides that 'Religious institutions shall be separate from the State', but 'Eastern Orthodox Christianity shall be considered the traditional religion';[253] nevertheless, the Bulgarian Constitutional Court has classified the republic as 'secular',[254] and sub-constitutional law provides for the autonomy of registered religious organizations.[255]

Needless to say, the three models offer only general categorizations of the postures of States towards religion.[256] National and established churches take many forms, through the foundation, recognition, protection, control, or financial support of a church by the State to a national ministry for all.[257] The same applies to separation: in 'structural separation' the State is independent of the control of institutional religion (which itself is independent of state control); and in 'transvaluing separation', state neutrality excludes religious influences from public life— religion is privatized. In turn, cooperation between State and religion may involve 'principled pluralism', when the State recognizes the public value of religion, or 'pragmatic pluralism', when the State collaborates with religion to achieve common goals.[258] Moreover, whilst the models surface at the constitutional level, they are less conspicuous in sub-constitutional laws. Here each State has at least some elements of all three models. State churches vary so greatly (in their strategic and operational autonomy) that it is difficult to find the defining element of the system; and within each state-church system, the State is separate from but cooperates with other religious organizations. Separation States are cooperative in so far as they facilitate the practice of religion. Hybrid systems have a basic separation but are like state-church systems in so far as the State favours particular religious organizations with formal agreements.[259] Indeed, as we shall see throughout this book, more

---

of this recognizes nine 'traditional religions' which are not required to register their statutes with the Ministry of Justice (Roman Catholic, Greek Catholic, Lutheran, Reformed, Orthodox, Jewish, Old Believers, Sunni Muslims, and Karaites); there are agreements with the Holy See (eg 16 September 2000).

[253] Const, Art 13.2–3; Art 13.1: religious freedom; Art 13.4: 'Religious institutions and communities and religious beliefs shall not be used to political ends.'

[254] CCt, Decision no 2/1998 (State Gazette (SG) 15/1998).

[255] RDA 2002 (SG 120/2002), Ch 3; Art 10 complements Const, Art 13.3 on the Orthodox Church.

[256] For other models proposed outside the field of law, see eg: A Hastings, *The Faces of God* (London: Geoffrey Chapman Publishers, 1976) ch 5 (a typology of church-state relations); for a geopolitical approach, see JTS Madeley, 'A framework for the contemporary analysis of church-state relations in Europe' in JTS Madeley and Z Enyedi (eds), *Church and State in Contemporary Europe* (London: Frank Cass, 2003) 23.

[257] See eg N Doe, 'The notion of a national church: a juridical framework' (2002) Law and Justice 77; and M Ogilvie, 'What is a church by law established' (1990) 28 Osgoode Hall LJ 179.

[258] For these models and their proponents see R Ahdar and I Leigh, *Religious Freedom in the Liberal State* (Oxford: OUP, 2005) ch 3; this also examines the neutrality model (in which the State does not intervene in religion and neither encourages nor discourages it), and the related competitive market model, in which the State considers religion to be a matter of private or individual choice.

[259] For critiques of classical doctrine, see R Sandberg, 'Church-state relations in Europe: from legal models to an interdisciplinary approach' (2008) Journal of Religion in Europe 329; S Ferrari, 'The new wine and the old cask: tolerance, religion and the law in contemporary Europe' (1997) 10(1) *Ratio Iuris* 75.

often than not cooperation is the dominant feature in all States of Europe through the provision of a host of facilities.[260]

Conclusion

The States of Europe regulate religion by means of constitutional law, sub-constitutional laws which implement or otherwise complement constitutional provisions, case-law, formal agreements which may be ratified by law, and in some instances through regional laws. International laws of the European Union, Council of Europe, and United Nations are also sources of national religion laws. The array of legal instruments used by States to regulate religion, and the diversity of subjects regulated, indicate well the pervasiveness of religion in society, the extent of the competence which States assume over religion, and the level at which such matters are best addressed. Whilst not all States define 'religion', those which do offer a spectrum of definitional forms, from the minimalist to the expansive— and all share an understanding of religion as belief in a transcendental worldview practised in teaching, worship, and norms of conduct for the lives of believers. The classical outlook is that there are three models of religion-state relations in Europe: the state-church system (in the Protestant north and Orthodox south-east); the separation system (in France, Ireland, and the Netherlands); and, the most prevalent, the hybrid or cooperation system (in the Catholic Mediterranean, Baltic and central-eastern Europe). However, whilst the models appear in constitutional texts, they are often blurred at sub-constitutional level; as we shall see, all States cooperate with religion on a host of matters. Nevertheless, several common principles emerge from the similarities between national laws in terms of sources, subject-matter, and systems: when the State regulates religion it should do so in accessible legal instruments; the State determines which religious matters it regulates (subject to religious freedom); national religion laws should satisfy international standards; religion involves belief in a transcendental worldview and its practice in teaching, worship, and observance; a State may adopt a particular national religion provided it guarantees religious freedom for others; a State is free from the control of institutional religion and vice versa; and a State may cooperate with religion to further common goals and tasks.

---

[260] Namely, in the provision of religious freedom, prohibitions against religious discrimination (Chs 2 and 3); the legal position, personality and autonomy of religious organizations (Chs 4 and 5); the protection of religious belief from defamation and of worship from disturbance (Ch 6); the protection of religious sites and the funding of religion (Ch 7); the provision of education, including religious education, and spiritual care in hospitals, prisons, and the armed forces (Ch 8); and permitting solemnization of religious marriages (Ch 9).

2

Religious Freedom and the Individual

Academic discussion of religious freedom in Europe has been dominated by the jurisprudence of the European Court of Human Rights on religious freedom under Article 9 of the European Convention on Human Rights (ECHR). The ECHR regime has without doubt set important standards for human rights and religion, and its adoption by States has helped to implement these. However, any assumption that the ECHR is the dominant force nationally is misplaced. As we have seen, all the States guarantee religious freedom in their constitutions and these are supplemented in many by sub-constitutional laws. Religious freedom is guaranteed regardless of the posture of the State towards religion—state-church systems, separation systems, and cooperation systems all provide formal protection for religious freedom. In several States, such protection appears in constitutional texts developed in the nineteenth century (and in some cases earlier), and in many States the fall of fascist or communist regimes in the twentieth century led to the introduction of new, or the restoration of earlier, constitutional guarantees of religious freedom. This chapter explores national laws on religious freedom, particularly as they apply to the individual (though their applicability to religious organizations is mentioned, this is more fully dealt with in Chapters 4 and 5). It does so within the context of the ECHR and Strasbourg jurisprudence. The principal focus is the right to hold any religious belief, the right to manifest that belief, and the authority of the State to limit the exercise of the right to manifest religion including the grounds on which it may do so. The study proposes that there is a formal convergence between national laws on religious freedom—sometimes this occurs independently of the ECHR, and sometimes Strasbourg jurisprudence has contributed, but in varying degrees, to unify national laws on this subject. That convergence generates several principles of religion law common to the States of Europe.

The scope and importance of religious freedom

The importance of religious freedom is reflected in its presence at the highest level of national laws in the constitutions of Europe,[1] not to mention its treatment in

---

[1] Austria: StGG, 1867, Art 14, B-VG, Art 149; Finland: Const, Art 11; Germany: GG Arts 4, 140, WRV, Arts 136–137, 141; Czech Rep: CFRF, Arts 15, 16; Estonia: Const, Art 40; Denmark: Const,

some States by dedicated religious freedom legislation.[2] Some constitutional provisions on religious freedom (particularly the early texts still operative today) are rudimentary and succinct, their focus being on freedom of public worship or the free expression of religious opinions, such as those of France,[3] Belgium,[4] Denmark,[5] and Austria.[6] More modern texts, though equally brief, protect 'the free profession and practice of religion' (Ireland),[7] or 'the freedom to profess a religious creed' (Germany),[8] in public or private (Slovenia),[9] or 'freedom of religious conscience' and worship (Greece).[10] At the other end of the spectrum, there are more complex provisions in which religious freedom embraces both individual and collective rights; for example: 'Everyone has freedom of religion and conscience' which 'entails the right to profess and practise a religion, the right to express one's own convictions and the right to be a member or decline to be a member of a religious community' (Finland);[11] or, again, the right 'freely to profess religious beliefs in any form, individually or with others, to promote them and to celebrate rites in public or in private, provided they are not offensive to public morality' (Italy).[12] Several constitutions refer in a comprehensive manner to the public and private exercise of religious freedom, its individual and collective

Art 67; Greece: Const, Art 13; Spain: Const, Art 16; Ireland: Const, Art 44; Italy: Const, Art 19; Hungary: Const, Art 60; Latvia: Const, Art 99; Lithuania: Const, Arts 25, 26; Malta: Const, Art 40; Netherlands: Const, Art 6; Poland: Const, Art 53; Slovenia: Const, 1991, Art 41.

[2] For States with sub-constitutional law on religious freedom, see France: Law of 1905, Art 1; Portugal: Law no 16/2001; Hungary: Act 4/1990; Romania: Law 489, 27 December 2006; Spain: Const, Art 16; and Constitutional Law no 7/1980, 5.7.1980; Slovakia: Law no 308/1991 Zb.

[3] France: Declaration of the Rights of Man and the Citizen 1789, Art 10: no one shall be disturbed for his religious opinions; see also Const 1946, Preamble, 5; Const, 1958, Art 1: equality is assured for all citizens without distinction of origin, race or religion and all beliefs shall be respected; Law of 1905, Art 1: the Republic guarantees liberty of conscience; CCl, Decision no 87 DC, 23 November 1977.

[4] Belgium: Const (1831), Art 19: 'Freedom of worship, public practice of the latter, as well as freedom to demonstrate one's opinions on all matters, are guaranteed, except for the repression of offences committed when using this freedom.'

[5] Denmark: Const, Art 67 (originating in the Const 1848): 'Citizens shall be at liberty to form congregations for the worship of God in a manner according with their convictions, provided that nothing contrary to good morals or public order shall be taught or done'.

[6] Austria: StGG, 1867, Art 14; (B-VG, 1920, Art 149(1)); Treaty of St Germain 1919, Art 63(2): 'All inhabitants of Austria have the right to exercise in public or private every kind of belief, religion or confession freely, insofar as their exercise is not incompatible with public order or good morals.'

[7] Ireland: Const, Art 44. 2.1: 'Freedom of conscience and the free profession and practice of religion are, subject to public order and morality, guaranteed to every citizen.'

[8] Germany: GG (1949), Art 4: 'Freedom of faith and of conscience, and freedom to profess a religious or philosophical creed, shall be inviolable.'

[9] Slovenia: Const (1991), Art 41.1: 'Religious and other beliefs may be freely professed in private and public life'; see also CCt, no U-I-68/98 (November 2001).

[10] Greece: Const (1975), Art 13.1 and 13.2: 'Every known religion is free and its related worship is practised unhindered under the protection of law. The practice of worship must not pose a threat to public order or morals.'

[11] Finland: Const (2000), Art 11; moreover: 'No-one shall be under any obligation to participate in the practice of a religion against his or her conscience.'

[12] Italy: Const (1948), Art 19.

character, and its manifestation in teaching and ritual (Hungary).[13] Several constitutional texts are modelled on, or otherwise inspired by, Article 9 ECHR.[14]

In any event, ratification of the ECHR means that its statement of religious freedom in Article 9 is now part of the national laws of Europe.[15] Moreover, States often make the same distinction as does Article 9 between the right to hold a religious belief as an absolute right and the right to manifest religion as a limitable right, as is the case in Portugal,[16] Greece,[17] Luxembourg,[18] and the United Kingdom.[19] The distinction is particularly clear in the constitutional laws of central and eastern Europe, such as in Romania,[20] Bulgaria,[21] Slovakia,[22] and the Czech Republic.[23]

---

[13] Hungary: Const, Art 60: '(1) [E]veryone has the right to freedom of thought, conscience and religion; (2) This right includes free choice or acceptance of religion or other conviction and the liberty to publicly or privately express or decline to express, exercise and teach such religions and convictions by way of religious actions, rites or in any other way, either individually or in a group'; see also LFCRC, Act 4/1990.

[14] Cyprus: Const, Art 18.4: 'every person is free and has the right to profess his faith and to manifest his religion or belief, in worship, teaching, practice or observance, either individually or collectively, in private or in public, and to change his religion or belief'; see also *AG v Ibrahim* [1964] CLR 195, 225; Czech Rep: Const, Arts 15 and 16 are almost identical to Art 9 ECHR with the exception of Art 16.2 which spells out the right of churches and religious societies to autonomy.

[15] ECHR, Art 9: '1. Everyone has the right to freedom of thought, conscience and religion; this right includes freedom to change his religion or belief and freedom, either alone or in community with others and in public or private, to manifest his religion or belief, in worship, teaching, practice and observance. 2. Freedom to manifest one's religion or beliefs shall be subject only to such limitations as are prescribed by law and are necessary in a democratic society in the interests of public safety, for the protection of public order, health or morals, or for the protection of the rights and freedoms of others.'

[16] Portugal: Const, Art 41.1: liberty of conscience, religion, and cult is inviolable; Art 41.2: no one can be harassed, deprived of rights, dispensed of obligations by reason of their convictions or religious practices; see also LORF (Law no 16/2001) Art 1: '... freedom of conscience or religion and of worship is inviolable and guaranteed to all in accordance with the Constitution, the Universal Declaration of Human Rights, the applicable international law and the present law'.

[17] Greece: Const, Art 13.1: 'Freedom of religious conscience is inviolable. The enjoyment of civil rights and liberties does not depend on the individual's religious beliefs'; Bulgaria, Const, Art 13: 'The practice of any religion shall be unrestricted'; but 'Religious institutions and communities, and religious beliefs shall not be used for political ends'.

[18] Luxembourg: the administrative court has invoked the US Supreme Court to support the distinction between freedom to believe, which may not be restricted, and freedom to manifest belief (by action) which may be restricted: CA 2-7-1998, no 10648C, *Bulletin Laurent* 2000, IV 20; see US SC, *Cantwell v Connecticut* 310 US 296, 20 May 1940; it also invoked *Kokkinakis v Greece* (1994) 17 EHRR 397.

[19] *R v SoS for Education, ex p Williamson* [2005] UKHL 15, paras 16–17: 'under article 9 there is a difference between freedom to hold a belief and freedom to express or "manifest" a belief. The former right, freedom of belief, is absolute. The latter right, freedom to manifest belief, is qualified'.

[20] Romania: Const, Art 29.1: 'Freedom of thought, opinion, and religious belief may not be restricted in any form whatsoever.'

[21] Bulgaria: CCt, no 5 of 1992, 11.6.1992 (just before ratification of ECHR): in the internal forum, choice of religion, is 'a sphere which by its nature is not subject to legal sanction'; the free exercise of religion includes the manifestation of religion through word, press, and association; the court recognized that religious freedom cannot be limited except under Const, Arts 13.4 and 37; the limitations in these articles 'cannot be extended or amended by law or interpretation'.

[22] Slovakia: CCt, Decision no PL U 18/95 (24 May 1995).

[23] Czech Rep: Const, Act no 1/1993 Sb, CFRF, Act no 23/1991 Sb (republished in Act no 2/1993 Sb), Art 15.1: everyone has freedom of thought, conscience, and religion, and the right to change his religion or faith or to be non-denominational; see also CCt, 27 November 2002, no Pl US 6/02; and CCt, 8 October 1998, no IV US 171/97.

In Estonia: 'Everyone has freedom of conscience, religion and thought . . . Everyone has the freedom to practise his or her religion, both alone and in a community with others, in public or in private, unless this is detrimental to public order, health or morals';[24] moreover, the right to manifest religion (along with the other constitutional rights) may be limited on the basis of the constitution and such laws as are consistent with it, by restrictions which are 'necessary in a democratic society', as long as they do not 'distort the nature of the rights and liberties'; also, in the exercise of constitutional rights, individuals must respect the rights and liberties of others.[25] There is debate as to whether the right to manifest beliefs, expressly included alongside religion in Article 9 ECHR, covers also a right to manifest all forms of thought and conscience.[26]

The European Court of Human Rights in Strasbourg pronounced famously in 1994 that:

> Freedom of thought, conscience and religion is one of the foundations of a 'democratic society' within the meaning of the Convention. It is, in its religious dimension, one of the most vital elements that go to make up the identity of believers and their conception of life, but it is also a precious asset for atheists, agnostics, sceptics and the unconcerned. The pluralism indissociable from a democratic society, which has been dearly won over the centuries, depends on it.[27]

This affirmation of the importance of religious freedom is echoed by national courts throughout Europe, even in jurisprudence pre-dating ECHR incorporation: in Bulgaria religious freedom is understood as 'a value of the highest order'—without which 'democratic society is unthinkable'.[28] The German Constitutional Court understands its importance in these terms: 'In a State in which human dignity is the supreme value and in which free individual self-determination is recognised to have a community-forming value, freedom of religion grants individuals a legal space free of state interference in which they can follow a way of life corresponding to their belief'; it 'thus embraces not just the (inner) freedom to believe or not, but also the outer freedom to manifest, profess and spread faith', allowing individuals 'to pattern their whole behaviour on the teachings of their faith and to act according to their inner beliefs'.[29]

For some national courts religious freedom involves religious tolerance. In the United Kingdom, for example:

---

[24] Estonia: Const, Art 40.
[25] Estonia: Const, Arts 3.1, 11, 19; these broadly mirror ECHR, Art 9.2; see also Bulgaria: Const, Art 37.1 and 37.2: 'Freedom of conscience, freedom of thought and the choice of religion or of religious or atheistic views shall be inviolable. The State shall assist in the maintenance of tolerance and respect between the adherents of different denominations, and between believers and non-believers'; but: 'Freedom of conscience and religion shall not be exercised to the detriment of national security, public order, public health and morals, or the rights and freedoms of others.'
[26] See R Sandberg, *Law and Religion* (Cambridge: CUP, 2011) ch 3.
[27] *Kokkinakis v Greece* (1994) 17 EHRR 397.
[28] Bulgaria: CCt, Decision no 5 of 1992, 11.6.1992; see also Plovdiv DC, Decision no 755 of 17.7.2006 in Case no 464/2006: religious freedom is not simply a matter of local significance within districts of a national State.
[29] Germany: CCt, BVerfGE, 98 (106).

Religious and other beliefs and convictions are part of the humanity of every individual. They are an integral part of his personality and individuality. In a civilised society individuals respect each other's beliefs. This enables them to live in harmony. This is one of the hallmarks of a civilised society. Unhappily, all too often this hallmark has been noticeable by its absence. Mutual tolerance has had a chequered history even in recent times. The history of most countries, if not all, has been marred by the evil consequences of religious and other intolerance.[30]

However, in other States, religious freedom 'is not to be confused with religious tolerance';[31] rather, 'religious freedom is more than religious tolerance, i.e. the mere condoning of religious confessions or non-religious beliefs'.[32] Indeed, the Romanian constitution provides that freedom of conscience itself 'must be manifested in a spirit of tolerance and mutual respect'.[33] As we have already seen, for the purposes of religious freedom, 'religion' itself is defined as transcendental belief in divinity and action based upon that belief in the visible world.[34]

The right to freedom of religious belief

As we have seen, in line with Strasbourg jurisprudence on Article 9 ECHR,[35] national laws in Europe make a clear distinction between the right to hold and change religious beliefs, which is an absolute right, and the right to manifest religious beliefs, which is qualified.[36] Strasbourg has developed a rich jurisprudence around the idea that 'Article 9 primarily protects the sphere of personal beliefs and religious creeds, i.e. the area which is sometimes called the *forum internum*'.[37] In the internal forum, the right to hold any religious belief embraces the duty on the State to refrain from religious indoctrination,[38] and to refrain from determining whether a particular religious belief is valid or not.[39] The right to change religious belief has been applied by Strasbourg in several landmark cases,[40] and it prohibits

---

[30] UK: *R v SoS for Education, ex p Williamson* [2005] UKHL 15, *per* Lord Nicholls.

[31] Cyprus: *Pitsillides v The Republic of Cyprus* [1983] 2 CLR 374: 'Tolerance as a legal concept is premised on the assumption that the State has ultimate control over religion and the churches, and whether and to what extent religious freedom will be granted and protected is a matter of state policy'.

[32] Germany: CCt, BVerfGE, 98 (106).

[33] Romania: Const, Art 29.2.

[34] See Ch 1 above.

[35] *Manoussakis v Greece* (1997) 23 EHRR 387; *Metropolitan Church of Bessarabia v Moldova* (2002) 35 EHRR 306; *Moscow Branch of the Salvation Army v Russia* App no 72881/01 (ECtHR, 15 October 2006).

[36] See above.

[37] *C v UK* App no 10358/83 (1983) 37 D&R 142.

[38] See eg *Darby v Sweden* (1991) 13 EHRR 774.

[39] *Metropolitan Church of Bessarabia v Moldova* (2002) 35 EHRR 306: '[In] principle, the right to freedom of religion as understood in the Convention rules out any appreciation by the state of the legitimacy of religious beliefs or of the manner in which these are expressed.'

[40] *Ivanova v Bulgaria* App no 52435/99 (ECtHR, 12 April 2007): the decision of the local Chief Education Inspector to dismiss a person if she did not cease membership of an Evangelical Christian group violated Art 9 ECHR on the basis, *inter alia*, that the State could not dictate what a person should believe or take coercive steps to make a person change their beliefs.

States both from penalizing apostasy and from the obstruction of free religious affiliation.[41] The right to hold religious belief also embraces the right not to declare religious belief.[42]

In addition to adoption of the Article 9 ECHR right by incorporation in national laws, the right to hold any religious belief is recognized in domestic legislation and/ or jurisprudence in many States across Europe—a person may 'hold whatever beliefs he wishes'.[43] The right is understood to be based, variously, on the maxim *lex non cogit ad impossibilia*—the law simply cannot control the minds of people,[44] freedom of choice,[45] the idea that beliefs without action do no concrete social harm,[46] and prohibitions against disclosure of religious belief.[47] Whilst some States, such as Italy, seem to have no explicit legislation on the right to change religious belief,[48] in most States, such as Lithuania, the right is implicit in the constitutional entitlement 'to choose any religion or faith'.[49] However, some States include the right explicitly in their constitutional order.[50] There are five principles associated with these rights—some generate free-standing rights, others generate correlative rights or duties.

First, there is the negative right of an individual not to be forced to hold or adopt a religious belief against their will. Though religious organizations (as we shall see in Chapters 3 and 5) may require their members (or classes of member) to hold the beliefs of that organization, the State 'may not require anyone, either directly or indirectly, to accept a certain religious or other belief'.[51] The right is buttressed by duties in constitutional law and/or criminal law; many States penalize interference with the enjoyment of freedom of religious belief; Czech law is typical: a person who, by using violence or threats of violence or other serious harm, 'prevents another from enjoying freedom of religion', is liable to imprisonment for up to one year.[52]

---

[41] *Buscarini v San Marino* (2000) 30 EHRR 208: it was held, *inter alia*, that 'requiring the applicant [who had been elected to parliament] to take the oath on the Gospels was tantamount to requiring [him] to swear allegiance to a particular religion, a requirement which is not compatible with Article 9'.

[42] The right not to declare religious belief may also be conceived as a form of manifestation.

[43] *R v SoS for Education, ex p Williamson* [2005] UKHL 15, paras 23–24, *per* Lord Nicholls.

[44] Lithuania: Valstybes zinios (OG), 95-01-27, no 9-199, p 6.

[45] Spain: CCt, Ruling no 180/1986, 21 February 1986, FJ2: freedom of religion 'implies freedom to have or adopt the religion or beliefs of a person's choice, and to practise them through worship, the celebration of rites, customs and teaching, in accordance with the terms of the [ECHR]'; see also no 19/1985, 13 February 1985, FJ2; 46/2001, 15 February 2001, FJ 4; 154/2002, 18 July 2002, FJ 6; 101/2004, 2 February 2004, FJ2.

[46] Belgium: Federal Act of 2 June 1998: beliefs translated by sects into indoctrination *are* harmful.

[47] Spain: Const, Art 16; Hungary: Act IV/1990, s 3.4; Slovenia: Const, Art 6.14. See below.

[48] Italy: Const Art 19 (religious freedom) makes no reference to the right to change religious belief.

[49] Lithuania: Const, Art 26.

[50] Czech Rep: CFRF, Art 15.1; Bulgaria: Const, Art 37; Hungary: Const, Art 60.2; Cyprus: Const, Art 18.4.

[51] Slovenia: CCt, Decision no U-I-92/01 (February 2002).

[52] Czech Rep: PC, s 236. See also France: Law of 1905, Art 31: intentional menaces or violence against freedom of religion or conscience is a crime; penalty, €15,000 and/or 6 days' to 2 months' imprisonment; Spain: PC, Art 522: this punishes acts against religious freedom by violence, intimidation, or any other unlawful pressure; the penalty is a fine or 4–10 months' imprisonment; see also Ch 6 below.

Secondly, the State cannot compel persons to engage in religious activities which offend their religious beliefs.[53] Whilst the right of association may more readily be understood as relating to the practice of religion (see below), some States consider the right to hold religious belief to include the right freely to choose religious affiliation in terms of membership (or not) of a religious group or organization; as the Slovenian Constitutional Court put it: 'freedom of religion as *forum internum* includes the right to affiliation or non-affiliation with a particular religion'; the state 'may not use coercive measures nor offer privileges regarding affiliation or non-affiliation with a particular religion or other belief';[54] it has also been held that disclosure in a book of the name of a Freemason violated the right of association (which prevailed in this case over freedom of expression).[55] In turn, States penalize conduct which coerces people to join religious organizations.[56] Several States (such as Cyprus) fix the age of competence to choose a religious profession or affiliation.[57]

Thirdly, many religious laws and traditions forbid apostasy (total repudiation or abandonment of a system of religious belief),[58] and schism (abandonment of religious affiliation).[59] Historically, even into the nineteenth century, several European States forbad apostasy, either from Catholicism, Protestantism, or Christianity in general.[60] Today, individuals have a civil law right to apostasy on the basis of the entitlement freely to change religion, as in the Czech Republic,[61] Bulgaria,[62] and Slovenia.[63] The Cypriot constitution prohibits 'the use of physical or moral compulsion for the purpose of preventing [a person] from changing his religion';[64] Spanish law forbids acts which force a person 'to change the beliefs which they profess';[65] and France protects freedom from psychological or physical pressure

---

[53] *Darby v Sweden* (1991) 13 EHRR 774, annex to Ct, para 51: Art 9.1 'protects everyone from being compelled to be involved in religious activities against his will'.

[54] Slovenia: CCt, Decision no U-I-92/01 (February 2002).

[55] Slovenia: SC, Decision no II Ips 460/97 (October 1998).

[56] France: Law of 1905, Art 31: intentional menaces or violence to make a person join a religious group or to contribute/abstain from contributing to its funds, is a crime.

[57] Cyprus: Const, Art 18.7: until a person attains the age of 16, the decision as to which religion is to be professed belongs to the parent or guardian. See more fully Ch 9 below.

[58] In Islam, there is no right to apostasy: Islamic Declaration of Human Rights, Art 10 (Cairo, 5 August 1990).

[59] Roman Catholic Code of Canon Law (1983), Canon 751 (heresy, apostasy, and schism).

[60] Hungary: Catholics who became Lutheran were punishable under Acts 54/1523 and 4/1525 and decrees from 1731 and 1751 (reaffirmed in 1844), but apostasy was abolished in 1848; Sweden: by a statute of 1734 citizens were forbidden to leave the Lutheran church, and apostasy from the 'true evangelical creed' was punished by expatriation and disinheritance; Austria: apostasy from Christianity led to exclusion from intestate succession until 1868; under the PC 1803 and 1852 inducing a Christian to apostasy, and heresy against Christianity, were punishable with imprisonment; the offences were repeated in the PC 1945; Portugal: apostasy under PC 1852, Art 135 was abolished by Decree 15 February 1911, Art 4; Spain: apostasy was abolished in 1835; Finland: apostasy was abolished in 1889.

[61] Czech Rep: CFRF, Art 15.1: 'The freedom of thought, conscience and religious confession is secured. Everybody has the right to change his religion or faith or to be undenominational.'

[62] Bulgaria: since 1878 there has been no law on apostasy, but it might have been relevant to the former (pre-1946) constitutional rule that the monarch had to be an Orthodox Christian.

[63] Slovenia: CCt, Decision no U-I-92/01 (February 2002): see above.

[64] Cyprus: Const, Art 18(5); but this has never been supplemented by law.

[65] Spain: CCt, Decision 369/1984, June 20 (on the basis of LORF, Arts 3 and 5).

imposed in order to prevent a person from abandoning membership of a sect.[66] States often criminalize conduct which prevents people from freely leaving religious organizations.[67]

Fourthly, some States used to forbid proselytizing.[68] However, as religious laws commonly impose on the faithful a duty to spread the faith,[69] so the majority of national laws have for a long time protected the right to proselytize.[70] Today, by reference to Strasbourg jurisprudence, the right to proselytize is recognized by the Constitutional Court in Spain,[71] and by the Parliamentary Constitutional Committee in Finland (which held a decision of the assistant parliamentary ombudsman, that a parish of the Evangelical Lutheran Church could not distribute religious literature intended for its members to non-member households,[72] to violate the constitutional right to freedom of expression and religion).[73] By way of contrast, in Greece: 'Proselytising is prohibited'.[74] Indeed, in all the States of Europe, if proselytizing involves criminal activity, it is forbidden. For example, Cypriot constitutional law prohibits physical or moral compulsion to make a person change or prevent him from changing his religion; but this has not been supplemented by law,[75] though if proselytizing involves coercion or threats, these may constitute a criminal offence.[76]

Fifthly, the constitutions of a small number of States confer a formal right not to declare religious belief,[77] which may have been developed in jurisprudence.[78] This is the case in Slovenia: 'No-one shall be obliged to declare his religious or other beliefs';[79] however, a census carrying data on religious beliefs was held compatible with this right, with religious freedom, and with the separation of State and religion, as the law governing the census did not require anyone to make a

---

[66] France: Law no 2001-504, 12 June 2001, Art 19: there is a right freely to leave a sect.

[67] France: Law of 1905, Art 31 (see n 56 above). It would be interesting to explore the extent, if any, to which State courts could challenge the enforcement by a religious organization of its internal disciplinary rules on apostasy in the light of the principle of religious autonomy; see Ch 5 below.

[68] Portugal: proselytizing for a religion disapproved by the Catholic Church was penalized by the PC 1852, Art 130 until abolished by Decree of 15 February 1911, Art 4; Finland: the offence was abolished in 1971 (see previously PC 1889/1894, Ch 10, s 5).

[69] See eg Roman Catholic Code of Canon Law 1983, Canon 781.

[70] This has been the position in Denmark since 1849, Bulgaria since 1878, and the Czech Rep since Acts 142/1867 and 49/1868 (Acts of the Austrian Empire).

[71] Spain: Judgment no 141/2000, 29 May 2000, FJ 4.

[72] Assistant Parliamentary Ombudsman, Decision 3851/4/05.

[73] Report 17/2006: this also referred to Art 9 ECHR: there was no justification to place more severe restrictions on the freedom of expression of parishes to circulate literature than on the distribution of advertising leaflets, newspapers, or political literature.

[74] Greece: Const, Art 13.2.

[75] Cyprus: Const, Art 18.5; Jehovah's Witnesses are a free religion under Const, Art 18.2: *Minister of Interior v Jehovah's Witnesses Congregation (Cyprus) Ltd* [1995] 3 CLR 78.

[76] Cyprus: PC, Art 91; see also France: Law (on sects) no 2001-504, 12 June 2001, Art 19.

[77] See also ECHR, Art 8: the right to respect for private (and family) life.

[78] Spain: Const, Art 16; Organic Law 15/1999 of 13 December, Art 7: 'no one may be forced to disclose details of his ideology, religion or beliefs. Only with the express written consent of the person concerned may personal data revealing ideology, trade union affiliation, religion or beliefs be processed'; see also CCt, Ruling 359/1985, 29 May 1985, FJ2 (using ECHR, Art 9, UDHR, Art 18).

[79] Slovenia: Const, Art 41.2; Estonia: Const, Art 42; Sweden: Const, Ch 2, Art 2; Hungary: Act IV/1990, s 3.4.

declaration in the census return about their religious belief—had it done so, this would have been unconstitutional.[80] Whilst in other States, too, religious data may be recorded in a national census,[81] provided the individual permits this in exercise of the right not to disclose religious beliefs,[82] in some States religious data must not be included in population registers.[83]

The law of the European Union has also had an impact in the field of religious privacy—and this has resulted in the creation of fundamentally uniform national laws across Europe on the collection of religious data relating to an individual.[84] Data relating to religion, such as on religious belief or affiliation,[85] is classified as sensitive data and may be processed only with the consent of the data subject,[86] and in accordance with prescribed data protection principles.[87] For example, an employer may request information on religious convictions for the accommodation of religious diet or holidays.[88] Indeed, in Latvia, religious discrimination is penalized more severely if committed with the use of an automated data processing system.[89] However, there are exemptions when the data is collected by a non-profit religious organization, in the course of its lawful activities, provided this only involves the organization's members or regular associates, and the data is not published without the consent of the person.[90]

In short, the right to hold and to change religious beliefs is an absolute right. The State cannot limit its free exercise—since it cannot control the thoughts of people. Five principles are associated with this right and these may be cast as duties imposed on the State and its citizens: individuals must not to be forced to hold or adopt a religious belief against their will; individuals must not be forced to engage in religious activities which offend their religious beliefs; individuals must not be forced to change their religious beliefs (the right to apostasy); individuals may encourage others by lawful means to change their religious beliefs (the right to

---

[80] Slovenia: CCt, Decision no U-I-92/01 (February 2002): provided that persons could freely declare their religion or decline to do so; the court also relied on ECHR Art 9.

[81] Ireland: there must be a census every 5 years; it includes data on religion.

[82] Romania: Law 489/2006: 'it is hereby forbidden to compel an individual to declare their religion, in any relationship with public authorities or private-law legal entities'.

[83] Latvia: Population Register Law 1998, Art 12.

[84] Directive (EC) 95/46 of 24 October 1995.

[85] Denmark: Act on Personal Data, no 429 of 31 May 2000, Act on Statistics, no 1189 of 21 December 1992; Cyprus: Processing of Personal Data Law 138(I)/2001; Bulgaria: Statistics Act, Protection of Personal Data Act; France: PC Arts 226-19; Germany: Federal Law on the Protection of Data; Sweden: Act 1998:2004; Ireland: Data Protection Act of 1988 and Data Protection (Amendment) Act 2003.

[86] Belgium: Federal Act of 8 December 1992 Art 6.1; Luxembourg: Law on Data Protection 2002; Czech Rep: Data Protection Law, s 4; Greece: Law 2472/1997, Art 2; Italy: Data Protection Act, Art 22 (Law no 675, 31 December 1996); Malta: Data Protection Act 2001, Art 12; Netherlands: Personal Data Protection Act, Art 16; Portugal: Law 67/98 of 26 October 1998, Art 7.1; Spain: Organic Law 15/1999 of 13 December, Art 7; Greece: Law 2472/1997.

[87] Estonia: Personal Data Protection Law 2007, Art 4; Finland: Personal Data Act (523/1999) ss 11 and 12—these principles include eg fairness, accuracy, and ensuring that information is up-to-date.

[88] Italy: Workers' Act (Act 1970/300), s 8.

[89] Latvia: Criminal Law (1998), s 149: a prison sentence of up to 2 years, mandatory community service, or a fine which is equal to no more than 50 times the minimum monthly wage.

[90] Poland: Act on the Protection of Personal Data; Romania: Law 677/2001, Arts 5, 7.

proselytize); and individuals must not be forced to declare their religious beliefs. These principles are often supported by criminal laws. However, the last two principles may be more appropriately conceived as manifestations of religion, to which we now turn.

The right to manifest religion

National laws in Europe generally mirror both Article 9 ECHR and Strasbourg jurisprudence as to the terms of the right to manifest religious belief. There is legislation and jurisprudence on what constitutes manifestation, the right to manifest religious belief in community or alone, in public or private, and in worship, teaching, practice, or observance. There are also special rules on waiver of the right to manifest when individuals voluntarily submit to a situation in which they acquiesce in restrictions on the free exercise of religion, as well as on conscientious objection.

The manifestation of religious belief

The manifestation must be of religion or belief, that is, a belief which must be coherent, serious and important, and consistent with human dignity.[91] According to early Strasbourg jurisprudence, there was no manifestation of belief if the activity in question was merely motivated by that belief.[92] This restrictive approach was heavily criticized,[93] and Strasbourg has since held that a manifestation exists if the action 'expresses' religious belief,[94] or is 'intimately linked' with religious belief,[95] as for example when a religious duty requires the action which constitutes manifestation.[96] Nor may a State determine whether the means of manifestation are 'legitimate'.[97]

---

[91] UK: *R v SoS for Education, ex p Williamson* [2005] UKHL 15, paras 23–24, *per* Lord Nicholls: 'when questions of "manifestation" arise . . . a belief must satisfy some modest, objective minimum requirements . . . . [it] must be consistent with basic standards of human dignity or integrity . . . . relate to matters more than merely trivial . . . possess an adequate degree of seriousness and importance . . . [and] it must be a belief on a fundamental problem . . . [and] coherent in the sense of being intelligible and capable of being understood. But, again, too much should not be demanded in this regard'.

[92] *Arrowsmith v UK* (1978) 3 EHRR 218: the Commission held that the term 'practice' in Art 9 'does not cover each act which is motivated or influenced by a religion or a belief'. Although the applicant was 'motivated or influenced' by pacifist beliefs she did not 'actually express the belief concerned'.

[93] R Sandberg, *Law and Religion* (Cambridge: CUP 2011) ch 3; S Knights, *Freedom of Religion, Minorities and the Law* (Oxford: OUP 2007) ch 2.

[94] eg *Knudsen v Norway* App no 11045/84 (1985) 42 D&R 247; see generally C Evans *Freedom of Religion under the European Convention on Human Rights* (Oxford: OUP, 2001) ch 6.

[95] *C v UK* App no 10358/83 (1983) 37 D&R 142.

[96] *X and Church of Scientology v Sweden* App no 7805/77 (1979) 16 D&R 68.

[97] *Manoussakis v Greece* (1997) 23 EHRR 387: '[The] right to freedom of religion as guaranteed under the convention excludes any discretion on the part of the State to determine whether religious beliefs or the means used to express such beliefs are legitimate.'

Whilst the constitutional laws of several States merely mirror the manifestation formula of Article 9 ECHR, most do not,[98] though some national courts do adopt the more recent Strasbourg approach on the relationship between the manifestation and the belief in question: the conduct, on 'objective standards', must be a 'direct expression' of religion or belief.[99] However, most national courts are not particularly exercised by the niceties of the Strasbourg distinctions on manifestation. More commonly, they use the much simpler notion of 'practice'—the practice of religious belief is, so to speak, their generic equivalent to manifestation: religious liberty 'implies freedom to have or adopt the religion or beliefs . . . and to practise them'.[100] Moreover, 'practice' does not refer to 'the observance of church prescriptions in the practice of every-day life' but 'to actions that according to their nature give expression to a religion or belief in any way'.[101] Therefore, as the German Constitutional Court puts it:

Religious practice does not just cover cultic actions and practices and the observance of religious customs such as worship, church collections, prayers, receiving the sacraments, processions, showing church flags, and ringing bells. It also extends to religious education, private religious and atheistic celebrations and expressions of the way of life connected to the religion or beliefs.[102]

In turn, across Europe, religious 'practices and observances' may include 'habits of dress and diet',[103] such as wearing religious headscarves,[104] the provision and receipt of pastoral care,[105] preaching,[106] parental imparting of religious beliefs to

---

[98] cf Lithuania: Const, Art 26: 'Every person has the right freely . . . either individually or with others, in public or in private, to manifest his or her religion or faith in worship, observance, practice or teaching' (and Cyprus: Const, Art 18.4; Czech Rep: Const, Art 15) and Italy: Const, Art 19: 'Everyone is entitled to freely profess religious beliefs in any form, individually or with others, to promote them and to celebrate rites in public or in private' (see nn 3 *et seq* above).

[99] Netherlands: Social Security Court, 23 May 2000, RSDV 2000, 175.

[100] Spain: CCt, Ruling no 180/1986, 21 February 1986, FJ2.

[101] Netherlands: HR 13 April 1960, NJ 1960, 436: a church minister refused conscientiously to pay a levy for his pension on the grounds that the financial care of church ministers was the responsibility of his church. Similar reasoning was applied to the slaughter of a goat at home without prior notification to the relevant public authorities as required under local law: see HR 4 November 1969, NJ 1970, 127.

[102] Germany: BVerfGE 24, 236 (246).

[103] Lord Walker, *R v SoS for Education, ex p Williamson* [2005] UKHL 15, para 62.

[104] Germany: BVerfGE 108, 282: a prohibition on teachers wearing a headscarf at school in the light of 'societal change linked to increasing religious pluralism' is a violation of the constitutional right to manifest religion; though social change 'may be an occasion for the legislator to redefine the admissible extent of religious [expressions] at school'. See Ch 8 below.

[105] Austria: VfSlg 15.592/1999: the law allowed prisoners to receive care from a pastor of their 'own religious belief'; a Jehovah's Witness prisoner requested pastoral care from another group of which he was not a member and the request was rejected on the basis of lack of formal membership of that group; however, it was held that the decision violated domestic religious freedom law and ECHR, Art 9.1: the requirement 'own religious belief' was satisfied in so far as the group was prepared to provide pastoral care even without formal membership; the right to manifest included receiving pastoral care.

[106] Bulgaria: a local law of Plovdiv required religious groups to register and it imposed fines for failure to do so; Jehovah's Witnesses were fined under the law for preaching without registration in a private home and a hired public hall—they claimed that this was a breach of national law and the ECHR. The Supreme Administrative Court upheld their conviction—the local law was within the

their children,[107] or the fulfilment of religious 'customs',[108] exhortations,[109] or duties, and the performance of religious rites,[110] such as burial rites,[111] as well as the practice of religious association (in organizations).[112] Some national courts distinguish between 'core' and 'peripheral' religious activities practised by small numbers of believers within a particular religious tradition or group;[113] the distinction has sometimes led to the protection only of the former, not the latter.[114] Above all, freedom of religious practice is 'to live and act according to one's own beliefs'.[115] In short, the practice of religion, the national equivalent to the Strasbourg concept of manifestation, is traditionally elucidated across Europe by reference to those elements of legal definitions of religion which were set out in Chapter 1.

Interference with the practice of religion

A key principle of Strasbourg jurisprudence is that States must not interfere with the manifestation of religion. This prohibition is deeply embedded in the national laws and jurisprudence of the States of Europe independently of their implementation of the ECHR. The prohibition may be illustrated by criminal laws which concern religious freedom, namely forcing a person to, or preventing a person from, the free practice of religion.[116] However, the rules of criminal law, analogous to the right to hold and to change religious beliefs, go well beyond the ECHR: this is

---

competence of the local council and did not violate religious freedom but merely placed legitimate restrictions on its exercise: Supreme Admin Ct, Cases no 7237/2000, no 2174/2000, no 5116/2003.

[107] Germany: BVerfGE 41, 29, 44, 47; 93, 1, 17. See more fully Ch 9 below.

[108] Spain: CCt, Ruling no 180/1986, 21 February 1986, FJ2: the practice of religion 'through worship, the celebration of rites, customs and teaching, in accordance with the terms of the [ECHR]'.

[109] UK: *R v SoS for Education, ex p Williamson* [2005] UKHL 15, para 62: 'Most religions require or encourage communal acts of worship of various sorts, preaching, public professions of faith.'

[110] Slovenia: CCt, Decision no U-I-111/04 (July 2004): 'freedom of religion ensures that the individual may freely profess their religion . . . by the fulfilment of religious duties . . . and the performance of religious rites . . . the so-called positive aspect of freedom of religion'; the court relied, *inter alia*, on *X and Church of Scientology v Sweden* App no 7805/77 (1979) 16 D&R 68.

[111] France: CE, 6 January 2006, no 260307.

[112] Germany: the constitutional right to 'Religious freedom . . . also includes freedom of religious association'; moreover: 'Freedom of religious association guarantees the freedom to form and organise a religious society': BVerfGE 83, 341. For religious association, see Ch 4 below.

[113] UK: *R v SoS for Education, ex p Williamson* [2005] UKHL 15, para 62, *per* Lord Walker: 'There will usually be a central core of required belief and observance and relatively peripheral matters observed by only the most devout. These can all be called manifestations of a religious belief.'

[114] UK: *R (on the application of Ghai) v Newcastle City Council* [2009] EWHC (Admin) 978: Hindus and Sikhs sought cremations on open air funeral pyres; the HC noted that 'the weight to be given to religious rights depends on how close the subject matter is to the core of the religion's values or organisation'; rejecting the submission that 'the determination of the core content of the Hindu religion is not a matter for the court', the judge held that Hindu belief about open air funeral pyres had 'the requisite degree of seriousness and importance' and was 'concerned with central rather than peripheral matters'; as to the Hindu claim, the court held that there had been interference, but that this was justified under Art 9.2 ECHR; as to the Sikh claim, the court held that the practice in Sikhism was a 'tradition' and not 'a dogma or belief'. The decision was upheld in the CA, but for other reasons.

[115] Germany: BVerGE, 31 May 2006–2 BvR 1693/04 (on GG, Art 4.10); see also BVerGE 32, 98, 106.

[116] Luxembourg: PC, Arts 142 and 143: violence and menaces against religious practices.

addressed to States whereas national criminal laws extend the prohibition to citizens. Spain is typical: the criminal law penalizes violence, intimidation, force, or any other illegitimate pressure, which either prevents 'a member . . . of a religion, from practices pertaining to the beliefs which they profess', or forces them 'to carry out acts of professing or not [professing] a religion'.[117] This formula is commonly used throughout Europe.[118] Criminal sanctions may be imposed for interference with, or coercion to engage in, for example, the performance of worship,[119] rituals, and services;[120] the celebration of religious festivals and holidays;[121] the performance of 'religious acts';[122] and the fulfilment of 'religious duties'.[123] The same applies to the coercion involved in the foundation of,[124] membership in,[125] contribution of funds to,[126] and the administration of property by a religious association.[127]

According to Strasbourg jurisprudence, there is no interference with the right to manifest religion under Article 9.1 ECHR, when a matter does not fall within the definition of belief; when the activity in question is not a manifestation of that belief; and when (in the field of civil law) the 'specific situation rule' applies. These are the so-called 'filtering devices', and are in reality limitations implicit in Article 9.1 distinct from the limitations explicit in Article 9.2, which justify State interference with the right to manifest religion (see below).[128] The specific situation rule recognizes that the right to manifest religion may be tempered by the particular situation of the individual who claims to exercise that right. The rule applies when an individual voluntarily submits themselves to a system of rules or other regulated environment, such as a prison,[129] military service,[130] a contract of employment (public[131] or

---

[117] Spain: PC, Art 522.

[118] Austria: PC, para 283; Belgium: PC, Art 142; Romania: PC, Art 318.2; Hungary: PC, para 174/A; Czech Rep: PC, s 236; Estonia, PC, Art 154.

[119] Spain: PC, Art 522; for judicial consideration of this, see CCt, Decree 369/1984, 20 June.

[120] For imprisonment for up to 1 year, see Bulgaria: PC, Art 165.1–2; Czech Rep: PC, s 236.

[121] Belgium: PC, Art 142: it is an offence to force or hinder anyone to practise a religion, including the celebration of certain religious festivities, and religious holidays; the punishment is a prison sentence of 8 days to 2 months and a fine. See also: Estonia: PC, Art 154.

[122] Slovakia: PC, Art 193.

[123] Greece: Military Penal Code, Art 158: any military officer arbitrarily preventing the reasonable exercise, within the limits imposed by the defined measures of order adopted by the military authority, of the religious duties of any prisoner, or insulting the religion of such prisoner in his/her presence, shall be sentenced to imprisonment for a maximum of 1 year.

[124] Estonia: PC, Art 159; it is punishable by a fine and/or prison.

[125] Estonia: PC, Art 154: there is no offence if the religious affiliation is detrimental to the morals, rights, or health of other people or violates public order; see also Art 155.

[126] France: Law of 9 December 1905, Art 31 (see n 56 above).

[127] France: CE, Decision, 25 August 2005, no 284307 (religious goods); 25.11.1994 (ritual slaughter, concerning the Israelite Cultuelle Association Ch'are Shalon Ve Tsedek (see n 134 below)).

[128] See R Sandberg, *Law and Religion* (Cambridge, 2011) ch 5.

[129] *X v UK* App no 5442/72 (1975) 1 D&R 41, 41–42.

[130] *Kalaç v Turkey* (1997) 27 EHRR 552.

[131] *Konttinen v Finland* App no 24949/94 (EComHR, 3 December 1996): dismissal by the State Railways of a member of the Adventist Church, absenting himself from work to observe holy days) without permission, did not breach Art 9: the right of resignation was the ultimate guarantee of religious freedom.

private),[132] or a university.[133] However, the rule has been softened in so far as it will only be applied when it is possible for a person in a specific situation to exercise their right to manifest religion in other ways.[134] Nevertheless, the specific situation rule has not had a great impact in more recent years in Strasbourg.[135]

The specific situation rule is commonly invoked in the States of Europe in contexts similar to those envisaged by Strasbourg, particularly in education. For example, in the Netherlands the rule has been applied to a director of a Catholic school who joined a Bhagwan community—he could not rely on religious freedom to escape a prohibition in the school against the wearing of orange gowns;[136] and in Luxembourg, it was applied to Seventh Day Adventist pupils who were required to attend school on Saturdays—there was no interference with their constitutional right to religious freedom.[137] Some States tend to the idea that whether there has been interference with the right to practise religion depends on the reasonableness of expectations of the individuals in such specific situations; and this pre-dates the development of the rule by Strasbourg.[138] Moreover, the rule has been applied in situations beyond those envisaged by Strasbourg. Three interesting examples come from the Netherlands: there was no interference with religious practice when a person who voluntarily placed himself in a traffic situation refused on religious grounds to undertake an obligatory blood test—he was convicted for the refusal;[139] there was no interference where a newly elected representative to the States Provincial refused on religious grounds to take the prescribed oath (as it contained a reference to 'Almighty') when an alternative oath was available;[140] similarly, if a

---

[132] *Stedman v UK* (1997) 23 EHRR CD168: the applicant was dismissed for refusing to accept a contract which meant she would have to work on Sundays. The Court held, *inter alia*, that there was no interference with her Art 9 right since she had not been pressured to change her religious views.

[133] *Karaduman v Turkey* App no 16278/90 (1993) 74 D&R 93: there was no interference because the applicant had chosen to pursue higher education in a secular university and had voluntarily submitted to university rules 'which may make the freedom of students to manifest their religion subject to restrictions as to place and manner intended to ensure harmonious coexistence between students of different beliefs'.

[134] *Jewish Liturgical Association Cha'are Shalom Ve Tsedek v France* App no 27417/75 (ECtHR, 27 June 2000): an 'alternative means of accommodating [the manifestation of] religious beliefs had . . . to be "impossible" before a claim of interference under article 9 could succeed'.

[135] S Knights, *Freedom of Religion, Minorities and the Law* (Oxford: OUP, 2007) 44; see also R Sandberg, 'The changing position of religious minorities in English law: the legacy of *Begum*' in R Grillo *et al* (eds), *Legal Practice and Cultural Diversity* (Aldershot: Ashgate, 2010) 267. See also *Sahin v Turkey* (2005) 41 EHRR 8: a university regulation banned a student from wearing a headscarf; although the rule was referred to (para 66), the court 'proceeded on the assumption that the regulations in issue, which placed restrictions of place and manner on the right to wear the Islamic headscarf in universities, constituted an interference with the applicant's right to manifest her religion'.

[136] Netherlands: AB 1983/277.

[137] Luxembourg: CCt, 20 November 1998: there was no breach of Const, Arts 19 and 20.

[138] UK: *Ahmad v Inner London Education Authority* [1978] QB 36: a full-time teacher claimed he was forced to resign after being refused permission to attend a Mosque during the hours of employment; the court held that there was no interference. See also *R v SoS for Education, ex p Williamson* [2005] UKHL 15, para 38: 'What constitutes interference depends on all the circumstances of the case, including the extent to which . . . an individual can reasonably expect to be at liberty to manifest his beliefs in practice'; the individual 'may need to take his specific situation into account'.

[139] Netherlands: HR, 9 June 1987, VR 1988, 60.

[140] Netherlands: Afdeling bestuursrechtspraak Raad van State, 16 January 2002, AB 2002, 77.

person fails to avail themselves of a legal exemption which would enable them to carry out a religious practice, they cannot then rely on religious freedom to challenge a restriction imposed on that conduct.[141]

As a result, some national courts now consider that the Strasbourg rule is one of general applicability. Therefore, it is now often difficult to establish interference in the exercise of the right to manifest religion.[142] For this reason, British courts have criticized the specific situation rule—the waiver of the right to the free practice of religion is inconsistent with the fundamental character of that right.[143] Finally, whereas Strasbourg has not applied the specific situation rule to a non-religious claimant who voluntarily puts themselves in a 'religious' situation,[144] national courts commonly hold that voluntary submission of a person (such as an employee) to the disciplinary regime of a religious association may result in limitations on the exercise of the religious freedom of that person. What might be styled the 'religious situation rule' (explored more fully in Chapter 3) has been deployed, for example, in Finland: a person who is employed by a religious organization and subsequently finds themselves in conflict with that organization on an issue of belief is deemed to have exercised his right to religious freedom in the act of undertaking that employment.[145]

Conscientious objection to military service

The interplay between the right to hold a religious belief and the right to manifest that belief is illustrated well by conscientious objection to military service. Whilst the notion of a right to conscientious objection is growing in international treaty law,[146] and in the Charter of Fundamental Rights of the European Union,[147] the classical stance of Strasbourg is that States are not obliged by Article 9 ECHR to recognize conscientious objection for the purpose of military service,[148] as this is

---

[141] Netherlands: HR, 16 January 1968, NJ 1969, 2: the case concerned a Quaker who sought to hold a protest march but had failed to apply for a permit and then, refused, relied on religious freedom.
[142] *R (on the application of Begum) v Headteacher and Governors of Denbigh High School* [2006] UKHL 15: a school's ban on wearing a *jilbab* was not an interference with the Art 9 right to manifest a pupil's religion on the basis of the specific situation rule; see also *R (on the application of X) v Y School* [2006] EWHC (Admin) 298 and *R (on the application of Playfoot (A Child)) v Millais School Governing Body* [2007] EWHC 1698; this approach has been much criticized: see M Hill and R Sandberg, 'Is nothing sacred? Clashing symbols in a secular world' (2007) Public Law 488–506.
[143] *Copsey v WBB Devon Clays Ltd* [2005] EWCA Civ 932, para 35, *per* Mummery LJ; Strasbourg had made 'repeated assertions [about the rule] unsupported by the evidence or reasoning that would normally accompany a judicial ruling'; the rule was 'difficult to square with the supposed fundamental character of [convention] rights'; Neuberger LJ also described the rule as 'surprising'.
[144] *Lautsi v Italy* App no 30814/06 (ECtHR, 3 November 2009): for discussion of the possible 'religious situation rule', see R Sandberg, *Law and Religion* (Cambridge: CUP, 2011) ch 10.
[145] Finland: Parliamentary Constitutional Committee, PeVL 22/1997, on a bill on the Orthodox Church.
[146] UNHRC (1993) General Comment 22: the ICCPR does not refer to 'a right to conscientious objection, but . . . such a right can be derived from article 18 . . . as the obligation to use lethal force may seriously conflict with the freedom of conscience and the right to manifest one's religion'.
[147] Art 10.2: 'The right to conscientious objection is recognised, in accordance with the national laws governing the exercise of this right.'
[148] *Grandrath v Germany* App no 2299/64, 10 YB ECHR 626 (1966).

not articulated in the ECHR.[149] However, Strasbourg is tending to the view that States may legitimately require strong evidence of genuine religious objections to justify exemptions from military service.[150] National laws employ various approaches to the matter.[151] First, there are those States which recognize that conscientious objection to military service is not protected under the ECHR, such as France[152] and the Netherlands,[153] which may be contrasted with conscientious objection in the field of health care.[154]

Secondly, there are those States which go beyond the ECHR and provide for conscientious objection to military service.[155] Slovakia is typical: 'No-one can be made to execute military service if it shall contradict his conscience or religious confession'; however, those wishing to use this right must exercise it within the deadlines prescribed by law (and these are justified to maintain preparedness for military action);[156] nevertheless, it is unconstitutional to revoke or refuse a gun licence to a person who, on religious grounds, lawfully refused military service—rights enjoyable equally by all citizens cannot be denied on the basis of a previous exercise of the right of religious freedom.[157] Portuguese law is unusual, as its treatment of military service is part of a general 'right to object to compliance with laws that contradict the imperative commands of one's own conscience, within the limits of the rights and duties imposed by the Constitution and under the terms of the law that may regulate the exercise of the conscientious objection'.[158] In Romania only monks, novices, and priests of registered religions are exempt from military service.[159]

---

[149] ECHR, Art 4.1.b: no one shall be required to perform forced or compulsory labour but this does not include 'any service of a military character or, in case of conscientious objectors *in countries where they are recognised*, service exacted instead of compulsory military service' (emphasis added).

[150] *N v Sweden* App no 10410/83 (1985) 40 D&R 203; *Raninen v Finland* App no 20972/92 (1996) 84-A D&R 17.

[151] See generally, *Conscientious Objection in the EC Countries*, PECCSR (Milan, 1992); Germany: Protestant and Catholic clergy and full-time ministers of other religions are exempt from military service, and ordinands may defer: WPflG, paras 11, 12; Latvia: Compulsory Military Service Law, Art 21.1.7; Netherlands: Military Conscription Act; Austria: Defence Act 1990, WehrG, s 18.3; Civilian Service Act 1986, ZivildienstG, s 13(a)(1); Poland: Main Administration Court, NSA Sygn III SA 1411/00 (19 September 2000); Portugal: Concordat with the Holy See, Art 17.

[152] France: CE, 8 June 1990, no 87195.

[153] Netherlands: SC, HR 9 June 1987, VR 1988, 60.

[154] See Ch 8 below, at n 142.

[155] Slovenia: Const, Art 46; Spain: the Constitutional Court has held that conscientious objection is a constitutional right of a non-fundamental nature when related to religious freedom: Judgment no 15/1982, 23 April 1982, FJ 6; and no 160/1987, 27 October 1987; no 161/1987, 27 October 1987, FJ 3.

[156] Slovakia: CCt, Dec no PL US 18/95 (24 May 1995); Civil Service Law, no 18/1992.

[157] Slovakia: CCt, Dec no PL US 18/97 (3 June 1998); the Law on Weapons and Ammunition which authorized this, breached Const, Art 12.4 (which prohibits denial of fundamental rights).

[158] Portugal: LORF, 16/2001, Art 12: 'The commands of conscience considered as imperative are those whose infringement involves a serious offence to one's moral integrity and . . . make any other behaviour non-mandatory'; and: 'Conscientious objectors to military service, without excluding those who also invoke a conscientious objection to civil service, have the right to civil service, which respects the commands of their conscience, as long as it is compatible with the principle of equality.'

[159] Romania: Law 46 of 1996, Art 6; Government Decree 618 of 1997 implements this.

Thirdly, there are those States which consider that alternative forms of service should be offered to those with conscientious objections. In some States this is found in legislation,[160] but in others in jurisprudence,[161] such as in Estonia, where courts have held that conscientious objection to military service on religious grounds does not include the right to refuse alternative civil service; all persons who refuse to serve in the defence forces for religious reasons must participate in alternative service.[162] The matter has particularly exercised Cypriot courts: the rule that no person shall be required to perform compulsory labour does not apply to 'any service of a military character if imposed or, in case of conscientious objectors, subject to their recognition by a law, any service exacted instead of compulsory military service'.[163] In one case a military court convicted two Jehovah's Witnesses for refusal to join the army. The Supreme Court held that religious beliefs and conscientious objection do not by themselves constitute a reasonable cause for exemption from compulsory military service, and these may be overridden by the political needs of the State.[164] Nevertheless, the court suggested the introduction of an exemption for conscientious objectors from compulsory military service and/or imposition of alternative service; the law was then reformed.[165] In another case a Muslim objected to military service on the ground that the National Guard was Christian Orthodox in character; the Supreme Court rejected this: the obligation applies to citizens and not to adherents of any particular religion, and the National Guard provides that non-Christians must be allowed to practise their religion.[166] Indeed, the Cypriot ombudsman held, in 2006, that the decision of the Council of Ministers to exempt three religious groups from military service violated the principle of equal treatment and constituted discrimination on grounds of religion—the Council reversed its decision.[167]

Limitations on the right to manifest religion

We have already met limits on the right to manifest religious belief which are implicit in the conditions required both for that right to be engaged and for there to

---

[160] Portugal: LORF, 16/2001, Art 12.3.

[161] Lithuania: two Jehovah's Witnesses sought to evade military service on religious grounds; the Commission of the Ministry for National Defence provided that alternative service should be offered; the Klaipeda Regional Court did not offer alternative service (2003); the DC held this to be unlawful (2004).

[162] Estonia: SC (Criminal Chamber), Case no 3-1-1-82-96; see Const, Art 124 on military service.

[163] Cyprus: Const, Art 10.3; this implements ECHR, Art 4.3.b.

[164] For the Supreme Court, Turkish occupation of 37% of Cyprus justified a limit of religious freedom by imposing compulsory military service and the law which did so was not unconstitutional.

[165] *Pitsillides v The Republic of Cyprus* [1983] 2 CLR 374: 'so long as the National Guard is used for the defence and security of the country, the Law imposing the obligation for military service on the citizens of Cyprus, irrespective of whether the right to religion and conscience is restricted, is not unconstitutional'; for the new Law 2/1992, see T Christodoulidou, 'Religious conscientious objection in Cyprus' (2006) 2 Cyprus and European Law Review 324.

[166] *Sarieddine v Cyprus* [2004] 3 CLR 572: so there was no breach of Const, Art 18 or ECHR, Art 9.

[167] Emilianides (2007) 49: the groups were the Maronites, Roman Catholics, and Armenians.

be an interference with its exercise. The right is not engaged if there is no manifestation of belief, and there is no interference when the specific situation rule applies. However, for Strasbourg, if the right is engaged and there has been interference with its exercise, the State may nevertheless (under Article 9.2 ECHR) justify interference with the right to manifest religion if the limitation is prescribed by law, serves a legitimate aim, and is necessary in a democratic society.[168] The limit is prescribed by law if it is authorized by 'written law', including parliamentary or secondary legislation,[169] and 'unwritten law', including judge-made law.[170] The restriction has a legitimate aim if pursued in the interests of public safety; the protection of public order, health, or morals; or the protection of the rights and freedoms of others.[171] The interference is justified on the basis that it is necessary in a democratic society if there is a 'compelling social need', and the restriction is proportionate.[172] The following explores the extent to which these limitations exist in the national laws of Europe.

The limitation models

There are four different, but closely related, approaches in national laws to substantive limitations on the right to manifest religion.[173] First, as we have seen, there are those States whose constitutions repeat the limitations found in Article 9.2 ECHR, such as the Czech Republic: the right to manifest religion may be limited by law, when this is necessary in a democratic society for the protection of public safety and order, health and morals, or the rights and freedoms of others;[174] this means the State may limit the exercise of the right but not deny its existence.[175] Indeed, one Constitutional Court considers that there is 'absolute harmony' between national law and the terms of Article 9.2 ECHR.[176] Secondly, there are States which repeat but add to the grounds appearing in the text of Article 9.2.[177]

---

[168] ECHR, Art 9.2 itself makes no reference to legitimate aim.

[169] *De Wilde, Ooms and Versyp v Belgium* (1979–80) 1 EHRR 373; rules of professional bodies made under delegated powers may also have the status of law: *Barthold v Germany* (1985) 7 EHRR 383.

[170] *Sunday Times v UK (No 1)* (1979–1980) 2 EHRR 245; the principle of legality requires this: Evans (n 94 above) 138.

[171] For Strasbourg this is often a formality: PM Taylor, *Freedom of Religion: UN and European Human Rights Law and Practice* (Cambridge, 2005) 301: it tends 'to accept rather than challenge the aim claimed by the State, and accordingly pass over this precondition with little detailed analysis'.

[172] *Serif v Greece* (2001) 31 EHRR 20. D Feldman, *Civil Liberties and Human Rights in England and Wales* (Oxford: OUP, 2nd edn, 2002) 57: this requires a 'balancing act' under which the court asks 'whether the interference with the right is more extensive than is justified by the legitimate aim'.

[173] Needless to say, while there are four approaches under native laws, the incorporation of the ECHR into national law renders the ECHR limitations also uniformly applicable under national laws.

[174] Czech Rep: CFRF, Art 16.4.

[175] Czech Rep: CCt, 27.11.2002, Coll of Decisions, no 4/2003 Sb.

[176] Spain: LORF, Art 3.1: see CCt, Judgment no 46/2001, 15 February 2001, FJ 11. See also Lithuania: Const, Art 26.4; and CCt, Valstybes zinios (OG), 95-01-27, no 9-199, p 6.

[177] Estonia: Const, Arts 40 and 41: religious practice may be restricted if its exercise is 'detrimental to public order, health or morals', if the restrictions are 'necessary in a democratic society', and do not violate the rights of others; France: Cass 13 December 1990, no 89-11713: this accepts a wide range of limits on the basis of the doctrine of State neutrality.

For example, Cypriot law allows restriction of the practice of religion on grounds of 'national security' and 'constitutional order': religious freedom may be restricted by such limitations as are prescribed by law and are necessary in the interests of: the security of the Republic; constitutional order; public safety; public order; public health; public morals; and the protection of the rights and liberties guaranteed to every person by the constitution.[178] Needless to say, any native additions to the grounds spelt out in Article 9.2 make it easier for States to limit the right to manifest religion. However, whilst national security and constitutional order may not appear as formal grounds in laws of other States, these would doubtless also constitute justifications to limit the right to manifest religion.

Thirdly, some national constitutions provide grounds for State interference which are narrower than those contained in the ECHR.[179] On the face of it, these would seem to make it more difficult for the State to restrict the free practice of religion. For instance, under Irish law: 'Freedom of conscience and the free profession and practice of religion are, subject to public order and morality, guaranteed to every citizen'; moreover, the property of any religious denomination or any educational institution shall not be diverted save for necessary works of public utility and on payment of compensation.[180] Extra-constitutional law, too, may add narrow grounds for restriction on specific issues related to manifestation of religious belief; in Portugal, for example, no one may be interrogated about their religion 'except for statistical surveys'.[181]

Fourthly, there are those States whose constitutions contain no explicit limitation of the right to manifest religion. Germany is a good example. The constitutional provision which carries the right to religious freedom does not contain express limitations on its exercise—but limits are found in other basic laws.[182] As there is no express reservation, the Federal Constitutional Court allows only those restrictions which apply to other constitutional rights through the balancing of religious freedom with these other rights: 'Since freedom of religion involves no reservation for the legislator, it may not be qualified by the general legal order, nor by an indeterminate clause about a threat to the continuance of the goods needed for state community, without this clause taking a constitutional law approach and without adequate constitutional security'. Rather, 'in the framework of the guarantee of freedom of religion, the possible conflict must be solved according to the fundamental value of order and considering the unity of this basic value system'— that is, any limit must represent a constitutional good.[183] Thus, under the constitution: 'Civil and citizens' rights and duties shall be neither defined nor restricted

---

[178] Cyprus: Const, Art 18.6.
[179] Belgium: Const, Art 19: freedom of worship cannot be used for 'the repression of offences'.
[180] Ireland: Const, Art 44.2.1 and 44.2.6.
[181] Portugal: LORF, Law no 16/2001, Art 9.
[182] Germany: GG, Art 4 (religious freedom): Art 2 (freedom of action), Art 5 (freedom of opinion), Art 8 (freedom of assembly) are not transferable to Art 4: see CCt, BVerfGE 32, 98 (107); 52, 223 (246).
[183] Germany: CCt, BVerfBGE 32, 98 (108).

by the practice of freedom of religion.'[184] In short: if religious freedom is involved, it takes precedence. In Austria, too, only 'public order' considerations will limit the right to manifest religion.[185]

In addition to these substantive limits on the practice of religion, there are also procedural limits (which do not formally appear in the ECHR) which restrict the free practice of religion by the individual.[186] These procedural limits in national laws are subject-specific. They may be explicit or implicit: if a group of individuals wishes to form a religious association with legal personality, it must satisfy the legal requirements such as registration or other form of recognition; if an individual wishes to criticize a religion publicly, this must not be done offensively; if a minister of religion seeks to deliver pastoral care at a prison, special permission must be obtained from public authorities; if parents seek religious education for their children in State schools (or withdrawal of their children from religious education), they must disclose their reasons for this; and if a couple wish to have a religious marriage, they must notify State authorities and satisfy the formalities laid down by State law. Procedural requirements such as these are explored more fully in later chapters.

Legal authority, legitimate aim, and democratic necessity

The extent to which the limitations on the free practice of religion provided by Article 9.2 ECHR are invoked in the countries of Europe varies from State to State. This may be justified by reference to the margin of appreciation enjoyed by States, the doctrine employed by Strasbourg to enable States to respond to their own national needs and so, in effect, fix different standards for the delivery of religious freedom.[187]

Legal authority: States agree that restrictions on the right to manifest religion must be 'prescribed by law': while some constitutions explicitly recognize this,[188] others do not.[189] This principle of legality (fundamental to the rule of law), that acts which restrict the exercise of the right to manifest religion must be legally authorized, is common in national jurisprudence. Courts often define the formula widely. Jurisprudence in the Netherlands has held that it is not confined to parliamentary legislation but includes other forms of law.[190] In the United Kingdom it has been held that the formula embraces limitations authorized by primary legislation (parliamentary statute), and secondary legislation or other regulatory instruments made on the basis of delegated authority, for example rules about a school uniform

---

[184] Germany: GG, Art 140; WRV, Art 136.1.
[185] Austria: VfSlg 15.394/1998. For the earlier view, see: VfSlg 2944/1955, VfSlg 3505/1959.
[186] Procedural requirements may also, of course, restrict the competence of the State.
[187] See eg P Taylor, *Freedom of Religion* (Cambridge CUP, 2005) 186–7, 307–10.
[188] See eg Czech Rep: CFRF, Art 16.4.
[189] Ireland: Const, Art 44.2.1.
[190] Netherlands: SC, HR, 25 June 1963, NJ 1964, 239; see also HR, 2 February 1990, NJ 1991, 289: a civil action against an evangelical couple who had allegedly made on religious grounds insulting remarks about homosexuals was justified on the basis of ECHR, Art 9.2; for an earlier case concerning remarks against Jews, see HR, 5 June 1987, AB 1988, 276.

policy.[191] By way of contrast, Estonia uses a stricter approach than Strasbourg: a restriction of religious liberty must be authorized by the constitution or such parliamentary laws as are in accordance with the constitution, not by delegated legislation; moreover, such laws as are used to authorize restrictions must themselves be clear and detailed.[192]

Legitimate aim: National courts commonly invoke the idea that a restriction on the right to manifest religion must serve a legitimate purpose. The interference must not be arbitrary. For instance, the principle was used by the Czech Constitutional Court to strike down a law providing that religious entities may use their income only for the religious mission of the entity: 'limiting churches and religious societies to make use freely of their lawfully obtained income only in the area of professing religious faith is arbitrary interference on the part of the State in the private law essence of these entities, and this interference is clearly not legitimized by any relevant public interest'.[193] The interests of public health, safety, order, and morals, and the rights of others, have all made their appearance in the jurisprudence of the States of Europe.

Interference justified by reference to *public safety and health* indicate well the inferiority of the right to manifest religion in the hierarchy of social values.[194] The pattern across Europe is that the threshold to establish the aim of public safety and health is not high. In the United Kingdom, the slaughter of a diseased sacred bullock was justified on grounds of public health.[195] In the Netherlands, restrictions on the religious use of a prohibited drug were justified on public health grounds,[196] and town and country planning decisions authorized by national law in relation to a place designated for agriculture over-rode objections to a programme on a site of religious pilgrimage.[197] In France, the principle of public safety and health has justified wearing seat belts regardless of religious objections,[198] controlling the inhumation and cremation of corpses,[199] administering a blood transfusion refused on religious grounds,[200] and protecting the welfare of children.[201] Health considerations often trump religious freedom when children are involved (for which

---

[191] UK: see respectively: *R v SoS for Education and Employment and others, ex p Williamson* [2005] UKHL 15 (statute); and *R (on the application of Begum) v Headteacher and Governors of Denbigh High School* [2006] UKHL 15: the school uniform rules were made under statutory authority.

[192] Estonia: Const, Arts 3.1, 11, and 19; Case no III-4/A-1/94 (RT III 1994, 8, 129); Case no 3-4-1-5-02 (RT III 2002, 28, 308); for Strasbourg, *De Wilde, Ooms and Versyp v Belgium* (1979), and *Barthold v Germany* (1985): for both Strasbourg cases see n 169 above.

[193] Czech Rep: CCt, 27 November 2002, no Pl US 6/02.

[194] Spain: CCt, Judgment no 154/2002, 18 July 2002, FJ 13.

[195] UK: *R (on the application of Swami Suryananda) v Welsh Ministers* [2007] EWCA Civ 893: the case concerned the decision of the Welsh Assembly Government to order the slaughter of Shambo, a bullock at a Hindu temple, which had tested positive for the bacterium that causes bovine tuberculosis.

[196] Netherlands: SC, HR, 9 January 2007.

[197] Netherlands: Supreme Administrative Court, 6 April 2005, AB 2005, 225: it was claimed that the Virgin Mary had appeared on the site; the local authority ordered the site cleared (including a chapel)—no building permit had been obtained and its use was contrary to its agricultural designation.

[198] France: Cass, 4 February 1998, no 97-83521.

[199] France: CE, 6 January 2006, no 260307: limit compatible with ECHR, Art 9.2.

[200] France: CE, 16 August 2002, no 249552; see also CE, 26 October 2001, no 198546.

[201] France: Cass, 22 February 2000, no 98-12338; Cass, 24 October 2000, no 98-14386.

see Chapter 9). For instance, in Cyprus it has been held that Jehovah's Witness parents' refusal on grounds of religious belief to consent to a blood transfusion for their child whose life was at risk were overridden by the protection of life and the welfare of the child; this was not a breach of either national law or the ECHR.[202] A similar conclusion has been reached by the Czech Constitutional Court where the child was placed in the care of public authorities of the State.[203]

Definitions of *public order* are rare, though the Austrian Constitutional Court understands the formula to embrace matters of 'essential importance' for 'peaceful living together'—previously, public order was synonymous with the 'embodiment of the prevailing fundamental thoughts and conceptions of the legal order'.[204] Reliance on this ground is generally successful. In Estonia, public order has justified restrictions on religious assembly and singing,[205] as well as on the wearing of religious headscarves in photographs taken for identification purposes.[206] Similarly, in France, a refusal to permit a Muslim time-off to attend the mosque was justified on the basis of the expeditious functioning of a public service,[207] and in Slovakia public order has been used to justify restrictions on the exercise of the right to conscientious objection to military service.[208] And a Portuguese court rejected a claim for breach of religious freedom in the case of failure by a defendant to attend a criminal trial on the basis of fulfilment of a promise to attend a pilgrimage to Fatima—under the constitution, legal duties cannot be dispensed with on the basis of religious practice.[209]

Claims to justify interference based on the protection of *public morals* have been rather less successful, due to difficulties around the subjectivity involved in their evaluation. For example, the Austrian Constitutional Court rejected the claim that 'public morals' would justify a ban on the ritual slaughter of animals; and that 'good morals' are those 'general fundamental ideas anchored in the population concerning a correct way of life, explicitly protected by a legal provision'.[210] Indeed, in Spain, the courts have cautioned that interference with the right to manifest religion on grounds of public morals must 'avoid a situation where an ethical concept, which has been incorporated into the ambit of the law, insofar as an ethical minimum is necessary for the existence of social life, is used to produce an unjustified restriction

---

[202] Cyprus: *Titos Charalambous* [1994] 1 CLR 396: Children Law, ss 3 and 4 (which it was held did not violate the Constitution, Art 15, or ECHR, Art 8).

[203] Czech Rep: CCt, 20 August 2004; transfer of a child to hospital care was authorized by the Civil Judicial Process Rules and this did not interfere with rights under the CFRF, Arts 16 and 32.

[204] Austria: VfSlg 15.394/1998. For the earlier view, see: VfSlg 2944/1955, VfSlg 3505/1959.

[205] Estonia: Harju County Court, Case no 4-05-936/1 (25 October 2006): a group singing religious songs at Tallinn railway station caused a disruption of public order which was contrary to the Public Meetings Act, s 7; neither ECHR, Art 9 nor 11 was invoked, nor Const, Art 40 or 47.

[206] Estonia: Government Reg no 79 (2005): there is a religious exemption but the face from the mandible to the upper forehead must remain uncovered.

[207] France: CE, 16 February 2004, no 264314; see also 16 December 1992, no 96459 (as to a member of the Adventist Church: held compatible with ECHR).

[208] Slovakia: CCt, Decision no PL US 18/95 (24 May 1995).

[209] Portugal: Second Instance Penal Tribunal of Porto, 26 June 1997, 9710063; Const, Art 41.2.

[210] Austria: VfSlg 15.394/1998: the court held that religious requirements on the ritual slaughter of animals do not offend public morals and these were protected by domestic law and ECHR, Art 9.

on fundamental rights and public liberties'.[211] However, the rights of others are commonly used as a ground of limitation,[212] particularly in the matrimonial sphere: for instance, the claimed religious freedom of a Muslim husband to chastise his wife (on the basis of the teaching of an imam) was limited by the woman's right to 'moral integrity'.[213] Similarly, a Portuguese court has pronounced a divorce in the case of a husband (a member of the Maná church) who tried to convert a Catholic wife whom he claimed was possessed of the devil; the court held that the exercise of religious freedom by the husband was limited by the religious freedom of the wife.[214]

Democratic necessity and proportionality: Courts throughout Europe often engage in determination of whether a restriction of the right to manifest religion is justified on grounds of necessity. They do so not only by reference to the criteria described above under legitimate aim, but also by reference to the doctrine of proportionality. As the Spanish Constitutional Court has pointed out, whether a limit on religious freedom is proportionate depends on whether 'the measures adopted are disproportionate for the defence of the juridical good that has given rise to the restriction'.[215] The doctrine of proportionality has been deployed extensively in the eastern States of Europe. Three contrasting cases illustrate its use. The Bulgarian Supreme Administrative Court considered that the provisions in Articles 13 and 37 of the Constitution, which set limits on freedom of religion and the system for recognition of denominations by the Bulgarian Council of Ministers, represent a 'necessary requirement not only to obtain the capacity of a legal entity of the denomination but also to carry out the activities and organised religious rituals by the respective communities'.[216] By way of contrast, the Czech Constitutional Court has struck down, on the basis of lack of proportionality, the law enabling the Minister of Culture to cancel authorization for religious legal entities to exercise special rights (including the solemnization of marriages, teaching religion at public schools, and appointing chaplains in the armed forces and prisons) when the religious entity had simply made an error in providing information required by the Minister.[217] Finally, in Slovenia, it was proportionate to forbid the carrying out of religious activities on the premises of public schools on the basis of the secular posture of the State.[218]

---

[211] Spain: Const Ct, Judgment no 62/1982, 15 October 1982, FJ 5.
[212] eg see above for proselytizing and the welfare of children.
[213] Spain: Criminal Court no 3 of Barcelona, 12 January 2004: the book (*La mujer en el Islam*) proposed that Muslim husbands ought to strike wives who after a reprimand fail to obey the husband.
[214] Portugal: SC, STJ, 16 May 2002, Process 02B1290.
[215] Spain: CCt, Judgment no 62/1982, 15 October 1982, relying on *Handyside v UK* (1979) 1 EHRR 337.
[216] Bulgaria: Supreme Administrative Court, Case 7237/2000.
[217] Czech Rep: CCt, 27 November 2002, no Pl US 6/02; the law was Act no 3/2002 Sb.
[218] Slovenia: CCt, Decision no U-I-68/98 (November 2001): 'in reviewing proportionality ... we must weigh ... the protection of the negative aspect of freedom of religion ... of non-believers [the right to have no religion] or the followers of other religions ... against the weight of the consequences

Conclusion

In a textual sense, there is full legal unity on religious freedom in the States of Europe through their incorporation of the ECHR (with its Article 9) in their national laws, but what seems to be a rather more piecemeal reception of Strasbourg jurisprudence on Article 9. However, alongside the ECHR, native laws and jurisprudence also protect religious freedom—and in many cases have done so for a long time—and they recognize its value both for social cohesion and the life and self-identity of the individual. In some States constitutional statements of religious freedom are succinct and in others they are more complex—in both cases these statements are either generally consistent with the text of Article 9 ECHR or they mirror it almost word for word. In so far as many States employ the criminal law to penalize violations of religious freedom, they go beyond the text of Article 9 ECHR. Clear shared principles may be induced from national laws and jurisprudence on religious freedom. Religious freedom should be protected. It involves two basic rights: the right to hold and change religious belief, and the right to manifest that belief in worship, teaching, practice, and observance—though the notion of practice is employed more usually than the Strasbourg notion of manifestation. The right to hold any religious belief is absolute, and the right to practise religious belief is qualified; and the specific situation rule is increasingly making its mark in national jurisprudence to the extent that when an individual waives the right to manifest religion, by voluntary submission to a restrictive environment, there will be no interference with that right. There is also agreement between national laws around the principle that interference with religious practice may be justified on grounds of public health, safety, order, and morals, and, though more rarely, the rights of others. However, States differ in the interpretation and application of these standards which themselves provide the framework for the enjoyment of religious freedom. It is these differences in interpretation or application, and the exercise of the margin of appreciation, that generate litigation for Strasbourg.

ensuing from an interference with the positive aspect of freedom of religion and the rights of parents' (under Const, Art 41.3): 'There is no proportionality if we generally prohibit any denominational activity' in a school, as this would only respect the negative religious freedom.

3

Religious Discrimination and Hatred

Global international law prohibits religious discrimination on the part of the State and private individuals as an integral aspect of its norms on religious freedom.[1] Moreover, the European Convention on Human Rights (ECHR) forbids States to discriminate on grounds of religion in the enjoyment of Convention rights.[2] The prohibition is particularly pertinent to the rights of religious minorities.[3] However, such discrimination is prohibited only if it 'has no objective and reasonable justification'; as such, preferential treatment afforded to one religious organization, such as a state church, may be justified provided it does not disable the enjoyment of religious freedom by others.[4] In addition, EU law prohibits discrimination on grounds of religion, particularly in some notable recent Directives.[5] The implementation of these Directives by Member States has had a profound effect on national laws in this field—it has generated an essentially unified (but complex) body of national laws on religious discrimination.[6] This chapter explores national civil laws which forbid religious discrimination, and exceptions enjoyed by organizations with a religious ethos. It also examines national criminal laws which prohibit religious discrimination, religious hatred, and associated religiously motivated crime.

---

[1] UNDID 1981, Art 2: 'No one shall be subject to discrimination by any State, institution, group of persons, or person on the grounds of religion or belief... "intolerance and discrimination based on religion or belief" means any distinction, exclusion, restriction or preference based on religion or belief and having as its purpose or as its effect nullification or impairment of the recognition, enjoyment or exercise of human rights and fundamental freedoms on an equal basis'. See generally PM Taylor, *Freedom of Religion: UN and European Human Rights Law and Practice* (Cambridge: CUP, 2005).

[2] ECHR, Art 14: 'The enjoyment of the rights and freedoms set forth in this Convention shall be secured without discrimination on any ground such as sex, race, colour, language, religion, political or other opinion, national or social origin, association with a national minority, property, birth or other status'; Art 1, Protocol 12 extends this to 'any right set forth by law'. See generally eg R Ahdar and I Leigh, *Religious Freedom in the Liberal State* (Oxford: OUP, 2005) 108.

[3] However, positive religious discrimination may be permitted in certain circumstances: see COE, Parliamentary Assembly, Res 1743 on Islam, Islamisms and Islamophobia in Europe, 23 June 2010, on prohibiting wearing the veil in order to promote the human dignity and freedom of Muslim women.

[4] Strasbourg: *Darby v Sweden* (1991) 13 EHRR 774. See more fully Ch 4 below.

[5] Directive (EC) 2000/43 and Directive (EC) 2000/78 (in the employment field); in July 2008 the Commission sought to extend this to the provision of goods and services, housing, education, social protection, social security and social advantage. For the EU, see Ch 10 below.

[6] The impact of EU law in the field of discrimination may be contrasted with that of the ECHR and Strasbourg jurisprudence in the field of religious freedom. As we saw in Ch 2 above, alongside common adoption of the ECHR, Strasbourg jurisprudence on ECHR, Art 9 seems to have had a more mixed reception in the national courts, perhaps because its fundamentals are already part of national laws.

Religious discrimination in civil law

National civil laws on religious discrimination deal with five basic issues: their foundation (the principle of equality); the grounds of discrimination (religion and related phenomena); the fields to which these laws apply (such as employment and the provision of goods and services); the types of discrimination (such as direct and indirect discrimination); and exceptions which permit discrimination. As well as enforcement of religious discrimination laws in State courts (by means of compensation, order or other civil remedy), a range of statutory and other bodies, such as ombudsmen,[7] commissions,[8] councils,[9] boards,[10] agencies,[11] and other authorities,[12] monitor implementation of the national legal standards, entertain cases of complaint, provide reports to government, and make recommendations for both law reform and the improvement of practice. Such bodies may be charged with the supervision of all forms of discrimination or religious discrimination in particular.[13]

The principle of equality

The foundation of national laws on religious discrimination is the principle of equality. The constitutions of most States explicitly provide for the equality of individuals before the law.[14] Some such constitutions expressly include religious equality in this principle. They do so regardless of their particular posture towards religion. The state-church systems of Denmark and Finland provide for equality.[15] The French separation system guarantees 'equality before the law to all citizens

---

[7] Lithuania: Equal Opportunities Ombudsman (EOO): Law on Equal Opportunities, 2003.

[8] Cyprus: Combating Racial and Some Other Forms of Discrimination (Commissioner) Law no 42(1)/2004; in 2008 there were 241 complaints, 3 of which concerned religion or belief: Cyprus Report 2008, European Network of Legal Experts in the Non-Discrimination Field, p 32; Bulgaria: Protection Against Discrimination Commission (Protection Against Discrimination Act 2004).

[9] Romania: National Council on Combating Discrimination (NCCD): Law no 324/2006.

[10] Denmark: Equal Treatment Board (Act no 387, 27 May 2008).

[11] Germany: General Law on Equal Treatment, 2006, AGG, 14 August 2006, Bundesgesetzblatt I 2006. Federal Anti-discrimination Agency (*Antidiskriminierungsstelle des Bundes*).

[12] Austria: Equal Treatment Commission (ETC): ETA, BGBl I no 66/2004; Belgium: Centre for Equal Opportunities and Opposition to Racism (Law of 15 February 1993, amended 10 May 2007): the centre may file judicial actions; France: High Authority against Discrimination and for Equality (HALDE) (Law no 2004-1486, 30 December 2004); Hungary: Equal Treatment Authority (Government Decree 361/2004); Estonia: Chancellor of Justice—however, complaints about natural persons or legal persons in private law do not fall within this jurisdiction if they 'concern professing and practising of faith or working as a minister of a religion in religious associations with registered articles of association': Law on the Chancellor of Justice, Art 355.2.

[13] eg the Finnish equality ombudsman has issued many statements about the applicability of equality principles to the Evangelical Lutheran Church (24 in 1991–2002).

[14] Cyprus: Const, Art 28.1: 'All persons are equal before the law, the administration and justice, and are entitled to equal protection thereof and treatment thereby.'

[15] Denmark: Const, Art 70: no Danish subject shall be deprived of his liberty because of his religious convictions; Art 71: no one shall be denied full enjoyment of any civil and political right by reason of his creed or descent nor for such reasons evade a legal duty; Finland: Const, Art 6.2.

without distinction based on origin, race or religion. She respects all beliefs'.[16] The same applies to cooperation systems: in Austria, 'All federal nationals are equal before the law. Privileges based upon birth, sex, estate, class or religion, are excluded';[17] and in Spain, the constitution provides that: 'Spaniards are equal before the law and may not in any way be discriminated against on the grounds of birth, race, sex, religion, opinion or any other condition or personal or social circumstance.'[18] Constitutions of central and eastern Europe are similarly explicit on the matter,[19] and national jurisprudence in some has developed on the basis that like be treated alike.[20]

In addition to statements that *individuals* are equal regardless of their religion, several constitutions expressly provide that *religions* are to be treated equally (presumably meaning Christianity, Islam, Judaism, and other religions, as opposed to religious groups or denominations within these traditions). For example, in Cyprus (with its Orthodox Christian majority) all religions are equal before the law and no legislative, executive, or judicial act shall discriminate against any religion or religious institution;[21] and in Romania (also with an Orthodox majority): 'All religions shall be free';[22] and the constitution expressly protects the religious identity of minorities.[23] The equality principle may also apply to *religious associations*, either explicitly, as in Italy (with its Catholic majority), where 'religious denominations are equally free before the law',[24] or Poland (also with a Catholic majority), where 'Churches and other religious organisations shall have equal rights';[25] and in Finland (with its Lutheran majority), equality before the law is a constitutional right which implies that all religious groups must be treated equally.[26] Equality of religions is also implicit in the cooperation systems of Catholic Spain, 'There shall be no state religion',[27] and Portugal: 'The State neither

---

[16] France: Const, 1958, Art 1; Preamble to Const, 1946: 'the French people reaffirms that each human being, irrespective of race, religion, or belief, possesses inalienable and sacred rights'; Netherlands: Const, Art 1: 'All . . . shall be treated equal in equal circumstances. Discrimination on the grounds of religion, belief, political opinion, race, sex or on any other ground shall be prohibited.'

[17] Austria: Const, Art 7.1.

[18] Spain: Const, Art 14; see also LORF (Law 7/1980 5 July), Art 1 (equal treatment before the law)—there is some speculation that a new statute might be brought before the Cortes in 2010.

[19] Lithuania: Const, Art 29: 'all people are equal before the law, courts and other state institutions and officers. A person's rights may not be restricted in any way and s/he may not be granted any privileges on the basis of his or her sex, race, nationality, language, origin, social status, religion, convictions or opinions'; see also Bulgaria: Const, Art 6.2; Romania: Const, Art 4; Slovenia: Const, Art 14.1.

[20] Estonia: SC, Case no 3-4-1-2-02, 3 April 2002, RT III 2002, 11, 108: but not every unequal treatment of equals amounts to a violation of the right to equality, provided such treatment is not arbitrary—unequal treatment is arbitrary if there is no reasonable cause for it.

[21] Cyprus: Const, Art 18.3.

[22] Romania: Const, Art 29.3.

[23] Romania: Const, Art 6: this 'guarantees the right of persons belonging to national minorities, to the preservation, development and expression of their ethnic, cultural, linguistic and religious identity'.

[24] Italy: Const, Art 8.1.

[25] Poland: Const, Art 25.1 see also Art 25.2: 'Public authorities . . . shall be impartial in matters of personal conviction, whether religious or philosophical, or in relation to outlooks on life, and shall ensure their freedom of expression within public life.'

[26] Finland: Const, Art 6.

[27] Spain: Const, Art 16.3.

adopts any religion whatsoever nor pronounces on religious issues.'[28] Once more, religious equality straddles religion-state models.

Prohibition of religious discrimination

To supplement their statements about religious equality as between individuals or groups, constitutions formally prohibit religious discrimination by both the State and by citizens within it. In some States the constitution forbids the State to discriminate simply on grounds of 'religion'; this is the case, for example, in the Netherlands,[29] Denmark,[30] Finland,[31] Poland,[32] Estonia,[33] and Cyprus (where every person shall enjoy all rights and liberties provided for in the constitution without any form of discrimination on grounds of, *inter alia*, religion).[34] By way of contrast, the Maltese constitution forbids discrimination on grounds, *inter alia*, of 'creed',[35] the Swedish, on grounds of 'religious affiliation',[36] the Czech, on grounds of 'religion or belief',[37] and the German, on grounds of 'religious views', 'faith', and 'belief'.[38] Moreover, the prohibition of religious discrimination is commonly seen as flowing from the right to religious freedom. Spanish jurisprudence is not untypical—religious freedom includes 'the right not to be discriminated against on grounds of religion or belief, so that different beliefs cannot sustain differences in juridical treatment'.[39]

A similar range of grounds is found in sub-constitutional laws which are designed to deal with discrimination in both the public and private spheres and to implement the Directives of the European Union. Discrimination is forbidden, *inter alia*, on grounds of: 'religion' in France, Ireland, Italy, Portugal, and Sweden;[40] 'religious

---

[28] Portugal: Const, Art 13: equality of religion; LORF (Law no 16/2001, DL 134/2003) Art 4.1.

[29] Netherlands: Const, Art 1; see also Portugal: Const, Arts 1, 8, 13, 15, 17, 58, 59, 69, 70–72.

[30] Denmark: see n 15 above.

[31] See the constitutions of Finland, Art 6.2; Bulgaria, Art 6.2; Romania, Art 4; Slovenia: Art 14.1.

[32] Poland: Const, Art 25.2; see n 25 above.

[33] Estonia: Const, Art 12: 'Everyone is equal before the law. No-one shall be discriminated against on the basis of origin, race, colour, sex, language, origin, religion, political or other opinion, property or social status, or on other grounds'; see also Hungary: Const, Art 70/A.

[34] Cyprus: Const, Art 28.2; this is autonomous and does not depend on discrimination in the exercise of other constitutional rights; cf ECHR, Art 14; Law 13(III) 2002, incorporating Protocol no 12 ECHR, provides a general prohibition: 'The enjoyment of any right set forth by law shall be secured without discrimination on any ground such as sex, race, colour, language, religion', etc.

[35] Malta: Const, Art 45.

[36] Sweden: Instrument of Government 1975, Art 2: 'Public power shall be exercised with respect for the equal worth of all and for the dignity of the individual' and (as amended 2002): 'The public institutions shall counteract discrimination against persons on grounds of.... religious affiliation.'

[37] Czech Rep: CFRF, Art 3.1.

[38] Germany: GG, Art 3.3: religious faith, belief; Art 33.3: religious views; Art 140 (with WRV, Art 136): religious faith.

[39] Spain: CCt, Judgment no 141/2000, 29 May 2000, FJ 4; and Ruling no 180/1986, 21 February 1986, FJ 2.

[40] France: Law of Social Cohesion, 30 December 2004; see also Law no 2008-496, 27 May 2008, and CCl, Decision no 910290, 9 May 1991; Ireland: Employment Equality Act 1998, Equal Status Act 2000, both as amended by the Equality Act 2004; Italy: Legislative Decree no 286, 25 July 1998; Portugal: LC 99/2003, Art 23; Sweden: Discrimination Act 2008:567.

conviction' in Latvia and Malta;[41] 'religion or belief' in Germany, Spain, Cyprus, the Czech Republic, Hungary, Slovenia, and the United Kingdom;[42] 'religion and belief' in Austria, Finland, Poland, and Luxembourg;[43] 'religion or faith' in Denmark and Bulgaria;[44] 'religious or other beliefs' in Greece;[45] 'religious, political or other beliefs' in Estonia;[46] 'religious or philosophical beliefs' in Belgium and the Netherlands;[47] and 'religious beliefs or convictions' in Lithuania.[48] On the face of it, these differences may have substantive significance: a rule which forbids discrimination on grounds of 'religion' (wide, to embrace practice) may afford greater protection than a prohibition on grounds of 'religious belief' (narrow).

As the term is not defined in the EU Directives, so 'religion' (and its associates outlined above) is left largely undefined in national laws on discrimination. Instead, understandings of religion from other areas of religion law are used—such as laws on religious associations,[49] or human rights jurisprudence;[50] and lack of religion or belief is also protected.[51] However, this is not always the case—for instance, for the purposes of Estonian discrimination law 'religion' (*usutunnistus*) refers to any belief which expresses a religious 'worldview'.[52] Jurisprudence on the definition of religion or belief in the discrimination field is especially rich in the Netherlands. On the one hand, 'religion' involves belief in a 'high authority', and it is not a 'mere opinion', or 'personal conviction';[53] but it is not necessary that a particular conviction (such as the need to wear a headscarf) is adhered to by all believers of a religion.[54] On the other hand, for the purposes of discrimination law, 'religion' includes both belief *and* the practice of that belief;[55] for example the practice of a

[41] Latvia: Labour Law 2002, Art 29; Malta: Employment and Industrial Relations Act 2002, and Legal Notice 461 of 2004 for 'religion or belief', and 54 of 2007 for 'religion or religious belief'.

[42] Germany: AGG, 2006, AGG, 14 August 2006; Federal Law on Civil Servants 1953, s 8.1; Spain: Law 62/2003, 30 December 2003, Art 27; Cyprus: Equal Treatment in Employment and Occupation Law no 58(1)/2004, Art 6; Hungary: ETA, Act CXXV 2003, Art 8; Slovenia: ETA 2004 (amended 2007), Art 1; UK: Equality Act 2010, ss 4–12.

[43] Austria: ETA 2004 (as amended 2008); Finland: Non-Discrimination Act 2004 (as amended 2009); Poland: Labour Code, Art 18; Luxembourg: Law of 28 November 2006.

[44] Denmark: Act no 1349, 16 December 2008; Bulgaria: Protection against Discrimination Act 2004.

[45] Greece: Law 3304/2005.

[46] Estonia: ETA, RT I 2008, 56, 315.

[47] Belgium: Act of 10 May 2007; Netherlands: GETA 1994 (as amended 2004); the Explanatory Memorandum to the amending Act uses *levensovertuiging* (philosophy of life), rather than *geloof* (belief), the term in Directive (EC) 2000/78; it is used alongside *godsdienst* (religion).

[48] Lithuania: ETA 2004 (as amended 2008).

[49] This is the case eg in Denmark, France, Germany, Poland, Portugal, Romania, Slovenia, and Spain.

[50] UK: *Grainger plc v Nicholson* EAT 0219/09/ZT; Equality Act 2010, Explanatory Notes, para 52.

[51] UK: Equality Act 2010, s 10.

[52] Estonia: Explanatory Notes to ETA 2008: Report, p 13, n 49.

[53] Netherlands: ETC, Opinion 2005-67: the complainant argued that she was not offered a job because the prospective employer suspected that she was a member of a 'religious group'—she was a member of Osho, the Bagwan Shree Rajneesh philosophy, and it was held that the employer had acted unlawfully on the basis of belief; see also ETC Opinion 2007-207 (personal conviction).

[54] Netherlands: ETC Opinion 2008-12.

[55] Netherlands: the right not to be discriminated against on religious grounds includes both the right to have a religious belief and the right to behave in accordance with it: ETC Opinions 1997-46, 2004-112, and 2004-148.

Muslim woman to refuse to shake hands with men is an expression of religious belief.[56] Whilst some national laws define 'religion' narrowly as 'religious belief',[57] others understand it more widely as 'religious convictions and practices',[58] and this echoes the ECHR distinction with regard to religious freedom between belief and its manifestation in worship, teaching, practice, and observance (see Chapter 2).

Accordingly, in spite of the focus in both constitutional and sub-constitutional laws on beliefs, the decisions of national courts and equal treatment agencies extend the prohibition against religious discrimination to both religious beliefs *and* practices. This is inevitable given the legal definitions of religion explored in Chapter 1 and the difficulties seen there in separating out religious belief from its practice. Thus, various beliefs and practices have been understood as being religious for the purposes of national discrimination laws. These include: the refusal of a Christian to register same-sex marriages (Netherlands);[59] religious fasting (Denmark);[60] the wearing of clothing appropriate to religious beliefs in a swimming pool (Romania);[61] the wearing of headscarves in fitness centres (Netherlands),[62] or at work (Belgium),[63] such as in a supermarket (Denmark),[64] or at school (Bulgaria);[65] the wearing of turbans or other religious garments in schools and in court (Belgium[66] and France).[67] They also include the performance of acts of worship under a leasing contract (France);[68] taking days off for religious holidays (Romania);[69] refusal by a Muslim to eat pork at work (Slovenia);[70] and having the status of a non-Orthodox teacher in a state school (Greece).[71] The lawfulness of decisions on individuals in such circumstances is another matter and these cases are explored below in the following section on types of religious discrimination.

Fields of religious discrimination

The prohibitions against religious discrimination in constitutional laws, and in sub-constitutional laws designed to implement EU law, apply to a wide range of fields in

---

[56] Netherlands: ETC, Opinion 2006-51; refusal to admit the woman to a school for training as a teaching assistant was unlawful; cf DC Rotterdam, 6 August 2008, LJN: BD9643 (n 117 below).

[57] Ireland: Employment Equality Act 1998, s 6(2)(e).

[58] Italy: Immigration Act 1998.

[59] Netherlands: ETC, 15 April 2008, Opinion 2008-40.

[60] Denmark: *A v B*, Eastern HC, 14 January 2008, Weekly Law Journal (U.2008.1028Ø).

[61] Romania: Case no 221, 21 September 2005.

[62] Netherlands: ETC, Opinion 2007-173; Opinion 2004-112; Opinion 2005-222.

[63] Belgium: Judgment of 14 January 2008 of the Labour CA of Antwerp.

[64] Denmark: Maritime and Commercial Court, 28 January 2008 (U.2008.1011S).

[65] Bulgaria: Protection against Discrimination Commission, 22 February 2008, Case no 37/2007.

[66] Belgium: Judgment of 25 June 2008, Court of Cassation.

[67] France: Administrative CA of Paris, 19 July 2005, Chamber no 1, Sect A, jurisdata no 2005-282552; HALDE 19 September 2005, Deliberation no 2005-26; 5 June 2006 no 2006-132.

[68] France: Court of Cassation, 3ème Chambre civile, 18 December 2002, no 01-00519.

[69] Romania: LC, Art 134.1: two days may be taken off each year for a religious holiday, provided that the faith of the employee is a State recognized religion under Law 489/2006; Spain: Workers' Statute, Art 37; Poland: Act of 17 May 1989, Art 42.

[70] Slovenia: Advocate of the Principle of Equality, 28 August 2008, UEM-0921-10/2008-3.

[71] Greece: COS, Proceedings, no 347/2002, 28 June 2002.

both the public and private sectors. The principal fields are employment and the provision of goods and services.[72] Some States have a single enactment on these subjects (which may consolidate earlier legislation), or a single enactment which is periodically amended,[73] but in most countries the implementation of the EU Directives has been piecemeal, achieved through a series of enactments.[74] Indeed, as religious discrimination is an aspect or requirement of the right to religious freedom, national laws which prohibit it seem to suggest that the Strasbourg specific situation rule does not apply to direct religious discrimination,[75] in relation to employment within or the provision of goods and services by secular entities in society.[76] In other words, a person cannot waive the right not to be discriminated against directly on religious grounds, because there is no defence to direct discrimination; this is so regardless of whether a person voluntarily submits to a restrictive regime.[77]

Employers in the private sector must not discriminate on grounds of religion,[78] a prohibition sometimes found in Labour Codes[79] in relation, for example, to access to employment, which embraces advertisements for jobs, candidature, recruitment, or selection.[80] Nor may they discriminate during the course of employment, with regard to the working conditions, wages, promotion, trade union membership, and dismissal of an employee.[81] Similarly, religious discrimination is forbidden in public sector employment, by means of national law[82] and provincial law,[83] or

---

[72] For a rare constitutional ban on religious discrimination in the field of employment, see France: Const, 1946, Preamble: 'Each has a duty to work and the right to obtain employment. No-one can be attacked in his work or employment by reason of his origins, opinions or beliefs.'

[73] Sweden: Discrimination Act 2008:567; UK: Equality Act 2010, ss 13, 19, 26, 29 and Parts 3–7.

[74] For examples of the plethora of amendments in this field, see n 78 below.

[75] For the specific situation rule, see Ch 2 above. For Strasbourg jurisprudence in the sphere of employment, see PM Taylor, *Freedom of Religion* (Cambridge: CUP, 2005) 138 *et seq.*

[76] As will be seen below, it may be that a variant on the specific situation rule is actually at the heart of exceptions to the duty not to discriminate for the purposes of entities with a religious ethos.

[77] Unless, that is, the exceptions apply; see below.

[78] Greece: Law 3304/2005; Italy: Law of 25 July 1998 no 286; Law of 20 March 1970, Art 15; Hungary: Act CXXV 2003; Germany: AGG, 2006, AGG, 14 August 2006; Work Constitution Act 1972 (amended 2006), s 75; Latvia: Labour Law 2002, Art 29; Finland: Non-Discrimination Act 2004 (amended 2007–9); Employment Contracts Act (amended 2004); France: Law of Social Modernisation, no 2002-73; Law of Social Cohesion, 30 December 2004; Law no 2008-496, 27 May 2008; Malta: Employment and Industrial Relations Act 2002, Legal Notice 461 of 2004 and 53 of 2007); Luxembourg: Law of 28 November 2006, Arts 1, 18; Spain: Workers' Statute, Art 17.1 (amended 2003).

[79] Poland: LC Art 18; Czech Rep: LC, Law no 262/2006, s 110; Portugal: LC, 99/2003, Art 23.

[80] Austria: ETA, BGBl I no 66/2004 (amended by BGBl I no 98/2008); Lithuania: ETA 2005 (amended to 2008), Art 11; Romania: Law no 324/2006; LC, Art 7; Slovenia: ETA, Arts 4, 6, Employment Relationship Act 2003 (amended 2007); Cyprus: Law no 58(1)/2004.

[81] Belgium: Act of 10 May 2007 (conditions, remuneration and dismissal); Italy: Law of 20 March 1970, Art 15 (dismissal); Romania: LC, Art 59 (dismissal); Denmark: Act no 1349, 16 December 2008.

[82] Czech Rep: Law no 219/2002; Law on Salaries (Law no 143/1992); Germany: Federal Law on Civil Servants 1953, s 8.1; Latvia: State Civil Service Law 2000 (amended 2006); Malta: Employment and Industrial Relations Act 2002 and Legal Notice 54 of 2007; Portugal: LC, 99/2003, Art 23.

[83] Austria: for public federal employment, see ETA, Federal Law Gazette no 100/1993 (amended by ibid no 97/2008); for the provinces, see eg Styrian ETA, Styrian Provincial Law Gazette no 24/

other form of regional law,[84] with respect to access to public employment, working conditions, promotion, trade union membership, remuneration, transfer, and dismissal.[85] In turn, providers of goods and services, in both the public and private sectors,[86] are forbidden to practise religious discrimination by national law, and sometimes by provincial or regional law.[87] The prohibition applies, *inter alia*, to the provision of housing,[88] social security,[89] health care,[90] vocational training,[91] education,[92] and military service.[93]

Types of religious discrimination

Discrimination is commonly defined in national laws as less favourable treatment, on the basis of a prohibited ground, afforded to a person than the treatment afforded to another person in a similar situation (that is, treating one person less favourably than another on a prohibited ground);[94] or as 'any distinction, exclusion or preference based on [*inter alia*] religion [or] beliefs . . . with the purpose or effect of impairing or nullifying the recognition, enjoyment or exercise in equal conditions of the human rights and fundamental freedoms or the rights recognised by law in the political, economic, social and cultural or any other field of public life'.[95] In implementation of EU law, national laws forbid religious discrimination by way of direct or indirect discrimination, instruction to discriminate, harassment, and victimization.[96] National laws define each of these forms of discrimination, often incorporating directly the definitions which are contained in EU law. The following deals with the terms of the prohibition in the employment sphere; education is dealt with in Chapter 8.

2004; Viennese Agricultural Labour Equal Treatment Act, Viennese Provincial Law Gazette Nr 25/1980 (amended by ibid no 38/2008).

[84] Belgium: see Decrees on the Flemish Community, 8 May 2002 and 10 July 2008; French-Speaking, 12 December 2008; Walloon, 6 November 2008; German-Speaking, 17 May 2004.

[85] Estonia: Law on Wages, Art 5; Belgium: Act of 10 May 2007; Denmark: Act no 1349, 16 December 2008: employment (dismissal, transfer, promotion, pay); Germany: GG, 2006, AGG, 14 August 2006, Bundesgesetzblatt I 2006 (trade union membership).

[86] Ireland: Equal Status Acts 2000–2004; Czech Rep: Anti-Discrimination Law 2009; Lithuania: ETA 2005 (amended 2008); Luxembourg: Law of 28 November 2006.

[87] Belgium: for national law see Act of 10 May 2007; see n 83 above for regional laws.

[88] France: Law of Social Modernisation, no 2002-73 and Law of Social Cohesion, 30 December 2004; Czech Rep: Ant-Discrimination Law 2009; Sweden: Discrimination Act 2008:567.

[89] Latvia: Law on Social Security 1995 (amended 2005); Hungary: Act CXXV 2003.

[90] Netherlands: GETA 1994, Law Gazette 1994, 230.

[91] Belgium: Act of 10 May 2007.

[92] UK: Equality Act 2010; see also Ch 8 below.

[93] Germany: Law on Equal Treatment of Soldiers, 2006.

[94] Ireland: Employment Equality Act 1998, s 6; Denmark: Act no 1349, 16 December 2008, s 1 (2); Greece: Law 3304/2005, Art 7.

[95] Romania: Anti-Discrimination Law 2006, Art 2.

[96] Poland: LC, Art 18; Romania: Law no 324/2006, Art 2; Slovenia: ETA 2004, Arts 4–6; Sweden: Discrimination Act 2008:567, s 4.

Harassment is any unwanted conduct related to protected grounds (including religion or belief) and manifested physically, verbally, or in any other manner,[97] that has the effect of violating the dignity of a person and of creating a hostile, offensive, or intimidating environment.[98] It may occur by way of association, as when employees are harassed not for their own religious beliefs but because of the religious beliefs of another person with whom they are associated.[99] For example, dismissal of a participant at an adult vocational training centre, who had been subjected to harassment whilst praying in a corridor was justified on the basis of the need to keep order at the centre (because it encouraged others to pray similarly).[100] Again, a thoughtless rather than a spiteful remark by a supermarket employee to a co-worker made in the presence of a customer about a religious headscarf, though derogatory, is lawful.[101] Victimization is less favourable treatment of a person who has undertaken or is presumed to have undertaken or is to undertake in the future any action for protection against discrimination.[102] In turn, incitement to discriminate occurs if a person in a position to influence others encourages them to discriminate.[103]

Direct discrimination is treating a person, on the grounds of their religion or belief, less favourably than another person is, has been, or would be treated in comparable circumstances. The victim must be in present, past, or assumed possession of a religion or belief; there is also direct discrimination if the victim is discriminated against on the grounds of the religion or belief of another person who is (or is presumed to be) associated with the victim. There is no defence of justification in cases of direct discrimination—but a general occupational requirement for employers with a religious ethos constitutes an exception (see below).[104] National courts have applied these rules to a variety of factual situations. Direct

---

[97] In the UK harassment is an offence in its own right under the Protection from Harassment Act 1997; see *Church of Jesus Christ Latter Day Saints v Price* [2004] EWHC Admin 325: an anti-harassment injunction was granted against an individual due to his continual harassment of the members (4,000 cold calls and preaching at them); *Singh v Bhaker* [2006] Fam Law 1026: after an arranged marriage, a female Singh moved to the home of her mother-in-law; she claimed to have been forced to do menial housework, kept as a virtual prisoner, not allowed to visit the local Sikh temple, and forced to have her hair cut, against her religious beliefs; the court found against the mother-in-law.

[98] Cyprus: Law 58(1)/2004, Art 6(1)(c); Denmark: Act no 1349, 16 December 2008, s 1(4); Estonia: ETA, Art 3.3; Luxembourg: Law of 28 November 2006, Art 18 (private sector) and Law of 29 November 2006, Art 5 (public sector); Malta: Public Services Management Code, s 7.1.3.4; Spain: Law 62/2003, Arts 28.1 and 37.2; UK: Equality Act 2010, s 26(1): see R Sandberg, 'Gods and services: religious groups and sexual orientation discrimination' (2008) 10 EccLJ 205–9.

[99] UK: *Saini v All Saints Haque Centre and ors* [2008] UKEAT/00227/08 (24 October 2008).

[100] Denmark: SC, Danish Law Weekly 2001, p 83.

[101] Denmark: *F v COOP Denmark A/S*, Maritime and Commercial Court, 28 January 2008, Weekly Law Journal (U.2008.1011S): in the presence of a customer, a supermarket employee called a co-worker with a religious headscarf a 'black-headed gull'; the dismissal of the employee was not justified.

[102] UK: Equality Act 2010, s 27: it occurs when A subjects B to a detriment because B is bringing proceedings, giving evidence, providing information, or making an allegation under the Equality Act.

[103] Bulgaria: Protection against Discrimination Act 2004; Spain: Law 62/2003, Art 28.2.

[104] Denmark: Act no 1349, 16 December 2008, s 1(2); France, Law no 2008-496, Art 1; UK: Equality Act 2010, s 13: it occurs when A treats B less favourably than A treats or would treat others because of a protected ground such as religion or belief.

discrimination occurs when an employer fails to remunerate an employee because he is a Muslim,[105] or prohibits 'religion-related clothing, such as headscarves and garments',[106] or does not short-list for a job a male Muslim who was as qualified as other short-listed candidates with equivalent or less experience,[107] or dismisses a temporary worker who would not join for lunch children with whom she worked on the basis of her religious commitment to fast during Ramadan.[108] In the provision of goods and services, denial of access to a swimming pool to a Muslim woman wearing a swimming costume appropriate to her religious beliefs, but seen by the swimming pool owners as 'casual clothing', amounted to discrimination.[109] On the other hand, dismissal of a nurse at a home for the elderly because she wished to engage in the traditional feasts of her church was not discriminatory—the employer would have been expected to treat a hypothetical comparator, refusing to carry out the same tasks for reasons other than religion, in the same way.[110] Indeed, that a claimant's reason for acting is religious does not necessarily mean that the respondent's action is based on religion.[111]

Indirect discrimination is putting a person, through an apparently neutral provision, criterion, or policy, at a disadvantage compared with other persons unless the provision, criterion, or policy is objectively justified by a legitimate aim and the means of achieving it are proportionate and necessary.[112] In short, differences in treatment on grounds of religion are prohibited unless justified as appropriate and necessary to realize a legitimate objective.[113] The case-law is rich. A book shop dismissed a female employee for wearing an Islamic headscarf in breach of an order of the employer based on clear company guidelines; the dismissal was justified as the policy applied to all employees without distinction and was designed to enhance the 'neutral' image of the company; and religious freedom may be limited where religious practices are 'likely to lead to chaos'.[114] The policy of a supermarket to be religiously neutral is a legitimate aim and a rule forbidding the wearing of a religious headscarf was an appropriate and necessary means of achieving

---

[105] Ireland: Equality Authority, DEC-S2006-004: *Hassan v Western Union*.

[106] Netherlands: ETC, Opinion 2007-173; it may have justified indirect discrimination if it was neutral.

[107] UK: *Bodi v Teletext* [2005] ET Case no 3300497/2005 (13–14 October 2005); however, most direct discrimination claims on grounds of religion fail: eg *Mohamed v Virgin Trains* [2005] ET Case no 2201814/2004 (12–14 October 2004; 20 May 2005); EAT (2006) WL 25224803 (30 August 2006); *McClintock v Department of Constitutional Affairs* [2007] UKEAT/0223/07/CEA (31 October 2007).

[108] Denmark: *A v B*, Eastern HC, 14 January 2008, Weekly Law Journal (U.2008.1028Ø).

[109] Romania: *D v N and Şofronea Swimming Pool*, NCCD, Case no 221, 21 September 2005.

[110] Sweden: Labour Court, 9 February 2005, Case 2005, no 21.

[111] UK: *Ladele v London Borough of Islington* [2009] EWCA (Civ) 1357: the threat to dismiss a registrar who refused on grounds of conscience to perform civil partnership ceremonies was lawful, as the council (for a non-religious reason) would have treated any such registrar in the same way.

[112] Bulgaria: Protection against Discrimination Act 2004; Denmark: Act no 1349, 16 December 2008, s 1(3); France, Law no 2008-496, Art 1; Malta: Equal Treatment in Employment Regs 2004; Spain: Law 62/2003, Art 28.1.

[113] Belgium: General Anti-Discrimination Federal Act, Art 7.

[114] Belgium: *EF v Club Corp*, Judgment of 15 January 2008, Labour CA.

that aim.[115] The same decision was reached in the case of dismissal of a woman wishing to wear a headscarf at work prior to introduction of a rule forbidding the wearing of religious signs.[116] Dismissal of a female Muslim teacher for failure on religious grounds to engage in shaking hands in a school was justified to prevent disorder,[117] as was dismissal of a teacher for wearing a religious headscarf in school.[118] Moreover, the rejection of an application for the position of registrar because the applicant Christian refused to register same-sex marriages was indirect discrimination but justified.[119] Such cases may be conceived as analogous to the Strasbourg specific situation rule—the individual voluntarily submits to a restrictive environment and thereby waives their right to manifest their religion; however, here there is justified interference whereas with the specific situation rule there is no interference with the right to manifest.[120]

By way of contrast, imprecise rules which forbid the wearing of religious dress by teachers will not justify religious discrimination.[121] The absence of a uniform in a school will enable the wearing of Islamic headscarves.[122] The policy of a bank to prohibit religious dress on its premises in order to protect security was discriminatory as it was not necessary to achieve security.[123] A prohibition against wearing a headscarf as a nurse in a Catholic hospital constitutes discrimination on the ground of religion as the nurse is capable of fulfilling her duties irrespective of her head garment.[124] A rule barring from a restaurant people wearing religious headscarves was not objectively justified and constituted indirect discrimination (the aim was legitimate but the means used to achieve it were not appropriate).[125] Rejection of a Muslim woman from training as an educational assistant because she refused to shake hands with men was not justified and constituted indirect discrimination.[126] The application of a rota to all employees, but which put Christians at a particular disadvantage by disabling them from attending church, was unjustified indirect

---

[115] Denmark: SC, U.2005.1265H: the clothing rule was not in breach of ECHR, Art 9.

[116] Belgium: *Centre for Equal Opportunities and Opposition to Racism v nv G4S Security Services and Samira Achbita*, Judgment of 14 January 2008, Labour CA of Antwerp.

[117] Netherlands: DC Utrecht, 30 August 2007, LJN: BB2648; DC Rotterdam, 6 August 2008, LJN: BD 9643: dismissal of a male Muslim customer manager (a civil servant at the Social Services Department) for refusing to shake hands was held necessary and proportionate on the basis that he had failed 'to observe the usual rules of etiquette and of greeting customs in the Netherlands'.

[118] Germany: Wuppertal Labour Court, 29 July 2008, 4 Ca 1077/08.

[119] Netherlands: ETC, Opinion 2008-40: it was justified on the basis of the rights of same-sex couples.

[120] They may also be conceived as the application of the maxim *volenti non fit injuria*.

[121] Belgium: Judgment no 175.886 of 18 October 2007, Administrative Section, COS: dismissal of a female Muslim teacher in a state school (for refusal to remove her headscarf contrary to a rule forbidding religious dress except for teachers of religion in the classroom) was suspended.

[122] Bulgaria: *Ramzie Shaib and ors v Vassil Vassilev and Anor*, PADC, 22 February 2008, Case 37/2007.

[123] France: HALDE 19 September 2005, Deliberation no 2005-26: a turbaned Sikh was refused access—also, the bank's directive was vague; HALDE asked the bank to review its policy.

[124] Germany: Cologne Labour Court, 6 March 2008, 19 Ca 7222/07: the parties settled at second instance: Cologne *Land* Labour Court, 3 December 2008, 3 Sa 785/08.

[125] Netherlands: ETC, Opinion 2004-112; see also ETC, Opinion 2005-222.

[126] Netherlands: ETC, Opinion 2006-51.

discrimination.[127] The principle which seems to emerge from these cases is simply that whether there is indirect discrimination depends entirely on the factual situation in question.

Some national laws impose on employers a general duty to make reasonable accommodation for the religious convictions and practices of employees in terms of working hours and rest days, particularly where 'this would not lead to excessive difficulties...and where it is possible to compensate for potential adverse consequences for the [business]'.[128] Most countries do not have a general duty to provide reasonable accommodation, but a duty might arise in relation to particular issues, such as time off for religious holidays,[129] and the provision of special meals to meet religious dietary requirements—and in one Slovenian case it was held that making dietary provision for Catholics and not for Muslims was discriminatory.[130] Such arrangements seem to prevail against the Strasbourg specific situation rule that those who voluntarily submit to secular environments waive their religious freedom.

Religious exceptions

Whilst the general rule is that direct discrimination on grounds of religion cannot be justified, and indirect discrimination may be justified, there is an exception to the prohibition against direct discrimination when religion represents a genuine occupational requirement.[131] A genuine occupational requirement may exempt an employer or a provider of goods and services from religious or other forms of generally prohibited discrimination.[132] For example, Cypriot law permits discrimination where 'due to the nature of activities or the framework within which they are exercised, the religion or belief constitutes a genuine, legitimate and justified occupational requirement'.[133] Various equivalent formulae appear in the laws of

[127] UK: *Williams-Drabble v Pathway Care Solutions* [2004] ET Case no 2601718/2004 (2 December 2004): the employer had failed to provide an 'adequate explanation' and show that the disadvantage was a 'proportionate means of achieving a legitimate aim'; *Fugler v MacMillan-London Hairstudios Ltd* [2005] ET Case no 2205090/2004 (21–23 June 2005): a 'no-Saturdays-off' rule was unjustified indirect discrimination against a Jewish employee—it was a legitimate aim but the employer should have considered how to accommodate the employee by rearranging duties; *Noah v Sarah Desrosiers (t/a Wedge)* [2008] ET Case no 2201867/07 (29 May 2008): termination of an interview for a job in a hairdressing salon when the applicant arrived with a headscarf was indirect discrimination.

[128] Bulgaria: Protection against Discrimination Act, Art 13.2; see also Sweden: Discrimination Act, Ch 3, s 4; Cyprus: Law 58(1)/2004, s 9; UK: Equality Act 2010, s 149: public authorities must pay 'due regard' to the need to 'remove or minimise disadvantages suffered by persons' on grounds of religion or belief, to take steps to meet their needs, and to encourage them to participate in public life.

[129] France: Ministerial Instruction, Ministry of Public Service, no 2106 of 14 November 2005; Ireland: Organisation of Working Time Act 1997; Poland: Act of 17 May 1989, Art 42; Romania: LC, Art 134.1: 2 days off per annum if the employee's faith is a State recognized religion under Law no 489/2006.

[130] Slovenia: Advocate of the Principle of Equality, 28 August 2008, UEM-0921-10/2008-3. However, preferential religious treatment is unconstitutional in Bulgaria: CCt, Dec. no 14 of 1992.

[131] See Directive (EC) 2000/78, Art 4.

[132] Belgium: General Anti-Discrimination Federal Act, Art 8; Denmark: Act no 1349, 16 December 2008, s 6; Estonia: ETA 2008, Art 10; Germany: AGG, s 9; Hungary: Act CXXV 2003, Art 22.

[133] Cyprus: Law on Equality of Treatment 2004, Art 7; see also Greece: Law 3304/2005, Art 9(2): religious beliefs should be a 'genuine, legitimate and justified occupational requirement'.

other States, such as 'significant and justified',[134] 'determining',[135] 'genuine and determining',[136] or 'legitimate and proportionate' requirements.[137]

Although several States make no reference to religious ethos,[138] in most States discrimination is lawful when an institution has a religious ethos. The right to discriminate may be enjoyed by, variously: 'religious institutions or organisations';[139] 'churches and other public or private organisations the ethos of which is based on religion or belief';[140] and 'religious associations and other public or private organisations'.[141] The same applies to religious communities, associations, and centres;[142] religious communities, facilities affiliated to them, or organizations which have united to practise a religion or belief;[143] 'establishments' with a religious ethos;[144] or 'institutions founded on religious principles'.[145] Such organizations may discriminate on the basis of religion,[146] sexual orientation,[147] and sex.[148] For example, in Austria, public or private organizations the ethos of which is based on religion or belief (such as faith schools), may engage in differential treatment against a person where, by reason of the activities involved (or the context in which they are carried out), the religion or belief of the person is a genuine, legitimate, and justified occupational requirement, having regard to the ethos of the organization.[149]

---

[134] Poland: LC, Art 18.

[135] Romania: Anti-Discrimination Law, Art 9; see also Luxembourg: Law of 28 November 2006, Art 18; Czech Republic: Anti-Discrimination Law; Italy: Decree, Art 3(5).

[136] Finland: Non-Discrimination Act 2004; France: Law no 2008-496, Arts 2.3 and 6.3.

[137] Malta: Legal Notice 461, 2004, Reg 4; Slovenia: ETA, Art 2: if the requirement is appropriate and necessary; see also Employment Relationship Act 2003 (amended 2007), Art 6.

[138] Finland, Portugal, Romania, and Spain have no provision in discrimination law on organizations with a religious ethos; the matter is governed by laws on genuine occupational requirements; but the Finnish Church Act 1054/1993, s 6.1.2 requires employees of the Evangelical Lutheran Church to be members of that church in order to engage in teaching, liturgical, or charitable activities. See Ch 5 below.

[139] Bulgaria: Protection against Discrimination Act, Art 7: differential treatment on grounds of religion is lawful when these constitute an essential and determining requirement in view of the nature of the organization (if the aim is legitimate and the requirement is necessary to achieve it).

[140] Cyprus: ETA 2004, Art 7; for a similar approach see Greece: Law 3304/2005, Art 9; Luxembourg: Law of 28 November 2006, Art 18; Slovenia: ETA, Art 2 (the same provision is in the FRA, Art 3.3).

[141] Estonia: ETA, Art 10; see also Latvia: Labour Law 2002 (as amended 2006).

[142] Lithuania: ETA, Art 3.

[143] Germany: AGG, Art 9; also Work Constitution Act, s 118: this does not apply to church hospitals; UK: Equality Act 2010 protects doctrines and members of organized religions, etc.

[144] Denmark: Act no 1349, 16 December 2008, s 6; Ireland: Employment Equality Act 1998–2007, s 37. For private and public institutions with a religious ethos, see: Belgium: General Anti-Discrimination Act, Art 13, and CCt, Decision no 17/2009 and no 39/2009.

[145] Netherlands: GETA, Art 5.

[146] Austria: ETA, s 20(2); Cyprus: ETA 2004, Art 7; Denmark: Act no 1349, 16 December 2008, s 6; Estonia: ETA, Art 10; Germany: AGG, Art 9; Greece: Law 3304/2005, Art 9(2); Hungary: ETA, Act CXXV 2003, Art 22; Italy: LD, Art 3(5); Lithuania: ETA, Art 3; Luxembourg: Law of 28 November 2006, Art 18.

[147] Bulgaria: Protection against Discrimination Act, Art 7; Netherlands: GETA, Art 5.

[148] Denmark: Act on Equal Treatment of Men and Women 2006.

[149] Austria: ETA, s 20(2); faith schools may use this exception in the appointment of teachers: Act on the Relations of Schools and [the Catholic] Church, BGBl no 48/1858; Schools Regulation, BGBl no 273/1962, s 3; Act on Religious Education, s 3; there is no case-law on this.

Exceptions to the general rule are justified on several grounds: to respect the religious freedom of the organization,[150] and to reflect the undertakings of those who have joined such organizations—a person who is employed by a religious organization and subsequently finds himself in conflict with that group on a religious issue is deemed to have exercised his right to religious freedom by undertaking that employment.[151] The latter represents an equivalent to the Strasbourg specific secular situation rule.[152] Exempted organizations have been allowed to discriminate in a wide variety of cases. An institution established to train ministers of religion may admit students of only one gender or religious belief.[153] A nursing home was entitled to dismiss an employee because she had left the church to which the home was affiliated—the dismissal was justified on the basis of breach of a duty of loyalty to that church.[154] A Christian church welfare institution (providing integration for migrants and financed by the State) was able to reject a Muslim for a position as a social educator on the basis of lack of a degree qualification, even though the employer had asked if the person would join the church in question.[155] A religious university may dismiss a theology student on the basis of his homosexuality.[156] An institute which trained ministers of a church was entitled to refuse admission of a former student for further study because he no longer fully believed the doctrines of that church—and he lived with his girlfriend; the rejection was lawful on the basis that the requirement that students should not have sexual relationships outside marriage was of central importance to the institute.[157] The exceptions also apply to the selection of pupils in religious schools (see Chapter 8).

By way of contrast, there are equally many cases in which the exception does not apply. A State law which required automatic resignation at the age of 75 from a church council of a recognized religion was found to be discriminatory on grounds of age—it was disproportionate in so far as it was based on an absolute presumption that such persons would no longer be capable of carrying out council functions.[158] Dismissal of a cleaner from a Christian humanitarian organization because he was

---

[150] Ireland: Employment Equality Act 1998–2007, s 37; see *Re Article 26 and the Employment Equality Bill 1996* [1997] 2 IR 321: 'it appears that it is constitutionally permissible to make distinctions or discrimination on grounds of religious profession, belief or status insofar as but only insofar as this may be necessary to give life and reality to the guarantee of the free profession and practice of religion contained in the Constitution'.

[151] Finland: Parliamentary Constitutional Committee, Statement (PeVL 22/1997) on the bill to alter the law on the Orthodox Church, s 16c.

[152] Indeed, Strasbourg itself accepts that the right to manifest religion which is enjoyed by a religious association may prevail over the rights of its employees: see PM Taylor, *Freedom of Religion* (Cambridge, 2005) 138 *et seq*; see eg *X v Denmark* App no 7374/76 (1976) 5 D&R 158.

[153] Ireland: Equal Status Act 2000, s 7.

[154] Germany: Rhineland-Palatine Labour Court, 2 July 2008, 7 Sa 250/08; the duty of loyalty is also found in legislation in some States: Portugal: LC, Art 121(1)(e).

[155] Germany: Hamburg Labour Court, 29 October 2008, 3 Sa 15/08.

[156] Hungary: SC, 8 June 2005 (Károli Gáspár Calvinist University).

[157] Netherlands: ETC, 20 July 2006, Opinion 2006-154.

[158] Belgium: CCt, Judgment no 152/2005 (5 October 2005): the court held there was no breach of ECHR, Art 9 or of Const, Arts 19 and 21 (on freedom of religion and religious autonomy).

not a member of the (national) Lutheran Church has been held unlawful.[159] Sexual orientation does not of itself permit a religious association to dismiss an employee.[160] A Muslim woman who applied for the post of a teacher of Arabic in a Muslim school was rejected because she refused to wear a headscarf; the Muslim school failed to establish that wearing a religious headscarf was a necessary condition in order to maintain or realize the religious founding principles of the school.[161] It has also been held in the Netherlands that a Christian school for professional education could not refuse entry to a person whose parents' moral views differed from those of the school.[162]

Crimes against the person motivated by religion

In 1996, the European Union required Member States to penalize 'public incitement to discrimination, violence or racial hatred in respect of a group of persons or a member of such a group defined by reference to colour, race, religion or national or ethnic origin'.[163] This has had a profound affect on national laws in Europe in the field of those criminal offences against the person which are motivated by religion.[164] This section deals with incitement to religious discrimination, violence, and hatred, as well as religiously aggravated crimes and the question of whether religion may mitigate criminal liability.

Incitement of religious discrimination and hatred

To underscore the seriousness of the social mischief, the laws of several European States criminalize religious discrimination (alongside discrimination on grounds of race, ethnicity, colour, sex, sexual orientation, age, and political opinions).[165] Various forms of conduct are penalized. Violation of the principle of equality is a criminal offence in, for example, Lithuania (if it occurs on the basis of religion),[166]

---

[159] Denmark: City Court Copenhagen, 1 September 2005 (unreported).
[160] France: Court of Cassation, 17 April 1991: the religious orientation of the employer (Fraternité Ste Pie) did not justify an exception to LC, Art L122-45 (now Art L1132-1).
[161] Netherlands: ETC, 15 November 2005, Opinion 2005-222.
[162] Netherlands: Amsterdam CA, 24 July 2007, LJN: BB0057.
[163] Council of the EU, Joint Action, 15 July 1996, on measures to combat racism and xenophobia (96/443/JHA), adopted on the basis of EU Treaty, Art K3), to prevent perpetrators of such offences exploiting the fact that xenophobic activities are classified differently in different States by moving countries to escape criminal proceedings. See also COE, Parliamentary Assembly, Rec 1805 (2007). Moreover, international law may also be incorporated in national laws; eg in the UK: International Criminal Court Act 2001, s 50(6), Sch 8: the offence of genocide includes acts committed 'with intent to destroy in whole or in part a . . . religious group'; moreover, a crime against humanity includes persecution against any identifiable group on religious grounds.
[164] Crimes which relate to religious belief and worship are dealt with in Ch 6 below.
[165] Latvia: Criminal Law, s 149; see also LORO, s 4.1; see also Bulgaria: PC, Art 162.
[166] Lithuania: PC, Art 169: 'Discrimination of the basis of . . . religion' is a crime: 'Any person who commits acts aimed at a certain group of people or a member thereof on account of that group's . . . religion with a view to interfering with their right to participate as equals in political, economical,

and Estonia (if it occurs on the basis of belief).[167] In some States religious discrimination is a civil offence when committed by private individuals, but a crime when committed by government officials; this is the case in Belgium[168] and Romania.[169] Moreover, religious discrimination may be punishable in the spheres of both public and private employment,[170] or in the provision of goods and services, as well as in the exercise of public functions: under Finnish law, a person who in the exercise of official authority, or in a trade, profession, service to the public, public amusement, or meeting, without justification 'places someone in an unequal or an essentially inferior position' on the basis of their religion is liable to a fine or imprisonment for up to six months.[171]

Incitement to religious discrimination is a criminal offence in Italy,[172] Belgium,[173] and Portugal: 'a person who in a public meeting, by writing proposed for publication or by any means of social communication...outrages a person, or a group of persons, on grounds of [*inter alia*] their...religion...intending to incite...religious discrimination or to encourage it, shall be punished with imprisonment from 6 months to 5 years'. Moreover, in Portuguese law, incitement to religious discrimination by private organizations is a more serious offence: a person who founds an organization or develops activities to incite religious discrimination, or who participates in such organizations or activities, is punishable with imprisonment for a term ranging from one to eight years.[174] In Latvia, too, the penalty for religious discrimination is more severe if it has been committed by a group of individuals, a senior representative of a company, enterprise, or other organization, or if it has been committed with the use of an automated data processing system; the rule also applies to government officials.[175]

Secondly, there are crimes of incitement to violence against the person on grounds of religion.[176] On the one hand, there are crimes of public incitement to

---

social, cultural or labour activity...shall be punished by community service or a fine, or detention, or imprisonment for a term of up to 3 years.'

[167] Estonia: PC, Art 152: 'Unlawful restriction of the rights of a person or granting unlawful preference to a person on the basis of his or her...belief...is punishable by a fine...or by detention.'

[168] Belgium: Act of 10 May 2007, Art 23: any public official, who discriminates against a person, group, community or its members in the exercise of his function is punishable with prison for 2 months to 2 years; when an official acts on the orders of a superior, only the superior is prosecuted.

[169] Romania: PC, Art 247.

[170] Spain: PC, Arts 314, 511, 512: if carried out in public or private employment, the penalty is prison for 6 months to 2 years or a fine; a civil servant who commits the offence may be barred from employment or public office for up to 4 years.

[171] Finland: PC, Ch 11, s 9; see also Luxembourg: PC Arts 454 and 455: licensing, employment.

[172] Italy: Law 85/2006, Art 13; the penalty is 1 to 6 months in prison or a fine of €6,000; and for violence or acts of provocation to violence, prison for 6 months to 4 years.

[173] Belgium: Law of 10 May 2007; BS, 30 May 2007, Art 22: incitement to religious discrimination may be punished with prison for between 1 month and 1 year and/or a fine.

[174] Portugal: PC, Art 240: the rule also applies to government bodies.

[175] Latvia: Criminal Law (1998), s 149: a prison sentence of up to 2 years, mandatory community service, or a fine which is equal to no more than 50 times the minimum monthly wage.

[176] As we saw in Ch 2, the criminal laws of States may penalize violence or threats of violence or other serious harm which prevents a person from exercising religious freedom; see eg Poland: PC, Art 194: '[Any person] who limits a person in his/her rights because of his/her religious affiliation or because of the lack of such an affiliation, shall be punished with a fine, limitation of freedom or

religious violence. In Austria, this occurs when a person publicly provokes or incites violence towards a church or religious community or towards a certain group belonging to such a church or religious community. The conduct must be calculated to endanger public order. The offence is punished with imprisonment for up to two years.[177] Incitement to religious violence is also considered a serious offence against public order in the Netherlands and Luxembourg.[178] On the other hand, French law forbids both public and private provocation to religious violence. It is an offence to provoke violence against a person or group by reason of their membership or non-membership of a determined religion; the provocation may be carried out through speech, menaces, writing, drawings, pictures, or images. The offence is punishable with imprisonment for up to one year and/or fines.[179] However, some States seem to make no distinction between public and private incitement to religious violence in the definitional elements of the offence, as is the case in the Czech Republic,[180] Bulgaria,[181] Italy,[182] and Lithuania: the production, possession to distribute, distribution or public demonstration of printed material, video, audio, or other products which propagate religious conflict (along with national and racial conflict), is punished by a fine.[183] Some groups in Lithuania have been subject to warnings about the possible commission of this offence, including groups in the film industry.[184]

Thirdly, there are offences of incitement to religious hatred. These have burgeoned in recent years.[185] The principal focus of the offence is incitement to hatred with regard to a person or a group by reason of their membership of a religious community.[186] The physical or external element of the offence (*actus reus*) may include, for example, words or behaviour; the display, publishing, or distributing of written material; the public performance of a play; distributing, showing, or playing

withdrawal of freedom for up to two years'; see also Czech Rep: PC, s 236; Spain: PC, Art 522; France: Law of 1905, Art 31; Bulgaria: PC, Art 165.

[177] Austria: PC, para 283.

[178] Netherlands: PC, Art 137d; Luxembourg: PC, Art 457-1; Spain: PC, Art 510.

[179] France: for public provocation see Law 72-546 of July 1972 (applying Law of 29 July 1881, Art 24); the fine is €45,000; for private provocation, see PC, R 625-7.

[180] Czech Rep: PC, s 196: 'a person, who uses violence against a group of citizens or an individual, or threatens them with death, a bodily injury or extensive damage, because of their... religion, or because they are non-denominational', shall be imprisoned for between 6 months and 3 years.

[181] Bulgaria: PC, Art 162: those who incite acts of violence against another because of his religion may be imprisoned for 1–6 years; those committing violence, to prison for up to 3 years.

[182] Italy: Laws 654/75, DL 122/1993 (Art 1)) and Law 85/2006, Art 13: those who provoke violence for religious reasons are liable to 1–6 months in prison or a fine of €6,000.

[183] Lithuania: Code of Misdemeanours in Administrative Law, Art 214-12; Hungary: PC, para 174/B.

[184] Lithuania: the authors of the website <http://www.satan.lt> (launched 2000), were warned in 2002 by the Security Department about possible commission of the offence, but no legal proceedings followed; the 'MTV Lietuva' channel was convicted, for showing *Popetown*, of inciting religious discrimination: Administrative Court of Vilnius District (2006).

[185] Hungary: PC, para 269: this penalizes incitement to national, ethnic, and racial hatred, but religious hatred may also be forbidden by analogy; the sentence is imprisonment for up to 3 years.

[186] Luxembourg: PC, Art 457-1; Latvia: LORO, s 4.1; Belgium, Act Combating Certain Types of Discrimination, 10 May 2007; BS, 30 May 2007, Art 22; Austria: PC, para 283; Bulgaria: PC, Arts 162.1; Czech Rep: PC, s 198A.

a recording; or broadcasting or including a programme in a programme service. It may also include the possession of written materials or recordings with a view to display, publication, distribution, or inclusion in a programme service.[187] The mental or internal element of the offence (*mens rea*) is usually intent to stir up religious hatred, or knowledge (actual or constructive) that this is the likely result of the action involved.[188] The penalties include imprisonment, but the term of imprisonment varies from State to State.[189] Most States classify incitement to religious hatred as a crime of public order,[190] or else as an offence to both public order and human dignity,[191] but in some States the offence may also be committed in private.[192] National laws provide for defences which are intended to protect the free and critical coverage of religion.[193]

It may be helpful to present the fundamentals of one national approach, that of Ireland. The offence of stirring up religious hatred was introduced in 1989 but it has been criticized as ineffective, with no prosecutions before 1995.[194] Hatred is defined as hatred against a group of persons, *inter alia*, on account of their religion. The elements of the offence cover a wide range of threatening, abusive, or insulting actions intended or likely to stir up religious hatred.[195] There is a defence in relation to published or distributed written material and recordings when there was no intent to stir up hatred. This is the case if the accused proves that he was not aware of the content of the material or recording and did not suspect, and had no reason to suspect, that the material or recording was threatening, abusive, or insulting. Moreover, it is a defence to show that, being in a private residence at the time, there was no reason to believe that the words, behaviour or material concerned would be heard or seen by a person outside the residence; or else, having shown that there was no intention to stir up hatred, 'to prove that he did not intend

---

[187] UK: Racial and Religious Hatred Act 2006, s 29.

[188] The Netherlands is typical: PC, Art 137e: the *mens rea* is knowledge or reasonable suspicion; in the case of a second offence; but no liability arises if the person was providing factual information.

[189] For imprisonment for up to 3 years, see Lithuania: PC, Art 170; Spain: PC, Art 510; Bulgaria: PC, Art 162.1; for up to 2 years in prison, see Poland: PC, Art 256 and Czech Rep: PC, s 198. cf Belgium, Act of 10 May 2007; BS, 30 May 2007, Art 22: prison for 1 month to 1 year and/or a fine; Italy: Law 654/75, DL 122/1993 (Art 1)) and Law 85/2006 (Art 13): 1–6 months' prison or a fine of €6,000; France: Law 72-546 of July 1972 (applying Law of 29 July 1881, Art 24) and PC, Art 625-7.

[190] Lithuania: PC, Art 170.1–170.3; UK: Racial and Religious Hatred Act 2006, s 29B, Explanatory Notes, para 14: there is no offence if the conduct occurs 'inside a private dwelling and there is no reason to believe that they can be heard or seen by a person outside that or any other private dwelling'.

[191] Poland: PC, Art 256.

[192] France: Law 72-546 of July 1972 (applying Law of 29 July 1881, Art 24), PC, R 625-7.

[193] UK: Racial and Religious Hatred Act 2006, s 29J, Explanatory Notes, 16: 'Nothing in this Part shall be read or given effect in a way which prohibits or restricts discussion, criticism or expressions of antipathy, dislike, ridicule, insult or abuse of particular religions or the beliefs or practices of their adherents, or of any other belief system . . . or proselytising or urging adherents of a different religion or belief system to cease practising their religion or belief system.'

[194] Ireland: National Consultative Committee on Racism and Interculturalism, 'Prohibition of Incitement to Hatred Act 1989: A Review' (August 2001).

[195] Ireland: Prohibition of Incitement to Hatred Act 1989, s 1; s 2: this covers written material and words and behaviour in public or in a private residence if the words, behaviour or material are heard or seen by persons outside it.

the words, behaviour or material concerned to be, and was not aware that they might be, threatening, abusive or insulting'.[196]

Criminal offences aggravated or mitigated by religion

In addition to incitement to commit crimes of discrimination, violence, and hatred motivated by religion, in most States religious motivation operates as an aggravating factor in relation to offences against the person when these are committed on the basis of hatred, contempt, or hostility towards that person because of their religion. Various approaches are used. It may be a factor taken into account by courts at sentencing (to increase a penalty), either on the basis of a discretionary practice or on the basis of formal law.[197] Alternatively, a religiously aggravated crime may be the religiously aggravated version of another offence, and that it is religiously aggravated would have to be proved as such prior to sentencing.[198] In some States religious aggravation applies to all offences,[199] but in others it will result in increased sentences in relation only to prescribed crimes, such as religiously aggravated homicide,[200] assault,[201] sexual offences,[202] coercion,[203] and discrimination.[204] Religious aggravation may also apply to offences against property, such as criminal damage[205] and theft.[206] Moreover, in some States a punishment may be increased if the accused is a minister of religion.[207] Sometimes, prosecutions for crimes committed against ministers of religion require the consent of the religious organization in question.[208]

---

[196] Ireland: Prohibition of Incitement to Hatred Act 1989, ss 2–4.

[197] A discretionary practice may be followed in States where there is no formal law on the matter (eg Cyprus and Hungary). cf the UK: Criminal Justice Act 2003, s 145: religion is a factor aggravating the seriousness of the offence in relation to all offences (except those listed below).

[198] UK: Scotland, 'offences aggravated by religious prejudice' are governed by the Criminal Justice (Scotland) Act 2003. cf Bulgaria: PC, Art 56: 'Extenuating and aggravating circumstances shall not be those which are taken into consideration by the law in defining the respective crime.'

[199] Spain: PC, Art 22.4: 'commission of an offence because of motives which are . . . anti-Semitic . . . [or due to] the religion or beliefs of the victim', is an aggravated offence and the penalty may be increased; Romania: PC, Art 75.1; Finland: PC, Ch 6, s 5; France: PC, Art 132–76.

[200] Portugal: homicide, imprisonment 12–25 years (PC, Art 132) instead of 8–10 years (Art 131).

[201] UK: England and Wales: Crime and Disorder Act 1998 (as amended by the Anti-Terrorism Crime and Security Act 2003), s 29, common assault (Criminal Justice Act 1988, s 39), actual bodily harm (Offences Against the Person Act 1861, s 47), causing grievous bodily harm (ibid s 20).

[202] Belgium: PC, Arts 372–377 (sex offences); other religiously aggravated offences include homicide (Arts 393–405); defamation (Arts 443–453); arson (Arts 510–514); and damage to buildings (Arts 521–525).

[203] Czech Rep: PC, s 235: imprisonment, 2–8 years if the offence is committed because of religious belief or because of being non-denominational (up to 3 years otherwise); see also religiously aggravated murder (s 219), bodily harm (s 221), and damage to property (s 257).

[204] Latvia: Criminal Law (1998), s 149: the penalty for religious discrimination and hatred is more severe if the offence has caused substantial harm or involved violence, fraud, or threats.

[205] Portugal: criminal damage 'linked to religious worship or the veneration of the memory of the dead or . . . in a place of worship or in a cemetery' (PC, Art 213) is punishable with prison for up to 5 years, or a fine instead of prison for up to 3 years, or a fine (Art 212); see also Austria: PC, para 126.

[206] Greece: PC, Art 374; and Austria: PC, para 128. See below Ch 6 below.

[207] Luxembourg: PC, Art 377: if a minister of religion commits rape, and has abused his position to do so, the sentence is increased; see also Art 380 for prostitution and exploitation.

[208] In Austria, if a criminal offence is committed against the honour of a spiritual adviser of a church or religious community during the exercise of office, the public prosecutor has to prosecute the perpetrator with authorization from the minister and the appropriate religious authority: PC, para 111.

The complexities of this area of law are well illustrated by the case of the United Kingdom.[209] In England and Wales, there are two offences of religious aggravation.[210] The first occurs if at the time of committing the offence, or immediately before or after doing so, the offender demonstrates towards the victim hostility based on the victim's membership (or presumed membership) of a religious group.[211] This does *not* require proof that the defendant was motivated by religious hostility;[212] the test is that the defendant formed the view that the victim was a member of a religious group and that the defendant demonstrated hostility based on that membership.[213] 'Membership' of a religious group includes 'association with members of that group' and 'presumed membership' means presumed by the offender.[214] The second occurs if the offence is motivated (wholly or partly) by hostility towards members of a religious group based on their membership of that group.[215] This requires proof that the defendant was motivated by religious hostility.[216] Religious aggravation may exist regardless of whether the defendant is of the same religious group as the victim.[217] For both types, it is immaterial whether or not the religious hostility of the offender is also based on any other factor.[218] 'Religious group' means 'a group of persons defined by reference to religious belief or lack of religious belief'.[219] 'Religious belief' is not defined. These crimes are based on pre-existing offences as religiously aggravated versions of them carrying a higher maximum punishment, namely: assault;[220] destroying or damaging property belonging to another;[221] and public order offences (fear or provocation of violence, intentional harassment, alarm, or distress) and harassment—there have been several cases involving religiously aggravated offences.[222] When a court

---

[209] See M Idriss, 'Religion and the Anti-Terrorism Crime and Security Act 2001' (2002) Criminal Law Review 890. See also n 201 above for religious aggravation taken into account at sentencing.

[210] R Card, *Card, Cross and Jones Criminal Law* (Oxford: OUP, 18th edn, 2008) para 7.102: 'The first type is "concerned" with the outward manifestation of . . . religious hostility, the other with the inner motivation of the offender': commenting on *Rogers* [2007] 2 AC 62, *per* Baroness Hale.

[211] Crime and Disorder Act 1998, s 28(1)(a). As the demonstration of hostility must be 'immediately' before or after the act, a demonstration 20 minutes after the act will not suffice; however, the victim need not be present at the demonstration: *Perry v DPP* [2004] EWHC 3112 (Admin).

[212] *DPP v Green* [2004] EWHC 1125 (Admin).

[213] Words used need not expressly identify the religious group: *AG's Reference (No 4 of 2004)* [2005] 1 WLR 2810 (CA)—on racial aggravation.

[214] Crime and Disorder Act 1998, s 28(2).

[215] ibid s 28(1)(b). Whereas proof of demonstration requires proof of what D did at the time of the offence, proof of motivation may be established by what D may have done or said on other occasions: *G v DPP; T v DPP* [2004] EWHC 183 (Admin): Card (n 210 above) para 7.113.

[216] Card (n 210 above) para 7.103.

[217] This has been applied to racial aggravation: *White* [2001] 1 WLR 1352 (CA).

[218] Crime and Disorder Act 1998, s 28(3).

[219] ibid s 28(5).

[220] Offences Against the Person Act 1861, ss 20, 47, and Crime and Disorder Act 1998, s 29(1).

[221] Crime and Disorder Act 1998, s 30 (under the Criminal Damage Act 1971, s 1); imprisonment for 14 years (10 years for the non-aggravated form) or a fine or both.

[222] Crime and Disorder Act 1998, ss 31 and 32, under the Public Order Act 1986, ss 4, 4A, and 5, and the Protection from Harassment Act 1997, ss 2, 4; *Norwood v DPP* [2003] EWHC 1564 Admin: displaying a poster in a window showing the events of 9/11 and the words 'Islam out of Britain' was a religiously aggravated offence under s 5, even though no Muslims had complained about it; *Hammond v DPP* [2004] EWHC Admin 69: an elderly, autistic evangelic protester who preached

considers the seriousness of an offence, if the offence was religiously aggravated, the court must treat that fact as an aggravating factor, and must state in open court that it was so aggravated; this should attract a heavier sentence.[223] In Scotland also, there are 'offences aggravated by religious prejudice'.[224]

By way of contrast, there is little evidence across Europe that religious motivation will constitute a mitigating factor which results in the reduction of a sentence, and indeed in Estonia this is expressly forbidden.[225] Usually such circumstances are allowed as a matter of judicial practice and discretion on the basis of special facts.[226] Spanish jurisprudence has accepted religious motivation as an extenuating circumstance in relation to Catholics who committed offences in a Protestant place of worship,[227] and to Jehovah's Witnesses preventing a blood transfusion.[228] In one Swedish case, a pastor of the Pentecostal Movement who preached a sermon disrespectful to homosexuals was prosecuted for agitation against a national or ethnic group; he was acquitted on the basis that his comments were made in the course of a religious ceremony and so protected by religious freedom.[229] Sometimes, legislation provides for explicit religious defences to what would otherwise be a criminal offence—such as carrying a blade in public for religious reasons,[230] or refusing to wear a crash-helmet on a motor cycle.[231] Whilst generally the religiously motivated consent of a victim will not excuse the perpetrator of the offence,[232] it may occasionally be the case that valid consent could be given to, for example, religious mortification, the infliction of pain on a penitent with his consent as part of religious repentance.[233]

---

on a Sunday afternoon while holding a large sign saying 'Stop Immorality. Stop Homosexuality. Stop Lesbianism. Jesus is Lord' was guilty under s 5; *Dehal v CPS* [2005] EWHC Admin 2154: a notice denouncing a president of a Gurdwara as a hypocrite, a liar and a 'mad dog' was not an offence under either s 4A or 5 since there was no real fear of public disorder.

[223] Criminal Justice Act 2003, s 145(1)–(2); s 145(3); Crime and Disorder Act 1998, s 28.

[224] Criminal Justice (Scotland) Act 2003, s 74.

[225] Estonia: Const, Art 41(2): 'beliefs shall not constitute an excuse for a legal offence'; see also PC, paras 57 and 58: no person is liable just because of his beliefs.

[226] This is the case in Belgium, Bulgaria, the Czech Republic, France, and Luxembourg.

[227] Spain: HC Ruling, 25 November 1955: a group of Catholics was convicted of attempting to burn Bibles at the altar when claiming to act in accordance with their 'deeply rooted Catholic beliefs' in protest against 'the intense and public propaganda of Protestant ideas' of the pastor and other members of the Protestant faithful—this 'hampered their sense of reason' and the penalty was reduced.

[228] Spain: HC Ruling, 27 March 1990: the defendant who pulled out the tube providing a blood transfusion (resulting in the death of the person) was found guilty of intentional homicide; 'the dogmatism and the rigidity of his ideas' was applied in mitigation; Ruling, 27 June 1997: parents who were Jehovah's Witnesses were guilty of homicide for refusing to allow their son to receive a blood transfusion when he was suffering from an advanced form of leukemia, subsequently dying from it; the intensity of the parents' religious convictions resulted in a lower sentence. See also Ch 9 below.

[229] Sweden: NJA 2005, p 805.

[230] UK: Criminal Justice Act 1988, s 139: it is an offence to have in a public place 'any article which has a blade or is sharply pointed'; it is a defence if the person had 'good reason or lawful authority' for having the article or is able 'to prove that he had the article . . . for religious reasons'.

[231] Road Traffic Act 1988, s 16 (originally Motor-Cycle Helmets (Religious Exemption) Act 1976): it is not a crime for a Sikh to wear a turban instead of a crash helmet for the purposes of road traffic law.

[232] Exceptions obviously include properly conducted sports and lawful surgical procedures.

[233] UK: *Brown* [1994] 1 AC 212, 267, *per* Lord Mustill.

National criminal laws on illicit sects represent a good example of the degree to which religion may not be used as a cloak to justify criminal conduct.[234] Recommendations about harmful sects have been made by both the Council of Europe[235] and the European Union.[236] Most European countries do not have laws specifically dealing with sects,[237] though as a general principle any religious group which contravenes the criminal law would be liable to prosecution,[238] or to dissolution as an illicit association.[239] However, a Slovakian ordinance defines a sect as:

...a destructive religious group, established on the basis of fanatical confession, ultimately on the basis of the deceitfulness of its founder, which depraves the development of the younger generation or violates the laws, and ultimately through their ideology and thoughts threatens lives, health or property and violates other generally legally binding statutes.[240]

European States which address the matter fall into three broad categories: those with anti-sect laws; those debating the matter; and those with bodies charged with the gathering of information on and the monitoring of sects.[241]

In France, a Law of 2001 defines a *mouvement sectaire* as one which pursues activities with the object of belief being to maintain or exploit the psychological or physical subjection of persons who participate in its activities—the law makes no express mention of religion.[242] Moreover, French law penalizes the circulation of materials aiming to promote the movement among young people, and the foundation and maintenance (or re-establishment if previously dissolved) of an entity for

---

[234] For the wider issues of new religious movements (NRMs) in Europe, see eg S Pastorelli, 'The European Union and the new religious movements' in LN Leustean and JTS Madeley (eds), *Religion, Politics and Law in the European Union* (London: Routledge, 2010) 187.

[235] The Parliamentary Assembly of the COE in 1992 considered 'major legislation on sects undesirable': Rec 1178; however, in 1999 it encouraged States to set up or support information centres on 'groups of a religious, esoteric or spiritual nature', to use the law against their illegal practices, to assist those who had been harmed by them, but 'to take firm steps against any action which is discriminatory or which marginalises religious or spiritual minority groups': Rec 1412.

[236] In 1984, the European Parliament expressed concerns about the recruitment and treatment of members of 'new organizations operating under the protection afforded to religious beliefs': Res 22 May 1984; it reaffirmed this in its 'Resolution on Cults in Europe' (March 1997) and Res 5 July 2001 (on cults which jeopardize the physical and psychological integrity of individuals); see generally JR Lewis (ed), *The Oxford Handbook of New Religious Movements* (Oxford: OUP, 2004).

[237] This is the case in Austria, Finland, Luxembourg, Portugal, Hungary, and Estonia.

[238] Czech Rep: PC, s 231: unlawful restraint; s 232: deprivation of personal freedom.

[239] Spain: LORF, Art 3.2: organizations involved in the study or practice of psychic or parapsychological phenomena, or other humanistic, spiritualistic, non-religious aims, are not protected by religious freedom; they may be classified as illicit associations, be dissolved, and their members punished: PC, Art 515; see also: *Iglesia de Scientology de España v Ministerio de Justicia* [2007] Audiencia Nacional, 11 October 2007 (No 0000352/2005): held lawful; Ireland: Defamation Act 2006: for the purposes of this statute, religion does not include an organization or cult the principal object of which is to make profit or that employs oppressive psychological manipulation of its followers.

[240] Slovakia: Home Office, Internal Ordinance no 2 (on extremism), Art 2; for criminal proceedings against the Church of Scientology in Italy, see: Tribunal of Milan, 2 July 1991; CA Milan, 5 November 1993, annulled by the Court of Cassation: Decision 163/1995.

[241] Estonia: before adoption of the CCA 2002, the Estonian Council of Churches' petition to the government to legislate on 'non-constructive religious communities' failed: PECCSR (2007) 73–4.

[242] France: Law no 2001-504 of 12 June 2001 (the so-called '*loi* About-Picard'), Art 1; the category *association cultuelle* (for which see Ch 4 below) is not generally applied to sects. See generally F Messner (ed), *Les 'sectes' et le droit en France* (Paris: Presses Universitaires de France, 1999).

the purpose of pursuing these objects.[243] It is also an offence to abuse fraudulently the vulnerable, namely those in a state of ignorance or feebleness (by virtue of age or infirmity), and to induce them to exercise their judgment so as to perform an act to their prejudice.[244] Latvia, too, has a so-called 'anti-sect' law: 'causing danger to public safety, order and the health of individuals while performing religious activities'; this may attract imprisonment for up to five years and/or a fine.[245] However, until 2008 there had been no prosecutions under this law.[246]

The second approach is the establishment of commissions on sects. For example, there is a Lithuanian commission to co-ordinate the activities of government departments to resolve issues raised by religious sects. Its functions are: to coordi-nate the investigation of the extent to which such groups comply with the law; to guarantee the exchange of information among state institutions; and to offer advice on action to be taken with respect to sects.[247] Finally, Belgium enacted legislation in 1998 to establish a centre to give advice on such organizations—indeed the Court of Arbitration has held that the centre cannot forbid the expression of an opinion by a religious or philosophical minority; but it may inform the public about the activities of such groups so that people may evaluate for themselves any dangers which may be associated with the group.[248] Nevertheless, Belgium is currently considering two new offences which may be applicable to such groups: the 'mental destabilisation of persons' and the 'abuse of persons' weakness'. The first offence consists of violating the fundamental rights of a person by acts of violence, threats, or psychological force, either by inducing fear in the individual that his family, goods, or work could be harmed, or by exploiting his credibility to convince him of the existence of false enterprises, imaginary powers, or non-existent events. The second offence is maliciously abusing the ignorance or weak-ened position of a person who is particularly vulnerable due to age, disease, physical or mental disability, or pregnancy; the offence is committed when the abuse seeks to force that person to act or fail to act in such a way as to result in their serious harm, or to incite a minor or other vulnerable person to suicide, resulting in actual suicide or a suicide attempt by that person.[249]

---

[243] France: PC, Art 434-43; penalty, 3 years' prison and €45,000.
[244] France: Law no 2001-504 of 12 June 2001, Art 223-15-2.
[245] Latvia: Criminal Law, s 227: or a fine of up to 100 times the minimum monthly wage.
[246] PECCSR (2008): National Report for Latvia, R Balodis.
[247] G Robbers (ed), *State and Church in the European Union* (Baden-Baden: Nomos, 2nd edn, 2005) 291–2; in Poland in 1997, the Prime Minister set up an inter-ministerial committee on new religious movements which reported in 2000: Order of 25 August 1997.
[248] Belgium: Law of 2 June 1998; Court of Arbitration, no 31/2000, 21 March 2000, *Moniteur belge*, 22 April 2000.
[249] Belgium, Chamber of Representatives, 2007–2008, Doc 0854/001, PC, Art 442. The first offence would be punishable with a prison sentence of 15 days to 2 years and/or a fine; the second offence with a prison sentence of 1 month to 4 years and/or a fine. A parliamentary report had been submitted to the Chamber of Representatives on 28 April 1997 with a list of sectarian organizations (Parliamentary Documents, Chamber, 1995–6, 313/8, p 227).

Conclusion

European Union law has been a major unifying influence in national laws on religious discrimination. All States in Europe have laws which address religious discrimination. Civil laws forbid discrimination variously on grounds of religion or belief in relation to employment and the provision of goods and services. The prohibition is against direct and indirect discrimination, incitement to discriminate, religious harassment, and victimization. There are exceptions for institutions with a religious ethos provided these act in a genuine, legitimate, and necessary fashion. There is an abundance of jurisprudence in relation to justifications for indirect religious discrimination and the statutory exceptions for bodies with a religious ethos. Recent years have also witnessed the emergence of criminal laws which prohibit religious discrimination, incitement to religious conflict, violence, and hatred, and religiously aggravated offences, though little case-law exists on these offences. Pronouncements of the Council of Europe and the European Union have led some States to legislate on religious sects and others to explore the phenomenon by way of advisory commissions and other such bodies, but the emergent laws on sects illustrate well the degree to which religiously motivated acts cannot justify breach of the criminal law. Several principles emerge from this comparison of national laws: religious discrimination is forbidden on the basis of the right to religious freedom; all individuals are equal and may not be discriminated against on grounds of their religion; a civil remedy should be available for religious harassment, victimization, direct discrimination, and indirect discrimination; direct religious discrimination may not be justified but indirect religious discrimination may be justified on the basis of a policy which is objective and necessary to achieve a legitimate aim; an entity may engage in direct discrimination on the basis of a special exception provided this is necessary to defend the religious ethos of that organization; States may penalize with criminal sanctions any person who engages in incitement to religious discrimination, violence, and hatred; and religion should not be used as a cloak for criminal activity.

4

The Legal Position of Religious Organizations

As we saw in Chapter 1, the principal focus of the three theoretical models of religion-state relations in Europe is the legal relationship between the State and institutional religion. In the state-church model, there is a close constitutional link between the State and a particular national, folk, or established church. In the separation model, the constitutional posture of the State is secular and institutional religion has no place in the public life of the State. In the cooperation model, a basic constitutional separation exists but the State collaborates with religious organizations over matters of common concern. This chapter examines the legal position of religious organizations within the three religion-state models. It explores the right to religious association, the legal categories of religious organization, and the acquisition and exercise of legal personality by religious organizations. Legal personality enables them to have a legal structure, to own property, and to sue (and be sued). The chapter also discusses the impact of national arrangements, with regard to the legal position of religious organizations, on the adequacy of the classical threefold understanding of religion-state models in Europe. As we have seen, all States cooperate with religion over religious freedom and discrimination—they also cooperate with religious entities over limited exceptions to anti-discrimination laws. This chapter proposes, similarly, that whilst there are structural differences in the models at the constitutional level, beneath this there is a basic unity between States as to the legal position and personality of religious organizations—all States cooperate, in various ways, with religion in this matter. It also suggests that common principles emerge from national laws on this subject.

The right of religious association

As seen in Chapter 2, the individual has a right to manifest religious belief *in community with others*.[1] Though initially Strasbourg confined the enjoyment of religious freedom to the individual,[2] it now takes the view that a religious organi-

---

[1] ECHR, Art 9.1: and the right may be exercised both publicly and privately.
[2] *Church of X v UK* (1968) 29 CD 70: the case brought by a church was dismissed as 'a corporation being a legal and not a natural person is incapable of having or exercising the [ECHR] rights'.

zation enjoys the right to religious freedom 'on behalf of' or as 'a representative of its members'.[3] This is at the heart of the notion developed in national laws of the collective right of religious freedom.[4] However, nowhere in Europe is a religious group required to have juridical personality under civil law. Religious groups may simply exist as unincorporated voluntary associations with no legal personality as such.[5] Individuals may form such groups on the basis of the right of association, a right expressly protected in the ECHR.[6] The right to associate may be cast without any specific reference to religion,[7] or it may rest on a general liberty in so far as the law does not prohibit association.[8] In some States, though, there is a specific formal right of religious association—to constitute religious communities,[9] or to belong to them.[10] The right of religious association is sometimes conceived as an aspect of religious freedom, as has occurred, for example, in Denmark[11] and Hungary.[12] Indeed, Cypriot law divides society itself into two basic religious groups: the Greek community, composed, *inter alia*, of 'members of the Greek Orthodox Church'; and the Turkish community composed, *inter alia*, of those 'who are Muslims'.[13]

The right to associate as a religious group exists irrespective of the religion-state model at work in a country.[14] The right of religious association exists when there is

[3] *X and Church of Scientology v Sweden* App no 7805/77 (1979) 16 D&R 68: 'the distinction between the Church and its members . . . is essentially artificial. When a church body lodges an application under the Convention, it does so . . . on behalf of its members. It should therefore be accepted that a church body is capable of possessing and exercising the rights . . . in its own capacity as a representative of its members'.

[4] The idea is well developed in Spain: Const, Art 16.1 protects the religious freedom of 'individuals and communities', natural and legal persons; see CCt, Judgments no 64/1988, 12 April 1988, FJ 2, no 107/1984, 23 November 1984, FJ 3; nos 141/2000, 29 May 2000, FJ 5; 154/2002, 18 July 2002, FJ 9.

[5] UK: *Forbes v Eden* (1867) LR 1 Sc & Div 568; Ireland: *State (Colquhoun) v D'Arcy* [1936] IR 641; France: Law of 2 January 1907 (see also Law of 1 July 1901); Belgium: the principal and most commonly used entity is the VZW/ASBL (Vereniging zonder winstoogmerk), which has existed since 1921.

[6] ECHR, Art 11: freedom of assembly and association.

[7] Germany: GG, Art 9; moreover, an unregistered private (religious) association has no legal personality: CC (BGB), Art 54; see also Malta, Const, Art 32.

[8] This is the position in common law in the UK.

[9] Poland: SFCR, 17 May 1989, Art 2; Slovenia: Const, Art 7.1 (separation), 7.2 (freedom to found a religious community); see also Art 42 (freedom of assembly); see also Latvia, Const, Art 99.

[10] Estonia: Const, Art 40: 'Everyone may freely belong to churches and religious associations'; freedom includes the right to practise religion 'in a community with others'.

[11] Denmark: Const, Art 67: 'Citizens shall be at liberty to form congregations for the worship of God in a manner which corresponds with their convictions, provided that nothing contrary to good morals or public order shall be taught or done'.

[12] Hungary: CCt, Decision 8/1990 (II.27) AB. cf Austria: it was unclear whether ECHR, Art 11 applied to religious groups (VfSlg 8387/1978); BGBl I 66/2002 clarified this.

[13] Cyprus: Const, Art 2.1 and 2.2: the Greek community comprises all citizens who are of Greek origin and whose mother tongue is Greek or who share the Greek cultural traditions or 'who are members of the Greek Orthodox Church'; *mutatis mutandis* the Turkish community comprises all those who are Turkish in origin, etc, or 'who are Muslims'; others shall 'opt to belong to either the Greek or Turkish community as individuals, but, if they belong to a religious group, shall so opt as a religious group and upon such option they shall be deemed to be members of such community'.

[14] Incorporation of the ECHR obviously means that Art 11 (right to associate) is part of national laws.

a state church,[15] or a traditional religion,[16] as well as in cooperation systems, where the law separates but allows collaboration between the State and religion,[17] and separation systems, when the State itself is forbidden to establish a religious community.[18] Moreover, the right to associate is to be enjoyed equally by all religious groups. As seen in Chapter 3, the principle of equality of religious groups, which has made its mark in Strasbourg jurisprudence,[19] is formally recognized in the laws of several States.[20] In Spain, for example, where the law provides that 'There shall be no State religion',[21] all faith communities may establish places of worship, commemorate feast days, appoint and train their ministers, promulgate and propagate their own beliefs, maintain relations with their own organizations or other religious faiths whether in Spain or beyond, and celebrate marriages.[22] In Germany religious equality is implicit in the notion of State neutrality towards religion.[23]

National laws use a range of essentially neutral expressions to signify structured religious groups, whether or not they have legal personality.[24] Sometimes the term 'religious organization' is applied to both established and non-established churches.[25] In the Irish separation system, a 'religious denomination' is 'a generic term wide enough to cover various churches, religious societies or congregations under whatever name they wished to describe themselves';[26] and a 'religious body' is 'an organised group of people members of which meet regularly for

[15] Iceland: Const, Art 63: 'All persons have the right to form religious associations and to practise their religion in conformity with their individual convictions. Nothing may however be preached or practised which is prejudicial to good morals or public order'.

[16] Bulgaria: Const, Art 13: ie Eastern Orthodox Christianity.

[17] Portugal: LORF (Law no 16/2001 and DL 134/2003), Art 3: 'Churches and other religious communities are separate from the State and are free in their manner of organisation.'

[18] Ireland: Const, Art 44.2.2 forbids endowment of religion including founding religious communities; see also *Campaign to Separate Church and State v Minister for Education* [1998] 2 ILRM 81.

[19] However, in *Iglesia Bautista and Ortega Moratilla v Spain* App no 17522/90 (1992) 72 D&R 256: preferential tax treatment for the Catholic Church over Protestant churches was justified due to its responsibilities (such as providing public access to its monuments and artefacts) under a Concordat with the State.

[20] Romania: Const, Art 29.3: 'All religions shall be free'; Italy: Const, Art 8.1: 'all denominations are equally free before the law'.

[21] Spain: Const, Art 16.3; Poland: Const, Art 25.1: 'Churches and other religious organisations shall have equal rights'; see, however, Hungary: 'treating the churches equally does not exclude taking the actual social roles of the individual churches into account' if relevant: Act IV/1990, s 15(3); see CCt, Decision 4/1993 (II.12) AB.

[22] Spain: LORF, 7/1980, 5 July 1980, Art 2.

[23] Germany: CCt, BVerfGE 24, 236 (247f).

[24] For 'sects', see Ch 3 above.

[25] UK: Human Rights Act 1998, s 13: 'religious organisation' with 'members'; and discrimination law speaks of 'organised religion' and 'organisations relating to religion' (see Ch 3 above); *Aston Cantlow and Wilmcote with Billesley Parochial Church Council v Wallbank* [2004] 1 AC 546, para 13, *per* Lord Nicholls: 'the Church of England remains essentially a religious organisation. This is so even though some of the emanations of the church discharge functions which may qualify as governmental' (such as church schools and the solemnization of marriage); see also Poland: Const, Art 25.1 and 25.5: 'churches and other religious organisations'.

[26] Ireland: *Re Article 26 and the Employment Equality Bill 1996* [1997] 2 IR 321; see also Sweden: Denominations Act 1998, s 2; cf Italy: 'denomination' is not defined, but jurisprudence tends to classify a religious group as a 'denomination' on the basis of objective criteria, not merely the subjective self-understanding of the group: CCt Decision no 467 of November 1992.

public worship'.[27] *Culte* denotes a religious group in Luxembourg, Belgium, and France.[28] Needless to say, a common label for an organized religious group is that of 'religious community' or 'religious association'; the usage is particularly prevalent in the States of central and eastern Europe.[29] Occasionally, laws define the aims of such groups; in Finland, a religious association is one which seeks 'to organize and support individual, corporate and public activities pertaining to religious profession and religious observance, based on confession of faith, scriptures or other individualised established sacred activities'.[30]

By way of contrast, the part played by Christianity in the juridical history of Europe (outlined in the Introduction) to some extent continues to shape legal vocabulary in the ecclesiastical titles used for religious associations whether or not they are Christian. In the separation system of the Netherlands, a 'church' has formal recognition as a 'structured organisation' which has as its purpose 'the worship of God on the basis of shared religious convictions'.[31] Portugal uses the more all-embracing formula 'churches and religious communities'—these are defined as 'organised social communities that promise a lasting existence in which believers can pursue the religious aims which their religion dictates'.[32] Much the same approach is used in central and eastern Europe. In Slovakia, a church or religious community is a voluntary association of persons of the same religious belief, in an organization with its own structures, bodies, internal regulations, and services.[33] Laws sometimes define units within a religious organization.[34] Estonian law has a plethora of titles for religious legal persons and each of them seems to reflect in equal measure the mixed religious demography of the country—episcopal Orthodox and congregational Protestant: a church (an association with an episcopal structure of at least three congregations);[35] a congregation;[36] an association of

---

[27] Ireland: Civil Registration Act 2004, s 45.

[28] Luxembourg: Const, Art 19; see below for France and Belgium.

[29] Lithuania: LORCA, Art 4: a 'religious community' is a group of individuals seeking to implement the aims of their religion, and 'a religious association' consists of two or more religious communities with a common leadership; a religious centre is the governing body of a religious association.

[30] Finland: FRA, 2003, s 7.1: this applies to registered religious associations; Sweden: Denominations Act 1998, s 2: a denomination is a community engaged in religious activities such as worship.

[31] Netherlands: HR, 23 July 1946, NJ 1947 1; HR, 31 October 1986, NJ 1987, 173 (organisation); in a series of opinions the ETC refused to treat the Roman Catholic Pension Fund as an 'independent unit' of the Catholic Church: Opinions 2002-111 and 2002-113 (2007, 173); see also UK: 'church' was also used to refer to an association for the advancement of Islam: *Ibrahim Esmael v Abdool Carrim Peermamode* [1908] AC 526, 535.

[32] Portugal: LORF, Art 20.

[33] Slovakia: Law no 308/1991 Zb (as amended 1992 and 2007).

[34] Latvia: LORO, 7 September 1995, Art 3: 'a "diocese" is a territorial and administrative unit of a certain organisational structure of a religious association in accordance with the canonical rules of a particular denomination, which is overseen by a bishop'; this describes eg Catholic dioceses.

[35] Estonia: for religious demography see Introduction above, at n 83; CCA 2002, Art 2.2, church: 'an association of at least three voluntarily joined congregations which has an episcopal structure and is doctrinally related to three ecumenical creeds or [has] at least three congregations and which operates on the basis of its statutes, is managed by an elected . . . board and is entered in the register . . . pursuant to the procedure [herein]'. This does not seem to be designed for Protestant churches.

[36] ibid Art 2.3, congregation: 'a voluntary association of natural persons who profess the same faith, which operates on the basis of its statutes, is managed by an elected or appointed board and is entered in the register in the cases and pursuant to the procedure prescribed by this Act'.

congregations;[37] a monastery;[38] and a religious society (such as a school or a hospital).[39] In short, any group of individuals with shared beliefs may come together for religious activity, on the basis either of a legal freedom to do so or a formal right to religious association; but such groups (while legally recognized) are not required to have legal personality.

Legal categories of religious organizations

States recognize a plethora of religious organizations in society. Generally, however, they differentiate between two basic classes: those without legal personality, and those with it. This section deals primarily with the latter. Whilst national laws enable religious groups to associate without legal personality, when such groups become legal persons (and acquisition is addressed in the next section), States arrange them in a variety of categories. Broadly, the forms of legal personality open to any common enterprise are also available to religious organizations— religious groups may become foundations, trusts, non-profit-making bodies, friendly societies, companies, or other types of association.[40] However, most States have legal personalities specifically designed for religious organizations. National laws are highly technical on this matter. The following examines these forms of legal personality in terms of five themes: (1) the legal terminology; (2) the vehicles by which the legal personality of religious organizations is recognized by the State; (3) the means by which the exercise of their legal personality is regulated (which commonly mirror modes of recognition in (2)); (4) the status of religious organizations in terms of public law and private law; and (5) whether the legal categories are distinctive of the three religion-state models of classical doctrine.[41]

---

[37] ibid Art 2.4: 'an association of at least three voluntarily joined congregations which profess the same faith and which operates on the basis of its statutes, is managed by an elected or appointed management board and is entered in the register pursuant to the procedure prescribed by this Act'.

[38] ibid Art 2.5: a monastery is 'a voluntary communal association of natural persons who profess the same faith, which operates on the basis of the statutes of the corresponding church or independent statutes, is managed by an elected or appointed superior of the monastery and is entered in the register in the cases and pursuant to the procedures prescribed by this Act'.

[39] ibid Art 4.1: 'a religious society is 'a voluntary association of natural or legal persons the main activities of which include confessional or ecumenical activities relating to morals, ethics, education, culture and confessional or ecumenical, diaconal and social rehabilitation activities outside the traditional forms of religious rites of a church or congregation and which need not be connected with a specific church, association of congregations or congregation'.

[40] Netherlands: foundation (*stichting*), association (*vereniging*); Cyprus: Law 118(1)/2002, Art 8.13: charitable trusts; Ireland: Friendly Societies Act 1896 (amended 1953); Estonia: Non-Profit Organizations Act 1996; Austria: Law of Associations 2002 (VereinsG); Belgium: Law of 13 May 2001, Art 4 (non-profit-making association); Germany: CC (BGB) Art 21 (registered association); Italy: CC, Arts 14–35 (recognized associations) and Arts 36–38 (non-recognized associations); Portugal: LORF 16/2001, Art 63 (private corporations on the National Register of Corporations).

[41] In so far as all States *constitute* religious organizations as religious entities with personality in civil law, it would be interesting to explore whether these religious organizations are all in a loose sense 'established' by the State, not as national religions, but as State-recognized religious organizations.

First, slightly different terminologies are used by States for religious associations with legal personality. The most common terminology, especially in States with either a general law on religious organizations or a national church,[42] is the twofold classification 'churches and religious societies',[43] 'churches and other religious communities',[44] 'churches and congregations',[45] and 'religious communities and associations'.[46] In turn, within these two broad categories religious associations may be further arranged in two,[47] three,[48] or more tiers.[49] In other States a single category seems to dominate (perhaps sub-divided into further categories), such as 'churches',[50] *cultes*,[51] *associations cultuelles*,[52] religious 'corporations',[53] 'denominations',[54] or religious trusts.[55] Moreover, a national or state church may have no legal personality as such, but units within it do, or else its links to the State supply legal personality.[56]

Secondly, across Europe, States use one or more of four basic instruments to recognize religious organizations: constitutions, statutes (that is, sub-constitutional laws), agreements (or covenants) and registers—and these in turn give rise to the categories 'constitutional', 'statutory', 'covenantal', and 'registered' religious communities. Indeed, several States employ expressly the category of 'recognised'

---

[42] Finland: Const, PL 76 (Lutheran Church), Law 521/1969, 179/1970 (Orthodox); for others, see FRA 2003, Ch 2, ss 7–28; Denmark: bodies other than the folk Church are religious entities (*trossamfund*).

[43] Czech Rep: Churches and Religious Societies Law 2002; Spain: LORF, 1980, Art 7.1; Latvia: Law on Religious Organizations, 7 September 1995, Art 3: church congregation, religious association, diocese; see also Slovakia: Law no 308/1991 Zb (as amended 1992 and 2007).

[44] Portugal: LORF 2001, Art 3; Poland: Const, Art 25.2, and SFCR, 17 May 1989, Art 2.

[45] Estonia: Churches and Congregations Act 2002: these are, in turn, a church, a congregation, an association of congregations, a monastery, and a religious society.

[46] Lithuania: Const, Art 43.1; Law on Religious Communities and Associations 1995.

[47] Poland: Const, Art 25.4: the Catholic Church (concordat and statute); 25.5: other churches and religious organizations (relations are determined by statutes ratifying agreements between their representatives and the Council of Ministers); Czech Rep: CRSL: religious associations with or without 'special rights'; Portugal: D-L 134/2003, 28 June 2005: religious associations may be 'settled' or 'non-settled'; Slovenia: FRA 2007, Art 6.1: religious communities are registered (with legal personality) or unregistered (without legal personality): see below.

[48] Italy: concordat with the Holy See (under Const, Art 7), statutorily approved agreements with other denominations (Const, Art 8), and registered religious organizations under Law no 1159 of 1929; Lithuania: LORCA 1995: the traditional religious communities; non-traditional state-recognized religious communities and associations; and other religious communities.

[49] Denmark: official church; recognized (by royal decree); approved (by the Ministry of Ecclesiastical Affairs); religious entities without recognition or approval; and those recognized by tax authorities.

[50] Austria: Const, Art 50; Hungary: Act IV/1990, s 9; UK: Methodist Church Act 1976; Luxembourg: Law of 23 November 1982 (Reformed Church); Netherlands: CC, Art 2.2.2.

[51] Belgium: Law of 19 July 1974 (on Islam); Luxembourg: Const, Art 19.

[52] France: for *associations cultuelles, associations culturelles, associations diocésaines*, and *congrégations* (religious orders) Laws of 1 July 1901, 9 December 1905, and 2 January 1907.

[53] Germany: for public religious corporations, see GG, Art 140; WRV, Art 137; for private religious corporations, see CC, Arts 21, 55–58.

[54] Bulgaria: RDA 2002 (SG 120/2002); Italy: Art 7: denominations or confessions (*confessioni religiose*) with agreements; for associations: CC, Arts 14–36.

[55] Cyprus: Const, Art 110: the Orthodox Church and Turkish Cypriot religious trust (*vakf*).

[56] UK, England: 'The Church of England is not itself a legal entity': *Aston Cantlow and Wilmcote with Billesley Parochial Church Council v Wallbank* [2004] 1 AC 546, para 84; Denmark: the Lutheran Church has no legal personality of itself but it does in so far as it is part of the fabric of the State.

religious organizations; for example, the Lithuanian constitution provides: 'Churches and religious organisations recognised by the State shall have the rights of legal persons'.[57] As seen in Chapter 1, the constitutions of several States expressly recognize the Catholic Church (with which they may have an agreement),[58] national Lutheran Churches,[59] and the Orthodox Church.[60] In several States, particular churches and religious organizations are recognized by parliamentary statutes dedicated to them individually,[61] perhaps on the basis of a prior agreement with the State,[62] or else by royal decree or ministerial ordinance.[63] Covenantal religious organizations are those which have a bilateral agreement with the State.[64] Recognition by entry on a register is the norm in many States.[65] The basis of recognition (and legal personality) may also in some States be a civil code.[66] Though many States have no formal category of 'recognized religions', the deployment of the instruments outlined above indicates that all States expressly or implicitly recognize religious organizations and they provide them with legal vehicles of recognition.

Thirdly, across Europe, States use one or more of three instruments to regulate the exercise of legal personality by religious organizations: statute or other particular law (either applicable to religious organizations generally or to specified ones); covenant (in the form of a concordat with the Holy See or other agreement in relation to religious organizations other than but also including the Holy See); and

---

[57] Lithuania: Const, Art 43.1; see also Austria: RCA 1874 (AnerkennungsG); ie the Catholic, Protestant, Greek Orthodox, Oriental Orthodox (Armenian, Syrian, and Coptic), Mormon, Old Catholic, and Methodist churches, and Jewish, Islamic, and Buddhist communities; Belgium: *culte reconnu*; France, Alsace-Lorraine: *cultes reconnus* (viz Lutheran, Reformed, and Catholic churches, and Jewish community); Cyprus, Const, Art 18.2: 'known religions' (those without secret beliefs, etc).

[58] Malta: Const, Art 2; Lichtenstein: Const, Art 37; Italy: Const, Art 7; Poland: Const, Art 25.4; Spain: Const, Art 16.1.

[59] Denmark: Const, Art 4; Finland: Const, Art 76; Norway: Const, Art 2; Iceland: Const, Art 62.

[60] Greece: Const, Art 3.1; Cyprus: Const, Art 110; Bulgaria: Const, Art 13.3: the Orthodox faith is the 'traditional religion'.

[61] Belgium: Catholic Church (Law of 8 April 1802), Protestant (Law of 8 April 1802), Anglican (Law of 4 March 1870), Islam (Law of 19 July 1974 amending Law of 1870), Greek and Russian Orthodox (Law of 17 April 1985, amending Law of 1870); Luxembourg: eg Law of 23 November 1982 (Reformed Church); UK: Dawat-e-Hadiyah (England) Act 1993 enables the Hindu sect to be a corporation sole for the holder of the office of Dal al-Mutlaq, Methodist Church Act 1976 provides for trusts for that church, Baptist and Congregational Trusts Act 1951, United Reformed Church Act 2000.

[62] Poland: Const, Art 25.5; see eg Polish Autocephalous Orthodox Church (Law of 4 July 1991), Protestant Reformed Church (Law of 13 May 1994), Methodist Church (Law of 30 June 1995).

[63] Denmark: religious entities (*trossamfund*) are those recognized by royal decree, approved by the Ministry of Ecclesiastical Affairs, or recognized by tax authorities; Austria: Law on the Recognition of Churches 1874: ministerial decree.

[64] For agreements with the Catholic Church, see Czech Rep: Agreement, 25 July 2002; Latvia: Agreement 2003; Slovenia: Agreement, 14 December 2001 (ratified by parliament, 28 January 2004); Lithuania: Agreement on Juridical Matters (2000); Poland: Concordat, 28 July 1993 (in force 25 March 1998); Portugal: Concordat 2004, Art 9: legal personality of the Episcopal Conference.

[65] Hungary: Act IV/1990, s 9; Spain: LORF, Art 7.1; Sweden: Denominations Act 1998, s 5; Germany: for registered private religious corporations, see CC, Arts 21, 55–58; Portugal: the Register of Religious Corporations was established by DL 134/2003, 28 June 2005; Czech Rep: CRSL, Act no 3/2002; Latvia: LORO, 7 September 1995, Art 13.

[66] Netherlands: CC, Art 2.2.2; Italy: CC, Arts 14–36: for non-covenantal associations.

a mixture of statute and covenant.[67] Constitutionally recognized religious organizations are regulated by statute in Greece[68] and Finland,[69] and individual (non-constitutional) churches are regulated by statute in Belgium, Luxembourg, and the United Kingdom, for example.[70] Registered religious denominations may be regulated by a general law on religious associations.[71] As to covenants,[72] there are concordats (treaties in international law) between the State and the Holy See in Austria, Spain, Italy, Poland, Portugal, Alsace-Lorraine (in France), and Luxembourg.[73] Agreements (short of concordats) with the Holy See have also been common in States more recently admitted to the European Union, generally those where Catholicism is the majority religious grouping.[74] The Czech Republic and Slovenia (with their small Catholic majorities), and Latvia (with similar numbers of Catholic and Orthodox) have concluded comprehensive agreements (not concordats) with the Holy See.[75] Lithuania, Slovakia, and Hungary (again with Catholic majorities) have also signed a set of agreements with the Holy See,[76] and in Estonia there is an agreement with the Catholic Church in the form of a 'verbal note'.[77] Agreements are also entered with religious organizations other than the Catholic Church (and some are subject-specific);[78] in Germany, for example, there are agreements between the *länder* and Protestant churches and Jewish

[67] As well as these regulatory instruments, there are also State institutions which oversee the affairs relating to religious organizations: see Ch 1 above.

[68] Greece: Orthodox: Law 590/1977; Jewish: Law 2455/1920; Muslim: Law 1920/1991.

[69] Finland: Const, s 76 (The Church Act): the organization and administration of the Evangelical Lutheran Church are laid down in the Church Act (which came into force on 1 March 2000).

[70] See n 61 above; and Finland: Law 521/1969 and 179/1970 (Orthodox Church).

[71] Bulgaria: RDA 2002 (SG 120/2002); Czech Rep: CRSL, Act no 3/2002S; Estonia: CCA 2002; Hungary: Act IV/1990; Portugal: D-L 134/2003, 28 June 2005; Slovenia: FRA 2007, Art 6.1; Spain: LORF 1980, Art 7.1; Latvia: LORO, 7 September 1995, Art 7; France: Laws of 1 July 1901, 9 December 1905, 2 January 1907; see also Netherlands: CC, Art 2.2.2.

[72] See R Puza and N Doe (eds), *Religion and Law in Dialogue: Covenantal and Non-Covenantal Cooperation between State and Religion in Europe* (Leuven: Peeters, 2006): some agreements have the status of law (concordats are treaties with the Holy See in international law), and others of administrative agreements or contracts.

[73] Austria: Const, Art 50, Concordat 1934; Spain: Const, Art 163, Concordat 1979; Italy, Const, Art 7, Concordat 1984, executed by Act no 121 of 1985—this has led to other agreements, on eg church holidays (1985), cultural and religious heritage (1996), and pastoral care in the police (1999); Poland: Const, Art 25.4; Concordat 1993; France, Alsace-Lorraine: the Napoleonic Concordat remains largely in force; Luxembourg: Concordat of 1801.

[74] See n 64 above; for the religious demography of these States, see Introduction above; but there are no agreements with the Holy See in other Catholic countries (eg Ireland and Belgium).

[75] Czech Rep: Agreement signed 25 July 2002; Latvia 2003; Slovenia, signed 14 December 2001 (ratified by parliament, 28 January 2004, after the Constitutional Court raised no objections).

[76] Lithuania, Agreement on Juridical Matters (2000), and Agreement on Pastoral Care of Catholics in the Army (2000); Slovakia: Basic Agreement (2001), and separate agreements on army chaplaincy (2002) and education (2003); Hungary: Agreement on Pastoral Care in the Army and Border Guard (1994), and Agreement on Financial Issues (1998).

[77] Estonia: this is a comprehensive agreement, signed 12 March 1999.

[78] Hungary: there are agreements with the Reformed, Lutheran, Baptist and Serb Orthodox churches, and the Alliance of Jewish Communities; in Slovakia there is an agreement with a small Christian Community (signed by the President and almost identical to that with the Holy See) and the Jehovah's Witnesses; Czech Rep: the Catholic Bishops' Conference and the Ecumenical Council of Churches has agreements with the Ministry of Defence (1998) and with the Prison Administration (1999); Lithuania: Const, Art 43.5: the State may conclude agreements with a religious association.

communities, as well as the Catholic Church.[79] Agreements also exist between States and alliances of religious organizations.[80] In turn, there may be mixtures of these approaches: religious entities are regulated statutorily on the basis of prior agreements with the State,[81] or by agreements based on pre-existing State legislation.[82] Thus, with the exception of constitutions and registers, the vehicles used to regulate religious groups with legal personality are basically the same as those used to recognize religious organizations.

Fourthly, religious organizations may have legal personality in either public law or private law. The public-private law divide transcends the modes of both recognition and regulation. Public law status is enjoyed variously by: recognized churches and religious communities (Luxembourg);[83] constitutionally recognized (but unregistered) religions (Greece);[84] state-churches (Finland);[85] concordat churches (Italy);[86] and registered public religious corporations (Germany).[87] In turn, private law status is enjoyed by, variously: registered religious communities (central and eastern Europe);[88] statutory churches (United Kingdom),[89] *associations cultuelles, associations diocésaines*, and *congrégations* (France).[90] Religious entities with statutorily approved agreements may also be private associations (Italy).[91] Indeed, a State may have a system of both public and private law personality: under Greek law, the Orthodox Church (and its dioceses, parishes, and monasteries), Jewish communities (with more than twenty Jewish families and a synagogue), and

---

[79] Germany: agreements exist between the Protestant church and the *länder*: eg Saxony-Anhalt (1993), Mecklenburg-West Pomerania (1994); agreements with the Catholic Church: Saxony (1996), Thuringia (1997), and Brandenburg (2003); and with smaller religious communities (eg in Lower Saxony, with the Free Religious Community of Lower Saxony (1970), and the Evangelical Methodist Church in North West Germany (1978)); see also Ch 1 above.

[80] Such as that in Poland with an alliance of the Lutheran, Orthodox, Polish Catholic, Evangelical Reformed, United Methodist, Old Catholic Mariavites Churches, and Baptist Union of Poland.

[81] Italy: Const, Arts 7, 8; Spain: RFA 1980, Art 7.1; Poland: Const, Art 25.5.

[82] Portugal: LORF 2001, Art 51: this applies to 'non-settled' religious communities; their agreements (with the government and/or municipalities) do not have to be ratified by a law.

[83] Luxembourg: Law of 23 November 1982: Reformed Protestant Church; Law of 10 July 1998: Israelite communities, Protestant Church, Greek Orthodox Church; Law of 11 June 2004, Anglican, Romanian, and Serbian Orthodox churches; Austria: RCA 1874 (AnerkennungsG).

[84] Greece: public law personality attaches to the Orthodox Church: Law 590/1977; Jewish community: Law 2455/1920; and Mufti offices: Law 1920/1991.

[85] Finland: Const, Art 76 (Lutheran); Law 521/1969 and 179/1970 (Orthodox Church).

[86] Italy: Const, Art 7 (Catholic Church).

[87] Germany: GG, Art 140 and WRV, Art 137.

[88] Austria: FLSCC 1998 (BeKGG); these include the Baha'I Religion, Federation of Baptist Communities in Austria, Hindu Mandir Society, Jehovah's Witnesses, Church of Seventh Day Adventists; Czech Rep: CRSL, Act no 3/2002; Estonia: CCA, 2002; Bulgaria: RDA 2002 (SG 120/2002); Hungary: Act IV/1990, s 9; Netherlands: CC, Art 2.2.2.

[89] UK: Methodist Church Act 1976; Belgium: Law of 19 July 1974 (Islam); Luxembourg: Law of 23 November 1982 (Reformed Church).

[90] France: Laws of 1 July 1901, 9 December 1905, and 2 January 1907; see also Latvia: LORO, 7 September 1995: a church congregation, a religious association, or a diocese; Estonia: CCA 2002, Art 2; Lithuania: LORCA: private law status is held by traditional (unregistered), recognized (but registered), and non-traditional/non-recognized (but registered) religious communities.

[91] Italy: Const, Art 8 (*intese* denominations); see also CC, Art 14–36: unregistered associations (non-recognized and recognized).

Mufti offices, are legal persons in public law;[92] all others are legal persons in private law (corporations or civil associations by judicial recognition);[93] and in Germany there are registered public religious corporations and registered private religious corporations.[94]

The arrangements outlined in this section dispel the myth that cooperation is just one of three European religion-state models. Cooperation transcends the national laws of all European States with regard to the legal personality of religious organizations. All States employ the terminology of religious association; most use the category church. All States provide vehicles which facilitate the recognition of religious organizations with legal personality. All States use legal instruments to regulate the exercise of legal personality by religious organizations. The only difference between States is the forms of the vehicles used and the identity of the religious organizations which enjoy the facility of legal personality. For example, in the Danish state-church system, alongside the national Lutheran church (which of itself does not have public law status) there are private religious entities which may be recognized or approved; but there is no registration.[95] Alongside the Finnish state Lutheran church with public law status, there is private law status for registered religious associations.[96] In the United Kingdom, with its national churches in Scotland and England (and units within these may have public law status), there are statutory churches with private law status as voluntary associations; whilst there is no register as such of religious organizations, there is a register of charities for the advancement of religion.[97] In the separation system of France, *associations cultuelles*, *associations diocésaines*, and *congrégations* enjoy status in private law, as do voluntary religious organizations in Ireland.[98] In hybrid States, cooperation over legal personality takes a number of forms. In some, legal personality is enjoyed by covenantal, recognized (public corporation) and registered (private association) religious organizations (Austria, Germany).[99] In others it attaches to unregistered religious organizations recognized by specific law applicable to them individually (Belgium),[100] or to unregistered but constitutionally recognized religions with private law status.[101] Similarly, in former communist States religious

---

[92] Greece: Orthodox: Charter (L 590/1977), Art 1.4; Jewish: Law 2455/1920; Mufti—these are so designated on the proposal of the Minister of Education and Cults: Law 1920/1991.

[93] Greece: Law 1363/1938 and Law 1672/1939. See also Strasbourg, *Canea Catholic Church v Greece* (1999) 27 EHRR 521: on the Catholic Church.

[94] Germany: GG, Art 140 and WRV, Art 137 (public); CC, Arts 21, 55–58 (private).

[95] Denmark: religious entities (*trossamfund*) approved by the Ministry of Ecclesiastical Affairs; there are also those without recognition or approval, and those recognized by tax authorities.

[96] Finland: Const, PL 76 (Lutheran Church), Law 521/1969 and 179/1970 (Orthodox Church), and for other registered religious associations FRA 2003, Ch 2, ss 7–28.

[97] UK: Methodist Church Act 1976; Charities Act 2006.

[98] France: Laws of 1 July 1901, 9 December 1905, 2 January 1907; Netherlands: CC, Art 2.2.2.

[99] Austria: Const, Art 50, Concordat with the Holy See 1934, Art 1; Germany: GG, Art 140, WRV, Art 137 (public); CC, Arts 21, 55–58 (private).

[100] Belgium: *culte reconnu* (eg Law of 19 July 1974—Islam); Luxembourg: Law of 23 November 1982 (Reformed Church).

[101] Cyprus: see Const, Art 110 for the Orthodox Church and the Turkish Cypriot religious trust (*vakf*); to enjoy private law status, other religious organizations must be a 'known' religion: Const, Art 18.2; Greece: public law personality attaches to the Orthodox Church, Jewish communities, and Mufti

organizations have private law status and they are registered as such.[102] Several States have a concordat church with public law status, covenantal religious organizations with private law status operating under statutorily approved agreements with the State, and registered religious associations with private law status.[103] In all three systems, the State *constitutes* religious organizations as legal persons in civil law—this constitutive act necessitates cooperation with the religions involved.

The conferral of legal personality

The principal procedures by which States confer legal personality on religious are: the enactment of legislation (for statutory religious organizations); the conclusion of a covenant (concordat or other cooperation agreement); the registration of religious organizations (which may be in the keeping either of executive or judicial authorities in the State); and (a hybrid form) the conclusion of cooperation agreements with registered religious organizations ratified by parliamentary statute. In that small number of States which do not have a legal form devoted exclusively to religious organizations, needless to say acquisition of legal personality is dependent on the general law applicable to the form sought.[104] The majority of States have forms of legal personality designed specifically for religious organizations. Their procedures all have in common requirements regarding the State body authorized to decide on the acquisition of legal personality, membership (particularly as to numerical size), doctrines and rituals, internal regulatory instruments, and institutional structures. The legal rules indicate well the keen interest which States have in the internal structures of religious organizations—their members, doctrine, ritual, and regulatory instruments. They also indicate that whilst religious organizations within particular legal categories may be treated equally, there is inequality of treatment as between those categories.

---

offices: Orthodox: Charter (Law no 590/1977) Art 1.4; Jewish: Law no 2455/1920; Mufti—these are designated by decree-law on the proposal of the Minister of Education and Cults: Law no 1920/1991.

[102] Czech Rep: CRSL, Act no 3/2002; Estonia: CCA Act 2002; Hungary: Act IV/1990, s 9; Latvia: LORO, 7 September 1995, Art 7; Bulgaria: RDA 2002 (SG 120/2002).

[103] Italy: Holy See, Art 7; *intese* denominations, Art 8; for associations, see CC, Art 14–36; Portugal: LORF 2001, Art 51: agreements with the 'non-settled' religions do not have to be ratified by law; Spain: LORF 1980, Art 7 (cooperation agreements); Poland: Const, Art 25.

[104] Ireland: in addition to the right to associate as unincorporated voluntary associations without legal personality, they may form public and private trusts, friendly societies, unlimited companies, statutory trusts, or registered companies: P Colton, 'Religious entities as legal persons—Ireland' in L Friedner (ed), *Churches and Other Religious Organisations as Legal Persons* (Leuven: Peeters, 2007) 132. For trusts, see eg the Irish Church Act 1869, s 22, for the Representative Church Body (incorporated by royal charter) of the (Anglican) Church of Ireland; Irish Presbyterian Church Act 1871; and Methodist Church in Ireland Act 1928. The Islamic Foundation of Ireland is registered on the basis of the Friendly Societies Act 1896 as amended; Spain: a religious group may register for legal personality as an association with the Ministry of the Interior under the general law on associations: Organic Law 1/2002, 22 March, Arts 5, 6, and 10.

The enactment of legislation

In those States with constitutionally or statutorily recognized religious organizations, national law is usually skeletal on the process of acquiring legal recognition.[105] It may be governed by administrative practice, law, or both.[106]
Constitutional recognition (with public law status) in Cyprus may be conferred if
a religious group is one made up of natural persons, ordinarily resident in Cyprus,
who profess the same religion and either belong to the same rite or are subject to the
same religious jurisdiction; it must have more than one thousand members (at the
date of the commencement of the constitution (1960)), at least five hundred of
whom became citizens of the republic on that date.[107] There are no formal legal
requirements for a religious group to become a statutory *culte reconnu* in
Belgium;[108] according to unwritten administrative practice, the group must be:
sufficiently large; well-structured; present in the territory for some decades; socially
important; and it must be such as not to threaten social order.[109]

By way of contrast, in Austria, the procedure for legal recognition is governed by
law rather than administrative practice. Churches and religious societies with public
law status are recognized as such by ministerial ordinance. The thresholds are
high—the group must have: existed for ten years, a membership of 0.2 per cent
of the population (ie around 16,000 people), forms of worship, statutes, and a
name which are not illegal or morally offensive; statutes dealing with appointment
to and competence of their board; assets to be used for religious purposes; a positive
attitude to society and the State; good relations with other religious organizations;
membership regulations; and a summary of its religious doctrines—an appeal lies
against non-recognition.[110] Greece is not dissimilar.[111] In the Netherlands, a

---

[105] The distinction between covenantal and statutory churches is artificial—even with recognition
by statute, there is a prior (informal) negotiated agreement which leads to the enactment of the statute.
[106] The constitutional recognition of national churches is the result of processes the description of
which is beyond the scope of this book.
[107] Cyprus: the constitutionally recognized groups are the Greek Orthodox Church, Turkish
Cypriot religious trust (for Muslims), Armenians, Maronites, and Latin Catholics; see Appendix E
of the Treaty of Establishment between the UK, Greece, Turkey, and Cyprus.
[108] See n 61 above for the statutory churches.
[109] Belgium: Questions and Answers, Chamber, 1999–2000, 4 September 2000, 5120 (Question
44, Borginon); Chamber, 1996–1997, 4 July 1997, 12970 (Question 631, Borginon). See R Torfs,
'Religious entities as legal persons—Belgium' in L Friedner (ed), *Churches and Other Religious
Organisations as Legal Persons* (Leuven: Peeters, 2007) 45, 47: 'There should be "enough" members;
probably some "tens of thousands". Yet no formal requirements exist. All norms are unwritten. They
are just informal guidance inspiring and steering administrative praxis'; there must be the cult of a
deity: CA Liège, 21 November 1949, Pasicrisie, 1950, II, 57: 'Antoinism' was a cult limited to its
members and was considered philanthropic, not religious.
[110] Austria: RCA 1874 (AnerkennungsG), as amended by BekGG 1998, s 11; the appeal lies to the
High Administrative Court; the recognized bodies include the Catholic Church, Protestant Church,
Greek Oriental Churches, Oriental Orthodox Churches (Armenian, Syrian, and Coptic), and
Jewish Religious Community.
[111] Greece: eg a Jewish community may obtain public law status if it consists of more than twenty
Jewish families and a synagogue; Mufti offices do so when designated by decree-law on the proposal of
the Minister of Education and Cults: Law 1920/1991.

church, its units, and united churches may acquire private law personality if they have their own statutes which are not in conflict with the law; general laws on legal entities may apply to a church, its units, and united churches unless the statutes of the church, etc conflict with these general laws—the statutes will prevail if they have been made in good faith in this regard on the part of the church, etc.[112]

Several other States recognize religious organizations by means of executive instruments issued within a statutory framework. In Denmark (where there is no registration system), the constitution provides that rules for religious bodies dissenting from the national church shall be laid down by statute.[113] In addition to the national church, pre-1970 recognized churches are now recognized by a royal decree administered through the Ministry of Ecclesiastical Affairs;[114] post-1970 approved religious entities (with rights to solemnize marriages) are approved by the same Ministry on a recommendation from a committee of experts in law and religion.[115] The practice seems to be that 'about 50 people' are required if it is an existing religion, and 150 people if it is not; the belief must not be contrary to good morals; it must have competent officers to represent the group before public authorities, and rules on membership (acquisition and departure); and the minister of religion who solemnizes marriages must be registered.[116] A system of executive recognition also operates in Greece as to places of worship.[117]

Not unlike Belgium and Austria, Lithuania operates a principle of longevity with regard to a religious group with the status of a 'traditional religion'; such communities need not register with the Ministry of Justice to acquire legal personality.[118] Moreover, the status of a religion 'recognized by the State' may be conferred on a religious community provided: (1) it is part of the historical, spiritual, and social heritage of Lithuania; (2) it is approved by the State; and (3) its doctrines and rites do not offend law and morality.[119] These religious communities may seek state recognition not less than twenty-five years after their registration as a registered religious community; recognition is granted by parliament on receipt of an opinion from the Ministry of Justice. If refused, the community may resubmit the application not less than ten years from the date of refusal; if successful the organization acquires legal personality.[120] In short, when the State confers legal personality on a

---

[112] Netherlands: CC, Art 2.2.

[113] Denmark: Constitution Act 1953, Part VII, s 66.

[114] Denmark: recognized churches are the Roman Catholic Church, Jewish Community, three reformed churches, Methodists, Baptists, and the Russian, Swedish, Norwegian, and Anglican communities.

[115] Denmark: these include the Salvation Army, Islamic communities, and Jehovah's Witnesses.

[116] *Forn Sidr* was approved in 2003; it worships the 'old Nordic gods' and has statutes and ceremonies (*blot*).

[117] Greece: private law religious associations or corporations need a permit from the Minister of Education and Cults to found a place of worship; the permit 'registers' the conditions: a minimum of 7 persons; a confession of faith (to ensure it is a 'known religion' (ie not secret)) which must not offend public order or good morals: Law 1363/1938 and Law 1672/1939.

[118] Lithuania: LORCA, Art 5; these include: Roman Catholic, Eastern Rite Catholic, Russian Orthodox, Old Believers, Lutherans, Reformed, Jewish, Sunni Muslim, and Karaite.

[119] Lithuania: LORCA, Art 6.

[120] ibid: in 2001, the Union of Evangelical Baptist Communities became state-recognized.

religious group by means of statute or executive instrument, it requires that group to satisfy criteria prescribed by law, administrative practice, or both, which are typically concerned with its size, beliefs, statutes, rites, and the compatibility of these with State law.

The conclusion of covenants

Similarly, where legal personality is based on a bilateral agreement ratified by specific law, sometimes the process is governed by informal administrative practice, sometimes by law, and sometimes by a mixture of these. In Luxembourg, a recognized cult (with public law status) is one with an agreement with the State approved subsequently by a specific law;[121] informal *de facto* criteria apply—the religious group must: represent a world religion; be officially recognized by another EU State; respect public order; have been present historically in Luxembourg; and have a sufficient number of members—it need not deposit its statutes but in practice each has its own regulatory instrument.[122] In Poland, relations between the State and churches and religious communities (other than the concordat Catholic Church) 'shall be determined by [parliamentary] statutes adopted pursuant to agreements concluded between their appropriate representatives and the Council of Ministers'; the process is governed by 'tradition and history', though the internal units of such churches and communities acquire legal personality by an ordinance issued by the Minister of the Interior and Administration. Poland also has a system of registration (see below).[123]

The interplay of legal process, political negotiation, and case-law is well illustrated by arrangements in Italy. Amendments to concordats with the Holy See must be agreed by both sides (but they need not follow the procedure prescribed for constitutional amendments); parliamentary ratification of such concordats is also subject to scrutiny by the Constitutional Court;[124] and further agreements may be made with the Catholic Episcopal Conference.[125] Though they have a constitutional right to associate on the basis of their own statutes (if not in conflict with the State law), for the making of agreements (*intese*) with other religious denominations,[126] according to recent case-law, the group must establish a prior

---

[121] Luxembourg: Const, Art 22: agreements with religious groups must be submitted to the Chamber of Deputies; see eg Law of 23 November 1982: Reformed Protestant Church; Law of 10 July 1998: Israelite communities, Protestant Church, Greek Orthodox Church; Law of 11 June 2004: Anglican, Romanian, and Serbian Orthodox churches.

[122] A Pauly, 'Entités religieuses comme personnes juridiques-Luxembourg' in L Friedner (ed), *Churches and Other Religious Organisations as Legal Persons* (Leuven: Peeters, 2007) 163, 166.

[123] Poland: Const, Art 25.5; SFCR, 17 May 1989; statutory churches include, the Eastern Old Rites Church (Law of 22 March 1928), Islamic Religious Community (Law of 21 April 1936), Polish Autocephalous Orthodox Church (Law of 4 July 1991), Protestant Reformed Church (Law of 13 May 1994), Methodist Church (Law of 30 June 1995), Baptist Union (Law of 30 June 1995), Union of Jewish Confessional Communities (20 February 1997); for the system of registration see below.

[124] Italy: Const, Art 7.1; CCt, Decision no 30 of 1971.

[125] Italy: Concordat of 1984, Art 13.2.

[126] Italy: Const, Art 8.3. These include the Confederation of Methodist and Waldensian Churches, Adventists, Assembly of God, Union of Jewish Communities, Baptists, Lutherans, Buddhist Union, Jehovah's Witnesses, Mormons, Orthodox Church of the Constantinople Patriarchate, and Hindus.

public recognition (explicit or implicit, national or local), as well as evidence of its religious nature on the basis of its internal regulatory instrument and/or on common perception.[127] There is no right to an *intesa*: the process is subject to political negotiation, and the support of the cabinet is required prior to subsequent approval by parliamentary law.[128] The position is similar in Spain for religious organizations which have a statutorily ratified cooperation agreement with the State; these agreements are then inscribed in the register of religious entities.[129] However, Catholic ecclesiastical units (for example dioceses and parishes) are legal persons under the concordat with the Holy See; they need not register but must simply inform the Bureau of Religious Affairs—but the Catholic Church's religious institutes must register.[130] Spain also has registration for religious organizations other than covenantal ones (see below). In other words, when a religious group acquires legal personality as a result of negotiating with the State a formal agreement subsequently ratified by parliamentary statute, the same basic criteria apply as in the case of acquisition solely by means of legislation. The only difference seems to be that in the former there is a formal agreement concluded prior to legislation, and in the latter negotiations prior to the enactment of legislation are not found in a formal agreement.

The registration of religious organizations

By way of contrast, when legal personality is acquired on registration of a religious organization, the procedure seems far more streamlined, and the criteria more precisely formulated, than those applying in relation to legal personality acquired by means of the enactment of legislation or the conclusion of formal covenants. Nevertheless, some registration systems are controversial. For example, the Bulgarian system of registration (supervised judicially),[131] has been criticized by Strasbourg for failing to specify criteria for registration, the grounds on which registration may be refused, the consequences of failure to register, or recourse in the case of refusal to register.[132] This is not the case in the majority of those States which have a registration system.

The registration authority: To register as a religious association with legal personality in private law, the registration authority may be executive or judicial, national or local. The norm is national administrative registration. In Poland registration is

---

[127] Italy: CCt, Decision no 195, 19 April 1993 (concerning Jehovah's Witnesses); see also Cassation Court, Decision no 1329, 8 October 1997.
[128] Italy: COS, Decision no 3048, 29 October 1997.
[129] Spain: LORF, Art 7; Protestant: Law 24/1992; 15 Jewish: Law 25/1992; 2 Muslim: Law 26/1992.
[130] Spain: Concordat 1979, Arts 1–3.
[131] Bulgaria: RDA 2002, ch 3; Hungary: registration was upheld in CCt, Decision 8/1993 (II.27) AB.
[132] The Legal Affairs Committee of the Assembly of the COE described Bulgarian RDA 2002 as 'an important step forward' but noted that many religious communities were unhappy with the special position of the Orthodox Church: Press Release, 15 December 2003; elements of the previous RDA (1949) were declared unconstitutional in the CCt, Decision no 2, 11 June 1992.

with the Ministry of the Interior and Administration,[133] in the Czech Republic with the Ministry of Culture,[134] in Austria with the Ministry of Education,[135] and in Finland with the National Patent and Register Board.[136] The Ministry of Justice is the registration authority in Lithuania (for a non-traditional and non-recognized religious community).[137] Other States have dedicated offices: Spain has a Register of Religious Entities in the Ministry of Justice,[138] in Slovakia registration is with the Church Department of the Ministry of Culture,[139] in Latvia with the Board of Religious Affairs (supervised by the Ministry of Justice),[140] and in Slovenia with the Office for Religious Communities.[141] In Portugal, settled religious groups are registered by the government on the basis of an opinion from the Commission for Religious Liberty.[142] By way of contrast, in Germany, Hungary, Estonia, and Bulgaria registration is with a local court,[143] and, in France, with the local authority.[144]

The numerical size of the group: For registration as a religious association with legal personality in private law, national laws commonly prescribe minimal numbers.[145] In some States the numerical threshold is low: in Germany, the group must have seven members;[146] in Hungary, ten (to register as an association, and 100 to register as a 'church');[147] in Estonia, twelve (for a congregation, thirty-six for

---

[133] Poland: SFCR 1989, Arts 30–34.

[134] Czech Rep: CRSL, Act no 3/2002 Sb; in 2002, 4 groups were registered without special rights (Czech Buddhist Society, Religious Society Hare Krishna, Christian Communities, and Community of Christians (Theosophy)); communities registered under the former Act of 1991 no 308/1991 Sb and listed in the CRSL Schedule have special rights (eg Roman Catholic, Anglican Congregation).

[135] Austria: FLSCC 1998 (BeKGG). The refusal of the Ministry of Education to register the Sahaja Yoga group in 1998 was upheld in the Constitutional Administrative Court.

[136] Finland: FRA 2003, s 10; see s 12 for the role of the Board.

[137] Lithuania: LORCA, Art 11; 140 non-traditional communities have legal personality; a non-traditional community may be registered within 6 months of submission of its statutes.

[138] Spain: LORF 1980, Arts 5 and 6; see CCt, Judgment no 46/2001, 15 February: an unjustified refusal to register violates religious freedom; the registration authority cannot control the beliefs of the applicant but must ensure that they are not inconsistent with Constitutional Law no 7/1980, 5 July, Art 3.2.

[139] Slovakia: Law no 308/1991 Zb (as amended 1992 and 2007).

[140] Latvia: LORO 1995, Arts 5.1 and 8.

[141] Slovenia: RFA 2007, Art 13.1.

[142] Portugal: LORF, Arts 34 *et seq.*

[143] Germany: CC, Arts 55–58 (magistrates' court); GG, Art 9.2; the register of public law corporations is with the education departments of the *länder*; Hungary: for associations, Act II/1989, s 3(4), for churches, Act IV/1990, s 9(1); Estonia: CCA 2002: religious societies are registered by a court as non-profit organizations; Bulgaria: registration is supervised by the Sofia City Court.

[144] France: an *association cultuelle* deposits its statutes at the *préfecture* to acquire legal capacity: Law of 1 July 1901; Catholic diocesan associations are recognized by the CE, Decision of 13 December 1923, as complying with the Laws of 1901 and 1905; this category was created as the church had been concerned that the category *association cultuelle* would lead to associations claiming to be Catholic when they were not: G Robbers (ed), *State and Church in the European Union* (Baden-Baden: Nomos, 2nd edn, 2005) 164. Law of 1901, Art 13 deals with *congrégations* (religious orders): in 1987, recognition was opened to non-Catholic orders, such as Buddhist, Orthodox, and Protestant.

[145] States which do not seem to do so include France, Portugal, and Sweden; decisions on the basis of numbers are forbidden in Spain, see LORF, Art 5; see also Royal Decree 142/1981, Arts 4.2 and 6.

[146] Germany: CC, Arts 55–58.

[147] Hungary: for associations, Act II/1989, s 3(4); for churches, Act IV/1990, s 9(1)(a).

a church);[148] in Lithuania, fifteen (to register as a non-traditional and non-recognized religious community);[149] in Finland, twenty;[150] and in Latvia, twenty (for a congregation, and for a religious association 200 (ten congregations)).[151] By way of contrast, there must be 100 adult members in Poland,[152] and Slovenia.[153] However, in Austria, the group must have at least 300 members, who must not belong to another recognized religious community.[154] Similarly, in the Czech Republic, the application must be signed by 300 adults resident in the republic, and a registered church or religious society may seek registration with 'special rights' if its membership reaches 0.1 per cent of the population (that is, more than 10,000 people).[155] At the other extreme, in Slovakia, the threshold is 20,000 adult members (about 0.37 per cent of the population).[156] In Germany, to register as a public law corporation, the religious community must have a membership of around one per 1,000 of the population of the relevant *land*.[157]

Name, aims, and headquarters: Not surprisingly, in applying for registration, the requirement across Europe is for a religious group to submit its name (which must be different from an existing one),[158] address,[159] aims,[160] or mission,[161] and, occasionally, the personal identification codes of the members of its management board.[162] Finnish law requires a statement that the religious association is domiciled in Finland as well as notification of the purposes of its activities.[163] French law requires the activities of an *association cultuelle* to be 'exclusively for the purpose of the church', and the objects of a religious order (*congrégation*) to be of public utility.[164] Under Spanish law, the group must submit its name and domicile, evidence its foundation in Spain, state its religious purpose, and declare that its activities do not breach public law or order.[165]

---

[148] Estonia: CCA 2002, ss 11–13; see Art 11 for names; boards may invite ministers outside Estonia to apply for a work and residence permit: Aliens Act, RT I 1993, 44, 637; RT I 2001, 58, 352.

[149] Lithuania: LORCA, Art 11.

[150] Finland: Freedom of Religion Act 2003, s 10; see s 12 for the role of the Board.

[151] Latvia: LORO, 7 September 1995, Art 7: for a congregation there must be 20 adult citizens or adults registered in the population register (including aliens) who share one confessional affiliation.

[152] Poland: SFCR 1989, Arts 30–34: they must be Polish citizens.

[153] Slovenia: FRA 2007, Art 13.1: citizens or aliens with permanent residence.

[154] Austria: FLSCC 1998 (BeKGG).

[155] Czech Rep: CRSL, Act no 3/2002 Sb; there are 21 registered groups with special rights (eg the Ecumenical Council of Churches in the Czech Republic and the Military Spiritual Service).

[156] Slovakia: Law no 308/1991 Zb (as amended 1992 and 2007): the threshold originally required them to be permanent residents in Slovakia; the Constitutional Court decided in February 2010 that the law was constitutional. Those operating before 1991 are automatically considered as registered.

[157] Germany: GG, Art 140; WRV, Art 137.5.2.

[158] Sweden: Denomination Act 1998, s 7–8: the Church of Scientology is registered; see also Portugal: LORF, Art 34.

[159] Lithuania: LORCA, Art 11; to register as a non-traditional and non-recognized religious community, the statutes of the group must include its name, main office, objects, and aims.

[160] Germany: CC, Arts 55–58; Hungary: Act IV/1990, ss 9–10; see also s 22: churches recognized prior to 1990 are registered automatically; Latvia: LORO, 7 September 1995, Arts 9 *et seq*.

[161] Slovakia: Law no 308/1991 Zb (as amended 1992 and 2007): the group must submit its name, office address, founders, and mission; Poland: SFCR 1989, Arts 30–34.

[162] Estonia: CCA 2002, ss 11–13; see Art 11 for name, etc.

[163] Finland: FRA 2003, ss 10 *et seq*.

[164] France: Law of 9 December 1905, Arts 4, 19.

[165] Spain: LORF, Art 5; see also RD 142/1981, Arts 4, 6.

The principle of longevity: A small number of national laws have requirements about the length of time the group has been present in the country. To register in Slovenia, a faith group must have been active there for at least ten years (but 'world religions' need not),[166] and in Czech law, a registered church or religious society may register with 'special rights' after ten years have elapsed since its original registration.[167] Germany has a 'durability guarantee': to register as a public law corporation the community must have existed or have been present there for at least thirty years.[168] However, under Portuguese law, to register as a settled religious corporation the group must have been in Portugal for at least thirty years or it must have been established abroad for sixty years or more.[169]

Connectedness with external community: Occasionally, national laws acknowledge that the applicant religious group is part of a wider religious organization. French law requires an *association cultuelle* to comply with 'the general organizational rules of the religion which the association is to advance',[170] and it recognizes that a Roman Catholic *association diocésaine* acts 'under the authority of the bishop, in communion with the Holy See and in conformity with the constitution of the Holy See'.[171] Similarly, in Lithuania a non-traditional and non-recognized religious community must have been established in accordance with the statutes of the religious association to which it belongs.[172] Indeed, Portuguese law enables a religious community organized internationally to register as a settled religious corporation.[173]

Doctrines and rituals: A common requirement is that the religious association must submit information about its beliefs and work, in the form of a confession of faith, which is sometimes problematic (Finland);[174] religious activities, doctrines, and rites (Poland);[175] doctrine, practice, and worship (Portugal);[176] or fundamental religious texts which describe its beliefs, doctrines, practices, rites, and activities (Slovenia).[177] Interestingly, under German law, to register as a public law corporation, the group must have competent hierarchies able to decide on internal matters of doctrine.[178] Commonly, national laws also require that the beliefs and work be compatible with prescribed standards. Various criteria are used. The doctrines and practices must be compatible with public safety, health, order or morals, or the

---

[166] Slovenia: RFA 2007, Art 13.1; Lithuania: Const, Art 43.2: the State 'shall recognise traditional Lithuanian churches and religious organisations, as well as other churches and religious organisations provided they have a basis in society and their teaching and rituals do not contradict morality or law'.
[167] Czech Rep: CRSL, Act no 3/2002 Sb.
[168] Germany: GG, Art 140; WRV, Art 137.5.2; loyalty to the State is not required: the Constitutional Court so decided in 2000 in relations to Jehovah's Witnesses.
[169] Portugal: LORF, Arts 34 *et seq*.
[170] France: Law of 9 December 1905, Arts 4, 19.
[171] France: Model Statutes, Art 1.
[172] Lithuania: LORCA, Art 11.
[173] Portugal: LORF, Arts 34 *et seq*.
[174] Finland: FRA 2003.
[175] Poland: SFCR 1989, Arts 30–34.
[176] Portugal: LORF, Art 35: this applies to non-settled religious communities not settled ones.
[177] Slovenia: FRA 2007, Arts 13 *et seq*.
[178] Germany: see n 168 above.

rights of others (Austria, Estonia);[179] or else the mission of the religious association and its basic articles of faith must not be contrary to human rights (Czech Republic).[180] In some States, the applicants must declare that the activities of the group comply with the constitution and law (Hungary),[181] or that they do not breach public law or order (Spain).[182]

Internal regulatory instruments: A standard requirement is that the religious association must have and submit its internal regulatory instruments. Moreover, these instruments must deal with prescribed matters—typically, the aims, name, and address of the association; membership (fees and termination); and the constitution of its governing bodies.[183] Various titles are given to these instruments. Statutes must be presented in Austria (for example dealing with board structures),[184] or a statute and memorandum of association (for example on the management board and its members) in Estonia[185] and Spain.[186] A charter must be submitted in Hungary,[187] Latvia,[188] and Slovenia.[189] In Portugal, the constitution of the religious organization must be submitted,[190] and in Sweden its by-laws (which deal, *inter alia*, with its purpose and decision-making structures).[191] Sometimes, the instrument must deal with its own amendment, as is the case in Poland,[192] Lithuania (as to the statutes of a non-traditional and non-recognized religious community),[193] and Finland (as to the charter of foundation and order of association);[194] or else, as in the Czech Republic, the law requires the religious association to notify the State of any changes to its statutes.[195]

Institutional organization: National laws deal in detail with the internal institutional structures of religious organizations applying for registration. These include, typically: management board structures;[196] the election or appointment and qualifications of board members;[197] financial accounting arrangements;[198] the governing

[179] Austria: FLSCC 1998 (BeKGG); see also Estonia: CCA 2002, ss 11–13.
[180] Czech Rep: CRSL, Act no 3/2202 Sb.
[181] Hungary: Act IV/1990, ss 9–10.
[182] Spain: LORF, Art 5; see also RD 142/1981.
[183] Germany: CC, Arts 55–58.
[184] Austria: FLSCC 1998 (BeKGG).
[185] Estonia: CCA 2002, ss 11–13.
[186] Spain: LORF, Art 5; see also RD 142/1981.
[187] Hungary: Act IV/1990, ss 9–10; see also s 22.
[188] Latvia: LORO, 7 September 1995, Arts 9 *et seq.*
[189] Slovenia: FRA 2007, Arts 13 *et seq.*
[190] Portugal: LORF, Arts 34 *et seq.*
[191] Sweden: Denomination Act 1998, ss 7–8: the Church of Scientology is registered.
[192] Poland: SFCR 1989, Arts 30–34.
[193] Lithuania: LORCA, Arts 11 *et seq.*
[194] Finland: FRA 2003, s 10; the charter must be signed by the founders along with an order of association; the order must identify its purposes.
[195] Czech Rep: CRSL, Act no 3/2202 Sb.
[196] Austria: FLSCC 1998 (BeKGG).
[197] Estonia: CCA 2002, s 14.
[198] Finland: FRA 2003, ss 10–11; the institutions of the association, the number of board members and auditors and their term of office, the accounting period and arrangements, fees, procedure to amend the order, dissolution of the association and the use of funds thereon (notification of dissolution must be sent to the National Patents and Register Board); see s 12 for the role of the Board.

body;[199] officers to act as competent partners of the State;[200] a democratic system of administration;[201] information on its leaders and administrative bodies;[202] the competence of its bodies and representatives;[203] the procedures for nomination and appointment of ministers and dissolution;[204] the dissolution of the religious association;[205] and the distribution of property in the event of liquidation.[206]

Membership: Standards are often imposed with respect to the members of the religious association. For example, the religious organization must have members (with funds provided by the faithful);[207] it should also have rules on membership and fees;[208] qualifications for membership;[209] admission to membership;[210] the rights and duties of members;[211] and the termination of membership.[212]

Refusals to register: National laws also deal with refusals to register: the grounds for refusal may be substantive or procedural. Some States confer a right on a religious organization to be registered (and a duty on the State to register) provided the requirements are met—this is the position in Germany where registration may be refused if the objects of the religious organization contravene criminal law, constitutional order, or the spirit of international friendship (for private corporations), or it does not acquiesce in civil obedience (for public corporations).[213] By way of contrast, in Estonia there is a duty on the State authority *not* to register the religious association if its doctrines or statutes do not comply with State law or if its activities will damage public order, health, morals, and the rights of others.[214] The Estonian

[199] Germany: CC, Arts 55–58.

[200] Germany: see n 168 above.

[201] Hungary: Act IV/1990, ss 9–10.

[202] Latvia: Law on Religious Organisations, 7 September 1995, Arts 9 *et seq*; additional rules apply to applications for registration by an educational establishment for clergy, a monastery, etc.

[203] Spain: LORF, Art 5; see also Royal Decree 142/1981, Arts 4.2 and 6.

[204] Poland: SFCR 1989, Arts 30–34.

[205] Portugal: LORF, Art 34.

[206] Lithuania: LORCA, Art 11.

[207] France: Law of 9 December 1905, Arts 4 *et seq*.

[208] Germany: CC, Arts 55–58.

[209] Finland: FRA 2003, s 3.

[210] Slovenia: FRA 2007, Arts 13 *et seq*; see also Administrative Court, Ljubljana, Case no U 1902/2004-13 (December 2005): the refusal to register the Church of Holy Simplicity because its statutes limited membership to those with a high school diploma and 10 years' work experience (allegedly in breach of the equality principle in Const, Art 14) was remitted to the registration authority for reconsideration.

[211] Lithuania: LORCA, Art 11; see also Portugal, LORF, Art 35.

[212] Poland: SFCR 1989, Arts 30–34.

[213] Germany: CC, Arts 55–58: private corporations; GG, Art 140; WRV, Art 137.5.2: public corporations—see CCt, Decision of 19 December 2000 (Az 2 BvR 1500/97): this raised questions about the loyalty of the Jehovah's Witness to the State in view of the organization's position on the State as part of the world of Satan: see R Puza, 'Relations between church and state in Germany in 2000' (2001) 8 EJCSR 35, 46; see also Austria: FLSCC 1998 (BeKGG): the refusal of the Ministry of Education to register the Sahaja Yoga group in 1998 was upheld in the Constitutional Administrative Court (15.9.2003): see B Schinkele, 'Church and state in Austria in 2003' (2004) 11 EJCSR 45, 55; for the right to registration, see also Spain: LORF, Art 5.

[214] Estonia: CCA 2002, ss 11–13; registration of the Church of Satanists has been refused.

grounds are typical and apply in Finland,[215] Hungary,[216] Lithuania,[217] and Portugal.[218] In Poland applications have been rejected due to 'danger for public security, order, health, public morals and freedoms and rights of citizens',[219] and because the applicant group lacks the 'features of religion'.[220] Registration may also be delayed if the applicant fails to furnish the required documents,[221] but delays in registration have been criticized by Strasbourg.[222] Unlawful refusals may be subject to challenge and there is a formal right of appeal against refusal in, for example, the Czech Republic,[223] Slovakia,[224] and Poland.[225] Moreover, registration may be withdrawn if the religious organization engages in activities in breach of the conditions operative for registration.[226] In Spain, a refusal to register the Unification Church was held to be in breach of religious freedom.[227]

The exercise of legal personality

Religious groups may be unable to avail themselves of legal personality, as they do not meet the conditions for its conferral—or else they may choose not to avail themselves of legal personality, perhaps for doctrinal reasons. Nevertheless, they enjoy the right to exercise freedom of religion, through their members individually or collectively—the latter, additionally, as we have seen, on the basis of the right to

---

[215] Finland: FRA 2003, s 10: law and good morals.

[216] Hungary: Act IV/1990, ss 9–11; see also s 22: constitution and law.

[217] Lithuania: LORCA, Art 12: refusal is lawful if a non-traditional and non-recognized religious community does not provide the required data or its activities violate human rights or public order.

[218] Portugal: LORF, Art 39: refusal is lawful if the group fails to satisfy the legal requirements, falsifies documents, or violates the constitutional limits of religious freedom.

[219] Poland: 48 applications were declined in the period 1995–2002; rejections for reasons of danger to security, etc were made in respect of eg the International Tantric Association 'Satori' 1995, Polish Evolutional Church 1995, Church of Believers of the Sign 1997.

[220] Poland: Church of Miracles—National Federation of Spiritual Healing Persons 1997, Church of Divine Grace 2001, Order of Contemplars of the Power 2002.

[221] Estonia: CCA 2002, s 14: if the application complies with the law, the court may suspend registration for 2 months and request the opinion of the relevant ministry or an expert from a competent agency; reasons for refusing to register must be given.

[222] *Religionsgemeinschaft Der Zeugen Jehovas and ors v Austria* App no 40825/98 (ECtHR, 31 July 2008), and *Verein Der Freunde der Christengemeinschaft and ors v Austria* App no 76581/01 (ECtHR, 26 February 2009): the 10-year waiting period for registered communities was unreasonable and in breach of ECHR, Art 14 (discrimination) taken in conjunction with ECHR, Art 9.

[223] Czech Rep: the CCt dismissed the Unification Church's appeal in 2004; see IRFR 2009.

[224] Slovakia: there are 60 days in which to appeal to the SC following refusal to register.

[225] Poland: appeal is to the Chief Administrative Court; eg Decision of the NSA 1999: the Ministry's decision was suspended to seek expert opinion on the Order of Knights of the Line of the Spiral Ring.

[226] Latvia: LORO, 7 September 1995, Art 11: registration may be withdrawn if the religious organization engages in religious intolerance or incitement to religious hatred, or violates or fails to observe its charter, or threatens state security, or public peace, health, or morals, or the rights of others.

[227] Spain: CCt Judgment 46/2001 of 15 February: the Unification Church challenged the refusal of the General Director for Religious Affairs (Ministry of Justice) of 22 December 1992 and the judgments of the National HC (30 September 1992) and SC (14 June 1996); it was held that the decisions violated religious freedom; see A Motilla, 'Church and state in Spain in 2000' (2001) 8 EJCSR 119, 123.

associate.[228] However, when a religious organization acquires legal personality, this generates additional rights whose enjoyment is facilitated and regulated by law. This occurs in various ways and to varying extents. These depend principally on whether the religious association is recognized constitutionally, by statute, or by register; whether it is regulated by legislation, covenant, or a mixture of these; and whether it has public or private law status. The following identifies the basic rights which flow from the acquisition of legal personality. The conditions under which these rights are exercisable are dealt with elsewhere in this book in each of the areas considered below. National laws on the exercise of legal personality tell us a great deal about the wide range of activities in which religious organizations may be engaged.[229]

First, legal personality enables a religious organization to alter its status in the juridical order. In a small number of those States which have a system of registration, a registered religious association has a right to seek a change in its status. For example, in Portugal, if registered as a settled religious community, it may conclude an agreement with the State, and so become a covenantal religious organization.[230] Similarly, in Spain a registered religious organization may seek conclusion of an agreement with the State in order to gain recognition as being 'firmly rooted in Spain'.[231] In the Czech Republic a registered church or religious community may seek to register as such with 'special rights' after ten years have elapsed since registration, if their membership is 0.1 per cent of the population (that is, more than 10,000).[232]

Secondly, legal personality affords a range of fiscal benefits, such as access to the taxation apparatus of the State: in Germany, for example, public corporation status entitles a religious organization to levy a church tax on its members which the State collects as a proportion of the income tax that the members pay.[233] Similarly, in other States, a religious legal person may be entitled to receive a portion of the income tax of its members: this is available for instance in France to the four *cultes reconnus* in the eastern *départements*.[234] Legal personality may attract tax exemptions for religious associations in relation to their non-profit religious (but not

---

[228] See above for unincorporated religious associations and Ch 5 below for autonomy.

[229] Estonia: CCA 2002, Arts 3.1 and 4.1: the main activities of a religious society include 'professing and practising their faith, primarily in the form of religious services, meetings and rites', 'confessional or ecumenical activities relating to morals, ethics, education, culture and confessional or ecumenical, diaconal and social rehabilitation activities outside the traditional forms of religious rites of a church or congregation'; Finland: FRA 2003, s 7.1: the life of a registered religious association involves 'individual, corporate and public activities pertaining to religious profession and religious observance, based on confession of faith, scriptures or other individualised established sacred activities'.

[230] Portugal: if they seek an agreement, negotiations are led by a commission appointed by the Ministry of Justice; it is then approved by the Council of Ministers, signed by the Prime Minister, and ratified by Parliament; see LORF, Arts 45–51.

[231] Spain: LORF, Art 7.

[232] Czech Rep: CRSL, Act no 3/2002 Sb; Romania has cults (long-established and large), which may receive financial support, religious associations (which could acquire the status of cults), and religious groups.

[233] Germany: GG, Art 140; WRV, Art 137.6; public law corporations include dioceses and parishes of the Catholic Church, and the Protestant *Landeskirchen*. See Ch 7 below.

[234] Spain: LORF, Arts 7 *et seq*; Sweden: Denominations Act 1998, s 16.

commercial) activities, such as exemptions from income tax and land tax.[235] Legal personality may also generate entitlements to State financial aid: recognized religions may receive state remuneration, pensions, and housing for their ministers.[236] Charitable and educational activities may also be carried out on the basis of legal personality.[237]

Thirdly, legal personality entitles religious organizations as such to own property,[238] to establish places of worship,[239] and to request state subsidies for the construction[240] or preservation of religious buildings of historical, cultural, and artistic value.[241] In France, for example, the ownership and repair of pre-1905 Catholic church buildings vests in the State, and post-1905 ownership and maintenance vest in the *associations diocésaines*.[242] In other States, registration of a place of public religious worship attracts tax benefits and enables the solemnization of marriages in it.[243] Legal personality may enable religious organizations to maintain cemeteries and crematoria (as is the case with public law religious entities in Finland, for example).[244] Religious organizations may enjoy certain exemptions from planning law applicable to places of religious worship, as occurs in Ireland.[245] Religious legal persons may also be entitled to restitution of property expropriated under previous political regimes.[246]

Fourthly, legal personality attracts the right to solemnize or bless marriages in accordance with religious rites. Registered religious associations in Spain may conclude agreements with the State to deal with civil effects of religious marriage.[247] Recognized cults in Luxembourg may (usually under their agreements with the State) bless marriages following a civil ceremony.[248] In Denmark the ministers of approved religious entities (such as the Salvation Army, Islamic communities, Jehovah's Witnesses) may perform marriages.[249] Registered religious

---

[235] Lithuania: CC, Bk II, Ch 4, Art 2.34; LORCA, Art 16 (tax); Hungary: Act IV/1990, s 19; Portugal: LORF 2001, Art 32 (tax); Sweden: Denominations Act 1998, s 9; Estonia: Income Tax Act, s 11.2 (RT I 1993, 79, 1184); Land Tax Act, s 4.5; Czech Rep: SCRL, Act no 3/2002 Sb; Denmark: approved religious groups receive tax benefits; France: Law of 9 December 1905.

[236] Belgium: Const, Art 181.

[237] Latvia: LORO, 7 September 1995, Arts 13–16; Lithuania: LORCA, Art 14; Hungary: Act IV/1990, s 19.

[238] France: Law of 9 December 1905: *associations cultuelles* may own property; Finland: FRA 2003, s 14: the order of association must cover the maintenance and inspection of its property; Latvia: LORO, 7 September 1995, Arts 13–16; Lithuania: LORCA, Art 13; Spain: CC, Art 38; Hungary: Act CXXV/2003, Art 22. See Ch 7 below.

[239] Slovakia: Const, Art 24; Lithuania: Const, Art 43.

[240] Belgium: Imperial Decree of 30 December 1809, Art 92.3; Law of 4 March 1870, Law 7 August 1931; Royal Decrees of 2 July 1949 and 1 July 1952.

[241] Lithuania: LORCA, Art 13. See Ch 7 below.

[242] France: Laws of 2 January 1907 and 3 April 1908: local authorities bear the cost of repair.

[243] UK: Local Government Finance Act 1988, Sch 5, s 11 (as amended 1992, Sch 10, s 2).

[244] Finland: Cemeteries Act (HE 204/2002), s 8.

[245] Ireland: Planning and Development Act 2000, s 4(2); Planning and Development Regulations 2001 (SI 2001/600), Art 10.

[246] Czech Rep: CRSL, Act no 3/2002 Sb.

[247] Spain: CC, Art 38. See Ch 9 below.

[248] Luxembourg: Const, Art 21.

[249] Denmark: Formation and Dissolution of Marriage Act 1969, as consolidated and amended by the Formation and Dissolution of Marriage Act 1999, s 21(3).

associations may solemnize marriages in Slovakia[250] and Sweden.[251] However, registration of itself may not enable the solemnization of marriage: in Cyprus the ministers of registered religions may perform religious marriages only if registered also with the Ministry of the Interior.[252] Sometimes the right is reserved to classes of registered religious association: in the Czech Republic only a religious body with special rights may solemnize marriages;[253] and in Finland, religious associations may solemnize marriages with permission from the Ministry of Education, but the Lutheran and Orthodox churches may do so on the basis of their public law status.[254]

Fifthly, legal personality enables religious organizations to enter contracts and employ personnel. For example, in Belgium legal personality is needed for a religious group to enjoy contractual capacity, as otherwise the physical persons who act in the name of the group will be personally liable.[255] This is also the case with registered religious associations in, for instance, Finland,[256] Greece,[257] Hungary,[258] Lithuania,[259] and Spain.[260] Whilst in Luxembourg recognized religions are not exempt from employment law,[261] in Estonia registered religious associations are (unless the statutes of the body provide otherwise).[262] In Germany, public religious corporations may employ civil servants under the public law employment regime, but registered (private) religious associations are subject to the general employment law.[263]

Finally, registration enables a religious association to establish schools[264] or educational institutions to train its ministers.[265] However, even in States where religious organizations as such have no legal personality, the law may allow for the establishment of denominational schools.[266] Registration may enable a religious association to provide its own religious education in state schools, as is the case, for example, in Hungary, Slovakia, Finland, and Portugal;[267] this also applies to the

---

[250] Slovakia: Const, Art 24.
[251] Sweden: Denominational Marriage Act, s 1 (this does not apply to the Church of Sweden: Marriage Code, Art 4.3).
[252] Cyprus: Marriage Law 104(I)/2003.
[253] Czech Republic: Churches and Religious Societies Law, Act no 3/2002 Sb.
[254] Finland: Matrimony Act (234/1929), s 14.
[255] Belgium: R Torfs, 'Religious entities as legal persons—Belgium' in F Friedner (ed), *Churches and Other Religious Organizations as Legal Persons* (Leuven: Peeters, 2007) 45, 47–48.
[256] Finland: FRA 2003, s 14.
[257] The Orthodox Church has its own Code on Church Employees: I Konidaris, 'Religious entities as legal persons—Greece' in L Friedner (ed), *Churches and Other Religious Organizations as Legal Persons* (Leuven: Peeters, 2007) 115, 117.
[258] Hungary: Act CXXV/2003, Art 22.
[259] Lithuania: LORCA, Art 17.
[260] Spain: CC, Art 38; LORF, Art 6.
[261] Luxembourg: Const, Art 21.
[262] Estonia: Labour Contract Act, s 7; RT I 1992, 15, 241; RT I 2000, 25, 144.
[263] Germany: GG, Art 140; WRV, Art 137.6: public law corporations.
[264] Slovakia: Const, Art 24. See Ch 8 below.
[265] Lithuania: Const, Art 43; Poland: see eg Law of 21 April 1936, Art 33 (Muslims); Law of 30 June 1995, Arts 14–15 (Methodists).
[266] Ireland: the Minister for Education enters the denomination on a register: Education Act 1998, s 8; however, the property would then be vested in trustees.
[267] Hungary: Act IV/1990, s 19; Slovakia: Const, Art 24; Finland: FRA 2003, s 13; Portugal: LORF 2001, Art 24.

cultes reconnus in eastern France.[268] The whole range of religious organizations—constitutional, statutory, covenantal, and registered—may also provide spiritual care in hospitals, prisons, and the armed forces on the basis of their recognition by the State.[269] The last word may be given to the Czech Republic and Spain. Czech law sums up the benefits enjoyed by religious associations with special rights: they may teach religion in public schools; establish their own schools; nominate chaplains for service in the armed forces and prisons; and receive state financial support for the salaries of pastors (a temporary right until restitution of property expropriated under communism).[270] Spanish law sums up the differences between religious associations with legal personality, and those without: all faith communities (registered or not) may establish places of worship; commemorate feast days; appoint and train ministers; propagate their beliefs; maintain relations with their own organizations or other religious faiths whether in Spain or beyond; and celebrate marriages. Those with legal personality may provide religious services in hospitals, military, prison, and community establishments, and religious instruction in state schools.[271]

Conclusion

A survey of national laws on the legal position of religious organizations indicates five facts: (1) States recognize a plethora of religious groups in society; (2) States enable religious organizations to acquire legal personality by means of a range of juridical facilities and forms; (3) States take a keen interest in the internal organization of religious communities before they confer legal personality upon them; (4) there is a formal inequality in the treatment of religious organizations as between the classes of religious legal persons and a substantive inequality in the conditions which must be satisfied to gain legal personality—generally these conditions favour structured religious groups; and (5) in the conferral of legal personality upon them, States cooperate directly with religious organizations regardless of the religion-state model they employ. Clear principles may be induced from the similarities between national laws. There is a right to religious association. This is a fundamental aspect of religious freedom. Religious groups are not required to have legal personality. States may use a variety of juridical vehicles in order to designate a religious group as a religious organization. They may also offer a range of legal categories which enjoy juridical personality under civil law. Legal personality may be recognized by means of the constitution, statutes, and registers. The exercise of legal personality may be regulated by statutes and covenants (concordats and other forms of agreement). In order to confer legal personality, States operate three basic systems: the enactment of legislation; the conclusion of covenants; and a mixture of

---

[268] France: this is the case in the three *départements* of Haut-Rhin, Bas-Rhin, and Moselle.
[269] See Ch 8 below.
[270] Czech Rep: CRSL, Act no 3/2002 Sb.
[271] Spain: LORF, Arts 2 *et seq.*

the two. National laws which require registration for the conferral of legal personality are the most complex. Once legal personality is acquired, national laws confer a range of benefits—in terms of their autonomy, property, and finance, and in the fields of education, spiritual care in public institutions, and marriage. Whatever its posture towards religion (state-church, separation, hybrid), the State constitutes religious organizations as legal persons in civil law (which is also a key aspect of the establishment of religion in its loosest sense)—this constitutive act necessitates cooperation. It would be instructive to examine political debate in national legislative processes prior to the enactment of the laws studied here (and the contribution of religious bodies to this debate) to help us to determine more precisely the role, if any, of the principle of cooperation in the development of national laws on the legal position of religious organizations.

5

The Autonomy and Ministers of Religious Organizations

The processes by which State authorities confer legal personality upon religious organizations necessitate a keen but general interest on the part of the State in some of the affairs of those organizations. As we have seen, to varying extents, States investigate the beliefs, rituals, membership, objects, institutional structures, and regulatory instruments of religious associations which seek legal personality. Those religious groups which do not seek legal personality need not navigate these intrusive procedures. Nevertheless, regardless of whether legal personality is acquired, national laws seek to protect the self-governance of religious organizations from intervention on the part of the State. This is the principle of autonomy—the subject addressed in this chapter. However, its protection in national laws is something of a paradox. The institutional independence of faith communities is dependent on the acquiescence of the State. On the one hand, it reflects the separation model of religion-state relations—States must not interfere in the internal affairs of religion. On the other hand, its enjoyment depends on cooperation between the State and religion. This chapter examines autonomy in the context of this ambiguity. It sets out the key elements of the principle of autonomy: its nature and rationale, and the limits which States may impose on its exercise. The chapter then deals with the institutional autonomy of religious organizations, in terms of their legislative, administrative, and judicial activities. It does so with particular reference to ministers of religion: their appointment, status, functions, and discipline, and the extent to which confidentiality laws protect the exercise of ministry. While it is often difficult to define the 'internal affairs' of faith communities, the chapter proposes that clear principles emerge from national laws with regard to religious autonomy.

The principle of autonomy

The principle of autonomy has been recognized by Strasbourg as being of fundamental importance to the freedom of religious organizations: 'the autonomous existence of religious communities is indispensable for pluralism in a democratic society and is thus an issue at the very heart of the protection which Article 9 affords'.[1] The duty of the State to respect the autonomy of religious organizations is also a core principle of national laws. It is articulated very clearly in Polish law: 'The relationship between the State and churches and other religious organisations shall be based on the principle of respect for their autonomy and the mutual independence of each in its own sphere.'[2] Moreover, this may be understood to apply to all religious organizations on the basis of the principle of religious equality.[3] Consequently, laws often expressly recognize the enjoyment of autonomy for religious organizations whether or not they have legal personality under civil law: this is the case, for example, in Slovenia,[4] Lithuania,[5] Portugal,[6] and Spain.[7] Equally, autonomy may be listed explicitly in legislation among the rights which attach to the conferral of legal personality on religious organizations whether they are constitutional,[8] statutory,[9] covenantal,[10] or registered.[11] More often than not, however, the principle is to be found in a developed form in case-law—though, as will be seen, this sometimes provides that some religious organizations may be more autonomous than others.[12]

The nature of autonomy

'Autonomy' means 'having one's own law' (*auto* meaning 'self', *nomos* meaning 'law'), or, for a body or institution, 'The right of self-government, of making its own laws and administering its own affairs'.[13] National laws echo this definition when speaking of the autonomy,[14] or the freedom,[15] of a religious organization in terms of its right to govern its own affairs.[16] States use a variety of terms

---

[1] Strasbourg: *Hasan and Chaush v Bulgaria* (2002) 34 EHRR 55, para 62.

[2] Poland: Const, Art 25.3; the assumption is that this applies to all religious organizations—Art 25.1: 'Churches and other religious organisations shall have equal rights.'

[3] For the principle of equality see Chs 3 and 4 below.

[4] Slovenia: FRA 2007, Art 6.1: 'The activities of churches and other religious communities are free regardless of the fact whether they are registered or non-registered.'

[5] Lithuania: Const, Art 43; see also LORCA, Art 7.

[6] Portugal, LORF 2001, Arts 20–23: this lists the rights of *all* denominations (not just registered, but unincorporated and corporate associations) and these include the right to 'free organisation'.

[7] Spain: LORF, 7/1980, 5 July 1980, Art 2: all faith communities (registered or not) may eg maintain relations with their own organizations or other religious faiths, whether in Spain or beyond.

[8] Greece: Const, Art 3.1: the (Orthodox) Church of Greece is self-governing and autocephalous; Art 105: the monastic communities of Mount Athos 'in accordance with its ancient privileged status, is a self-governing part of the Hellenic State'.

[9] Poland: eg Law of 21 April 1936, Arts 1–2 (Muslim); Law of 30 June 1990, Art 3 (Baptist).

[10] Spain: Agreement with the Holy See 1979, Art 1: 'The Spanish State recognizes the right of the Catholic Church to carry out its apostolic mission and guarantees the church free and public exercise of those activities inherent to it, especially worship, jurisdiction and teaching'.

[11] Estonia: CCA, Art 10.2; Slovakia: Law no 308/1991 Zb.

[12] Hungary: CCt, Decision 8/1990 (II.27) AB: registered churches enjoy autonomy and the State cannot interfere in their internal affairs; but registered associations do not enjoy autonomy to the same degree.

[13] *Oxford English Dictionary* (Oxford: OUP, 2nd edn, 1989). See generally the studies in G Robbers (ed), *Church Autonomy* (Frankfurt am Main: Peter Lang, 2001).

[14] Slovakia: Const, Art 24.

[15] Bulgaria: Const, Art 13.1; Art 13.2: the religious institutions are separate from the State.

[16] Czech Rep: CFRF, Art 16.2: churches and religious societies are free to govern their own affairs.

for religious autonomy, such the right to 'self-governance' (Hungary),[17] 'self-regulation' (Spain),[18] 'self-administration' (Greece),[19] and 'self-organisation' (Italy).[20] German constitutional law speaks of their 'independence': 'Religious communities shall regulate and administer [their] own matters independently within the limits of the law that applies to all'; they are independent regardless of whether they are public law corporations or civil law associations.[21] Moreover, it has been held by the German Federal Constitutional Court that: 'The guarantee of the right to organize and administer their affairs independently... adds to the freedom of religious life and work of churches and religious communities'; as such, the independence of a faith community is a constitutional right.[22] Similarly, the Italian constitution recognizes the special position of the Catholic Church as 'sovereign and independent in its own order'.[23]

Typical statements of the nature of autonomy as the right to self-governance are found in Portugal, Austria, and Cyprus. Under Portuguese law, in relation to all faith communities: 'Churches and other religious communities are separate from the State and are free in their manner of organisation and in the exercise of their activities and worship.'[24] Similarly, though it is expressed here only for the purposes of religious organizations with legal personality, the Austrian constitution states:

Every church and religious society recognised by law has the right to public religious practice, to arrange and administer its internal affairs autonomously, and to retain possession and enjoyment of its institutions, endowments and funds devoted to worship, instruction and welfare, but it is like every society subject to the general laws of the land.[25]

Statements of autonomy may include the right of a religious organization to legislate for itself. For example, the Cypriot constitution recognizes the 'autocephaly' (ie that it is its own head) of the Orthodox Church of Cyprus and the autonomy of the Turkish Cypriot religious trust (*vakf*)—both have the right to regulate and administer their internal affairs and property in accordance with their own internal regulations.[26]

As will be seen later in this chapter, the ways in which this general principle is applied in practice to particular religious organizations vary from country to country. So much so, in fact, that some commentators (such as Minnerath) propose that there are five forms of religious institutional autonomy in Europe within the

---

[17] Hungary: LFCRC (1990), Art 8: 'religious denomination or church... with self-governance'.
[18] Spain: LORF 1980, Arts 5–6.
[19] Greece: Law 590/1977, Art 9; for the self-governance of the Holy Synod of the Hierarchy, see Arts 4 and 6; Const, Art 3.1.
[20] Italy: Const, Art 8.2: 'The non-Catholic denominations have the right to organize themselves according to their own statutes, in so far as they are not in conflict with Italian law'—this applies to religious groups which have an agreement (*intesa*) with the State.
[21] Germany: GG, Art 140; WRV, Art 137.3; see also n 2 above for the use of the idea of 'independence' in Poland: Const, Art 25.3.
[22] Germany: BVerfGE 53, 366 (401); 72, 278 (289); for religious freedom, see GG, Art 4.
[23] Italy: Const, Art 7.1.
[24] Portugal: LORF, Art 3.
[25] Austria: StGG, Art 15.
[26] Cyprus: Const, Art 110.

three classical models of religion-state relations (state-church, separation, and cooperation). Where there is a state religion (for example Malta, Catholicism), or a national religion (for example Greece, Orthodoxy), the state church has more or less full autonomy, whereas in countries with a national church (Scandinavia, Lutheran) or established church (England) the autonomy of that church is more limited (or very limited, as is the case in Denmark). In countries with 'recognized' *cultes* (for example Belgium and Luxembourg), the autonomy of religious organizations is strong. Where there is separation without recognition or institutional cooperation (for example France), there is an absence of formal State recognition of institutional religious autonomy but it may exist in practice. Other States have a formal system of institutionally autonomous but cooperating religious communities (for example in central and eastern Europe, as in Germany and Austria). Then there are States with a system of more or less full autonomy based on religious independence and cooperation agreements (for example Portugal, Spain, and Italy).[27] However, as is suggested below, significant qualifications need be made to this analysis, particularly with regard to the key duty which flows from the principle of autonomy—the prohibition against State intervention in the internal affairs of religious organizations and the details of laws on their institutional autonomy. The extent of their autonomy and permissible State intervention both depend on the precise activity involved.

The rationale for autonomy

Around the overarching idea that the State and religion have two distinct identities and spheres of operation, States across Europe employ a variety of justifications for the autonomy of religious organizations. The most common, needless to say, is the collective right to manifest their religious freedom in practice. The treatment of institutional religious autonomy by national laws devoted to freedom of religion is an obvious indication of this.[28] National jurisprudence also justifies autonomy in the same way; for example in characteristically European fashion, the constitution of Ireland provides that: 'Every religious denomination shall have the right to manage its own affairs, own, acquire and administer property, movable and immovable, and maintain institutions for religious or charitable purposes';[29] the Irish courts have held that 'the primary aim of [this] constitutional guarantee is to give vitality, independence and freedom to religion'.[30] Several States justify institutional religious self-governance on the basis of the separation of State and religion; for instance, autonomy and separation are juxtaposed in Slovenian law: 'The State and religion are separate. Religious communities enjoy equal rights and freedom of activity.'[31] Similarly, sometimes States justify autonomy by reference to 'the

---

[27] R Minnerath, 'Church autonomy in Europe' in Robbers (n 13 above) 381.

[28] Hungary: LFCRC (1990), Art 8: Czech Rep: CFRF, Art 16.2; Spain: LORF, 7/1980 of 5 July; Luxembourg: Const, Art 19 (*cultes*); Lithuania: Const, Art 43.

[29] Ireland, Const, Art 44.22.5.

[30] Ireland: *McGrath and Ó Ruairc v Trustees of Maynooth College* [1979] ILRM 166, 187.

[31] Slovenia: Const, Art 7; see also Portugal: see n 24 above; and Bulgaria: CCt, Decision no 5 1992.

mutual independence' of the State and religious organizations in their respective fields.[32]

Another standard justification is that religious organizations are private bodies and as a result the State has no part to play in the administration of their internal affairs. Obviously, this approach is particularly prevalent in those States where religious associations have juridical personality in private law. For example, in the Czech Republic autonomy has been justified by the Constitutional Court on the basis of the 'private law essence' of religious associations.[33] The idea is particularly well developed in France[34] and in the United Kingdom: when the public law remedy of judicial review is sought to question decisions made within faith communities, the courts have consistently seen the exercise of autonomy by voluntary religious associations as a private matter with which the State generally cannot interfere;[35] the courts also invoke the principle of separation,[36] and the notion that the affairs of religion are not the business of government.[37] Equally, however, this does not mean that religious associations with public law status do not enjoy autonomy: religious public corporations are autonomous in, for example, Luxembourg, Austria, and Greece.[38] Their autonomy is sometimes justified on the basis that they are not 'organs of the State' (in the case of the Orthodox Church of Cyprus),[39] or 'departments of State' (in the case of the established Church of England).[40]

A somewhat less common justification is the self-understanding of religious organizations: a faith community is autonomous because this is how it may conceive of itself in terms of its own doctrine and religious law—and the State should defer to this.[41] For example, Austrian jurisprudence requires the State to

---

[32] Poland: Const, Art 25.3: see n 2 above; this echoes the outlook of the (Catholic) Second Vatican Council in *Gaudium et spes* (1965) para 76.3: 'in their own domain, the political community and the Church are independent from one another and autonomous' and should develop a 'healthy cooperation'.

[33] Czech Rep: CCt, 27 November 2002, no Pl US 6/02.

[34] France: Law of 9 December 1905: 'The Republic does not recognize...any religious denomination.'

[35] *R v Provincial Court of the Church in Wales, ex p Williams* (1998) 5 EccLJ 217: this church is 'a body whose authority arises from consensual submission to its jurisdiction, with no statutory or... governmental function. It is analogous to other religious bodies which are not established as part of the State. This Court has consistently declined to exercise jurisdiction over such bodies'.

[36] *R v Chief Rabbi of the United Hebrew Congregations of Great Britain and the Commonwealth, ex p Wachmann* [1992] 1 WLR 1036: 'the court is hardly likely to regulate what is essentially a religious function—the determination whether someone is morally and religiously fit to carry out the spiritual and pastoral duties of his office. The court must inevitably be wary of entering so self-evidently sensitive an area, straying across the well-recognised divide between church and state'.

[37] *R v Disciplinary Committee of the Jockey Club, ex p Aga Khan* [1993] 1 WLR 909.

[38] Luxembourg: Law of 23 November 1982 (Reformed Church); Law of 10 July 1998 (Israelite Community); Greece: Law 590/1977 (Orthodox), Law 1920/1991 (Mufti); Austria: StGG, Art 15.

[39] Cyprus: *Autocephalous, Holy, Orthodox and Apostolic Church of Cyprus v House of Representatives* (1990) 3 CLR 338: ie in the sense of Const, Art 139.

[40] This was applied to the established Church of England: *Marshall v Graham* [1907] 2 KB 112; *Aston Cantlow and Wilmcote with Billesley Parochial Church Council v Wallbank* [2004] 1 AC 546, para 13.

[41] See eg UK: HC Deb, 29 October 1987, vol 121, cols 405–407: 'The religious communities have made clear that elements of their slaughter requirements are fundamental obligations, forming part of

respect the self-understanding of a religious organization when a question arises which concerns the exercise of its autonomy.[42] Likewise, in Irish case-law: 'each religious denomination should be respected when it says what its ethos is'.[43] However, the German Constitutional Court does not go quite this far: 'the State would violate the autonomy granted to churches and communities of faith and conviction, and their independence in their own sphere, if it did not consider their own self-understanding when interpreting the practice of religion resulting from a specific belief or worldview'.[44] This subjective approach is perhaps but a small step from justifying religious autonomy on the basis of a claim by a religious organization to its inherent right of self-governance. Such a claim is made by the Catholic Church.[45] In turn, agreements between a State and the Holy See come close to recognizing this claim as the basis of the autonomy of that church; the concordat between Poland and the Holy See is typical: 'The Republic of Poland and the Holy See reaffirm that the State and the Catholic Church are, each in its own domain, independent and autonomous, and that they are fully committed to respecting this principle in all their mutual relations and in co-operating for the promotion of the benefit of humanity and the good of the community.'[46] The same claim is recognized by parliamentary statute in the United Kingdom to justify the autonomy of the national Presbyterian Church of Scotland.[47]

These justifications for religious autonomy, and doubtless there are many more, are related one to another in so far as through them States generally acknowledge an essential difference between the secular and the spiritual spheres—their separateness. However, the principle of autonomy, and justifications for it, together represent something of a paradox: autonomous religious organizations are independent of the State, but that independence is dependent in large measure on the State and its cooperation with religion in this matter. As religious organizations are dependent on the State for the conferral and acquisition of legal personality (see Chapter 4), so they depend on the State for protection of their institutional

---

their religious law which it is not open to them to alter'; therefore: 'We do not believe that we would be justified in imposing such a burden on these communities.'

[42] Austria: for Constitutional Court decisions on this, see: VfSlg 6102/2001; VfSlg 3657/1959 (ÖAKR 32/1981, p 426); VfSlg 7801/1976 (ÖAKR 32/1981, p 556); VfSlg 7982/1977 (ÖAKR 32/1981, p 559); VfSlg 11574/1987 (ÖAKR 37/1987/88, p 353).

[43] Ireland: *Re Article 26 and the Employment Equality Bill 1996* [1997] 2 IR 321.

[44] Germany: CCt, BVerfGE 24, 236 (247f).

[45] For the Catholic Church on its 'inherent right' to discipline the faithful, see Code of Canon Law, c 1311; this derives from the nature of the church 'as a visible organisation': *Lumen gentium*, 8. For the approaches of faith communities to their own autonomy, see eg Robbers (n 13 above).

[46] Poland: Concordat 1993 (in force 1998), Art 1; see also the Agreement on Legal Affairs with Croatia (1996), Art 1: this carries an identical formula; the idea of inherent authority may surface in other forms—Spain: Concordat 3 January 1979 (ratified 4 December 1979), Art 1: this guarantees 'the church free and public exercise of those activities inherent to it, especially worship, jurisdiction and teaching'; see also Lithuania: Agreement on Legal Affairs (2000), Art 4: 'The Republic of Lithuania shall recognise the freedom of the Catholic Church to carry out its pastoral, apostolic and charitable mission.'

[47] UK: Church of Scotland Act 1921, Schedule, Articles Declaratory, Art IV: the church receives from Christ 'the right and power subject to no civil authority to legislate and to adjudicate finally, in all matters of doctrine, worship, government, and discipline in the Church'.

autonomy. Moreover, the justifications also raise difficult questions as to whether religious autonomy may be conceived as *given* by States or as *inherent* in the very character of a faith community in terms of its own theological and juridical self-understanding. The legal evidence outlined above suggests that States tend to the former view.[48] In any event, the autonomy of faith communities is not absolute but qualified: and to this we now turn.

State intervention and the limits of religious autonomy

Autonomy is both a relational and a jurisdictional concept. A body is autonomous only in relation to other jurisdictions within the wider community in which it functions. It is thus chiefly with regard to the State that a religious organization is autonomous. Romanian law captures the idea succinctly: 'religious communities shall be autonomous from the State'.[49] However, this raises complex questions about the precise scope of religious autonomy. In the exercise of its jurisdiction, a State may choose not to entertain matters which concern the internal affairs of a religious organization at all (complete autonomy), or it may defer to the religious organization (its norms or authorities), or it may intervene on the basis of a limitation prescribed by law (limited autonomy); in short: '"Autonomy" is only the label we attach to one side of a necessarily two-sided encounter between normative worlds'—here, the State and religion.[50] States across Europe employ all three approaches to religious autonomy—and which approach is used depends on the particular religious activity in question.

As a starting point, a fundamental element of the principle of autonomy is the duty of the State not to interfere in the internal affairs of a religious organization. This prohibition may be understood as correlative to or implicit in the right to self-governance. It is also spelt out expressly in case-law. The jurisprudence of the Bulgarian Constitutional Court is typical: 'State interference and governmental interference in the internal organisational life of religious communities and institutions as well as in their public manifestation are inadmissible save for those performed on the grounds of [the] Constitution.'[51] On the one hand, therefore, as a general principle, a State cannot interfere in the affairs of a faith community: to restrict expenditure of its lawful income to activities connected solely with professing its faith;[52] to control it in matters of doctrine, government, discipline,[53] worship, or those which have 'spiritual and purely religious content';[54] to exclude

---

[48] See generally N Doe and A Jeremy, 'Justifications for religious autonomy' in R O'Dair and A Lewis (eds), *Law and Religion*, in the series Current Legal Issues (Oxford: OUP, 2001) 421.
[49] Romania: Const, Art 29.5; see also Slovenia: Const, Art 7.
[50] P Dane, 'The varieties of religious autonomy' in Robbers (n 13 above) 147.
[51] Bulgaria: Decision no 5, 11 June 1992, Case no 11/92, SG no 49, 16 June 1992.
[52] Czech Rep: CCt, 27 November 2002, no Pl US 6/02.
[53] Ireland: *State (Colquhoun) v D'Arcy* [1936] IR 641: 'an un-established religious association is free from State control as regards doctrine, government and discipline'; UK: *Blake v Associated Newspapers* [2003] EWHC 1960: on the definition of 'bishop'.
[54] Greece: COS, Decision no 491/1940, 583/1940: the spiritual suitability of a person for ordination.

members if they 'fail to fulfil a decision of . . . an authority . . . or upon other weighty reasons';[55] or to upset the exercise of lawful discretion by a minister of a national church concerning the administration of baptism and the suitability of (unmarried) candidates for the office of godparent.[56] Such cases are generally in line with Strasbourg case-law, which also prohibits State interference in, for example, the appointment of a mufti,[57] ecclesiastical property disputes,[58] and engineering the unification of two rival Islamic groups.[59]

On the other hand, a State may legitimately intervene in the affairs of a religious organization on the basis of explicit or implicit limitations prescribed by law. Explicit limits are those which appear in legislation. As a general principle—rooted in the rule of law—religious organizations must comply with the law of the State. This principle often accompanies constitutional statements of religious autonomy; Germany is typical: religious communities are autonomous 'within the limits of the law that applies to all'.[60] Moreover, as already seen (Chapter 4), to acquire and retain legal personality, the activities, doctrines, rituals, and statutes of religious associations must comply with public order, health, morals, and the rights of others.[61] Consequently, the State may intervene if a faith community engages in religious intolerance or hatred;[62] if it fails to comply with an order to restore the lawfulness of its activities, its registration may be cancelled;[63] and in Bulgaria, religious organizations cannot use their autonomy for political ends.[64] However, State intervention is permitted only if it is lawful, proportionate, and necessary; this is a fundamental requirement of Article 9 ECHR as to the exercise of the collective right to manifest religion in practice.[65]

Implicit limits are generally those recognized by the courts. An assertion of religious autonomy will fail if the activity in question is not religious in an objective way. This is clearly articulated in German jurisprudence: whilst the view of the community on the proximity of the activity to its central mission must be

---

[55] Estonia: SC, Case no 3-4-1-1-96: 'Membership of such societies is a matter of religious belief. No authority can oblige any person to surrender his or her religious beliefs.'

[56] Finland: CA Decision no 2792, 13 October 1989 (KKO 1998:122); see also, for the refusal of a bishop to ordain a woman as a priest, Chancellor of Justice, Resolution 561/24/5/1989.

[57] *Agga v Greece*, nos 3 and 4 App no 32186/02 (ECtHR, 13 July 2006); see also *Serif v Greece* (2001) 31 EHRR 20.

[58] *Holy Synod of the Bulgarian Orthodox Church (Metroplitan Inokentiy) and ors v Bulgaria* App nos 412/03 and 35677/04 (ECtHR, 22 January 2009).

[59] *Supreme Holy Council of the Muslim Community v Bulgaria* App no 39023/97 (ECtHR, 16 December 2004).

[60] Germany: GG, Art 140; WRV, Art 137.III; Austria: StGG, Art 15: like 'every society [they are] subject to the law of the land'; Romania: Const, Art 29.3: 'All religions shall be free and organised in accordance with their own statutes, under the terms laid down by law.'

[61] eg Spain: Const, Art 16.1: religious autonomy is limited by public law, health, morals, and order; Finland: FRA 2003, ss 21–23: a registered religious organization (or its founders) may request inspection of the order of association (or alterations in it), which may involve a committee of experts to examine whether its activities are lawful, particularly with regard to human rights.

[62] Latvia: LORO, 7 September 1995, Art 11; Romania: Const, Art 29.4: religious enmity.

[63] Hungary: Act IV/1990, Art 16(2); Czech Rep: Act no 3/2002, ss 21 and 22.

[64] Bulgaria: Const, Art 13.4.

[65] Czech Rep: CCt, 27.11.2002, no Pl US 6/02; Bulgaria: Decision no 5, 11 June 1992, Case no 11/92, SG no 49, 16 June 1992; see Ch 2 above for ECHR, Art 9.

considered,[66] the activity itself must be religious 'in terms of spiritual content and external appearance'.[67] The same approach has been used, for example, in Cyprus: refusal to grant a permit to a religious organization to purchase property for the vacations of its members did not violate its *religious* freedom.[68] Moreover, a State court may intervene if a decision is made by a religious authority in violation of its own rules with regard to property, finance, or the enforcement of civil rights,[69] or when the religious authority lacks competence under those rules or otherwise fails to comply with relevant State law.[70]

However, there is currently debate on the applicability of human rights *within* religious organizations—whether they (like the State) must respect the ECHR.[71] The issue is particularly relevant to state churches and those with public law status. On the one hand, it has been held that a parochial church council of the Church of England is not a public authority and so not obliged to meet human rights law standards as to chancel repair liability;[72] and in Belgium it has been held that a faith community must discipline its ministers 'within the norms of the religion concerned' but in so doing need not comply with Article 6 ECHR (on fair trials).[73] On the other hand, for Strasbourg, there was a violation of Article 6 ECHR when an Italian court failed to ensure a fair hearing in the tribunal of the Roman Rota of the Catholic Church before authorizing enforcement of its judgment in a marriage case; it has also applied similar ECHR standards to the national Church of Finland.[74] Likewise, the dismissal by the Catholic Church of an organist (separated from his wife) on grounds of adultery and bigamy was in breach of Article 8 ECHR (the right to family and private life);[75] but there is no breach of this right when an officer of a religious organization is aware or should have been aware of its standards on marriage on admission to the office held.[76]

---

[66] Germany: BVerfGE 53, 346 (401); 66, 1 (22); 72, 278 (289).

[67] Germany: BVerfGE 84, 341; see also BVerfGE 24, 236 (247f). See also Austria: VfSlg 6102/2001; VfSlg 3657/1959 (ÖAKR 32/1981, p 426); VfSlg 7801/1976 (ÖAKR 32/1981, p 556); VfSlg 7982/1977 (ÖAKR 32/1981, p 559); VfSlg 11574/1987 (ÖAKR 37/1987/88, p 353).

[68] Cyprus: *Church of the Nazarene International Ltd v Minister of Interior* [1996] 3 CLR 3091.

[69] Ireland: *McGrath and Ó Ruairc v Trustees of Maynooth College* [1979] ILRM 166.

[70] Greece: for supervision of the Holy Synod on appointment of members: COS, Decision no 1175/1975; dismissal by a metropolitan of a parish priest: Decision no 4625/1985; refusal of a metropolitan council to grant credit for payment of wages to a parish priest: Decision no 669/1949.

[71] This is similar to the question as to whether State discrimination law applies within religious organizations: see Ch 3 above for exceptions allowing them to discriminate.

[72] UK: *Aston Cantlow and Wilmcote with Billesley PCC v Wallbank* [2004] 1 AC 546.

[73] See R Torfs, 'Autonomy of churches in Belgium' in H Warnink (ed), *Legal Position of Churches and Church Autonomy* (Leuven: Peeters, 2001) 83, 87 et seq.

[74] *Pellegrini v Italy* App no 30882/96 (ECtHR, 20 July 2001); *Launikari v Finland* App no 34120/96 (ECtHR, 5 October 2000): right to a fair trial in the Evangelical Lutheran Church.

[75] *Schüth v Germany* App no 1620/03 (ECtHR, 23 September 2010): whilst ECHR, Art 9 protects its autonomy (with Art 11, right to associate), his contract with the church 'could not be interpreted as an unequivocal undertaking to live a life of abstinence in the event of separation or divorce'.

[76] *Obst v Germany* App no 425/03 (ECtHR, 23 September 2010): there was no breach of ECHR, Art 8 (right to private and family life) when the Director of Public Affairs for Europe of the Church of Jesus Christ Latter-Day Saints (Mormon) was dismissed by it (a legal person of public law) after confessing an extra-marital affair, on the basis that he was aware (or should have been) when signing a contract of employment of the importance of marital fidelity and the duties of loyalty to the church.

Institutional autonomy

As well as the right to freedom from State interference in their internal affairs, religious organizations enjoy a wide range of rights associated with their institutional autonomy, rights which have also been enumerated in global international law.[77] They may establish institutions of governance, and to acquire legal personality must usually do so (see Chapter 4 for boards of management), which in turn generally exercise legislative, administrative, and judicial functions.[78] What follows outlines the key elements of national laws as they enable and regulate the exercise of institutional religious autonomy. The study also indicates how difficult it is to define the 'internal affairs' of a religious organization, in terms of its core subject-matter jurisdiction, beyond the broad categories of legislation, administration, and adjudication.

Legislative autonomy

Religious organizations regulate their internal affairs on the basis of a variety of legislative instruments. These fall into two broad categories. On the one hand, many religious organizations function under external regulatory instruments enacted or otherwise approved for them by the State. As seen in Chapter 4 with regard to the legal position and personality of religious organizations, these instruments include parliamentary statutes, covenants (sometimes ratified by statute), and 'internal' statutes (of faith communities) approved by State registration authorities. Such instruments are the result of general cooperation between the State, in an exercise of its sovereignty, and religious organizations, in an exercise of their autonomy. However, when faith communities have to submit their internal statutes to State authorities in such circumstances, their legislative autonomy is of course limited by the procedural requirement of State approval and by the substantive requirement that such statutes be consistent with the laws of the State. On the other hand, religious organizations also function under a wider range of internal instruments properly so-called—instruments created or adopted by and within those organizations without recourse to the authorities of the State. These include systems of Christian law (for example canon law or other polity of church order), Islamic law, Jewish law, and other systems of 'religious law'.[79] It is with regard to this category of internal religious law that faith communities enjoy greater procedural legislative autonomy—national laws do not formally require State approval for these types of religious law.

---

[77] UNDID, Art 6: see Ch 1 above, at n 79.

[78] Many faith communities use this tripartite distribution of functions in their governmental organization, though in very different and varied ways; see eg for the Catholic Church, Code of Canon Law 1983, c 135: 'The power of governance is divided into legislative, executive and judicial power'. For the approaches of Christian churches, see eg N Doe, 'Modern church law' in J Witte and FS Alexander (eds), *Christianity and Law: An Introduction* (Cambridge: CUP, 2008) 271, 279.

[79] For 'religious law', see A Huxley (ed), *Religion, Law and Tradition* (London: Routledge, 2002).

Indeed, States often recognize the autonomy of religious organizations to create or adopt internal regulatory instruments whether they have legal personality or not—provided such instruments are generally consistent with the law of the State. This is the case regardless of the religion-state model adopted. Among the cooperation systems of central and eastern Europe, Romania is typical: 'All religions shall be free and organised in accordance with their own statutes, under the terms laid down by law';[80] in those of the Mediterranean, Spain is equally typical: religious entities 'shall be fully independent and may lay down their own organisational rules, internal and staff by-laws'.[81] The same applies in separation systems, such as that of the Netherlands: a church, its units, and united churches may have their own statutes provided these do not conflict with the law of the State.[82] Likewise, in countries which have a national or established church, both that church and other faith communities may have their own internal rules.[83] Occasionally, State courts recognize that such regulatory instruments both facilitate and order the institutional lives of faith communities.[84]

Consequently, many States explicitly recognize religious laws.[85] Again, they may do so regardless of the religion-state model at work. In cooperation States the canon law of the Roman Catholic Church may be recognized formally in an agreement with the Holy See;[86] in the Irish separation system and the English state-church system, Catholic canon law is classified by case-law as a species of 'foreign law' and it must be proved in State courts by the evidence of expert witnesses.[87] The Cypriot constitution recognizes the Holy Canons of the Orthodox Church.[88] Jewish law

---

[80] Romania: Const, Art 29.3; see also Lithuania: Const, Art 43; LORCA, Art 7: they may freely organize themselves in accordance with their religious polity and manage their internal affairs by statutes; Estonia: CCA 2002, s 10.2; Slovakia: Law no 308/1991 Zb (as amended 1992 and 2007).

[81] Spain: LORF, Art 6.1; Italy: Const, Art 8.2: 'non-Catholic denominations may organize themselves according to their own statutes, in so far as they are not in conflict with Italian law'.

[82] Netherlands: CC, Art 2.2; see the decision HR, 15 March 1985, NJ 1986, 191: this case concerned a church minister who challenged his dismissal.

[83] UK: Welsh Church Act 1914, s 13(1): the disestablished Church in Wales may frame constitutions and regulations; for the competence of other (but non-statutory) voluntary associations to legislate, see eg *Forbes v Eden* (1867) LR 1 Sc & Div 568; see below for the established Church of England.

[84] Germany: BVerfGE 66, 1 (19); 70, 138 (165); BVerfGE 57, 220 (243f): a religious organization may take 'all measures, which have to be made in pursuit of charitable tasks determined by the fundamental mission of the church, [eg] the specification of structural types, the choice of personnel and the precautions to guarantee the "religious dimensions" of the operation'.

[85] Equally, religious organizations sometimes formally recognize the applicability of State law to them; see eg the Catholic Code of Canon Law 1983, c 22: 'When the law of the Church remits some issue to the civil law, the latter is to be observed with the same effects in canon law, insofar as it is not contrary to divine law, and provided it is not otherwise stipulated in canon law.'

[86] Lithuania: Agreement with the Holy See on Legal Affairs 2000, Art 4: 'The Republic of Lithuania shall recognise the freedom of the Catholic Church to carry out its . . . activities in accordance with Canon Law and the procedure prescribed by the laws of the Republic of Lithuania.'

[87] Ireland: *Colquhoun v Fitzgibbon* [1937] IR 555; see also *O'Callaghan v O'Sullivan* [1925] 1 IR 90; UK: *Buckley v Cahal Daly* [1990] NIJB 8.

[88] Cyprus: Const, Art 110: the Orthodox Church may regulate its affairs 'in accordance with the Holy Canons and its Charter'; see also Art 111: marriages of the Orthodox Church or another church 'shall be governed by the law of the Greek Orthodox Church or of the Church of such religious group'.

and Islamic law are formally recognized in Spain,[89] as are elements of Islamic family law in Thrace (in Greece).[90] Other States enable religious laws to be invoked in civil law arbitrations.[91] The rules of religious associations without legal personality may be recognized in private law. Ireland is typical: such rules are terms of a contract entered by the members.[92] Thus, as is the case in the United Kingdom: 'A Court of Law will not interfere with the rules of a voluntary [religious] association unless to protect some civil right or interest which is said to be infringed by their operation'; moreover: 'Save for the due disposal and administration of property, there is no authority in the Courts ... to take cognizance of the rules of a voluntary association.'[93] In Slovenia, for example, it has been held that State courts may consider the provisions of canon law to determine whether the Catholic Church has violated its own rules.[94]

By way of contrast, in state-church systems, the State is more directly involved in the law-making processes of national and established churches. However, the degree of involvement varies from country to country and from one type of ecclesiastical legislation to another. The Charter of the Orthodox Church of Greece is approved by parliament,[95] but its church-made Holy Canons (recognized in the statutory charter) are invulnerable to challenges under State law as to matters of doctrine and liturgy.[96] The Finnish parliament enacts law for the Evangelical Lutheran Church but it may only approve or reject an ecclesiastical bill—the General Synod of the church has exclusive control over its content; the church also has a Church Ordinance;[97] but the government may alter bills applicable to the Orthodox Church without its consent prior to their approval by parliament.[98]

---

[89] Spain: Law 25/1992, 10 November, Art 6: Jewish law; Law 26/1992, 10 November, Art 6: Islamic law.

[90] Greece: Treaty of Lausanne 1923, ratified by DL 25/25 August 1923.

[91] UK: Arbitration Act 1996: see R Sandberg, *Law and Religion* (Cambridge: CUP, 2011) 184.

[92] Ireland: *State (Colquhoun) v D'Arcy* [1936] IR 641, 650.

[93] UK: *Forbes v Eden* [1867] LR 1 HL Sc & Div 568, 588; relied on in *Buckley v Cahal Daly* [1990] NIJB 8: the case concerned the effects of incardination under Roman Catholic canon law.

[94] Slovenia: HC, Ljubljana, no II Cp 490/2002 (May 2002): the case concerned the laicization of a priest; the court overturned the decision of a lower court which decided that the matter was not justiciable on the basis of lack of civil jurisdiction in the matter.

[95] Greece: the Charter is ratified in Law 590/1977; see also Const, Art 3.1; Const, Art 105: Mount Athos, under the jurisdiction of the Ecumenical Patriarchate of Constantinople, is governed by its 20 monasteries and a Charter drawn up by the monasteries and ratified by the Greek parliament and the Ecumenical Patriarchate, which came into force in 1927.

[96] Greece: there are two views about its canons—one is that any state law contrary to them is unconstitutional (the church holds this view and some jurists); the other is that this applies only to doctrinal canons and not to those on the administration of the church; the Council of State in 1967 tended towards the former view: 'the legislator ... cannot ... bring about fundamental changes to the basic administrative institutions which have been deeply entrenched and long established within the Orthodox Church': Ch K Papastathis, 'Religious self-administration in the Hellenic Republic' in Robbers (n 13 above) 425, 434.

[97] Finland: Church Law, Ch 2, s 2 and Ch 15, s 2; s 76 (Church Act) of the Constitution came into force on 1 March 2000: 'The legislative procedure for enactment of the Church Act and the right to submit legislative proposals relating to the Church Act are governed by the specific provisions in that Code.'

[98] Finland: Law 521/1969 (a skeleton law) and the (supplementary) Law 179/1970; new legislation applicable to the Orthodox Church was due to come into force in 2007; see J Seppo, 'Finland's policy

The legislative autonomy of the Church of England is not dissimilar. A Measure of the General Synod of the Church of England must receive both parliamentary and royal approval to acquire the same authority and invulnerability to judicial challenge as an Act of Parliament; a Canon must receive royal assent (but not parliamentary approval) and be consistent with common law, statute, and prerogative; by convention, parliament does not legislate for the church without its consent; and the church has other instruments created with no State involvement at all (for example Acts of Synod).[99] At the other end of the spectrum, the Danish national church has little legislative autonomy: the Ministry of Ecclesiastical Affairs is its governing body; its Canons are promulgated by parliament—but by convention church legislation will only be enacted with cross-party agreement.[100]

In short, there is little difference in principle between the States of Europe in the matter of the legislative autonomy of religious organizations. All religious communities are free to legislate as long as, one way or another, their rules are approved by the State explicitly or implicitly. Ultimately, the rules of all religious organizations must not be inconsistent with State law—provided, that is, State law complies with the standards set by the ECHR. Moreover, certain classes of instrument of national or established churches (in state-church systems) must be approved by parliament, just as the instruments of public or private religious associations (in separation and cooperation systems) must be approved by State institutions through parliamentary statutes, or covenants (perhaps ratified by statute), or in the process of registration. Importantly, however, some sources of religious law, especially those of fundamental and doctrinal significance, need no State approval.

Administrative and ministerial autonomy

Most of the activities of religious organizations may be classified as administrative (or executive). They include the formulation of policy (for which they enjoy strategic autonomy) and its implementation (for which they enjoy operational autonomy) in relation to a host of matters, such as their mission, proclamation of the faith (in teaching and practice), worship and ritual, ministry to their members, charitable and educational work, and the administration of property and finance. As seen elsewhere in this book, national laws protect the rights of religious organizations to engage in these activities as a feature of their internal autonomy, and the acquisition of legal personality may generate additional rights exercisable

on church and religion' in L Christoffersen, KÅ Modéer, and S Andersen (eds), *Law and Religion in the 21st Century—Nordic Perspectives* (Copenhagen: Djøf Publishing, 2010) 89, 91.

[99] UK: Church of England Assembly (Powers) Act 1919 (measures); Synodical Government Measure 1969 (canons); Lord Sainsbury, 19 July 2005, GC 192–3 (convention); for the great variety of other regulatory instruments employed by the church (such as an Act of Synod), which do not involve any participation by the State, see N Doe, *The Legal Framework of the Church of England* (Oxford: OUP, 1996) ch 1; the Presbyterian Church of Scotland enjoys greater autonomy: Church of Scotland Act 1921.

[100] Denmark: Constitution Act 1953, Part 1, s 4; Part VII, s 66: the constitution of the church is to be set down by statute (this has not been done).

externally in the milieu of the public institutions of the State (with the attendant qualifications to autonomy that these may entail).[101] The members of a religious organization also enjoy the right to participate in the activities of religious organizations on the basis of their individual religious freedom,[102] and membership itself (and eligibility for it) is a matter of internal autonomy,[103] though controversially Finland forbids simultaneous membership of more than one religious community.[104] This section deals with a fundamental aspect of the administrative autonomy of a religious organization—the collective right to operate a system of ministry—its ministerial autonomy.

The appointment of ministers of religion: It is a general principle of religion law in Europe that the State must not interfere in the appointment of ministers of religion to offices within religious organizations.[105] The same applies to decisions about their status within a faith community or the conferral of a particular religious character upon them (such as through ordination).[106] The Belgian constitution provides in unequivocal terms that: 'The State does not have the right to intervene either in the nomination or in the installation of ministers of any religion whatsoever.'[107] Similarly, in Germany, religious communities 'shall confer their offices without the participation of the state or the civil community'; this applies

[101] For rights which flow from legal personality, see Ch 4 above; for doctrine and worship, see Ch 6 below; for property and finance, see Ch 7 below; for education and spiritual care in public institutions, see Ch 8 below; and for marriage, see Ch 9 below.

[102] To acquire legal personality, many national laws require a religious organization to have a membership, as well as (in some States) rules about the rights and duties of the members: see Ch 4 above; the right to join is also a fundamental aspect of individual religious freedom: see Ch 2 above.

[103] Finland requires religious organizations to have registers of their members: Freedom of Information Act 2003, s 11; for the Lutheran church, Church Law, Ch 16, s 2; see also Orthodox Church Act, s 12; Austria: VfSlg 16.998/2003; cf VwGH 29.6.2004, 2003/01/0576: under the Law on Personal Status, s 24.2, only members of registered religious organizations are entitled to have their membership entered in personal status documents; Jehovah's Witnesses sought this in their marriage certificates on the basis of their status as a registered religious community (since 1998); this was refused; the Constitutional Court upheld the refusal—their religious freedom had not been violated.

[104] Finland: in 1999 the Committee on Freedom of Religion proposed to abolish the prohibition (in the FRA) as conditions of membership were a matter for the religious communities themselves; the move was opposed by several churches, including the Evangelical Lutheran Church (because a religious conviction was by nature exclusive), and the Orthodox Episcopal Meeting of Finland (which proposed an explicit ban in its own legislation on dual membership): see J Seppo, 'Church and state in Finland in 2000' (2001) 8 EJCSR, 241, 244.

[105] Spain: LORF 1980, 7/1980, 5 July 1980, Art 2; Lithuania: Const, Art 43; Latvia: LORO, Art 14; Slovenia: HC, Ljubljana, Decision no 1 Cp 101/2006 (February 2006): the State cannot interfere in the appointment of a mufti. The process is usually set out in their regulatory instruments, eg Catholic Code of Canon Law 1983, c 523: 'appointment to the office of parish priest belongs to the diocesan bishop, who is free to confer it on whomsoever he wishes'; Cyprus: Orthodox archbishops and metropolitans are elected by an Electoral Assembly of clergy, monks, and laity (Charter 62–63).

[106] UK: *Buckley v Cahal Daly* [1990] NIJB 8: the case concerned the effects of the incardination of a priest under Roman Catholic canon law; for the right to ordain, see eg Czech Rep: CFRF, Art 16.2; ordination is generally dealt with by their internal instruments: Cyprus: Charter, Art 63. However, for a rare definition of 'clergy', see Austria: VwGH (Slg 9491/1913): 'a person who is a teacher of religious doctrine and advisor in religious matters, who supervises the services and rituals, who is entrusted with the office of preaching, the administration of services and decisions in ritual questions, and who finally has to administer the register, is to be regarded as clergy'.

[107] Belgium: Const, Art 21.

whether they are public law corporations or civil law associations.[108] Nevertheless, alongside this freedom there may occasionally be a duty on the religious organization to notify the State of prescribed appointments—but this is rare. For example, in Austria, whereas there is no State involvement in the appointment of ministers by the Protestant Church,[109] the Catholic Church must notify the Federal government as to the name of the candidate to be appointed to a bishopric—but the State cannot veto the appointment.[110]

By way of contrast, in a small number of countries certain senior religious appointments must be approved by the State: for instance, the bishop of the single Catholic diocese in Luxembourg must be a citizen nominated by the Pope but approved by the government.[111] State approval is more prevalent in national or established churches—but even here, the churches enjoy a degree of autonomy in the form of a right to nominate. The clergy of the Danish folk church are appointed by the Minister for Ecclesiastical Affairs after nomination by a parish council.[112] Bishops and other senior clergy in the Church of England are nominated by the church but appointed by the Monarch on prime ministerial advice; yet there is greater autonomy with respect to the appointment of parish clergy—here the State is not involved.[113] However, in Finland, bishops of the national Evangelical Lutheran Church are no longer appointed by the President but by a process of election carried out within the church;[114] moreover, the Finnish courts have upheld the refusal of a diocesan chapter to appoint a curate on the basis of his opposition to the ordination of women as priests.[115] Appointment disputes in the Orthodox Church often arise in State courts in Greece.[116] The State is far more

[108] Germany: GG, Art 140; WRV, Art 137.3.
[109] Austria: ProtestantG 1961.
[110] Austria: Concordat, Art 4: the government may impose conditions, but if no agreement is reached, the Holy See may freely appoint the candidate. See also Poland: eg the Orthodox Church must notify (Law 4 July 1991) as must the Pentecostal Church (Law 20 February 1997); agreements with the Holy See in Estonia, Latvia, Lithuania, Poland, and Slovakia also provide for notification to the State of the free appointment of bishops by the Pope.
[111] Luxembourg: Law of 1873; the bishop has legal personality: Law of 13 May 1981; the diocese was raised to an archbishopric by the Pope in 1988. Moreover, the Catholic Archbishop of Strasbourg and the Bishop of Metz (in the eastern departments) are appointed by the head of state in France.
[112] Denmark: Act on Civil Servants, no 678/1998; bishops are crown appointees on election by the church.
[113] England: Appointment of Bishops Act 1533; Suffragan Bishops Act 1534; for cathedral deans, see Cathedrals Measure 1999; for parish clergy, see Patronage (Benefices) Measure 1986.
[114] Finland: Act to Amend Church Act 2001, Ch 6, s 1; offices are held only by Evangelical-Lutherans.
[115] Finland: the chapter ruled that the candidate was unsuitable as a vicar in a parish where 3 of the 8 ministers were women; this was upheld due to the constitutional principle of sexual equality which also applied to the State church: Supreme Administrative Court, 23 September 2001 (Deposit no 2260); see also SC, 19 January 2001 (no 88/DNo S 99/1215); and Turku Administrative Court, 13 June 2007 (no 00362/07/2302).
[116] Greece: COS, Decision no 1175/1975; appointment of an abbot and regulation of monastery administration: Decision no 2403/1965; decision of the Permanent Holy Synod to reject an appeal against the election of an abbot: Decision no 688/1977. However, after notification to the Minister of Education and Cults, the election of archbishops is published by presidential decree.

involved in the appointment of ministers of religion who provide spiritual care in public institutions (see Chapter 8).

The civil law status of ministers of religion: There are three basic approaches to the status of ministers of religion for the purposes of State employment law. Each approach is directly relevant to the issue of autonomy. At one end of the spectrum are those States in which ministers of religion are not considered to be employees and do not function under a contract of employment. This allows a considerable amount of autonomy for religious organizations with respect to the conditions of service applicable to their ministers of religion. It is a long-settled matter that a minister of religion does not function under a contract of employment in the separation systems of France, Ireland, and the Netherlands.[117] In the Netherlands, ministers of religion have traditionally been regarded as office-holders not employees, on the basis that the essential element of subordination is absent; however, whilst this position has been affirmed by the Supreme Court,[118] Islamic imams have been treated by the courts as employees,[119] and ministers in public institutions (such as the armed forces or prisons) have been held to be civil servants.[120] A similar trend is discerned in the state-church system of the United Kingdom over the classical common law doctrine that religious ministry and the existence of a contract of employment are incompatible.[121] Today, ministers of both established and non-established religions may be employees if there is a clear contractual intent as to their terms and conditions of service, though religious doctrine may be relevant to determine whether such intent exists;[122] and this may represent 'a growing loss of autonomy on the part of religious bodies'.[123]

Secondly, there are national laws which allow for the existence of contracts of employment for ministers of religion if their religious organizations choose the structures of civil employment law in this regard. This is the case in States of central and eastern Europe. Secular employment law may apply on the basis of religious organizations opting in to the civil system. For example, Estonian employment law applies to ministers of religion provided this is prescribed by the statutes of their religious organization.[124] There are similar special employment regimes applicable

---

[117] France: so the courts are not competent to review decisions of a bishop in suspending a priest: *Cour de Cassation*, 1912—no citation: G Robbers (ed), *State and Church in the European Union* (Baden-Baden: Nomos, 2nd edn, 2005) 175; Ireland: *Wright v Day* [1895] 2 IR 337; *O'Dea v O'Briain* [1992] ILRM 364; *Millen v Presbyterian Church in Ireland* [2000] ELR 292.

[118] Netherlands: HR, 30 May 1986, NJ 1986, 702 (imam); HR, 14 June 1991, NJ 1992, 173.

[119] Netherlands: HR, 17 June 1994, RVDW 136.

[120] Netherlands: Rb Assen, 23 March 1993 (unreported). See generally Ch 8 below.

[121] UK: *Re Employment of Church of England Curates* [1912] 2 Ch 563; *President of the Methodist Conference v Parfitt* [1984] QB 368; *Davies v Presbyterian Church of Wales* [1986] 1 WLR 323.

[122] UK: *Percy v Board of National Mission of the Church of Scotland* [2006] 1 AC 28; and *New Testament Church of God v Stewart* [2008] ICR 282.

[123] J Rivers, *The Law of Organized Religions* (Oxford: OUP, 2010) 146: it may also represent 'religious partiality on the part of the State in favour of those religions which share the predominant secular values and against those which are more traditional or just different'. See J Duddington, 'God, Caesar and the employment rights of ministers of religion' (2007) Law and Justice 129 for recent developments concerning the application of employment rights to all ministers of religion.

[124] Estonia: Employment Contracts Act 1992, RT I 1992, 15, 241; RT I 2000, 25, 144, Art 7; clergy of the Evangelical Lutheran Church do not have employment contracts; their stipends are paid

to religious organizations in Lithuania, Hungary, and Slovakia.[125] Such arrangements are not entirely incompatible with religious autonomy in so far as entry into them represents an exercise of autonomy. However, opting into a civil employment regime may expose a religious organization to intervention on the part of the courts of the State in the administration and enforcement of such contracts. Nevertheless, in Austria, which has this system, the courts will generally uphold the freedom of the religious organization in the formation of employment contracts, they will enforce ministerial contracts, and they will interpret them with respect for its autonomy, internal statutes, and self-understanding of the ministry in question.[126] National insurance benefits for ministers of religion are also common across Europe.[127]

Thirdly, in a small number of States, some clergy have the status of civil servants. This is the case in some northern state-church systems such as Denmark, where clergy of the national church are classified as civil servants, and their employment relations are governed by special law.[128] The same applies in Finland to ministers of the national Lutheran and Orthodox churches,[129] and in Greece the State pays the salaries of the ministers of the Orthodox Church and in Thrace those of three official Muslim religious leaders.[130] At the same time, however, countries without a state church also use this model: in Luxembourg ministers of religion are civil servants and are paid salaries and pensions by the State.[131] In such cases autonomy is, on the face of it, less visible in so far as religious organizations are dependent on the State for the status and remuneration of their ministers. As will be seen in Chapter 8, the State is far more involved in its own contractual relations with, and

by the Board of Congregation; see also Cyprus: clergy may be employed and there are rules on their salaries: eg Charter of Orthodox Church, Arts 52, 75–79.

[125] Lithuania: LORCA; Hungary: Act 80/1997, s 26; Slovakia: Labour Code (Act no 311/2001 Zz).

[126] Austria: OGH Arb coll 9490/1976, OGH, 16 September 1987, 9 Ob A 71/87; conflicts between a religious organization and its ministers as to employment contracts may be entertained by State courts, but all preliminary matters (such as the validity of removal from office, retirement, discipline, and transfer) are excluded from the jurisdiction of the court: OGH SZ 47/135/1974, SZ 60/80/1987; for interpretation in the light of Const, Art 15 (autonomy), see ArbVG, s 132.4; the law on industrial relations is not applicable to the denominational purposes of recognized religious societies.

[127] Lithuania: Law of 1 January 2000; Hungary: Act 80/1997, s 26; Slovakia: Labour Code (Act no 311/2001 Zz); Portugal: social security benefits: Regulation-Decree no 5/83, 31 January 1983; see also Austria: ASVG-Social Security Act 1955, s 5.1.7; Ireland: *Mulloy v Minister for Education* [1975] IR 88: the Supreme Court held that a minister of religion, like any other person, may count service teaching overseas towards his pension; denial of this was a breach of Const, Art 44.2.3.

[128] Denmark: Act on Civil Servants, no 678/1998; see also Act on Employment in Positions in the Folk Church, no 310/1990.

[129] Finland: for Lutherans, Church Code, Part II, chs 5 and 6; see also Act to Amend the Church Act 2001, Ch 6, s 1; and Orthodox Act no 179 1970; in both churches ministers are in 'full-time permanent employment' (not under contract); Orthodox Church ministers are civil servants of the Central Church Board but there is a proposal for them to have contracts of employment.

[130] Greece: Treaty of Lausanne 1923.

[131] Luxembourg: Const, 1868, Art 106, pensions, and Art 126, salaries; see also Germany: ministers of religious public corporations are civil servants.

remuneration of, ministers of religion who provide spiritual care externally, that is, in its public institutions.

The functions of ministers of religion: Unsurprisingly, States do not generally have a great deal of interest in the operational activities of ministers of religion.[132] However, occasionally national laws impose duties on the State and its citizens which are specifically owed to ministers of religion in the performance of aspects of their functions, such as a prohibition on the State preventing them from corresponding with their superiors,[133] or an obligation on others not to obstruct or hinder them in the exercise of their spiritual functions.[134] Sometimes national laws may also confer specific political rights, exercisable by ministers of religion outside their faith communities in wider civil society. One such right is the freedom to engage in politics, which may include the right to be elected to parliament;[135] though it has been held by the German Federal Constitutional Court that a religious organization may freely deny its own ministers the right to stand for public office while they exercise religious ministry.[136] However, in Belgium ministers of religion cannot be admitted to parliament or other public office,[137] and in Portugal they cannot hold political appointments.[138] There are also sometimes special exemptions (or privileges) for ministers of religion, such as relief from the fulfilment of legal duties incompatible with their spiritual functions,[139] attendance in court to give evidence,[140] jury service (in States with jury systems),[141] and compulsory military service.[142]

Equally, ministers of religion are only occasionally the object of special disabilities under civil law. France is notable in this regard, but the disabilities date from

---

[132] Ministerial functions are left to the regulatory instruments of religious organizations; eg Portugal, LORF, Arts 20–23: all faith communities may designate functions for their ministers. See, however, Ch 9 below for laws on ministers and their solemnization of marriages.

[133] Belgium: Const, Art 21.1.

[134] UK: Offences Against the Person Act 1861, s 36; Criminal Law Act 1967, s 1: it is an offence to obstruct, by threats or force, any clergyman or other minister in or from celebrating divine service or otherwise officiating in any church or other place of divine worship; see also Luxembourg: PC, Art 145; Netherlands: PC, Art 147; Belgium: PC, Art 145.

[135] UK: the House of Commons (Clergy Disqualification) Act 1801was repealed by the House of Commons (Clergy Disqualification) Act 2001 thereby allowing clergy to serve; see also Government of Wales Act 1998, s 13(1)(b); Scotland Act 1998, s 16(1)(b); Denmark: Const, Art 30.2: this applies to clergy of the national church—but normally the person must apply for leave to serve: Act on Civil Servants, s 58; Ireland: there is no exclusion under Electoral Act 1992, s 41.

[136] Germany: CCt, BVerfGE 42, 312; for the civil right: GG, Art 33.3.

[137] Belgium: Const, Art 181 (parliament); Law of 12 January 1973, Art 107 (local councils); Law of 28 June 1983, Art 35 (office of auditor); for judicial office, see CCP, Art 293.1, and European Commission for Human Rights, *Demeester v Belgium*, Journal des Tribunaux, 1982, p 524; in Italy they are ineligible for the office of mayor.

[138] Portugal: Law 14/79, 16 May, Art 6.1; DL 701-B/76, 20 September.

[139] Poland: Law of 1989, Art 12.

[140] Spain: Act of Criminal Procedure, Art 263: 'in relation to information that they were privy to in the exercise of their functions in their ministry'; Austria: Criminal Procedure Law, s 151.1; Civil Procedure Law, s 320.2; General Administration Procedure Law, s 48.2.

[141] Belgium: CCP, Art 224.6; Ireland: ministers are excused from jury service: Juries Act 1976; Portugal: jury service (Concordat 2004, Art 6).

[142] See Ch 2 above.

earlier periods of anti-clericalism: ministers of religion cannot receive gifts or legacies from sick persons for whom they provide spiritual care during a final illness; celebrate a religious marriage prior to a civil one; conduct burials without State administrative authorization; or baptize a child without the consent of the parents concerned.[143] Similarly, whilst they may be prosecuted in the same way as any citizen, sometimes criminal laws specifically address ministers of religion and forbid them, for example, to provoke resistance to the State and its law;[144] to engage in acts of public disorder[145] or other forms of civil disobedience;[146] to agitate against human rights;[147] or to abuse clerical office (particularly in relation to ministry which involves work with children).[148] Rules of this sort point once more to the ambiguity of the principle of autonomy. On the one hand, such rules indicate the limits of religious autonomy. On the other, the paucity of such rules in the national laws, or their general silence on the day-to-day pastoral functions of ministers of religion, indicates clearly the indifference of States towards these matters. It also reflects the operational autonomy of ministers of religion and the extent to which faith communities are free to regulate the activities of their ministers in accordance with their own internal regulatory instruments.

Judicial and quasi-judicial autonomy

All religious organizations employ processes for the resolution of internal disputes, whether through a system of courts or tribunals or some form of quasi-judicial process.[149] A particularly fruitful area to gauge the judicial and quasi-judicial autonomy of religious organizations is that of the discipline of ministers of religion. In state-church systems, the tribunals of the national church may be subject to the supervisory jurisdiction of the courts of the State to ensure that the principles of

---

[143] France: CC, Art 909; a case from Liège, 5 May 1909, DP II.2.364: a grandmother had a child baptized without the consent of the widowed father and was ordered to pay token damages. Nor can ministers teach in primary schools: Laws of 1882, 1886, and 1904; CE, 10 May 1912: held that a cleric be barred from the competition for qualification as a teacher in public secondary schools—the decision dealt with education not employment, at the height of anti-clericalism of the Third Republic.

[144] France: Law of 9 December 1905, Art 35.1; see Cass Crim, 17 May 1907: DP 1907, 1, p 273; see also Cass Crim, 4 January 1912: Bull Crim, no 2; Cass Crim, 5 August 1915: Bull Crim, no 168; defamation by a minister of cult of a citizen charged with a public service is a crime punishable with a fine of €25,000 and/or imprisonment for up to 1 year: Law of 1905, Art 34.

[145] France: PC, Alsace-Moselle, Art 130.

[146] Luxembourg: PC, Art 268: any minister who in a public assembly, or in written pastoral instructions, attacks the government, law, or other act of a public authority, is punishable with imprisonment for 8 days to 3 months and a fine of €251–5,000; Belgium: PC, Art 268: this is identical—there were no prosecutions during the 20th century; some see it as incompatible with ECHR, Arts 9 and 10.

[147] Czech Rep: the Ministry of Culture may withdraw the registration of any denomination engaged in systematic agitation against human rights: Act no 3/2002, ss 21 and 22.

[148] Greece: PC, Art 196 (abuse of office), Art 342.1 (child abuse); Spain: Concordat 1976, Art II: a Catholic bishop must be notified if a cleric is charged with a crime.

[149] For Christian churches, see eg N Doe, 'Modern church law' in Witte and Alexander (n 78 above) 279 *et seq*; see eg Catholic Code of Canon Law 1983, cc 1400–1752 (processes, trials and tribunals); in Judaism, the *bet din* (literally 'house of law') is a court composed of rabbis, and Islam has its *mahkamah* (or place of judgment).

natural justice are satisfied in ministerial discipline cases; this is the position in England[150] and Denmark,[151] but disciplinary processes in the Finnish national church have been subject to criticism by Strasbourg.[152] In Greece, the Council of State has a supervisory jurisdiction over the Orthodox Church in matters which concern administration; it may determine the competence of the church body to decide the matter and ensure that the decision complies with State law.[153] However, the Council of State has no jurisdiction over matters which relate to doctrine or worship, or those which have 'spiritual and purely religious content' (such as a decision about the suitability of a candidate for ordination).[154] The Council of State has held that the decisions of the ecclesiastical courts are reviewable in so far as they are disciplinary bodies,[155] and it has reviewed cases involving the transfer and dismissal of clergy.[156]

Even countries with a separation or cooperation system of religion-state relations are not wholly indifferent to the practices of religious courts and other bodies with quasi-judicial functions in the field of ministerial discipline.[157] The general principle is that religious organizations may discipline their ministers in accordance with their own statutes or other internal regulatory instruments.[158] If a religious disciplinary body violates these, its decision may be reviewed by the courts of the State; this has occurred in Belgium.[159] The matter may be addressed within the framework of employment law; for instance the Slovakian Constitutional Court has held that labour law disputes between a Catholic priest and the church come under the jurisdiction of the State courts.[160] Indeed, in the separation system of the

---

[150] UK: for the Church of England, Clergy Discipline Measure 2003: clergy misconduct; for doctrine cases and other proceedings, under the Ecclesiastical Jurisdiction Measure 1963, and the extent to which the church courts are subject to the supervisory jurisdiction of the HC, see M Hill, *Ecclesiastical Law* (Oxford: OUP, 3rd edn, 2007) chs 6–7.

[151] Denmark: cases are brought in the Episcopal court eg on doctrinal discipline; its decisions may be challenged in the HC (with three theological experts); in other matters trial is in a Priests' Court whose members are chosen by lot from a list prepared by the Minister for Ecclesiastical Affairs; cases on bishops are tried in the HC with appeal to the SC: Act on Doctrinal Cases, no 336/1992; see also P Garde, 'Triple loyalties of a clergyman in the national church of Denmark' (2001) 8 EJCSR 21.

[152] *Launikari v Finland* App no 34120/96 (ECtHR, 5 October 2000).

[153] See Ch K Papastathis, 'Religious self-administration in the Hellenic Republic' in Robbers (n 13 above) 427.

[154] Greece: COS, Decision nos 491/1940, 583/1940: the Council declined jurisdiction to question refusal of a metropolitan to ordain a person on the basis of spiritual unsuitability; if a matter has both an administrative and a spiritual dimension, its administrative aspects are reviewable: no 5456/1978.

[155] Greece: COS, Decision nos 195/1987, 825/1988; no 1534/1992: annulling a bishop's court decision.

[156] Greece: COS, Decision no 5761/1974: transfer; no 824/1949: discharge; no 1665/1949, 507/ 1983, and no 4625/1985: dismissal; see also no 669/1949: refusal of a metropolitan council to grant credit for the payment of wages to a parish priest; no 688/1977: decision of the Permanent Holy Synod which rejected an appeal against the election of an abbot.

[157] Indeed, some formally recognize their matrimonial jurisdictions: eg Cyprus: Const, Art 111: matters which relate to the marriage discipline of its members are governed by the law of the Greek Orthodox Church and are subject to the jurisdiction of its tribunals: see Ch 9 below.

[158] Latvia: LORO, Art 14; Cyprus: the Holy Synod of the Orthodox Church, acting as a tribunal, may depose clergy: Charter, Art 22.

[159] See n 73 above.

[160] Slovakia: CCt, Decision no III US 64/00 (31 January 2001).

Netherlands the decision of a religious authority to dismiss a minister of religion is unlawful if made in bad faith.[161] By way of contrast, the Czech Constitutional Court has rejected the claim that State courts have jurisdiction in disputes about the dismissal of clergy and other pastoral workers of religious communities; the matter is regulated by the internal rules of the religious communities themselves and it is for the relevant authorities of these communities to determine the capacity of their officers for ministry.[162] The same reluctance is found in the United Kingdom in relation to voluntary religious associations, on the basis that ministerial discipline in these is a private law matter.[163] An agreement with the Holy See is the basis for State deference to discipline within the Catholic Church in Spain: 'The Spanish State recognizes and respects the exclusive legal authority of the Church Courts over those offences which exclusively violate an ecclesiastical law in accordance with Canon Law. Civil authorities shall have no right to appeal sentences served by Church Courts.'[164]

Autonomy and confidentiality

Needless to say, the administration of the internal affairs of a religious organization often necessitates the passing of confidential information;[165] and some Christian churches forbid the disclosure of secrets obtained by a priest in the rite of confession.[166] The extent to which religious organizations enjoy freedom to control such confidential information goes to the heart of their autonomy. However, national laws on this subject illustrate well the balance which States may need to strike between their respect for religious autonomy and the limits sometimes placed on it.

States generally forbid the disclosure of secrets obtained in the exercise of religious ministry. Whilst this is consistent with religious autonomy, the basis on which they do so differs from country to country. The prohibition is often found in laws specifically applicable to ministers of religion. This is the case, but not

---

[161] Netherlands: HR, 15 March 1985, NJ 1986, 191.

[162] Czech Rep: CCt, 26 March 1997 no I US 211/96: but they may hear cases on ministerial salaries (Civic Judicial Process Rules (Act no 99/1963 Sb)); see also *Dudová and Duda v Czech Republic*, App no 40224/98 (ECtHR, 30 January 2001); see also Hungary: CCt, Decision 32/2003 (VI.4) AB: the courts cannot intervene in a dispute between a bishop and a pastor: see B Schanda, 'Church and state in Hungary in 2003' (2004) 11 EJCSR 99.

[163] UK: *R v Chief Rabbi, ex p Wachmann* [1992] 1 WLR 1036: the court declined to intervene by way of public law judicial review in a discipline case concerning a rabbi as it was a private matter.

[164] Spain: Agreement with the Holy See, 28 July 1976 (ratified 19 August 1976), Art II.4; cf the position in Italy: see n 74 above.

[165] For the processing of data by religious organizations, see Ch 2 above.

[166] See eg the Catholic Church, Code of Canon Law 1983, c 983: 'The sacramental seal is inviolable. Accordingly, it is absolutely wrong for a confessor in any way to betray the penitent, for any reason whatsoever, whether by word or in any other fashion'; for the seal of the confession in Anglicanism, see N Doe, *Canon Law in the Anglican Communion* (Oxford: OUP, 1998) 291 *et seq*; for private confession in Orthodoxy, see T Ware, *The Orthodox Church* (London: Penguin Books, 1991) 295 *et seq*; for a recent report in the Lutheran Church of Sweden, see *Ett skyddat rum: tystnadsplikt I Svenska kyrkan* (*A Safe Place: Professional Secrecy in the Church of Sweden*), Church of Sweden Reports 2010:3.

exclusively, in countries with a state church. In Finland, a priest of the Lutheran church is forbidden to reveal a secret received in confession and in the course of pastoral counselling; a similar rule applies to Orthodox priests.[167] In Denmark, the same prohibition applies both to clergy of the national church (on the basis that they are civil servants), and to ministers of other religions (when they perform public functions).[168] Priests of the former established Church of Sweden used to be subject to a similar rule,[169] but this was abolished in 2000.[170] Likewise, Portuguese law used to protect the seal of the confessional in the Catholic Church, but this special protection was abolished in 1982.[171] The general prohibition is also found in States with no state church: in Estonia, Romania, and the Czech Republic ministers of religion must not disclose information received in the course of private confession or pastoral conversation, nor must they disclose the identity of the person providing it.[172] However, the majority of States protect religious secrets by rules applicable to professional secrets generally, which may also cover ministers of religion. This is the case in the separation system of France,[173] and in most cooperation systems.[174]

Moreover, in a small number of States ministers of religion may be exempt from the duty to report crimes to the relevant public authorities when they have knowledge of these on the basis of information gained as a result of religious ministry. This is the case in the Czech Republic,[175] and in Austria there is a defence to breach of the duty to report for those who learn of such crimes through information confided to them in their capacity as spiritual advisers.[176] By way of contrast, according to Finnish law, if a Lutheran priest learns about a serious offence, the priest must encourage the penitent to inform the relevant authorities; if the penitent does not do so, the priest must inform the victim or the police but without indicating the identity of the penitent.[177]

Similarly, the duty to testify as a witness in court is often relaxed with regard to information received in the course of religious ministry.[178] Various approaches are

---

[167] Finland: Church Law 1993, Ch 5, s 2; and PC, Ch 38, s 1.
[168] Denmark: Strfl, para 152 b, stk 1; see also Greece: PC, Art 371.1: breach of confidentiality.
[169] Sweden: PC (BrB), 20:3; Church Act 1992:300, 36:1.
[170] Sweden: Church of Sweden Act 1998:1592, Art 2.
[171] Portugal: PC, 1852, Art 136 § 1; Law no 4/71 created a new crime of violation of religious secrecy applicable to any religion (Art 20); this was abrogated by DL no 400/82 (Art 6.2).
[172] Estonia: CCA, Art 22; Czech Rep: CRSL, Act no 3/2002 Sb; Romania: Law no 489/2006.
[173] France: PC, Art 226-13; Cass Crim, 4 December 1891, *Fay*: Bull Crim, no 239; DP 1892, 1, p 139. For other cases, see the studies in J Flauss-Diem (ed), *Secret, Religion, Normes Étatiques* (Strasbourg: Presses Universitaires de Strasbourg, 2005) Part 1.
[174] Spain: PC, Art 199: disclosure is penalized by a prison sentence of 1 to 3 years, and/or a fine; Italy: PC, Art 622; C Cass no 8635/1996; Code of Criminal Procedure, Art 200; Bulgaria, PC, Art 145 (1); the penalty is imprisonment for up to 1 year or a fine of 300 BGN; Hungary: PC, para 177; see also Act 4/1978, 137.2.j; Belgium: PC, Art 458: this forbids disclosure by 'persons who because of their function or profession have knowledge of secrets that have been confided to them'; Luxembourg: PC, Art 458: penalty—6 months in prison and/or a fine of €500–5,000.
[175] Czech Rep: PC, s 167; Hungary: PC, para 177; Spain: Law of 14 September 1882, Art 263.
[176] Austria: PC, para 286; see also France, PC, Arts 234, 434, 226.
[177] Finland: Church Law 1993, Ch 5, s 2; and PC, Ch 38, s 1.
[178] Bulgaria: RDA, Art 13: 'The confidentiality of confession is inviolable. No clergyman shall be forced to testify or disclose information about facts and circumstances that became known during confession'; Czech Rep: CRSL (Act no 3/2002); Slovakia: CCP, para 130 (Law n 301/2005); Spain: Law of 14 September 1882, Arts 417.1 and 707.

used. In some States the courts and other public authorities are forbidden to examine ministers of religion. This is the case in Portugal for Catholic priests on the basis of an agreement with the Holy See: they 'may not be asked by magistrates or other authorities about facts and things of which they obtained knowledge because of their ministry'; a similar rule is found in the law applicable to ministers of other religions.[179] The same basic position applies to religious organizations which have an agreement with the State (for example in Italy), and those with statutes applicable to them (for example in Latvia and Poland).[180] Indeed, in Austria, spiritual advisers must not be interrogated as witnesses in criminal, civil, administrative, or taxation proceedings, or in proceedings of the Constitutional Court or High Administrative Court, with regard to information obtained in confession or in their capacity as spiritual advisers. What constitutes a 'spiritual adviser' for these purposes is determined on the basis of the self-understanding of the religious organization concerned, and any examination which interferes with these provisions is either void or a ground of appeal.[181] In each of these States the law provides a very high level of ministerial autonomy.

However, under Belgian law, if ministers of religion are summoned to testify in court or before a parliamentary committee of investigation, the law obliges them to disclose religious secrets; failure to do so may lead to a prison sentence (of eight days to six months) and a fine.[182] Similarly, in Finland the general prohibition against disclosure by a priest of the national Evangelical Lutheran Church may be overridden in criminal proceedings if the offence to which the disclosure relates is one which carries a minimum sentence of six years' imprisonment; there are no rules prohibiting disclosure for other ministers of religion, nor protection against testifying in court.[183] Under Estonian law, clergy must testify if their testimony is requested by the accused or is not related to ministerial or professional activities of support staff.[184] In the United Kingdom, too, priest-penitent communications are not privileged;[185] but in criminal proceedings, it is unlikely that a trial judge would require evidence of a confession made to a priest.[186]

Nevertheless, even in States which protect religious secrets, the law may allow the person confessing to consent to disclosure by the cleric.[187] Moreover, in Lithuania

---

[179] Portugal: Concordat, Art 5; LORF, Law no 16/2001 of 22 June, Art 16.2; see also Lithuania: Agreement with the Holy See, Art 8; and Slovakia: Concordat with the Holy See, Art 8.

[180] Italy: Code of Criminal Procedure, Art 200; Latvia: Seventh Day Adventist Church, Law no 93 (3669), 12 June 2007; CCP, s 106; Law on Criminal Procedure, s 121; Law on Administrative Procedure, s 163; Poland: Code of Criminal Procedure, Art 178; CA Krakow, Decision of 1 January 1995, II Akz 237/95, KZS 1995/6/36; SC, 1 KZP 1/91, OSNKW 1992, 7–8/46.

[181] Austria: CCP, Art 320 (for appeal, Art 321); Code of Criminal Procedure, Art 151 (for nullity, Arts 281, 345); see also Luxembourg: Cass Crim, 21 March 1957, P 17, p 43.

[182] Belgium: PC, Art 458.

[183] Finland: Church Law 1993, Ch 5, s 2; PC, Ch 38, s 1.

[184] Estonia: Code of Criminal Procedure, Art 72; RT I 2003, 27, 166.

[185] Hill (n 150 above) para 5.62.

[186] Police and Criminal Evidence Act 1984, ss 76, 78, 82(3): there is a discretion to admit/exclude.

[187] Ireland: *Cook v Carroll* [1945] IR 515; *Forristal v Forristal and O'Connor* (1966) 100 ILTR 182; *ER v JR* [1981] ILRM 125; *Pais v Pais* [1970] 3 DPP 830; Law Reform Commission Report on Contempt of Court (LRC 47–1994) para 4.21; *Johnson v Church of Scientology* [2001] 1 IR 682,

the agreement with the Holy See provides that: 'Upon the instigation of criminal procedures against a member of the clergy, the relevant [secular] legal institutions, in consideration of the pastoral responsibility [of the religious organization] for the faithful, shall inform the competent ecclesiastical authority thereof, provided it does not negatively affect the investigation process.'[188] Under Polish law, protection against disclosure does not apply when the priest is the accused or a suspect.[189] Some States have special provisions applicable to disclosures which concern children. In Belgium, when a minor is the victim of listed crimes and confides in a minister of religion, and a serious and imminent danger exists for the mental or physical integrity of the child, from which the child cannot protect himself (either alone or with the help of others), the minister is allowed to report the offence to the public prosecutor.[190]

Conclusion

All States in Europe recognize the autonomy of religious organizations. Moreover, all States must respect the autonomy of a religious organization regardless of its legal position and whether it has or does not have legal personality. National laws are agreed that autonomy is the right of a religious organization to govern its own internal affairs. The rationale for autonomy varies from State to State: its foundation in most is the collective right to religious freedom, and in many it is rooted in the separation of state and religion; but the private character of religion and the self-understanding of the religious organization may also act as the basis of autonomy. States generally tend to the view of religious autonomy as conceded rather than inherent. This leads to an apparent paradox: the independence of religious organizations is dependent in large measure on the State and its cooperation with religion in this matter. Above all, the principle of autonomy forbids the State to interfere in the internal affairs of religious organizations. But this is not an absolute duty: the State may intervene on the basis of explicit and implicit limits which are lawful, necessary, and proportionate; and there is growing debate as to whether human rights apply within religious organizations.

It is often very difficult to identify what constitutes the internal affairs of a religious organization for the purpose of defining its autonomy. So often those affairs are of a type in which the State has an interest. However, as a general

---

[2001] 2 ILRM 110. Sweden: the decision of the Svea Appeal Court to hear a priest as to a confession on the request of a defendant was criticized by the Justice Ombudsman: Decision of 16 June 1993.

[188] Lithuania: Agreement with the Holy See, Art 8; Latvia, Agreement with the Holy See, Art 7.

[189] Poland: Code of Penal Procedure 1997, Art 178; Code of Civil Procedure 1964, Art 261; Decision of the Appeal Court in Kraków, 1 January 1995, II Akz 237/95, KZS 1995/6/36; as defined by the Supreme Court (I KZP 1/91, OSNKW 1992, 7–8/46); CCP, Art 261.2.

[190] Belgium: PC, Art 458: the offences against minors are sexual assault, rape, murder, manslaughter, offences involving bodily harm, female genital mutilation, abandonment, and neglect.

principle, religious organizations enjoy institutional autonomy. They are free to legislate: regardless of the religion-state model at work, some of their regulatory instruments require express State approval or else tacit State approval in the sense that generally they must not be inconsistent with State law; but systems of religious law (for example Canon Law, Jewish Law, or Islamic Law) need no State approval. They are free in the field of administration: all religious organizations may freely appoint their ministers of religion, or, in the case of some state-churches, nominate these for appointment by State authorities; States differ when they classify ministers of religion as office-holders, employees, or civil servants; and States do not have a great deal of interest in the operational functions of ministers of religion. They are also free to adjudicate on matters of ministerial discipline, but States differ as to whether this is subject to review in State courts. There is generally a high level of autonomy as to ministerial confidentiality; they must not disclose confidential information gained in the course of ministry, and in most States they are under no legal duty to reveal such information in proceedings in State courts—but this may be qualified. In short, the extent to which religious organizations are autonomous depends in part upon the religion-state model at work in a country, but more usually upon the activity for which the faith community claims its autonomy. The fundamental principle which emerges is that religious organizations are autonomous to the extent permitted by the law of the State. Autonomy is but one aspect of the mutual inter-dependence of State and religion.

6

The Protection of Doctrine and Worship

Doctrine and worship are of central importance to most religious faiths. Doctrine may be understood as beliefs, tenets of faith, or teaching derived from or contained in a sacred text itself conceived as a deposit of revelation. Worship is reverence to a deity, acts of devotion, and other rituals generated by religious faith and doctrine. Earlier chapters have shown that States of Europe are not indifferent to religious doctrine and worship. Both have a pivotal role in the definitions of religion in national laws. The intellectual acceptance of doctrine is part of the right to hold a religious belief. Freedom to teach and to worship is fundamental to the right to manifest religion. Discrimination on grounds of religious belief is unlawful. Bodies with a religious ethos may discriminate in prescribed circumstances on doctrinal grounds. To acquire legal personality, a faith community may be required to satisfy the State that its doctrine and worship are not offensive to public order. The autonomy of religious organizations covers their doctrine and worship. This chapter explores the extent to which national laws in Europe protect the doctrines and worship of faith communities from attacks on them by the State, its citizens, and the media. Its principal focus is the criminal law. It draws out the similarities and differences between national laws in terms of their purpose, definitional elements for liability, defences, and penalties. The chapter also explores the ways in which the media is regulated in its portrayal of religion. National laws which seek to protect religious doctrine and worship tell us much about the value placed on religion by States, and the high level of juridical convergence in this field in terms of common principles. They also raise questions about whether attacks on religion should be subject to a system of punishment. Moreover, crimes against religious doctrine and worship are important not only for the implications they have for freedom of expression, but also for the repercussions they may cause on the wider national and international canvas.[1]

---

[1] The publication in Denmark in 2006 of cartoons depicting the Prophet Mohammed resulted in public disorder and loss of life around the world. Responding to these events, Manuel Barroso, Chair of the European Commission, spoke of the value and non-negotiability of both religious freedom and freedom of expression, as well as the 'clear distinction between politics and religion' in Europe (15 February 2006).

Crimes against religious belief and doctrine

Historically, throughout Europe, criminal laws forbad blasphemy against the Christian religion.[2] The offence still exists in several States.[3] However, in some its survival is a matter of current debate, and in many it has been abolished, to be replaced with the offence of defamation of religion. The objective of these offences is the protection of religious belief and doctrine, though in some countries the law explicitly protects religious feelings. As we have seen with crimes which restrict freedom to hold or manifest religious belief, incitement to religious hatred, and crimes aggravated by religion,[4] in the majority of States offences against religious belief and doctrine are found mainly in Criminal or Penal Codes which may be supplemented by case-law—though there is little jurisprudence in this field.[5] What follows also explores reasons underlying legal reforms on this subject: these often include considerations of free speech—yet Strasbourg has held that although freedom to manifest religion does not entitle religious faith to be exempt from all criticism, freedom of speech contains 'a duty to avoid expressions that are gratuitously offensive to others and profane'.[6] However, what follows does not suggest that criminal offences against the vilification of religion are justified by prohibitions of blasphemy in systems of religious law.[7]

The offence of blasphemy

European States fall into three groups with regard to blasphemy: those with such an offence; those which have abolished it; and those currently discussing abolition. Several States have an offence of blasphemy against God or sacred beliefs. The offence is almost exclusively used in countries with a State church.[8] A common feature of these is that the blasphemy must be public and intentional, and,

---

[2] See generally the introductions to each national report in M Kotiranta and N Doe (eds), *Religion and Criminal Law in Europe*, PECCSR (Leuven: Peeters, 2011).

[3] See, however, the Parliamentary Assembly of the COE, Res 1805 (2007) para 4: 'blasphemy, as an insult to religion, should not be considered a criminal offence'; '[e]ven though today prosecutions in this respect are rare in member states, they are legion in other countries of the world'.

[4] See Chs 2 and 3 above.

[5] However, in the UK the category 'religious offences' is known in Parliament, but not in statute: House of Lords Select Committee on Religious Offences in England and Wales, Report 2003.

[6] *İA v Turkey* App no 42571/98 (ECtHR, 13 September 2005), para 28: 'Those who choose to exercise the freedom to manifest their religion, irrespective of whether they do so as members of a religious majority or a minority, cannot reasonably expect to be exempt from all criticism. They must tolerate and accept the denial by others of their religious beliefs and even the propagation by others of doctrines hostile to their faith'; and para 24; see also *Otto-Preminger Institute v Austria* (1995) 19 EHRR 34.

[7] Blasphemy is forbidden in many religions; see eg the Catholic Church, Code of Canon Law 1983, c 1369; for *birkat ha-shem* (literally 'blessing [euphemism for cursing] the Name [of God]' by a *megaddef* (blasphemer) in Jewish law: L Jacobs, *Concise Companion to the Jewish Religion* (Oxford: OUP, 1999) 19; for *kufr* (a *kāfir* or unbeliever) in Islam: J Schacht, *An Introduction to Islamic Law* (Oxford: OUP, Reprint, 1991) 131; moreover, Christian churches have a system of doctrinal offences.

[8] For separation systems: Netherlands: PC, Art 147: 'scornful blasphemy'; see below for Ireland.

generally, all religions are protected, not simply Christianity. Various formulations are used. In Greece, it is an offence to insult God, publicly and with malicious intent—an insult (which may be oral, written, or in pictures or gestures) consists of lack of respect or contempt for God expressed in a particularly offensive manner; it is not an offence to question the existence of God. All religions are protected.[9] Similarly, in Denmark, 'a person, who publicly mocks or insults the creed or form of worship of any religious community lawfully present in the country, is to be fined with a maximum of 4 months' imprisonment'.[10] In Finland, where the law was reformed in 1998, the penalty for blasphemy against God and blasphemy against sacred beliefs is imprisonment for six months, and this is treated as an offence against public order. Blasphemy against God does not require proof of specific intent on the part of the perpetrator, but proof of specific intent is required for blasphemy against sacred beliefs.[11] However, whereas in Greece and Denmark all religions are protected, it has been understood that in Finland the offence of blasphemy against God applies only to the God of Christianity and not, for example, the many gods of Hinduism—though Hinduism would be protected by the law of blasphemy against sacred beliefs; the case-law is limited, but two cases from the 1960s and 1970s led to convictions.[12]

However, in most States the offence of blasphemy has been abolished. This has happened mainly, but not exclusively, in countries which have a system of separation or cooperation between State and religion. Sometimes abolition has accompanied a move towards separation. Blasphemy against the Catholic religion was abolished in Portugal in 1911 following the introduction of republicanism and a system of separation.[13] By way of contrast, in predominantly Protestant Sweden, blasphemy was abolished in 1970, well before disestablishment of the national church there (in 2000), on the basis that it offended freedom of expression and because religion was in any event protected through other offences.[14] The offence was removed from Austrian law in 1975,[15] and from in Spanish law in 1988;[16] both countries are predominantly Catholic in terms of their religious demography,

---

[9] Greece: PC, Art 198(1).

[10] Denmark: Strfl, para 140; there were several unsuccessful prosecutions in the 1970s and 1980s; the offence originated in a law of 1683.

[11] Finland: PC, Ch 10, 'Breach of the sanctity of religion' (563/1998): 'a person who (1) publicly blasphemes against God, or, for the purpose of offending, publicly defames or desecrates what is otherwise held to be sacred by a church or religious community, as referred to in the Act on the Freedom of Religion (267/1998) . . . . shall be sentenced for a breach of the sanctity of religion to a fine or to imprisonment for at most six months'. Inclusion of a reference to God was hotly debated: Report of the Law Committee, 3/1998; Report of the Constitutional Committee, 23/1997.

[12] K Nuotio, 'Religion in the criminal law of Finland' in M Kotirinata and N Doe (eds), *Religion and Criminal Law* (Leuven: Peeters, 2011) 63, 66; the case of *Hannu Salama* concerned the description of the sexual fantasies of a priest, and that of *Harro Koskinen* the painting of a pig crucified: ibid 68.

[13] Portugal: PC 1852, Art 130; Decree of 15 February 1911, Art 4: this forbad outrage against any dogma, act, or object of the Catholic religion, if made in public or by means of any publication.

[14] Official Government Report—SFS 1970:225. Since 1948 the title of the offence has been 'a crime against the peace of creeds': NJA II 1948, p 359.

[15] Austria: Penal Law Amendment Act 1975.

[16] Spain: Organic Law 5/1988, June 5: this effected abolition through reform of the Penal Code.

and in Spain the definition of blasphemy in case-law reflected this vividly; it involved 'uttering injurious words against God, the Virgin Mary or the Saints'.[17] However, as we shall see below, in all of these States the offence of blasphemy has been replaced by defamation of religion.

On the other hand, in several countries of central and eastern Europe, blasphemy was abolished during communist rule on the basis of its essentially atheistic ideology. The former offence of blasphemy was not then reinstated following the collapse of communism. This occurred, for example, in Hungary, where blasphemy was forbidden by a law of 1878 but abolished in the years of the communist regime by a law which is still operative today.[18] Much the same happened under Bulgarian law, where there was an offence of blasphemy from 1896–1951.[19] Indeed, the Czech Republic justifies its absence of a blasphemy law on the basis of its constitutional prohibition that the State may not align itself to any particular ideology, including religion.[20] Political revolution and the demise of the Catholic Church were also the stimulus for the French abolition of blasphemy in 1791; however, in the eastern department of Alsace-Moselle, a person who causes scandal through public blasphemy against God, or otherwise publicly outrages Christian cults or an established religious community recognized as a corporation, or per-forms injurious and scandalous acts in a place dedicated to religious assemblies, is punishable by up to three years in prison.[21]

However, the abolition of blasphemy has not been confined to countries with a separation or cooperation system of religion-state relations. This is shown in the case of the state-church system of the United Kingdom. Whilst dormant in Scotland,[22] for the purposes of England and Wales blasphemy was abolished by statute in 2008.[23] The position prior to, and the debate ending with, the statute illustrate the very wide range of issues involved in the abolition of the offence of blasphemy. It is for this reason worth devoting a little space to these. At common law, blasphemy was 'an offence to God and to religion, [and] a crime against the laws, state and Government'; since 'Christianity is parcel of the Laws of England', it followed that 'to reproach the Christian religion [was] to speak in subversion of the law'.[24] The offence consisted of publishing 'blasphemous' material in conflict with the tenets of the Church of England and in indecent or offensive terms likely to outrage the feelings of the general body of Church of England believers.[25] The

---

[17] Spain: HC, Circular of 31 January 1945; and HC, Ruling of 24 June 1954.

[18] Hungary: Act V/1878, para 190; see now, Act IV/1978 (PC) para 269/A (national symbols).

[19] See the first Bulgarian Penal Act (1896), Art 204.

[20] Czech Rep: Const, Art 2.

[21] France: Alsace-Moselle, PC, Art 166; the Roman Catholic Church, Reformed Church, the Church of the Augsburg Confession, and Judaism are the four recognized cults to which this applies.

[22] G Maher, 'Blasphemy in Scots law' (1977) SLT 257; the last prosecution was in 1843.

[23] UK: Criminal Justice and Immigration Act 2008, s 79: 'The offences of blasphemy and blasphemous libel under the common law of England and Wales are abolished.' For the process, see R Sandberg and N Doe, 'The strange death of blasphemy' (2008) 71 MLR 971.

[24] *Taylor's Case* (1676) 1 Vent 293. See HL Select Committee Report 2003, Vol I, App 3, para 2.

[25] It could be written or verbal: *R v Gott* (1922) 16 CR App R 87; *R v Ramsay and Foote* (1883) 15 Cox CC 231: blasphemy did not arise 'if the decencies of controversy are observed, even the fundamentals of religion may be attacked'; see also *Bowman v Secular Society Ltd* [1917] AC 406.

extent to which the law protected Christian denominations other than the Church of England was an open question.[26] There was no requirement that the defendant had to intend to blaspheme.[27] On several occasions, claims that the blasphemy law was incompatible with the ECHR were unsuccessful in Strasbourg.[28] However, a report of 2003 concluded that: the offence was a dead-letter; there was no assurance it would continue to be in the 'margin of appreciation' of the United Kingdom and thus compatible with the ECHR; it was uncertain whether the offence applied to the Church of England or Christianity; and it might be discriminatory and its penalties disproportionate.[29] Nevertheless, it was held in 2007 that: the offence still existed; it could be accurately stated; and it was ECHR-compliant (under Article 10 (2))—but statute already prevented prosecution for blasphemy in respect of a play.[30] On 5 March 2008, the Government proposed that the law 'has fallen into disuse' and there was anyway 'new legislation to protect individuals on the grounds of religion and belief' (namely the Racial and Religious Hatred Act 2006).[31] The motion was passed by 148 votes to 87 by the House of Lords and then by 378 votes to 57 in the House of Commons. Blasphemy was abolished.

The possible abolition of the offence of blasphemy is currently on the political agenda in several States. In Denmark, following publication of cartoons depicting Mohammed, there has been recent debate about its abolition,[32] and in Italy, the Catholic Church no longer enjoys special protection with regard to its doctrine.[33] An interesting development comes from Ireland. The constitution provides that the publication or utterance of blasphemous, seditious, or indecent matter is an offence punishable in accordance with law.[34] A film may also be banned as unfit for general exhibition in public by reason of its being blasphemous; this also applies to advertisements for films.[35] Similarly, the composition, printing, or publication of a blasphemous libel is an offence (but 'blasphemous' is not defined).[36] However, prosecutions are rare, and the Irish Constitution Review Group recommended in

[26] Other denominations were protected 'to the extent that their fundamental beliefs [were] those which are held in common with the established Church': *Gathercole's Case* (1838) 2 Lewin 237.

[27] *R v Lemon, R v Gay News* [1979] AC 617.

[28] *Gay News Ltd v UK* (1983) 5 EHRR 123; *Choudhury v UK* (1991) 12 HRLJ 172: 'no State authority or any body under which the United Kingdom Government may be responsible under the Convention, directly interfered in the applicant's freedom to manifest his religion or belief'; see also *Wingrove v UK* (1997) 24 EHRR 1.

[29] HL Select Committee, Report, Religious Offences in England and Wales 2003, App 3, paras 12 and 15.

[30] *Green v The City of Westminster Magistrates Court* [2007] EWHC 2785 (Admin); Theatre Act 1968, s 2(4); see also the Broadcasting Act 1990, Sch 15, para 6 (applicable to the BBC).

[31] HL Hansard (5 March 2008) col 1118.

[32] Denmark: Law 90 2007–08, 2; it is also being debated whether to widen PC, Art 266b on defamation of religion if blasphemy is abolished; see n 1 above concerning the cartoons: no blasphemy prosecution took place.

[33] Italy: CCt, Decision nos 168/2005; 327/2002; 508/2000; 329/1997; 440/1995; see also D Jouvenal, 'Church and state in Italy in 2000' (2001) 8 EJCSR 205, 212 (on PC, Art 402).

[34] Ireland: Const, Art 46.

[35] Censorship of Films Act 1923–1992, s 7; Censorship of Films (Amendment) Act 1925, s 3. Monty Python's *Life of Brian* seems to have been refused a certificate as blasphemous.

[36] Ireland: Defamation Act 1961, s 13(1). That Act also repealed the following relevant legislation: Criminal Libel Act 1819; Law of Libel Amendment Act 1888.

1996 that the constitutional offence of blasphemy should not be retained.[37] Moreover, the Supreme Court held in 1999 that there was no legislative definition of blasphemy and no mechanism to institute a prosecution.[38] Consequently, in debate on the Defamation Bill 2006 there were calls variously for the abolition of blasphemy or for a referendum on whether the constitutional reference to blasphemy should be deleted—neither of these occurred.[39] Instead, under the Defamation Act 2009 it is now a crime to publish or utter blasphemous material grossly abusive or insulting in relation to matters held sacred by any religion, thereby causing outrage among a substantial number of the adherents of that religion; intent to cause such outrage must be proved. It is a defence to prove that a reasonable person would find genuine literary, artistic, political, scientific, or academic value in the material.[40]

Defamation of religion

Rather than an offence of blasphemy, most States today have a wider offence of defamation of religion.[41] Often the rationale for protection of religious doctrine by way of defamation of religion is that of public order rather than overt recognition of any value inherent to the religious doctrine attacked. Moreover, the offences of defamation of religion transcend the three classical models of religion-state relations. Of interest here is that administration of the offences may necessitate an enquiry into the doctrines of religious organizations. Needless to say, in so far as one purpose of these criminal offences is to protect religion, the necessity for such an investigation would not seem to violate the principle of autonomy outlined in Chapter 5, but on the face of it such enquiries would appear to qualify the principle of separation. As with the offence of blasphemy, national laws across Europe use a range of formulations for the defamation of religion. They fall into four basic groups: those which protect all religious doctrines; those which protect the doctrines of prescribed religious organizations; those which do not specify religion as such, but religion comes within the umbrella of general laws on defamation; and those which expressly prohibit defamation against a group or individual on grounds of their religious beliefs.

Austrian law carries an offence of 'disparaging religious doctrines': a person who disparages or derides in public a religious doctrine, and does so in circumstances

---

[37] Ireland: Report of the Constitution Review Group (Dublin 1996) 291–304; see also P O'Higgins, 'Blasphemy in Irish Law' (1960) 23 MLR 151; Law Reform Commission 'Consultation Paper on the Crime of Libel' (August 1991), and 'Report on the Crime of Libel' (LRC 41–1991) (December 1991); see also N Cox, *Blasphemy and the Law in Ireland* (New York: Edwin Mellen Press, 2000).

[38] Ireland: *Corway v Independent Newspapers Ltd* [2000] 1 ILRM 426, 436–7.

[39] In a speech on 20 May 2009 to the Select Committee on Justice, Equality Defence and Women's Rights, the Minister of Justice proposed reform of the law <http://www.justice.ie>.

[40] Ireland: Defamation Act 2009, s 36: religion does not include an organization or cult whose principal object is profit or which uses oppressive psychological manipulation of its followers or recruits.

[41] The UK does not, nor does Cyprus, though there are 'Offences injurious to the public in general: Offences relating to religion', which protect certain religious manifestations: PC, Part IV, Ch 154.

likely to give rise to public nuisance, is punishable with imprisonment;[42] it has been held by Strasbourg that the Austrian crime of disparaging religious doctrines does not offend Article 9 or 10 ECHR.[43] By way of contrast, the laws of some States prohibit defamation only of specified or recognized religions. This is the position in Greece: there is an offence of 'insulting religions', namely, the Eastern Orthodox Church or any other 'known religion' (ie one whose doctrines are not secret). The object of such insult can be any person considered 'sacred' by any religion as well as any ceremony of worship.[44] There is also an offence of insulting acts committed in places of worship.[45] Other States restrict defamation of religion to attacks on the beliefs of religious organizations recognized by the State. Under Italian law, any person who offends a religious confession in public and outrages those who profess it, is to be punished by a fine, which is higher if the outrage is against a minister of religion.[46] Only those religious confessions which have an agreement with the State, or public recognition in an administrative measure, a judicial decision, or by 'common consideration', enjoy this protection; philosophical associations do not enjoy it.[47]

Some States have no specific offence of defamation of religion, though this may be covered indirectly by other laws on defamation.[48] Estonia is typical: there are no provisions specifically dealing with religion; defamation is sufficiently covered by provisions dealing with specific circumstances (for example activities which publicly incite to hatred, violence, or discrimination on the basis of religion).[49] Similarly, Romanian law carries no crime of defamation of religion but the law on insult and libel may be used to protect religion as part of human dignity,[50] as might the law which prohibits acts, words, or gestures in public which affront good morals, cause public scandal, or disturb public peace and order.[51] However, Romanian law on religious freedom and denominations prohibits all forms of slander against religion, as well as public actions offensive to religious symbols; but this legislation provides no sanctions in the event of breach of these prohibitions;[52] the provision on religious symbols was introduced during parliamentary debates.[53] Whilst there is

---

[42] Austria: PC, para 188: imprisonment for up to 6 months or a fine of up to 360 daily rates; see also Germany: PC, para 166: insulting faiths and religious organizations.

[43] Austria: for cases on PC, s 188, see OGH, 19 June 1970, 10 Os 36/70; OGH, 19 December 1985, 11 Os 165/85; in *Otto-Premiger Institut v Austria* (1995) 19 EHRR 34 a wide margin of appreciation for Austria was accepted and it was held that there was no breach of ECHR, Art 10.

[44] Greece: PC, Art 199.

[45] Greece: PC, Art 200(2); see below.

[46] Italy: PC, Art 403: €1,000–1,500, and €2,000–6,000 for an offence to a minister of religion.

[47] Italy: CCt, Decision no 195/1993.

[48] Belgium: ie if it falls under PC, Art 22; Lithuania: PC, Ch 20: crimes against religious liberty.

[49] Estonia: PC, Art 151.1.

[50] Romania: PC, Arts 206–207; due to criticism of these as too restrictive of free speech, the offences were abolished by Law no 278/2006, but this latter law was held unconstitutional: CCt, Decision no 62/2007—as such, both offences continue in force.

[51] Romania: PC, Art 321: proof of intent is required; for distribution, etc of obscene matter, Art 325.

[52] Romania: Law no 489/2006, Art 13.2.

[53] Romania: Opinion 354/2005, adopted at the 64th plenary session, October 2005; see also Reply from Romania, Study no 406/2006 of the European Commission for Democracy through Law

no specific offence of defamation of religion in Luxembourg, defamation of a minister of religion in the exercise of ministry is punishable by sentences ranging from eight days to three months in prison and a fine; it must be proved that the perpetrator intended to defame.[54]

Another approach is to punish defamatory statements against a group or a person made on grounds of their religious beliefs. Once more, offences of this type straddle religion-state models. In the state-church system of Denmark, this offence is in addition to the crime of blasphemy; Danish law criminalizes defamatory statements about a group of persons on the grounds of, *inter alia*, their religion or personal beliefs.[55] This is also the position in Finnish law.[56] The same offence has survived disestablishment of the national church in Sweden.[57] Likewise, in the Dutch separation system the criminal law penalizes as 'serious offences against public order' defamatory statements about a group of persons on the grounds of, *inter alia*, their religion or personal beliefs. The statements must be made 'publicly' and 'intentionally' and may be made orally, in writing, or by image.[58] Nor is the prohibition against both public and private defamation of religion inconsistent with the principle of *laïcité* in France. French law forbids intentional public defamation against a person or group of persons by reason of their membership or non-membership of a determined religion;[59] this also applies to sects, but a simple allegation of membership of a sect does not constitute defamation.[60] The definitional elements of private defamation are almost identical.[61] Private injury (such as by letter) against a person or group by reason of their membership or non-membership, true or supposed, of a determined religion is also punishable in France.[62]

Defamation of a person or group on grounds of their religion is also criminalized in the cooperation systems of central and eastern Europe. The Czech Republic affords this protection to members of denominations whether or not they are registered by the State: a person who publicly defames 'a group of inhabitants of the Republic because of their political conviction, religion or because they are non-denominational, shall be sentenced to a term of imprisonment of up to two years'.[63] Much the same applies in Lithuania, where the law also forbids ridicule

---

(Venice Commission), Annex II to the preliminary report on national legislation in Europe, concerning blasphemy, religious insults, etc: Strasbourg, 23 March 2007, p 67.

[54] Luxembourg: PC, Art 145: by deeds, words, gestures etc; outrage is understood in a general sense: Cour, 5 February 1979, Pasicrisie 24, p 230.

[55] Denmark: Strfl, para 266b; see above for blasphemy under PC, para 140.

[56] Finland: PC, Ch 11, s 8; see above for blasphemy under PC, Ch 10.

[57] Sweden: PC (BrB) 16:8.

[58] Netherlands: PC, Art 137c.

[59] France: Law 29 July 1881 (on the liberty of the press), Art 32; the penalty is imprisonment for up to 1 year and/or a fine of €45,000.

[60] France: CA Paris, 15 May 2002: Juris-data no 180609.

[61] France: PC, Art R 624–3; the penalty is €750; see also Law of 29 July 1881, Art 33.3.

[62] France: PC, Art R 624–4; penalty, €750.

[63] Czech Rep: PC, Ch V, s 198.

on the basis of religion.[64] On the other hand, defamation of religion has been held by the Hungarian Constitutional Court to represent a disproportionate limitation on freedom of expression.[65] Indeed, whilst it accepts that religion must be respected in the exercise of freedom of expression, Strasbourg has held that a conviction under a law on defamation of religion in Slovakia was excessive in the limits it placed on freedom of expression.[66]

Outrage to religious feelings

Far more controversial are those criminal laws in Europe which penalize conduct which offends religious feelings. The incidence of such laws is widespread—and once more it is not distinctive of a particular religion-state model. Religious feelings may be afforded protection on the basis of a law on either blasphemy or defamation of religion. The former is the position in the separation system of the Netherlands: public statements offensive to religious feelings, made orally, in writing, or in images, are penalized as a serious offence against public order. Likewise, ridiculing a church minister in the lawful exercise of his office is penalized.[67] The concept of 'outrage' in Irish blasphemy law also implies conduct offensive to religious feelings.[68] Countries with a cooperation model of religion-state relations generally protect religious feelings by means of defamation of religion. Some Italian commentators justify the prohibition on the basis that religious feelings are part of the 'moral patrimony' of Italy.[69] The Portuguese Penal Code has a section specifically devoted to 'crimes against religious feelings'—these are justified on the basis that they protect both religious liberty and public peace:[70] 'a person who in public offends another person or mocks [them] on grounds of [their] belief or religious practice, in a way likely to disturb public peace, shall be punished with imprisonment up to 1 year or a fine [at the prescribed rate] up to 120 days'.[71] It is understood that this provision was inspired by Swiss law.[72]

As has already been suggested, the administration of these offences may necessitate an enquiry by the courts into religious doctrine. It may also require a court to identify which doctrines are protected and which religious feelings are offended. These matters have been the subject of consideration by the Spanish courts. Spain has a special category of defamation of 'religious sentiments': the law punishes

---

[64] Lithuania: PC, Art 170.1–3; this reinforces Const, Art 25.4: 'Freedom to express convictions and to impart information shall be incompatible with criminal action—incitement of national, racial, religious, or social hatred, violence and discrimination, with slander and misinformation.'

[65] Hungary: CCt, Decision 30/1992 (V 26) AB.

[66] *Klein v Slovak Republic* App no 72208/01 (ECtHR 31 October 2006).

[67] Netherlands: PC, Art 147; see also PC, Art 429: the display of such material on public roads.

[68] Ireland: Defamation Act 2009, s 36; see above.

[69] Italy: PC, Bk II, title IV; for the justification, see E Vitali, 'Religion et droit penal en Italie', in Kotiranta and Doe (n 2 above) 155.

[70] J de Figueiredo Dias (ed), *Comentário Conimbricense do Código Penal. Parte Especial*, II (Coimbra: Coimbra Editora, 1999) 637.

[71] Portugal: PC, Art 251. This version of the article was introduced in 1995.

[72] Portugal: J de Sousa e Brito, 'Religion and criminal law in Portugal', in Kotiranta and Doe (n 2 above) 215, 217.

intentional public defamation, through words, documents, or other written texts, of the dogmas and beliefs of religions so as to offend religious sensibilities.[73] It has been held that this provision applies to religious feelings only in relation to core doctrine—public verbal vilification of 'the dogma, rites, or ceremonies, that is, the true fundamentals, rules of worship and the external acts of religious practices' is forbidden.[74] However, serious, scientific, and profound theological study is permitted, but not 'antireligious rebuffs, scoffing or the mockery of basic dogmas'.[75] For example, it is an offence to mock the confessional;[76] to exhibit on a toilet door in a private dwelling (accessible to the public) a drawing which parodies a temple and depicts the Virgin Mary being sexually assaulted;[77] or to publish in a university gazette obscene drawings of monks, nuns, or the Holy Trinity.[78] In one case, the constitutionality of the draft law on defamation of religion and its protection of religious feelings was challenged on the ground that it violated both religious freedom and the separation of state and religion. This argument was rejected by the Constitutional Court on the basis that the crime actually derives from the right to religious freedom and that the State must under the constitution 'take into account the religious beliefs of Spanish society'.[79]

A small number of States protect religious feelings by extending defamation of religion beyond attacks on beliefs to offence caused by attacks on places of worship and religious objects. In Poland, any person who intentionally offends the religious feelings of other persons by public vilification of an object of religious devotion or a place used for carrying out religious rites, is to be punished with a fine or detention for up to two years.[80] In 1995, the Constitutional Court recognized the importance of religious sentiments and justified their protection on the basis of religious freedom: 'Religious feelings, due to their character, are the subject of special protection. They are directly connected with freedom of conscience and religion, which is "a constitutional value".'[81] Criticisms of a religious community or the statements of religious leaders are not punishable. Only two cases have come before

---

[73] Spain: PC, Art 525; this was introduced on the basis of Organic Law 10/1995 of November 23, II.II.3: 'criminal offences against freedom of conscience, religious sentiments, and respect for the deceased'.

[74] Spain: HC, Ruling of 14 February 1984.

[75] Spain: HC, Ruling of 26 November 1990.

[76] Spain: HC, Ruling of 11 October 1973: when a priest was portrayed as saying to a penitent: 'That will be 345.70 pesetas and a donation'.

[77] Spain: HC, Ruling of 1 July 1975.

[78] Spain: HC, Ruling of 19 February 1982.

[79] Spain: CCt, Decree, 180/1986, of February 21: 'it is unimaginable how a precept which aims to guarantee respect for religious convictions of all citizens can affect the right to religious freedom and the religion of each individual ... The lay nature of the State does not imply that the religious beliefs and sentiments of society cannot be the object of its protection'; for the duty to take into account the religious beliefs of Spanish society, see Const, Art 16.3.

[80] Poland: PC, Art 196: it may be oral, written or by gestures; see also Netherlands, PC, Art 147: ridiculing objects dedicated to worship at the place and time of lawful worship; Cyprus: PC, Art 138; damage to religious property with intent to insult religion is punished; Ireland: Defamation Act 2009, s 36: conduct which insults matters 'held sacred' might include sacred objects and places.

[81] Poland: CCt, Decision K 17/93, OTK 1994, cz I, it 11, p 90.

the courts,[82] though Polish laws on defamation of religion have been upheld in Strasbourg.[83]

The paucity of cases before the courts in recent years across Europe for offences against religious feelings may be due in part to the availability of prosecution for incitement to religious hatred.[84] It may also be due to the substantive and procedural difficulties in bringing a successful prosecution. Not only are the definitional elements of such offences complex and difficult to prove, procedural safeguards may also serve to deter vexatious prosecutions. The point is illustrated by Cypriot law on the subject. Any person who with the deliberate intention to wound the religious feelings of any person utters any word or makes any sound in the hearing of that person, or makes any gesture in the sight of that person, or places any object in the sight of that person, is guilty of a misdemeanour and is liable to imprisonment not exceeding one year. The conduct may also consist of an offensive publication: any person who publishes a book, pamphlet, article, or letter which any class of persons considers as a public insult to their religion, with intent to vilify such religion or to shock or insult its believers, is guilty of a misdemeanour. Intent to wound the religious feelings is required. The law seeks to protect both public order and religious feelings. The offence applies to all religions. Moreover, a prosecution may not be commenced except by or with the consent of the Attorney-General of Cyprus.[85]

A comparison of the offences

The points of similarity between national laws on the protection of religious belief and doctrine are clear. The majority of States consider that vilification of religion is a criminal act which threatens public order. To forbid it, they use the offence of blasphemy or (often replacing blasphemy) its modern equivalent, defamation of religion. Both may forbid conduct offensive to religious feelings. Blasphemy predominates in countries with a state church, but not invariably—and its recent revival in Ireland seems exceptional. Defamation of religion transcends all religion-state models. All religions are protected, but prosecutions are rare and difficult, perhaps due to the complexities of the offences. Sacred doctrines, persons, ceremonies, places, and objects (and feelings based on them) may all be protected from vilification (and outrage). However, reasonable criticism of religion is permissible. The principle which emerges is that individuals must not vilify religious beliefs or doctrines but may do so to the extent this is not likely to threaten public order.

---

[82] Poland: one case about a poster of a film, *Scandalist Larry Flint* was discontinued (2004); in another an artist who depicted male organs on a cross was sentenced (2004) by a Gdańsk court to 6 months' limitation of freedom—this was overruled on appeal: see M Rynkowski, 'Religion and criminal law: Poland' in Kotiranta and Doe (n 2 above) 205, 207.

[83] ibid 213: the weekly *Wprost* published an image of a 'Black Madonna' wearing a gas mask; the European Commission on Human Rights held the application inadmissible as the image simply sought to bring attention to environmental issues about air pollution.

[84] See Ch 3 above.

[85] Cyprus: PC, Art 141, Cap 154; for the consent of the A-G, see Art 142.

On the other hand, national laws diverge in their justifications for these offences. This divergence often produces dissonance. The abolition or abandonment of blasphemy is justified on the basis of, variously: dissatisfaction about its historical association with the protection of Christianity; an inheritance from former political regimes (especially communist); the introduction of a system of separation of church and state; the rarity of prosecutions; and the restrictive effects of the offences on freedom of speech. Justifications for the offences of blasphemy, defamation of religion, and insult to religious feelings, are by no means consistent. Whilst in all States the offences exist to prevent public disorder, in some they are justified because religious feelings are somehow 'special' or part of the 'moral patrimony' of a country, or because their protection is required by religious freedom. Another possible rationale for the offences, which does not surface in laws, is the right to hold any religious belief *free from insults to that belief.*[86] However, the most common criticism of the offences of blasphemy and defamation of religion is their potential to restrict freedom of expression—freedom of expression and a prohibition against the vilification of religion are mutually incompatible. It is suggested that this view is largely misplaced. What laws actually seek is a balance between the freedom and the prohibition (a) at the level of principle and (b) in terms of the limits applicable to them: freedom of expression is exercisable unless it jeopardizes public order; vilification of religion is forbidden if it jeopardizes public order. Yet it is difficult to see why religious feelings, and not, for example, political feelings, should enjoy special protection.[87]

Crimes against religious worship

As seen in Chapter 2, Article 9 ECHR protects the individual and collective right of freedom of worship. This may be exercised in public or in private. The freedom is fundamental to the right to manifest religion in practice—and States have a positive obligation to protect freedom of worship.[88] At the national level, freedom of worship often enjoys formal constitutional or other legal protection either as a right of the individual,[89] or of a religious organization (on the basis of its autonomy), provided its exercise does not contravene the limits imposed on it by law.[90]

---

[86] If this is correct, the offences of blasphemy and defamation of religion (including outrage to religious feelings) provide more extensive protection than that afforded by Art 9 ECHR: see Ch 2 above.

[87] For an excellent summary of criticisms, see J Rivers, 'The question of freedom of religion or belief and defamation' (2007) 2 Religion and Human Rights 113.

[88] *Kosteski v The Former Yugoslav Republic of Macedonia* App 55170/00 (ECtHR, 13 April 2006): religious worship unlawfully disrupted is a breach of ECHR, Art 9.

[89] Denmark: Const, Arts 67, 68; Sweden: Instrument of Government, Ch 2; Belgium: Const, Arts 19, 20; Italy: Const, Art 20; Luxembourg: Const, Art 19; Malta: Const, Art 40.

[90] Greece: Const, Art 13: 'Every known religion is free and its related worship is practised unhindered under the protection of the law. The practice of worship must not pose a threat to public order or morals'; Cyprus: Const, Art 18.4; Hungary: Const, Art 60.2; Czech Rep: Const, Art 15; Portugal: Const, Art 41 and LORF, Art 1.

One of the ways in which national laws seek to honour this freedom is through the use of a series of criminal offences and sanctions. The protection offered is generally more extensive than that afforded by Article 9 ECHR in so far as it is applies to a number of religious activities not expressly covered by the Article. National laws forbid three forms of conduct: disturbance to worship; disturbance of religious meetings; and disturbance to funerals.[91] It is also important to note that these prohibitions further extend the principle of autonomy for religious organizations beyond non-interference by the State in their affairs to non-intervention by citizens.[92] What follows outlines legal similarities and differences.

Disturbance of religious worship

Blasphemy, defamation of religion, and outrage to religious feelings do not generally involve direct physical harm—their principal focus is religious belief and sentiment and the likelihood of public disorder, which itself may include physical harm. Crimes which relate to worship are somewhat materially different. They involve disruption to religious conduct and their commission may involve physical harm. Moreover, prosecutions for offences to freedom of worship seem to be more common than those which relate to doctrine. However, like crimes against religious doctrine, crimes against worship generally have the character of public order offences, and usually they afford protection to all religions. Similarly, like doctrine offences, worship offences consist of various definitional formulations with regard to the *actus reus*, but intent is generally required in terms of the *mens rea*. Once again, the offences straddle the tripartite classical understanding of religion-state models.

The law of the state-church Danish system criminalizes only disturbances to 'religious services or other public religious functions'.[93] However, Greek law punishes acts which prevent the preparation, commencement, or continuation of a gathering of believers for the purposes of worship, in public or private, indoors or outdoors.[94] The Irish separation system penalizes riotous, violent, or indecent behaviour during the celebration of divine service in places of public worship of any religious denomination; it has been held that the conduct must be 'highly indecent and improper'.[95] The Cypriot cooperation system forbids the disturbance of any assembly lawfully engaged in the performance of religious worship or ceremony.[96] In Lithuania the crime of 'disturbance of religious ceremonies or celebrations' distinguishes but protects state-recognized and other religious groups: 'Any person who, through violent acts, noise-making, or similar acts disrupts a service or other rites of a church or religious community recognised by the State or a

---

[91] In Ch 7 below it is seen that the civil law is also used to protect religious property.

[92] See Ch 5 above for the non-intervention of the State in the affairs of religious organizations.

[93] Denmark: Strfl, para 137, stk 2; see also Finland, PC, Ch 17, s 11.

[94] Greece: PC, Art 200(1).

[95] Ireland: Ecclesiastical Courts Jurisdiction Act 1860, ss 2 and 3; *Worth v Torrington* (1845) 13 M&W 781, 795.

[96] Cyprus: PC, Art 139; see also Portugal, PC, Art 252.

celebration of a religious group'.[97] But in Polish law 'disturbance of the performance of a public religious act' seems only to apply to a registered church or religious community.[98] The principle which emerges is that individuals must not engage in conduct which disrupts religious worship; differences between national laws relate to the scope of this prohibition in terms of whether it applies to public and/or private worship and whether it applies to all or simply to some recognized religious organizations.[99]

States often extend their protection of religious worship by means of criminal sanctions to other more general forms of religious activity which may or may not be associated with worship, such as religious practices, classes, and meetings. For example, Belgium forbids disrupting, hindering, or interrupting the practice of religion, through disturbance or disorder, in a place serving the religion or during its public ceremonies. The punishment is imprisonment for between eight days and three months and a fine. This protects all religions (not only recognized ones). Intent to disrupt must be proved.[100] Similarly, French law penalizes preventing, delaying, and interrupting religious practices, and this prohibition has been applied to the administration of the sacraments as well as classes on sacred premises for catechetical formation.[101] The criminal law of Luxembourg also prohibits the disruption of religious festivals and days of religious observance.[102] Other States prohibit disturbances to the performance of 'religious rituals'; this is the case in Latvia.[103] Special provisions protect the ritual slaughter of animals for religious purposes.[104]

---

[97] Lithuania: PC, Art 171. However, in a recent case of a woman who disrupted a Catholic Mass as it was in Latin not Lithuanian, since disruption was minimal, the court used the Code of Misdemeanours of Administrative Law, Art 174 with a fine for breach of public order, rather than PC, Art 171.

[98] Poland: PC, Art 194; other religious groups may be protected by the law on meetings in Art 260.

[99] In countries where the law formally restricts its scope to public worship, this would seem to be at odds with ECHR, Art 9: this, of course, recognizes freedom of worship in both public and private.

[100] Belgium: PC, Art 143.

[101] France: Law of 9 December 1905, Art 32; Cass Crim, 6 November 1909, *Proc gen, CA Amiens c Waguet*: DP 1910, 1, p 377; see also Alsace-Moselle: PC, Art 167.

[102] Luxembourg: PC, Arts 142; see also Arts 143 and 268: breach of the peace in a place of worship or on the occasion of religious worship is punishable.

[103] Latvia: Criminal Law, s 15: 'a person who commits intentional interference with religious rituals, if the same are not in violation of the law', is liable to community service or a fine; see also R Balodis, 'Legal protection of religion in the Republic of Latvia' in Kotiranta and Doe (n 2 above) 163, 168: a letter from the Ministry of the Interior (29 May 2008) to Professor Ringolds Balodis indicated that barring members of the Grebenschikov Old Believers at Riga from entering their place of worship might have been the subject of a prosecution.

[104] S Ferrari and R Bottoni, 'Legislation regarding religious slaughter in the EU, candidate and associated countries', Report 2010, <http://www.dialrel.eu> see eg UK: Slaughterhouses Act 1974, Part II and Welfare of Animals (Slaughter or Killing) Regulations 1995 (SI 1995/731): these protect slaughter according to Jewish and Muslim methods; Spain: 'The slaughter of animals in accordance with Jewish law must abide by health standards in force' (Agreement, Art 14, ratified by Law 25/1992 of 10 November); see also Agreement with the Islamic Communities (ratified by Law 26/1992 of 10 November), Art 14; France: a Jewish association challenged a law (under ECHR, Art 9) which did not permit the slaughter of animals in accordance with Jewish ritual: *Jewish Liturgical Association Cha'are Shalom Ve Tsedek v France* (2000) 9 EHRR 27: it was held there was no breach as the applicants could have been supplied from Belgium, but if the law had made it impossible for them to eat meat in accordance with Jewish practice, there would have been a breach; see also Ireland: Slaughter of Animals Act 1935, s 15; Slovenia: Animal Protection Act 1999, Art 5; Estonia: Animal Protection Act 2000, Art 10.

The seriousness of these offences is reflected in the penalties which may be imposed upon their commission. The location of the crime and the means used to commit it may also affect the penalty. In Spanish law those who 'with violence, threats, tumult or other conduct, impede, interrupt or disturb the acts, functions, ceremonies or demonstrations of the religions inscribed in the public registry of the Ministry of Justice or the Interior', may be punished with six months' to six years' imprisonment, if the act is committed in a place of worship, or a fine at the prescribed rate for four to ten months if it occurs in any other place.[105] In Italy, the offence of disturbing the offices, ceremonies, or practices of a religious confession, in the presence of a minister of religion or in a place of worship, a public place, or one open to the public is penalized with two years' imprisonment; if the conduct is accompanied by violence or menaces, it attracts imprisonment for up to three years.[106] Under Finnish law, 'a person who employs or threatens violence, so as unlawfully to prevent worship, ecclesiastical proceedings or other similar religious proceedings arranged by a church or a religious community' (one that is recognized) may be punished with a fine or imprisonment for up to two years;[107] the same applies in Austria,[108] and in Bulgaria the sentence is up to one year.[109]

In the event that a person insults religion through acts which disturb religious worship, such person may be liable to prosecution for defamation of religion or outrage of religious feelings. Defamation of worship is an offence in the state-church systems of Greece[110] and Finland.[111] It is also an offence in the cooperation system of Portugal: as well as that of intentionally disturbing religious worship, there is an offence of vilifying or mocking in public any act of religious worship; this is punishable by imprisonment for up to one year and a fine.[112] Similarly, in Austria, a person whose conduct is calculated to give rise to public nuisance at a place dedicated to the lawful practice of a church or religious community, during a sacred service, or an act of worship, may be imprisoned for six months or fined.[113] The equivalent offence in Spain has led to a number of prosecutions. Spanish law punishes public defamation of the rites or ceremonies of religions and public harassment of those who profess or practise religion (intent must be proved).[114] It also penalizes any person who 'in a place of worship or during religious ceremonies carries out acts of profanation offending legally protected religious sentiments'.[115] The latter has led to several cases which involved, variously, spitting on, exhibiting irreverently, pocketing, and burning the host used at Holy

---

[105] Spain: PC, Art 523.   [106] Italy: PC, Art 405.
[107] Finland: PC, Ch 17, s 11; see also Lithuania: PC, Art 171: the penalties are community service, a fine, restriction of liberty, or detention.
[108] Austria: PC, para 189.1.
[109] Bulgaria: PC, Art 165.1–2.
[110] Greece: PC, Art 199: insulting worship of the Orthodox Church or other known religion.
[111] Finland: PC, Ch 10(2).
[112] Portugal: PC, Art 252; fine at the prescribed rate for up to 120 days.
[113] Austria: PC, para 189.2.
[114] Spain: PC, Art 525; HC Ruling of 14 February 1984.
[115] Spain: PC, Art 524.

Communion.[116] A related offence in Hungary is that of conduct which causes public scandal on premises designated for the purposes of the ceremonies of a registered church;[117] though in one case of a religious procession disrupted by a driver forcing believers to let his car pass along the road, the criminal offence of the 'violation of the Freedom of Conscience and Religion' was applied.[118]

By way of contrast, in other States, there is no law specifically devoted to the penal protection of religious worship but there is no shortage of alternatives. Disruption of worship could fall under the general law on public order; this is the position, for example, in Romania[119] and Sweden.[120] The same applies in the Czech Republic: a person who in a public place behaves in a grossly indecent manner or causes disorder, or disrupts an assembly of citizens or ceremony is punishable with imprisonment for up to two years or a fine.[121] Alternatively, communal religious activity may be covered by general offences which seek to protect the right of association, such as in Bulgaria[122] and the Netherlands.[123] Or else disruption to religious worship may be dealt with by crimes which address unlawful entry on property (as has occurred in Ireland).[124] However, in some countries disruption of religious worship may constitute the offence of hindering religious freedom (see Chapter 2),[125] or a specific offence of interfering in the functions of ministers of religion (see Chapter 5).[126]

As has been seen, unlike crimes against religious doctrine, greater use tends to be made of offences against worship. The United Kingdom is a case in point. In England and Wales, under the Ecclesiastical Courts Jurisdiction Act 1860 it is a criminal offence to commit 'riotous, violent or indecent behaviour' in the course of lawful liturgical action.[127] The offence may be committed in any cathedral, church, or chapel of the Church of England or in any chapel of any religious denomination

---

[116] For profanation as lack of respect, see HC Rulings of 11 December 1950, 10 December 1982, and 25 March 1993; for spitting on the host, Ruling of 22 December 1913; Ruling of 15 July 1982; for exhibiting the host disrespectfully, Ruling of 31 December 1896; for opening a tabernacle, Ruling of 27 February 1929; for pocketing the host, Ruling of 15 July 1982; for burning the host, Ruling of 10 December 1982.

[117] Hungary: Act 69/1999 (on misdemeanours), para 150.

[118] Hungary: BH 1999.292.

[119] Romania: PC, Art 324.

[120] Sweden: PC (BrB), Art 16:4; see NJA II 1970, p 553.

[121] Czech Rep: PC, s 202.

[122] Bulgaria: PC, Art 174a.

[123] Netherlands: PC, Arts 145, 146; see also Criminal Procedures Act, Art 123.

[124] Ireland: in 2006 several Afghan refugees entered Saint Patrick's Cathedral in Dublin and went on hunger strike; their occupation disrupted the routine worship of the Cathedral; although proceedings against them were ultimately dropped, they were initially charged under the Prohibition of Forcible Entry and Occupation Act 1971: 'Church of Ireland pleads with men to leave Cathedral' *Irish Times*, 20 May 2006; 'Peaceful end to Afghan Protest' *Irish Times*, 22 May 2006; 'DPP drops Afghan Hunger Striker Charges' *Irish Times*, 6 June 2006.

[125] eg Romania: PC, Art 318.

[126] Sweden: PC (BrB) 16:4.

[127] UK: Ecclesiastical Courts Jurisdiction Act 1860, s 2; indecency simply means creating a disturbance: *Abrahams v Cavey* [1968] 1 QB 479; *Jones v Catterall* (1902) 18 TLR 367 'idolatory' called out during the service was held to be 'indecent'. In Scotland, disturbance of public worship is punishable under the common law as a breach of the peace: *Dougall v Dykes* (1861) 4 Irvine 101.

or in any certified place of religious worship,[128] during the celebration of 'divine service' or at any time, and in any churchyard or burial ground.[129] Moreover, it is a crime to molest, disturb, vex, or trouble (or by any other unlawful means to disquiet or misuse) any preacher duly authorized to preach or any clergyman in holy orders ministering or celebrating any sacrament or any divine service, rite, or office.[130] The offence may be committed by a clergyman acting in an indecent or violent way in his own church or churchyard.[131] Also, a person may be removed for disturbing divine service even though no part of that service is actually proceeding at the time.[132] During the period 1997 to 2002, there were sixty prosecutions under this Act and twenty-one convictions.[133] Indeed, according to 'National Churchwatch' there were 6,829 crimes against places of worship in twelve (of forty-two) police areas in the year ending in April 2002.[134] Recently, a parliamentary committee stated that the penalties in the Act are of little deterrence value and that the Act itself is archaic—but it is not obsolete and still sends an important message.[135]

Freedom to conduct worship and associated collective religious activities is a qualified right and may be subject to restriction by the State.[136] As stated above, behaviour which may otherwise actually disrupt worship will not be punishable if the definitional elements of the relevant crimes are not made out—for example if the disruption is minimal, unintentional, unlikely to cause public disorder, or, when it is also a species of defamation of religion, does not insult religion. Moreover, whilst Article 9 ECHR protects both public and private worship (which themselves may be limited under Article 9.2), some national criminal laws restrict their protection to disruption of *public* worship or that of recognized religions. Similarly, protection will not be afforded if the worship itself is unlawful or violates public order, health, morals, and the rights of others.[137] As such, preaching may be forbidden if a religious organization fails to register,[138] or if it

---

[128] Places of Worship Registration Act 1855.

[129] See also Burial Laws Amendment Act 1880, ss 7, 8.

[130] Ecclesiastical Courts Jurisdiction Act 1860, s 2; *Cope v Barber* (1872) LR 7 CP 393, see *Matthews v King* [1934] 1 KB 505; 'clergyman in holy orders' normally excludes a minister not episcopally ordained: *Glasgow College v AG* (1848) 1 HL Cas 800, 819, 823.

[131] *Vallancey v Fletcher* [1897] 1 QB 265.

[132] *Williams v Glenister* (1824) 2 B&C 699.

[133] HL Select Committee, Religious Offences in England and Wales, First Report 2003, para 58.

[134] ibid para 26: of these, 186 were violent crimes, and 2,866 incidents of criminal damage.

[135] ibid para 134; see para 132 for the claim that the UK is not 'a secular state'.

[136] As worship is a manifestation of religion, the right to it is a qualified under ECHR, Art 9.1 and therefore subject to the limits set out in Art 9.2: see Ch 2 above.

[137] Poland: Const, Art 53.5: 'The freedom to publicly express religion may be limited only by means of statute and only where this is necessary for the defence of State security, public order, health, morals or the freedoms and rights of others'; Greece: Const, Art 13: 'Every known religion is free and its related worship is practised unhindered under the protection of the law. The practice of worship must not pose a threat to public order or morals'; Cyprus: Const, Art 18; Czech Rep: Const, Art 15; Portugal: Const, Art 41 and LORF, Art 1; Austria: RCA 1874; FLSCC 1998; Lithuania: LORCA, s 6; Estonia: CCA 2002, Arts 11–13; Hungary: Const, Art 60.2; Spain: LORF, Art 5;

[138] Bulgaria: registration was required by a local regulation in Plovdiv—this was upheld, in relation to Jehovah's Witnesses by Plovdiv DC and the Supreme Administrative Court, Cases no 7237/2000,

is likely to agitate resistance to the State,[139] civil disobedience,[140] or violation of human rights.[141] However, in Sweden the conviction of a Pentecostal minister who preached a public sermon against homosexuals was overturned on the basis of freedom of religion.[142] Nevertheless, in Austria in 1998, a meeting at a cemetery to commemorate the killing of Jews by the Nazis which was to coincide with a meeting to commemorate German soldiers killed in the Second World War was banned on grounds of possible public disorder; the ban was upheld by the Constitutional Court in the face of claims of restraint of religious freedom on the basis of possible public disorder.[143]

Disruption of funerals

Whilst the disruption of funerals in several States would be prohibited by general laws applicable to religious freedom,[144] in many States special protection is afforded by the criminal law to the administration of funeral rites. This is the case, for example, in Belgium,[145] Luxembourg,[146] and Portugal.[147] The foundations for the offence vary as between States. The administration of funeral rites may be protected on the basis of freedom of worship (Spain),[148] public nuisance (Austria),[149] or because disruption constitutes contempt for the dead (Lithuania),[150] or impiety (Hungary).[151] Cypriot law uses defamation of religion: any person who with intent to wound the feelings of any person or to insult their religion causes disturbance to others assembled for funeral ceremonies is liable to punishment.[152] In Finland, it is a breach of the sanctity of religion if a person 'by making a noise, acting threateningly or otherwise, disturbs . . . a funeral'; this is punishable by fine or up to six

no 2174/2000, no 5116/2003, but struck down in a later case (Case no 464/2006) as in violation of ECHR, Art 9, Const, Art 37, and RDA, Arts 5 and 7.

[139] France: Law of 9 December 1905, Art 35.1; see Cass Crim, 17 May 1907: DP 1907, 1, p 273; see also Cass Crim, 4 January 1912: Bull Crim, no 2; Cass Crim, 5 August 1915: Bull Crim, no 168.

[140] Luxembourg: PC, Art 268; Belgium: PC, Art 268.

[141] Czech Rep: the Ministry of Culture may withdraw the registration of any denomination engaged in systematic agitation against human rights: Act no 3/2002, ss 21 and 22.

[142] Sweden: SC, *Prosecutor v Åke Green*, HD Mål nr B 1050–05, NJA 2005:87, 805 *et seq.*

[143] Austria: VfSlg 15.680/1999; cf VfSlg 16.054/2000; *Ollinger v Austria* App no 76900/01 (ECtHR, 29 June 2006): it was held that the authorities had given too little weight to the applicants' and cemetery visitors' interests (who traditionally visited the cemetery on the day of the event, 1 November 1998 (All Saints' Day)); Art 11 ECHR on freedom of assembly had been violated.

[144] Latvia: Criminal Law, s 151; Bulgaria: PC, Art 165(1).

[145] Belgium: PC, Art 143.

[146] Luxembourg: PC, Art 143.

[147] Portugal: PC, Art 253: 'A person who through violence or menace of serious harm hinders or disturbs a funeral procession or ceremony' is punishable by imprisonment for up to a year or a fine.

[148] Spain: LORF, Art 2.1.b; PC, Art 523.

[149] Austria: PC, para 191.

[150] Lithuania: PC, Art 313–1: 'Any person who, seeking to express contempt for the deceased, disturbs the peace at a funeral, commits a misdemeanour, and shall be punished by community service or a fine or restriction of liberty, or detention'.

[151] Hungary: PC, para 181.

[152] Cyprus: PC, Art 140 of Ch 154.

months in prison.[153] A similar crime of malicious disturbance of a funeral, or other mourning ceremony or rites, exists in Poland, where the funeral need not be religious, and may be in public or private.[154]

There is a great deal of ancient law on the subject in the United Kingdom. First, it is an offence to 'play at any game or sport, or discharge firearms, save at a military funeral' in any cemetery or to 'wilfully and unlawfully disturb any persons assembled in the cemetery for the purposes of burying a body' or to 'commit any nuisance within' a cemetery.[155] This now applies only to private cemeteries. As to cemeteries administered by local authorities, it is an offence wilfully to create any disturbance or nuisance in such a cemetery or wilfully to interfere with any burial taking place or with any grave, vault, tombstone, or other memorial or any flowers, or plants, or any such matter or to play any game or sport therein.[156] Secondly, as to burials 'with or without a religious service', it is an offence to engage in 'riotous, violent, or indecent behaviour' at any burial, and to 'bring into contempt or obloquy the Christian religion, or the belief or worship of any church or denomination of Christians, or the members or any minister of any church or denomination, or any other person'.[157] It is also an offence to obstruct, by threats or force, any minister in the performance of a duty in the lawful burial of the dead in any churchyard or other burial place.[158]

The portrayal of religion in the media

One field in which the tensions between freedom of religion and freedom of expression are particularly evident is that of religion and the media.[159] Protected by the ECHR,[160] freedom of expression is a fundamental right in national laws and these sometimes set out its purposes, which may include enabling the media to convey to society ideas and information,[161] to develop public opinion,[162] and to

---

[153] Finland: PC, Ch 10(2).

[154] Poland: PC, Art 195.1.

[155] UK: Cemeteries Clauses Act 1847, s 59.

[156] UK: Local Authorities' Cemeteries Order 1977: SI 1977/204, Art 18.

[157] UK: Burial Laws Amendment Act 1880, s 7: there is no definition of 'any other person'; for objections to s 7, see HL SC, Religious Offences, 2003, para 29.

[158] UK: Offences against the Person Act 1861, s 36; Criminal Law Act 1967, s 1.

[159] See generally N Doe (ed), *The Portrayal of Religion in Europe: The Media and the Arts* (Leuven: Peeters, 2004).

[160] ECHR, Art 10.1: 'Everyone has the right to freedom of expression. This right shall include freedom to hold opinions and to receive and impart information and ideas without interference by public authority and regardless of frontiers. This article shall not prevent States from requiring the licensing of broadcasting, television or cinema enterprises'; Art 10.2 authorizes limits prescribed by law and necessary in a democratic society in the interests, *inter alia*, of national security, health, and morals.

[161] Germany: GG, Arts 5 and 19: freedom of expression is exercisable both by individuals and by corporations as a guarantee to limit legislative, executive, and judicial power on the part of the State.

[162] Ireland: Const, Art 40.6: 'The education of public opinion [is] . . . a matter of . . . grave import to the common good'; see also Spain: CCt, 12/1982, 31 March.

facilitate intellectual[163] and artistic creativity.[164] Needless to say, the exercise of freedom of religion may seek both to utilize and to limit freedom of expression in order to enable the profession of religious ideas,[165] without distinction between religious beliefs or practices,[166] and to prohibit discrimination on grounds of religion;[167] and it may include for religious groups the right to communicate the faith and to create mass media for this purpose.[168] The assumption by the State of competence over the media is a commonplace.[169]

The press and religion

State laws in Europe may protect freedom of the press by means of the constitution,[170] or by a designated body of press law, or both.[171] However, freedom of the press is not unlimited; Ireland is typical: the State shall endeavour to ensure that the press 'whilst preserving [its] rightful liberty of expression, including criticism of Government policy, shall not be used to undermine public order or morality or the authority of the State'.[172] Occasionally national media laws have provisions on religion—but this is rare: in the Netherlands the State has a Press Fund to provide financial aid for the reorganization of secular periodicals; but: 'Their publication or distribution may not be connected with membership or sponsorship of or participation in an association, religious society or other organisation';[173] and in Austria, a media employee has a right to refuse to participate in schemes which offend his or her religious convictions.[174]

   More usually, in general terms, States do not employ the civil law to regulate press coverage of religion nor do they require by law equal treatment of different

---

[163] Portugal: Const, Art 37: 'the right to express and publicise thoughts freely, by words, images or other means, and the right to impart, obtain and receive information without hindrance or discrimination'; the exercise of this right must not be prevented by any form of censorship.
[164] Finland: Constitutional Freedom of Expression Act, Art 12: no distinction is made between religious, political, artistic, scientific or other forms of expression or communication.
[165] Luxembourg: Const, Art 19: freedom of religion embraces the right to manifest religious opinions; see also Strasbourg: *Hakånsson v Sweden* (1983) 5 EHRR, 297: when national law on disturbing the peace was applied to a man who shouted 'like a trumpet' about the sinfulness of alcohol and pornography, the Commission held this to be a breach of ECHR, Art 9.1; cf *Van Den Dungen v Netherlands* App 22838/93 (1995) 80-A D&R 147, 150: the case of a man outside an abortion clinic displaying pictures of foetal remains alongside images of Christ fell outside Art 9.1.
[166] Germany: GG, Art 4.
[167] Ireland: Const, Art 44.2.1: 'the free profession and practice of religion, subject to public order and morality', are guaranteed to everyone.
[168] Spain: Const, Art 16; see also Art 20: freedom of expression.
[169] Spain: Const, Art 149.1.27: the State has exclusive jurisdiction over the press, radio, and television and all other media without prejudice to the powers of the autonomous (regional) communities.
[170] Italy: Const, Art 21; Greece: Const, Art 14; Belgium: Const, Art 25.
[171] France: Law of 1 August 1986; Portugal: Const, Art 38 and Law of 26 February 1975: freedom of editorial direction does not apply in relation to media of a 'doctrinal or denominational character'.
[172] Ireland: Const, Art 40.6.
[173] Netherlands: Media Act 1987, s 129; see also Sweden: Const, Ch 2, Art 13: 'particular regard shall be paid to the importance of the widest possible freedom of expression . . . in . . . religious matters'.
[174] Austria: Media Act, s 2.

religions in this.[175] The press is free to choose topics and express opinions on any religion, though it is of course subject to proceedings for the criminal offences outlined above in relation to blasphemy, defamation of religion, and outrage to religious feelings, as well as incitement to religious hatred and associated offences (see Chapter 3). All of these offences may restrict the portrayal in the press of both religious beliefs and worship. In addition, informal mechanisms may be used to regulate press coverage of religion. These may focus on journalistic practice. Some are bilateral. For example, collaborative dialogue between associations of journalists and religious groups is sometimes formalized in the internal structures of such associations, as is the case in France.[176] Needless to say, religious organizations have press offices active in the provision of information to the media and they may collaborate in this field, as occurs in Finland, Britain, and the Netherlands.[177] Similar arrangements may be found in Spain,[178] where, moreover, an agreement with the Holy See provides: 'Safeguarding the principles of religious freedom and freedom of expression, the State shall ensure that its social media shall respect the feelings of Catholics and shall establish [other] agreements concerning these matters with the Spanish Episcopal Conference.'[179]

Moreover, codes of practice are frequently used as a form of self-regulation with regard to journalistic ethics and practice. These are indispensable instruments to underscore and convey directly the standards of the criminal law as they apply to the press.[180] The Irish Code of Conduct of the National Union of Journalists forbids journalists to encourage discrimination, ridicule, prejudice, or hatred on grounds of religion,[181] and it prohibits advertisements which may cause offence on grounds of religion;[182] the Austrian Code of Ethics for the Press forbids mockery of religious doctrines or of recognized churches and religious communities;[183] and in

---

[175] It would be interesting to explore the extent to which the media is subject to national civil laws which prohibit discrimination on grounds of religion in the provision of services: see generally Ch 3 above.

[176] France: Professional Association of Journalists on Religion; Netherlands: in 1968 the Organisation of Catholic Journalists merged with the Netherlands Association of Journalists and in 1973 the Catholic Press Agency became part of the religious department of the General Press Agency.

[177] Finland: the Evangelical Lutheran Church has its own General Communication Centre which disseminates information to the press and monitors press coverage; in Britain, the Churches Media Council was set up in September 2003 as a forum for church leaders and journalists; in the Netherlands, Catholics and Protestants have formed a Christian Contact for Publicity which also works with the ecumenical Inter-church Organisation for Communication.

[178] These exist for the Federation of Evangelical Religious Entities of Spain, Israelite Communities of Spain, and Islamic Commission of Spain. The Episcopal Committee of the Media, of the Roman Catholic Church, is governed by its own statutes.

[179] Spain: Agreement on Education and Cultural Affairs, 3 January 1979 (ratified 4 December 1979), Art 14.

[180] Luxembourg: Law of 20 October 1979: the Press Council is a statutory body which has issued a code of practice prescribing that it is the responsibility of journalists and editors to consider the effect of laws on the portrayal of religion concerning defamation, incitement, and discrimination.

[181] Ireland: NUJ Code of Conduct, para 10.

[182] Code of Advertising Standards of the Advertising Standards Authority for Ireland (2001) paras 2.14, 2.16: advertisements should respect the dignity of all persons, should avoid causing offence on grounds of religion, and should not ridicule or exploit religious beliefs, symbols, rites, or practices.

[183] Austria: Code of Ethics for the Austrian Press, Art 5.5 and 5.6.

Germany a code of practice recommends against 'publications, in words or pictures, which could, by their form or content, seriously offend the moral or religious feelings of a group' or discriminate on grounds of religion.[184] Complaint systems and remedial action are common; the United Kingdom is typical: the Press Complaints Commission may address publications offensive to religion and its code of practice forbids pejorative reference to religion.[185] Individual newspapers may also have unilateral policies which aim to ensure fair coverage of the affairs of majority and minority religions.[186]

Religion, radio, and television

EU law prohibits the transmission of advertisements during the broadcast of religious ceremonies, but the EU rule which prohibited the broadcasting of material which is offensive to religious beliefs has recently been abandoned.[187] As with the press, the laws of most European States explicitly recognize a right to freedom in broadcasting;[188] and broadcasters are subject to the same criminal laws (outlined above) as the press. However, in most States broadcasting services have no specific duty to cover religious matters, they are free to do so, as a matter of their own discretion, but in some, prescribed television channels are under a specific duty to cover religion, as is the case in Ireland.[189] Whatever the legal regime for broadcasting, it is often the case that national laws safeguard religious pluralism in programmes. A common feature of national laws is the duty on public broadcasting entities to adopt a pluralistic, impartial, and objective approach to religious programmes.[190] However, Spanish law also requires private radio and television channels to respect 'the political, religious, social, cultural and linguistic pluralism' of the country.[191] Laws may also impose on radio and television companies a duty to

---

[184] Germany: Code of Conduct, Principles 10–12; this is monitored by the German Press Council.
[185] UK: Code of Practice, Art 12: the press 'must avoid prejudicial or pejorative reference to a person's . . . religion . . . It must avoid publishing details of a person's . . . religion'.
[186] See N Doe, 'Religion and media in Europe: a comparative study' in Doe (n 159 above) 287, 293.
[187] Council Directive (EC) 2007/65; this amended Directive (EEC) 89/552, Art 12: 'Television advertising shall not be offensive to religious . . . belief'; see R McCrea, *Religion and the Public Order of the European Union* (Oxford: OUP, 2010) 178, n 102: the directive is likely 'to benefit well-established majority religions whose services are far more likely to be the subject of television broadcasts than the services of minority or non-mainstream faiths'.
[188] France: Law of 30 September 1986.
[189] Ireland: Broadcasting Authority Act 2001, s 28: the national broadcasting service must provide programmes to cover religious activities; see also UK: BBC Licence Agreement, cl 3.2(c): the BBC is required to include in its services 'programmes of an educational nature' which are defined to include 'religious programmes'.
[190] Austria: ORF Act 1984 (as amended in 2001), Art 4.1: one of the duties of public radio is to consider adequately the importance of the recognized churches and religious communities; Belgium: Law of 24 July 1997, Art 3: programming on the public service RTBF must reflect the different religious traditions in society; Netherlands: Media Act 2000, s 51b: the Programme Service Foundation (NPS) must provide programmes which represent 'a balanced reflection of the social, cultural, religious and spiritual diversity in the Netherlands'; Ireland: Broadcasting Authority Act 2001, s 28: coverage of religious activities must cater for both majority and minority interests; see also Radio and Television Act 1988, s 9: impartiality.
[191] Spain: Law 4/1980, Art 4c.

respect religious feelings and show tolerance towards religious difference,[192] as well as specific duties not to incite religious hatred, as is the case in France and Greece.[193]

Many States have statutory agencies, or other bodies,[194] charged with oversight of broadcasting in relation to religious topics; this is the position in the United Kingdom: one of the functions of the Office of Communications (OFCOM) is to ensure that 'the proper degree of responsibility is exercised with respect to the content of programmes which are religious programmes'; these must not involve 'any exploitation of any susceptibilities of the audience for such a programme; or any abusive treatment of the religious susceptibilities of those belonging to a particular religion or religious denomination'.[195] It is frequently the case that religious groups are represented on the boards of broadcasting authorities, sometimes as a matter of practice,[196] or else as a requirement of law.[197] However, in Spain, the law does not provide directly for religious representation on television and radio boards, but it does provide for the establishment of advisory committees to these.[198] There is an Advisory Committee of Catholic Programming which assists the administration board of the national RTVE (Spanish Radio-Television): with six members appointed by the director general, the board advises on the direction, content, scheduling, and identity of religious programmes.[199] No other religious group in Spain has an equivalent body.

Whilst religious organizations may of course have their own television and radio channels,[200] national laws do not generally confer on religious groups a right of direct access to public broadcasting services and transmission. There are, however, exceptions. Once more, Spain is notable. Here, social groups and political parties have a constitutional right of access to the media so as to exercise their freedom

---

[192] Italy: Law 223/1990 and 249/1997.

[193] France: Law of 1 August 2000; Greece: Law 2328/1995, ss 2 and 14; Luxembourg: Law of 27 July 1991.

[194] Portugal: Law 43/98.

[195] UK: Communications Act 2003, s 319; see also OFCOM Broadcasting Code 2008, s 4. See also Ireland: RTE Programme Makers Guide (2002) 35: 'As religious beliefs are so central in Irish society, RTE news and programmes will deal with religious topics on a regular basis. RTE in all its broadcasting that relates to religious issues should respect the values and loyalties of citizens and promote tolerance'; programmes should not give 'unintentional offence' and should reflect in 'a non-judgmental way the diversity of beliefs that exist in Ireland'.

[196] In Portugal, representatives from 12 religious groups are members, as a matter of practice, of the public service commission which deals with the religious content of programmes; see also UK: the Central Religious Advisory Committee (CRAC) advises the BBC and OFCOM 'on religious broadcasting policy and to comment on programmes once broadcast'; membership of the committee is 'both clerical and lay and drawn from the main Christian denominations and from other world religions, which are part of the fabric of British religious life'.

[197] Austria: ORF Act 1984, ss 28, 30: this provides for representation from the Catholic, Lutheran, and Calvinist churches on the Audience Council of ORF; in turn, the council nominates 6 members to the Foundation Council, 1 of whom must be from the recognized churches and religious communities; Luxembourg: recognized religious groups are represented on the National Council for Programmes: Law of 27 July 1991, Art 32.

[198] Spain: Law 4/1980.

[199] Spain: this was set up at the request of the Spanish Episcopal Conference, 25 November 1982.

[200] Austria: Private Radio Act 2001; Portugal: Law 31-A/99 of 17 July, Art 3.1; this is the case provided they have legal personality: Law 4/2001 of 23 February.

of expression.[201] Whilst the law on religious freedom does not specifically mention religion, registered religious groups are understood to share this right.[202] At the request of the administration board of the public entity RTVE, the Advisory Committee on Freedom of Religion clarified criteria which would entitle a religious group to gain access to the media on the basis, *inter alia*, of its significance in Spanish society, history, culture, and welfare. The Evangelical, Jewish, and Islamic communities all have agreements with the State on this.[203] Access to transmission time is also provided for in France,[204] Germany,[205] and Portugal.[206]

State laws deal in a variety of ways with advertising and religion on radio and television. Some States forbid all forms of religious advertising.[207] In line with EU law on the subject, advertising during the transmission of religious services is forbidden.[208] In the Netherlands, advertising is forbidden on Sundays immediately before or after a religious programme, unless there are no objections from religious organizations participating in the programme.[209] However, the laws of some States expressly provide that advertising must not be offensive to religious beliefs; in Ireland this is achieved by a ministerial code (where also the law admits limited advertising of religious literature and events);[210] and in Austria, the law forbids the public radio ORF to broadcast advertisements which offend human dignity, discriminate on grounds of religion, or offend religious convictions.[211]

Conclusion

The opinion has recently been expressed that the general policy of the States of Europe has been characterized by a fundamental assumption that religious freedom

---

[201] Spain: Const, Art 20.3.   [202] Spain: Law 4/1980.

[203] Spain: Report of 10 February 1984: see J Rossell, 'Religious denominations and the media in Spain' in Doe (n 159 above) 231, 248.

[204] France: Law of 30 September 1986, Art 56.

[205] Germany: Interstate Broadcasting Treaty, Art 42: the regime for public stations is similar to that for private ones, which provides: 'The Protestant Churches, the Catholic Church and the Jewish Community shall, upon request, be granted fair time for the transmission of religious programmes; the broadcaster may demand reimbursement for costs'.

[206] Portugal: Law 16/2001 22-1, Art 25; see also Netherlands: Media Act, s 50.

[207] France: Decree of 27 March 1992; Ireland: Radio and Television Act 1988, s 10: this ban was challenged unsuccessfully in *Murphy v Independent Radio and Television Commission* [1998] 2 ILRM 360; Austria: ORF Act, Art 13.5: this does not ban religious advertising on radio, but it bans commercial advertising on radio on Good Friday, All Saints' Day, and Christmas Eve.

[208] Luxembourg: Law of 27 July 1991, Art 268; Austria: ORF Act, Art 15.6.

[209] Netherlands: Media Act 2000, s 41.

[210] Ireland: Code of Standards (1995) para 5.1(iii); Broadcasting Act 2001, s 65: nothing prevents 'the broadcasting of a notice of the fact (a) that a particular religious newspaper, magazine or periodical is available for sale or supply, or (b) that any event or ceremony associated with any particular religion will take place, if the contents of the notice do not address the merits or otherwise of adhering to any religious faith or belief or of becoming a member of any religion or religious organisation'.

[211] Austria: ORF Act, Art 14.1; Spain: Law 34/1988, 11 November; and Res of 17 April 1980, and Res of 22 January 2001 of General Director of the Mass Media approved by RTVE (issued on the basis of Law 4/1980).

is not the domain of the criminal law.[212] This is clearly not the case. Nevertheless, national laws which protect religious doctrine and belief do not signal that the State recognizes the value of religious doctrine per se, but they do recognize its value for those who hold and adhere to it. Some might consider that this is tantamount to indirect or implicit recognition of the value of religion, but what States acknowledge is the value of religious doctrine in terms of the potential of attacks upon it for social conflict. Blasphemy is still an offence in several States—predominantly those with a state church, though in these it aims to protect the doctrines of all religions. However, in most States it has been abolished. Usually this has occurred as a result of dissatisfaction about its historical association with the protection of Christianity, the rarity of prosecutions for it, or a process of separation of State and religion— though in Ireland recent debate has resulted in its retention. The offence of defamation of religion is more common. Outrage to religious feelings may also be an aspect of both blasphemy and defamation of religion but their special protection is not easy to justify. Nevertheless, the principle which emerges is that individuals who insult religion in such a way as to jeopardize public order may be the subject of criminal proceedings. A similar principle may be induced from national laws with regard to crimes against worship: individuals should not disrupt the lawful exercise of worship or other associated activities of a faith community (including funeral rites), and if they do so criminal proceedings may be instituted against them. Once more, States do not seem to value religious worship per se but simply the right to religious freedom of which worship is a manifestation. Whilst crimes against worship are more common, crimes against doctrine rarely come before the courts. It is tempting to speculate on the reasons for this. The former usually involve a more visible expression of physical harm than the latter. Freedom of expression is more at stake in the latter than the former. Moreover, it might be that codes of practice and the like on the coverage of religion in the media are proving to be an effective mechanism to ensure compliance with the standards of the criminal law (which they often mirror) in this field. In any event, it is a general principle of religion law common to the States of Europe that freedom of expression does not extend to the unjustified vilification of any religion.

---

[212] M Kotiranta, 'The relation between religion and criminal law as a topic of discussion throughout Europe: an introduction to the national reports' in Kotiranta and Doe (n 2 above) 3: 'Although there has been a desire in modern Europe to keep legislation on religious freedom outside the domain of the criminal law, the multicultural character of the society in which we live has raised, once again, and in a new form, the issue of whether particular protection should be granted for religious feelings.'

7

The Property and Finances of Religion

Issues which relate to the property and finances of religion are commonly the subject of public debate and controversy—from the mineral exploitation of sacred mountains, through the slaughter of sacred animals, to the construction of minarets.[1] With regard to religious property, this chapter examines the right of religious organizations to acquire, administer, and dispose of property. It also studies the restitution of religious property confiscated under former political regimes, and the protection of sacred places, objects, vesture, and human remains. As to religious finances, all States in Europe fund religion, to lesser or greater extents, either directly or indirectly or both. The following examines the so-called church tax, deductions from tax liability for religious purposes, compensation for the confiscation of religious property, direct subsidies by the State to fund religious activities, and tax exemptions for religion. Such arrangements have a profound effect on the classical understanding that there are three models of religion-state relations in Europe—they suggest that in relation to both property and finance, though possibly more markedly with regard to finance, national laws produce intimate links between the State and religion. With property and finance, the dominant model of religion-state relations across Europe is that of cooperation. Moreover, there is perhaps no better area of law to illustrate the value which States place on religion and its activities than laws which facilitate their preparedness to spend money on them. What follows also seeks to articulate the principles of religion law on property and finance common to the States of Europe.

The property of religious organizations

Religious organizations need property to carry out their worship and ritual, to transact their administrative business, and to accommodate a host of other activities associated with their charitable and educational objects. The States of Europe treat

---

[1] Ireland: *Tara Prospecting Ltd v Minister for Energy* [1993] ILRM 771: the court upheld a government decision to prohibit mineral exploitation on a mountain associated with St Patrick; Wales: *R (on the application of Swami Suryananda) v Welsh Ministers* [2007] EWCA Civ 893: the court upheld an order by the Welsh Assembly Government to slaughter (since it had tested positive for the bacterium causing bovine tuberculosis) a sacred bullock at a Hindu temple; Switzerland: following much debate, and a referendum on 29 November 2009 (at which 57% voted in favour), the federal constitution was amended: 'The construction of minarets is prohibited': Art 72.3.

religious property by means of both civil law and criminal law. Civil law deals with the acquisition, administration, disposal, and restitution of the property of religious organizations. Criminal law penalizes offences with regard to places of worship, objects of religious devotion, the use of clerical vesture, and memorials to the dead. Civil and criminal laws on religious property may be justified on the basis of several values—and sometimes these may be in tension with each other. From the religious perspective, the peaceful enjoyment of property is a fundamental aspect of both religious freedom and the right of faith communities to institutional autonomy. From the secular perspective, given that much religious property in Europe is of historical, architectural, and cultural importance, States have a direct interest in its protection as part of the national heritage. The right to the peaceful enjoyment of property under the ECHR is a limited one,[2] but Strasbourg has recognized the importance of the free enjoyment of property to the exercise of religious liberty.[3]

The right to acquire, administer, and dispose of property

National laws across Europe provide for the right of religious organizations to acquire, administer, and dispose of property in a number of different ways. Much of the time, the right is implicit in the general property law or in laws applicable to religious autonomy,[4] but occasionally it is found expressly in constitutions or in laws at the sub-constitutional level, particularly those which deal with the legal personality of faith communities. Constitutional statements of the right straddle the various religion-state models of Europe. In the state-church system of Greece, for example, the constitution makes special provision for the property rights of the Orthodox Church of Greece—it recognizes that the monasteries of the Ecumenical Patriarchate and the property of the Orthodox Patriarchate of the Middle East cannot be alienated,[5] and that the territory of Mount Athos belongs to its monasteries.[6] In the separation system of Ireland, the constitution provides for both the right and the limitations which may be placed on its free exercise: 'Every religious denomination shall have the right to . . . own, acquire and administer property, movable and immovable'; however: 'The property of any religious denomination . . . shall not be diverted save for necessary works of public utility and on payment of compensation.'[7]

---

[2] ECHR, Protocol 1, Art 1: 'Every natural or legal person is entitled to the peaceful enjoyment of his possessions. No one shall be deprived of his possessions except in the public interest and subject to the conditions provided for by law and by the general principles of international law'; but this does not impair 'the right of a state to enforce such laws as it deems necessary to control the use of property in accordance with the general interest or secure the payment of taxes or other contributions or penalties'.

[3] C Evans, *Freedom of Religion under the European Convention on Human Rights* (Oxford: OUP, 2001) 107.

[4] For the former, see eg Slovenia: the right to property of all citizens (Const, Art 33) applies by implication to religion; for the latter, see Ch 5 above.

[5] Greece: Const, Art 18.8; the Court of Appeal in Thessaloniki has held that this also applies to Roman Catholic monasteries: Decision 1161/1983.

[6] Greece: Const, Art 105.2.   [7] Ireland: Const, Art 44.2.5 and 6.

The right is also guaranteed constitutionally in the cooperation systems of Germany and Austria, in brief terms,[8] and Cyprus, in very fulsome terms: there shall be no deprivation, restriction, or limitation on the right to acquire, own, possess, enjoy, or dispose of any movable or immovable property belonging to any See, monastery, church, or any other ecclesiastical corporation; moreover, no rights over such property shall be exercised without the written consent of the appropriate ecclesiastical authority; a similar rule applies to Muslim *vakfs* and mosques.[9] The Polish constitution seems unique: it justifies the right as one required by religious freedom to satisfy the needs of believers and for others to benefit from religious services; and this is supplemented by rules in statutes applicable to faith communities individually.[10]

It is more common for States to recognize the right to acquire, administer, and dispose of property in laws and other instruments operative at sub-constitutional level as a function of the legal personality of a religious organization.[11] Once more, national arrangements transcend the three classical religion-state models. The separation system of France enables *associations cultuelles* to own and administer property, as may Catholic *associations diocésaines*, but Catholic churches built before 1905 vest in the State (which must maintain them).[12] In the state-church system of the United Kingdom, where a place of public worship may be registered,[13] the trustees of religious organizations have a right to acquire, administer, and dispose of property, sometimes on the basis of statutes applicable to those organizations individually.[14] Much the same applies in Greece, where the right to own extends beyond the Orthodox Church,[15] and in Finland, where, moreover, the national churches and other faith communities may administer cemeteries[16] and crematoria.[17] The right is also explicit in countries with a cooperation system of religion-state relations; this is the case in Latvia, Hungary, and Slovakia,[18] and in Romania

---

[8] Germany: 'Property rights and other rights of religious societies or associations in their institutions, foundations, and other assets intended for purposes of worship, education, or charity shall be guaranteed': WRV, Art 138.2 and GG, Art 140; for a similar formula see Austria: Constitutional Act, Art 15; Art 6.2: the State may limit the right for the public good.

[9] Cyprus: Const, Art 23.9; and Art 23.10: no rights shall be exercisable over the objects and property of mosques or other religious institutions without the consent of the Turkish Communal Chamber.

[10] Poland: Const, Art 53.2: 'Freedom of religion shall also include possession of sanctuaries and other places of worship for the satisfaction of the needs of believers as well as the right of individuals, wherever they may be, to benefit from religious services'; see eg Law of 13 May 1994, Art 33: Lutherans; see also Lithuania: Const, Art 43.3: prayer houses; and LORCA, Art 13.

[11] Again, one basis for such rights is the constitutional guarantee of religious freedom.

[12] France: Laws of 2 January 1907 and 3 April 1908; see also Law of 1905, Arts 12 *et seq.*

[13] See generally J Rivers, *The Law of Organized Religions* (Oxford: OUP, 2010) ch 5.

[14] See eg Baptist and Congregational Trusts Act 1951; for legislation applicable to the Church of England see M Hill, *Ecclesiastical Law* (Oxford: OUP, 3rd edn, 2007) ch 7.

[15] Strasbourg: *Canea Catholic Church v Greece* (1999) 27 EHRR 521.

[16] Finland: FRA 2003, s 14; Cemeteries Act (HE 204/2002) s 8; see Church Law (1055/1993) for Lutherans, and Orthodox Church Act (179/1970); see also Sweden: Funeral Act 1990, Ch 2, ss 6–7.

[17] Finland: Environmental Protection Act (86/2000).

[18] Latvia: LORO, 7 September 1995, Art 16; Hungary: Act CXXV/2003, Art 22; Slovakia: Act no 308/199.

the Orthodox Church and other religious groups have the exclusive right to produce and sell religious objects.[19]

The need for cooperation between the State and religion is the hallmark of national laws on the construction of places of worship. Some States recognize in religious organizations a formal legal right to establish places of worship.[20] The law may also confer rights to request state subsidies for this purpose.[21] However, the approval of public planning authorities is generally required for the construction of places of worship. A particularly restrictive regime operated in Greece, where a religious group had to obtain the consent of the local Orthodox Church for the construction of a place of worship—the Greek courts considered this compatible with Article 9 ECHR,[22] but Strasbourg did not;[23] and today the law provides: 'The permit or opinion of the local authorities of the Greek Orthodox Church is not required for the establishment, construction or operation of a temple or church of any religion or doctrine, with the exception of the Greek Orthodox Church.'[24] Moreover, the decision in Slovenia to call a referendum on the construction of an Islamic mosque was defeated on the basis of religious freedom: 'it is crucial for the exercise of the right to free profession of religion that religious communities are allowed to build their own buildings which correspond to their way of religious worship, religious rites, and customs'.[25] The refusal of a planning authority to permit the construction of a minaret attached to an Islamic centre was also overturned by the Swiss Federal Supreme Court on similar grounds; however, following a referendum on the matter in 2009, the Swiss constitution was amended to prohibit the erection of minarets, largely on the basis of the view that minarets were symbols of political rather than religious significance.[26]

Sacred places may also be the subject of civil law protection as monuments of cultural importance;[27] this may even include natural sites which have a particular

---

[19] Romania: Law 103 of 1992.

[20] Spain: LORF, Art 2: religious freedom covers 'the right of churches, faiths and religious communities to establish places of worship or assembly for religious purposes'; Portugal: Law 16/2001, 22 June; Slovakia: Const, Art 24.

[21] Belgium: Imperial Decree of 30 December 1809, Art 92.3; Law of 4 March 1870, Law of 7 August 1931; RD, 2 July 1949 and 1 July 1952; see more fully below.

[22] Greece: Law 1363/1938, Art 1; SC, Decision no 421/1991.

[23] *Manoussakis and ors v Greece* (1997) 23 EHRR 387; *Pentidis and ors v Greece* App no 23238/94 (ECtHR 9 June 1997); see also *Vergos v Greece* App no 65501/01 (ECtHR, 24 June 2004): refusal to designate an area to construct a prayer-house was interference with the right to manifest religion 'through worship and observance'.

[24] Greece: Law 3467/2006, Art 27; such applications must be submitted to the Ministry of National Education and Religious Affairs not to the local authorities of the Orthodox Church.

[25] Slovenia: CCt, Case no U-I-111/04 (July 2004).

[26] Switzerland: Const, Art 72.3: 'The construction of minarets is prohibited'; the Swiss government, Federal Commission on Racism, Catholic Bishops' Conference, Federation of Swiss Protestant Churches, and Federation of Jewish Communities, *inter alia*, opposed the ban on grounds of religious freedom: see M Stüssi, 'Banning minarets: addressing the validity of a controversial Swiss popular initiative' (2008) 3(2) Religion and Human Rights (2008) 135–53; the ban was also criticized by the UN Human Rights Council in March 2010.

[27] Portugal: Law no 107/2001, 8 September, Art 4; Poland: Law of 17 May 1989, Art 17; Luxembourg: they may be seen as public buildings: COS, Decision of 13 July 1938.

religious association.[28] Latvia is typical: places of worship may be listed as monuments of historical and architectural importance and officially recognized and
protected as such; moreover, the agreement with the Holy See singles out the
special significance of one such site.[29] Consequently, States employ a variety of
mechanisms which seek to strike a balance between the free use of such buildings by
religious organizations and their protection by the State as part of the national
heritage. For example, States sometimes formally require religious organizations to
make available to society their historic, artistic, and documentary patrimony.[30] In
some States religious buildings of cultural significance may be altered only with the
consent of the relevant public authority,[31] on which religions may be represented.[32]
In others religious organizations may enjoy limited exemptions from planning law
with regard to work on their places of worship; this is the position in Ireland[33] and
the United Kingdom—in England and Wales places of public religious worship
may be registered,[34] and there is a limited exemption from the requirement for
listed building consent in relation to ecclesiastical buildings which are used for
ecclesiastical purposes.[35] Again, there is sometimes provision for the transfer of
religious buildings to the State when they are no longer used for religious purposes,[36] or for their demolition on grounds of public health and safety, usually with
the consent of the religious organization in question.[37]

Property disputes within or between religious organizations often come before
the courts (though they may also be resolved through legislation) and the State must

[28] Ireland: *Tara Prospecting Ltd v Minister for Energy* [1993] ILRM 771: the mountain site had been
associated with St Patrick; it was held that it is lawful for the government to prohibit mineral
exploitation activities on a site when the activity would be 'offensive on religious grounds'.

[29] Latvia: Law of 1995; Agreement with the Holy See, Art 11: 'The Shrine of Aglona is part of the
cultural and historical heritage of the Republic . . . and as such is protected by existing legal provisions.'

[30] Spain: Agreements with the Holy See, on Education and Cultural Affairs 1979, Art 15:
availability; on Legal Affairs 1979, Art 1.5: demolition; and Art 1.6: respect for archives.

[31] Sweden: Cultural Heritage Act, Lagen (1988:950).

[32] Austria: from December 2009 protection is afforded to monuments owned by recognized
churches and religious communities only on declaration by the State of the monument as one of
public interest: DenkmalschutsG 2001, s 2.1; no alterations are permitted without the consent of the
Federal Authority for Monuments (s 5) but those for worship are allowed if there is a compelling
liturgical reason; there are religious representatives on the Council for Historic Monuments:
Denkmalbeirat-VO 1979, s 5.

[33] Ireland: the law also imposes controls over changes to the interior of places of worship: Planning
and Development Act 2000, s 4(2); Planning and Development Regulations 2001, SI 600/2001,
Art 10; see s 52(2) of the Act of 2001 for interior changes. See also National Monuments Act 1930 (as
amended 1954 to 2004): many religious sites are covered by this.

[34] UK, England and Wales: Places of Worship Registration Act 1855; a place of worship is 'a place
of which the principal use is as a place where people come together as a congregation or assembly to do
reverence to God': *R v Registrar General, ex p Segerdal* [1970] 2 QB 679, 707; registration attracts local
tax exemption (see below), but if the public is excluded it is not eligible for registration: *Gallagher
(Valuation Officer) v Church of Jesus Christ of Latter-day Saints* [2008] UKHL 56.

[35] UK, England and Wales: Planning (Listed Buildings and Conservation Areas) Act 1990, s 60(1);
it extends to the Church of England, Church in Wales, Roman Catholic Church, Methodist
Church, Baptist Union, and United Reformed Church.

[36] Malta: Act IV 1992; Act of 2002, Art 52: Catholic cultural property is to come within
the exclusive control of the Catholic Cultural Heritage Commission (with similar provision for
other religious groups) rather than under the supervision of the Superintendent of Cultural Heritage.

[37] Portugal: LORF 2001 22 June Law 16/2001; also the State may appropriate Catholic places of
worship of historical importance but the church may retain the right to use them: Concordat, Art 22.1.

not be in breach of its duty of neutrality in such cases.[38] However, a particularly remarkable case from Cyprus illustrates the limits of the competence of religious organizations with regard to personal property. In a case dealing with the question of whether relatives of a deceased Orthodox monk had a right to his property, the Supreme Court held that: (1) the exclusive right of the Orthodox Church to regulate and administer its property (in accordance with its Charter) does not extend to the personal property of its monks; (2) the property of its monks is not to be assumed to be the property of the church; (3) each monk continues to enjoy the right to his own property, as safeguarded by the constitution; and (4) as a monastery does not have the right to such property, the relatives of the monk were considered to be his heirs with a right of succession to his personal property. The decision has been much criticized: the court did not give due weight to the claim of the monastery to religious freedom, to the fact that the monk had voluntarily submitted himself to the Charter of the Orthodox Church which provides that the property of all monks belongs to the monastery, or to Cypriot succession law which safeguards the rights of religious organizations.[39]

By way of contrast, many States provide for the restitution of religious property confiscated under former political regimes. France made provision to remedy confiscation of religious property following the revolution,[40] as did both Germany[41] and Austria,[42] following the Second World War. Today, provision is made for restitution of religious property confiscated under communism in, for instance, the Czech Republic,[43] Bulgaria,[44] Lithuania,[45] Poland,[46] and Slovakia.[47]

---

[38] See eg UK: *General Assembly of the Free Church of Scotland v Lord Overtoun, Macalister v Young* [1904] 515; *Varsani v Jesani* [1999] Ch 219; *Dean v Burne* [2009] EWHC 1250; Strasbourg: *Holy Synod of the Bulgarian Orthodox Church (Metroplitan Inokentiy) and Ors v Bulgaria* App nos 412/03 and 35677/04 (ECtHR 22 January 2009): the State must not breach its neutrality in the resolution of religious property disputes. For resolution by statute, see eg Estonia: RT I 2003, 3, 18; RT I 2004, 1, 1: these authorized schemes to resolve a dispute between the Estonian Apostolic Orthodox Church and the Russian Orthodox Church based on a settlement of 4 October 2002.

[39] Cyprus: *Holy Monastery of Mahairas v Maria Papasavva* Civil Appeal, no 12193, 4/4/2007; the court relied principally on Const, Art 23; whilst it did not consider Succession Law, Art 53, the court acknowledged that the Orthodox Church had the exclusive right under Const, Art 110.1 to administer its own affairs and property in accordance with the Holy Canons and its Charter, but that this did not extend to the property of monks: see A Emilianides, 'The constitutional position of the Charter of the Orthodox Church of Cyprus' (2005) 1 *Nomokanonika* 41 (in Greek).

[40] France: under the *ancien régime* the Catholic Church possessed large estates; by a Decree of 2 November 1789, these were nationalized and in return the State undertook to pay stipends for ministers of the four recognized cults (Lutheran, Reformed, Catholic, Jewish); this is still much the same today in the eastern departments; but Law of 1905, Art 2 ended ministerial salaries from public funds; see also UK: the Welsh Church Act 1914 disendowed the Church of England in Wales and redistributed funds to various bodies, but the Church in Wales retains ownership of church buildings.

[41] Germany: the government pays €3m to the Central Jewish Council; there are similar agreements between the *länder* and Jewish communities: eg Saxony-Anhalt pays €750,000 pa.

[42] Austria: Austrian State Treaty, Art 26; see n 186 below.

[43] Czech Rep: Act no 298/1990 Sb and 338/1991 Sb restored the property of 170 religious houses.

[44] Bulgaria: the Labour Land Law Property Act of 12 March 1946 was repealed by the Law of 1992, SG, no 15, 21 February 1992 and the religious property of legal persons restored.

[45] Lithuania: Law on the Restoration of Prayer Houses etc, February 1990 (repealing Decree of 6 June 1948).

[46] Poland: Law of 1989 Dz U 1990, no 61, item 354.

[47] Slovakia: nationalization was compensated by State-funded salaries to clergy: Act no 218/1949 Coll; restitution was effected by Act no 298/1990 Coll; Act no 282/1991; Act no 161/2005.

The issue is still very much alive, and has led to much litigation in Romania, where in 1948 the State declared itself owner of all religious property and transferred the right to use the properties of the Greek-Catholic Church to the Romanian Ortho-dox Church.[48] Much property has been returned but there are still claims for about 300 churches outstanding and Strasbourg has condemned delays in resolution of the matter as contrary to Articles 6 (fair trial) and Article 13 (effective remedy) ECHR.[49] Moreover, in Hungary six religious organizations have agreed to abandon their restitution claims for an annual allowance; such agreements are then ratified by law.[50] Similarly, in Slovenia the State must return in kind religious property confiscated under communist nationalization programmes, or if this is not possible they must pay compensation; a law of 1991 suspending for three years the restitution of farmlands and forest was declared unconstitutional.[51] In short, that States must restore confiscated religious property is but one application of the wider principle shared by all European countries that faith communities have a right to acquire, administer, and dispose of their own property, subject to such lawful limits as may be imposed in the public interest and to preserve the national heritage.

The protection of sacred places and objects in criminal law

Alongside laws which penalize restraint of religious freedom, incitement to religious hatred, defamation of religion, and disturbance of religious worship (see Chapters 3 and 6), the criminal laws of Europe penalize attacks on, or misuse of, religious property, namely: places of worship, sacred objects, religious vesture, and human remains. Like the rules of civil law on the preservation of religious property of historical, architectural and cultural significance, these crimes usually directly protect the temporal value of such properties—only indirectly, if at all, might they be understood to recognize the value of the religious activities associated with them.[52]

Sacred places: In most States, attacks on places of worship do not constitute a specific offence but are forbidden by the general law on criminal damage to property.[53] However, in some States, desecration of a sacred place is a distinct crime. For instance, Portuguese law penalizes intentionally 'desecrating a place of worship in a manner likely to disturb public peace'.[54] In other States, desecration is

---

[48] Romania: Decree 177 of 1948 was repealed by Decree 9 of 1989; Decree 126 of 1990 sets out a procedure and commission for restitution; disputes sometimes arise: see eg CA, Cluj, Decision 156/ 1996.
[49] *Sfântul Vasile Polonă Greek Catholic Parish v Romania* App no 65965/01 (ECtHR, 7 April 2009); also, a court refusal to hear a petition of a Greek Catholic parish for an order requiring an Orthodox parish to allow it to hold services in its former church was held to be in breach of ECHR, Art 6: *Sâmbata Bihor Greek Catholic Parish v Romania* App no 48107/99 (ECtHR, 12 January 2010).
[50] Hungary: Act 32/1991; see also CCt, Decision 4/1993 (II. 12) AB.
[51] Slovenia: CCt, Decisions and Rulings, OdlUS V, 174 (Decision no U-I-107/96, 5 December 1996).
[52] In this sense, such rules may be distantly related to religious freedom; it would be instructive to examine the legislative processes leading to the enactment of the criminal laws studied here in order to determine what role, if any, concepts of religious freedom played in their justification.
[53] See eg UK: Criminal Damage Act 1971, s 1; Romania: PC, Art 217; Sweden: PC (BrB), 12:1.
[54] Portugal: PC, Art 251; see also Spain: PC, Art 613.

included within the offence of defamation of religion; in Cypriot law it is an offence if any person destroys, damages, or defiles any place of worship with the intention of insulting religion (or with knowledge that such will result).[55] Moreover, Greece penalizes acts which demonstrate contempt for the sacred character of a place of worship in such a way as to offend the religious feelings of the faithful.[56] However, Austria classifies a criminal offence against places of worship as one of public nuisance.[57] Sometimes, agreements with the Catholic Church affirm the duty of the State to ensure respect for sacred places; this is the case, for example, in Lithuania.[58]

Sacred objects: Whilst in many States the general law on criminal damage applies *mutatis mutandis* to religious objects,[59] in several States such objects attract special penal protection; these include States which have no specific law dedicated to desecration of places of worship. The purposes of protection and the definitional elements of the offences vary as between the States. Three approaches seem to be used. In the separation system of France, the basis of protection is that of heritage: the law criminalizes the destruction, degradation, or deterioration of objects of patrimony, an archaeological discovery, or cultural goods from a place of worship;[60] the same applies in Luxembourg, where the destruction or degradation of monuments, statues, and other artefacts placed in churches and temples is prohibited.[61] However, Portugal criminalizes intentional desecration of an object of worship or religious veneration when this is done in a way likely to disturb public peace.[62] Other States use the ubiquitous defamation of religion. In Italy it is an offence intentionally to destroy, plunder, daub, or damage objects intended for religious practice; the conduct is more serious if it causes offence to the religious confession in question; it is also a crime to insult religious objects without their physical damage.[63] The penalties vary considerably: in Belgium a person who, through acts, words, gestures, or threats, offends religious objects (either in places for religious practice, or during public religious ceremonies) is punishable with prison for fifteen days to six months and a fine;[64] but in Greece, removal of objects of divine worship from a place intended for such worship is aggravated theft punishable with prison for up to ten years.[65]

Similar crimes have recently been introduced in some countries of central and eastern Europe following the fall of communism; for example Hungarian law

---

[55] Cyprus: PC, Art 138 (Ch 154); this applies to sacred places of known religions: Const, Art 18.2; see also Poland: PC, Art 196; Ireland: Defamation Act 2009, s 36: matters 'held sacred'.

[56] Greece: PC, Art 200(2).

[57] Austria: PC, para 189, para 2: this deals with offences at places of worship.

[58] Lithuania: Agreement of 5 May 2000, Art 7.

[59] See n 53 above and eg Romania: PC, Art 360: destruction of, *inter alia*, great libraries, archives of historical or scientific value, works of art, manuscripts, is punishable with 5–20 years' imprisonment.

[60] France: PC, Art 322–3; see also Denmark, Strfl, para 139; see Netherlands: PC, Art 147.

[61] Luxembourg: PC, Art 526; imprisonment and a fine may be imposed; see also Art 144.

[62] Portugal: PC, Art 251.

[63] Italy: PC, Art 404; see also Cyprus: PC, Art 138 (Ch 154).

[64] Belgium: PC, Art 144; see also Italy: PC, Art 404.

[65] Greece: PC, Art 374.

penalizes a person who desecrates objects of religious worship or objects used for conducting the ceremonies on or outside premises designated for the purposes of ceremonies of a registered religious organization.[66] By way of contrast, in Ireland, laws specifically protecting religious property have been replaced by general offences of criminal damage. The crime of sacrilege was abolished in 1976; moreover, churches, chapels, meeting houses, and other places of divine worship, and objects within them, had been specifically protected by the Malicious Damage Act 1861.[67] Indeed, in 1986 three men were indicted under the Act for maliciously damaging a statue of the Virgin Mary located in a grotto, but the judge directed the jury to acquit the accused because it had not been proven that the grotto was a place of divine worship.[68] Such crimes were replaced in 1991 by a general offence of criminal damage to property.[69]

Clerical vesture: Several States used to have criminal laws forbidding the misuse of clerical vesture but these have since been abolished; this is the case, for example, in Portugal[70] and France (with the exception of Alsace-Moselle).[71] Today in the majority of States the offence of fraud would cover the unauthorized use of religious garments worn in order to impersonate ministers of religion.[72] However, some States specifically penalize such conduct. For example, under Estonian law, only a person to whom a religious association has granted such permission may wear the professional attire of a minister of religion as prescribed in the statutes of that religious association. The rule does not apply if the attire of the minister of religion is ordinary clothing.[73] The same applies in Romania.[74] Similarly, in Luxembourg, any person who publicly wears a costume, uniform, decoration, ribbon, or other insignia of an order to which he does not belong is punished by a fine. It has been held that this provision includes the official garments of ministers of religion; the conduct must be fraudulent—namely, to persuade others that the person possesses the status conveyed in wearing the item.[75]

The offence is most prevalent in state-church systems where the criminal law protects the use of clerical vesture by the national or established churches in relation to the exercise of public ministerial functions. In the United Kingdom, a person

---

[66] Hungary: Act 69/1999, para 150.

[67] Ireland: Criminal Law (Jurisdiction) Act 1976.

[68] Ireland: under s 39 of the Act: 'Gang damages "moving" statue etc' *Irish Times*, 1 November 1985.

[69] Ireland: Criminal Damage Act 1991, ss 2–5.

[70] Portugal: PC, 1852, Art 134 (as amended in 1911): 'a person who pretending to have the quality of a minister of a religion exercises publicly any of the acts of the same religion', shall be penalized; this was abrogated by DL no 400/82 of 23 September.

[71] France: see the pre-1905 PC, Art 259; in Belgium, prohibitions on the unauthorized public use of clothing which expresses an officially-recognized function apply to clerical garb: PC, Art 228.

[72] Czech Rep: PC, ss 209, 250; Hungary: PC, para 318; Ireland: Criminal Justice (Theft and Fraud Offences) Act 2001, ss 4, 6, and 7; see also: 'Sex attacker seen posing as priest' *Irish Independent*, 30 July 2007; Cyprus: PC, Art 109 (Ch 154).

[73] Estonia: CCA 2002, Art 21; it may also be an aggravating factor: PC, para 58: 'taking advantage of an official uniform or badge in order to facilitate commission of the offence'.

[74] Romania: Law no 489/2006; Art 23(4); see also PC, Art 281.

[75] Luxembourg: PC, Art 228; Trib Corr Diekirch, 21 December 1962, Pas 19, 148.

who knowingly and wilfully solemnizes a marriage according to the rites of the Church of England falsely pretending to be in Holy Orders is liable to imprisonment for a term not exceeding fourteen years; the offence also applies to marriages solemnized in the disestablished Church in Wales.[76] It is also unlawful (but no longer a crime) for a minister of religion to assume the name, style, or title of archbishop of any province, bishop of any diocese, or dean of any deanery already settled as titles operative in the Church of England.[77] In similar fashion, Denmark criminalizes the misuse of religious garments of the national church in the exercise of prescribed public functions on the basis that the garments belong to Danish public authorities.[78] However, more extensive protection is afforded in Greece beyond the national church: any person wearing in public, without being entitled to do so, the robes of a religious official of the Greek Orthodox Church or of any other known religion in Greece is liable to be sentenced to imprisonment for up to six months or to a fine.[79]

Human remains and memorials to the dead: As seen in Chapter 6, national laws commonly protect the administration of funeral rites. Similarly, most States penalize the abuse and removal of human remains.[80] Whilst some classify the offence as 'profanation of a corpse' (Luxembourg),[81] or breach of the sanctity of a grave (Finland),[82] for several States the offence is one of dishonouring the dead. Portugal is typical: a person who without authorization abducts, destroys, or hides a corpse or part of it, or ashes of a deceased person, or desecrates such corpse or ashes, through acts offensive of the respect due to the dead is punishable with imprisonment or a fine.[83] Spain has a similar offence, and if the offence is committed with the religion of the deceased in mind this is treated as an aggravating factor for the purposes of sentencing;[84] moreover, the offence is committed if the feelings of loved ones are injured,[85] as is also the case in Cyprus.[86] The sanctions for such offences reflect their seriousness: as well as fines, prison sentences which may be imposed range from two years in Portugal, Sweden, and Lithuania[87] to three years

---

[76] UK: Marriage Act 1949, s 75(1)(d); also s 78: the Church of England includes the Church in Wales.

[77] UK: Ecclesiastical Titles Act 1871; this also abolished the crime.

[78] Denmark: Strfl, para 132, stk 1, nr 1.

[79] Greece: PC, Art 176; with respect to the Church of Greece, the clergy's robe is described in the PD of 21 January 1931; for usurpation of functions, see PC, Art 175.2.

[80] Austria: PC, para 190; see also Denmark: Strfl, para 139; Czech Rep: PC, s 202a; Italy: PC, Arts 407–413; UK: *R v Sharpe* (1857) Dears & B 160.

[81] Luxembourg: PC, Art 453.1.

[82] Finland: PC, Ch 17, s 12.

[83] Portugal: PC, Art 254.

[84] Spain: PC, Art 526: a person who 'profanes a cadaver or its ashes', is 'liable to imprisonment for 12–24 weekends and fined [at the prescribed rate] for 3–6 months'; for the aggravated offence, see PC, Art 22.4.

[85] Spain: HC, Ruling of 26 November 1984: on the basis of an equivalent provision in previous law, it was held that such conduct involved 'disturbing the eternal rest and peace of the dead, as well as respect due their memory and the sentiments of their friends and loved ones'.

[86] Cyprus: PC, Art 140 (Ch 154): the offence is committed by a person who with intent to wound the feelings or insult the religion of any person offers indignity to a human corpse.

[87] Portugal: PC, Art 254; Sweden: PC (BrB), Art 16:10; Lithuania: PC, Arts 311, 312.

in Romania,[88] and up to eight years in Poland.[89] The lawful removal of human remains from consecrated ground may also require the consent of the religious body which owns that ground; this is the case in England.[90]

When States penalize the desecration of a tomb or memorial, they do so on the basis of similar foundations. The most common is disrespect for the dead,[91] or the memory of the dead; for example, under Spanish law a person who fails to show due respect to the memory of the deceased, violates gravesites or tombs, or wilfully outrages, destroys, alters, or damages funeral urns, pantheons, gravestones, or tombs, is liable to imprisonment and a fine; if the offence is motivated by religion the sentence is greater.[92] However, Swedish law penalizes disturbance to 'the peace of a tomb' by causing damage to a coffin, urn, grave, or other resting-place of the deceased or at a sepulchral monument without authorization.[93] The basis of a similar offence in Finland and Denmark is the sanctity of a grave.[94] The sanctions vary as between States: in Austria a person who abuses a burial, resting, or memorial place is to be punished with imprisonment for up to six months or a fine,[95] in Romania for up to three years in prison,[96] and in Bulgaria theft from a grave is punishable with imprisonment for one to ten years.[97] The laws of Belgium and France double the sentence when desecration of a sepulchre is motivated by religion.[98] In other countries, there is no specific offence with regard to desecration of memorials to the dead but such conduct is covered by the general law on criminal damage.[99] From the legal evidence outlined above, it seems to be a principle of religion law common to the States of Europe that sacred places, religious objects, clerical vesture, human remains, and memorials to the dead must be respected by States and citizens alike.

---

[88] Romania: PC, Art 318.

[89] Poland: PC, Art 262.

[90] See eg UK: Burial Act 1857, s 25: if the corpse is buried in consecrated ground of the Church of England, a faculty is required from the diocesan court, and if reburial is to be in un-consecrated ground, a licence from the Home Office is also required.

[91] Portugal: PC, Art 254: a person who desecrates a place where there is a resting place or memorial, through acts offensive of the respect due to the dead, is punished with imprisonment up to 2 years or a fine [at the prescribed rate] for up to 240 days; Poland: PC, Art 262; Italy: PC, Arts 407–413; Latvia, Criminal Law (1998), s 228.

[92] Spain: PC, Art 526; see also Art 22.4; see also Cyprus: PC, Art 140 (of Ch 154).

[93] Sweden: PC (BrB), Art 16:10: 2 years' prison; Lithuania, PC, Arts 311–312: prison for up to 1 year.

[94] Finland: PC, Ch 17, s 12: a fine or prison for up to 1 year; Denmark: Strfl, para 139.

[95] Austria: PC, para 190: the fine is 360 daily rates.

[96] Romania: PC, Art 318.

[97] Bulgaria: PC, Art 195(1),(8).

[98] Belgium: PC, Art 453; see also Art 526 for destruction of a tomb; France: PC, Art 225-17; penalty, up to 1 year in prison and €15,000; for religious motivation, the penalty is up to 3 years prison and €45,000; Spain: PC, Art 526; Cyprus: PC, Art 140 (of Ch 154).

[99] Hungary: PC, para 271; Ireland: Criminal Damage Act 1991; *Bennett v Bonaker* (1828) 2 Hag Eccl 25; 3 Hag Eccl 17; *Adlam v Colthurst* (1867) LR 2A and E 30.

Financial support for religion

One way or another, all the States of Europe fund religion directly or indirectly. This has long been a feature of European religion-state relations, and some speculate that today State financial support has a quasi-contractual character which underscores the mutual interdependence of State and religion.[100] This would seem to be an accurate generalization. What follows seeks both to substantiate the claim on the basis of the details of national laws and to suggest that there is a high level of cooperation between State and religion in this field regardless of the particular posture adopted by States in terms of their religion-state relations. At the same time, however, States employ a wide range of *general* approaches to the public financing of religion—from those which are restrictive to those which are facilitative. In a small number of States the law prohibits the endowment of any religion; this is the position under the Irish constitution—but the courts have held that the prohibition only applies to 'permanent financial provision' for a favoured religion;[101] neutral or impermanent financial aid is lawful.[102] French law, too, provides: 'The Republic does not recognize, fund or subsidise any religion'—but there are exceptions;[103] and Danish law prescribes that no one shall be obliged to contribute to the financial support of religion.[104]

Elsewhere a constitutional prohibition is understood to be implicit in the principle of the basic separation of State and religion;[105] and in Spain it has been held that the constitutional principle of cooperation does not impose a duty on the State to fund religion.[106] At the other end of the spectrum there are States in which funding is required by the constitution, as is the case in Denmark in relation to the national church,[107] or more usually by sub-constitutional law, as is the case in

---

[100] R Torfs, 'Church financing—towards a European model?' in B Basdevant-Gaudemet and S Berlingò (eds), *The Financing of Religious Communities in the European Union* (Leuven: Peeters, 2009) 343: in the 19th century, States funded religion to compensate for the nationalization of religious property; in the 20th century, with the growth of the welfare state, cooperation with religion led to support on the basis of partnership; and today, aid incentivizes religious groups to respect the State and its values; indeed, financial support itself affects the neutrality of the State towards religion.

[101] Ireland: Const, Art 44.2.2: 'The State guarantees not to endow any religion'; *Re Article 26 of the Constitution and the Employment Equality Bill* [1997] 2 IR 321, 354.

[102] Ireland: *Campaign to Separate Church and State Ltd and Murphy v Minister for Education* [1998] 3 IR 321: 'there is no reason in principle why the State . . . should not confer benefits on religious denominations, provided . . . that in doing so it remains neutral and does not discriminate in favour of particular religions' (*per* Keane J); thus, it is lawful to fund a Roman Catholic seminary (*McGrath and Ó Ruairc v Trustees of Maynooth College* [1979] ILRM 166) and chaplains in denominational schools (*Campaign to Separate Church and State Ltd and Murphy v Minister for Education* [1998] 3 IR 321).

[103] France: Law of 19 December 1905, Art 2: 'there can be included in these budgets . . . the expenses [as] to chaplaincy services designed to ensure the free exercise of religion in public establishments such as secondary schools, colleges, schools, nursing homes, asylums and prisons'.

[104] Denmark: this is implicit in the principle that no one shall be obliged to support the worship of any God other than his own with financial contributions: Const, Art 68.

[105] Estonia: this is the case on the basis that there is no state church (Const, Art 40).

[106] Spain: CCt, Decision 146 of 21 January 2001.

[107] Denmark: Constitution Act 1953, Part 1, s 4: the Evangelic Lutheran Church shall be 'supported' by the State. Other churches are funded from donations; in relation to specific areas of

Hungary with regard to registered religious organizations.[108] There are also States where the law formally allows[109] or facilitates[110] funding,[111] in order to enable the exercise of religious freedom.[112] In turn, State financial support may be the subject of agreements;[113] for example the agreement between Spain and the Holy See provides: 'The State promises to collaborate with the Catholic Church in the obtaining of adequate economic support, absolutely respecting the principle of religious freedom.'[114] But quasi-contractual support has proved controversial in Estonia as regards its financial agreement with the Estonian Council of Churches.[115]

However, the norm in most, but not all,[116] States is that religious organizations are self-funding.[117] The entitlement of religious organizations to acquire and administer their own finances is obviously implicit in their right to hold and acquire property, but often it is expressly recognized by national laws,[118] sometimes in the form of a right to receive collections from the faithful.[119] Some States

potential funding, see Romania: religious organizations shall enjoy support from the State including facilitation of religious assistance in the army, hospitals, prisons, homes, and orphanages: Const, Art 29.5.

[108] Hungary: LFCRC 1990, Art 19.1: 'the State shall provide a rate of subsidies from the central budget corresponding to that received by similar state institutions, defined in a normative way, for the operation of the educational, teaching, social and health care, sports, children's and youth protection institutions of a church legal entity'; see also Act on the Financial Conditions of Religious and Public Activities of Churches, Act 124/1997; CCt, Decision 22/1997 (IV.25) AB: this requires equal funding.

[109] Germany: WRV, Art 137 VI: this provides for the church tax: see n 128 below.

[110] Sweden: the State 'shall contribute to create the prerequisites of the [registered] religious communities to carry out an actively and long-term directed religious activity in the form of worship, pastoral care, education and care': Law on Support to Religious Communities, SFS 1999:932.

[111] Netherlands: for political debate on the matter see Kamerstukken II, 1989–1990, 20 868, no 2 and II, 1990–91, 20 868, no 3; UCV 47, 22 June 1992, Handelingen II, 1991–92: G Robbers (ed), *State and Church in the European Union* (Baden-Baden: Nomos, 2nd edn, 2005) 384.

[112] The facilitation of religious freedom by means of financial support is an idea invoked in Italy, for example, on the basis of Const, Art 3: the State must 'remove all economic and social obstacles that, by limiting the freedom and equality of citizens, prevent full individual development and participation of all workers in the political, economic and social organisation of the country': D Durisotto, 'Financing of churches in Italy' (2010) 165 Law and Justice 159.

[113] Hungary: as well as the agreement with the Holy See 1997 on financial issues, there are agreements on fiscal issues with the Reformed, Lutheran, Baptist, Serb Orthodox, and Alliance of Jewish Congregations in 1998 (eg funding for rural clergy); Slovakia: Agreement with the Holy See (no 326/2001) and with other registered churches etc (no 250/2002).

[114] Spain: Agreement with the Holy See on Economic Affairs 1979, Art 2.5: the church 'declares its intent to obtain sufficient resources for its needs of its own accord'. The agreements with other religious organizations do not deal with state financial support.

[115] Estonia: in 2004 the Council received about €314,103 (RT I, 2004, 1, 1) whereas in 1999 it was €128,000 (RT I, 1999, 3, 49). The constitutionality of this has been questioned (on the basis of inequality) by non-Christian religious communities; however, Reg of 18 January 2005 allows contracts to be entered with recipients of state subsidies, and the Council and the Ministry of Internal Affairs signed such a contract on 13 April 2006: Robbers (n 111 above) 110.

[116] With its traditions of state funding, private funding is weak in eg Belgium.

[117] France: today they are funded privately and by indirect support; religious cultural associations (but not *associations cultuelles*) may receive state funding.

[118] Austria: church funds are protected by StGG, Art 15.

[119] Slovenia: Acts, nos 15/1976, 42/1986, and 22/1991; see also Spain: Agreement with the Holy See on Economic Affairs 1979, Art 1: 'The Catholic Church may freely obtain payment from the faithful, organise public collections and receive alms and offerings.'

authorize religious organizations to charge fees for the provision of selected religious rituals such as marriage and burial.[120] Nevertheless, as seen in Chapter 4, one common condition of legal recognition is that religious organizations ensure financial accountability with respect to their internal management boards, accounting arrangements, membership fees, and liquidation.[121] Needless to say, a religious association may organize not-for-profit activities, such as hospital, charitable, educational, publishing, or broadcasting work;[122] and some States make express provisions for Islamic financial practices.[123] In any event, under national laws there are five different forms of direct or indirect State financial support for religion: the so-called 'church tax'; tax allocations or deductions; subsidies for the public services performed by religion; compensation for confiscation of and damage to religious property; and tax exemptions or concessions.

The church tax

Whilst most States do not have this facility, the so-called church tax system is used in some countries with a State church.[124] In Finland the members of the Evangelical Lutheran Church and the Orthodox Church pay to these churches part of their income tax; the churches reimburse the State for the cost of collection and those who do not wish to pay the tax must resign from their church;[125] also, private companies must pay part of their corporation tax to the parishes of the Lutheran Church—this generates an annual income of about €1000 million; in 2005 the parish share of the corporation tax was 1.94 per cent.[126] Similarly, in Denmark, the church tax is payable only by members of the national church and it accounts for three-quarters of the budget.[127] However, the system is also employed in some cooperation countries, though only in the central and eastern part of Europe. In Germany, public corporation status entitles a religious organization to

[120] England: Ecclesiastical Fees Measure 1986: this applies to the established Church of England; for Scotland, see the (national) Church of Scotland (Property and Endowments) Act 1925 (as amended).

[121] Finland: FRA 2003, s 10; Estonia: CCA, Art 26; Lithuania: LORCA, Art 11.

[122] Ireland: *Governors of Barrington's Hospital v Minister for Health* [1988] IR 56: the State is not obliged to provide funds for such hospitals; Lithuania: LORCA, Art 14: publishing; Latvia: LORO, 7 September 1995, Arts 13–16: for broadcasting. However, in Denmark a parish council in the national church cannot donate money for the activities of voluntary Christian organizations without the consent of the Ministry of Ecclesiastical Affairs: Act on the Participation of the Folk Church in Inter-church Cooperation (334/1989); see also Act on the Economy of the Folk Church (537/1997).

[123] UK: Finance Act 2005: this allows mortgages that do not offend Islamic prohibitions on usury.

[124] There is no church tax in England: the Church of England is largely self-funded through voluntary payments from the faithful: N Doe, *The Legal Framework of the Church of England* (Oxford: OUP, 1996) 477 *et seq.*

[125] Finland: the church tax is determined on the basis of taxable income in municipal taxation; the church's share of the tax collection expenses is 4.7%. The operational expenditure of the central and diocesan administration of the Orthodox Church is paid mainly from state funds. Other registered religious communities receive no financial state aid but fund themselves (from donations or fees).

[126] Finland: Income Tax Act 1535/1992, s 1.2; in 2003 the Lutheran Church expenses were €67m for cemeteries; the Orthodox parishes receive 0.08% of the tax return.

[127] Denmark: 85% of its income is from members; 15% of its expenditure (eg ministers' salaries) is paid by the State (Const Act 1953, Part 1, s 4: the church shall be 'supported' by the State).

levy a church tax (*kirchensteuer*) on its members which the State collects as a proportion of the income tax they pay.[128] Approximately 80 per cent of the budgets of the Protestant and Catholic churches in Germany are funded by the church tax; the State collects this as a proportion of the income tax at rates of 8 to 9 per cent of the income tax liability of a person, and for doing so it charges a fee (currently 3 to 4 per cent of the sum collected).[129] The Federal Administrative Court has confirmed the legality of the church tax.[130] There is also a system of church tax in Austria, where similarly the adult members of the recognized religious communities must pay (a duty recoverable in State courts) a proportion of their tax and the State collects, but no religious community makes use of the system.[131] The right of the Church of Sweden to levy a tax ended on its disestablishment in 2000, but the church may now impose a public-law charge (*kyrkoavgift*) which the State authorities must collect for the church; this system to collect members' fees is also available to a registered religious community if it 'contributes to the fundamental values on which society is founded, maintained and strengthened' and if it is 'stable and has its own vital power'.[132] The Lutheran Church in Poland has recently introduced an internal tax—but this is not collected through the State tax apparatus.[133]

Allocations from tax liability

Whereas with the church tax, a religious organization is empowered by civil law to tax its members, and the tax is collected by the State, some States expressly entitle individuals to allocate voluntarily a portion of their income tax (collected by the State) to a selected religious or related object; the State then assigns the sum to that object.[134] This is the case in Portugal in relation to settled religious communities,[135] and in the eastern departments of France with regard to the four

---

[128]   Germany: WRV, Art 137.6: 'Religious societies that are corporations under public law shall be entitled to levy taxes on the basis of the civil taxation lists in accordance with Land law'; and Art 138.1: 'Rights of religious societies to public subsidies on the basis of a law, contract or special grant shall be redeemed by legislation of the *Länder*.'

[129]   But only about 35% of the population pays the tax.

[130]   Germany: (1994) File no 1 BvL 8/85.

[131]   Austria: Church Funding Act of 1 May 1939: religious groups recognized under RCA 1874 may enjoy the facility; contributions are classified as private membership fees (which seems to contradict their public law status); the churches can recover the fees by recourse to civil courts. The Greek Orthodox Church has this facility under Law of 23 June 1967 but no law has been made to implement this.

[132]   Sweden: Denominations Act 1998, s 16; Act on Levies to Religious Denominations, Lagen (1999:291, 1999:932).

[133]   Poland: the Catholic Church receives income from collections, donations, and quasi-fees for baptisms, marriages, and burials, and from the pastoral parish visit (just after Christmas) called the *kolęda* (literally 'Christmas carol').

[134]   UK: religious charities receive tax benefits eg through the Gift Aid Scheme; income tax paid by donors on the money that they donate to charity may be reclaimed by the recipient charity.

[135]   Portugal: LORF: they may receive 0.5% of the income tax of a member; the community must apply for this, and the taxpayer must declare its use for religious or charitable aims, and choose a particular community (Art 32); the Concordat with the Holy See, Art 27 also deals with tax deductions.

cultes reconnus.[136] In Italy, the Holy See and religious communities with an agreement with the State may request that voluntary donations from their members are assigned to them (0.8 per cent of their income tax); in the tax declaration the payer ticks a box to enable the money to be used for: the Italian State for extraordinary measures against famine in the world, natural disasters, aid to refugees, conservation of cultural monuments; the Catholic Church, for the purpose of worship (for the benefit of the population), support of the clergy, welfare measures which benefit the national community or third world countries. One denomination with an agreement with the State—the Christian Evangelical-Baptist Union—does not make use of this scheme.[137] A similar system operates in Spain; however here taxpayers may assign (by way of deduction) 0.7 per cent of their income tax to the Catholic Church or to social interest activities decided by the government; there is no provision for such a sum to be assigned to other religious organizations; in 2003, the sum assigned to the Catholic Church was €135 million.[138]

Such arrangements have also been introduced in countries of central and eastern Europe following the demise of former communist regimes. In Hungary a taxpayer who is a member of a registered religious association may donate 1 per cent of income tax to that association and receive a consequential tax deduction; the State supplements the money from the assignment by up to 0.9 per cent of the revenue from income tax according to the proportion assigned.[139] Similarly, in Poland taxpayers may deduct from their tax liability donations to an institution of 'public interest' for up to 10 per cent of their income; however, while churches are not on the list of public interest organizations, church-affiliated bodies are; in the tax declarations for 2005, only 1,156,480 taxpayers used the facility, generating €16 million.[140] In Slovakia, every taxpayer may assign up to 2 per cent of taxable income to an eligible legal entity including churches and religious organizations,[141] and in Slovenia a taxpayer may allocate up to 0.5 per cent of their income tax to a specific religious community for the purpose of the general good.[142] Latvian law offers much the same facility.[143] There is neither a church tax nor provision for tax allocations or deductions in Malta. In short, the system of allocations from the income tax liability of individuals is generally reserved to recognized or registered, and statutory or covenantal, religious organizations with legal personality.

---

[136] Namely the Lutheran, Reformed, Catholic, and Jewish communities.
[137] Italy: the Agreement with the Holy See on Church Entities and Property 1984 (ratified by Law no 222 of 20 May 1985); another system in Italy for both the Catholic Church and religious organizations with agreements is to off-set donations from taxable income to the Catholic Central Institute for the Support of the Clergy or equivalent bodies in other denominations (eg Seventh-Day Adventist Church, Law no 516, 22 November 1988, Art 29).
[138] Spain: Agreement with the Holy See on Economic Affairs 1979, Art 2.2.
[139] Hungary: Act 129/1996.
[140] Poland: Law on Organisations of Public Interest 2003, OJ, Dz U 2003, no 96, item 873.
[141] Slovakia: Act no 595/2003 (income tax).
[142] Slovenia: Personal Income Tax Act, OG, no 117/2006, Art 142.
[143] Latvia: Law on Residents' Income Tax, Ch 10.1.3.

Direct subsidies for religious objects

The principal religious objects under national laws to which States make direct
financial contributions are: the maintenance of historic religious sites; the salaries of
ministers of religion; chaplaincies in hospitals, prisons and the armed forces; the
delivery of religious education in schools; and the educational and other charitable
work of religious organizations. In practice, the enjoyment of State aid is based not
only on the acquisition of legal personality by a religious organization but also on a
host of political and other factors, such as the size and place of the religious group in
society. Needless to say, therefore, the distribution of State aid to faith communities
is not infrequently the subject of debate concerning claims about equality of
treatment.[144]

Places of worship and other religious property: States commonly provide financial
support for the preservation of places of worship of importance to the national life
and heritage. They may do so typically either on the basis of laws, as is the case in
Belgium and Luxembourg,[145] or of agreements, such as in Estonia with respect to
the Estonian Council of Churches.[146] Sometimes aid is extended beyond the
maintenance of historic buildings to that of religious artefacts and archives,[147]
which may also be of educational value.[148] Generally, such funds are enjoyed by
prescribed religious communities; in Lithuania the traditional religions are beneficiaries of funds for the preservation of their monuments allocated under an annual
government resolution,[149] and in Romania, registered religious associations may
receive similar funding.[150] In addition, national laws may provide for other forms
of financial aid. In Italy the State may loan real property to religious bodies and
charge low rents for such property.[151] In France, as well as allocating sums for the
preservation of monuments (and its maintenance of pre-1905 Catholic
churches),[152] the State may guarantee sums borrowed by *associations cultuelles*

---

[144] See eg n 111 above.
[145] Belgium: Law of 13 July 2001; for aid towards the construction of places of worship, see eg Law
of 7 August 1931; RD, 2 July 1949 and 1 July 1952; Luxembourg: the State may maintain Catholic
churches: Decree of 30 December 1809, as public buildings: COS, Decision of 13 July 1938.
[146] Estonia: Protocol of Common Concerns, 17 October 2002; see also Preservation and Development of Sacred Buildings, Government Policy Doc, 11 March 2003: this is the basis of State support
for 2004–2013 for religious sites of historic, communal, and cultural value.
[147] Hungary: Act 124/1997, s 7(1).
[148] Greece: eg there is an annual award to Athens Cathedral: Law 2844/1954; the Patriarchate of
Jerusalem and Monastery of Mount Sinai are entitled to funds for educational purposes: Law
590/1077, Art 1; also, monasteries which transfer to the State forest and pasture receive an annual
subvention: Law 1811/1988 (but the scheme under this law has not yet been implemented).
[149] Lithuania: between 0.8m and 4m LTL is allocated to these to preserve their monuments.
[150] Romania: Law 72 of 1997 and Government Decree 1030 of 2000; Slovenia funds 30–50% of
repair costs; in 2005 funding amounted to €2,484,630; Poland: in 2003, €150,000 was granted for
restoration projects.
[151] Italy: Law no 390 of 1986.
[152] France: Law of 1905, Art 19; Law of 13 April 1908; Law of 25 December 1942; see also CE, 19
June 1914, Vital Pichon: Rec CE, 1914, p 726.

and Catholic diocesan associations for the construction of new places of worship.[153] Grants for the restoration of religious sites are made from a variety of public funds in Ireland[154] and the United Kingdom,[155] where, in England and Wales, a registered place of public religious worship is also exempt from council taxes.[156]

Remuneration for ministers of religion: Most States do not have a system of financing ministers of religion; in France such a system was abolished in 1905 and in the Netherlands it ended in 1983.[157] However, there is a strong tradition of State remuneration for ministers of religion in Luxembourg[158] and in Belgium: here the State pays the salaries and pensions of the ministers of the recognized religious organizations,[159] as well as providing appropriate housing for them.[160] Similarly, in Greece, the State assumes responsibility for a very wide range of expenses related to the clergy of the Orthodox Church, including their training, salaries, pensions,[161] and expenses incurred in the administration of the sacraments and other rituals at homes, hospitals, and cemeteries;[162] it also covers the remuneration of lay employees of the church,[163] and, in Thrace, the salaries of the three official Muslim religious leaders.[164] Likewise, Cyprus pays the salaries of Orthodox clergy who minister in rural areas and (since 1999) those of ministers of three other recognized religious organizations.[165] In 2000, the Ecclesiastical Fund (*kyrkofonden*) was set up

---

[153] France: *départements, communes* and the Finance Ministry may do so: Law of 29 July 1961, Art 11.

[154] Ireland: eg the National Development Plan; in 2005 Irish Aid provided €12m to the Irish Missionary Resource Service (which consists of 82 individual Catholic missionary organizations).

[155] UK: grants may be made by the State for the Churches Conservation Trust under the Redundant Churches and Other Religious Buildings Act 1969; in 2005–6 the English Heritage/Heritage Lottery Fund made grants of over £24m for the repair of churches.

[156] UK: Local Government Finance Act 1988, Sch 5, s 11 (as amended 1992; Act, Sch 10, s 2).

[157] France: Law of 1905, Art 2 ended the payment of ministerial salaries; Netherlands: State payments towards clergy stipends and pensions ended in 1983; S van Bijsterveld, 'The financing of religious communities in the Netherlands' PECCSR (2009) 269.

[158] Luxembourg: Const, Art 106.

[159] Belgium: Const, Art 181: 'The State awards remuneration and pensions to religious leaders; those amounts are to be included in the budget'; this was widened in 1993: 'The wages and pensions of representatives of organisations recognised by law who extend moral services, on the basis of non-confessional philosophy of life, are to be paid by the State.' The State finances eg Catholic ministers (Law of 8 April 1802), Protestant (Law of 8 April 1802), Jewish (Law of 4 March 1870), Muslim (Law of 19 July 1974), and Orthodox (Law of 17 April 1985); in 2009, this amounted to €106m (with €5.2m going to Islamic groups), and the Minister for Justice announced a reform to enable financial support to both recognized and non-recognized religions: the report was due 1 October 2010.

[160] Belgium: 'appropriate' means 'in accordance with his social status': COS, 2 April 1953, *Rechtskundig Weekblad*, 1952–1953, 1691; this is chargeable to the municipalities or provinces.

[161] Greece: eg for the salaries and pensions of prelates: Law 1041/1980; for training and salaries, see originally FL 536/1945 and FL 469/1968; the State makes grants to the Welfare Fund of the Orthodox Parish Clergy of Greece for pensions: Law 2084/1992; the sum for salaries in 2005 was €157m.

[162] Greece: Decision 106/1962 Preliminary Taxation Court of Patra; Law 574/1977, Art 2.3 (funerals, paid by the local authority); LD 3097/1954, Art 3 (hospital ministry, paid by the hospital).

[163] Greece: Law 1476/1984; monks and nuns engaged in agricultural work are insured and granted pensions: Law 4169/1961; clergy may engage in other employment (eg as teachers): Law 1256/1982 and Law 1400/1983.

[164] Greece: in relation to the Turkish-speaking Muslim minority, under the Treaty of Lausanne 1923.

[165] Cyprus: in 2005, over £2m was paid to these four religious organizations.

by the State in Sweden in order, *inter alia*, to remunerate the clergy of the disestablished Church of Sweden.[166]

A similar pattern of state-funded ministerial remuneration is found in central and eastern Europe with regard to ministers of recognized or registered religious organizations,[167] sometimes as compensation for restrictive practices towards religion under former political regimes.[168] For example, in Slovakia registered religious communities may claim on a monthly basis from the Ministry of Culture for the salaries of clergy engaged in pastoral care and church administration; they may also claim for their travel and removal expenses, and for premiums for health, social, and employment insurance—an annual report must be submitted to the Ministry of Culture on the use of these funds.[169] Elsewhere, ministers of religion are funded mainly by sums derived from the church tax or allocations from income tax. However, direct State funding of chaplains in the armed forces, prisons, and hospitals is more widespread across Europe. This occurs, for example, in the separation systems of France and Ireland,[170] the cooperation systems of Poland and Spain,[171] and the state-church system of the United Kingdom.[172] Chaplaincy funding is considered in more detail in Chapter 8.

Schools: The vast majority of States in Europe provide for some form of religious education in public schools. As will be seen in Chapter 8, various models are used with complex arrangements for opting in or opting out. Suffice it to say here, however, that the State funds compulsory classes in (mainly) Christianity in Scandinavia and the United Kingdom.[173] In countries with compulsory denominational religious education, either of a single denomination or a choice of denominations, the State funds teachers from that denomination to deliver the classes.[174] In countries with optional denominational education, once again the State funds the delivery of classes by the denomination in question.[175] The State funds optional

---

[166] Sweden: PECCSR (2009) 319, 323.

[167] Lithuania: Law on State Social Insurance, Art 4; Romania: Law 142 of 1999; Czech Rep: Act no 3/2002, s 7: religious communities with special rights can access State funds for clergy salaries but few do; Slovenia: FRA, Arts 27–28; in 2002, this amounted to €1,253,422 but in 2005, only €21,708.

[168] Austria: eg Protestant Act, s 20, 6 July 1960/1; cf Czech Rep: payments under Act 217/1949, 1 November 1949 (on the forfeiture of religious property) for (low) clergy salaries ceased on 31 December 1999.

[169] Slovakia: Const, Art 24; Act no 218/1949, as amended by Acts nos 16/1990, 522/1992, and 467/2005; Government Ordinance no 578/1990; but 4 groups do not claim these subsidies (Jehovah's Witnesses, Christian Congregations, Seventh-Day Adventists, New Apostolic Church).

[170] France: Law of 19 December 1905, Art 2; COS, 16 March 2005, Decision no 26 5560; Ireland: 'A health board shall make arrangements with the appropriate authorities for the performance of religious services in each hospital, sanatorium and home maintained by it': Health Act 1970, s 39.

[171] Poland: see eg Law of 13 May 1994, Arts 22–23: hospitals and prisons (Lutherans); Czech Rep: Agreement with the Catholic Church 2002, Art 14; Hungary: Government Decree 61/1994 (IV.20) (army); Minister of Justice Decree 13/2000 (VII.14) (prisons).

[172] UK: full-time hospital chaplains are paid by the NHS; the total cost of chaplaincy services to the armed forces is £30m/€43.5m: HC Deb, 24 July 2006, vol 449, col 768W.

[173] eg Denmark: Primary Schools Act (730/2000).

[174] Catholic education in Malta; Orthodox education in Greece and Cyprus; there is a choice of denominations in Austria, Germany, and Belgium.

[175] eg Spain: the State pays the salaries of teachers of the Catholic religion in all publicly-funded schools, and for teachers from the Evangelical, Islamic, and Jewish federations; see Agreement with

non-denominational religious education in countries with this system.[176] However, in France there is no religious education and in Slovenia denominational education is catered for in limited circumstances but it is not state-funded.[177] States also contribute directly to the costs of running faith schools—this is a common pattern across Europe,[178] even in the separation systems of France[179] and Ireland, where most schools are faith schools.[180]

Charities: Religious organizations engage in a wide range of charitable activities. States may also contribute financially to these. Hungarian law is typical: 'the State shall provide a rate of subsidies from the central budget corresponding to that received by analogous state institutions . . . for the operation of the educational, teaching, social and health care, sports, children's and youth protection institutions of a church legal entity, and subsidies shall be granted from the funds allocated for the above purposes'.[181] Moreover, provision for religious charity work transcends all three European models of religion-state relations. For example, in the Irish separation system, state agencies may provide financial support for youth organizations;[182] in the German cooperation system, the State funds private faith-related hospitals;[183] and in the Greek state-church system, there is special state funding for the charitable work of the Orthodox Church's *Apostoliki Diakonia*—the size of the sum is determined by a joint decision of the Minister of Education and Cults and the Minister of Finance.[184]

Compensation for the confiscation of religious property

In addition to restitution (see above), national laws commonly seek to provide compensation for the confiscation of religious property during former political

---

Holy See 1979 on Education and Cultural Affairs, Art 7; see Art 10 of each of the Agreements with the Evangelical, Jewish, and Islamic Communities; the public Foundation for Pluralism and Coexistence in 2005 contributed €649,000 to the Islamic Commission.

[176] eg Estonia: Education Acts 1992 and 2003.

[177] France: Law of 1905; however, Art 2: see n 170 above; Slovenia: Education Act 1996.

[178] Germany: eg in 2006, 9,300 Catholic kindergartens were funded; see PECCSR (2009) 171; Estonia: Private Schools Act, Art 22; Lithuania: LORCA, Art 14 and Law on Education, Arts 1, 20, and 32.

[179] France: *Loi Debré* of 21 December 1959: the State may fund private schools (which are part of public service education under the control of the State) when they have signed a contract with the State.

[180] Ireland: the Minister of Education and Science must support recognized religious schools financially: Education Act 1998, ss 7 and 12.

[181] Hungary: LFCRC 1990, Art 19.1; see also Act on the Financial Conditions of Religious and Public Activities of Churches, Act 124/1997; Lithuania: LORCA, Art 14; this empowers but does not oblige the State to contribute; and Slovenia: Humanitarian Organization Act, Art 2.4, OG, no 98/2003.

[182] Ireland: Youth Work Act 2001, s 34: the Church of Ireland Youth Development receives €220,000 annually from the Youth Affairs Section of the Department of Education and Science.

[183] Germany: in 2004, 36% of hospitals were private (2,157 hospitals); approximately 38% of these are Catholic or Protestant; the latter run 270 hospitals; see PECCSR (2009) 171.

[184] Greece: FL 976/1946, Art 24.1; Law 1155/1981; also, the Ministry for Public Health and Social Welfare subsidizes activities for children sponsored by the dioceses, and the State funds the Nursing Foundation of the Church, a state-owned hospital for Orthodox clergy: Pr D 124/1985.

regimes. This compensation may in turn be used for the objects discussed in the previous section. For example, the German government pays €3 million annually to the Central Jewish Council in Germany under an agreement with that community; there are similar agreements between the *länder* and Jewish communities (for example Saxony-Anhalt pays €750,000 per annum).[185] Similarly, in Austria, the State provides for compensation where property was confiscated by national socialist measures in relation to Catholic, Protestant, and Old Catholics' property, as well as for the destruction of Jewish property (synagogues, cemeteries, objects).[186] Parallel trends are to be found in former communist countries. For instance, in Lithuania, the State is given the option of either restitution or compensation,[187] in Slovenia such property is to be returned unless this is not possible, in which case compensation must be paid,[188] and in Hungary, six religious organizations agreed to abandon restitution claims in favour of an annual allowance instead.[189] The compensation process in Poland is administered by committees composed of representatives from the Ministry of the Interior and the churches and other religious communities. These committees function as arbitration bodies and their decisions are binding. There are five such committees: one each for the Catholic, Lutheran, and Orthodox churches, and the Jewish communities, and a general committee for others (such as the Methodist and Reformed churches). There has been debate recently about abolition of the fund.[190] However, in Slovakia, nationalized religious property was returned in its existing condition with no compensation for any damage that may have been done to it.[191]

Tax exemptions and concessions for religious organizations

Once more, the extensive provision for tax benefits in national laws indicates the very high level of cooperation between States and religion in Europe, regardless of the religion-state posture of the country in question. Acquisition of legal personality may entitle a religious organization to a wide range of tax exemptions and

---

[185] Germany: see also n 41 above.

[186] Austria: under agreements of 1960, the Catholic Church today receives an annual payment of about €14m; Protestants, around €898,000, Old Catholics, €41,000, and Jewish, around €248,600.

[187] Lithuania: Law on the Restoration of Prayer Houses etc, February 1990: this obliges local authorities to sign an agreement with religious communities either defining the terms of restitution or compensating.

[188] Slovenia: Denationalization Act 1991; a statute suspending restitution for 3 years was held unconstitutional as to cases where the return of more than 200 hectares of farmlands and forests were requested by an individual claimant: CCt, OdlUS V, 174 (Decision no U-I-107/96, 5 December 1996).

[189] Hungary: Act 32/1991; CCt, Decision 4/1993 (II. 12) AB; Czech Rep: CRSL, Act no 3/2002 Sb.

[190] Poland: Law of 1989 Dz U 1990, no 61, item 354; the general committee is governed by an Ordinance of the Minister of the Interior and Administration, 9 February 2000; the budget for 2004 was in the region of €19m; in that year a group of Senators proposed abolition of the fund: Document 771 from 29 July 2004; the Catholic Church receives 87% of the fund.

[191] Slovakia: Act no 298/1990 Coll; Act no 282/1991; Act no 161/2005.

concessions in relation to their non-profit-making activities.[192] They are enjoyed, for example, by registered religious associations,[193] religious associations with 'special rights',[194] registered religious charities,[195] religious organizations which have agreements with the State,[196] *associations cultuelles*,[197] and former national churches.[198] There are extensive provisions for exemptions from income tax on their non-profit activities. For example, no tax is paid on income derived from donations made to religious organizations,[199] whether in the form of a collection from the faithful (for example during the time of worship),[200] an *inter vivos* donation,[201] a bequest on the death of a donor,[202] the sale of property (the proceeds of which are to be used for religious or charitable purposes),[203] or other capital gain,[204] or corporate revenue.[205] Occasionally laws provide expressly that religious organizations may receive unlimited donations for their religious and charitable activities,[206] or else they limit the tax relief of the donor.[207] Sometimes income tax exemption is the subject of litigation.[208]

---

[192] eg in Poland religious organizations are liable to income tax on their economic activities, and clergy are liable to a general quarterly tax based on the size of their parish: Law of 20 November 1998; see also Chief Administrative Court, Decision of 31 August 1999, ONSA 2000, no 3, 119.

[193] Lithuania: CC, Bk II, Ch 4, Art 2.34; LORCA, Art 16 (tax); Hungary: Act IV/1990, s 19; Estonia: Income Tax Act, s 11.2 (RT I, 1993, 79, 1184); Portugal: LORF 2001, Art 32; Sweden: Denominations Act 1998, s 9.

[194] Czech Rep: CRSL, Act no 3/2002 Sb.

[195] UK: Charities Act 2006, s 2(2); Cyprus: Law 118(1)/2002, Art 8.13; See also Appendix E of the Treaty of Establishment between the UK, Greece, Turkey, and Cyprus: Robbers (n 111 above) 247.

[196] Spain: Protestant: Law no 24/1992; Jewish: Law 25/1992; Muslim: Law 26/1992; they are exempt from transfer tax and stamp duty and property tax (for places of worship): Acts 10 November 1992; LORF 1980, Art 7.2: 'Subject to the principle of equality, [the] Agreements ... may confer upon churches ... the tax benefits applied by ordinary legislation to non-profit entities'; for the general law on such foundations, see Law 30/1994 of 24 November; Agreement with the Holy See 1979, Art 5.1: 'The Church may carry out its own charitable or welfare activities.'

[197] France: Law of 1905.

[198] In 2000, the Church of Sweden was given tax exemption for 10 years: PECCSR (2009) 323.

[199] Romania: Law 27 of 1994; Estonia: Income Tax Act, Art 11(2) (RT I, 1993, 79, 1184) and Regulation no 89 21 March 2000 (RT I 1996,48, 946); Slovakia: Act no 595/2003 Coll.

[200] Poland: collections for religious aims 'in places and during times regarded as customary according to local tradition' are exempt from public collections law: Law of 1932, Dz U 1932, no 22, item 162.

[201] Portugal: Concordat 1940 provided a general exemption; the Concordat 2004 preserves this: Art 26; LORF 2001, Art 31(1) and (2); those registered are exempt from municipal tax for property used for ritual or religious aims and for property transactions *inter vivos* and on death: Art 32.

[202] Greece: Law 2238/1994, Art 99; Law 2961/2001, Arts 25 and 43.

[203] Lithuania: LORCA 1995, Art 16: eg if proceeds from sale are intended for the construction, repair, or restoration of places of prayer, charity, culture, and education; for exemption for charitable donations, see Law on Charitable and Sponsorship Funds 2000, no 61-1818.

[204] Ireland: Taxes Consolidation Act 1997, s 609: they are exempt from capital gains tax.

[205] Austria: Federal Revenues Act, s 38: this applies to religious organizations with public law status.

[206] Poland: see eg Law of 20 February 1997, Art 18 (Jewish); legal persons can deduct up to 10%: Law on Personal Income Tax, Dz U 2000, no 14, 176.

[207] Latvia: Law on Corporate Income Tax, Art 20: private companies may make donations to religious organizations and with the permission of the Ministry of Finance may claim tax relief of 85%.

[208] Cyprus: Income Tax Law 118(1)/2002, Art 8.13: 'the income of a religious, charitable, or education institution of public character' is exempt; there is no definition of 'religious institution' and so all known religions, not just recognized ones, can benefit; but the Orthodox Archdiocese of Cyprus has been involved in protracted litigation about this—see eg *Archdiocese of Cyprus v Republic of Cyprus*, Decision of 5 July 2002: the church relies on its right to property under Const, Art 23.

There are also extensive tax exemptions and relief with regard to transactions which relate to the acquisition, use, and transfer of real property. Hungary is typical: religious associations are exempt from real estate tax when they acquire land by purchase, inheritance, or gift.[209] Exemptions from real estate tax may equally apply to the transfer of land,[210] and this may include relief from payment of stamp duty,[211] or relief from taxes payable on rents.[212] Places of worship of registered denominations are exempt from local taxes in, for example, Bulgaria,[213] Hungary,[214] Italy,[215] Romania,[216] and Slovakia;[217] the same applies to monasteries in Greece.[218] Similarly, in the United Kingdom, in England and Wales, registration as a place of public religious worship (or a church hall or similar building used in connection with it) generates exemption from local council tax provided the site is open to the public.[219] There is also relief on the payment of value added tax; for example, in Estonia, religious organizations may purchase electricity for places of worship at a rate of 5 per cent VAT instead of the required 18 per cent.[220] Finally, relief may arise on export duties[221] or import taxes; for instance, in Cyprus, all construction materials, fittings, and furniture for churches or mosques and all vestments and other articles which are imported for religious purposes by religious authorities are eligible for relief from import duties.[222]

Conclusion

Throughout Europe, national laws on religious property and finance represent a high level of cooperation between States and religion. Such laws are the result of

---

[209] Hungary: Act XCIII/1990, Art 5.1; no local tax on property: Act C/1990, Art 3.2; Act 100/1990, s 3(2); Act 93/1990, s 5 (on fees); see also Estonia: Land Tax Act, s 4.5.

[210] Romania: Law 27 of 1994; Latvia: Law on Real Estate Tax; Italy: Concordat, Arts 13 and 14.

[211] Spain: places of worship are exempt from transfer tax, stamp duty, and property tax: agreements with the Evangelical Entities, Israelite Communities, and Islamic Commission (Laws of 10 November 1992).

[212] Greece: Law 2238/1994, Art 99: the Orthodox Church and other known religious communities are exempt from real estate tax; tax is payable on 10% of the rent from property belonging to places of worship; exemption for large real estates: Law 2459/1997, Art 3 for Orthodox Church, Israelite community, and Muslims; all known religions are exempt from community real estate tax: Law 2130/1949, Art 24.7; special tax exemptions for Mount Athos: Const, 105.

[213] Bulgaria: Local Taxes and Fees Act, s 241.

[214] Hungary: Act 100/1990, s 3(2); Act 93/1990, s 5.

[215] Italy: DL no 504, 30 December 1992, Art 7; Portugal: LORF, Art 65.1.

[216] Romania: whilst Law 27 of 1994 does not expressly list them, the Ministry of Finance has exempted them: Note 90561, 17 April 1997; they are also exempt from real estate transfer, inheritance, and donation taxes: Law 27 of 1994.

[217] Slovakia: Act no 582/2004 (local taxes).

[218] Greece: LD 3432/1955.

[219] UK: Local Government Finance Act 1988, Sch 5, s 11 (as amended by the Local Government Finance Act 1992, Sch 10, s 3); if the public is excluded it is not eligible for registration: *Gallagher (Valuation Officer) v Church of Jesus Christ of Latter-day Saints* [2008] UKHL 56.

[220] Estonia: RT I 2001, 64, 368 (until 2005); see also Italy: DPR no 633, 26 October 1972, Art 68.

[221] Greece: products exported from Mount Athos are exempt: Charter of Mount Athos, Art 168.

[222] Cyprus: Customs and Excise Regulations 2004, 380/04, s 3, Class P of Annex 1.

keen political negotiation between States and faith communities, irrespective of the particular posture of a country towards its religion-state relations. This field also yields a wide range of principles of religion law common to the States of Europe. In terms of civil law, all religious organizations have the right to acquire, administer, and dispose of property—though they need legal personality to do so. States must not arbitrarily confiscate religious property, and if they do so they must provide for schemes of restitution or, where this is not possible, compensation. Moreover, freedom of religion entitles faith communities to construct places of worship. However, the exercise of these rights may be subject to limitations prescribed by law. This is nowhere more evident than in relation to religious buildings which are of historical, architectural, and cultural importance. States may require religious organizations to satisfy rules which ensure that such properties are protected for enjoyment as part of the national heritage. Such rules underscore the limits of the autonomy of religious organizations. Nevertheless, sacred places, religious objects, clerical vesture, human remains, and memorials must all be respected. Failure to do so will lead to the imposition of penal sanctions which in themselves reflect well the seriousness with which States treat damage to or misuse of religious property.

The entanglement of States with religion is especially conspicuous in the realm of finance—politically, religious organizations have secured for themselves extensive legal benefits to financial assistance from government. Either directly or indirectly all States provide financial support to religion. Considerable public funds are spent on making available the taxation apparatus of the State in the administration of the church tax and allocations of income tax liability, which themselves confer valuable monetary benefits on religion on the basis of the personal choice of the taxpayer. States commonly subsidize the maintenance of historic religious sites, the remuneration of ministers of religion, the provision of chaplaincy services, and religious education in public institutions, and they contribute to the charitable activities of faith communities. States compensate religious organizations for the confiscation of property under former restrictive political regimes—and they involve religious bodies directly in its computation. They also confer on them a wide range of tax exemptions and other forms of relief as to income and the enjoyment of real property. Such schemes may tend to generate assumptions that religious organizations have, by virtue of their activities, a right to be beneficiaries of State financial aid. It is therefore not surprising that equality in State-funding is often on the political agenda in the States of Europe. In any event, the national laws studied here, and the shared principles which may be induced from them, indicate a material benevolence on the part of States towards religion. This also implies that States value religion to the extent that they are prepared to support it financially. However, a thorough examination is needed of the political dialogue that has occurred between States and religious bodies, prior to the enactment of the laws outlined above, to uncover the reasons and justifications for State benevolence in this field. Typically, such assumptions are not expressly articulated in the laws themselves.

8

Religion, Education, and Public Institutions

Throughout Europe, the presence of religion in the public sphere is topical and controversial, particularly the display of religious symbols in public places, such as schools and government offices.[1] As has already been seen, the regulation of religion in public institutions has also made its mark on those national laws in Europe which relate to the right of the individual to manifest religion publicly, the duty on public authorities not to discriminate on grounds of religion or belief, the portrayal of religion in the media, and the facilities which States provide to support religion from public funds.[2] What follows extends this theme to religion in schools, hospitals, prisons, and the armed forces, all of which are key public institutions and services of the State.[3] As to education, in the context of global international law and Strasbourg jurisprudence on this subject, the chapter compares national laws on the provision of religious education in public State schools, and the rights of pupils, parents, and teachers, as well as the legal regulation of private (but often publicly funded) faith schools. As to hospitals, prisons, and the armed forces, the chapter examines national laws on the provision of religious assistance in these, comparing the respective legal regimes applicable to each public institution. As with national laws on property and finance in religion, so the laws of Europe on religion in these public institutions transcend in a fundamental way the classical understanding of state-religion models in Europe: an examination of laws on religion in these public institutions reveals but one dominant system across Europe—that of cooperation. However, often there is an inequality of treatment as between

---

[1] On 20 July 2010, the Spanish Parliament rejected proposals for a ban on the wearing of the Islamic *burqa* in public places by 183 to 162 votes, with 2 abstentions; Strasbourg: *Lautsi v Italy* App no 30814/06 (ECtHR, 3 November 2009): the presence of a crucifix in public schools was held incompatible with ECHR, Art 9; in Poland, a resident of Łódź saw, in a TV broadcast of a session of the city council, a cross hanging in the council chamber; the Chief Administrative Court (NSA) held that the resident's right to freedom of conscience or religion was not violated and that no form of discrimination had taken place: M Rynkowski, 'Religion and criminal law: Poland' in M Kotiranta and N Doe (eds), *Religion and Criminal Law in Europe* (Leuven: Peeters, 2011) 205, 209, n 9; see also: COE, Parliamentary Assembly, 'Islam, Islamism and Islamophobia in Europe', Rec 1927 (23 June 2010), s 3.1.3: this called on Member States 'not to establish a general ban of the full veiling or other religious or special clothing, but to protect women from all physical and psychological duress as well as their free choice to wear religious or special clothing and ensure equal opportunities for Muslim women ... in public life'; it also invited 'states to guarantee women's freedom of expression by penalising, on the one hand, all forms of coercion, oppression or violence that compel women to wear the veil or the full veil'.

[2] See Ch 2 (right to manifest), Ch 3 (discrimination), Ch 6 (media), Ch 7 (finance).

[3] See also Ch 2 above for conscientious objection to military service.

religions in this field. The chapter also induces and articulates from the national legal systems principles of religion law common to the States of Europe, and it seeks to highlight possible areas for further research.

Religion and education in state schools

The relationship between religion and education is addressed in some detail in the instruments of the United Nations, the Council of Europe, and the European Union. They deal with the right of parents and guardians to the religious education of their children, the right of the State to provide in its schools neutral and objective religious education, and the duty of the State to provide for exemptions when parents (or children) do not wish to receive religious education. These represent important international standards against which national laws in Europe may be measured in the context of public education,[4] which itself often grew out of the work of churches.[5]

According to the United Nations, education should 'promote understanding, tolerance, and friendship among all nations and all racial, ethnic or religious groups'.[6] In its provision, States must respect the freedom of parents to ensure the religious and moral education of their children in conformity with their own convictions.[7] Thus: 'Every child shall enjoy the right of access to education in the matter of religion or belief in accordance with the wishes of the parents [or] guardians, and shall not be compelled to receive teaching on religion or belief against [their] wishes . . . the best interests of the child being the guiding principle.'[8] However, 'instruction in subjects such as the history of religion and ethics' is permissible 'if it is given in a neutral and objective way', and instruction in a particular religion must provide for non-discriminatory exemptions or alternatives which accommodate parental wishes.[9] Similarly, for the Council of Europe,[10] the ECHR provides: 'No person shall be denied the right to education. In the exercise of any functions which it assumes in relation to education and to teaching, the state shall respect the rights of parents to ensure such education and teaching in

---

[4] For the right to education, see eg Luxembourg: Const, Art 23; Malta: Education Act 1998, Art 3; Spain: Const, Art 27.3; Bulgaria; Const, Art 53; Germany: GG, Art 7(1); WRV, Art 149; France: CCl, 23 November 1977, AJDA 1978, p 565; CCl 18 January 1985, RFDA 1985, p 633; Laws of 28 March 1882 and 30 October 1886 deal with the *laïcité* of public primary schools, for example.

[5] Ireland: Report of the Constitutional Review Group 1996, p 377; UK: A Bradney, *Law and Faith in a Sceptical Age* (Abingdon: Routledge-Cavendish, 2009) 120–30.

[6] ICESR, Art 13.1; see also UNESCO Convention 1960, Art 5.1(a); UN Convention on the Rights of the Child (CRC), 1989, Art 29. Such education should be compulsory.

[7] ICCPR, Art 18.4.

[8] UNDID, Art 5; see Ch 9 below.

[9] General Comment no 22 on Art 18, adopted 30 July 1993; see *Leirvag v Norway* Communication no 1155/2003.

[10] Education is defined as: 'the whole process whereby in any society adults endeavour to transmit their beliefs, culture and other values to the young, whereas teaching or instruction refers in particular to the transmission of knowledge and to intellectual development': *Campbell and Cosans v UK* (1982) 4 EHRR 293: the case concerned corporal punishment in Scottish schools.

conformity with their own religious and philosophical convictions.'[11] In turn, the Parliamentary Assembly of the Council of Europe invites States 'to promote education about religions', their values, history, and traditions,[12] at State primary and secondary schools, in an impartial manner in order to engender respect for different faiths.[13] For the Strasbourg court, therefore, the State may provide religious education and it enjoys a wide margin of appreciation in this regard. However, the State must ensure that knowledge is conveyed in 'an objective, critical and pluralistic manner'.[14] For example: there is to be no indoctrination;[15] pupils must not be required to learn sacred scriptures by heart;[16] parents may set up their own religious schools;[17] and parents may seek admission to such schools if dissatisfied with State religious education.[18] Equally, there are limits to permissible objections to State religious education when this is general and neutral,[19] and when denominational education and exemptions from it are reasonable;[20] indeed, when university students voluntarily submit themselves to an educational regime they may waive their right to manifest their religion—that is, when the specific situation rules applies.[21] The European Union, too, recognizes the right of parents to ensure the education of their children in conformity with their religious and philosophical convictions.[22] The European Union also recommends that the Member States 'ensure that religious instruction in schools respects cultural pluralism' and that they make provision for teacher training to this effect.[23]

At the national level, the laws of all States in Europe deal with religious education in public schools run by the State. The issues which these laws address include: whether the State must provide religious education itself or merely provide *for* religious education by others; the types or forms of religious education (such as Christian, denominational, and non-denominational, or general religious knowledge);[24] the design of the curriculum; who delivers and funds the teaching

---

[11]   ECHR, First Protocol, Art 2.

[12]   Rec 1396 (1999) adopted 27 January 1999.

[13]   Rec 1720 (2005) adopted 4 October 2005.

[14]   Strasbourg: *Kjeldsen, Busk Madsen and Pedersen v Denmark* (1979) 1 EHRR 711.

[15]   *Ciftci v Turkey* App no 71860/01 (ECtHR, 17 June 2004): the ban on teaching the Koran to pupils in the final years of primary education to avoid indoctrination was not itself indoctrination; see also *CJ, JJ and EJ v Poland*, App no 23380/94 (1996) 84-A D&R 46 (1996).

[16]   *Hasan and Eylem Zengin v Turkey* App no 1448/04 (ECtHR, 9 October 2007).

[17]   Art 2 of the First Protocol ECHR includes the right to set up and run a private school subject to conditions laid down to ensure a proper educational system as a whole: *Jordebo v Sweden* App no 11533/85 (ECtHR, 6 March 1987). However, there is no state duty to fund private schools: see eg *X v UK* App no 7782/77 (1978) 14 D&R 179, 180.

[18]   *Jimenez Alonso and Jimenez Merino v Spain*, App no 51188/99 (ECtHR, 25 May 2000).

[19]   *Valsamis v Greece* [1997] 24 EHRR 294.

[20]   *Bernard and ors v Luxembourg*, App no 17187/90 (1993) 75 D&R 57.

[21]   See Ch 2 above for *Sahin v Turkey* (2005) 41 EHRR 8 and *Karaduman v Turkey* App no 16278/90 (1993) 74 DR 93. It has also been applied to a teacher seeking to absent himself to attend prayers (he had not notified the employer): *Ahmad v UK* (1981) 4 EHRR 126.

[22]   EU: Charter of Fundamental Rights, Art 14.

[23]   EU: General Policy Rec no 5, 'Combating intolerance and discrimination against Muslims', CRI, 2000, 21, 27 April 2000.

[24]   Sometimes a distinction is made between religious education, ie religious studies, and religious instruction in the beliefs, etc of a particular religious denomination.

(the State, religious organizations, or both); and arrangements for opting in to or out of religious education by parents or, depending on their age, by children themselves.[25] Each State in Europe adopts one or other of five basic approaches to these issues: (1) compulsory Christian knowledge which the State designs, teaches and funds, but from which parents or pupils may opt out; (2) compulsory denominational education which religious organizations design (perhaps in collaboration with the State) and teach but which the State funds and from which pupils may opt out; (3) opt-in denominational education which religious organizations design (perhaps in collaboration with the State) and deliver but the State funds; (4) opt-in non-denominational education which the State designs, delivers, and may fund; and (5) the prohibition of religious education on the premises of State schools but the State makes provision for pupils to receive religious education externally.[26] States often allow pupils time off for religious reasons.[27]

Compulsory Christian religious education

In the first category, public schools must provide Christian religious education, the curriculum is designed, delivered, and funded by the State, and attendance is mandatory but pupils have a right to withdraw. The category is most prevalent in the state-church systems of northern Europe. 'Christian knowledge' is taught in Danish primary and secondary schools, where it covers the history of Christianity and the Reformation; in grammar schools the wider subject of religion is compulsory only in the last three years of study. Children may be withdrawn on a request from their parents and the child may withdraw at the age of 15; teachers can also request exemption from teaching Christianity.[28] In Finland, compulsory religious education is broadly Christian but pupils in comprehensive and senior secondary schools may elect to take worldview studies or denominational education paid for by the school and delivered on the basis of a curriculum approved by the national Board of Education.[29]

---

[25] The decision of the parent, rather than that of the child, usually determines whether pupils may be exempt from religious education; but as will be seen below, ages are generally fixed by law to enable the child to decide without parental consent. Under international law, parental wishes alone might violate the rights of the child: UN Doc CRC/C/SR.625 (2000) 55.

[26] For a helpful overview of COE countries, see *Hasan and Eylem Zengin v Turkey* App no 1448/04 (ECtHR, 9 October 2007).

[27] See eg Austria: SchZG, Arts 2 and 13; however, Luxembourg: a law permitting schools to require Saturday attendance was challenged by Seventh Day Adventists for whom the day is sacred but upheld by the national courts as not in breach of ECHR, Art 9 or Const, Arts 19 and 20: Administrative Tribunal, TA 16-2-1998, no 9360 and 9430, *Bull Laurent* 2000, IV, 5, 2–7–1998, no 10648C, *Bull Laurent* 2000, IV, 20; CCt, 20 November 1998. Strasbourg held this to be a justified limit on the right to manifest religion: *Casimiro and Ferreira v Luxembourg* App no 44888/98 (ECtHR, 27 April 1999).

[28] Denmark: in primary schools Christian knowledge is taught to prepare children for confirmation; it is delivered by clergy of the national church as civil servants: Act on the Primary School (730/2000).

[29] Finland: EA, 628/1998 (as amended by 454/2003), s 13 and Law on Secondary Education, 629/1998 (as amended by 455/2003), s 9; the right of parents to ensure religious education of their children: FRA 453/2003; for discussion of former systems based on a law of 1922, see *Hartikainen v Finland* (Comm no 40/1078) UN Doc A/34/40, Decision of 9 April 1981.

For the United Kingdom, in state-maintained schools in England and Wales, the State must provide compulsory religious education which in turn must 'reflect the fact that the religious traditions in Great Britain are in the main Christian' whilst taking account of the teaching and practices of the other principal religions represented in Great Britain.[30] If a parent requests a pupil to be 'wholly or partly excused', that pupil is to be so excused.[31] No syllabus shall provide religious education by means of any catechism or formulary distinctive of a particular denomination (but they may be studied); and teachers are not to be treated less favourably as to remuneration or promotion by reason of the fact that they do or do not teach religious education.[32] Moreover, schools must provide a daily act of collective worship 'wholly or mainly of a broadly Christian character' which 'reflects the broad traditions of Christian belief without being distinctive of any particular Christian denomination'; parents may withdraw children and pupils in the final two years of secondary school may do so themselves.[33] However, the requirement that worship be mainly Christian may be disapplied.[34] It is also unlawful to disadvantage a person in terms of employment, remuneration, or promotion at a school by reason of their religious opinions or for not attending daily worship; refusals to allow teachers time off during school hours to attend prayers have been upheld as being consistent with the ECHR and domestic law.[35]

Compulsory denominational education

With the second category, public schools must provide for denominational religious education, usually on the basis of a curriculum designed in partnership with the denominations concerned; it is funded by the State but delivered either by public teachers or by the denominations; pupil attendance is mandatory but there are exemptions. This model straddles both state-church and cooperation systems of religion-state relations. In Malta, religious education is Catholic, and in Greece and Cyprus, Orthodox. In addition to the Maltese constitutional principle that the Catholic Church has the duty and entitlement to teach right from wrong: 'Religious teaching of the Roman Catholic Apostolic Faith shall be provided in all State

---

[30] UK: EA 1996, s 375; SSFA 1998, s 69; there is a reservation to ECHR, Protocol 1, Art 2 to provide efficient instruction and avoid unreasonable public expenditure: see S Knights, *Freedom of Religion Minorities and the Law* (Oxford: OUP, 2007) para 4.27.

[31] UK: EA 1996, s 390.

[32] UK: each Local Education Authority (LEA) must establish a Standing Advisory Committee for Religious Education (SACRE) to monitor this; it consists of groups 'to represent such Christian denominations and other religions and denominations of such religions as [in the view of the LEA] reflect the principal religious traditions in the area'; the Church of England must be represented; EA 1996, s 392; SSFA 1998, Sch 19; s 59: teachers.

[33] UK: ibid s 70 and Sch 20; s 71: the right to withdraw.

[34] UK: EA 1996 s 391; s 394: SACRE may do so having regard to family backgrounds, etc. Worship which 'reflected Christian sentiments' is lawful even if there 'was nothing in [it] which was explicitly Christian': *R v Secretary of State for Education, ex p R and D* [1994] ELR 495, 502.

[35] UK: SSFA 1998, s 59; *Ahmad v Inner London Education Authority* [1978] QB 36: ECHR; *Mayuuf v Governing Body of Bishop Challoner Catholic Collegiate School and anor* [2005] ET Case no 3202398/04 (21 December 2005): discrimination.

Schools as part of compulsory education.' The State pays for this—the Minister for Education must provide for the curriculum on the basis of representations from the Catholic bishops,[36] and the teachers may be required to be Catholic.[37] However, parents may withdraw their children and pupils can opt out themselves at the age of 16.[38] In Greece and Cyprus, teaching in Orthodox Christianity must be provided by the State. Greek public education must contribute to the development of a 'religious consciousness' formed by the Orthodox religion.[39] The syllabus is approved by the Ministry of Education in consultation with the Orthodox Church and the teachers are appointed and paid by the State.[40] Pupils may be exempt from religious education classes on the basis of a declaration by parents or guardians, but no declaration of their religion is required to enable this; there is also provision for daily prayer and attendance at church.[41] Much the same applies in Cyprus;[42] however, compulsory attendance for Cypriot Orthodox pupils has been criticized by the United Nations,[43] and the Cypriot equality body has criticized a teacher for sending to the library a Jehovah's Witness pupil who had opted out—a more a creative activity should have been provided.[44]

Unlike Malta, Greece, and Cyprus, in Austria, Germany, and Belgium, the duty of the State to provide for religious education is not confined to instruction in the teaching of a single denomination. Under Austrian law, denominational (or confessional) religious instruction is compulsory for all pupils of a recognized church or religious community in primary schools and secondary schools.[45] The denomination designs the syllabus and the Ministry of Education must publish it but cannot veto its content; classes are then delivered by teachers appointed by each denomination but paid and supervised by the State.[46] Pupils under 14 may be withdrawn by parents (on written request to the head teacher in the first ten days of the school year) and pupils over 14 may withdraw themselves by written request but there are

[36] Malta: Const, Art 2.2 and 2.3; EA 1988, s 20: the duty of the Minister of Education.

[37] Malta: 'A requirement . . . that the Roman Catholic Religion be taught by a person professing that Religion shall not be held to be inconsistent with or in contravention of this section': Const, Art 45.9.

[38] Malta: Const, Art 40.2.

[39] Greece: Const, Art 16; Law 1566/85, Art 1.1: one aim of primary and secondary education is 'to have faith to the country and the genuine elements of the Orthodox Christian tradition'; and Art 6.1: 'to realize the deeper meaning of the Orthodox Christian ethos'.

[40] Greece: the aims of religious education in primary schools include knowing what it means to be an active Orthodox Christian, and in secondary school understanding the multi-religious character of modern societies: Ministerial Decision of 2003; the total exclusion of non-Orthodox teachers from single-post state schools contravenes Const, Art 13(1): COS, Decision no 347/2002, 28 June 2002.

[41] Greece: Law 1566/85, Art 17.4; withdrawal and daily prayer are also governed by Circulars of the Ministry of National Education and Religious Affairs; see also Data Protection Authority, Decision 77A/2002 no 5 and Strasbourg: *Alexandridis v Greece* App no 19516/06 (ECtHR, 21 February 2008).

[42] Cyprus: *Arvanitakis v The Republic* [1994] 3 CLR 859: refusal to exempt a Jehovah's Witness pupil from religious education classes was held to be unlawful.

[43] UNCRC, *Summary record of the 310th meeting: Cyprus* UN Doc CRC/C/SR.310 (1996) 9 and 47.

[44] Cyprus: Report no 31/2005, 2 November 2005.

[45] Austria: StGG, Art 17(4); RelUG, Art 1; SchOG 1962, s 2(1): to gain respect for religious values.

[46] Austria: RelUG, Art 2; for teachers, see Arts 3–6; denominational teachers are subject to the discipline of their denomination: CCt, VfSlg 2507/1953.

no alternative classes. No provision exists for prayers but pupils and teachers may attend school religious services organized by the denominations at the beginning and end of the year.[47] In Germany: 'Religious instruction shall form part of the regular curriculum in state schools, with the exception of non-denominational schools. Without prejudice to the State's right of supervision, religious instruction shall be given in accordance with the tenets of the religious community concerned. Teachers may not be obliged against their will to give religious instruction';[48] the state pays for it.[49] However: 'Parents and guardians shall have the right to decide whether children shall receive religious instruction', and accordingly, they may withdraw their children until they reach 12, when the parental wish must not conflict with that of the child; at 14 the child decides.[50] The content is decided by the denomination and if six to eight pupils of the same denomination seek confessional education, it must be provided as a constitutional right; for those opting out, many *länder* have introduced ethics classes.[51] A similar system exists in Belgium with regard to the (six) recognized religious organizations.[52]

Optional denominational religious education

In the third category, public schools must provide for denominational religious education, designed, funded, and delivered either by the State or by the denomination, with a right to opt in for pupils. The arrangement operates in the cooperation systems of Italy, Spain, and Portugal and in many central and eastern European States. In Italy there must be two hours each week of state-funded Catholic religious education in play and primary schools and one hour per week in senior schools; parents must declare whether their children up to the age of 13 will attend or not, and if they decline, the children take part in other subjects or take time off school.[53] The syllabus is jointly agreed by the Minister for Public Education and the Catholic Bishops' Conference.[54] The teacher is chosen by the diocesan bishop, who may withdraw permission if the teacher does not comply

---

[47] Austria: StGG, Art 17(4); RelUG, Arts 1 *et seq*; prayers were abolished in 1993.

[48] Germany: GG, Art 7.3; see also WRV, Art 149: cooperation in education.

[49] Germany: a denomination is under no duty to take a pupil from another denomination in classes it provides, but may admit them: Federal CCt, BVerfGE 68, 16 (19 *et seq*); 74, 244 (253 *et seq*).

[50] Germany: GG, Art 7.2; Religious Education of Children Act 1921; see also CCt, BVerfGE 41, 29.

[51] Germany: ibid; an Islamic association may provide instruction in public schools in Berlin: Federal Administrative Court, 23 February 2000, BVerwGE 326.

[52] Belgium: Law of 29 May 1959 (*pacte scolaire*), Art 8: there must be two hours of religious or ethical education each week provided by the recognized religions; Const, Art 24: pupils have the right to religious education at the expense of the community; pupils who opt out may take classes in ethics: COS, 14 May 1985, no 25.326; COS, 10 July 1990, no 35.442; for religious education in Luxembourg see eg the Law of 6 February 2009.

[53] Italy: Concordat 1984, Art 9: it is justified by the 'value of the religious culture' and the 'historic patrimony of the Italian people'; in 2008/9, €800m were spent on it; whilst problems remain about the declaration and religious privacy, the system was upheld in CCt, Decision no 13 of 1991.

[54] Italy: PD no 751, 16 December 1985.

with the moral standards of the church.[55] A denomination with an agreement (*intesa*) may assign its own teachers if the pupils, parents, or the school apply for classes in a particular religion or in 'the phenomenon of religion and its implications'; this is funded by the denomination. Denominations with no agreement have no such right.[56] A similar system operates in Spain (where there are also optional classes in the history and culture of religions) with regard to teaching the Catholic religion,[57] and the State pays for Protestant, Jewish, and Islamic education designed by the denominations and delivered by their teachers if at least ten pupils opt in—if fewer than ten opt in, the denomination funds the teaching.[58] Portuguese public education must be non-confessional,[59] but the State provides for the teaching of Catholic morals and religion (*in* school not *by* the school) delivered by state-funded teachers appointed as civil servants on the nomination of the Church and using materials prepared by it—the pupil or parent must make an opt-in declaration.[60] Other faith entities may deliver denominational education if at least ten pupils request it or their parents declare they wish it; the entity sets the syllabus, and trains and nominates the teachers who are engaged by the State.[61]

The countries of central and eastern Europe follow the pattern employed in Italy, Spain, and Portugal. Lithuania is typical: public education must be secular, open, tolerant, and available for all regardless of religion. However, at the request of parents (until the child is 15, when the child decides), religious instruction designed by the traditional religions must be given at public schools; it is delivered by teachers authorized by those religions but trained and paid by the State; pupils who do not opt in may take ethics classes.[62] Denominational religious education requested by parents or pupils and delivered by denominational teachers paid by

---

[55] Italy: for withdrawal due to the pregnancy of an unmarried teacher, see Court of Cassation, 24 February 2003, no 2803; see also Decree of 9 July 2003, no 216: if withdrawn the teacher is assigned to another subject or given a different job in the public sector.

[56] Italy: see eg the agreement with the Jewish community 1989, Art 11; the Netherlands also has an opt-in system: Const, Art 23.3: public education must have 'regard to everyone's religion or belief'; Primary Education Act, Art 51: public schools host education provided by religious organizations.

[57] Spain: pupils may elect for teaching of the Catholic religion which is offered in all publicly funded schools (public and private-subsidised); Agreement with the Holy See on Education and Cultural Affairs 1979, Art 1: 'the education provided in public schools will be respectful towards Christian values'; Art 2: teaching the Catholic religion 'in conditions equal to those of the basic subjects'; Art 3: nomination of teachers by the diocesan bishop, but 'No-one shall be compelled to teach religion'; Art 6: the syllabus designed by the Episcopal Conference is approved by the Ministry of Education; Art 7: funding; the system was upheld in CCt, Decisions 38/2007, 15 February 2007, and 51/2011, 14 April 2011, on the basis of the cooperation principle in Const, Art 16 and Art 27.3: the rights of parents to religious education for their children; see also SM Monelos, 'Some recent problems concerning religious education in Spain' (2000) 8 EJCSR 125.

[58] Spain: see Art 10 of each Agreement; Law 24/1992 of 10 November: 'evangelical religious classes'; Law 25/1992 of 10 November: 'Jewish religious classes'; Law 26/1992 of 10 November: 'Islamic religious classes'. For the history and culture of religions, see Organic Law 2/2006 of 3 May.

[59] Portugal: Const, Art 43(3); for the facility for all denominations, see CCt, Decision 423/1987.

[60] Portugal: Law 46/1986, Art 47; DL no 323/83 of 5 July implementing Concordat 2004, Art 19; Ordinance no 344A/88, 31 May: parents must declare their wish; see also CCt, Decision 174/1993.

[61] Portugal: for others, DL no 329/98 of 2 November; this is consolidated in LORF, Art 24.

[62] Lithuania, Const, Art 40.1; EA, 1-1489, 25 June 1991, Art 31.1.5.

the State is also provided in Poland,[63] Hungary,[64] Romania,[65] and Slovakia[66] in relation to statutory, covenantal, or registered religious denominations. Moreover, in Latvia the Christian religion must be taught in state and municipal schools to the children of those parents who have requested it by written application if the child is under the age of 14; the curriculum is approved by the Ministry of Education and Science (it cannot include Judaism or Islam). It may be taught by teachers of the Lutheran, Catholic, Orthodox, Old believers, and Baptist denominations (registered churches) if not fewer than ten students in the school seek it. The teachers are selected by the religious authority and approved by the Ministry of Education and Science. Such teaching is funded by the State, with ethics being offered as an alternative.[67]

Non-denominational religious education

A fourth approach is optional non-denominational religious education with or without State funding.[68] Sweden has an opt-out system: the State must provide and fund education about religion; pupil attendance is mandatory but there is provision for pupils to opt out.[69] Estonia has an opt-in system: the State is under no duty to provide religious education but it must do so if at least fifteen pupils so elect, in which case non-confessional religious education is delivered around a syllabus determined by the Ministry of Education. Various religions are studied; in primary schools, the parents decide and in secondary schools, the pupils decide independently.[70] Bulgarian public education must be secular, but religions may be studied in the context of compulsory lessons in ethics, history, and philosophy; optional education in religion is available if there are at least thirteen pupils seeking it and it is taught on the basis of materials authorized by the Ministry of Education but there is no state funding for this.[71]

---

[63] Poland: Const, Art 53: Ordinance, Minister for National Education, 14 April 1992 (amended 1999): there must be 7 pupils requesting it and the school may request payment from the denomination; see also CCt, Decision of 20 April 1993 K 11/90: this upheld the constitutionality of the system; and Strasbourg: *Grzelak v Poland* App no 7710/02 (15 June 2010): this criticized the lack of alternatives for pupils who opt out.

[64] Hungary: Act 79/1993, s 4; see also Czech Rep: School Act no 561/2004.

[65] Romania: Const, Art 32.7; pupils may choose which state-registered religion is to be studied; the curriculum is set by the religious association and is approved by the Ministry of Education; EA, Law 84 of 1995, Art 9; Law 128 of 1997: state funding; see also CCt, Decision 72, 18 July 1995.

[66] Slovakia: Const, Art 23; see also Act no 29/1984 and Act no 308/1991 Zb, the agreement with the Holy See (2004) and with the registered religions (13 May 2004); at the age of 15 the child decides.

[67] Latvia: EA 1998, Arts 32–35; LORO, Art 6.

[68] Non-denominational religious education may also operate alongside opt-in denominational education: see above eg for Spain.

[69] Sweden: EA (800:2010) ss 6–7; formerly, Christianity was taught on the basis of a reservation from ECHR, Protocol 1, Art 2; see *Angelini v Sweden* (1988) 10 EHRR 123.

[70] Estonia: EA, (RT I 1992, 12, 192); (RT I 2003, 78, 526), Art 4.4; Act on Basic Schools and Gymnasia, (RT I 1993, 63, 892); (RT I, 1999, 42, 497), Art 38.8; (RT I 1999, 24, 358); the aims include understanding religion in life, moral development, tolerance, and making personal choices; children decide at 15.

[71] Bulgaria: Law of Public Education, Art 5; Ministry of Education Guidance, 18 December 2000.

The prohibition against religious education

The fifth category is where the State forbids religious education on state-school premises but allows pupils to receive it elsewhere. This occurs in the separation system of France and the cooperation system of Slovenia. Except in the eastern departments,[72] French public education is secular: primary schools must reserve a day each week for religious education outside the school (it cannot occur within the school), and Wednesdays are the norm—but 'moral and civic' (rather than moral and religious) education is provided.[73] However, in secondary schools chaplaincies may be appointed by the head teacher at the request of parents and on the nomination of a religious authority—the State has no duty to fund them and they are funded by the parents and the relevant faith community.[74] It is unlawful to 'deny to pupils who request it such individual leave of absence as may be necessary for worship or celebration of a religious festival, at least in so far as their absence is compatible with performance of the tasks entailed by their studies and with the maintenance of public order in the school'.[75] A slightly more flexible approach is employed in Slovenia. Whilst public schools cannot provide religious education,[76] it may be delivered on the premises in extra-curricular form by the registered religious communities if the Minister of Education so permits and there are no other 'appropriate premises'.[77] Whilst France and Slovenia are exceptional, there is a general juridical consensus across Europe that the State should provide for religious education in public schools.

The display of religious symbols and dress

Most States have no law about religious symbols on school premises.[78] However, a cross must be displayed in Austrian public and public-status private schools in classes where religious instruction is compulsory, if the majority of the pupils belong to a Christian denomination.[79] Crucifixes are displayed in Italian classrooms (which may be blessed each year by a Catholic priest),[80] but Strasbourg has held that this was incompatible with the state duty of neutrality towards religion in

---

[72] France: in the three eastern departments, religious education is part of the curriculum in primary and secondary schools; teachers are paid by the State; and parents may withdraw their children.

[73] France: Law of 28 March 1882.

[74] France: Decree of 22 April 1960, Order of 8 August 1960, Ministerial Circular, 22 April 1988; see also Law of 1905, Art 2: this prohibits funding of chaplaincies in schools by the State.

[75] France: CE, 14 April 1995, no 15765-3: this involved the Central Consistory of Israelites of France.

[76] UN Doc CRC/C/SR.938, para 50 (2004).

[77] Slovenia: EA 1996, Art 72; but elementary schools must provide non-religious lessons on religion and ethics as elective courses: Elementary Schools Act, Art 17.2; see also the case of *Mihael Jarc et al* no U-1-68/98 (November 2001): the prohibition against denominational activities in public schools (EA, Art 72) was constitutional and consistent with ECHR, Protocol 1, Art 2.

[78] The public use by the State of religious symbols more generally and outside the field of education (eg the deployment of crosses on national flags) is beyond the scope of this study.

[79] Austria: RelUG 1949, s 2(b)(1).

[80] Italy: Decree of the Ministry of Public Education 1992: but participation in ritual is voluntary.

the provision of education.[81] Nevertheless, crucifixes in Spanish schools have been classified as both religious and cultural symbols and their presence on school premises is a matter of discretion for the relevant school authorities;[82] in Slovakia, too, they are lawful.[83] Moreover, one Romanian court has recently held that the display of religious symbols in schools was lawful, but another court has held it unlawful,[84] however, a ban on crucifixes in German classrooms has been upheld by the Constitutional Court.[85] There is therefore little legal evidence of a clear consensus on this subject around Europe.

Religious dress has proved more problematic.[86] On the one hand, the Austrian Education Minister has decided that the wearing of Islamic headscarves is a religious precept and thus a ban on headscarves in public schools is unlawful.[87] The Bulgarian discrimination commission has held that Muslim girls were allowed to wear headscarves when there was no uniform policy in place in the school.[88] In Sweden, too, it is permissible to wear a headscarf on the basis of religious freedom, though headscarves may be banned for reasons of school order and security, but not without dialogue about common values, gender equality, and democracy.[89] Indeed, it has been held in Germany that bans in some *länder* on the wearing of headscarves by all civil servants, including teachers, may represent a disproportionate limit on religious freedom.[90] For example, the rejection for a post in a school in (mainly Catholic) Baden-Würtemburg of a Muslim candidate who insisted on wearing a headscarf was unlawful, as there was no formal legal ban in place there; also, wearing the headscarf was a personal statement, not a manifestation of the State; nor did it impede German educational values or state neutrality.[91]

---

[81] Strasbourg: *Lautsi v Italy* App no 30814/06 (ECtHR, 3 November 2009): this constituted a breach of ECHR, Protocol 1, Art 2 in conjunction with ECHR, Art 9.

[82] Spain: SC of Madrid, Decision of 15 October 2002 and SC Castilla-Leon, Decision of 20 September 2007; however, the latter court decided on 14 December 2009 that a crucifix may violate the negative right to freedom of religion of parents and children and so must be removed if the parents so request.

[83] Slovakia: National Council, Decision no 1845 of 10 December 2009: the 'placement of religious symbols in schools and in public institutions is the full right of each member State of the European Union'.

[84] Romania: HC of Cassation, 11 June 2008: lawful; Bucharest CA: unlawful.

[85] Germany: the display of a crucifix in classrooms in Bavaria (with its majority Catholic population) was challenged by a theosophist parent: CCt, BVerfGE 93, 1 (1995): in a 5 to 3 decision it was held that the display of a crucifix was in breach of the principle of neutrality in GG, Art 4.1.

[86] UNHCR: the right to manifest religion includes 'wearing of distinctive clothing or head covering': General Comment 22 (1993).

[87] Austria: Decree of 23 June 2004, Zl 20.501/3-III/3/2004.

[88] Bulgaria: Discrimination Commission, 22 February 2008, Case no 37/2007.

[89] Sweden: National Board of Education, Decision no 52-2006:689; see also Decision no 58-2003:2567; a ban was also upheld in the UK in *R (on the application of Begum) v Headteacher and Governors of Denbigh High School* [2006] UKHL 15; but a ban on wearing a Sikh *kara* was held to be discriminatory in *R (on the application of Watkins-Singh) v The Governing Body of Aberdare Girls' High School* [2008] EWHC (Admin) 1865.

[90] Germany: CCt, BVerfGE, 108, 282.

[91] Germany: CCt, BVerfGE, 108, 282. Baden-Würtemburg then passed a law to ban it; when Bavaria did likewise its Constitutional Court upheld the ban. Berlin, too, has banned all religious symbols in public schools; see also Wuppertal Labour Court, 29 July 2008, 4 Ca

On the other hand, French law forbids the wearing of religious dress: 'In state primary and secondary schools, the wearing of signs or dress by which pupils overtly manifest a religious affiliation is prohibited. The school rules shall state that the institution of disciplinary proceedings shall be preceded by dialogue with the pupil.'[92] Under quasi-legislation, this ban applies to, for example, the Islamic veil, Jewish *kippa*, or Christian cross of excessive dimensions; it also extends to parents who accompany their children to school on the basis that the parents are voluntarily contributing to the public service—but the French equality authority has requested the latter to end.[93] The ban has been held compatible with *laïcité* as its aim is to balance social integration with freedom; thus there is no discrimination when a Sikh pupil is expelled for wearing a turban in school.[94] The UN Committee on the Rights of the Child has criticized the law as inconsistent with both religious freedom and the best interests of the child,[95] but a ban on the use of headscarves by Swiss primary school teachers was upheld in Strasbourg.[96]

Faith and other religious ethos schools

National laws about faith schools illustrate well the extent to which the State and religion cooperate. Faith schools are found in all States regardless of their posture on religion-state relations: they exist in the separation systems of France[97] and Ireland (where the vast majority of schools are faith schools),[98] in state-church systems,[99] and in cooperation systems,[100] and, for instance, in Belgium there are more

---

1077/08: a teacher who after a warning not to wear a headscarf continued to do so was lawfully dismissed.

[92] France: Law of 15 March 2004 (no 2004-228); for proceedings see Education Code (L 141-51) added by the 2004 law; there were 494 to 36 votes in favour of the Law of 2004 in the Assembly and 276 to 20 in the Senate; see D Glendenning, *Religion, Education and the Law: A Comparative Approach* (Dublin: Tottel Publishing, 2008) 216.

[93] France: Administrative Instruction, 18-5-2004; HALDE Deliberation no 2007-117, 14 May 2007.

[94] France: CE no 364893 (27 November 1989); the turban case: Administrative CA of Paris, 19 July 2005.

[95] UNCRC, *Summary Record of the 967th meeting: France* UN Doc CRC/C/SR.967 (2004), paras 26, 35, and 42; *Summary Record of the 968th meeting: France* UN Doc CRC/C/SR.968 (2004), para 82; and *Concluding Observations: France* UN Doc CRC/C/15/Add.240 (2004), paras 25–26.

[96] *Dahlab v Switzerland* App 42393/98 (ECtHR, 15 February 2001): but 'it is very difficult to assess the impact that a powerful external symbol such as the wearing of a headscarf may have on the freedom of conscience and religion of very young children' (ibid 4–8); see D McGoldrick, *Human Rights and Religion: The Islamic headscarf debate in Europe* (Oxford: Hart, 2006) p 131.

[97] France: 18% of pupils are in private education, of which 90% are in Catholic schools.

[98] Ireland: Const, Art 42.4: the State may provide education with due regard 'for the rights of parents, especially in the matter of religious and moral formation'; about 98% of first-level schools are denominational (around 94% are Catholic); Netherlands: two-thirds of primary schools are denominational.

[99] Denmark: Act on Free Schools and Private Primary Schools (619/2002); but there are no folk church schools; there are also very few faith schools in Finland: eg the English school in Helsinki is Catholic; Greece: see eg PD1025/1977 and PD73/2001.

[100] Hungary: 10% of secondary schools are religious; Slovenia: 3% of secondary schools; Poland: around 1% of pupils are educated at these (mainly Catholic); Spain: 11.1% of all schools, public and

Catholic schools than State schools.[101] What follows deals with their private and/or public status, foundation, State financial support, the adoption of admissions criteria, and their provision of education, including religious education and discipline.[102]

Most States distinguish between public and private schools.[103] Generally, faith schools have the status of private schools.[104] However, in some States faith schools may have public status. This is the case in Germany, with its tradition of public Christian Communal Schools and private schools (which may also be confessional);[105] and in Austria there is a presumption that the schools of recognized churches and religious communities have public status.[106] Sometimes, though, faith schools are difficult to categorize as private or public. For example, in Hungarian law 'church schools' are a distinct category which is neither public nor private.[107] Similarly, in the United Kingdom, faith schools in England are either independent or maintained, and of the latter, foundation and voluntary schools may be designated as schools with a 'religious character' when established by a religious body or for religious purposes.[108] The public-private distinction in the field of education is also blurred in the case of jointly established state-faith schools,[109] and, above all, by virtue of the public funding regimes applicable to faith schools (see below).[110]

National laws often confer rights on religious organizations with legal personality to found a school. Once again, the right transcends the religion-state models of Europe. In cooperation systems, the right to found a school may be enjoyed by registered,[111] statutory,[112] or covenantal religious organizations.[113] The freedom to establish and administer denominational schools is found in the separation system

private, are Catholic; Czech Rep: eg 88 Catholic, 22 Protestant; Sweden: eg of 4,660 primary schools, 709 are private and around 9% of these are religious; Italy: around 5–6% of all schools are Catholic (2008).

[101] Belgium: nationwide 60% of schools are Catholic; in 1989 the first Islamic school was set up (in Brussels).

[102] For parental choice, see eg Denmark: Act on Free Schools and Private Primary Schools (619/2002); every child has a right to free education: Const, Art 76; Belgium: Const, Art 24.

[103] Slovenia: EA 1996 (amended 2002); Estonia: Const, Art 37.

[104] As is the case in Bulgaria and France.

[105] Germany: the Christian Communal School (*christliche Gemeinschaftsschule*) was the norm following the 1970s; the CGS was consistent with the Basic Law: Federal Ct, Decision of 17 December 1975 BVerfGE 41, 29; 42, 65 and 41, 88; School Law of Lower Saxony, Arts 129 *et seq.*

[106] Austria: CCt, 5063/1965 in OAKR 32/1981, p 482.

[107] Hungary: Act 4/1990; see also: CCt, Decision 4/1993 (II.12) AB.

[108] UK, England and Wales: SSFA 1998, s 69(3); the order must state the religion or denomination: s 69(4); the procedure is governed by secondary legislation: s 142.

[109] Lithuania: provision exists for joint state/municipal and traditional religion schools: EA, Art 10; see also CCt Ruling, no 49–1424, 13.6.2000: such schools are classified as secular.

[110] Czech Rep: State schools are established by municipalities, regional authorities, or occasionally the Ministry of Education; faith schools are often integrated into this system and faith groups rarely use the category of private schools as such (which must be registered with the Ministry of Education).

[111] Lithuania: Const, Art 40; EA, Art 10; LORCA, Art 14; Bulgaria: Public Education Act 1991, Art 30; Romania: EA, Law 84 of 1995, Art 9.4; Slovenia: EA 1996 (as amended 2002); Latvia: Agreement with the Holy See 2002, Arts 16 *et seq.*

[112] Poland: Law of 1989, Art 21.

[113] Portugal: Concordat 2004, Art 21; and LORF, Art 27(a).

of the Netherlands.[114] The Maltese state-church system prescribes that when the Catholic Church seeks a licence to establish a school, the application signed by the diocesan bishop cannot be refused by the Minister of Education (provided the legal conditions are met).[115] Private individuals from a particular faith group may also establish their own faith schools.[116] However, in Denmark, the refusal of a local council to make a building available for a free school for the children of parents from the Church of Scientology has been upheld by the courts as consistent with Article 9 ECHR.[117]

States make extensive provision for their financial support of faith schools.[118] In Ireland, faith schools recognized by the Minister for Education may receive funding and the State must not discriminate on religious grounds in this regard.[119] Equally, German private faith schools have a right to state funding equal to that of public schools.[120] This is also the case in Hungary, though here equal funding includes a bar against charging tuition fees.[121] In Austria, the State may subsidize human resources for public status private schools run by recognized churches or religious societies, but not for non-denominational public status private schools; such favourable treatment is not in breach of the ECHR, on the basis that faith schools assist the State to discharge its responsibility for the provision of education.[122] State funding is also permitted in the separation system of France: a private school (which includes a faith school) may enter with a public authority a contract for the State to pay for staffing costs at the school in a manner similar to the financial support of public schools.[123] However, no State funds are payable to (private) religious schools in, for example, Bulgaria.[124]

National laws generally permit faith schools to operate their own criteria for the admission of pupils, which may or may not include religious criteria.[125] Two

---

[114] Netherlands: see G Robbers (ed), *State and Church in the European Union* (Baden-Baden: Nomos, 2nd edn, 2005) 379, n 31.

[115] Malta: EA, Act XXIV 1988, Art 8.2.

[116] Italy: Const, Art 33; the Catholic Concordat and *intese* with other religious organizations repeat this; see also Hungary: Const, Art 67; Portugal: Const, Arts 43 and 75.

[117] Denmark: High Court, VLD 12/1 1999.

[118] Luxembourg: Law of 31 May 1982; Estonia: Private Schools Act, Art 22; Lithuania: LORCA, Art 14; Slovenia: EA 1996, Art 86; Italy: Law of 10 March 2000, no 62.

[119] Ireland: EA 1998, ss 10, 12; Const, Art 44.2.4: 'Legislation providing State aid for schools shall not discriminate between schools under the management of different religious denominations, nor be such as to affect prejudicially the right of any child to attend a school receiving public money without attending religious instruction at that school'; the property of educational institutions shall not be diverted 'save for necessary works of public utility and on payment of compensation': Art 44.2.6; funding is compatible with the endowment ban in Art 44.2.2: *Campaign to Separate Church and State v Minister for Education* [1998] 3 IR 321.

[120] Germany: BVerfGE 75, 40 and 90, 128; 9,300 Catholic kindergartens were funded in 2006.

[121] Hungary: Act 4/1990, s 19(1): the State grants equal funding for state and church schools but formally the school is maintained by the church—equal funding entails a bar against tuition fees.

[122] Austria: PrivatschulG, s 17; VfGH 27.2.1990, B 1590/88; *Verein & Gemeinsam Lernen v Austria* (1995) 20 EHRR CD 78: there was no breach of ECHR, Protocol 1, Art 2 read with ECHR, Art 14, because of the relief they provided for state expenditure.

[123] France: *loi* Debré, 21 December 1959.

[124] Bulgaria has signed Protocol 1 ECHR with a declaration which rejects any financial commitments to educational institutions with a religious orientation: H/INF (92) 3, p 1.

[125] Slovenia: EA 1996 (as amended 2002); Ireland: Equal Status Act 2000, s 7.

contrasting approaches to the admission of pupils to a Jewish school come from the Netherlands and the United Kingdom. As to the former, a boy was refused admission to an orthodox Jewish school on the basis that the mother was a convert to a liberal Jewish community by means of a form of conversion not recognized by the orthodox Jewish community as an alternative to the normal requirement for Jewish matrilineal descent; the Supreme Court declined to interfere in the decision of the school on the basis that the parental right in Article 2 of the First Protocol to the ECHR to religious education for their children, applies only to public and not to private schools.[126] The general rule in England and Wales is that state-maintained religious schools, when oversubscribed, may impose admission criteria based on religion.[127] However, in an English case with almost identical facts to that from the Netherlands, it was held that a Jewish school's admission requirement which restricted entry to Jews recognized as such by the Office of the Chief Rabbi (namely through matrilineal descent or recognized conversion) constituted unlawful racial discrimination.[128] Indeed, in France, religious schools which operate under a contract with the authorities of the State must admit pupils without any distinction of either race or religion.[129] Criteria may also be set for the appointment and dismissal of teachers at faith schools.[130]

Faith schools must generally comply with the national curriculum of the State.[131] However, different provisions may apply with respect to religious education, which is usually in accordance with the tenets of the religion concerned.[132] For example, in Ireland religious instruction in primary faith schools is designed to enable 'the child to develop spiritual and moral values and to come to a knowledge of God'—it is taught by national school teachers, and parents may withdraw their children;[133] but secondary schools provide religious instruction supervised by the religious authorities concerned, and parents may withdraw their children.[134]

---

[126] Netherlands: HR, 22 January 1988, NJ 1988, 891: ECHR, Protocol 1, Art 2 'gives parents a fundamental right *vis-à-vis* the State to respect of their choice of education of a specific character, but does not give a right that can be enforced *vis-à-vis* a private organisation that provides such education'.

[127] UK: England and Wales: Equality Act 2010, s 85(1); but exclusion of pupils on grounds of religion is forbidden by s 82(2)(e) and (f); attendance at Sunday school or worship cannot be a condition: EA 1996, s 398.

[128] UK, England and Wales: *R (on the application of E) v Jewish Free School Governing Body* [2009] UKSC 15: however, the SC was divided—5 justices held that there was direct racial discrimination; 2 that there was indirect racial discrimination; 2 that there was no racial discrimination but legitimate selection on grounds of religion.

[129] France: *loi* Debré, 21 December 1959.

[130] Ireland: Employment Equality Act 1998–2004, s 37; *Flynn v Power* [1985] IR 648; Netherlands: GETA, Art 5; dismissal of a female Muslim teacher who refused to shake hands with men on religious grounds was lawful: DC Utrecht, 30 August 2007, LJN: BB2648.

[131] Hungary: Act 4/1990; Luxembourg: Law of 31 May 1982; Greece: Law 3432/2006: supervised by the Ministry of National Education and Religious Affairs.

[132] UK: England and Wales: SSFA 1998, Sch 19, paras 3 and 4; S Petchey, 'Legal issues for faith schools in England and Wales' (2008) 10 EccLJ 174.

[133] Ireland: Revised Curriculum for Primary Schools 1999, p 58.

[134] Ireland: EA 1998, ss 9, 30; *Campaign to Separate Church and State v Minister for Education* [1998] 3 IR 357: 'A child who attends a school run by a religious denomination different from his own may have a constitutional right not to attend religious instruction at that school but the Constitution does not protect him from being influenced, to some degree, by the religious 'ethos' of the school.

In France the provision of religious education in private confessional schools is not compulsory under State law.[135] The Slovenian constitutional separation of State and religion is understood to prohibit religious activities at private faith schools unless such activities are extra-curricular.[136] A Dutch Muslim school may impose requirements as to the dress of staff if this is necessary in order to maintain the ethos of the school,[137] but a prohibition against wearing a headscarf on religious grounds in the first year at a Swedish private school was held contrary to the requirement that the school be 'open to all pupils'.[138] In summary, faith schools are a distinctive feature of the both the public but more usually the private educational landscape of Europe; religious groups may seek the foundation of faith schools—such schools may enjoy the financial support of the State, their own criteria for the admission of pupils, and the discipline of staff to the extent permitted by law, and they may provide for education in accordance with the tenets of religion. These arrangements indicate a high level of cooperation between State and religion.

Religion in prisons, hospitals, and the armed forces

Global and European international laws recognize the right of prisoners to the free exercise of religion without discrimination;[139] so far as practicable, this includes access to religious care, literature, and services.[140] Spiritual care in hospitals is also regulated by guidance at European level,[141] and medical personnel have rights not to participate, on grounds of religion, in procedures for abortion.[142] According to Strasbourg, religious freedom is also exercisable in the armed forces, though

---

A religious denomination is not obliged to change the general atmosphere of its school merely to accommodate a child of a different religious persuasion who wishes to attend that school.'

[135] France: *loi* Debré, 21 December 1959; for opting out see also the Dutch Primary Education Act, Art 41.

[136] Slovenia: EA 1996 (as amended 2002).

[137] Netherlands: ETC, 15 November 2005, Opinion 2005-222.

[138] Sweden: National Board of Education, Decision no 52-2006:689 of 22 May 2006 (which invoked the School Act, Ch 9, s 2); there must be good reasons rather than a general blanket prohibition.

[139] ICCPR, Art 10(1); UN General Assembly, UN Doc A/Res/45/111 (14 December 1990), Appendix: 'There shall be no discrimination on the grounds of . . . religion . . . It is . . . desirable to respect the religious beliefs and cultural precepts of the group to which prisoners belong, whenever local conditions so require'; for the ECHR, see below. See generally NS Rodley, *The Treatment of Prisoners under International Law* (Oxford: OUP, 1999).

[140] UN Standard Minimum Rules for the Treatment of Prisoners 1955, r 41-2; *Boodoo v Trinidad and Tobago* Communication no 721/1997; UN Doc A/57/40, vol 2 (2002) p 76: prohibiting without explanation a prisoner from access to Muslim prayer services and confiscation of his prayer books violated ICCPR, Art 18.

[141] European Network of Health Care Chaplaincy, *Standards for Health Care Chaplaincy* (2002).

[142] Denmark: Consolidated Act on Induced Abortion, s 10(2), Lovbekendtgørelse 2006-06-16 no 541: 'doctors, nurses, midwifes and social and health assistants . . . for whom it is contrary to their ethical or religious beliefs to perform or assist in induced abortion, may . . . be granted exemption'; Austria: Strafgesetzbuch, s 97: this bans discrimination against one who refuses conscientiously to perform a lawful abortion; see also FortpflanzungsG, s 6 for a similar rule as to medically assisted procreation; Spain: CCt, Judgment no 161/1987, 27 October, FJ 3; UK: Abortion Act 1967, s 4.

voluntary submission to military discipline may result in waiver of elements of the right to manifest religion.[143] At national level, States across Europe facilitate spiritual assistance in hospitals, prisons, and the armed forces. Some have a single provision on hospitals, prisons, and the armed forces,[144] or provisions on these applicable to individual faith communities.[145] Others take prisons and hospitals together,[146] or they couple prisons and the armed forces,[147] or else they have separate treatment of prisons,[148] hospitals,[149] and the armed forces.[150] The subject may also be dealt with in agreements.[151] In any event, laws address the right to spiritual care; the process of appointing ministers of religion to provide it; their status, salaries, and supervision; and the religious activities which may be undertaken as part of spiritual assistance.

The provision of spiritual assistance

The entitlement of religious organizations to provide for the spiritual needs of prisoners, patients, and members of the armed forces transcends the classical religion-state postures of Europe, but the facility is usually reserved to prescribed religions. In the separation system of France, for example, the traditional practice of the armed forces is for Catholic, Protestant, and Jewish military chaplains.[152] In state-church systems, the principal provider of chaplaincy ministry is the national church, as is the case in Finland and the United Kingdom.[153] In cooperation systems, the right is confined to recognized religious communities, as in Austria,[154] Germany,[155] and Belgium.[156] Catholic chaplains have a covenantal right of access

---

[143] *Kalac v Turkey* (1997) 27 EHRR 552. See Ch 2 above for conscientious objection to military service.

[144] Estonia: CCA 2002, Art 9.1; Lithuania: LORCA, Art 8; Portugal: LORF, Art 13; Slovakia: Act 308/1991 Zb, Art 9.

[145] Poland: for hospitals: Jewish Communities, Law of 20 February. 1997, Art 14; prisons: Methodist Church, Law of 30 June 1995, Arts 19–20; military: Orthodox Church, Law of 4 July 1991, Art 23.

[146] Austria: StrafvollzugsG 1969; France: Law of 1905, Art 2.

[147] Latvia: LORO, Art 1(8); Council of Ministers, Regs on the Chaplaincy Service, 2 July 2002.

[148] Belgium: eg for hospitals, RD, 23 October 1964; Bulgaria: Penalty Performance Act 1998, s 70; UK: Prison Act 1952 and Prison Rules 1999.

[149] Hungary: Act 4/1990, s 6 and Act 154/1997, s 11; Slovenia: ALPRC, Art 16: retirement homes.

[150] Denmark: Act on Personnel of the Defence Forces (249/2001); Romania: Law 195 of 2000, Art 2; United Kingdom: Army Chaplains Act 1868, s 2.

[151] Italy: Concordat with the Holy See, Art 11; Spain: Agreements ratified by Law 24/1992 of 10 November (Evangelical); Law 25/1992 of 10 November (Israelite); Law 26/1992 of 10 November (Islamic).

[152] France: this is the case under the Law of 8 July 1880.

[153] Finland: eg there is a state-funded Lutheran Chaplain General to the armed forces who has 25 full-time and 13 part-time army chaplains; Orthodox and others are part-time; UK: Queen's Regulations for the Army 1961, paras J1432–J1142; Army Chaplains Act 1868, s 2.

[154] Austria: StrafvollzugsG 1969, s 85 deals with the religious activities of prisoners.

[155] Germany: see WRV, Art 141 for cooperation in relation to chaplaincies.

[156] Belgium: for prisons, RD, 21 May 1965 (as amended), Arts 16, 36, 55; see Arts 50, 52 for Catholic clergy; see also RD, 23 March 2001; for hospitals, RD, 23 October 1964; for the military, RD, 17 August 1927.

to Italian prisons, hospitals, and the armed forces, as do ministers of the denominations with *intese*, though ministers of religious organizations without an agreement have access for those who request it.[157] Much the same applies in Spain for covenantal religious organizations,[158] in Poland for the statutory religious entities,[159] in Romania for registered religious associations,[160] and in Bulgaria for the traditional religions.[161]

Whilst these arrangements generate an implicit right in the members of religious organizations to such ministry,[162] some States recognize a formal right to spiritual assistance vested in the individual.[163] For instance, the doctrine of *laïcité positive* is the basis in France upon which a person unable to practise religion freely and privately may access spiritual care in prisons, hospitals, and asylums;[164] and in Portugal the State must provide 'adequate conditions' for the individual to have spiritual care from their faith communities in hospitals, prisons, and the armed forces.[165] A right in the individual is particularly well developed in the countries of central and eastern Europe. Estonia is typical:

Persons staying in medical institutions, educational institutions, social welfare institutions and custodial institutions, and members of the Defence Forces have the right to perform religious rites according to their faith unless this violates public order, health, morals, the rules established by these institutions or the rights of others staying or serving in these institutions.[166]

This approach is echoed in Hungary, Slovakia, Slovenia, Latvia, and Lithuania.[167]

As has been seen, many States confer on the individual the right not to disclose their religious identity.[168] However, some States require the religious affiliation of a prisoner to be recorded on admission to the prison. This is the case in the

---

[157] Italy: Concordat with the Holy See, Art 11; see also RD, February 1930, Arts 5 and 6 (for denominations recognised under Law no 1159 of 1929).

[158] Spain: Agreement with the Holy See on Legal Affairs 1979, Art 4; and Agreement 1979 on Religious Assistance in the Armed Forces; as to the other communities: 'The exercise of the right to religious assistance is guaranteed for persons in prisons, hospitals, welfare or other similar public centres or establishments, provided by ministers designated by the respective' bodies; Art 9 of each agreement: Law 24/1992 of 10 November (Evangelical); Law 25/1992 of 10 November (Israelite); Law 26/1992 of 10 November (Islamic). For the military, see Article 8 of each agreement.

[159] Poland: provision is made for chaplains in hospitals as to the statutory religious associations and the Holy See (but these are not paid for by the State); see eg for hospitals: Jewish Communities, Law of 20 February 1997, Art 14; prisons: Methodist Church, Law of 30 June 1995, Arts 19–20; military: Orthodox Church, Law of 4 July 1991, Art 23.

[160] Romania: Law 195 of 2000, Art 2.

[161] Bulgaria: Penalty Performance Act 1998, s 70.

[162] The exercise of such a right would of course depend on the terms of religious law.

[163] There may be such a right in any event under ECHR, Art 9.

[164] France: Law of 1905, Art 2.

[165] Portugal: LORF, Art 13.

[166] Estonia: CCA 2002, Art 9.1.

[167] Hungary: Act 4/1990, s 6, Act 154/1997, s 11; Slovakia: Act 308/1991 Zb, Art 9; Slovenia: Military Service Act 2002, Art 1, Military Service Rules; Latvia: LORO, Art 14(5); Council of Ministers, Regs on the Chaplaincy Service, 2 July 2002; Lithuania: LORCA, Art 8; Penitentiary Code, Art 60 (Ministry of Justice, no 172, 16 August 2000); Agreement with the Holy See, Arts 1 *et seq*.

[168] See Ch 2 above.

United Kingdom.[169] The requirement has been held by Strasbourg to be consistent with the ECHR.[170] But prisoners may not 'invent' a religion in order to gain privileges to which they would not otherwise be lawfully entitled.[171] Nevertheless, the Austrian Constitutional Court has held that the right to spiritual care from a religious group specified by a prisoner does not depend on proof adduced by the prisoner of formal membership of that group; prisoners have a right to such care from a minister of their 'own religious belief'—these words refer to the outward appearance of inner values and not to formal religious membership (here in relation to a Jehovah's Witness).[172]

The appointment of ministers of religion in the public sector

Ministers of religion who serve in prisons, hospitals, and the armed forces are commonly styled chaplains. Their appointment is a collaborative process between the State and religion: a religious organization nominates and a public body appoints.[173] The approach is similar to that on the delivery of denominational education in public schools. For example, hospital and prison chaplains are nominated by the religious entity and appointed by the State in Italy,[174] Spain,[175] and Austria where, moreover, chaplains to nursing homes may be appointed with the consent of the competent religious authority (such as the Catholic diocesan bishop or the governing body of the Protestant Church).[176] Needless to say, the public and religious authorities involved in the process depend on the type of institution in question. The appointment of hospital chaplains is a local matter of collaboration between the religious organization and the relevant authorities of the hospital itself; Ireland is typical: 'A health board shall make arrangements with the appropriate authorities for the performance of religious services in each hospital, sanatorium and home maintained by it';[177] but only ministers requested by a patient are allowed access to Belgian hospitals.[178]

---

[169] UK: England and Wales: Prison Act 1952, s 10(5).

[170] Strasbourg: *X v UK* App no 7291/75 (1977) 11 D&R 55: there was no evidence that a prison refusing to register the prisoner as being of the Wicca religion violated his right to manifest religion; registration was merely an administrative act on the part of the prison.

[171] *McFeeley and ors v UK* (1980) 3 EHRR 161.

[172] Austria: Law on Execution of Imprisonment (BGBl 144/1969 as amended), s 85; CCt, VfSlg 15.592/1999: the court invoked Art 14 StGG, Art 63 Treaty of St Germain, Art 9 ECHR.

[173] Poland: see n 159 above.

[174] Italy: Concordat with the Holy See, Art 11: the pastoral care of patients is the responsibility of Catholic clergy; they are appointed by state authorities on the nomination of the church; the same arrangement is used with *intese* religious entities; see also RD, February 1930, Arts 5 and 6 for denominations recognized under Law no 1159 of 1929: ministers from these are appointed on request.

[175] Spain: see Art 9 of each agreement as ratified by Law 24/1992 of 10 November (Evangelical); Law 25/1992 of 10 November (Israelite); Law 26/1992 of 10 November (Islamic).

[176] Austria: StrafvollzugsG 1969.

[177] Ireland: Health Act 1970, s 39; France: Ministerial Circular of 26 July 1976; Portugal: Ordinance no 603/82 of 18 June; UK: England, Department of Health, NHS Chaplaincy, Meeting the Religious and Spiritual Needs of Patients and Staff (2003).

[178] Belgium: RD, 23 October 1964.

However, in view of the issues of security which can arise, the appointment of prison chaplains may involve central (and local) government. Under the French separation system, prison chaplains are appointed by the Ministry of Justice after consultation with the relevant and competent religious authority.[179] Central government is also involved in the state-church regimes of Denmark, Finland,[180] and the United Kingdom: in England and Wales there must be a Church of England chaplain (or in Wales, Church in Wales chaplain) appointed by the Secretary of State and acting under licence from the diocesan bishop; the Secretary of State may also appoint a prison minister of other denominations if the number of prisoners requires this.[181] In the cooperation system of Estonia, prison chaplaincy is coordinated jointly by the prison service and the Lutheran Church but only clergy from churches of the Estonian Council of Churches may serve;[182] indeed, in Latvia the Prison Board and the Board of Religious Affairs collaborate on the matter.[183] The appointment of a prison chaplain is sometimes the subject of judicial proceedings; this has occurred in Ireland.[184]

For similar reasons, the collaborative process of religious nomination and public appointment is more complicated in relation to military chaplains. For example, in Austria there is a Catholic bishop to the armed forces appointed solely by the Pope on the recommendation of the Federal government; chaplains are chosen by the bishop with the consent of the Defence Ministry and are appointed by the State; the Protestant Military Superintendent is nominated by the Protestant Church Council and appointed by the Defence Secretary; and chaplains are nominated by the church, appointed by the State, and authorized to minister by the church.[185] Austria is not untypical: in the United Kingdom, military chaplains are appointed by the Secretary of State for Defence on the recommendation of the Chaplain General to the Armed Forces, following nomination by an accredited representative of the religious organization concerned.[186] In Spain, Catholic assistance is provided

---

[179] France: Decree of 12 September 1972; Belgium: RD, 21 May 1965; and RD, 23 March 2001.

[180] Denmark: the Ministry of Ecclesiastical Affairs appoints prison and hospital chaplains; Finland: the church licenses chaplains; the Swedish Christian Council organizes chaplaincy for the national prison service—it has close links with Jewish and Islamic organizations; every prison must have two chaplains, one being from the Church of Sweden.

[181] England and Wales: Prison Act 1952, ss 7, 9, 53 (chaplains) and s 10 (ministers); Prison Service Chaplaincy: Prison Service Standing Order 7A.

[182] Estonia: Code of Enforcement Procedure, Art 171; ministers from the other denominations may serve at the request of prisoners; Czech Rep: Agreement between the Prison Administration and the Ecumenical Council of Churches, and with the Catholic Bishops' Conference.

[183] Latvia: Council of Ministers, Regs on the Chaplaincy Service, 2 July 2002.

[184] *Irish Prison Service v Morris* ADE/06/10, Determination no 074, 28 February 2007, FTC/06/10, Determination no 073, 2 March 2007; DEC-S 2002–015: the court rejected a claim of religious discrimination by a prison chaplain under the Employment Equality Acts (alleging less favourable treatment as to promotion); the difference in treatment was grounded on the office or position which the complainant held rather than the religion he professed or practised.

[185] Austria: for Catholics, see Concordat, Art 8; for Protestants, see ProtestantenG, s 17; Germany: there is an Evangelical Church Office for the Defence Forces for Protestant military chaplains, and a Catholic bishops' military office; Belgium: RD, 17 August 1927; Denmark: Act on Personnel of the Defence Forces (249/2001); France: Law of 8 July 1880.

[186] UK: Church of England, the bishop; Church of Scotland, the Committee for Chaplaincy to HM Forces; chaplaincy functions are governed by Queen's Regulations for the Army 1961, paras J1432–J1142; chaplain is a commissioned chaplain in holy orders: Army Chaplains Act 1868, s 2.

by the military vicariate and its bishop is appointed by joint agreement of church and State; the bishop authorizes a team of clergy to deliver the service; and non-Catholic assistance is provided on the basis of the agreements (and royal decrees).[187] Arrangements in the countries of central and eastern Europe are very similar; Romanian military chaplaincy, for instance, is coordinated by the Ministry of Defence, Ministry of the Interior, and Ministry of Justice.[188] There are also several agreements with the Holy See on this subject.[189]

The status, salaries, and supervision of chaplains

As with appointment, legal rules concerning the status, salaries, and supervision of public sector chaplains vary depending on the institution involved. Generally, permanent hospital chaplains are employed by the relevant hospital authority and paid on that basis.[190] There is greater variety, though, as to the status and payment of prison chaplains. In some States (such as Bulgaria) prison chaplains are employed by the prison authorities and paid on that basis;[191] but in others (such as in England and Wales) they are public officials or civil servants remunerated by the State.[192] However, in France ministers of religion who serve in prisons do not have contracts but are subject to special rules as non-established public officials and they are paid by the State as such;[193] in Italy, too, Catholic clergy serving in prisons are not classified as regular State employees even if paid by the State.[194] Occasionally, the chaplains of some religious organizations are paid by the State, and those of others are not; in Spain, for instance, the expenses of Catholic ministry in prisons (and in hospitals) are met by the State but ministry provided by the three religious federations which have agreements with the State are met by those organizations.[195] In turn, Latvian prison chaplains are jointly funded by the State and the denomination,[196] but in Poland hospital and prison chaplains (unlike military chaplains) are not paid by the State.[197]

---

[187] Spain: Agreement with the Holy See 1979; see also Italy: Concordat, Art 11; the appointment of military chaplains from *intese* denominations is governed by Presidential Decree; for denominations recognized under Law no 1159 of 1929, see RD, 28 February 1930.

[188] Romania: Law 195 of 2000, Art 2; Law 80 of 1995, Arts 9 *et seq*; Slovenia: Military Service Act 2002, Art 1 and Military Service Rules; Poland: see eg Law of 21 April 1936, Art 22 for Muslim military chaplaincy; Lithuania: LORCA, Art 8; Slovakia: Act 308/1991 Zb, Art 9.

[189] Latvia: Agreement with the Holy See on Religious Assistance in the National Armed Forces, Arts 23–29; Lithuania: Agreement, Arts 1–3; Slovakia: Agreement ratified in Law 648/2002 Zz.

[190] France: payment is made on the basis of the Law of 1905, Art 2.

[191] Bulgaria: Penalty Performance Act 1998, s 70; only ministers of the traditional religions may be employed at a prison; Czech Rep: prison chaplains have been paid by the State since 2002; Finland: in 1999, there were 17 full-time Lutheran clergy in prisons and one Orthodox.

[192] UK: Prison Act 1952; Estonia: Code of Enforcement Procedure; Hungary: Act 6/1996 (VII.12) IM, ss 93–99; in Finland, Denmark, and Greece ministers of the national churches are in any event classified as civil servants, as are ministers of religion in Luxembourg: see Ch 5 above.

[193] France: Decree of 12 September 1972 (prisons); payment is made on the basis of the Law of 1905, Art 2.

[194] Italy: Concordat with the Holy See, Art 11.

[195] Spain: Art 9 of each agreement: Law 24/1992 of 10 November (Evangelical); Law 25/1992 of 10 November (Israelite); Law 26/1992 of 10 November (Islamic).

[196] Latvia: LORO, Art 1(8); Council of Ministers, Regs on the Chaplaincy Service, 2 July 2002.

[197] Poland: prisons: Methodist Church, Law of 30 June 1995, Arts 19–20; military chaplaincies: Orthodox Church, Law of 4 July 1991, Art 23.

Military chaplains have the rank of, or are equivalent to, officers and are salaried as such by the State in, for example, the Czech,[198] Hungarian,[199] British,[200] and Finnish armed forces.[201] The same applies in Italy, in relation to Catholic chaplains,[202] and France, in relation Catholic, Protestant, and Jewish chaplains.[203] However, Estonian military chaplains (drawn only from the Estonian Council of Churches) are state-paid civil servants,[204] and German military chaplains, too, are state officials (on contracts), though they have no military rank,[205] but Belgian military chaplains are *not* classified as civil servants.[206] Whilst military chaplains are also state-funded in Portugal[207] and Poland,[208] in Spain Catholic military chaplaincy only is state-funded through contracts on a permanent or temporary basis paid from public funds.[209] By way of contrast, Latvian army chaplains are jointly funded by the State and the relevant religious denomination,[210] and in the Romanian armed forces ministers of religion may be hired on a temporary basis.[211] Needless to say, volunteers who provide spiritual assistance in the armed forces by way of occasional visits are not paid from public funds.

The supervision of military chaplaincy rests on the basic principle that ministers of religion who serve in the armed forces have a double subordination: to the military and to the religious authorities. For example, in Austria Catholic military chaplains are subject in temporal matters to the authorities of the armed forces (and ultimately the Ministry of Defence) and in spiritual matters to the bishop and Protestant clergy to the Protestant Military Superintendent.[212] Similarly, in Latvia military chaplains are supervised by the Chief Chaplain of the National

---

[198] Czech Rep: Agreement between the Ministry of Defence and the Ecumenical Council of Churches and the Bishops' Conference, 3 June 1998.

[199] Hungary: chaplains of the Catholic Church, Reformed Church, Lutheran Church, and Alliance of Jewish Communities are financed by the State: Government Decree 61/1994 (IV.20) Korm.

[200] UK: the Church of England chaplain is a commissioned chaplain in holy orders: Army Chaplains Act 1868, s 2; see also: Sweden: the Church of Sweden (by agreement) must make payments for the services of a military dean who is a member of the staff of the commander-in-chief and appointed by the armed forces in consultation with the church; the dean supervises part-time chaplains from either the Church of Sweden or other church; there are no Islamic or Jewish chaplains.

[201] Finland: there is a state-funded Lutheran Chaplain General who has 25 full-time and 13 part-time army chaplains; Orthodox and others are part-time.

[202] Italy: under a Presidential Decree; Concordat, Art 11.

[203] France: Law of 8 July 1880; there are also chaplains engaged in a civil capacity on contracts of employment, and unpaid (volunteers).

[204] Estonia: CCA, Art 9.

[205] Germany: see WRV, Art 141 for the basis of cooperation.

[206] Belgium: RD, 17 August 1927; for their non-civil servant status, see Cour de Cass, 23 November 1957, I, p 983.

[207] Portugal: LORF, Art 13; DL no 93/91 of 26 February; for Catholic chaplains, Concordat 2004, Art 17.

[208] Poland: see eg Orthodox Church, Law of 4 July 1991, Art 23.

[209] Spain: each Agreement, Art 9, ie Law 24/1992 of 10 November (Evangelical); Law 25/1992 of 10 November (Israelite); Law 26/1992 of 10 November (Islamic).

[210] Latvia: LORO, Art 14; Council of Ministers, Regs on the Chaplaincy Service, 2 July 2002, para 4; also, Agreement with the Holy See on Religious Assistance in National Armed Forces, Arts 23–29.

[211] Romania: Law 195 of 2000, Art 12.

[212] Austria: for Catholics, see Concordat, Art 8; for Protestants see ProtestantenG, s 17.

Armed Forces, who is subject to the Commander of the Armed Forces;[213] in Slovakia the Military Deanery of the Army General Headquarters is charged with administration of the system and is accountable to the Ministry of Defence.[214] A small number of States impose additional restrictions on military chaplains: for instance, Romanian military chaplains cannot marry a person who is not a Romanian citizen, participate in political or trade-union meetings, travel abroad, or express publicly their political convictions.[215] States with a Catholic military ordinariate may have further religious tiers of accountability; Lithuania is typical: a military chaplain is subordinate canonically to the Vicar General as senior military chaplain, who in turn is responsible to the Military Ordinary, himself accountable to the Pope.[216] Other religious entities may have similar schemes.[217]

The accommodation of religious activities

The States of Europe seek to accommodate a range of religious activities for patients, prisoners, and military personnel. With regard to hospitals, provision may be made for visits by a minister of religion to deliver spiritual care, personal devotions, collective worship or other rites, spiritual literature, religious diet, ministration to the dying, and funeral rites.[218] Permissible religious activities in prisons are spelt out in some detail in the laws of central and eastern Europe. Latvia, Bulgaria, and Lithuania are typical. Latvian prison chaplains may provide pastoral support, spiritual advice, and moral education; and all prisoners may see a cleric once a month.[219] Bulgarian prisoners have the right to engage in 'religious practices' (and chaplains may assist them to do so),[220] and Estonian prisoners in 'religious rites', unless these violate public order, health, morals, or the rights of others.[221] In one case, a prison confiscated candles from a Buddhist prisoner on grounds of security; the prisoner claimed the use of candles was required by his religion and that confiscation violated his constitutional right to religious freedom; the court held that there had been no violation—it recognized that candles are an important aspect of Buddhist ritual but that Buddhism did not require the prisoner

---

[213] Latvia: Council of Ministers, Regs on the Chaplaincy Service, 2 July 2002; see also Agreement with the Holy See on Religious assistance to Catholics in the National Armed Forces, Arts 23–29.

[214] Slovakia: Act 308/1991 Zb.

[215] Romania: Law 195 of 2000, Art 18.

[216] Lithuania: Agreement with the Holy See, Arts 1 *et seq.*

[217] UK: Church of England military chaplains are responsible to a bishop, and Church of Scotland chaplains to the Committee for Chaplaincy to HM Forces.

[218] Spain: see Art 9 of each agreement ratified by Law 24/1992 of 10 November (Evangelical); Law 25/1992 of 10 November (Israelite); Law 26/1992 of 10 November (Islamic); but there is no mention of funerals in the agreement with the Evangelicals; Art 14.4 of Islamic Communities Agreement: 'attempts should be made to adapt the food to interns in public centres or establishments and military premises, as well as to Muslim pupils in public and agreed subsidised private educational institutions to Islamic religious precepts and to mealtimes during the Ramadan fast'.

[219] Latvia: LORO, Art 14; Council of Ministers, Regs on Chaplaincy Service, 2 July 2002.

[220] Bulgaria: Penalty Performance Act 1998, s 70; Austria: StrafvollzugsG 1969, s 85; Slovakia: Act 308/1991 Zb, Art 9; Slovenia: Military Service Act 2002, Art 1 and Military Service Rules.

[221] Estonia: CCA 2002, Art 9.

to burn them in his cell.[222] Estonian prisoners may also subscribe at their own expense to religious publications.[223] Lithuania has similar rules,[224] but here a claim that a prison catered inadequately for religious diet was rejected on the basis that provision for such diets was impractical.[225]

Extensive provision is also made for English and Welsh prisons in the United Kingdom as to clerical visits, services, holy days, books, and religious diet.[226] However, aspects of these arrangements have generated recourse to Strasbourg.[227] The European Commission on Human Rights has decided that a prison rule which applied generally to all prisoners, requiring them to clean their cells, was justified, when a high-caste Sikh prisoner complained that it was against his religion to clean the floor of his cell; the claim was rejected but the Commission accepted that the belief was genuinely held.[228] Strasbourg has also accepted as justified on grounds of security or practicality a refusal by a prison to allow a high-risk prisoner to attend Sunday worship for fear that he would cause disorder at the event,[229] confiscation of a religious book on the basis that it contained a chapter on the martial arts,[230] a refusal to allow a prisoner to wear religious clothes,[231] and the supply of what was claimed to be an inadequate kosher diet (on the basis that the prisoner failed to exhaust the domestic remedies).[232] Similarly, Strasbourg has rejected the petition of a Swiss prisoner, who claimed to be a light worshipper, not to be held in a dark cell (on the basis that this was not a genuinely held belief),[233] the request of a Buddhist prisoner in Austria to use a prayer chain (on the basis that this was not a core element of his religion),[234] and the complaint

---

[222] Estonia: Tartu DC, Case no 3-07-701 (2 May 2007); Const, Art 40.

[223] Estonia: Code of Enforcement Procedure, Art 98.

[224] Lithuania: Penitentiary Code, Art 60 (Minister of Justice, no 172, 16 August 2000).

[225] Lithuania: in 1999 the ombudsman examined a discrimination complaint of inadequate provision for the religious diets of prisoners, patients, and military personnel; the Ministries of Health and of National Defence argued that the diet was based on physiological, age, and health factors, not on religion; also, only 0.16% of prisoners had special dietary needs so it was not practical to change the relevant regulations.

[226] England and Wales: Prison Rules 1999, r 14-1; they are expected to wear prison clothing but must be allowed to wear obligatory religious dress as agreed between the religious body and the prison service headquarters: ibid, r 23; Prison Service Order 4550: Religion Manual.

[227] It may be noted that the litigation pre-dates changes effected by the instruments cited above.

[228] *X v UK* App no 8231/78 (1982) 28 D&R 5: the prisoner claimed unsuccessfully that imposing prison clothing was degrading as he recognized no authority between himself and his god.

[229] *X v UK* (1983) 5 EHRR 289; *Childs v UK* (1983) 5 EHRR 513.

[230] *X v UK* App no 6886/75 (1976) 5 D&R 100; *X v UK* App no 5442/72 (1975) 1 D&R 41, 42: a Buddhist prisoner who had been refused permission to publish in a Buddhist magazine failed 'to prove that it was a necessary part of this practice that he should publish articles in a religious magazine'.

[231] *McFeeley v UK* (1980) 3 EHRR 161.

[232] *DS and ES v UK* App no 13669/88 (1990) 65 D&R 245; see also *Jakóbski v Poland* App no 18429/06 (ECtHR, 7 December 2010): failure to meet Buddhist dietary needs violated ECHR, Art 9.

[233] *Omkarananda and Divine Light Zentrum v Switzerland* App 8118/77 (1981) 25 D&R 105: it was held that this was not a genuinely held belief.

[234] *X v Austria* App no 1753/63 (1965) 8 YB ECHR 174: the Commission accepted only 'necessary expressions' of religion and questioned whether the prisoner's use of a prayer chain (and growing a beard) was 'an indispensable element in the proper exercise of the Buddhist religion'; refusal was justified on the basis of the prisoner's health and discipline, and as to growing a beard, because of difficulties in identifying him (even though he would have been the only one with a beard).

by a German prisoner that the prison provided inadequate access to Anglican clergy.[235]

National laws cater for similar needs in the armed forces.[236] Accommodation is made for clerical visits, the celebration of religious services, and the teaching of religion on military sites.[237] However, in Bulgaria, religious practices may be carried out only outside and not on military sites;[238] the same applies in Slovenia, and here the military authorities must post a list of local places of worship.[239] Spain deals with the subject in some detail in its agreements with the Catholic Church, and the Evangelical, Jewish, and Islamic communities.[240] For example, the agreement with the Islamic Commission provides: 'all military personnel of the Muslim faith...[are entitled] to receive Islamic spiritual support and to participate in religious activities and rites inherent to Islam, subject to authorisation by their superiors, who shall endeavour that these be compatible with the needs of the service, facilitating the places and suitable means for this purpose'. Moreover: 'Muslim servicemen unable to comply with their religious obligations, in particular collective prayer on Friday, because there is no mosque or, as appropriate, oratory in the place they are stationed, may be authorised to comply therewith in the closest mosque in the vicinity, service permitting.' Finally: Islamic religious assistance shall be dispensed by imams or others designated by the Islamic Commission and authorized by army commanders who shall lend such aid as needed so that they can perform their duties under the same conditions as those ministers of other denominations with agreements with the State.[241]

Conclusion

National laws on religion in schools, hospitals, prisons, and the armed forces reveal a high level of cooperation between European States and religion, a general consonance between national standards and those of international law in this field, and a wide range of important principles common to the States of Europe irrespective of their particular postures to internal religion-state relations. All States recognize the value to pupils of education about religion during their time in public schooling. Parents and guardians have a right to the religious education of their

---

[235] *X v Germany* App no 2413/65 (1966) 23 CD 1: the Commission held that there was no evidence to support the prisoner's claim under Art 9 that there were inadequate facilities for both pastoral care by an Anglican priest and Anglican worship even though Protestant facilities were provided.

[236] Portugal: LORF, Art 13: 'adequate conditions' must be provided. See also Belgium: RD, 10 March 2009, *Moniteur Belge*, 27 July 2009: this allows Muslim women who are members of the Civil Forces to wear the veil.

[237] Lithuania: LORCA, Arts 8 *et seq*; Slovakia: Act 308/1991 Zb, Art 9.

[238] Bulgaria: Defence and Armed Forces Act, s 196.

[239] Slovenia: Military Service Act 2002, Art 1; Military Service Rules.

[240] Spain: Art 8 of the Agreements ratified by Law 24/1992 of 10 November (Evangelical); Law 25/1992 of 10 November (Israelite); see also Agreement with the Holy See 1979.

[241] Spain: Agreement ratified by Law 26/1992 of 10 November (Islamic), Art 8.

children, and children themselves have a right to decide on this when they reach the age of maturity. The State should provide for neutral and objective religious education. The State may provide, or provide for, classes in Christian knowledge, denominational education, or non-denominational education either in school or outside. The State may design the syllabus alone or in collaboration with religious organizations or it may allow religious organizations to design denominational education. Religious education may be delivered by State teachers or by teachers chosen by religious organizations in the case of denominational education. The State may fund religious education regardless of the way in which it is delivered. Attendance at religious education may be compulsory or optional. However, the State should provide for exemptions when parents or mature children so wish. Moreover, teachers should not be obliged to provide religious education against their wishes. However, it is difficult to identify a juridical consensus in Europe about religious dress and symbols in public schools—regulation of the matter is in the process of development. Schools with a religious ethos exist in varying numbers in all States and are a feature of both the public but more usually the private educational landscape of Europe. Religious groups have a right to seek the foundation of faith schools. States may fund these schools but should not discriminate in doing so. Faith schools may operate their own criteria for the admission of pupils and the discipline of staff to the extent permitted by law. They may also provide education in accordance with the tenets of religion.

National laws on religion in hospitals, prisons, and the armed forces are less complicated than those on religion in education. Yet they, too, yield shared principles. Individuals have a right to the free practice of religion in hospitals, prisons, and the armed forces, and religious organizations are entitled to assist in this. The appointment of chaplains and other ministers of religion to provide religious assistance in these institutions is a collaborative exercise between the State and religion. The State should, so far as is practicable, contribute financially to the provision of spiritual care for patients, prisoners, and military personnel. The State in partnership with religious organizations should adequately supervise public sector chaplaincy. Spiritual assistance should accommodate pastoral care and religious practices in hospitals, prisons, and the armed forces. All these principles indicate that religion has a distinctive part to play in the public institutions of the State. However, further study is needed to understand the role of quasi-legislation in this field, in the form of ministerial and other circulars, codes of practice, and guidance, as well as how these, alongside the national laws and the principles outlined above, are actually implemented in the day-to-day administration of religion laws in these public sectors.

9

Religion and the Family:
Marriage and Children

Recent years have seen considerable public debate about religion and private life, particularly with regard to the recognition of religious laws on marriage.[1] The protection of children in religious contexts is also topical.[2] Debates of this sort raise a host of associated issues about how national laws in Europe address marriages conducted in accordance with religious rites, and the religious upbringing of children. These subjects also tell us much about the degree to which the law impinges upon essentially private matters of family life and whether religion and the family are properly matters of concern to the State. The first part of the chapter explores national laws which deal with religious marriages—their formation, dissolution, and annulment—and, briefly, laws on civil partnerships and same-sex marriages as they touch upon religion. The second part examines parental rights with respect to the religious upbringing of children, limitations which may be placed on these, and rules about the religious autonomy of the child. These subjects are examined in the context of international law. For example, the ECHR provides a qualified right to respect for private and family life,[3] and states that men and women of marriageable age have the right to marry and to found a family, in

---

[1] In February 2008, the Archbishop of Canterbury, Dr Rowan Williams, stated in a public lecture that it seemed 'unavoidable' that aspects of Islamic law on eg marriage would be recognized by UK law: R Williams, 'Civil and religious law in England: a religious perspective' (2008) 10 EccLJ 262. The lecture provoked outrage from many. However, Lord Philips of Worth Matravers gave qualified support for the idea: see his 'Equality before the law' (2008) 161 Law and Justice 75; see also A Shachar, 'Entangled: state and religion and the family' in R Ahdar and N Aroney (eds), *Shari'a in the West* (Oxford: OUP, 2010) ch 8.

[2] eg in relation to concerns about child abuse in the Catholic Church: see eg the article by Bente Clausen in the Danish *Kristeligt Dagblad*, 22 March 2010, p 7; for litigation, see eg UK: *Raggett v Society of Jesus Trust of 1929 for Roman Catholic Purposes and anor* [2010] EWCA (Civ) 1002 (27 August 2010): where school governors had accepted vicarious liability for the conduct of a Jesuit teacher alleged to have sexually abused a pupil and there was evidence of such abuse, it was a proper exercise of discretion by the first instance judge to allow the action to proceed even though it was outside the limitation period and time-barred (under the Limitation Act 1980, s 33); see also *Maga v Trustees of the Birmingham Archdiocese of the Roman Catholic Church* [2010] EWCA (Civ) 256 (16 March 2010).

[3] ECHR, Art 8: the exercise of the right may be limited by law if necessary for a democratic society and to protect national security, public safety, the economic well-being of the country, the prevention of disorder and crime, the protection of health and morals and the rights of others.

accordance with the national laws governing the exercise of this right.[4] Moreover, Strasbourg has held that freedom of religion does not override national judicial proceedings instituted in order to protect a minor who has suffered as a result of entry into a marriage permitted under religious law.[5] The chapter also seeks to elucidate common principles of religion law in this field.

Religion and marriage

Historically in Europe religious marriages were the norm.[6] However, over the course of the past two hundred years, States have introduced civil marriage devoid of any religious component. This occurred during the nineteenth century in some States,[7] and in the twentieth century in others.[8] Nevertheless, States continue to protect the institution of marriage,[9] and sometimes its value is affirmed in agreements with the Holy See.[10] Needless to say, marriage itself is traditionally defined by the State as a quasi-contractual voluntary and lifelong monogamous union between a man and a woman (though, as will be seen, some States now recognize same-sex marriages).[11] Faith communities also offer religious marriages and these represent an important feature of life in European society. In turn, national laws across Europe deal in considerable detail with the formation of religious marriages,

---

[4] ECHR, Art 12; Art 14 on discrimination may also be relevant.

[5] *Khan v UK* App no 11579/85 (1986) 48 D&R 253: the abduction of and unlawful sexual intercourse with a 14-year-old girl were not justified on the basis that these took place during a marriage permitted under Islamic law; that an action etc is 'permitted' by religion does not render it a lawful manifestation of religious freedom; see P Taylor, *Freedom of Religion* (Cambridge: CUP, 2005) 213.

[6] See generally *Marriage and Religion in Europe*, PECCSR (Milan: Dott A Giuffré Editore, 1992).

[7] UK: England and Wales: Marriage Act 1836; Ireland: Marriages (Ireland) Act 1844; Italy: civil marriage was introduced under the Civil Code 1865 as the only form of marriage recognized by the State; much criticized by the Catholic Church, recognition of Catholic marriages was restored by the Lateran Concordat 1929, Art 34 (ratified in Law no 847 of 1929), the so-called *matrimoni concordati*; Hungary introduced civil marriage in 1895.

[8] Finland: Laws on Civil Marriage 1917; Malta: Marriage Act 1975: previously only Catholic marriages were recognized; Greece: Law 1250/1982.

[9] Ireland: Const, Art 41: 'the State pledges itself to guard with special care the institution of Marriage on which the family is founded, and to protect it against attack'; Poland: Const, Art 18: 'marriage . . . shall be placed under the protection and care of the Republic of Poland'.

[10] Spain: Agreement with the Holy See on Legal Affairs 1979, Art 6: 'The Holy See reaffirms the permanent value of its doctrine concerning marriage and reminds those who celebrate marriage in accordance with canon law of the serious obligation they assume to abide by the canonical rules regulating marriage and, especially, to respect their essential meaning.'

[11] UK: *Hyde v Hyde* (1866) LR 1 P&D 130, 133: 'marriage, as understood in Christendom, may . . . be defined as the voluntary union of one man and one woman to the exclusion of all others'; cf *Sheffield City Council v E and S* [2005] 1 FLR 965, 1000: marriage is 'a secular institution whose duties and obligations are regulated by the secular courts of an increasingly secular society. For, although we live in a multi-cultural society of many faiths, it must not be forgotten that as a secular judge my concern is with marriage as a civil contract, not a religious vow'; Scotland: Marriage (Scotland) Act 1977, s 2; Denmark: Marriage Act (147/1999); also, if a marriage is involuntary or one of convenience to acquire residence, it will not be recognized: Aliens Act (608/2002); a forced marriage would be an aggravated form of crimes of coercion: Law no 316 of 30/04/2008.

to a lesser extent with their termination, and increasingly with civil partnerships and same-sex marriages.[12]

The formation and recognition of religious marriages

While the decision to marry is obviously a private matter, the formation of a marriage has a direct effect on the public status of a couple in civil law. In their laws on marriages conducted in accordance with religious rites, the States of Europe either enable or disable the intrusion of religion in this particular public sphere in so far as they may or may not recognize such religious marriages. Whilst all States permit the celebration of a religious ceremony following a civil marriage, countries fall into three broad categories in terms of the formation and recognition of religious marriages: (1) States which recognize the validity and public effects of certain religious marriages formed at the time of their ritual celebration, provided the conditions of civil law are met; (2) States which recognize Catholic marriages as religious marriages with civil effect from the time of their ritual celebration but recognize the marriages conducted by ministers of other faith communities as essentially civil marriages merely solemnized in a religious context and formed on subsequent civil registration; and (3) States which do not recognize religious marriages at all, but may permit a religious ceremony subsequent to a civil marriage, or indeed penalize their solemnization under criminal law if conducted prior to a civil marriage.[13] Models (1) and (2) recognize the autonomy of faith communities in this matter; model (3) does so to a far lesser extent.

First, there are the countries in which religious marriage ritual generates public marital status: religious marriages are recognized by the State from the moment of their solemnization, provided the conditions of civil law are met; as such, parties may choose between a civil or religious marriage.[14] This approach transcends the religion-state postures found in Europe. In state-church systems, marriages solemnized by the national church are recognized on the basis of its constitutional position, and the ministers of other recognized religious organizations may solemnize marriages on the basis of permission from the State.[15] In Denmark, a marriage

---

[12] Other than in cases of divorce (see below), laws do not usually deal with the religious conduct of spouses; however, see eg Spain: a book by an imam proposed that a Muslim husband ought to strike his wife if after a reprimand she fails to obey him; it was held that the husband's religious freedom was limited by the woman's right to moral integrity: Criminal Court no 3 of Barcelona, 12 January 2004.

[13] Indeed, where former communist regimes had forbidden religious marriages, several States today recognize these as an alternative to civil (secular) marriage, provided the conditions of civil law are satisfied: see OA Khazova, 'Family law on post-soviet European territories: a comparative overview of some recent trends', *Electronic Journal of Comparative Law* <http://www.ejcl/141/art141-3.doc>; Czech Rep: Family Act 1963: this prohibited religious marriages but was amended by Act no 234/1992 Sb; Estonia: Personal Status Act 1926 abolished in 2001: RT I 2001, 53, 307.

[14] Austria: marriages by legally recognized churches and religious societies are acknowledged as a lawful manifestation of religion under Constitutional Act, Art 15; Law on Personal Status 1937, Art 67.

[15] Finland: the Lutheran and Orthodox churches may conduct marriages on the basis of their constitutional positions and permission may be given to other (but only registered) religious entities by the Education Minister: Marriage Act (234/1929), s 14; see also FRA 1992; Malta: for Catholic

may be solemnized in a place of worship of the folk church (if one of the parties is a member) or of another recognized religious community if its minister is so authorized by the State; parish clergy of the folk church act as civil registrars, and other religious entities may have marriage registers and issue marriage certificates if recognized by royal decree or approved by the Minister of Ecclesiastical Affairs.[16] Similarly, in England and Wales, a marriage solemnized according to the rites of the Church of England (which includes for this purpose the disestablished Church in Wales) is valid in civil law;[17] and a person having a qualifying connection with the parish has a right to be married in its church.[18] Moreover, marriages may be conducted according to the usages of the Society of Friends and Jews (but only between two professing the Jewish religion);[19] civil and religious marriages are also recognized in Scotland (but no special position is accorded to the national church).[20] Much the same applies in Greece with regard to an Orthodox marriage, which requires a licence from the metropolitan (analogous to a civil licence);[21] in Thrace, each of the three Islamic muftis have jurisdiction to apply Islamic law in relation to the formation of marriage;[22] but marriages may not be solemnized on Mount Athos, as no female may enter into that territory.[23]

The so-called separation system of Ireland also recognizes the validity of marriages from the moment of solemnization in accordance with religious rites, and most marriages are of this type. However, the conditions of civil law must be satisfied. Religious organizations may apply to the civil Registrar General for their ministers to be entered on the Register of Solemnizers. Three months' notice of a marriage must be submitted by the parties to the civil registrar—without notice the marriage is invalid. After the issue of a marriage registration form by the civil registrar, the marriage is solemnized by a registered solemnizer and then

---

marriage, Agreements of 3 February 1993 and 6 January 1995, appended to the Marriage Law Amendment Act 1995.

[16] Denmark: 'the rules of procedure governing marriage ceremonies in the Danish National Church . . . shall be laid down by the Minister of Ecclesiastical Affairs . . . recognised religious communities shall be subject to their own special rules. For other religious communities marriage . . . shall be approved by the Minister of Ecclesiastical Affairs': Formation and Dissolution of Marriage Acts 1969 and 1999, s 21(3); 90 religious communities other than the folk and recognized churches are so authorized (including, as from 2003, the Nordic gods' community): G Robbers (ed), *State and Church in the European Union* (Baden-Baden: Nomos, 2nd edn, 2005) 71.

[17] UK: Marriage Act 1949, Part II, s 26; places of worship may be registered for the solemnization of marriage: Marriage Act 1949, ss 41–42; and Places of Worship Registration Act 1855.

[18] UK: Church of England Marriage Measure 2008; the special status of the church may be at odds with ECHR, Art 14: *R (Baiai, Trzcinska, Bigoku and Tilki) v Secretary of State for the Home Department* [2006] EWHC 823, subsequently approved [2008] UKHL 53; see also J Humphreys, 'The right to marry in the parish church: a rehabilitation of *Argar v Holdsworth*' (2004) EccLJ 405.

[19] UK: Marriage Act 1949, s 47 (Quakers), s 26 (Jews).

[20] Scotland: marriages by habit and repute constitute valid marriages if begun before 2006: Family Law (Scotland) Act 2006; civil and religious marriages are governed by the Marriage (Scotland) Act 1977.

[21] Greece: refusals are subject to judicial review: COS, Decision 390/1971; the same applies to ecclesiastical dissolution: Decision 2635/1980; CC, Art 1371: mixed marriages may be celebrated; Law 1250/1982: this abolished many impediments which the Orthodox Church has retained.

[22] Greece: Treaty of Lausanne 1923; and Law 2345/1920 (as amended since).

[23] Greece: Statutory Charter, Art 186 (with LD 10 of 16 September 1926, Art 43b).

registered—but failure to register does not invalidate the marriage.[24] The model is also used in the cooperation systems of Cyprus, Lithuania, and Sweden. Under Cypriot law, the formation of marriages in recognized religious entities is governed by their own laws;[25] whereas formerly members of the Orthodox Church could not enter a civil marriage (unless it was contracted overseas),[26] today Orthodox Christians may choose either civil or religious marriage,[27] and the church's Charter deals with betrothal.[28] Similarly, Lithuania acknowledges marriages conducted by recognized and registered religious organizations.[29] Confessional marriage has civil effect from the moment of its religious celebration if it is: without impediments as to age and free will; celebrated according to the order and rules of the organization; and recorded in the civil register within ten days of the rite—the date of the marriage is that of the religious celebration unless it is not registered within the ten days, in which case it is the date of its registration in the civil register.[30] Sweden has much the same approach.[31] In each case, the religious rite alone constitutes the marriage for the purpose of civil law.

Secondly, there are States which recognize Catholic marriages as having civil effect from the moment of their religious celebration, but other religious marriages as having civil effect at the moment of their civil registration. In short, marriages conducted by non-Catholic ministers are essentially civil marriages solemnized in a religious context and formed on subsequent civil registration. This model predominates in States with a cooperation system of religion-state relations. Portugal, Spain, and Italy are in this category. Under Portuguese law the State recognizes Catholic marriages and, as a result of recent reform, those of the settled religions, but not those of registered religious entities.[32] The same applies in Spain: 'marriage contracted according to the rules of [Catholic] Canon Law' has civil effect at the moment of its celebration (but must be registered in the civil registry on presentation

---

[24] Ireland: Civil Registration Act 2004; s 54: solemnizers may be duly nominated ministers of religion or State officials; registration of a solemnizer may be cancelled eg if requested, or if the person is no longer fit and proper, but there is a right of appeal; places for the solemnization of marriages are not registered; the marriage registration form will declare the capacity of the parties.

[25] Cyprus: Const, Art 111: 'any matter relating to betrothal [or] marriage . . . of the Greek Orthodox Church or of a [recognized] religious group . . . shall be governed by the law of the Greek Orthodox Church or of the Church of such religious group, as the case may be, and shall be cognizable by a tribunal of such Church'; this applies to the Orthodox, Maronite, and Catholic churches.

[26] Cyprus: *Metaxa v Mita* (1977) 1 CLR 1.

[27] Cyprus: Const, First Amendment (Law 95/1989); and Law 21/1990.

[28] Cyprus: Charter, Arts 217 *et seq*.

[29] Lithuania: Const, Art 38.4; this does not apply to marriages contracted before the constitution came into force: CCt, Ruling no 31-562 of 27 April 1994.

[30] Lithuania: CC, Art 3: these marriages 'entail the same legal consequences as those entailed by the formation of a marriage in the Register Office'; the civil registrar registers them and issues a certificate; for Catholic marriages, see Agreement with the Holy See on Legal Matters 2000, Art 13.

[31] Sweden: Act on Marriages in Denominations other than the Church of Sweden, 1993:305; around 40 denominations have this right; for the disestablished Church of Sweden, Marriage Code, Ch 4, s 3.

[32] Portugal: Concordat 2004, Arts 13 and 14 (Catholic); DL 324/2007, 28 September 2007 (settled); LORF 2001, Art 19 (registered).

of the church marriage certificate),[33] but Protestant, Jewish, and Islamic marriages are recognized once registered in the civil registry (not from the moment of celebration)—prior to the ceremony, the parties must obtain a certificate from the civil registry as to their capacity to marry (delivered to them by the solemnizing minister); the ceremony must be in the presence of the minister and two adult witnesses within six months of issue of the certificate; once celebrated, the minister records the marriage (and the names of witnesses) in the civil certificate; a copy of this must be sent immediately to the civil registry for registration with a copy being kept by the minister.[34] Italy has a similar system for Catholic marriages (valid at celebration),[35] those conducted by ministers of *intesa* denominations without prior administrative State authorization (essentially civil marriages operative on civil registration), and those of other denominations with prior executive State authorization (likewise civil marriages valid on registration).[36]

Several States in central and eastern Europe adopt the same model. Provided there are no civil impediments and they are subsequently registered civilly, Catholic marriages are recognized as having civil effect from the moment of celebration, in, for example, Latvia,[37] Poland,[38] and Slovakia.[39] However, different rules apply to other religious organizations. Latvian couples may be married before a minister of a registered religious organization who must, within fourteen days, report the ceremony for entry in the civil marriage register.[40] Ministers require authorization from their religious organization to solemnize the marriage, and they do so on behalf of the State.[41] Similarly, after confirmation from the civil registry that the proposed marriage is lawful, Polish marriages solemnized in accordance with the rites of the statutory religious entities are certified by the officiating minister prior to

---

[33] Spain: CC, Art 60; repeated in the Agreement with the Holy See on Legal Affairs, 3 January 1979, Art 6.1: this continues: 'Canonical marriage is considered legal under civil law from the moment of celebration. For full recognition of these effects, the marriage must be registered in the Civil Registry; this may be done with the presentation of the church certificate of the existence of the marriage.'

[34] Spain: Agreement ratified by Law 24/1992, 10 November (Evangelical), Art 7.1: 'The civil effects of marriages celebrated before the ministers of Churches belonging to the Federation of Evangelical Religious Entities of Spain are recognised. For full recognition of these effects, the marriage must be registered in the Civil Registry Office'; see also Agreement, Law 25/1992, 10 November, Art 7: marriages under 'Jewish rules'; Agreement, Law 26/1992, 10 November, Art 7: marriages under 'Islamic law'.

[35] Italy: Concordat, Art 8 (recognition); the Catholic minister may issue a marriage certificate submitted to the municipal registry but the marriage is valid at the point of celebration not on delivery of the certificate; the agreement also allows for the operation of canonical impediments, and banns for marriage must be published at the town hall (as they must for civil marriage).

[36] Italy: ie religious groups which operate under Law no 1159 of 1929.

[37] Latvia: Agreement 2000, Art 8; the marriage must be registered with the civil authorities.

[38] Poland: 'From the moment [Catholic] canonical marriage is concluded it has the same effect as a marriage concluded according to Polish law': Concordat, Art 10.

[39] Slovakia: the agreement with the Holy See 2000, Art 10, permits the solemnization of Catholic marriages 'in accordance with canon law'.

[40] Latvia: Civil Law, s 53: 'a marriage shall be solemnized by the registrar of a General Registry office or a minister of the denominations set out in Section 51 if the provisions regarding the entering into of marriage have been complied with'; these include Evangelical Lutheran, Orthodox, Old Believers, Methodist, Baptist, Seventh Day Adventist ceremonies; see ibid s 58 for liability.

[41] Latvia: Law on Civil Status 1993, Art 13.2; also: Civil Law, s 40.

submission, within five days, to the civil statistics office.[42] Slovakian couples may marry in the presence of two witnesses before a State or a religious authority—the latter form must be administered by a person authorized by a registered religious organization in accordance with a religious form of service; the religious authority or minister must deliver a certificate of the marriage to the civil registry.[43] Marriages in the Czech Republic conducted by ministers of denominations registered with 'special rights' also have civil effect when registered after notification, within three days, to the municipal registry; the marriage ceremonies of other religious organizations are not recognized civilly.[44] As with the first model, this model, too, produces a fundamental inequality between religions; Catholic marriages are state-recognized religious marriages valid at the point of celebration; others are essentially civil marriages administered spiritually and certified by a minister of religion, and are validated by the State when registered. However, in Estonia, both Catholic marriages and those of other registered religious organizations are solemnized by their ministers in accordance with spiritual rites on behalf of the State—both types of marriage are recognized by the State but only on registration and the issue of a certificate of marriage by the relevant civil authority.[45]

Thirdly, there are States which do not recognize religious marriages at all—but parties may nevertheless undergo a religious ceremony after the civil marriage.[46] Moreover, in some of these States it is a criminal offence for a minister of religion to solemnize a religious 'marriage' prior to a civil marriage. Such crimes straddle the religion-state models of Europe. In the French separation system, religious marriages are not recognized in civil law, so the parties must contract civil marriage before a religious matrimonial ceremony—the latter alone does not constitute a marriage.[47] Every minister of religion who habitually conducts religious ceremonies of marriage without prior authorization from the civil authorities commits an offence punishable with imprisonment and/or a fine. This applies to all religions. There must have been a celebration of the marriage (not simply a benediction) and proof of intent is required. However, there is provision for such ceremonies in the case of the danger of death of one of the parties and there is a defence if the parties present the minister with a false certificate of civil marriage.[48] The same approach is used in the Dutch separation system and the criminal liability of a minister of religion in such circumstances has been upheld by the Supreme Court as a justified restriction of religious freedom.[49]

---

[42] Poland: Family Code, Law of 24 July 1998.
[43] Slovakia: LORF, 1 September 1991.
[44] Czech Rep: Act no 91/1998 Sb; Minor Offences Act, s 42c.
[45] Estonia: Family Law Act 1994, s 130 (as amended 2004): they must be authorized by the Ministry of Internal Affairs; Agreement with the Holy See 1999, Art 8: 'marriages celebrated in the Catholic Church, upon registration and for which a certificate of marriage has been issued by the civil registry office, have civil effect'.
[46] Religious ceremonies may also precede or follow a civil marriage in the other two models in relation to those religious groups whose religious marriages have no civil law effect.
[47] France: moreover, despite the Catholic canonical requirement of celibacy, the (secular) marriage of a priest is valid in civil law: C Cass Civ, 25 January 1888; this is not affected by the Law of 1905.
[48] France: PC, Arts 199, 200, and 433; the penalty is up to 6 months' prison and a fine of €7,500.
[49] Netherlands: CC, Art 168; PC, Art 449; SC, HR, 22 June 1971, NJ 1972, 31.

Several cooperation systems also do not recognize the civil effects of a religious marriage. Some criminalize religious marriage ceremonies prior to a civil marriage, others do not. On the one hand, Belgian law provides: 'A civil wedding should always precede nuptial benediction except in cases established by law, should this be necessary.'[50] Any minister of religion who celebrates a marriage before the civil marriage ceremony has been performed will be punished with a fine; but, as occurs in France, there is a defence if one of the parties to the marriage was in danger of death, and any postponement could have made the celebration impossible.[51] Luxembourg follows suit, and here the penalty for celebration of a religious marriage before a civil marriage is a fine of €500–5,000 and/or imprisonment.[52] On the other hand, whilst in Germany religious organizations have no competence over marriage, which is an entirely civil matter conducted in a registry office— religious marriages have no civil effect—a religious wedding must not precede a civil marriage although there are no sanctions for breach of this rule. A religious marriage with civil effects may be contracted only between foreigners before a body recognized by their home State.[53] Indeed, on the basis that they violate religious liberty and the right of religious organizations to autonomy, such offences have been abolished in, for example, Austria,[54] Portugal,[55] Bulgaria,[56] and Hungary.[57] In these States a religious marriage may precede a civil marriage but it is not recognized as having civil effects—the parties remain unmarried. The same applies in the secular system of Slovenia.[58]

Nevertheless, in several States which recognize the civil effect of religious marriages, the failure of ministers of religion to satisfy conditions laid down by civil law may constitute a punishable offence. For example, under Spanish law, '[a] person who authorizes a marriage in which there is some cause for nullity or there exists a claim for such, will be punished with a prison term of six months to two years, and will be banned from office for two to six years in the case of a public employee or public figure'; this applies equally to Catholic, Evangelical, Jewish, and Muslim marriages.[59] In the Czech Republic the failure of a minister of a denomination with special rights to notify the civil registry within three days of celebration may result in payment of a fine by the minister.[60] There are also several interesting

---

[50] Belgium: Const, Art 21, para 2.

[51] Belgium: PC, Art 267; the minister may also be imprisoned for 8 days to 3 months.

[52] Luxembourg: PC, Art 267; imprisonment for 8 days to 3 months.

[53] For discussion of the law in Germany, see CCt, Judgment, 18 July 2001, Az 1 BvQ 23/01, 1 BvQ 26/01; see R Puza, 'Relations between church and state in Germany in 2000' (2001) EJCSR 35, 38.

[54] Austria: celebration of a religious marriage ceremony prior to civil marriage is a lawful manifestation of religion on the basis of Constitutional Act, Art 15 and the Treaty of St Germain, Art 63.

[55] Portugal: the crime under PC 1852, Art 136.2 was abolished by DL no 400/82, Art 6.1.

[56] Bulgaria: PC, Art 176(3); repealed—SG 51/2000; the punishment was prison for up to 1 year.

[57] Hungary: Act XXXI/1894; DL 10/1962. Religious marriages recognized by States in which they were contracted are recognized by Hungary as a matter of private international law.

[58] Slovenia: Const, Art 53; the agreement with the Holy See does not deal with the matter.

[59] Spain: PC, Art 291. There have been no court cases in which clerics or ministers of other religions have been prosecuted for or convicted under this law.

[60] Czech Rep: Family Law Act, s 42c; but a minister of a religious community not registered 'with special rights' is not punished for celebrating a marriage ceremony as this has no civil effect; Latvia: Civil Law, s 58: failure to notify in 14 days has the same result.

criminal offences in England and Wales which relate to the solemnization of religious marriages.[61] For instance, it is an offence if any person knowingly and wilfully solemnizes a marriage outside the prescribed hours, without publication of banns (in cases of marriage by banns), pretending to be in holy orders,[62] in an unauthorized place,[63] without registering the marriage, or registering any marriage which is void.[64] An offence has recently been created in relation to the marriage of persons whose gender has been re-assigned. The general rule is that a minister of religion is not obliged to solemnize the marriage of a person if the minister reasonably believes that the gender of the person is an acquired gender. However, an unauthorized disclosure of information relating to the 'gender history' of the person is a criminal offence.[65] The rule applies only to those who have gained information in an official capacity but this may include receipt of information in connection with a religious organization. There are exceptions for prescribed religious purposes: disclosure is permitted to enable a person to make a decision whether to officiate at or permit the solemnization of a marriage.[66] The position is broadly the same in Scotland.[67] Finally, in Austria the failure of the registrar to include the religion of a Jehovah's Witness, a *registered* religious community, in the marriage certificate was not unlawful or discriminatory when national law provided only for entry of membership of *recognized* religions in the marriage certificate.[68]

The termination of religious marriages

The States of Europe do not generally recognize as having civil law status a divorce (the dissolution of an otherwise valid marriage) pronounced under religious law;[69] nor do they recognize a religious re-marriage if the prior civilly recognized marriage has not been civilly dissolved. Nevertheless, religion may play a part in the civil dissolution of both civil marriages and civilly recognized religious marriages.[70] For

---

[61] See also Ireland: Civil Registration Act 2004, s 69.

[62] UK: Marriage Act 1949, s 75(1)(a)–(d); s 78: the rule about hours applies to marriages in the Church of England and the Church in Wales, but it does not apply to a marriage by special licence, or Quaker and Jewish marriages; pretending to be in holy orders may result in imprisonment for up to 14 years.

[63] UK: Marriage Act 1949, s 75(2): the same rules apply as to s 78 (see n 62 above).

[64] UK: ibid s 76.

[65] UK: Gender Recognition Act 2004, s 22: the disclosure is punishable by a fine of up to £5,000.

[66] UK: Gender Recognition (Disclosure of Information) (England, Wales and Northern Ireland) (No 2) Order 2005, SI 2005/916: disclosure is also permitted as to appointment of a person as a minister, to any employment for the purposes of the religion, to admission to a religious order, or to determine 'whether the subject is eligible to receive or take part in any religious sacrament, ordinance or rite, or take part in any act of worship or prayer, according to the practices of an organised religion': Art 4.

[67] UK: Gender Recognition (Disclosure of Information) (Scotland) Order 2005 (SSI 2005/125).

[68] Austria: VfSlg 16.998/2003: Law on Personal Status BGBl 60/1983 (as amended), s 24(2); it was held that this was allowed by the margin of appreciation and did not conflict with ECHR, Arts 9 and 14.

[69] For divorce in eg Judaism and Islam, see J Neusner, T Sonn, and JE Brockopp, *Judaism and Islam in Practice: A Sourcebook* (London: Routledge, 2000) 112–25.

[70] Portugal: Supreme Court of Justice, 16 May 2002, Process 02B1290: the court pronounced a divorce when a husband (from the Maná church) tried to convert a Catholic wife whom he claimed to be possessed; the exercise of religious freedom by the husband was limited by that of the wife.

example, under French law,[71] the courts may take into account the excessive religious practices of a spouse in relation to divorce proceedings and they have held that this is not contrary to religious freedom under Article 9 ECHR.[72] Thus, refusal by a spouse following (a civil) marriage to undergo a religious marriage ceremony to which he had agreed prior to that (civil) marriage is a ground for divorce; the same approach has been applied to a wife taking religious vows during marriage.[73] Equally, a court may refuse a divorce which one party opposes on religious grounds if this would cause that party 'exceptional hardship' given that party's commitment to religious teaching on the indissolubility of marriage.[74] Likewise, a Jewish husband who refuses to issue a *get* (a pronouncement of divorce) may be ordered to pay compensation to the wife—but the court has no authority (due to *laïcité*) to order a positive religious action by the husband.[75] However, in one case pressure exerted on a husband to issue a *get* was upheld by the European Commission on Human Rights.[76] Civil divorce law also has religious aspects in the United Kingdom: clergy of the Church of England and the Church in Wales may refuse on grounds of conscience to solemnize the marriage of divorced persons whose former marriages have been dissolved but whose former spouse is still living.[77] Moreover, the civil law recognizes the existence (but not the civil binding effect) of Jewish divorce—the court may refuse to issue a civil decree absolute until a *get* has been granted by the Jewish husband to his wife.[78]

For centuries in western Christendom annulment of marriage was the preserve of the Catholic Church. However, this slowly changed with the development of civil dissolution and annulment.[79] Today, the vast majority of States in Europe make no provision for recognition of the annulment by a religious authority of a religious marriage, either in those States which recognize religious marriages, or, needless to

---

[71] France: for annulment, see TGI Le Mans, 7 December 1981, JCP 1986, 20573; for dissolution, Law of 11 July 1975; civil divorce has only civil effects; religious nullity has no civil effects.

[72] France: Cass, 21 May 1990, no 89-12512 (Catholic); Cass, 9 October 1996, no 95-10461 (Jehovah's Witness).

[73] France: CA Amiens, 3 March 1975, DS 1975, p 706 (the vows case).

[74] France: the hardship clause under CC, Art 240; Civ, 2, 23 October 1991, D 1993, p 193.

[75] France: Cass, 15 June 1988, Bull Civ II, no 146; Cass, 21 November 1990, D 1991, 434, n E.

[76] *D v France* App no 10180/82 (1983) 35 D&R 199, 202: the applicant failed to persuade the Commission that pressure to repudiate a marriage entered under 'Jewish law' would oblige him to act against his conscience; he claimed that his refusal was a manifestation of his religion; the Commission stated: 'he alleges only that by reason of his family's special status he would forfeit for all time the possibility of re-marrying his ex-wife, for the Mosaic law provides that a Cohen may not marry a divorced woman, whether his ex-wife or anyone else's'.

[77] UK: England and Wales: Matrimonial Causes Act 1965, s 8.

[78] UK: Divorce (Religious Marriages) Act 2002 (adding a new s 10A to the Matrimonial Causes Act 1973): this provides that where a marriage was solemnized under the usages of the Jews (or any other prescribed religious usages—but none has been), the court may refuse a decree absolute until a *get* has been granted by the husband; this seeks to solve the problem of a husband who prevaricates over the *get*, but it does not address the problem where the wife seeks divorce: M Freeman, 'Is the Jewish get any business of the State?' in R O'Dair and A Lewis (eds), *Law and Religion* (Oxford: OUP, 2001) 365.

[79] eg Ireland: the Matrimonial Causes and Marriage (Amendment) Act 1870 abolished the matrimonial jurisdiction of the courts of the Anglican Church (and in England it had been abolished by the Matrimonial Causes Act 1857). Dissolution of marriage in Ireland was forbidden constitutionally but is now permitted on the basis of Const, Art 41.3.2 under the Family Law (Divorce) Act 1996.

say, in those which do not recognize such marriages. Similarly, the agreements between the Holy See and States of central and eastern Europe on the recognition of Catholic marriages do not generally deal with the ecclesiastical annulment of such marriages; where such annulments do take place, they enjoy no status in civil law.[80] Indeed, the Lithuanian and Slovakian agreements with the Holy See simply require the authorities of the Catholic Church to report such annulments to the State.[81]

However, Catholic annulments have civil law status in Portugal,[82] Malta,[83] Spain, and Italy. The Spanish agreement with the Holy See provides: 'Those parties contracting matrimony, in accordance with the provisions of Canon Law, may resort to the Ecclesiastical Courts, requesting a declaration of annulment or requesting a papal decision in relation to a valid but unconsummated marriage. At the petition of either party, the said ecclesiastical decisions shall have full legal effect under civil law if they are declared to be in accordance with State Law.'[84] However, the failure of a spouse to appear in a nullity trial in the Catholic tribunals, either voluntarily or involuntarily (due to failure to cite the party), will bring into question the legality of the ecclesiastical process.[85] In Italy (where civil divorce was introduced in 1970), the agreement with the Holy See recognizes the annulment jurisdiction of Catholic tribunals,[86] and their decisions are valid once recognized (in accordance with a summary procedure) by a State court of appeal. The parties petition the civil court to obtain recognition of the Catholic annulment (or dissolution); the civil court must establish that the church court had jurisdiction, that the ecclesiastical process complied with Italian law, and that the other conditions for the recognition of 'foreign judgments' have been met.[87] Strasbourg has held that the recognition by the State court of appeal of the marriage annulment process in a Catholic matrimonial tribunal is subject to the fair trial standards contained in Article 6 ECHR.[88] The Italian courts have also held that State courts as well as Catholic tribunals are competent to declare annulment of Catholic marriages on the basis of civil rules as to capacity.[89]

---

[80] This is the case in the Czech Republic, Estonia, Hungary, Latvia, Poland, and Slovenia.

[81] Lithuania: decisions of Catholic tribunals on nullity and decisions of Rome on dissolution must be reported to the relevant State authorities: Agreement with the Holy See on Legal Affairs, Art 13; Slovakia: Agreement of 2000, Art 10.

[82] Portugal: the Church may dissolve Catholic marriages under civil law; they may also be declared void by church tribunals under canon law subject to confirmation by a State court; and dispensation may be provided if the marriage has not yet been consummated: Concordat 2004, Arts 13 and 14.

[83] Malta: Agreements of 3 February 1993 and 6 January 1995, appended to Marriage Law Amendment Act 1995.

[84] Spain: Agreement on Legal Affairs with the Holy See, Art 6.2.

[85] Spain: SC, Judgment of 27 June 2002, FJ 1: the failure prevents the concession of effectiveness under civil law to matrimonial decisions taken by the church tribunals.

[86] Italy: Treaty of Villa Madama 1984.

[87] Italy: ie those conditions laid down in the Code of Civil Procedure, Art 797.

[88] Strasbourg: *Pellegrini v Italy* App no 30882/96 (ECtHR, 20 July 2001): it was held that the recognition by the Court of Appeal of Florence of a Catholic court annulment of a concordat-marriage violated Art 6.

[89] Italy: Court of Cassation, Decision of February 1993.

The Orthodox Church has also attracted special treatment in Greece and Cyprus, where religious decisions as to the termination of marriage enjoy limited status in civil law. For example, whilst in Greece the Orthodox Church may declare the dissolution and annulment of Orthodox marriages, such declarations are not binding on the State, and the refusal of a metropolitan to grant an ecclesiastical dissolution is subject to judicial review by the Council of State.[90] Moreover, each of the three Islamic muftis of Thrace have jurisdiction to apply Islamic law in relation to divorce among Muslims there.[91] However, in Cyprus, all matters relating to divorce, judicial separation, or restitution of conjugal rights or to family relations of the members of the Orthodox Church are under the jurisdiction of a family court. In divorce cases the court is presided over by a cleric with two lay judges, but if the church does not appoint a presiding judge the (civil) Supreme Court appoints. A similar provision applies to members of the Maronite, Catholic, and Armenian churches.[92]

Civil partnerships and same-sex marriages

The rise of same-sex partnerships under national laws in Europe, and in some States same-sex marriages, has not yet led Strasbourg to recognize a right to same-sex marriage—principally because of a lack of consensus among the States of Europe on this matter.[93] However, same-sex marriages have been introduced in, for example, the Netherlands,[94] Belgium,[95] and Finland.[96] But in some States, such as Poland, the introduction of same-sex marriages would necessitate constitutional reform,[97] and in Spain it has been held that there is no right to same-sex marriage.[98] Also, same-sex partnerships have been introduced in Germany, where the constitutionality of the Federal Registered Life Partnership Act (coming into force in 2001) has been upheld as not changing the nature and consequences of marriage.[99]

---

[90] Greece: Council of State, Decision 2635/1980.

[91] Greece, Thrace: they also have jurisdiction over guardianship, wills and testaments, and intestacy among Muslims there: Treaty of Lausanne 1923; and Law 2345/1920 (as amended).

[92] Cyprus: Const, Art 111; see also Law 95/1989; the family courts for Orthodox Christians were established under Law 23/1990; those for the other three churches by Law 87/1994; for irretrievable breakdown, see Law 46(I)/1999.

[93] *Schalk and Kopf v Austria* App no 30141/04 (ECtHR, 24 June 2010): ie under ECHR, Art 12.

[94] Netherlands: CC, Art 1.30; this has been the position since 2002, before which 'registered partnerships' were possible.

[95] Belgium: CC, Art 143: 'Two persons of different sexes or of the same sex may contract marriage'.

[96] Finland: Act 950/2001; as to whether the national church may prohibit its personnel from entering such relationships, the Chancellor of Justice has opined that 'the church ordinance and ecclesiastical law cannot contain regulations that are at variance with the Constitution': *Kotima*, 11 January 2002.

[97] Poland: Const, Art 18: marriage is heterosexual. However, the refusal of the mayor of Warsaw to allow a demonstration against discrimination toward homosexuals whilst allowing 6 demonstrations against homosexuality violated ECHR, Art 11: *Bączkowski and ors v Poland* App no 1543/06 (ECtHR, 3 May 2007).

[98] Spain: Law no 13/2005, 1 July; see also Supreme Court, 5 July 1988, FJ 11; 3 March 1989, FJ 3; 19 April 1991, FJ 3; 6 September 2002, FJ7.

[99] Germany: Federal CCt, Judgment of 18 July 2001—Az 1 BvQ 23/01, 1 BvQ 26/01.

Law in the United Kingdom illustrates well how religion might impact on same-sex civil partnerships.[100] This allows two people of the same sex to enter a civil partnership which operates 'when they register as civil partners of each other'.[101] The law provides that: 'No religious service is to be used while the civil partnership registrar is officiating at the signing of a civil partnership document'; moreover, the place at which partners may register the partnership must not be premises 'used solely or mainly for religious purposes'.[102] In turn, it has been held by the courts that: a registrar may lawfully be required to register civil partnerships despite her religious objections;[103] a Christian counsellor may lawfully be dismissed if he fails, for religious reasons, to give an unequivocal commitment to counsel same-sex couples;[104] and a justice of the peace who resigned because he could not in conscience place children with same-sex couples was unsuccessful in a claim of religious discrimination because he had never made it plain that his objection was conscientious or religious.[105] Much the same applies to the celebration of civil marriages.[106]

Religion and children

The religious dimensions of the life of a child are well-documented.[107] However, there is considerable debate about the stage at which children develop the capacity for autonomous religious discernment as well as the influences on their choices in

---

[100] However, in the past Strasbourg has held several pieces of UK legislation to be discriminatory against homosexuals: *Dudgeon v UK* (1981) 4 EHRR 149; *Sunderland v UK* (1997) 24 EHRR 22; *Smith and Grady v UK* (2000) 29 EHRR 493. UK law is increasingly recognizing homosexual family life: *Ghaidan v Godin Mendoza* [2004] UKHL 30.
[101] UK: Civil Partnership Act 2004, s 1(1); restrictions on who may enter a civil partnership are the same as for marriage but for the sex: ss 3 and 4; it is terminated (like marriage) on death, dissolution or annulment: 1(3); adultery is a ground for marital divorce, not dissolution of a civil partnership nor annulment for non-consummation (as might a marriage: Matrimonial Causes Act 1973, s 12); see M Hill, 'Church, State and civil partners: establishment and social mores in tension' in N Doe and R Sandberg (eds), *Law and Religion: New Horizons* (Leuven: Peeters, 2010) 57.
[102] UK: Civil Partnership Act 2004, s 295 (religious service) and s 6 (religious premises).
[103] UK: *Ladele v London Borough of Islington* [2009] EWCA (Civ) 1357.
[104] UK: *McFarlane v Relate Avon Ltd* [2010] EWCA (Civ) 880: 'The promulgation of law for the protection of a position held purely on religious grounds cannot therefore be justified. It is irrational, as preferring the subjective over the objective'; for a critical analysis, see R Sandberg, 'Laws and religion: unravelling *McFarlane v Relate Avon Ltd*' (2010) 12 EccLJ 361.
[105] UK: *McClintock v Department of Constitutional Affairs* [2007] UKEAT/0223/07/CEA.
[106] Marriage Act 1836, s 45A(4); a building with a recent religious association cannot be an approved premises: Marriage and Civil Partnership (Approved Premises) Regulations 2005/3168, Sch 1.
[107] J Piaget, *The Child's Conception of the World* (London: Routledge & Kegan Paul, 1929); R Goldman, *Religious Thinking from Childhood to Adolescence* (London: Routledge & Kegan Paul, 1964); for parental and religious community influences, see the studies in EC Roehlkepartain, PE King, L Wagener, and PL Benson (eds), *The Handbook of Spiritual Development in Childhood and Adolescence* (Thousand Oaks, Cal: Sage Publications, 2005).

this regard.[108] The subject is treated in skeletal form in global international law.[109] For the United Nations, children have an independent right to freedom of thought, conscience, and religion,[110] and parents (and guardians) must direct the child in the exercise of this right in a manner consistent with the evolving capacities of the child.[111] But in all actions concerning children (public or private) 'the best interests of the child shall be a primary consideration'.[112] The instruments of the United Nations also provide that: parents have the right to organize family life in accordance with their religion;[113] a child has the right to religious education in accordance with parental wishes (see Chapter 8);[114] and there must be no religious discrimination against children.[115] Due account must be taken of the child's wishes in religious matters when not under parental care (the child's best interests being 'the guiding principle'),[116] on the basis that a child has a right to be heard.[117] Moreover: 'Practices of a religion or belief in which a child is brought up must not be injurious to his physical or mental health or to his full development.'[118] What follows examines how the States of Europe address these issues and, where appropriate, Strasbourg jurisprudence developed in this field. The study does not,

---

[108] G Van Bueren, 'The right to be the same, the right to be different: children and religion' in T Lindholm, WC Durham, and BG Tahzib-Lie (eds), *Facilitating Freedom of Religion or Belief: A Deskbook* (Leiden: Martinus Nijhoff Publishers, 2004) 699–719, 715. Children 'indoctrinated' by their parents in religious matters are hindered from growing as autonomous adults: H LaFollette, 'Freedom of religion and children' (1989) 3(1) Public Affairs Quarterly 75–87.

[109] S Langlaude, *The Rights of the Child to Religious Freedom in International Law* (Leiden: Martinus Nijhoff Publishers, 2007) especially ch 2 for theories; see ibid ch 3 for the approach of religions to children.

[110] Convention on the Rights of the Child 1989: UNGA Res 25(XLIV), UN Doc GA Res 44/25 (1989), Preamble, para 5: the family is the fundamental social unit; Art 14.1: 'States Parties shall respect the right of the child to freedom of thought, conscience and religion.'

[111] ibid Art 14.2: 'States Parties shall respect the rights and duties of the parents and, when applicable, legal guardians, to provide direction to the child in the exercise of his or her right in a manner consistent with the evolving capacities of the child'; Art 14.3: 'Freedom to manifest one's religion or beliefs may be subject only to such limitations as are prescribed by law and are necessary to protect public safety, order, health or morals, or the fundamental rights and freedoms of others.'

[112] ibid Art 3.

[113] UNDID 1981, Art 5(1): 'The parents or, as the case may be, the legal guardians of the child have the right to organize the life within the family in accordance with their religion or belief and bearing in mind the moral education in which they believe the child should be brought up.'

[114] ibid Art 5(2): 'Every child shall enjoy the right of access to education in the matter of religion or belief in accordance with the wishes of the parents or . . . legal guardians, and shall not be compelled to receive teaching on religion or belief against the wishes of his parents or legal guardians, the best interests of the child being the guiding principle.'

[115] ibid Art 5(3): 'The child shall be protected from any form of discrimination on the ground of religion or belief. He shall be brought up in a spirit of understanding, tolerance, friendship among peoples, peace and universal brotherhood, respect for freedom of religion or belief of others, and full consciousness that his energy and talents should be devoted to the service of his fellow men.'

[116] ibid, Art 5(4): 'In the case of a child who is not under the care either of his parents or of legal guardians, due account shall be taken of their expressed wishes or of any other proof of their wishes in the matter of religion or belief, the best interests of the child being the guiding principle.'

[117] UNCRC, *Summary Record of the 283rd meeting: Finland*, UN Doc CRC/C/SR.283, p 38 (1996).

[118] Convention on the Rights of the Child, Art 5(5).

however, deal with national structures for the protection of children within religious organizations.[119]

The religious upbringing of children: parental rights

It is a principle of religion law in Europe that the parents have a right to bring up their children in accordance with their own religion. The right is presented as one which derives from religious freedom in, for example, Romania,[120] Slovenia,[121] Cyprus,[122] Germany,[123] Portugal,[124] and Spain.[125] It is generally understood that the right is to be exercised jointly by the parents. France is typical: as spouses may change their religion freely, so the parents should together choose the religious upbringing of their children—but the courts should take into account the capacity of children to discern their own choices in such matters.[126] In Ireland an express or implied agreement between parents on the religious upbringing of a child binds both parties and may not be unilaterally revoked by either party.[127] Similarly, in Austria, parents may agree on the religious upbringing of their children before they reach the age of majority; the agreement ends on the death of either spouse.[128] Whereas it was the case historically in the United Kingdom that the right to

---

[119] Needless to say, religious organizations may make decisions in relation to children and religion; eg Cyprus: religious courts may settle cases involving family relations: see Law 95/1989 and Law 23/1990 (Orthodox); Law 87/1994 (Maronite, Armenian, and Catholic churches); Greece: in Thrace, the three Islamic muftis have a similar jurisdiction; Finland: it is lawful for a minister of the national church to refuse to accept an unmarried couple as godparents for a child on the basis that the couple did not satisfy the requirements laid down in the Ecclesiastical Law of 1964, s 36; the SC overruled the Eastern CA in its decision no 2792, 13 October 1989 (KKO 1989:122) which cautioned the minister.

[120] Romania: Const, 29.6: 'Parents or legal guardians have the right to ensure, in accordance with their own convictions, the education of the minor children whose responsibility devolves on them.'

[121] Slovenia: Const, Art 41.3: 'Parents have the right to provide their children with a religious and moral upbringing in accordance with their beliefs. The religious and moral guidance given to children must be appropriate to their age and maturity, and be consistent with their free conscience and religious and other beliefs or convictions'; see also Poland: Const, Art 53.3.

[122] Cyprus: Const, Art 18.7: decisions on the child's religion shall be taken by the lawful guardian.

[123] Germany: 'it is a matter for parents to teach their children beliefs in questions of faith and conviction (cf BVerfGE 41, 29, 44, 47f) and not to impart to them views they do not share (cf BVerfGE 93, 1, 17)': BVerfGE, Decision of 31 May 2006—BvR 1693/04.

[124] Portugal: LORF, Law no 16/2001, Arts 8 and 11; see also Finland: FRA 453/2003.

[125] Spain: it has been held that 'family' includes families originating in marriage: Const, Art 39.1; CCt, Judgment no 45/1989, 20 February, FJ 4; but not exclusively so, provided the union is stable and effective: CCt, Judgment no 184/1990, 15 November (with a dissenting judgment citing ECHR *Markcx v Belgium* App no 6833/74 (ECtHR, 13 June 1979); and *Johnston v Ireland* (1986) Series A, no 112).

[126] France: CC, Art 371-2; Cass Civ 1, 11 June 1991, D 1991, 521; if there is disagreement or a divorce, the court will uphold a prior agreement: Paris CA, 6 April 1967, JCP 1967, II, 15100.

[127] Ireland: *Re Tilson* [1951] IR 1; *Re May* [1959] IR 74. Failure to bring up a child in accordance with a prior matrimonial agreement may be a ground for divorce if this constitutes conduct under which 'the respondent has behaved in such a way that the applicant cannot reasonably be expected to live with the respondent': Judicial Separation and Family Law Reform Act 1989, s 2.

[128] Austria: SC, OGH, 3 September 1986, 1 Ob 586/86 (ÖAKR 37/1987, p 104); see also OGH, 12 May 1993, 3 Ob 521/93 (ÖAKR 42/1993).

determine the religious upbringing of a child vested in the father,[129] today the law recognizes the right of both parents to be involved in decisions concerning the religious upbringing of the child (though there is no parental duty in this regard),[130] and this parental entitlement continues until children reach sufficient understanding to make their own decision: the welfare of the child is paramount.[131]

Therefore, following the breakdown of relations between parents, the parent with lawful custody may decide on the religious upbringing of the child and the parent without custody merely has a right to comment on the matter. Nevertheless, the decision to grant custody to one or other parent may itself involve consideration of the religion of the parents. The right to religious freedom and the prohibition against religious discrimination may both have a part to play in the determination of cases in such circumstances. One Austrian case has resulted in a landmark decision at Strasbourg on this subject. The Austrian court held that it was in the best interests of the child not to grant custody to a mother on the basis that she was a Jehovah's Witness opposed to blood transfusion.[132] However, Strasbourg held that membership of a religious group does not of itself provide a ground on which to refuse parental custody; the Austrian court had violated the right to family life under Article 8 ECHR and it had discriminated on grounds of religion under Article 14 in holding against the mother on this basis, among other factors associated with the child's welfare.[133]

Consequently, in a series of cases against France, Strasbourg has held that there must be direct and concrete evidence that the religious influences of a parent will be detrimental to the welfare of a child before a decision is made not to grant custody to that parent.[134] In other words, the decision to place a child must not be based solely on the religious affiliation of a parent but on the best interests of the child.[135] Indeed, it is permissible for national courts to require a parent to whom custody of a child is given to undertake not to involve the child in the religious activities of

---

[129] UK: *Hawksworth v Hawksworth* (1871) LR Ch App 539; for qualifications to the paternal right, see *Ward v Laverty* [1925] AC 101, 108, and *Shelley v Westbrook* (1817) Jac 266: the poet Shelley was denied custody of his child on the basis that he was an atheist. The rule was abolished by the Guardianship of Infants Act 1925: courts 'should pay serious heed to the religious wishes of parents' but this should not infringe the welfare of the child.

[130] UK: 'A person with parental responsibility has the right to determine the child's religious education, though there is no duty to give the child a religious upbringing': *Re J (Specific Issue Orders: Child's Religious Upbringing and Circumcision)* [1999] 2 FLR 678, 685.

[131] UK: *Gillick v West Norfolk and Wisbech Area Health Authority* [1986] AC 112. The welfare of the child is paramount and a court must have regard to the background of a child including the child's religious and cultural heritage: Children Act 1989, s 1(3)(d).

[132] Austria: see n 128 above; the District Court decided that the mother's membership of a religious group should not be the sole reason to refuse custody; it recognized that the religious ban on blood transfusion, the rejection of communal celebration of customary holidays, and impaired social integration, could all have a negative effect on the children—but this was overridden by the psychological effect of separating the children from the mother; the Regional Court underlined how Jehovah's Witnesses were not outlawed in Austria; however, the Supreme Court considered that the lower courts' decisions failed to give due consideration to the welfare of the children.

[133] Strasbourg: *Hoffmann v Austria* (1994) 17 EHRR 293.

[134] *Palau-Martinez v France* App no 64927/01 (ECtHR, 16 December 2003), para 13.

[135] *Schmidt v France* App no 35109/02 (ECtHR, 26 July 2007).

that parent.[136] Once more, such restrictions on the religious freedom of a parent granted custody may be justified on the basis of the best interests of the child.[137] However, the Strasbourg Commission has declared admissible the complaint of a Bulgarian mother against the decision of a national court that her involvement with the Warriors of Christ had been a relevant factor in denying her custody; this was a breach of Article 9 ECHR.[138]

This Strasbourg approach has now made its way into national jurisprudence; for example, in Spain, restrictions on access to a child by the father solely because the father was a member of the Christian Gnostic Movement are not permitted, on the basis of religious freedom.[139] Similarly, it has been held in the United Kingdom that it would be a breach of the ECHR for a court to deny a parent the care of a child simply because of that parent's religious beliefs—those beliefs need to be balanced against the welfare of the child and the rights of the other parent.[140] The best interests of the child may also be relevant in cases of divorce when these have a religious dimension. For instance, in Luxembourg, a husband refused to allow the child to have religious education and first communion in the Catholic Church, even after he and his spouse had undergone a religious marriage ceremony and after the baptism of the child. The wife sought divorce but the husband objected on grounds of freedom of conscience. It was held that the exercise of freedom of conscience and religion under the national constitution and the ECHR can never constitute in themselves a ground for divorce under the Luxembourgeois civil code, but it may be relevant to establish the grounds for divorce listed in that code—the wife was granted a divorce.[141]

Limitations on the religious freedom of parents

As we have seen from the custody cases, the religious freedom of parents with regard to the nurture of their children is not absolute but qualified.[142] The protection of children from what may be the harmful religious postures and practices of parents has generated a great deal of case-law across Europe, particularly on medical treatment, spiritual chastisement, religious affiliation, and adoption. The fundamental principle is that the religious freedom of the parents is inferior to the well-being of the child. As such, the refusal of Jehovah's Witnesses, on religious grounds, to medical treatment in the form of blood transfusions for their children is consistently denied on the basis of the welfare of the child. This has occurred in

---

[136] *FL v France* App no 61162/00 (ECtHR, 3 November 2005): restrictions on the custodial mother's involvement with the Raelian movement were justified and not in breach of ECHR, Arts 8 and 9.
[137] *Deschomets v France* App no 31956/02 (ECtHR, 16 May 2006): restriction was justified and there was no breach of ECHR, Arts 8 and 9; the mother was a member of the Brethren church.
[138] *MM v Bulgaria* App no 27496/95 (ECom (Report), 9 July 1997).
[139] Spain: CCt, Judgment no 141/2000, 29 May, FJ 7 (citing Hoffmann).
[140] UK: *Re J (Specific Issue Orders: Child's Religious Upbringing and Circumcision)* [1999] 2 FLR 678 (upheld by the CA: [2000] 1 FLR 571).
[141] Luxembourg: CA 7-7-1999, *AW v GE*, nos 22552 and 22766; CC, Art 229.
[142] See Ch 2 above for general limitations on the right to manifest religion.

the Netherlands,[143] the Czech Republic,[144] and Cyprus—particularly when the life of a child is at risk. Protection of the child in such cases offends neither national law nor ECHR rights to religious freedom.[145] Indeed, 'risks to health in general' will trump religious freedom in Spain[146] and Austria.[147] However, in France the court must be satisfied that there is a concrete likelihood of harm to a child before it restricts the religious rights of parents;[148] if this is established, it is not a breach of religious freedom for a doctor to administer a blood transfusion to save life.[149] Considerations of child health have also been invoked by Strasbourg to restrict religious chastisement by parents: when parents in the Protestant Free Church in Sweden sought to chastise their children, due to their belief that corporal punishment of children was required by the bible, the State's prohibition of this was upheld on the basis of the health and vulnerability of the child.[150] A similar stance is used in the United Kingdom with regard to corporal punishment desired by parents on religious grounds at faith schools.[151]

Moreover, parents may be required to undertake not to involve their children in potentially harmful activities of prescribed organizations. For example, in Austria this has happened in relation to parents who are members of the Church of Scientology,[152] and the Sahaja Yoga movement.[153] Nor may religious freedom extend in adoption cases to the insistence by the natural parents that their child will be placed with adoptive parents who share the same religion as the natural parents. This is the position in Great Britain.[154] Otherwise, however, adoption agencies by statute 'must give due consideration to the child's religious persuasion, racial origin and linguistic background'.[155] Indeed, the courts will not automatically assume in

---

[143] Netherlands: *ARR v S*, 20 January 1983, AB 1983, 389: refusal to allow a married couple of Jehovah's Witnesses to adopt a child was justified on the basis of their stance towards blood transfusion; there was no breach of ECHR, Art 9.

[144] Czech Rep: CCt, Decision of 20 August 2004, no III. ÚS 459/03: an order made to override the refusal of Jehovah's Witness parents to allow medical treatment for their child in imminent danger by way of blood derivatives was justified and did not violate CFRF, Arts 32.4 and 16.1.

[145] Cyprus: *Titos Charalambous* [1994] 1 CLR 396: Children Law, ss 3 and 4 (which it was held did not violate the Constitution, Art 15, or ECHR, Art 8).

[146] Spain: Const Ct, Judgment no 154/2002, 18 July 2002, FJ 13.

[147] Austria: OGH, 4 June 1996, 1 Ob 601/95.

[148] France: Cass 12 December. 2006, no 05-22119 (Church of Scientology); Cass 19 February 2002, no 99-19954 (Brothers); but see Strasbourg: *Palau Martinez v France* App no 64927/01 (ECtHR, 16 December 2003).

[149] France: CE, 26 October 2001, Case no 198546 (Jehovah's Witness), 16 August 2002, Case no 249552; see also Cass, 22 February 2000, Case no 98-12338; and Cass, 24 October 2000, no 98-14386.

[150] *Seven Individuals v Sweden* App no 8811/79 (1982) 29 D&R 104.

[151] *R v Secretary of State for Education, ex p Williamson* [2005] UKHL 15: EA 1996, s 548 prohibits corporal punishment.

[152] Austria: OGH, 13 August 1996, 2 Ob 2192/96h; see also n 158 below for the UK.

[153] Austria: OGH, 30 January 1996, 1 Ob 623/95; see also UK: *Wright v Wright* [1980] 2 FLR 276; *Buckley v Buckley* (1973) 3 Fam Law 106: parents must not indoctrinate or cause social isolation for their children; *Re H* [1981] 2 FLR 253: a Jehovah's Witness mother was required to allow the child to take part in school activities and celebrate Christmas and Easter.

[154] UK: *Re P (A Minor) (Residence Order: Child's Welfare)* [1999] 2 FLR 573: this case concerned a Downs Syndrome child born to Orthodox Jews and fostered by practising Roman Catholics.

[155] UK: Adoption and Children Act 2002, s 1(5); moreover, a local authority cannot cause a child in its care 'to be brought up in any religious persuasion other than that in which he would have been brought up had the order not been made': Children Act 1989, s 33(6)(a).

adoption cases that a child has the religion of the natural parent, unless the child is very young.[156] They will also seek to enable children to continue their own religious practices with the adoptive parents but not if this is, in the view of the court, detrimental to the welfare of the child.[157] However, as a general principle, with adoption (and custody) the 'Courts must not pass any judgment on the religious beliefs of the parents where they are socially acceptable and consistent with a decent and respectable life'.[158]

The religious autonomy of the child

A key limitation on parental rights concerning the religious upbringing of their children is the religious autonomy of the child, a fundamental of international law (see above). Sometimes national laws expressly provide for this; in Slovenia: 'Parents have the right to provide their children with a religious and moral upbringing in accordance with their beliefs. The religious and moral guidance given to children must be appropriate to their age and maturity, and be consistent with their free conscience and religious and other beliefs or convictions'.[159] The religious autonomy of the child is also articulated well in Spanish law: 'minors have the right to freedom of ideology, conscience and religion' and 'the parents and guardians have the right and the duty to cooperate in order that the minor exercises this freedom in such a way as to contribute to his or her integral development'.[160] However, States differ as to the age at which children enjoy religious autonomy. For example, Austrian children are free to choose their own religion at the age of 14,[161] and Cypriot children at the age of 16.[162] Moreover, in Dutch law, parental refusal on religious grounds to consent to the marriage of a child (with capacity under civil law) is held to be unlawful.[163]

The religious autonomy of the child is particularly important with regard to their membership of religious organizations.[164] Once more, the ages vary as between

---

[156] UK: *Re J (Specific Issue Orders: Child's Religious Upbringing and Circumcision)* [1999] 2 FLR 678 (a decision upheld by the Court of Appeal: [2000] 1 FLR 571); for the exception, see *Re P Section 91 (14) Guidelines (Residence and Religious Heritage)* [1999] 2 FLR 273.

[157] UK: *Re R (A Minor) (Residence; Religion)* [1993] 2 FLR 163; *Re S (Minors) (Access: Religious Upbringing)* [1992] 2 FLR 313: 'if a court were bound by [the child's] religious beliefs it would . . . amount to an abandonment of the duty imposed upon it by Parliament, to decide what [the child's] welfare, viewed objectively, requires'; see also *Re T and M* [1995] FLR 1.

[158] UK: *Re T (Minors) (Custody: Religious Upbringing)* [1981] 2 FLR 239; *Re B and G (Minors) (Custody)* [1985] FLR 134: the court ruled against a parent belonging to the Church of Scientology which the judge described as 'immoral and socially obnoxious' and 'corrupt, sinister and dangerous'; see A Bradney, *Law and Faith in a Sceptical Age* (London: Routledge-Cavendish, 2009) ch 5.

[159] Slovenia: Const, Art 41.3.

[160] Spain: Constitutional Law no 1/1996, 15 January, Art 6.1–2; see also CCt, Judgments nos 141/2000, 29 May, FJ 5; 154/2002, 18 July, FJ 9.

[161] Austria: BundesG über die religiöse Kindererziehung, s 4; InterkonfG 1868, s 4.

[162] Cyprus: Const, Art 18.7.

[163] Netherlands: Ktr Gorinchem, 8 November 1982, NJ 1983, 383.

[164] See Ch 2 above for the right of religious affiliation. Children must be allowed to choose a religion or join a religious organization and States ought to provide minimum information on age: Report of the Secretary-General, UN Doc HRI/GEN/2/Rev.3, p 71 (2006).

States. For example, in Germany, at the age of 10 children must be heard before there is a change in their membership of a religious denomination, and at 14 they are free to determine their own religious affiliation; but the United Nations' Committee on the Rights of the Child has expressed concern as to what happens in practice when a child of 10 makes a choice about religious affiliation which is contrary to the wishes of the parents.[165] The age at which this freedom is enjoyed in the Czech Republic is 15 (until then the choice is that of the parents), in Iceland that of 16 or 18, but this has been criticized by the United Nations' Committee on the Rights of the Child,[166] which has also criticized Finland where, again, the age is 18 (and 15 with parental consent).[167] In any event, Strasbourg has not yet directly considered the freedom of minors to act against parental wishes in the matter of religious affiliation, but it has decided that once majority is reached, the individual may freely choose his or her religion.[168] However, a claim that the rules of a monastic order of the Macedonian Orthodox Church were unconstitutional, on the basis that they prevented monks from looking after their parents in illness or old age, was rejected by the Constitutional Court of Macedonia on the ground of the religious freedom of their children (who had entered the order without parental consent) and on the basis that the court could not examine the constitutionality of internal religious rules or violate the autonomy of the church; Strasbourg rejected the case as the domestic remedies had not been exhausted.[169] As seen in Chapter 8, the religious autonomy of the child also applies to the provision of religious education in public or State schools; in this field also, the ages at which the child may withdraw from religious education vary from State to State.

In short, the concept of the religious autonomy of the child surfaces in national laws, but there would appear to be no juridical consensus as to the age at which this autonomy arises. It may be that this can be justified on the basis of the margin of appreciation as to what is in the best interests of the child. In any event, diversity between countries seems in keeping with the fluidity of the concept of the evolving capacity of the child which plays such a prominent part in global international law.

Circumcision and female genital mutilation

National laws may permit but control the circumcision of male children (practised in Judaism and Islam) when necessary to protect the welfare of the child. The

---

[165] Germany, UN Doc CRC/C/11/Add, p 13 (1994) and Summary Record of the 244th meeting: Germany, UN Doc CRC/C/SR.244, p 57 (1995).

[166] The CRC was unclear whether it was 16 or 18, but in any event these ages were too high: UN CRC, Summary Record of the 856th meeting: Iceland, UN Doc CRC/C/SR.856, p 16 (2003); also, a Belarus rule which prevented minors under the age of 15 from participating in religious rituals without parental consent was too high: CRC, SR of 786th meeting: Belarus, UN Doc CRC/C/SR.786, para 70 (2002).

[167] Finland: EJCSR 2001, Vol 8, 246; see also Summary Record of the 1068th meeting: Finland, UN Doc CRC/C/SR.1068, para 17 (2005).

[168] *Riera Blume and ors v Spain* App no 37680/97 (ECtHR, 14 October 1999).

[169] *Šijakova and ors v The Former Yugoslav Republic of Macedonia* App no 67914/01 (ECtHR, 6 March 2003): the court rejected the complaint for non-exhaustion of domestic remedies.

approach of Bulgaria to parental rights to circumcise their children for religious purposes has been the subject of particular concern to the United Nations.[170] In the United Kingdom circumcision is assumed to be lawful,[171] but if both parents cannot agree, it must not be performed without a court order and such order may be made only if in the best interests of the child.[172] The issue became topical in Ireland in 2003 when a circumcision with a razor blade carried out at a home by a medically unqualified individual resulted in the death of a 4-week-old baby.[173] The subsequent case and acquittal of the man who performed the procedure raised awareness nationally of unregulated male circumcision.[174] As a result, the Minister for Children and Youth Affairs at the Department of Health and Children established a Committee on Cultural Male Circumcision, which reported in 2006 and which recognized the spiritual reasons for male circumcision in some religions. The Report also acknowledged that Orthodox Jewish circumcisions in Ireland are performed by trained Rabbis: 'these circumcisions are carried out with parental consent, are deemed to be in the interest of the child, and are competently performed'.[175] Interestingly, under Cypriot law, any person who holds or is responsible for a Muslim feast in connection with a circumcision (or a marriage) or is the occupier of premises on which it is held, and engages (with or without pay), or permits a dancing girl to dance or sing at such feast, is liable to a fine not exceeding €128.15, or to imprisonment for one month.[176]

Whilst there is debate as to whether female circumcision is a religious or cultural practice,[177] the European Parliament passed a resolution in 2001 on female genital mutilation; this called on the Member States to 'regard any form of female genital mutilation as a specific crime, irrespective of whether or not the woman concerned has given any form of consent, and to punish anybody who helps, encourages, advises or procures support for anybody to carry out any of these acts on the body of a woman or girl'.[178] Whilst several States have no express law on the subject, in some it is covered by general offences against the person,[179] and in Ireland a recent

[170] Circumcision may be linked to UNDID 1981, Art 5; UN Doc E/CN.4/1988/45, p 4 (1988): 'Some Islamic practices have allegedly been penalized, especially the circumcision of infants'; Bulgaria responded (p 10): 'Circumcision is not prohibited in Bulgaria'.

[171] UK: *R v Brown* [1994] 1 AC 212, 231; this is so whether or not it is performed by a doctor: Law Commission, *Consent in the Criminal Law*, Consultation Paper no 139 (1995) para 9.2.

[172] UK: *Re J (Child's Upbringing and Circumcision)* [2000] 1 FCR 307, CA. For the argument that the approach is incompatible with the duty to prevent harm to children, see H Gilbert, 'Time to reconsider the lawfulness of ritual male circumcision' (2007) EHRLR 279.

[173] 'Man Charged with Illegal Circumcision' *Irish Independent*, 21 November 2003.

[174] 'Jury clears Nigerian man involved in circumcision death case' *Irish Independent*, 8 October 2005; see also 'Gardai investigate alleged backstreet circumcision' *Irish Times*, 19 August 2004.

[175] Cultural Male Circumcision, Report of Committee 2004–5, p 11.

[176] Cyprus: PC, Art 97 of Cap 154.

[177] C Hamilton, *Family, Law and Religion* (London: Sweet & Maxwell, 1995) 148.

[178] Res 2001/2035; see also Res of 12 April 1999 on female genital mutilation, and Res 1247 of the Parliamentary Assembly of the Council of Europe (2001).

[179] Portugal: it is an offence to 'deprive or affect in a serious way the capacity of another person to sexual fruition': PC (Law no 59/2007 of 4 September, Art 144b) was altered; in Law Proposal 98/X the addition was justified on the basis that 'it would forbid such practices as female genital mutilation'; see also Bulgaria: PC, Art 129(2); PC, Art 222; Czech Rep: PC, s 222.1; Poland: PC, Art 157, para 1).

attempt to criminalize it failed on this basis.[180] Sometimes it may be treated as an aggravated crime.[181] However, in many States female genital mutilation is a distinct criminal offence, introduced relatively recently,[182] and Italy treats it as a crime against the fundamental rights to personal integrity and the health of female children and women.[183] National laws do not explicitly refer to religion in definitions of the offence.[184] For example, in Belgium, it is defined as the execution, facilitation, or promotion of any type of mutilation of the genitals of a person of the female sex, regardless of her consent; the punishment which may be imposed is more severe in the case of minors, and when the mutilation is committed by parents or guardians.[185] Much the same applies in Austria.[186] In Spain it may be prosecuted if performed abroad,[187] and in Sweden it is penalized even if it is not an offence in the country where it was performed.[188] However, in the United Kingdom, in England and Wales there is no offence of female genital mutilation if performed in a surgical operation necessary for physical or mental health;[189] similar provisions exist in Scotland.[190]

Conclusion

National laws which affect religious marriages and the religious upbringing of children point to a fundamental reciprocity with regard to the public and private aspects of religion in society. On the one hand, as with the intrusion of religion in schools, hospitals, prisons, and the armed forces, so the marriage laws of many States facilitate the entry of religion into public life in so far as religious marriage

---

[180] Ireland: for the Prohibition of Female Genital Mutilation Bill 2001, see *Irish Independent*, 7 March 2001; the fear of female genital mutilation in other countries has been used as an argument in deportation cases: see eg *A v Minister for Justice and anor* [2007] IEHC 169; *Obende v Minister for Justice and anor* [2006] IEHC 162; *D and anor v Refugee Appeals Tribunal and ors* [2008] IEHC 19; *Okeke v The Minister for Justice and ors* [2006] IEHC 46.

[181] Romania: PC, Art 182, para 3; it may be punished with 3 to 12 years' imprisonment.

[182] Denmark: introduced in 2003, it is punishable with 6 years' imprisonment: Strfl, para 245a.

[183] Italy: Law no 7/2006; PC, Art 583; Const, Arts 2, 3, and 32.

[184] Cyprus: PC, Art 233A of Ch 154; the penalty is imprisonment not exceeding 5 years.

[185] Belgium, PC, Art 409: if committed on a minor, the penalty is 5–7 years' imprisonment; if on an adult, 3–5 years; if it leads to permanent disablement, 5–10 years, and death, 10–15 years; if performed by a parent or other person with parental responsibility, the minimum sentence may be increased.

[186] Austria: PC, para 90.1: consent is no defence; the penalty is imprisonment for 1–10 years (depending on the circumstances of the case).

[187] Spain: PC, Art 149.2: the punishment is 6–12 years in prison; if the victim is a minor or disabled, punishment may include disqualification from the exercise of guardianship for 4–10 years; for the offence committed abroad, see Organic Law of 1 July 1985, Art 23.4.

[188] Sweden: Act to Ban Female Genital Mutilation, 1982:316, s 1; NJA II 1982, p 423, NJA II 1998, pp 378 *et seq*: the punishment is imprisonment from 2–10 years; consent does not excuse the act.

[189] UK: Female Genital Mutilation Act 2003, s 1(2); the penalty is imprisonment not exceeding 14 years or a fine (or both).

[190] UK: Female Genital Mutilation (Scotland) Act 2005.

ritual often generates a public marital status in civil law. National laws also indicate, once more, a high level of cooperation between States and religions in this field. On the other hand, laws on the religious upbringing of children reflect the degree to which the State may intrude in the private religious affairs of the family in so far as they have a direct interest in regulating the rights of parents and children with regard to religion. Moreover, national laws disclose a number of fundamental principles common to the States of Europe in these two areas. Individuals are free to celebrate religious marriage ceremonies on the basis of the right to religious liberty. All States permit religious groups to mark a civil marriage with a ritual ceremony after a civil marriage, but many forbid this before the civil event. However, the State may recognize a marriage conducted in accordance with religious rites as having civil effect either from the moment of its ritual celebration or from the moment of its civil registration. The State may confine this recognition to prescribed religious organizations. The conditions set out in civil law must be satisfied by religious organizations authorized to conduct such marriages. Equally, the State has the right not to recognize the civil status of religious marriage ceremonies. Religious dissolution of marriage is not generally recognized in Europe, though in a small number of States declarations of annulment of Catholic marriages by the tribunals of the church may be recognized in civil law if confirmed by the courts of the State. These laws indicate that, once more, the autonomy of religious organizations is not absolute and that often religious organizations are treated unequally in this field.

   That parents and guardians have the right to bring up their children in their own religion is a general principle of religion law across Europe which is consistent with international law. The parents should decide jointly on the religious nurture of their children. A decision to grant custody to one parent should not be based solely on the parent's membership of a religious organization. However, the religious practices of parents may be limited by what is determined to be in the best interests of the child. This is particularly so in cases of custody and adoption, medical treatment, and spiritual chastisement: religious freedom is inferior to the welfare of the child; and parents may be required to make undertakings as to religious affairs affecting children. Moreover, a child acquires religious autonomy to act against parental wishes with regard to religion at ages which vary across Europe. This applies to the adoption of religious beliefs, the membership of religious organizations, and withdrawal from religious education in public schools. Male circumcision seems to be permitted (subject to the best interests of the child) in most European countries, but female genital mutilation is forbidden. However, further study would be useful on the incidence of religious marriages prior to civil marriage, the incidence of convictions in States which forbid religious marriage ceremonies prior to civil marriage, and child protection mechanisms in Europe applicable to religious organizations.

10

The Religion Law of the European Union

All the earlier Chapters concentrate on laws at the national level. The focus of this Chapter is the European Union (EU) itself. In recent years there has been a profound increase in the treatment of matters which affect religion by the laws and other regulatory instruments of the EU.[1] This has occurred to such an extent that commentators today speak of the category 'European law on religion' among the several branches of law emerging alongside the development of the EU, its institutions, and the fuller economic, political, and social integration of its Member States.[2] This chapter suggests that the posture of the EU towards religion is characterized by seven fundamental principles: the value of religion; subsidiarity, the principle that national religious affairs are primarily the concern of each Member State; religious freedom; religious equality (and non-discrimination); the autonomy of religious associations; cooperation with religion; and the special protection of religion by means of privileges and exemptions. These principles may be induced from the laws and other regulatory instruments of the EU—its treaties, regulations, directives, jurisprudence, and other formal sources.[3] However, the Union also claims as one of its material or inspirational sources the category 'general principles common to the laws of the Member States'.[4] It is proposed here that the principles articulated from national religion laws in the previous chapters may themselves represent the fundamentals of this latter EU category—namely the

---

[1] There seem to be three broad phases: 1957–c 1975, a general absence of norms on religion; 1976–1992, the side-effects of economic law on religion and the emergence of interest in religion (illustrated by eg Case 130/75 *Prais v Council of Ministers* [1976] ECR 1589); 1992 to the present, from Maastricht to Lisbon, characterized by a growing body of substantive norms on religion. The following suggests that the next period might involve a more rigorous and critical understanding and articulation of the 'general principles of community law' on religion in Member States of the Union.

[2] G Robbers, 'Diversity of state-religion relations and European Union unity' (2004) EccLJ, 304, 312: 'the fundamental principles of European law on religion' include regionality, neutrality, and equality; see also M Ventura, *La Laicità dell'Unione Europea: diritti, mercato, religione* (Turin: G Giappichelli Editore, 2001); for a sociological approach, see eg G Davie, *Religion in Modern Europe* (Oxford: OUP, 2000).

[3] See generally R McCrea, *Religion and the Public Order of the European Union* (Oxford: OUP, 2010): this suggests that the EU seeks a balance between its religious, humanist and cultural elements.

[4] Treaty of Rome, Art 215(2); Lisbon Treaty 2007, Amending the Treaty on European Union and Treaty Establishing the European Community, signed at Lisbon, 13 December 2007; Art 6.3: rights in the ECHR which result from 'the constitutional traditions common to the Member States, shall constitute general principles of the Union's law'; see also eg Case 2/69 *Stauder v City of Ulm* [1969] ECR 419: fundamental rights are 'enshrined in the general principles of law and protected by the Court'.

general common principles induced from similarities between the national religion laws of the Member States.[5]

The value of religion

The first of the principles of EU religion law is the value of religion. The extent to which religion, especially Christianity, has influenced both the idea and identity of Europe historically is a common theme among scholars.[6] This persists today. Like the ill-fated draft constitution of 2004, in its (much debated) preamble,[7] the European Union Reform (or Lisbon) Treaty 2007 (EURT), amending the Treaty on European Union and the Treaty Establishing the European Community, provides that the EU draws 'inspiration from the cultural, religious and humanist inheritance of Europe, from which have developed the universal values of the inviolable and inalienable rights of the human person, freedom, democracy, equality and the rule of law'.[8] The Treaty also recognizes the 'specific contribution' of *churches* to Europe.[9] Whilst this provision describes the normative role of religion in European life, the principle of the value of religion is not new in EU law—and a reference to the European 'spiritual heritage' appears in the EU Charter of Fundamental Rights (CFR).[10] It is occasionally recognized in some EU regulatory instruments which acknowledge explicitly, but in a somewhat general manner, the significance of the 'religious and philosophical values of society',[11] or 'spiritual welfare'.[12] Moreover, it has been suggested by the European Court of Justice that

---

[5] What follows develops themes proposed in N Doe, 'Towards a "common law" on religion in the European Union' in LN Leustean and JTS Madeley (eds), *Religion, Politics and Law in the European Union* (London: Routledge, 2010) 141.

[6] See eg J Le Goff, *The Birth of Europe* (Malden, MA: Blackwell, 2005); however, for the secularization of Europe, see S Bruce, *From Cathedrals to Cults: Religion in the Modern World* (Oxford: OUP, 1996) 230.

[7] See R Potz *et al*, 'God in the European Constitution', Opinions of Members of the European Consortium for Church and State Research, ECCSR, *Newsletter*, 4–110; eg Pope John Paul II called for the inclusion of 'a reference to the religious and in particular Christian heritage of Europe': *Ecclesia in Europa*, 28 June 2003, para 114 (see Commission of European Bishops' Conferences (COMECE), *The Treaty Establishing a Constitution for Europe: Elements for Evaluation*, 11 March 2005); COMECE suggested, therefore, that: in order 'to facilitate citizens' identification with the values of the European Union, and to acknowledge that public power is not absolute, the COMECE secretariat recommends that a future Constitutional Treaty of the European Union should recognise the openness and ultimate otherness associated with the name of God. An inclusive reference to the transcendent provides a guarantee for the freedom of the human person'.

[8] EURT, Preamble. See also JHH Welier, *Un'Europea Cristiana: Un saggio esplorativo* (Milan: BUR Saggi, 2003), cited in McCrea (n 3 above) 58: Weiler argues that the failure of the Preamble to mention God or Christianity represented an 'EU-enforced *laïcité* on European public life'; see also AJ Menendez, 'A review of a Christian Europe' (2005) 30(1) ELR 133.

[9] EURT: Treaty on the Functioning of the EU (TFEU), Art 17.3; see also draft Const (2004), Art 52.3.

[10] EURT: CFR, Preamble: 'Conscious of its spiritual and moral heritage, the Union is founded on the indivisible, universal values of human dignity, freedom, equality and solidarity.'

[11] Directive (EC) 2006/123, Preamble, para (40).

[12] Directive (EEC) 77/388: tax exemptions may be enjoyed for 'supplies of staff by religious or philosophical institutions for medical, welfare, child protection and educational purposes with a view

religion may be a defining characteristic of nationhood within Member States: a 'nation' is 'the totality of individuals linked by the fact of sharing traditions, culture, ethnicity, religion and so on'.[13] Similarly, the Seventh Framework Programme directive, in the context of European citizenship, recognizes that 'religions' (plural), along with cultural heritage, institutions and legal systems, history, language and values, are a 'building element' of European multicultural identity and heritage.[14]

Needless to say, like the draft constitution of 2004, the Lisbon Reform Treaty does not specify *which* spiritual or religious heritage is inspirational; indeed, Article 22 of the Charter of Fundamental Rights provides that the Union must respect 'religious diversity'.[15] This expresses the neutrality of the Union towards different religions,[16] and is consistent with both the foundational instruments of the Community and the practice of functional regulatory instruments. They expressly recognize the category 'religious diversity',[17] the need to work with 'religious pluralism',[18] and the growth of interaction between religions in Europe and beyond.[19] Consequently, the value of *religions*, of their diversity-plurality, is known to the EU legal order. The decision on Specific Programme Cooperation accepts that 'appreciation and understanding of differences between value systems of different religions or ethnic minority groups lay foundations for positive attitudes'.[20] And the year of equal opportunities programme seeks to facilitate and celebrate diversity, and highlights 'the positive contribution that people, irrespective of religion or belief, can make to society as a whole'.[21] The EU also recognizes the categories 'public morality'[22] and 'principles of morality'.[23]

Significantly, the Union adopts an essentially neutral approach to its understanding of religion in a definition which appears in a directive on refugees, third

to spiritual welfare'; also Regulation (EC) 1781/2006, Art 18: exemptions for organizations carrying out non-profit charitable, religious, and cultural purposes.

[13] Case C-300/04 *Eman v College van Burgemeester en Wethouders van den Haag* [2006] ECR I-9583.

[14] Council Decision (EC) 1982/2006.

[15] Draft Const (2004), Art 82; but EURT: TEU, Art 3 refers only to 'cultural and linguistic diversity'.

[16] See Robbers (n 2 above) 314 for argument in favour of neutrality; see also McCrea (n 3 above) for the 'principle of balance' between religious, cultural and humanist influences which underpin the public order of the EU.

[17] Decision (EC) 2006/320 [2006] OJ L118/9, 13.

[18] Decision (EC) 1982/2006 [2006] OJ L412/1, 24; see also Common Position 2006/795/CFSP.

[19] Decision (EC) 1983/2006, Preamble (European Year of Intercultural Dialogue): EU enlargement, increased mobility in a single market, old and new migratory flows, exchanges with the rest of the world through trade, education, leisure, and globalization in general, is increasing interaction between peoples, cultures, languages, ethnic groups, and religions in Europe and beyond.

[20] Decision (EC) 2006/971.

[21] Decision (EC) 771/2006, Art 2 (on the basis of Directive (EC) 2000/78).

[22] EURT, Art 30: 'The provisions of Articles 28 and 29 shall not preclude prohibitions or restrictions on imports, exports or goods in transit justified on grounds of public morality, public policy or public security'; see also Art 55.

[23] Case C-377/98 *Netherlands v Council* [2001] ECR I-7079, para 96: 'The Community Trade Mark Regulation and the Trade Marks Directive both provide for the refusal of registration or invalidity of a mark which is contrary to public policy or to accepted principles of morality.'

country nationals who have well-founded fears of religious persecution in their own country:

The concept of religion shall in particular include the holding of theistic, non-theistic and atheistic beliefs, the participation in, or abstention from, formal worship in private or public, either alone or in community with others, other religious acts or expressions of view, or forms of personal or communal conduct based on or mandated by any religious belief.[24]

Needless to say, there would seem to be no obvious Christian bias in this definition of religion. Moreover, neutrality, in terms of recognition of the value of religion, is also consistent with the principle of equality (see below): under the regulation (for example) to establish a Community code on rules governing the movement of persons across borders, border guards must 'fully respect' human dignity irrespective of religion or belief.[25] However, at the same time, EU instruments recognize the dangers posed by 'the radicalisation of religious groups'.[26] Indeed, the EU has a specific interest in the movement of ministers of religion in this context.[27]

The Union is not alone, of course, in a European context, in its recognition of the value of religion and the associated values of religious diversity and neutrality. These are of fundamental importance in the wider Council of Europe. They appear, for instance, in recommendations of the Parliamentary Assembly of the Council of Europe,[28] as well as in Strasbourg jurisprudence.[29] The Member States, too, at national level may be assumed to recognize its value in terms of the many benefits they confer upon it.[30] Typically, courts assume (for example) that 'some benefit accrues to the public from the attendance at places of worship of persons who live in this world and mix with their fellow citizens'.[31] Moreover, the value of religion to European life and development is recognized, unsurprisingly, by religious groups themselves,[32] many of which espouse similar values to those of the EU: for instance the Ecumenical Charter (2001), entered between the Conference

---

[24] Directive (EC) 2004/83, Art 10(b).

[25] Regulation (EC) 562/2006, Art 6 (Schengen Borders Code).

[26] Common Position 2005/304, Art 11: in dealing with conflict prevention, management, and resolution in Africa, the EU must evaluate possible cooperation at national and international levels, 'to address the problem of the relationship between the radicalisation of religious groups and their vulnerability to terrorist recruitment, in a conflict prevention and peace building perspective'.

[27] Based on an action plan of 2005, a paper urges governments to monitor 'travelling imams inciting to violence, talent spotters, recruiters and other leading figures and their movements within the European Union'; it calls on States to support the training of imams in language and teaching skills and modern Islamic literature to 'counteract the effect of the radical message and stress the incompatibility of such a message with the main principles and values of Islam': Melander, 'EU calls for plan to tackle radical imams' (Reuters Report) *Irish Times*, 6 February 2007; see D Glendenning, *Religion, Education and the Law: A Comparative Approach* (Dublin: Tottel Publishing, 2008) 82.

[28] Rec 1202, 2 February 1993: 'The recourse to religion [as a source of values] has, however, to be reconciled with the principles of democracy and human rights.'

[29] *Kokkinakis v Greece* (1994) 17 EHRR 397: religion is 'one of the most vital elements that go to make up the identity of believers and their conception of life'; and pluralism is 'indissociable from a democratic society'.

[30] As has been seen, however, it is often difficult to determine whether States value religion per se or whether they value its value to those whose religious freedom they protect: see eg Chs 7, 8, and 9 above.

[31] UK: *Neville Estates v Madden* [1962] Ch 832.

[32] eg Papal Exhortation: *Ecclesia in Europa* ('Jesus Christ . . . the source of hope for Europe' (2003)).

of European Churches and the Roman Catholic Commission of Episcopal Conferences in Europe, provides: 'Christianity constitutes an empowering source of inspiration and enrichment for Europe'; the parties undertake to participate in 'the building of Europe', and to work for 'a humane, socially conscious Europe, in which human rights and the basic values of peace, justice, freedom, tolerance, participation and solidarity prevail'.[33] This approach is not dissimilar to the instruments of a number of religious alliances which have formed in recent years around Europe.[34] Furthermore, the definition of 'religion' appearing in the EU directive on refugees mentioned above also accords fully with the understanding of religion in the national laws of Europe, particularly in terms of its inclusive reference to non-theistic and atheistic beliefs.[35] In short, the principle of the value of religion in EU law is deeply rooted in the juridical instruments of the Council of Europe and in the national laws of each State.

Subsidiarity in religious matters

The second principle in EU religion law is that of subsidiarity. This is a principle which seeks to ensure that in areas which do not fall within its exclusive competence, the Union will not take action unless the objectives of the proposed action cannot be adequately achieved by the individual Member States.[36] Based on a Declaration appended to the Treaty of Amsterdam 1997,[37] Article 17.1 EURT provides: 'The Union respects and does not prejudice the status under national law of churches and religious associations or communities in the Member States'. Needless to say, interpreted literally, this does not present (or protect) the competence of Member States to operate their own systems of religion law in general—it merely recognizes the right of a State to determine the legal position of religious organizations within it. However, commentators often discuss this provision in the context of the principle of subsidiarity.[38] The key point is that for the EU the regulation of religion is primarily a matter for Member States at national level.[39]

The examples of the application of the principle of subsidiarity, in terms of the non-intervention of the EU in national religious affairs, are well known. The Union respects the special status of Mount Athos under the Greek Constitution for

---

[33] *Charta Oecumenica* (2001) III.7: the alliance commits itself: 'to seek agreement...on the substance and goals of our social responsibility, and to represent in concert...the concerns and visions of the churches vis-à-vis the secular European institutions; to defend basic values against infringements of every kind; to resist any attempt to misuse religion and the church for ethnic or nationalist purposes'.

[34] N Doe, 'Protestantism in Europe: juridical perspectives' (2008) III *Derecho y Religion* 91.

[35] See Ch 1 above.

[36] It first appeared in the Maastricht Treaty, Art 3A (but had a long history in Catholic Canon Law).

[37] Treaty of Amsterdam 1997, Appendix: Declaration on the Status of Churches and Non-Confessional Organisations; see also draft Const (2004), Art 52.

[38] See eg McCrea (n 3 above) ch 3.

[39] The regulation of religion is not expressly listed among the competences of the EU, though subjects associated with religion are, such as culture and education: see eg TFEU, Art 6.

reasons of 'a spiritual and religious nature'.[40] 'Religious factors' may be important in decision-making within Member States (exercising their margin of appreciation) on the regulation of gambling.[41] That a person maintained washing machines in a Bhagwan community was irrelevant to the question of whether he was engaged in 'economic activity'.[42] Religious and ethical issues about abortion were irrelevant to determine the legality of restrictions on the provision by student associations of information about abortion services.[43] Much the same approach has been used in relation to the morality of prostitution.[44] Sunday trading questions, and restrictions of the free movement of goods, are matters for national law.[45] The attempt to make Sunday the Europe-wide day of rest failed.[46] Subsidiarity is also used in Strasbourg jurisprudence in terms of the margin of appreciation it allows to States in religious matters, as well as, for instance, the recognition or establishment of state-churches—subject to the proviso that States protect the exercise of religious freedom by the other faith communities in their territories,[47] and ensure impartiality towards religion in this.[48]

---

[40] Declaration on the Status of Mount Athos 1979 (on Art 105 of the Hellenic Constitution).

[41] Case C-260/04 *Commission of European Communities v Italy* [2007] ECR I-07083, para 35; see also Case C-338/04 *Placanica* [2007] ECR I-1891, and Case C-65/05 *Commission of European Communities v Greece* [2006] ECR I-10341; and EFTA Surveillance Authority Decision 336/94: decision-making in Member States as to the administration of amusement machine operations may not be justified on religious grounds alone; see also Case C-275/92 *Her Majesty's Customs and Excise v Schindler* [1994] ECR I-1039, para 60: it was 'not possible to disregard the moral, religious or cultural aspects of lotteries, like other types of gambling in member States'.

[42] Case 196/87 *Steymann v Staatssecretaris van Justitie* [1988] ECR 6159: the question that the Dutch referred to the court was: 'Can activities which consist in, and are entirely centred around, participating in a community based on religion or belief or on another form of philosophy and in following the rules of life of that community, whose members provide each other with benefits, be regarded as an economic activity or as a service for the purposes of the Treaty establishing the European Economic Community?'; it was held that: 'Article 2 of the EEC Treaty must be interpreted as meaning that activities performed by members of a community based on religion or another form of philosophy as part of the commercial activities of that community constitute economic activities in so far as the services which the community provides to its members may be regarded as the indirect *quid pro quo* for genuine and effective work': ibid para 14.

[43] Case C-159/90 *Society for the Protection of Unborn Children (SPUC) v Grogan* [1991] ECR I-4685, paras 19, 20: 'Whatever the merits of those arguments on the moral plane, they cannot influence the answer to the national court's first question. It is not for [this] Court to substitute its assessment for that of the legislature in those Member States where the activities in question are practised legally.'

[44] Case C-268/99 *Jany and ors v Staatssecretaris van Justitie* [2001] ECR I-8615, para 56: 'So far as concerns the question of the immorality of that activity, raised by the referring court, it must be borne in mind that, as the Court has already held, it is not for the Court to substitute its own assessment for that of the legislatures of the Member States where an allegedly immoral activity is practised legally.'

[45] Case C-145/88 *Torfaen BC v B&Q plc* [1989] ECR I-3851.

[46] Case C-84/94 *UK v Council of Ministers* [1996] ECR I-5755.

[47] *Darby v Sweden* (1991) 13 EHRR 774; *Dödsbo v Sweden* App no 61564/00 (ECtHR, 17 January 2006).

[48] *Refah Partisi (Welfare Party) v Turkey* (2003) 37 EHRR 1: 'The court has frequently emphasised the state's role as the neutral and impartial organiser of the exercise of various religions, faiths and beliefs, and stated that this role is conducive to public order, religious harmony, and tolerance in a democratic society. It also considers that the state's duty of neutrality and impartiality is incompatible with any power on the state's part to assess the legitimacy of religious belief and that it requires the state to ensure neutral tolerance between opposing groups.'

Nevertheless, matters within the economic competence of the Union may have a religious dimension. For example, under rules on the procurement of public works contracts, national authorities must apply domestic procedures adapted to the relevant EU law which might include provisions about the 'structures of the church'.[49] There are provisions on the export of cultural goods, including elements of them which form an integral part of 'religious monuments'.[50] Rules on objects containing precious metals cover both secular and religious items.[51] A regulation on statistics on income and living conditions applies to 'institutions', which includes 'religious institutions (convents, monasteries)'.[52] Moreover, under the decision to establish the European Year of Equal Opportunities, actions in relation to religion (along with race, ethnicity, disability, age, and sexual orientation) must take full account of gender differences.[53]

However, the internal treatment of religion within the affairs of a non-Member State may be a matter of direct interest to the institutions of the EU in terms of its external relations with that State. This would seem to be a qualification to the principle of subsidiarity. For example, one function of the special representative of the EU for Afghanistan is to advise on 'respect for human rights of all Afghan people, regardless of gender, ethnicity or religion'.[54] Some directives refer explicitly to the religious affairs departments of non-Member states.[55] The decision on principles, priorities, and conditions in the Accession Partnership with Turkey includes the requirement that Turkey guarantees 'in law and practice' the full enjoyment of human rights and freedoms by all without discrimination on grounds of religion or belief.[56] Similarly, the regulation which establishes a financing instrument for the promotion of democracy and human rights worldwide enables Community assistance in the fight against discrimination based on religion or belief.[57] By way of contrast, that religion properly falls within the competence of a State is implicitly assumed rather than spelt out explicitly in the constitutions of States in Europe—though the principle of subsidiarity is used formally in relation to the governance of some religious matters which are considered best dealt with at local instead of national level.[58]

It has been suggested that one reason for the deference of the EU to the principle that religion is best dealt with at the national level is that the EU lacks a strong cultural identity of its own.[59] On the one hand, it is commonly proposed that the

---

[49] Directive (EEC) 71/305, Art 2; Directive (EEC) 92/456, Annex 1 (ie 'church councils' in Belgium); see also Directive (EC) 2004/18.
[50] Regulation (EEC) 3911/92, Annex, Art 1.2.
[51] Common Customs Tariff 1999/L 278/1, 508.
[52] Regulation (EC) 1982/2003, Annex 1(f).
[53] Decision (EC) 771/2006, Preamble (2).
[54] Council Joint Action 2007/106/CFSP, Art 3(e).
[55] Directive (EC) 2006/97 on the accession of Bulgaria and Romania.
[56] Council Decision (EC) 2006/35 [2006] OJ L22/34, 37.
[57] Regulation (EC) 1889/2006, Art 2.1(b)(iii).
[58] See Ch 1 above for religion and regionalism, Ch 7 above for historic sites and local government, Ch 8 above for religious entities and local schools and hospitals, and Ch 9 above for marriage and local registry offices.
[59] See below for the 'Soul for Europe' initiative of former Commission President Jacques Delors.

approaches of the Member States to religion are heavily influenced by particular religious traditions reflected in their religious demography, and that the views of States about religion and its role in society are based on shared historical and cultural assumptions.[60] On the other hand, McCrea argues: 'The European Union, by contrast, lacks a strong cultural identity of its own and is still in the process of developing its political institutions. The weakness of its identity means that the Union lacks the authority to effect fundamental change in the relationship between religion, law, and the state in Europe.'[61] However much one may speculate on the reasons for the principle, subsidiarity means that national religious affairs are not directly within EU competence but are primarily the concern of the Member States; the EU must not intervene in these affairs; and the EU respects the status under national laws of religious organizations within Member States. Nevertheless, the EU may decide on matters falling within its competence even if indirectly these have a religious dimension within a Member State, and it has a direct interest in the treatment of religion in non-Member States with which it is engaged in external relations.

Religious freedom

The third principle of EU religion law is religious freedom. In its respect for 'human dignity as a general principle of law',[62] under the EURT, the EU recognizes the rights, freedoms, and principles set out in the Charter of Fundamental Rights 2000, which charter shall have 'the same legal value as the Treaties' (and it is consolidated with them).[63] The Charter states: 'Everyone has the right to freedom of thought, conscience and religion. The right includes freedom to change religion or belief and freedom, either alone or in community with others and in public or in private, to manifest religion or belief, in worship, teaching, practice and observance.'[64] This mirrors Article 9 ECHR, and there is provision in the Lisbon Treaty for accession to the ECHR,[65] though the EU Court of Justice has for some time consulted and paid the highest respect to the jurisprudence of the Strasbourg European Court of Human Rights.[66] The principle, associated with many

---

[60] See JTS Madeley and Z Enyedi (eds), *Church and State in Contemporary Europe: The Chimera of Neutrality* (London: Frank Cass Publishing, 2003).

[61] McCrea (n 3 above) 3; but nevertheless the EU employs a 'principle of balance' between the sometimes competing claims of religion, culture, and politics.

[62] Case C-36/02 *Omega Spielhallen* [2004] ECR I-9609, para 34: 'the Community legal order undeniably strives to ensure respect for human dignity as a general principle of law. There can therefore be no doubt that the objective of protecting human dignity is compatible with Community law, it being immaterial in that respect that, in Germany, the principle of respect for human dignity has a particular status as an independent fundamental right'; para 35: 'Since both the Community and its Member States are required to respect fundamental rights, the protection of those rights is a legitimate interest which, in principle, justifies a restriction of the obligation imposed by Community law'.

[63] EURT: Treaty on European Union (TEU), Art 6.1.

[64] CFR, Art 10; see also draft Const (2004), Art 70.1; both have same wording as ECHR, Art 9.

[65] EURT: TEU, Art 6.2: the Union shall accede to the ECHR.

[66] Case C-109/01 *Akrich v Secretary of State for the Home Department* [2003] ECR I-9607.

other rights,[67] but which does not appear expressly in the Rome or Maastricht treaties, was in the early jurisprudence of the European Court of Justice understood to be a feature of Community polity.[68] The principle is also embedded in the EU in numerous regulatory instruments, such as the directive on the equal treatment of men and women in the supply of goods and services: 'it is important to respect other fundamental rights and freedoms, including... the freedom of religion'.[69] Some provisions are facilitative: respect for religious freedom appears in the directive on freedom of movement of EU citizens,[70] the Council Code on cross-border movement has rules on journeys for religious events, along with political, scientific, cultural, and sports events.[71] Other rules are prohibitive: for example, staff appointments to the European Defence Agency must not refer to the religious beliefs of candidates.[72]

The principle is particularly evident in the administration of justice. A decision on extradition cooperation provides that a Member State has *no* duty to extradite if that State has 'substantial grounds' to believe that the request has been made to prosecute or punish a person on religious grounds, or would 'cause prejudice' to the position of that person for this reason.[73] The framework decision on the mutual recognition of financial penalties enables a Member State to refuse to execute a decision or financial penalty if it believes (objectively) that these aim to punish a person on grounds of religion.[74] Another framework decision, on the mutual recognition of confiscation orders, provides that a Member State may refuse to confiscate property if confiscation is to punish or prosecute a person on account of their religion or belief.[75] An agreement between the EU and Iceland and Norway provides that the latter may refuse to surrender a person if they believe the arrest warrant was issued to prosecute or punish that person on grounds of religion or belief.[76] Similar rules exist as to the transit of third county nationals or stateless persons when a Member State refuses transit if such persons run the risk of torture,

---

[67] CFR, Art 7 (privacy and family life); Art 8 (data protection); Art 9 (marriage and the family); Art 11 (expression); Art 12 (association); Art 13 (the arts and academic freedom); Art 14 (education including religion); Art 17 (property); Art 21 (discrimination); Art 23 (gender equality); Art 24 (children); Art 25 (the elderly and their right to participate in social and cultural life); and Art 26 (disability): all potentially concern religion.

[68] Case 130/75 *Prais v Council of Ministers* [1976] ECR 1589: while the law on community officials (1968) forbade religious discrimination, it was held that scheduling an examination on a Friday in the case of a Jewish candidate was not in breach of freedom of religion; para 19: 'In so far as the Defendant, if informed of the difficulty in good time would have been obliged to take reasonable steps to avoid fixing for a test a date which would make it impossible for a person of a particular religious faith to undergo the test, it can be said that the defendant in the present case was not informed of the unsuitability of certain days until the date for the test had been fixed, and the defendant was in its discretion entitled to refuse to fix a different date.'

[69] Directive (EC) 2004/113, Preamble (3).

[70] Corrigendum to Directive (EC) 2004/58, Preamble (32); see also Decision (EC) 2004/513.

[71] Regulation (EC) 562/2006, Annex I(d) (in accordance with the Treaty of Rome, Art 251).

[72] Decision (EC) 2004/676, Art 36.

[73] Decision (EC) 2004/579 [2004] OJ L261/69, 76.

[74] Council Framework Decision (EC) 2005/214, Preamble (5).

[75] Council Framework Decision (EC) 2006/783, 13 (in accordance with TEU, Art 6 and CFR, Ch VI).

[76] Agreement [2007] OJ L129/2, Art 1(4).

inhuman or degrading treatment or punishment, the death penalty, or persecution because of religion (but not belief).[77]

As we have already seen, alongside a host of criteria which concern respect for democracy, the rule of law, and human rights,[78] the EU commonly makes religious freedom or equality a condition in its policies on external relations with non-Member States.[79] The regulation to establish a financing instrument for democracy and human rights worldwide enables Community assistance in the fight against discrimination based on religion or belief.[80] The Accession Partnership with Turkey includes the requirement that Turkey guarantees 'in law and practice' the full enjoyment of human rights and freedoms by all, irrespective of religion or belief. It also requires Turkey to 'adopt and implement provisions concerning the exercise of freedom of thought, conscience and religion by all individuals and religious communities' in line with the ECHR, as well as to take into account recommendations of the Commission against Racism and Intolerance, an institution of the Council of Europe.[81] Needless to say, Strasbourg jurisprudence, and the myriad micro-principles which it has developed about the terms of religious freedom under Article 9 ECHR, will become very important in the elaboration of religious freedom within the EU and its institutions. Moreover, as seen in Chapter 2 and elsewhere, religious freedom is a well-developed element of the constitutional traditions common to the States of Europe independently of their incorporation of the ECHR in their own national legal systems; and the EU should have regard to these.[82]

Religious equality and discrimination

The fourth principle of EU religion law is that of religious equality. Article 21 of the EU Charter of Fundamental Rights provides that: 'Any discrimination based on any ground such as sex, race, colour, ethnic or social origin, genetic features, language, religion or belief, political or other opinion, membership of a national

---

[77] [2007] OJ L129/40; see also Directive (EC) 2005/85, Art 27(1).

[78] See eg the Copenhagen Criteria: 'Membership requires that [a] candidate country has achieved stability of institutions guaranteeing democracy, the rule of law, human rights and respect for [the] protection of minorities, the existence of a functioning market economy as well as capacity to cope with competitive pressure and market forces within the Union': European Council in Copenhagen, 21–22 June 1993, Conclusions of the Presidency, SN 180/1/93 REV 1: see McCrea (n 3 above) 94.

[79] Common Position on Nigeria, 2002/401.

[80] Regulation (EC) 1889/2006, Art 2.1(b)(iii).

[81] Council Decision (EC) 2006/35 [2006] OJ L22/34, 37, 38.

[82] See also Case 5/88 *Wachauf v Bundesamt für Ernährung und Fortwirtschaft* [1989] ECR 2609: 'The Court has consistently held ... that fundamental rights form an integral part of the law, the observance of which is ensured by the Court. In safeguarding those rights, the Court has to look to the constitutional traditions common to the Member States, so that measures which are incompatible with the fundamental rights recognised by the Community may not find acceptance in the Community. International treaties concerning the protection of human rights on which the Member States have collaborated or to which they have acceded can also supply guidelines to which regard should be had in the context of Community law.'

minority, property, birth, disability, age or sexual orientation, shall be prohib-ited.'[83] This is declaratory of the existing foundational laws of the Union.[84] Indeed: 'Non-discrimination is a fundamental principle of the European Union' and provides for action to combat discrimination on account of religion and belief, in accordance with Article 13(1) of the Treaty of Rome and Article 21 of the Charter of Fundamental Rights.[85] It is a 'general principle of Community law'.[86] Non-discrimination is based on the principle of equal treatment,[87] which itself is 'a basis for democracy'.[88] Another reason for it is social cohesion: non-discrimination on grounds of religion or belief expresses a 'basic principle of social cohesion' and should be incorporated in all levels of the strategic approach to cohesion.[89]

The prohibition against religious discrimination appears in a multitude of EU regulatory instruments, with a marked increase in recent years,[90] and is applied in many contexts. First, Community officials are themselves beneficiaries of the principle. Discrimination on grounds of religion or belief is prohibited in the recruitment of Union personnel,[91] and specifically for staff of the European Defence Agency.[92] Secondly, third country nationals: Member States must imple-ment the directive on admitting third country nationals for the purpose of scientific research without discrimination on grounds of religion or belief;[93] the same applies to third country nationals for study, pupil exchanges, unremunerated work, and voluntary service.[94] Thirdly, families: Member States must apply the directive, on the right of EU citizens and their families to move and reside freely in the territories of the Member States, without discrimination on account of religion or belief.[95]

The principle is applied in relation to health care. One regulation promotes health care services for lower income population groups and marginalized groups, including 'persons belonging to groups suffering religious discrimination'.[96] It is also applied in relation to the application of funds. The regulation on the European Regional Development Fund, the European Social Fund, and the Cohesion Fund

---

[83] See also EURT (TEC), Art 10; and draft Const (2004), Arts 81, 118.

[84] Treaty of Rome (Nice Version), Art 13: 'the Council, acting . . . on a proposal from the Commis-sion and after consulting the European Parliament, may take appropriate action to combat discrimina-tion based on sex, racial or ethnic origin, religion or belief, disability, age or sexual orientation'.

[85] Decision 1672/2006, Preamble (8); see Directive (EC) 2000/78.

[86] Case C-144/04 *Mangold v Helm* [2005] ECR I-9981; see also Case C-43/05 *Commission of European Communities v Federal Republic of Germany* [2006] ECR I-33: the case concerns the failure to transpose Directive (EC) 2000/78 into German law.

[87] Case C-411/05 *Palacios de la Villa v Cortefiel Servicios SA* [2007] EU ECJ (16 October 2007); for discrimination and religion, see also Case C-13/05 *Chacon Navas v Eurest Colectividades SA* [2006] ECR I-06467; Case C-276/06 *El Youssfi v Office National de Pension* [2007] EU ECJ (17 April 2007).

[88] Decision (EC) 2006/971.

[89] Decision (EC) 2006/702, Preamble (15) and Introduction to Guidelines for Cohesion Policy.

[90] Regulation (EC) 1974/2006, Annex II, para 15.2.

[91] Decision (EC) 2002/621 (Personnel Selection Office).

[92] Decision (EC) 2004/676, Art 5.

[93] Directive (EC) 2005/71, Preamble (4); see also Recommendation (EC) 2005/251.

[94] Directive (EC) 2004/114; see also Directive (EC) 2004/38.

[95] Corrigendum to Directive (EC) 2004/58, Preamble (32).

[96] Regulation (EC) 1905/2006, Art 5(2).

provides for Member States to take appropriate steps regarding access to and implementation of the funds without discrimination on grounds of religion or belief.[97] The same applies with regard to the European Agricultural Fund for Rural development.[98] The regulation which establishes the European Globalisation Adjustment Fund, to support redundant workers affected by major structural changes in world trade, provides that the Council and Member States must ensure that the fund is administered without discrimination on grounds of religion.[99] And the regulation to establish a financing instrument to promote democracy and human rights worldwide enables Community assistance in the fight against discrimination based on religion or belief.[100]

Moreover, soft-law regulatory instruments provide educative mechanisms to encourage the fight against discrimination. The Culture Programme aims to contribute to the elimination of religious discrimination.[101] The decision establishing the Youth in Action Programme links the promotion of active citizenship with the fight against discrimination on grounds of religion and belief.[102] The objective of the year of equal opportunities programme is to raise awareness of the right to equality: all people are entitled to equal treatment irrespective of religion or belief.[103] According to this programme, the Union will take into account the different ways in which men and women experience discrimination on grounds of religion.[104] The provision which forbids religious discrimination in the ECHR is somewhat similar in width to that developed in EU law: it prohibits state discrimination on grounds of religion in the exercise of convention rights and 'any rights set down by law'.[105] As seen in Chapter 3, the implementation of EU directives on discrimination has led to uniformity on this subject at national level.

The autonomy of religious associations

The fifth principle of EU religion law is the autonomy of religious organizations. However, neither the Treaty of Rome nor the Maastricht Treaty expressly provides for the right of religious associations to self-governance. Nevertheless, it is possible that the principle of religious autonomy is implicit in Article 17 of the Lisbon Reform Treaty on the status of religious associations, and as seen in Chapter 5, it is

---

[97] Council Regulation 1083/2006, Preamble (30) and Art 16; see also Regulation (EC) 1080/2006.
[98] Council Regulation (EC) 1698/2005, Art 8.
[99] Regulation (EC) 1929/2006, Art 7.
[100] Regulation (EC) 1889/2006, Art 2.1(b)(iii).
[101] Decision (EC) 1855/2006, Art 12(d).
[102] Decision (EC) 1719/2006, Art 2(3).
[103] Decision (EC) 771/2006, Art 2 (on the basis of Directive (EC) 2000/78).
[104] Decision (EC) 771/2006, Art 4.
[105] ECHR, Art 14: 'The enjoyment of [Convention] rights and freedoms . . . shall be secured without discrimination on any ground such as . . . . religion'; and Protocol 12, Art 1. Also: *Moscow Branch of the Salvation Army v Russia* App no 72881/01 (ECtHR, 15 October 2006): on the registration of religious bodies.

certainly a necessary aspect of religious freedom.[106] In any event, respect for and protection of religious autonomy has been assumed in many other regulatory instruments over the years. For instance, the Turkey accession partnership decision requires Turkey to establish conditions for the functioning of religious communities, including legal and judicial protection—*inter alia*, through legal personality of the communities, their members, and assets, teaching, appointment and training of clergy, and enjoyment of property rights in line with Protocol 1 ECHR.[107] However, one condition in the EU partnership with the former Yugoslav Republic of Macedonia is that the latter is to 'ensure the full implementation of the constitutional principle of the separation of religious communities and groups from the State', as well as to review 'the legal framework for religious communities and groups'.[108]

Importantly, the Union sometimes explicitly allows the operation of duties which people may assume under their own systems of religious law.[109] For example, Member States could grant exemptions from the restrictive measures against Iraq (introduced for security reasons), to prevent the entry or transit through their territories of prescribed persons, where the State decides that travel is justified on the grounds of 'urgent humanitarian need, including religious obligation'.[110] The same 'religious obligation' formula was also used in relation to persons seeking entry into a Member State at the same time that EU restrictions were operative against the Republic of Congo,[111] in relation to persons suspected of involvement in the assassination of a former Lebanese Prime Minister,[112] and in relation to nationals of the Côte d'Ivoire.[113] However, the Court of Justice did not engage in discussion about the implications for the religious autonomy of the Church of Scientology in a case concerning French laws which restricted its financial freedom; but it did intervene to strike down the French law because of its lack of precision and on the basis of its breach of legal certainty.[114]

Perhaps the most well-known juridical expression of the autonomy principle relates to the freedom of religious organizations to discriminate on grounds of religion in the employment sphere.[115] One directive prohibits direct and indirect discrimination on grounds of religion or belief (along with disability, age, or sexual orientation).[116] However, religious discrimination may be permitted in 'the case of

---

[106] EURT, Art 15b repeats the draft Const (2004), Art 52.
[107] Council Decision (EC) 2006/35 [2006] OJ L22/34, 38.
[108] Decision (EC) 2006/57 [2006] OJ L35/57, 60.
[109] See eg Case C-434/05 *Horizon College* [2007] ECR I-4793.
[110] Council Common Position 2007/140.
[111] Common Resolution 2005/440/CFSP.
[112] Common Position 2005/888/CFSP.
[113] Common Position 2004/852.
[114] Case C-54/99 *Association Église de Scientologie de Paris and Scientology International Reserves Trust v The Prime Minister* [2000] ECR I-1335: the organization had requested repeal of a French law which enabled public authorities to require prior authorization for all international financial transactions deemed by the government to represent a 'threat to public policy [and] security'; the law was struck down as 'the system established is contrary to the principle of legal certainty'.
[115] For national laws on this subject see Ch 3 above.
[116] Directive (EC) 2000/78, Art 4(1).

occupational activities within churches and other public or private organisations the ethos of which is based on religion or belief'. This applies 'where, by reason of the nature of these activities or the context in which they are carried out, a person's religion or belief constitute a genuine, legitimate and justified occupational require-ment, having regard to the organisation's ethos'.[117] Nevertheless, provided that its rules are otherwise complied with, 'this Directive shall thus not prejudice the right of churches and other public or private organisations, the ethos of which is based on religion or belief, acting in conformity with national constitutions and laws, to require individuals working for them to act in good faith and with loyalty to the organisation's ethos'.[118] Similarly, a working time directive enables states to dero-gate from prescribed requirements, if there is proper regard for workers' safety and health, in relation to workers officiating in religious ceremonies in churches and religious communities.[119]

An important by-product of the exercise of religious autonomy is the juridical integration of decision-making by religious authorities into the European regula-tory regime; religious authorities may be assigned tasks of carrying out public EU functions. Several instruments on foodstuffs deal with 'legislative or administrative decisions or customs' of Member States 'relating . . . to religious rites'.[120] Ritual slaughter, now within the scope of EU law,[121] is exempt from the requirement to stun animals before slaughter.[122] In the Member States, 'the religious authority on whose behalf slaughter is carried out shall be competent for the application and monitoring of the special provisions which apply to slaughter according to religious rites'.[123] Incidentally, evisceration (removal of organs) must be carried out no later than forty-five minutes after stunning or, 'in the case of ritual slaughter, half an hour after bleeding'.[124] A regulation on foodstuffs hygiene provides that food business operators of slaughterhouses must ensure the trachea and oesophagus remain intact during bleeding, except in the case of the slaughter 'according to a religious custom'.[125]

Other examples of the legal recognition of decisions taken by religious bodies in an exercise of their autonomy include the following. The decisions of church tribunals in matrimonial cases operative under concordats between the Holy See and Portugal, Spain, and Italy are afforded recognition by the Union for the

---

[117] ibid Art 4(2): also: 'This difference of treatment shall be implemented taking account of member states' constitutional provisions and principles, as well as the general principles of Community law, and should not justify discrimination on another ground'.

[118] ibid. For criticism of this (as a description of a rule rather than a rule), see J Rivers, 'In pursuit of pluralism: the ecclesiastical policy of the European Union' (2004) 7 EccLJ 285.

[119] Directive (EC) 93/104, Art 17.

[120] Directive (EC) 2001/88, Preamble (1).

[121] Previously, under Directive (EEC) 74/577, Art 4, national provisions relating to ritual slaughter were exempted from the European requirement to stun before slaughter.

[122] Directive (EC) 93/119; for national laws, see Ch 6 above n 104.

[123] Directive (EC) 93/119.

[124] Directive (EEC) 83/90.

[125] Corrigendum to Regulation (EC) 853/2004, Ch IV, 7(a); see also C321 E/314, Protocol no 33 (1997) on animal welfare: 'while respecting the legislative or administrative provisions and customs of the Member States relating in particular to religious rites, cultural traditions and regional heritage'.

purpose of determining the personal marital status of individuals.[126] Rules on the description and presentation of wines permit recommendations to the consumer concerning the acceptability of the wine for religious purposes;[127] such recommendations may be indicated 'only if the wine . . . has been produced in accordance with the special rules laid down by the religious authorities concerned, and those authorities have given their written approval as to such indication'; moreover, such recommendations may be indicated only in trade with the religious authorities concerned.[128] Rules prohibit the processing of personal data revealing religious or philosophical beliefs; but there are exceptions for processing by a foundation, association, or any other non-profit-making body with a religious or philosophical aim (political or trade union aims are also covered) carried out in the course of their legitimate activities, provided the processing relates solely to the members of the body or persons having regular contact with it in connection with its purposes—disclosure is subject to data subject consent.[129] As seen in Chapter 5, the autonomy of religious organizations is a key feature of both national laws and Strasbourg jurisprudence. It may very well be, therefore, that this fundamental of EU law is a very good example of the use by the EU of the principles of religion law common to the Member States as material or inspirational sources for its stance on this subject. Further research would be needed to verify this.

Cooperation with religion

The sixth principle of EU religion law is that of cooperation with religion. The principle of the value of religion, in its programmatic acknowledgement of the contribution of religion to European values, as well as the arrangements described above in relation to the exercise of autonomy, illustrate mutual collaboration between the EU and religion. However, the Lisbon Treaty goes further; Article 17.3 EURT provides: 'Recognising their identity and their specific contribution, the Union shall maintain an open, transparent and regular dialogue with these churches and organisations'.[130] Cooperation between the EU and associations which might include religious bodies has been on the political agenda for

---

[126] Regulation (EC) 1347/2000, Art 40.

[127] Regulation (EEC) 3201/90, Art 10(1).

[128] ibid Art 10(2): however, the terms Kosher wine, Passover kosher wine, Kosher wine for Passover and their translations may appear without this restriction (in Art 10(2) provided that the rule in Art 10(1) on recommendation of acceptability of use for religious purposes is satisfied).

[129] Directive (EC) 95/46; for national laws on religion and data protection, see Ch 2 above.

[130] See also EURT, Art 136a for promoting the role of the social partners at EU level and dialogue between them; Art 17b: the right to petition EU institutions (also Charter of Fundamental Rights, Art 22); and Art 8b: EU institutions shall give 'representative associations' the opportunity to make known and publicly exchange their views in all areas of Union action; maintain an open, transparent and regular dialogue with these; and consult them. Under Art 256a, the Economic and Social Committee consists of representatives of civil society organizations (including cultural ones); see also draft Const (2004), Art 52.3.

some time:[131] in a declaration appended to the Maastricht Treaty on charitable associations responsible for welfare programmes and services;[132] in an opinion on the role of civil society organizations in the building of Europe;[133] and in a call for a structured channel for feedback, criticism, and protest in European governance.[134] Indeed, the database of Consultation, the European Commission and Civil Society (CONECCS), carries information about formal consultative bodies and civil society organizations, with a great number of religious organizations being listed.[135] The Catholic Church, the Protestant Churches, and Jewish, Muslim, Orthodox, and other religious groups all have full-time representation in Brussels.[136]

The principle of cooperation with churches and religious organizations may be justified on the basis of their particular expertise in, for example, moral and social affairs, and enhancement of legitimacy in governance.[137] It may also represent a pragmatic response to the fact that, as some maintain, religions have refused to accept the marginal role which they have been assigned as a result of the adoption in most States of the constitutional separation of State from religion.[138] The Catholic Church, for example, commonly pronounces on matters of public concern;[139] indeed, in his address to the European People's Party in 2006, Pope Benedict XVI stated: 'As far as the Catholic Church is concerned, the principal focus of her intervention in the public arena is the protection and promotion of the dignity of the person, and she is thereby consciously drawing particular attention to principles which are not negotiable', namely, the protection of life at all its various stages, the natural structure of the family (and marriage), and the right of parents to educate their children.[140]

---

[131] In 1992 Commission President Jacques Delors set up a scheme called 'A Soul for Europe' the aim of which was 'giving a spiritual and ethical dimension to the European Union'; in an address Delors explained: '[w]e won't succeed with Europe solely on the basis of legal expertise or economic know-how ... If in the next ten years we have not managed to give a soul to Europe, to give it spirituality and meaning, the game will be up'; the Bureau of European Policy Advisers (BEPA) was given responsibility for the initiative 'A Dialogue with Religions, Churches, Humanisms'; the White Paper, *European Governance*, COM (2001) 428 final, Brussels, 25 July 2001, also acknowledged the role for religious perspectives in policy-making by recognizing the 'particular contribution' of 'churches and religious communities': for these see McCrea (n 3 above) 65 *et seq*.

[132] Declaration no 23; see also COM/97/0241; see also 'Building a Stronger Partnership', COM (2000) 11. In 1999, under President Romano Prodi, one section of the European Commission's Group of Policy Advisers was assigned the task of 'dialogue with religions, churches and humanisms'.

[133] 1999/C 329/10.

[134] COM (2001) 428, 2001/C 287/01.

[135] These include the Church and Society Commission of the Conference of European Churches, Catholic European Study and Information Centre, European Humanist Federation, and *Centre Européen Juif d'Information*: <http://www.europa.eu.int/comm/civil_society/connecs/index.htm>.

[136] See M Rynkowski, 'Remarks on Art I.52 of the Constitutional Treaty: new aspects of the European ecclesiastical law' (2005) 6(11) German Law Journal 343.

[137] See Rivers (n 118 above) 286–7.

[138] See eg J Casanova, *Public Religions in the Modern World* (Chicago: University of Chicago Press, 1994).

[139] See eg D Yamane, *The Catholic Church in State Politics: Negotiating Prophetic Demands and Political Realities* (Lanham, MD: Rowman and Littlefield Publishers, 2005).

[140] Papal Address of 30 March 2006, quoted in McCrea (n 3 above) 26.

In any event, the principle merely articulates existing practices and procedures under EU law.[141] The provision which establishes a high level advisory group on social integration, to examine the participation of ethnic minorities in the labour market, mentions religion.[142] The EU Agency for Fundamental Rights must cooperate closely with non-governmental organizations (NGOs) and institutions of civil society active in combating racism and xenophobia at national, European, and international levels; one of the functions of the agency is to establish a 'cooperation network' (the Fundamental Freedoms Platform), which is to include 'religious, philosophical and non-confessional organisations'.[143] The principle is also employed in the context of EU external relations. One function of the special EU representative for Central Africa is to contribute, in cooperation with the Organisation for Security and Co-operation in Europe (OSCE), to the prevention and resolution of conflict by developing close contacts with authorities and other local actors which include 'religious groups and their leaders', NGOs, political parties, and minorities.[144]

The principle has been extended to financial support for religion. For the purposes of expenditure, religion is included in the classification of non-profit institutions.[145] The regulation for a financing instrument for development cooperation provides that 'churches and religious associations and communities' are eligible for funding.[146] Under the instrument for nuclear safety cooperation, non-state actors eligible for financial support include 'churches and religious associations and communities' likely to contribute to the development or the external dimensions of internal Union policies.[147] Similarly, churches and religious associations and communities are eligible for funding to implement action and joint cross-border cooperation programmes under the European Neighbourhood and Partnership Instrument.[148] The regulation which establishes the Instrument for Stability Abroad also provides that churches, religious associations, and communities are eligible for financial support.[149] Indeed, there are several religious alliances, such as the Conference of European Churches, whose constitutions provide for direct engagement with the EU.[150]

---

[141] Decision (EC) 1983/2006, Preamble (see n 19 above).
[142] Decision (EC) 2005/85 (implementing Treaty of Rome, Art 13).
[143] Regulation (EC) 168/2007.
[144] Council Joint Action 2007/113, Art 3(1)(d).
[145] Regulation (EC) 113/2002.
[146] Regulation (EC) 1905/2006, Art 24; see also Regulation (EC) 625/2004.
[147] Council Regulation (Euratom) 300/2007, Art 7(2).
[148] Regulation (EC) 1638/2006, Art 14(1)(h)(viii).
[149] Regulation (EC) 1717/2006, Art 10(2).
[150] It has an office in Brussels for its Church and Society Commission. The Commission has working groups on EU legislation. There are seven members: Church of England, Church of Denmark, Church of Finland, the Netherlands Council of Churches, Council of Protestant Churches of Portugal, Lutheran Church of Slovakia, and the EKD. CEC is 'an ecumenical fellowship of churches in Europe which confess the Lord Jesus Christ as God and Saviour according to the Scriptures and seek to fulfil together their common calling to the glory of the one God, Father, Son and Holy Spirit' (Constitution). See also (eg) the European Network of Health Care Chaplaincy.

The Lisbon Treaty obligation under Article 17.3 EURT to cooperate in dialogue with religions, and the consequential right of religious associations to such dialogue, goes beyond the requirements of the ECHR—it does not appear in the Convention—though the Council of Europe has expressed the value of dialogue and cooperation between States and religion.[151] The Treaty also goes beyond the constitutional laws of most Member States: the constitutions of States do not generally impose a *duty* on those States to engage in dialogue and cooperate with religions. However, there is a principle which may be induced from the national laws of Europe, that States have a *right* to establish facilities for dialogue with religion—and of course covenants, concordats, and other agreements have proliferated in church-state relations within national borders on this basis. Moreover, as we have seen time and time again in this book, cooperation is facilitated by national laws at sub-constitutional level in relation to a host of matters of common concern to the State and religious organizations: the acquisition of legal personality; non-interference by the State in the internal affairs of religious organizations; the protection of doctrine and worship; the preservation of historic religious sites; the financing of religion; provision for religious education in public schools; spiritual assistance in hospitals, prisons, and the armed forces; and the administration of religious marriage ceremonies. In other words, when the EU accords 'religious perspectives a particular degree of recognition and facilitation in policy-making', under which 'religious bodies are recognized as elements of civil society with which the union will maintain a dialogue',[152] this simply reflects a basic principle of religion law common to the States of Europe.

The special protection of religion

The seventh principle of EU religion law is the special protection of religion by means of privileges and exemptions. This principle is more prevalent in the functional instruments of the EU rather than its treaties. However, the EU Charter of Fundamental Rights has provisions which imply special protection for particular religious activities. Article 10.2 provides: 'The right of conscientious objection is recognised, in accordance with the national laws governing the exercise of this right.'[153] Article 14.3 states:

The freedom to found educational establishments with due respect for democratic principles and the right of parents to ensure the education and teaching of their children in conformity with their religious, philosophical and pedagogical convictions shall be respected, in accordance with national law governing the exercise of such freedom and right.[154]

---

[151] See Ch 1 above, at n 171.

[152] McCrea (n 3 above) 68: in so doing, the EU 'implicitly identifies religious perspectives as a legitimate and necessary element of policy formation. Furthermore, the recognition of the right of religious bodies to be consulted by law-making institutions in a separate article [in the EURT] from that dedicated to civil society in general, characterizes this religious contribution to law-making as distinctive and particularly important'.

[153] See also draft Const (2004), Art 70.2; see Ch 2 above for national laws on this subject.

[154] See also draft Const (2004), Art 74.3; see Ch 8 above on religious education and faith schools.

As with religious autonomy, the provision of special protection would seem to be a micro-principle of religious freedom: the basic idea is that people cannot practise their religion freely if rules of general applicability disadvantage them in particular ways due to their religious needs.[155]

The concept of special protection is not new. It is based on the current EU juridical practice in various fields.[156] First, special protection may be afforded to religious *associations*. A Member State may provide that a trade mark shall not be registered, or if registered, shall be liable to be declared invalid, where the trade mark covers 'a sign of high symbolic value, in particular a religious symbol'.[157] Advertisements must not be inserted in any broadcast of a 'religious service', and 'religious programmes' of less than thirty minutes must not be interrupted by advertisements.[158] Secondly, special protection may be afforded to *individuals*. Member States must satisfy the directive on electronic commerce but may derogate if necessary for public policy to assist in 'the fight against any incitement to hatred on grounds of... religion'.[159] The personal files of temporary staff of the European Defence Agency shall not refer to their 'religious activities and views'.[160] The system to protect personal data in the passenger name records of air passengers transferred to the US Bureau of Customs and Border Protection prohibits the use of sensitive information on religious beliefs.[161] However, such sensitive religious data may be processed if this is necessary for criminal investigations.[162]

Thirdly, special protection may apply to religious *property*. There are provisions on the export of cultural goods forming an integral part of 'religious monuments'.[163] The return of cultural objects unlawfully removed from a Member State includes objects found in the inventories of ecclesiastical institutions.[164] Some provisions are explicitly designed for the 'protection of cultural and religious sites',[165] or 'the rehabilitation of damaged and destroyed properties... including historic and religious sites'.[166] One regulation prohibits dealing in Iraqi cultural

---

[155] However, some argue that the justification of laws or policy on religious grounds is inconsistent with a liberal constitutional order; see eg J Habermas, 'Religion in the public sphere' (2006) 14(1) *European Journal of Philosophy* 1, 4: 'the self-understanding of the constitutional state has developed within the framework of a contractualist tradition that relies on "natural" reason, in other words solely public arguments to which supposedly all persons have equal access. The assumption of a common human reason forms the basis of justification for a secular state that no longer depends on religious legitimation'; this draws heavily from J Rawls, *Political Liberalism* (New York: Columbia University Press, 1993).

[156] For a discussion about the 'protection of religion from the market', see McCrea (n 3 above) 147.

[157] Directive (EEC) 89/104, Art 3(2)(b).

[158] Directive (EEC) 89/552 (amended by (EC) 97/36), Art 11(5); see Ch 6 above.

[159] Directive (EC) 2000/31, Art 3(4)(a); for national laws, see Ch 3 above.

[160] Decision (EC) 2004/676, Art 32; for national laws, see Ch 2 above.

[161] Decision (EC) 2004/535. For a challenge to and judicial consideration of the directive, see Case C-317/04 *European Parliament v Council of the European Union* [2006] ECR I-4721.

[162] Decision (EC) 2002/187, Art 15(4).

[163] Regulation (EEC) 3911/92, Annex, Art 1.2.

[164] Directive (EEC) 93/7.

[165] Council Joint Action 2006/304 [2006] OJ L112/19, 19 (in Kosovo).

[166] Decision (EC) 2006/56: conditions for EU partnership with Serbia and Montenegro.

property and items of 'religious importance', and protects inventories of Iraqi 'religious institutions'.[167]

Fourthly, special protection is extended to *food*. In a regulation on foodstuffs, an applicant seeking authorization to trade in genetically modified food or feed (different from its conventional counterparts with respect to composition, nutritional value, and intended use) must send with the application 'a reasoned statement that the food does not give rise to ethical or religious concerns'; moreover, labelling of such genetically modified food or feed must include information on whether the modification 'gives rise to ethical or religious concerns'.[168] Similarly, export refunds on beef and veal should be granted for third countries which, 'for cultural or religious reasons, traditionally import substantial numbers of animals for domestic slaughter'.[169]

A related practice in the EU is the conferral of special religious privileges or extraordinary rights. This has not been articulated formally in the foundational instruments of the Union. First, EU law commonly exempts religion directly from prescribed requirements. 'Mobile churches' enjoy exemptions from requirements of vehicle harmonization.[170] Tax exemptions may be enjoyed in relation to 'supplies of staff by religious or philosophical institutions for medical, welfare, child protection and educational purposes with a view to spiritual welfare'.[171] By way of contrast, the Turkey accession partnership decision provides that Turkey may not privilege the Muslim community over non-Muslims; Turkey must:

Adopt a law comprehensively addressing the difficulties faced by non-Muslim religious minorities and communities in line with the relevant European standards. Suspend all sales or confiscation of properties which belong or belonged to non-Muslim religious community foundations by the competent authorities pending adoption of the abovementioned law.[172]

Secondly, enjoyment of the privilege is at the discretion of a Member State. Exceptions to working time requirements may be made for those officiating at religious ceremonies.[173] The directive on equal treatment of men and women in employment does not limit the right of a Member State to exclude from its field of application those occupational activities and, where appropriate, prior training, for which, by reason of their nature or the context in which they are carried out, the sex of the worker constitutes a determining factor.[174] The directive on harmonization of aspects of copyright enables Member States to have exceptions for reproductions by the press, communication to the public, or making available articles on 'religious

---

[167] Regulation (EC) 1210/2003, Art 3 and Annex II.
[168] Regulation (EC) 1829/2003, Preamble (22), Arts 5 and 13.
[169] Regulation (EC) 2000/2005; see also Regulation (EC) 393/2005; Regulation (EC) 1254/99, Art 33.
[170] Directive (EC) 2001/85, Annex 1, para 1.3.2.
[171] Directive (EEC) 77/388.
[172] Council Decision (EC) 2006/35 [2006] OJ L22/34, 37.
[173] Directive (EC) 2003/88, Art 17(1)(c). See also Case C-14/04 *Dellas v Premier Ministre* [2005] ECR I-10253 on Directive (EC) 93/104 on derogations for workers officiating at religious ceremonies.
[174] Directive (EEC) 76/207, Art 2(2).

topics' and materials for 'use in religious celebrations'.[175] As to consultation with and information for employees, Member States may set special provisions for religion.[176] Likewise, Member States may exempt payment service providers from requirements about the provision of information on the payer accompanying transfers of funds to organizations carrying out non-profit charitable, religious, and cultural purposes, provided such organizations are subject to external reporting and audit.[177] As seen in earlier chapters, the concept of a special privilege or exemption for religion has long been a feature of national laws in relation to a very wide range of matters—such as conscientious objection to military service, exceptions for bodies with a religious ethos to discriminate on grounds of religion, exemptions from planning law requirements for religious sites, tax benefits for religious purposes, and withdrawal of pupils from compulsory religious education in State schools.[178]

Conclusion

The enlargement of the EU, in composition and competence (economic, political, and social), has produced an expansion in the volume of EU laws and other regulatory instruments dealing with religion. A wide range of religious phenomena are now expressly recognized in EU law: religious associations, groups, authorities, leaders, rules, customs, obligations, beliefs, teaching, ceremonies, rites, worship, observance, practice, and education—all are EU juridical categories. An examination of its regulatory instruments tells us much about the posture of the EU in terms of its own religion-Union relations. The details of its laws indicate that the EU shares characteristics most in common with the so-called cooperationist model of religion-state relations, though the language of separation is also employed. Needless to say, the EU is not a state-church system nor is it an exclusively secular institution. Rather, the religion law of the EU recognizes: the value of religion in the life of Europe; the subsidiarity in religious matters enjoyed by the Member States; cooperation with religion in the form of a duty to engage in dialogue with churches and religious associations; religious freedom; the autonomy of religious associations; religious equality; and the special protection from market forces and privileges afforded to religion. The Lisbon Reform Treaty and the Charter of Fundamental Rights provide a convenient presentation and summary of the seven principles. However, these principles have not been articulated *de novo* by the EU in its recent reforms. They may be found in, and perhaps represent the motivating force behind, a host of pre-existing legal instruments of the EU. Some of

---

[175] Directive (EC) 2001/29, Art 5(3)(c) and (g).
[176] Directive (EC) 2002/14, Art 3(2).
[177] Regulation (EC) 1781/2006, Art 18.
[178] See McCrea (n 3 above) 164, dealing with discrimination law in the EU: 'This approach suggests that EU law recognizes religion as an exceptional phenomenon whose communal rights and public role are entitled to broad recognition not accorded to other kinds of bodies'.

them, of course, are also to be found in the ECHR and the jurisprudence of Strasbourg.

Needless to say, the implementation of EU religion law by the Member States, notably in the protection of religious data and the prohibition of religious discrimination (see Chapters 2 and 3), has produced an obvious juridical uniformity at national level. Equally, however, the EU principles are themselves mirrored in national religion laws. This has occurred without any identifiable influence on the part of the EU (or indeed the ECHR). Further research is needed to determine whether the development of the seven EU principles has been influenced by the general principles of religion law common to the States of Europe articulated in this book. If their development has been so influenced, this may be justified on the basis that the 'general principles of law common to the Member States' are, according to the EU, a material or inspirational source for its own law. The principles induced from national religion laws may also serve as a yardstick by which to measure the legitimacy of future developments in EU law on religion, and perhaps to help to administer the idea that treaty/charter rights are to be interpreted in harmony with the common constitutional traditions of Member States.

General Conclusion

Law is a place where religion and politics meet. All the States of Europe possess laws which affect religion. A comparison of these national laws reveals profound similarities between States in their treatment of religion. From these similarities emerge principles of religion law common to the States of Europe. This is a category which has not hitherto been suggested by scholarship in this area. The existence of these shared principles may be factually established as a result of careful observation. Each State contributes through its own legal system to this store of principles. The principles themselves have strong persuasive authority and are fundamental to the self-understanding of States in their postures towards religion. The principles contain within themselves the possibility for further development. Moreover, the existence of the principles both demonstrates and promotes juridical unity in Europe in terms of its continental approach to religion in society. The principles seem to rest on three fundamental maxims: people may practise religion freely; States must treat religions equally; and religion is of social value. These maxims would seem to underlie the vast majority of legal arrangements addressed in this book. Flowing from these maxims about freedom, balance, and utility, the principles themselves are capable of articulation as general normative propositions which operate in relation to a very wide range of subjects. A tentative statement of these is proposed in the Appendix.

Classical scholarship understands that there are three basic models at work with regard to religion-state relations in each of the countries of Europe. The state-church system is marked by close constitutional links between government and a particular church. The separation system is one in which, constitutionally, religion has no place in the public life of the State. The cooperation system is rooted in the constitutional separation of State and religion but facilitates cooperation between them in relation to matters of common concern. The studies in this book suggest that beneath the level of constitutional law such distinctions cannot so easily be made. At this level, the dominant model in the States of Europe is that of cooperation between the State and religion. Cooperation occurs in the shape of formal or informal pacts between the institutions of government and religious organizations, the protection of religious freedom, and the prohibition of religious discrimination. Collaboration takes place with respect to the conferral of legal personality on religious groups seeking this, State restraint from interference in the internal affairs of religious organizations, and the protection of religious doctrines from vilification and worship from disruption. It also surfaces in relation to the preservation of religious sites of historic value, financial support for religious initiatives, provision for religious education in or outside public schools, the provision of spiritual care in hospitals, prisons, and the armed forces, and the ability to celebrate marriage in a religious context. However, cooperation at sub-constitutional level comes at a price—its enjoyment often requires religion to satisfy a multitude of substantive and procedural conditions set by law.

By and large national religion laws, and the principles induced from the similarities between them, are indigenous—developed on the basis of the particular historical, political, cultural, and religious forces which have shaped the countries domestically. It is these same forces which contribute to the many juridical differences between countries which exist at the constitutional level in terms of the programmatic postures of States towards religion. However, more often than not, at the sub-constitutional level these differences exist in terms of the detailed conditions under which States particularize shared overarching principles to concrete cases. All States allow religious groups to seek legal personality, but the conditions vary; all States confer tax benefits on prescribed religious activities, but the amounts vary. All States allow religious ceremonies to mark a marriage, but countries differ on whether those ceremonies generate a marriage with civil status. Equally, some States provide for denominational religious education in public schools, others do not—but all make provision for the religious education of pupils either on or off school premises. At the same time, however, often national laws are unified by common compliance with global international law, the ECHR or EU law. This is particularly evident in relation to the religious education and upbringing of children (UN), religious liberty (ECHR), and religious discrimination (EU). Indeed, the principles of religion law common to the States of Europe may represent a blueprint for those who advocate modernization of the ECHR, as well as for the EU in its determination of the general principles of law and common national traditions when it legislates on religion in the future.

A study of national religion laws may also benefit from, and perhaps contribute to, disciplines outside the field of law. Sociology of religion, for instance, provides fundamental propositions about the contemporary role of religion in society. These propositions may be used to understand religion law more deeply in its social contexts. Equally, national religion laws and the principles which flow from them may be used to substantiate or refute the propositions of sociology of religion, given that law itself, of course, is like religion a social phenomenon. On the one hand, classical sociology of religion proposes that secularization has resulted in a decline in both institutional religion and its influence in the public sphere—if correct, this would explain the rise of the constitutional separation of State and religion. Post-modern sociology has also claimed that there has been an increase in religious pluralism and new forms of religiosity in recent years—if correct, this might help to explain the increase in State laws which seek to accommodate both religious diversity and, for example, new religious movements. On the other hand, sociology proposes that religion has retreated from the public into the private sphere. Granted, in most States religious organizations have private law status. But national laws which accommodate religion in public institutions seem to undermine this thesis, and States have a direct interest in problems associated with the upbringing of children in the private sphere of the family. Also, sociology proposes that religion has both a cohesive and divisive role in society. The value of religion is certainly recognized implicitly in national laws—and State recognition of its potential for division is illustrated well in public order criminal laws which relate to religious hatred and defamation of religion. Indeed, for those sociologists who still see the influence of religion on society, the emergent EU law on religion, and its duty of dialogue, may be of particular interest and significance.[1]

This book does not purport to be an exhaustive study of law and religion in Europe; it is merely a preliminary comparative introduction. A number of important matters have emerged which are in need of a great deal of further comparative study and reflection. One such matter is the geographical coverage of the book. Its principal focus has been the Member States of the European Union with material from a small selection of States outside the Union, mainly when these have been the subject of proceedings under the ECHR at Strasbourg. A more ambitious study of all the States represented in the Council of Europe would be an important contribution to the secondary literature in this field. Another matter is the legislative history of national laws on religion, particularly debate which immediately preceded their enactment—and the contribution, if any, of religious organizations to this debate. This would provide the much-needed political context for laws, including the reasons for them in terms of their intended purpose and justification. This would enable a more comprehensive and rigorous evaluation of national laws at the political level. Similarly, further study is needed on the application and enforcement of laws in several areas, particularly with a view to determining the extent to which States actually treat different religions equally. Empirical research would be invaluable to uncover the practical difficulties which, for example, religious groups face in seeking legal personality, and which parents and pupils face in opting out of religious education, and the incidence of convictions for the celebration of religious marriages before civil marriage in those States which criminalize this. Related to this is the need for a general religious perspective on national laws and the issues they address. The book has merely presented the perspective of the State. A religious perspective could tell us about the impact which national laws have on the internal lives of religious organizations, the degree to which they meet standards set by the State, and how pluralism and other developments in wider civil society affect their own religious laws and other regulatory instruments. Above all, a religious perspective could stimulate debate as to whether religious laws and the values they express are represented in the principles of religion law common to the States of Europe.

---

[1] For suggestions for an interdisciplinary approach, see N Doe, 'A sociology of law on religion—towards a new discipline: legal responses to religious pluralism in Europe' (2004) 152 Law and Justice 68; for examination of key sociological themes and their applicability to law and religion, see R Sandberg and R Catto, 'Law and sociology: toward a greater understanding of religion' in N Doe and R Sandberg (eds), *Law and Religion: New Horizons* (Leuven: Peeters, 2010) 275.

The Principles of Religion Law Common
to the States of Europe

A principle of religion law common to the States of Europe is understood here to be a foundational proposition of general applicability which has a strong dimension of weight, is induced from the similarities between the legal systems of States, derives from its constitutional traditions, expresses a basic democratic value, and is about, is implicit in, or underlies national religion law.

1. The State is free to choose its own general posture toward religion in terms of its place in public life and government subject to respect for human rights.
2. The State may recognize a national or established church provided it facilitates the exercise of religious freedom for those who do not belong to that church.
3. The State may prohibit its adoption of a State religion.
4. The State may provide for its cooperation with religion.
5. The State must meet the standards of international law as they affect religion.
6. Religion involves beliefs in a transcendental worldview practised in worship, teaching and norms of conduct for the lives of believers.
7. The State may not limit the right to hold any religious belief.
8. There is no obligation to declare a religious belief publicly.
9. Everyone may worship, teach, observe or practise religion publicly or privately.
10. Everyone may worship, teach, observe or practise religion alone or in community.
11. Everyone has a right to free religious affiliation and association.
12. Religious proselytising may be engaged in freely.
13. Everyone may abandon the right to manifest religion by voluntary waiver.
14. No person is compelled to engage in military service contrary to their religion.
15. The manifestation of religion may by limited by law for a legitimate aim.
16. All are equal and no discrimination may occur on the basis of religion or sex.
17. A religious organization may discriminate on grounds of religion and sex when this is genuinely necessary in order to fulfil its religious purposes and doctrine.
18. No person may stir up hatred against or violent conflict between religions.
19. A religious group may associate freely to manifest its beliefs.
20. The State may recognize religious organizations by means of the constitution, statutes, agreements or registration.
21. A religious group may seek legal personality and must satisfy such conditions for its acquisition as may be prescribed by law.
22. A religious organization is autonomous, and the State cannot intervene in its internal affairs.
23. A religious organization should comply with its internal rules which must not be inconsistent with the law of the State.
24. The State may limit the exercise of religious autonomy only when this is necessary for the preservation of public order, health and morals.

25. Ministers of religion may function as office-holders, under contracts of employment or other status recognized by law.
26. Religious organizations may freely appoint their ministers of religion or, in the case of state-churches nominate these for appointment by the State.
27. The discipline of ministers is a matter for the religious organization to which they belong, save to the extent that the law provides for recourse to the courts of the State.
28. No-one may in public intentionally defame religious doctrines.
29. No-one may intentionally disturb worship and ritual in a public sacred place.
30. The State may penalize with criminal sanctions the vilification of religion and the disruption of religious worship.
31. The media should respect religion in its coverage of religious affairs.
32. A religious organisation may freely acquire, administer and dispose of property.
33. The State must not arbitrarily confiscate religious property lawfully held and if it does so it must provide for restitution or where this is not possible compensation.
34. The State may impose such restrictions on the construction and preservation of religious sites as are necessary to protect the national and cultural heritage.
35. Sacred places should not be damaged with the intention to insult religion.
36. The State should provide for tax allocations to religious purposes, remuneration for ministers who provide spiritual care in public institutions, tax exemptions for religion, and compensation for confiscation and damage to religious property.
37. Parents are free to provide for the religious education of their children.
38. The State may provide or provide for the religious education of pupils in public schools by way of Christian knowledge, denominational education, and non-denominational education, either in or outside public school premises.
39. The State must provide for exemptions when parents or mature children wish to withdraw from religious education in public schools when this is compulsory.
40. Teachers in public schools must not be compelled to provide religious education.
41. Religious organizations are free to seek to establish religious schools and the State must not interfere in the admission of pupils to and the administration of such schools save to the extent permitted by law.
42. A person has the right to the free practice of religion in hospitals, prisons and the armed forces and the State must make provision for this.
43. Ministers of religion may minister to patients, prisoners and military personnel.
44. The State should provide financial support for spiritual assistance which accommodates pastoral care and religious practices in hospitals, prisons and the armed forces so far as is practicable.
45. Religious symbols and dress may be freely displayed or worn in public to the extent permitted by law.
46. The State must permit the celebration of marriage in a religious context following a civil marriage.
47. The State may recognize a marriage conducted in accordance with a religious rite as having civil effect either from the moment of its ritual celebration or from the moment of its civil registration provided the conditions set down by law are met.
48. Religious organizations should be free to administer matrimonial dissolution or annulment but without any effect in civil law.
49. Parents and guardians may bring up their children according to their own religious convictions subject to the overriding welfare of the child.
50. A child who reaches the age of discretion is free to choose his or her religion.

Select Bibliography

The following lists works in the English language used for this book. See Further Reading for literature in the native languages of the countries studied.

Ahdar, R, and Leigh, I, *Religious Freedom in the Liberal State* (Oxford: OUP, 2005)

Balodis, R, 'State and church in Latvia' in Robbers, G (ed), *State and Church in the European Union* (Baden-Baden: Nomos, 2nd edn, 2005) 253

—— 'Religious entities as legal persons—Latvia' in Friedner, L (ed), *Churches and Other Religious Organisations as Legal Persons* (Leuven: Peeters, 2007) 149

—— 'The financing of religious communities in Latvia' in Basdevant-Gaudemet, B and Berlingò, S (eds), *The Financing of Religious Communities in the European Union* (Leuven: Peeters, 2009) 235

Basdevant-Gaudemet, B, 'State and church in France' in Robbers, G (ed), *State and Church in the European Union* (Baden-Baden: Nomos, 2nd edn, 2005) 157

—— and Berlingò, S (eds), *The Financing of Religious Communities in the European Union* (Leuven: Peeters, 2009)

Berend, N, *Christianization and the Rise of Christian Monarchy: Scandinavia, Central Europe and Rus' c 900–1200* (Cambridge: CUP, 2007)

Blanco, MR, 'Religion and law in dialogue: covenantal and non-covenantal cooperation of state and religions in Spain' in Puza, R and Doe, N (eds), *Religion and Law in Dialogue* (Leuven: Peeters, 2006) 197

Bonnici, UM, 'State and church in Malta' in Robbers, G (ed), *State and Church in the European Union* (Baden-Baden: Nomos, 2nd edn, 2005) 347

—— 'The financing of religious communities in Malta' in Basdevant-Gaudemet, B and Berlingò, S (eds), *The Financing of Religious Communities in the European Union* (Leuven: Peeters, 2009) 261

Bradney, A, *Law and Faith in a Sceptical Age* (Abingdon: Routledge Cavendish, 2009)

Bruce, S, *From Cathedrals to Cults: Religion in the Modern World* (Oxford: OUP, 1996)

Brundage, JA, *Medieval Canon Law* (London: Longman, 1995)

Cameron, E, *The European Reformation* (Oxford: Clarendon Press, 1991)

Canas, V, 'State and church in Portugal' in Robbers, G (ed), *State and Church in the European Union* (Baden-Baden: Nomos, 2nd edn, 2005) 439

Cane, P, Evans, C, and Robinson, Z (eds), *Law and Religion in Theoretical and Historical Context* (Cambridge: CUP, 2008)

Card, R, *Card, Cross and Jones Criminal Law* (Oxford: OUP, 18th edn, 2008)

Casanova, J, *Public Religions in the Modern World* (Chicago: University of Chicago Press, 1994)

Casey, J, 'State and church in Ireland' in Robbers, G (ed), *State and Church in the European Union* (Baden-Baden: Nomos, 2nd edn, 2005) 187

Chadwick, H, *East and West: The Making of a Rift in the Church* (Oxford: OUP, 2003)

Christodoulidou, T, 'Religious conscientious objection in Cyprus' (2006) 2 Cyprus and European Law Review 324

Christoffersen, L, 'The financing of religious communities in Denmark' in Basdevant-
    Gaudemet, B and Berlingò, S (eds), *The Financing of Religious Communities in the
    European Union* (Leuven: Peeters, 2009) 129
—— Kjell, ÅM and Andersen, S (eds), *Law and Religion in the 21st Century—Nordic
    Perspectives* (Copenhagen: Djøf Publishing, 2010)
Colton, P, 'Religion and law in dialogue: covenantal and non-covenantal cooperation of
    state and religions in Ireland' in Puza, R and Doe, N (eds), *Religion and Law in Dialogue*
    (Leuven: Peeters, 2006) 93
—— 'Religious entities as legal persons—Ireland' in Friedner, L (ed), *Churches and Other
    Religious Organisations as Legal Persons* (Leuven: Peeters, 2007) 125
—— 'The financing of religious communities in Ireland' in Basdevant-Gaudemet, B and
    Berlingò, S (eds), *The Financing of Religious Communities in the European Union* (Leuven:
    Peeters, 2009) 203
Cox, N, *Blasphemy and the Law in Ireland* (New York: Edwin Mellen Press, 2000)
Cranmer, F, 'Religion, human rights and the Council of Europe: a note' (2009) 162 Law
    and Justice 36
Cross, FL and Livingstone, EA (eds), *The Oxford Dictionary of the Christian Church*
    (Oxford: OUP, 3rd edn revised, 2005)
Dane, P, 'The varieties of religious autonomy' in G Robbers (ed), *Church Autonomy*
    (Frankfurt am Main: Peter Lang, 2001) 117
Davie, G, *Religion in Modern Europe: A Memory Mutates* (Oxford: OUP, 2000)
Doe, N, *Fundamental Authority in Late Medieval English Law* (Cambridge: CUP, 1990)
—— *The Legal Framework of the Church of England* (Oxford: Clarendon Press, 1996)
—— *Canon Law in the Anglican Communion* (Oxford: Clarendon Press, 1998)
—— 'Ecclesiastical quasi-legislation' in Doe, N, Hill, M, and Ombres, R (eds), *English
    Canon Law* (Cardiff: University of Wales Press, 1998) 93
—— *The Law of the Church in Wales* (Cardiff: University of Wales Press, 2002)
—— 'The notion of a national church: a juridical framework' (2002) 149 Law and
    Justice 77
—— (ed), *The Portrayal of Religion in Europe: The Media and the Arts* (Leuven: Peeters,
    2004)
—— 'Religion and media law in Europe: a comparative study' in Doe, N (ed), *The Portrayal
    of Religion in Europe: The Media and the Arts* (Leuven: Peeters, 2004) 287
—— 'The concordat concept as constitutional convention in church-state relations in the
    United Kingdom' in Puza, R and Doe, N (eds), *Religion and Law in Dialogue* (Leuven:
    Peeters, 2006) 237
—— 'Protestantism in Europe: juridical perspectives' (2008) III *Derecho y Religion* 91
—— 'Towards a 'Common Law' on Religion in the European Union' in Leustean, LN and
    Madeley, JTS (eds), *Religion, Politics and Law in the European Union* (London:
    Routledge, 2010) 141
—— and Sandberg, R (eds), *Law and Religion: New Horizons* (Leuven: Peeters, 2010)
Dübeck, I, 'State and church in Denmark' in Robbers, G (ed), *State and Church in the
    European Union* (Baden-Baden: Nomos, 2nd edn, 2005) 55
—— 'Non-covenantal cooperation of state and religion in Denmark' in Puza, R and Doe, N
    (eds), *Religion and Law in Dialogue* (Leuven: Peeters, 2006) 39

Durham, WC and Ferrari, S (eds), *Laws on Religion and the State in Post-Communist Europe* (Leuven: Peeters, 2004)

Durisotto, D, 'Financing of churches in Italy' (2010) 165 Law and Justice 159

Edge, PW, *Legal Responses to Religious Difference* (Dordrecht: Kluwer Law International, 2001)

—— *Religion and Law: An Introduction* (Aldershot: Ashgate, 2006)

Emilianides, A, 'State and church in Cyprus' in Robbers, G (ed), *State and Church in the European Union* (Baden-Baden: Nomos, 2nd edn, 2005) 231

—— 'Religion and state in dialogue: Cyprus' in Puza, R and Doe, N (eds), *Religion and Law in Dialogue* (Leuven: Peeters, 2006) 19

—— 'Religious entities as legal persons—Cyprus' in Friedner, L (ed), *Churches and Other Religious Organisations as Legal Persons* (Leuven: Peeters, 2007) 49

—— 'The financing of religious communities in Cyprus' in Basdevant-Gaudemet, B and Berlingò, S (eds), *The Financing of Religious Communities in the European Union* (Leuven: Peeters, 2009) 111

Evans, C, *Freedom of Religion under the European Convention on Human Rights* (Oxford: OUP, 2001)

Evans, MD, *Religious Liberty and International Law in Europe* (Cambridge: CUP, 1997)

Feldman, D, *Civil Liberties and Human Rights in England and Wales* (Oxford: OUP, 2nd edn, 2002)

Ferrari, S, 'The new wine and the old cask: tolerance, religion and the law in contemporary Europe' (1997) 10(1) *Ratio Juris* 75

—— 'Church and state in post-communist Europe' in Ferrari, S and Durham, WC (eds), *Law and Religion in Post-Communist Europe* (Leuven: Peeters, 2003) 411

—— 'State and church in Italy' in Robbers, G (ed), *State and Church in the European Union* (Baden-Baden: Nomos, 2nd edn, 2005) 209

—— and Durham, WC (eds), *Law and Religion in Post-Communist Europe* (Leuven: Peeters, 2003)

Freeman, M, 'Is the Jewish get any business of the State?' in O'Dair, R and Lewis, A (eds), *Law and Religion* (Oxford: OUP, 2001) 365

Friedner, L, 'Church and state in Sweden in 2000' (2001) 8 EJCSR 255

—— 'The portrayal of religion in Sweden: the media and the arts' in Doe, N (ed), *The Portrayal of Religion in Europe: The Media and the Arts* (Leuven: Peeters, 2004) 259

—— 'State and church in Sweden' in Robbers, G (ed), *State and Church in the European Union* (Baden-Baden: Nomos, 2nd edn, 2005) 537

—— 'Covenantal and non-covenantal cooperation of state and religions in Sweden' in Puza, R and Doe, N (eds), *Religion and Law in Dialogue* (Leuven: Peeters, 2006) 231

—— (ed), *Churches and Other Religious Organisations as Legal Persons* (Leuven: Peeters, 2007)

—— 'Religious entities as legal persons—Sweden' in Friedner, L (ed), *Churches and Other Religious Organisations as Legal Persons* (Leuven: Peeters, 2007) 217

Garde, P, 'Triple loyalties of a clergyman in the national church of Denmark' (2001) 8 EJCSR 21

Germann, M, 'The portrayal of religion in Germany: the media and the arts' in Doe, N (ed), *The Portrayal of Religion in Europe: The Media and the Arts* (Leuven: Peeters, 2004) 77

Gilbert, H, 'Time to reconsider the lawfulness of ritual male circumcision' (2007) 3 EHRLR 279

Glendenning, D, *Religion, Education and the Law: A Comparative Approach* (Dublin: Tottel Publishing, 2008)

Goldman, R, *Religious Thinking from Childhood to Adolescence* (London: Routledge & Kegan Paul, 1964)

González del Valle, JM and Hollerbach, A (eds), *The Teaching of Church-State Relations in European Universities* (Leuven: Peeters, 2005)

Goodman, MD, *Mission and Conversion: Proselytizing in the Religious History of the Roman Empire* (Oxford: OUP, 1994)

Grillo, R, *et al* (eds), *Legal Practice and Cultural Diversity* (Aldershot: Ashgate, 2010)

Habermas, J, 'Religion in the public sphere' (2006) 141 European Journal of Philosophy 1

Hamilton, C, *Family, Law and Religion* (London: Sweet & Maxwell, 1995)

Hartley, T, *The Foundations of European Union Law* (Oxford: OUP, 7th edn, 2010)

Hastings, A, *The Faces of God* (London: Geoffrey Chapman, 1976)

Heikkilä, M, Knuutila, J, and Scheinin, M, 'State and church in Finland' in Robbers, G (ed), *State and Church in the European Union* (Baden-Baden: Nomos, 2nd edn, 2005) 519

Helmholz, RH, *Roman Canon Law in Reformation England* (Cambridge: CUP, 1990)

—— *The Spirit of Classical Canon Law* (Athens, GA and London: University of Georgia Press, 1996)

Herrin, J, *Byzantium: The Surprising Life of a Medieval Empire* (London: Allen Lane, 2007)

Hill, M, *Ecclesiastical Law* (Oxford: OUP, 3rd edn, 2007)

—— 'The financing of religious communities in the United Kingdom' in Basdevant-Gaudemet, B and Berlingò, S (eds), *The Financing of Religious Communities in the European Union* (Leuven: Peeters, 2009) 327

—— 'Church, state and civil partners: establishment and social *mores* in tension' in Doe, N and Sandberg, R (eds), *Law and Religion: New Horizons* (Leuven: Peeters, 2010) 57

—— and Sandberg, R, 'Is nothing sacred? Clashing symbols in a secular world' (2007) Public Law 488

—— Sandberg, R and Doe, N, *Religion and Law in the United Kingdom*, in the series *International Encyclopaedia of Laws* (Amsterdam: Kluwer Law and Business, 2010)

Humphreys, J, 'The right to marry in the parish church: a rehabilitation of *Argar v Holdsworth*' (2004) EccLJ 405

Hussey, JM and Louth, A, *The Orthodox Church in the Byzantine Empire* (Oxford: OUP, 1986)

Huxley, A (ed), *Religion, Law and Tradition* (London: Routledge, 2002)

Ibán, IC, 'State and church in Spain' in Robbers, G (ed), *State and Church in the European Union* (Baden-Baden: Nomos, 2nd edn, 2005) 139

—— 'The financing of religious communities in Spain' in Basdevant-Gaudemet, B and Berlingò, S (eds), *The Financing of Religious Communities in the European Union* (Leuven: Peeters, 2009) 313

Iordache, RE, 'Church and state in Romania' in Ferrari, S and Durham, WC (eds), *Law and Religion in Post-Communist Europe* (Leuven: Peeters, 2003) 239

Ivanc, B, 'The financing of religious communities in the Republic of Slovenia—legal aspects' in Basdevant-Gaudemet, B and Berlingò, S (eds), *The Financing of Religious Communities in the European Union* (Leuven: Peeters, 2009) 303

Jacobs, L, *Concise Companion to the Jewish Religion* (Oxford: OUP, 1999)

Janis, M, Kay, R, and Bradley, A, *European Human Rights Law* (Oxford: OUP, 2nd edn, 2000)

Jouvenal, D, 'Church and state in Italy in 2000' (2001) 8 EJCSR 205

Kalb, H, 'The financing of religious communities in Austria' in Basdevant-Gaudemet, B and Berlingò, S (eds), *The Financing of Religious Communities in the European Union* (Leuven: Peeters, 2009) 87

Khazova, OA, 'Family law on post-soviet European territories: a comparative overview of some recent trends' (May 2010) 14(1) Electronic Journal of Comparative Law <http://www.ejcl.org/141/art141-3.pdf>

Kiviorg, M, 'State and church in Estonia' in Robbers, G (ed), *State and Church in the European Union* (Baden-Baden: Nomos, 2nd edn, 2005) 95

—— 'Religious entities as legal persons—Estonia' in Friedner, L (ed), *Churches and Other Religious Organisations as Legal Persons* (Leuven: Peeters, 2007) 67

—— 'The financing of religious communities in Estonia' in Basdevant-Gaudemet, B and Berlingò, S (eds), *The Financing of Religious Communities in the European Union* (Leuven: Peeters, 2009) 137

Klausen, J, *The Islamic Challenge: Politics and Religion in Western Europe* (Oxford: OUP, 2005)

Knights, S, *Freedom of Religion, Minorities and the Law* (Oxford: OUP, 2007)

Konidaris, I, 'Religious entities as legal persons—Greece' in Friedner, L (ed), *Churches and Other Religious Organisations as Legal Persons* (Leuven: Peeters, 2007) 115

Kotiranta, M, 'The legal position of religion and the media in Finland' in Doe, N (ed), *The Portrayal of Religion in Europe: The Media and the Arts* (Leuven: Peeters, 2004) 41

—— 'Religious entities as legal persons—Finland' in Friedner, L (ed), *Churches and Other Religious Organisations as Legal Persons* (Leuven: Peeters, 2007) 79

—— 'Financing churches and religious associations in Finland' in Basdevant-Gaudemet, B and Berlingò, S (eds), *The Financing of Religious Communities in the European Union* (Leuven: Peeters, 2009) 145

—— and Doe, N (eds), *Religion and Criminal Law in Europe* (Leuven: Peeters, 2011)

Kuznecoviene, J, 'State and church in Lithuania' in Robbers, G (ed), *State and Church in the European Union* (Baden-Baden: Nomos, 2nd edn, 2005) 283

—— 'Religious entities as legal persons—Lithuania' in Friedner, L (ed), *Churches and Other Religious Organisations as Legal Persons* (Leuven: Peeters, 2007) 157

—— 'The financing of religious communities in Lithuania' in Basdevant-Gaudemet, B and Berlingò, S (eds), *The Financing of Religious Communities in the European Union* (Leuven: Peeters, 2009) 241

LaFollette, H, 'Freedom of religion and children' (1989) 3(1) Public Affairs Quarterly 75

Langlaude, S, *The Right of the Child to Religious Freedom in International Law* (Leiden: Martinus Nijhoff Publishers, 2007)

Le Goff, J, *The Birth of Europe* (Malden, MA: Blackwell, 2005)

Lesaffer, R (trans by J Arriens), *European Legal History* (Cambridge: CUP, 2009)

Leustean, LN and Madeley, JTS (eds), *Religion, Politics and Law in the European Union* (London: Routledge, 2010)

Lewis, JR (ed), *The Oxford Handbook of New Religious Movements* (Oxford: OUP, 2004)

Machado, JEM, 'Media and religion in Portugal' in Doe, N (ed), *The Portrayal of Religion in Europe: The Media and the Arts* (Leuven: Peeters, 2004) 209

Madeley, JTS, 'A framework for the contemporary analysis of church-state relations in Europe' in Madeley, JTS, and Enyedi, Z (eds), *Church and State in Contemporary Europe: A Chimera of Neutrality* (London: Frank Cass, 2003) 23

—— and Enyedi, Z (eds), *Church and State in Contemporary Europe: A Chimera of Neutrality* (London: Frank Cass, 2003)

Martinez-Torrón, J, 'Religious liberty in European jurisprudence' in Hill, M (ed), *Religious Liberty and Human Rights* (Cardiff: University of Wales Press, 2002) 99

Martinková, J, 'Religious entities as legal persons—Slovakia' in Friedner, L (ed), *Churches and Other Religious Organisations as Legal Persons* (Leuven: Peeters, 2007) 191

—— 'The financing of religious communities in Slovakia' in Basdevant-Gaudemet, B and Berlingò, S (eds), *The Financing of Religious Communities in the European Union* (Leuven: Peeters, 2009) 295

McClean, D, 'State and church in the United Kingdom' in Robbers, G (ed), *State and Church in the European Union* (Baden-Baden: Nomos, 2nd edn, 2005) 553

—— 'Religious entities as legal persons—United Kingdom' in Friedner, L (ed), *Churches and Other Religious Organisations as Legal Persons* (Leuven: Peeters, 2007) 223

McCrea, R, *Religion and the Public Order of the European Union* (Oxford: OUP, 2010)

Menendez, AJ, 'A review of a Christian Europe' (2005) 301 ELR 133

Messner, F, 'The autonomy of religious confessions in France' in Warnink, H (ed), *Legal Position of Churches and Church Autonomy* (Leuven: Peeters, 2001) 111

Minnerath, R, 'Church autonomy in Europe' in G Robbers (ed), *Church Autonomy* (Frankfurt am Main: Peter Lang, 2001) 381

Modéer, KA, 'The financing of religious communities in Sweden' in Basdevant-Gaudemet, B and Berlingò, S (eds), *The Financing of Religious Communities in the European Union* (Leuven: Peeters, 2009) 319

Monelos, SM, 'Some recent problems concerning religious education in Spain' (2001) 8 EJCSR 125

Moravčiková, M, 'State and church in the Slovak Republic' in Robbers, G (ed), *State and Church in the European Union* (Baden-Baden: Nomos, 2nd edn, 2005) 491

Morris, RM (ed), *Church and State in 21st Century Britain: The Future of Church Establishment* (London: Palgrave Macmillan, 2009)

Motilla, A, 'Church and state in Spain in 2000' (2001) 8 EJCSR 119

—— 'Religious entities as legal persons—Spain' in Friedner, L (ed), *Churches and Other Religious Organisations as Legal Persons* (Leuven: Peeters, 2007) 209

Mückl, S, *Europäisierung des Staatskirchenrechts* (Baden-Baden: Nomos, 2005)

—— 'Religious entities as legal persons—Germany' in Friedner, L (ed), *Churches and Other Religious Organisations as Legal Persons* (Leuven: Peeters, 2007) 109

Mulík, P, 'Covenantal and non-covenantal cooperation of state and religions in Slovakia' in Puza, R and Doe, N (eds), *Religion and Law in Dialogue* (Leuven: Peeters, 2006) 165

Neusner, J, Sonn, T, and Brockopp, JE, *Judaism and Islam in Practice: A Sourcebook* (London: Routledge, 2000)

O'Connell, MR, *The Counter Reformation 1559–1610* (London: Harper and Row, 1974)

O'Dair, R and Lewis, A (eds), *Law and Religion* (Oxford: OUP, 2001)

O'Dowd, J, 'Religion in arts and media: Ireland' in Doe, N (ed), *The Portrayal of Religion in Europe: The Media and the Arts* (Leuven: Peeters, 2004) 129

Ogilvie, M, 'What is a church by law established?' (1990) 28 Osgoode Hall Law Journal 179

O'Higgins, P, 'Blasphemy in Irish Law' (1960) 23 MLR 151

Padover, SK, *The Revolutionary Emperor Joseph II of Austria 1741–1790* (London: Archon Books, 2nd edn, 1967)

Papastathis, CK, 'Religious self-administration in the Hellenic Republic' in Robbers, G (ed), *Church Autonomy* (Frankfurt am Main: Peter Lang, 2001) 425

—— 'State and church in Greece' in Robbers, G (ed), *State and Church in the European Union* (Baden-Baden: Nomos, 2nd edn, 2005) 115

—— 'The financing of religions in Greece' in Basdevant-Gaudemet, B and Berlingò, S (eds), *The Financing of Religious Communities in the European Union* (Leuven: Peeters, 2009) 177

Parker, G (ed), *The Thirty Years' War* (London: Routledge, 1984)

Pauly, A, 'State and church in Luxembourg' in Robbers, G (ed), *State and Church in the European Union* (Baden-Baden: Nomos, 2nd edn, 2005) 305

—— Entités religieuses comme personnes juridiques-Luxembourg' in L Friedner (ed), *Churches and Other Religious Organisations as Legal Persons* (Leuven: Peeters, 2007)

Pauly, RJ, *Islam in Europe: Integration or Marginalisation?* (Aldershot: Ashgate, 2004)

Petchey, S, 'Legal issues for faith schools in England and Wales' (2008) 10 EccLJ 174

Peteva, J, 'Church and state in Bulgaria' in Ferrari, S and Durham, WC (eds), *Law and Religion in Post-Communist Europe* (Leuven: Peeters, 2003) 37

Philips, Lord, 'Equality before the law' (2008) 161 Law and Justice 75

Piaget, J, *Child's Conception of the World* (London: Routledge & Kegan Paul, 1929)

Potz, R, 'State and church in Austria' in Robbers, G (ed), *State and Church in the European Union* (Baden-Baden: Nomos, 2nd edn, 2005) 391

—— 'Covenantal and non-covenantal cooperation of state and religions in Austria' in Puza, R and Doe, N (eds), *Religion and Law in Dialogue* (Leuven: Peeters, 2006) 11

—— et al, 'God in the European Constitution' Opinions of Members of the European Consortium for Church and State Research, ECCSR, (2004) 4 *Newsletter* 4–110

Prepeluh-Magajne, U, 'Religious entities as legal persons—Slovenia' in Friedner, L (ed), *Churches and Other Religious Organisations as Legal Persons* (Leuven: Peeters, 2007) 197

Puza, R, 'Relations between church and state in Germany in 2000' (2001) 8 EJCSR 35

—— and Doe, N (eds), *Religion and Law in Dialogue: Covenantal and Non-covenantal Cooperation between State and Religion in Europe* (Leuven: Peeters, 2006)

Rawls, J, *Political Liberalism* (New York: Columbia University Press, 1993)

Rivers, J, 'In pursuit of pluralism: the ecclesiastical policy of the European Union' (2004) 7 EccLJ 267

—— 'The question of freedom of religion or belief and defamation' (2007) 2 Religion and Human Rights 113

—— *The Law of Organized Religion* (Oxford: OUP, 2010)

Robbers, G (ed), *Church Autonomy* (Frankfurt am Main: Peter Lang, 2001)

—— 'Diversity of state-religion relations and European Union unity' (2004) 7 EccLJ 304

—— (ed), *State and Church in the European Union* (Baden-Baden: Nomos, 2nd edn, 2005)

Robbers, G (ed), 'State and church in Germany' in Robbers, G (ed), *State and Church in the European Union* (Baden-Baden: Nomos, 2nd edn, 2005) 77

—— 'State and church in Europe' in Robbers, G (ed), *State and Church in the European Union* (Baden-Baden: Nomos, 2nd edn, 2005) 577

—— 'Treaties between religious communities and the state in Germany' in Puza, R and Doe, N (eds), *Religion and Law in Dialogue* (Leuven: Peeters, 2006) 59

—— 'Financing religion in Germany' in Basdevant-Gaudemet, B and Berlingò, S (eds), *The Financing of Religious Communities in the European Union* (Leuven: Peeters, 2009) 169

Rodley, NS, *The Treatment of Prisoners under International Law* (Oxford: OUP, 1999)

Roehlkepartain, EC, King, PE, Wagener, L, and Benson, PL (eds), *The Handbook of Spiritual Development in Childhood and Adolescence* (Thousand Oaks, Cal: Sage Publications, 2005)

Rossell, J, 'Religious denominations and the media in Spain' in Doe, N (ed), *The Portrayal of Religion in Europe: The Media and the Arts* (Leuven: Peeters, 2004) 231

Rynkowski, M, 'State and church in Poland' in Robbers, G (ed), *State and Church in the European Union* (Baden-Baden: Nomos, 2nd edn, 2005) 419

—— 'Remarks on Art I-52 of the Constitutional Treaty: new aspects of the European ecclesiastical law' (2005) 6(11) German Law Journal 343

—— 'Religion and law in dialogue: Poland' in Puza, R and Doe, N (eds), *Religion and Law in Dialogue* (Leuven: Peeters, 2006) 135

—— 'Religious entities as legal persons—Poland' in Friedner, L (ed), *Churches and Other Religious Organisations as Legal Persons* (Leuven: Peeters, 2007) 177

—— 'The financing of churches and religious communities in Poland' in Basdevant-Gaudemet, B and Berlingò, S (eds), *The Financing of Religious Communities in the European Union* (Leuven: Peeters, 2009) 277

Sandberg, R, 'Church-state relations in Europe: from legal models to an interdisciplinary approach' (2008) 1 Journal of Religion in Europe 329

—— *Law and Religion* (Cambridge: CUP, 2011)

—— and Doe, N, 'The strange death of blasphemy' (2008) 71 MLR 971

—— and Catto, R, 'Law and sociology: toward a greater understanding of religion' in Doe, N and Sandberg, R (eds), *Law and Religion: New Horizons* (Leuven: Peeters, 2010) 275

Shachar, A, 'Entangled: state and religion and the family' in Ahdar, R and Aroney, A (eds), *Shari'a in the West* (Oxford: OUP, 2010) ch 8

Schacht, J, *An Introduction to Islamic Law* (Oxford: OUP, Reprint, 1991)

Schanda, B, 'State and church in Hungary' in Robbers, G (ed), *State and Church in the European Union* (Baden-Baden: Nomos, 2nd edn, 2005) 323

—— 'Religion and law in dialogue: covenantal and non-covenantal cooperation of state and religions in Hungary' in Puza, R and Doe, N (eds), *Religion and Law in Dialogue* (Leuven: Peeters, 2006) 79

—— 'Covenantal cooperation of state and religions in the post-communist member countries of the EU' in Puza, R and Doe, N (eds), *Religion and Law in Dialogue* (Leuven: Peeters, 2006) 251

—— 'Religious entities as legal persons—Hungary' in Friedner, L (ed), *Churches and Other Religious Organisations as Legal Persons* (Leuven: Peeters, 2007) 119

—— 'The financing of religious communities in Hungary' in Basdevant-Gaudemet, B and Berlingò, S (eds), *The Financing of Religious Communities in the European Union* (Leuven: Peeters, 2009) 195

Shatter, A, *Family Law* (Dublin: Butterworth, 4th edn, 1997)

Schinkele, B, 'Church and state in Austria in 2003' (2004) 11 EJCSR 45

—— 'Religious entities as legal persons—Austria' in Friedner, L (ed), *Churches and Other Religious Organisations as Legal Persons* (Leuven: Peeters, 2007) 37

Sousa e Brito, J de, 'Covenantal and non-covenantal cooperation of state and religions in Portugal' in Puza, R and Doe, N (eds), *Religion and Law in Dialogue* (Leuven: Peeters, 2006) 155

—— 'Religious entities as legal persons—Portugal' in Friedner, L (ed), *Churches and Other Religious Organisations as Legal Persons* (Leuven: Peeters, 2007) 183

Šturm, L, 'State and church in Slovenia' in Robbers, G (ed), *State and Church in the European Union* (Baden-Baden: Nomos, 2nd edn, 2005) 469

—— 'Religion and law in dialogue: Slovenia' in Puza, R and Doe, N (eds), *Religion and Law in Dialogue* (Leuven: Peeters, 2006) 189

Stüssi, M, 'Banning minarets: addressing the validity of a controversial Swiss popular initiative' (2008) 32 Religion and Human Rights 135

Sullivan, RE, *Christian Missionary Activity in the Early Middle Ages* (Aldershot: Variorum, 1994)

Tamm, D, 'Religious entities as legal persons—Denmark' in Friedner, L (ed), *Churches and Other Religious Organisations as Legal Persons* (Leuven: Peeters, 2007) 61

Taylor, PM, *Freedom of Religion* (Cambridge: CUP, 2005)

Torfs, R, 'State and church in Belgium' in Robbers, G (ed), *State and Church in the European Union* (Baden-Baden: Nomos, 2nd edn, 2005) 9

—— 'Religious entities as legal persons—Belgium' in Friedner, L (ed), *Churches and Other Religious Organisations as Legal Persons* (Leuven: Peeters, 2007) 45

—— 'Church financing—toward a European model?' in Basdevant-Gaudemet, B and Berlingò, S (eds), *The Financing of Religious Communities in the European Union* (Leuven: Peeters, 2009) 343

Tretera, J, 'State and church in the Czech Republic' in Robbers, G (ed), *State and Church in the European Union* (Baden-Baden: Nomos, 2nd edn, 2005) 35

—— 'Concordatarian agreements and public agreements in the Czech state ecclesiastical law' in Puza, R and Doe, N (eds), *Religion and Law in Dialogue* (Leuven: Peeters, 2006) 33

—— 'Religious entities as legal persons—Czech Republic' in Friedner, L (ed), *Churches and Other Religious Organisations as Legal Persons* (Leuven: Peeters, 2007) 35

—— and Horák, Z, 'The financing of religious communities in the Czech Republic' in Basdevant-Gaudemet, B and Berlingò, S (eds), *The Financing of Religious Communities in the European Union* (Leuven: Peeters, 2009) 119

Ullmann, W, *Law and Politics in the Middle Ages: An Introduction to the Sources of Medieval Political Ideas* (London: Sources of History Limited, 1975)

van Bijsterveld, S, 'State and church in the Netherlands' in Robbers, G (ed), *State and Church in the European Union* (Baden-Baden: Nomos, 2nd edn, 2005) 367

—— 'Religious entities as legal persons—Netherlands' in Friedner, L (ed), *Churches and Other Religious Organisations as Legal Persons* (Leuven: Peeters, 2007) 171 van Bijsterveld, S, 'The financing of religious communities in the Netherlands' in Basdevant-Gaudemet, B and Berlingò, S (eds), *The Financing of Religious Communities in the European Union* (Leuven: Peeters, 2009) 269

van Bockxmeer, H, 'The portrayal of religion in the Netherlands: the media and the arts' in Doe, N (ed), *The Portrayal of Religion in Europe: The Media and the Arts* (Leuven: Peeters, 2004) 185

van Bueren, G, 'The right to be the same, the right to be different: children and religion' in Lindholm, T, Durham, WC, and Tahzib-Lie, BG (eds), *Facilitating Freedom of Religion or Belief: A Deskbook* (Leiden: Martinus Nijhoff Publishers, 2004) 699

van Caenegem, RC, *Judges, Legislators and Professors: Chapters in European Legal History* (Cambridge: CUP, 1987)

von Campenhausen, A, 'Conventional cooperation between state and religion: Germany' in Puza, R and Doe, N (eds), *Religion and Law in Dialogue* (Leuven: Peeters, 2006) 5

Ventura, M, 'Religion and law in dialogue: covenantal and non-covenantal cooperation of state and religions in Italy' in Puza, R and Doe, N (eds), *Religion and Law in Dialogue* (Leuven: Peeters, 2006) 115

Ware, T, *The Orthodox Church* (London: Penguin Books, 1991)

Warnink, H (ed), *Legal Position of Churches and Church Autonomy* (Leuven: Peeters, 2001)

Watt, WM, *The Influence of Islam in Medieval Europe* (Edinburgh: Edinburgh University Press, 1994)

Weatherhead, JL (ed), *The Constitution and Laws of the Church of Scotland* (Edinburgh: Board of Practice and Procedure, 1997)

Wieshaider, W, 'Communicating religion in Austria: the media and the arts' in Doe, N (ed), *The Portrayal of Religion in Europe: The Media and the Arts* (Leuven: Peeters, 2004) 5

White, RCA, and Ovey, C, *Jacobs, White and Ovey: The European Convention on Human Rights* (Oxford: OUP, 5th edn, 2010)

Williams, R, 'Civil and religious law in England: a religious perspective' (2008) 10 EccLJ 262

Witte, J, *Law and Protestantism: The Legal Teachings of the Lutheran Reformation* (Cambridge: CUP, 2002)

—— and Alexander, FS (eds), *Christianity and Law: An Introduction* (Cambridge: CUP, 2008)

Yamane, D, *The Catholic Church in State Politics: Negotiating Prophetic Demands and Political Realities* (Lanham, MD: Rowman and Littlefield Publishers, 2005)

Young, J, 'Regulation of the representation of religion in the media in the United Kingdom' in Doe, N (ed), *The Portrayal of Religion in Europe: The Media and the Arts* (Leuven: Peeters, 2004) 287

FURTHER READING

The following are key texts in languages other than English.

Europe-wide studies

Berlingò, S (ed), *Code Européen: Droit et Religions* (Milan: Dott A Giuffré Editore 2001)

Fernández-Coronado González, A (editor in chief), *El derecho de la libertad de conciencia en el marco de la Unión Europea: pluralismo y minorías* (Madrid: Editorial Colex, 2002)

Ferrari, S and Ibán, IC, *Diritto e religione in Europa occidentale* (Bologna: Il Mulino, 1997)

Flauss-Diem, J (ed), *Secret, Religion, Normes Étatiques* (Strasbourg: Presses Universitaires de Strasbourg, 2005)

Margiotta Broglio, F, Mirabelli, C, and Onida, F, *Religioni e sistemi giuridici: introduzione al diritto ecclesiastico comparato* (Bologna: Il Mulino, 1997)

Messner, F (ed), *Les 'sectes' et le droit en France* (Paris: Presses Universitaires de France, 1999)

Mückl, S, *Europäisierung des Staatskirchenrechts* (Nomos: Baden-Baden, 2005)

Ventura, M, *La Laicità dell'Unione Europea: Diritti, Mercato, Religione* (Turin: G Giappichelli Editore, 2001)

Country-by-country

What follows is a selection of leading texts in the native languages of the countries studied. For a fuller list, see the bibliographies at the end of each national report in Robbers, G (ed), *State and Church in the European Union* (Baden-Baden: Nomos, 2nd edn, 2005).

Austria: Gampl, I, Potz, R, and Schinkele, B, *Österreichisches Staatskirchenrecht: Gesetze, Materialien, Rechtsprechung* (2 vols, Vienna: Orac, 1990, 1993)

Belgium: De Pooter, P, *De rechtspositie van erkende erediensten en levensbeschouwingen in Staat en maatschappij* (Brussels: Larcier, 2003)

Denmark: Espersen, P, *Kirkeret* (Copenhagen: Almindelig Del, 1993)

France: Messner, F, Prélot, P-H, and Woehrling, J-M (eds), *Traité de droit français des religions* (Paris: LITEC, 2003)

Germany: Winter, J, *Staatskirchenrecht der Bundesrepublik Deutschland* (Neuwied: Luchterhand Verlag, 2001)

Hungary: Schanda, B, *Magyar állami egyházjog* (Budapest: Szent István Társulat, 2nd edn, 2003)

Italy: Finocchiaro, F, *Diritto ecclesiastico* (Bologna: Zanichelli, 2003)

Lithuania: Kuznecoviene, J, *Religijos Lietuvoje* (Siauliai: Nova Vita, 1999)

Luxembourg: Held, L, *Staatsrecht und Kirchenrecht im Grossherzogtum Luxembourg* (Luxembourg: Sankt-Paulus-Drukerei, 1984)

Netherlands: Hirsch Ballin, EMH, *et al*, *Kerk en Staat* (Baarn: Amboboeken, 1987)

Poland: Krukowski, J, and Warchałowski, K, *Polskie prawo wyznaniowe* (Warsaw: Lexis Nexis, 2000)

Portugal: Adragão, PP, *A Liberdade Religiosa e o Estado* (Coimbra: Almedina, 2002)

Slovenia: Šturm, L, *Cerkev in država* (Ljubljana: Nova Revija, 2000)

Spain: González del Valle, JM, and Blanco, M, *Derecho eclesiástico español* (Madrid: Civitas, 2002)

Sweden: Edqvist, G, Friedner, L, Lunqvist-Norling, M, and Tibbling, P, *Kyrkoordning för Svenska kyrkan* (Stockholm: Verbum, 2009)

See also the website of EURESIS—European Studies on Religion and State Interaction, for documents, surveys, and links in this field see <http://www.euresisnet.eu>

Index